Ricky Ponting played cricket professionally from 1992 to 2013 and is one of the greatest players to have worn the baggy green. He holds more records than any other player in Australian history, and is the country's highest run-scorer in Test and ODI cricket. Under his leadership the Australian team won a historic 5–0 Ashes victory, achieved back-to-back World Cup wins in the ODI format, amassed 48 victories from 77 Tests and equalled the world record of 16 straight Test wins.

Pontingfoundation

Off the field, Ricky and his wife Rianna have raised over $10 million since 2002 to help young Australians and their families beat cancer, and in 2008 they established the Ponting Foundation. Your purchase of this book contributes to the work of the **pontingfoundation.com.au**.

PONTING

at the close of play

HarperSport

An Imprint of HarperCollinsPublishers

HarperSport
An imprint of
HarperCollins*Publishers*
77–85 Fulham Palace Road
Hammersmith, London W6 8JB

www.harpercollins.co.uk

First published by HarperCollins*Publishers* 2013
This paperback edition 2014

1 3 5 7 9 10 8 6 4 2

PB ISBN 978-0-00-754476-9
EB ISBN 978-0-00-754477-6

Typeset in Sabon LT by Kirby Jones
Printed and bound in Great Britain by
Clays Ltd, St Ives plc

For my beautiful wife Rianna and
our gorgeous children Emmy and Matisse
And for Mum, Dad, Drew and Renee
Thanks to you all for always being there for me

Contents

Insights

ACKNOWLEDGMENTS

WRITING MY AUTOBIOGRAPHY was a pretty daunting thing to do and required support from so many people who I now want to thank. Normally these thanks and acknowledgments are placed at the back of a book but I wanted these pages to be at the front, as my story wouldn't exist if it wasn't for this long list of amazing people who have all played a part in my career.

My family means the world to me. Rianna has worked tirelessly on this book and has had the most profound influence on my life. I cannot thank you enough, sweetheart, for everything you do for us and for everything that we share. Emmy and Matisse — I can't wait to share everything together, now that I have retired from travelling the world playing cricket. We are going to have so much fun together. Mum and Dad — words cannot express my thanks for absolutely everything that you taught me and gave me the opportunity to do. My brother Drew and sister Renee — I am so proud of you and your families. Brian, Leanne and the whole extended Cantor family — thank you for making me so welcome in your family. I want to make special mention of Natalie for being a great sister-in-law, nanny and friend. We couldn't have led the lives we have without you. To our extended families on both sides, thank you for your love and support.

My story is predominantly about cricket. It wouldn't have happened without my team-mates, coaches and support staff who have been with me right through my career. Many of you are named in this book, but to everyone I played with or against, thanks for the contest, camaraderie and shared passion for the game.

This book has been a long time in the making. We made the decision back in 2009 to have HarperCollins publish it, and we have been working together on it ever since. The biggest credit must go to Geoff Armstrong, who has worked with me since my *Captain's Diary* in 2006. Geoff, you did a mountain of work to bring my story to life and I hope you're as proud of the finished copy as I am — thank you for your professionalism, quality work and mateship.

I also want to make special mention of Peter Lalor and my manager, James Henderson, who worked very closely with me over the final months of writing. We had a looming deadline and both of you gave me more than I could have asked for to get this book to the printer. Thank you to you both. James, you've been an incredible mate and manager. Your guidance in all aspects of our lives will always be cherished.

To the whole team at HarperCollins — I am very proud of our long relationship and the books that we have published together. Thank you for letting me tell my story over the years and for the wonderful package of this book.

Finally, I want to thank all of the other people who have been a part of this story, including: my initial manager, Sam Halvorsen; all the team at DSEG, especially James, Jo Henderson and Richard King; my personal sponsors and confidants who have always been there for me; the cricket media for building the exposure of our game; and the volunteers and fans of Australian cricket, who are the backbone of all that we do. You have all been a part of my career and I thank you for being in my story.

Ricky Ponting
September 2013

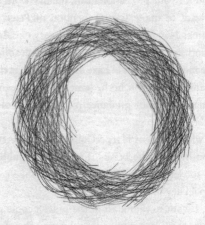

Pontingfoundation

The Ponting Foundation

How the Ponting Foundation makes a difference

The Ponting Foundation is dedicated to doing everything possible to help young Australians and their families beat cancer.

It provides funding for a wide range of essential services that comfort and nurture young Australians with cancer, while providing emotional support and financial assistance for their family.

Through alliances with some of Australia's leading cancer charities and research groups, Ricky has used his profile to influence widespread community engagement to raise important incremental funds for specific charity programs, hospitals and ground-breaking research projects engaged in the fight against cancer in Australia's children and youth.

The Foundation also funds programs that assist in the care and well-being of the wider family unit as they support their child through illness.

How you can help

Make a donation

Visit www.pontingfoundation.com.au and make an online donation. Donations of $2 or more are fully tax deductable for Australian residents.

Get Involved with the Biggest Game of Cricket

The Biggest Game of Cricket is the Ponting Foundation's major annual fundraising activity. Harnessing the pride of Australia Day, BGOC is a community based event with thousands of games being played and events all around Australia. Visit www.biggestgameofcricket.com.au for all the details.

Corporate partners — building pride through great partnerships

The Ponting Foundation sincerely appreciates the generous support of its corporate partners and invites interested companies to join the corporate team.

Become a Ponting XI member

A key pillar for the long-term success of the Ponting Foundation has been the creation of the 'Ponting XI'.

The substantial donations made by members of the Ponting XI have ensured the Foundation remains fully self-sufficient, allowing funds raised by other means to be distributed to the Foundation's beneficiaries.

By joining this thoughtful and generous group of leading philanthropists, you will be partnering with the Foundation and importantly, the wider healthcare community, in helping young Australians and families beat cancer.

Please contact the Ponting Foundation at info@pontingfoundation.com.au for more details.

With Prof Murray Norris and Prof Michelle Haber AM at the Ricky and Rianna Ponting Molecular Diagnostic Laboratory, Children's Cancer Institute, at the University of NSW, Sydney.

Giving back

The issue of childhood cancer is something very dear to the hearts of Rianna and myself since a hospital visit we made together back in 2002. Phil Kearns, a good friend who was involved at the Children's Cancer Institute Australia (CCIA) invited us to visit the Sydney Children's Hospital to meet with some of the many children and their families in the oncology ward. Listening to each family's story was one of the most emotional experiences of our lives. We were deeply saddened by the stories we heard but at the same time overwhelmed by the commitment of the families, doctors and nurses to help these children fight the biggest battle of their young lives. Following our visit, we sat outside the Children's Hospital and with tears in our eyes made a commitment to one another to do everything possible to improve the lives of young Australians with cancer and their families. We worked as ambassadors of the CCIA helping to raise money to fund research into Acute Lymphoblastic Leukaemia, the most common cancer in children.

It was through our work with the CCIA that we realised we were in a unique position to make a real difference. After very careful consideration, we decided to establish the Ponting Foundation with the aim of raising funds for the benefit of young Australians with cancer and their families. Since 2008, we have been steadily doing our best to give back to those most in need. We have partnered with a variety of incredible organisations, including the CCIA, Redkite, the Murdoch Children's Research Institute, the David Collins Leukaemia Foundation and the National Institute of Integrative Medicine, to spread our fundraising to the areas that we believe need the most focus. We visit hospitals regularly, spending time with the children and their families as well as meeting doctors, researchers and nurses, who always teach us something new about the issues of childhood cancer.

With my retirement from cricket, we intend to become even more active in our work, not only from a fundraising perspective but just as importantly, from an advocacy and awareness point of view. We need to do more for our children to protect their future. Cancer is the major killer of our children and we have to do everything we can to increase the survival rates especially around the uncommon forms of cancer. Rianna and I couldn't do this on our own. We have an incredible Board that includes some of Australia's most respected business people, including Trevor O'Hoy, Stephen Roberts, Ray Horsburgh, Ian Foote, Katie McNamara, Steven Ivak and James Henderson. Our founding Chairperson, Margaret Jackson, was an amazing contributor as are our Ponting XI members, including Christian Johnston, Peter de Rauch, Sir Ron Brierley, Philip Allison, Sir Michael Parkinson, Honey Bacon, and David and Kelli Lundberg.

My routine

Here's a simple summary of the routine that I went through every time I batted for Australia.

Last thing the night before a game or when I expected to bat

- Write a list of what I needed to do out in the middle
    - Watch the ball
    - Play straight
    - Loud calls
    - Be patient
    - Be positive in attack and defence
    - Bat for a long time
    - Make 100
    - Be man of the match
    - Be man of the series
- Read this list out loud after writing it, underline each item when read and visualise each point for tomorrow
- Write a list of each bowler and how they will try to bowl
    - Visualise how they will try to get me out
- Then switch off the light and go to sleep

Before going out to bat

- Get ready the same way each and every time
- Sit down and watch the openers with my gear all in same positions around me — ready to go
- Sit with a bottle of water and chew three pieces of gum
- Sip the water when needed
- As soon as a wicket falls, remove the gum and put it aside. Drink water and leave for the middle

Walking out to the middle

- Display energy and walk to the middle fairly quickly
- Do three or four butt kicks with each leg
- Play a number of shadow 'straight drives' while walking
- Flick my wrists with bat in hand — both hands

On arrival at the crease

- Take guard and get middle
- Clear all the rubbish on the wicket around the crease line — must be perfectly clear
- Walk down and look closely at the wicket
- Identify the *area* that I think the bowler can bowl a good ball
- Make sure that area is totally clear
- Move to the side of the pitch and do my hamstring stretches with bat in both hands
- Walk back to the crease while observing the field placement
- Take my grip and take my stance in the crease

Bowler's run-up and delivery

- Say 'watch the ball' to myself twice — halfway through run-up and just before release of the ball
- Look at the identified *area* down the wicket and look up at the bowler's release of the ball
- Then whatever happens, happens
- Switch my mind off completely until bowler is back near top of run-up
- Switch back on and start this delivery routine again

PONTING

INVERMAY PARK

Launceston, February 2, 2013

SO MUCH OF WHO I AM is where I came from.

It started here and in a lot of ways it's right that it ends here in these dressing rooms. I'm two months retired from Test cricket and back playing for the Mowbray Eagles. Back where it all began.

I entered these rooms as a boy and left them 30 years later. I wore the baggy green cap at the crease and the Australian captain's jacket at the toss. I wore one-day colours too in an era when we were unbeatable at World Cup cricket. I wore them all with pride, at all times striving to be the best I could, but if you stripped all that away you would find what matters most and what kept me going: cricket.

It is simple really. I loved the game, the rituals, the fierce competition and the equally fierce mateship it promoted.

Dressing rooms, hotels, cricket grounds and aeroplanes are the places where my life has been lived.

The rooms are our refuge. For Test players they're a place away from the cameras, journalists, crowds and constant glare. For club cricketers they're a sanctuary where you can be with your mates away from work and the grind of daily life. You check in Saturday morning and you check out Saturday night a little wobbly from the long day and a few drinks after the game.

Every club cricketer has got a dressing room routine, sometimes it's hard to pick the pattern in the mess, other times it's obvious. Me? I'm not neat, I take the bats out and stand them up to clear some room in the jumble of the kit bag. The gloves are numbered, but in no order and as the game goes on things spread out further. Matthew Hayden said I spread my gear round like a 'scrub turkey' but he was almost as bad; Justin Langer, Mike Hussey they were like me; others were neat as pins. Damien Martyn was, and Michael Clarke and Brad Haddin verge on the obsessive, everything laid out like it's a display in a store window. Marto would mark the edges of his territory with tape and warn us not to let our mess trespass within. In different grounds we had different seating patterns that established themselves over the years.

Spreading the bats and placing your bag somewhere is about marking your turf, setting out the boundaries of your space.

From the time I was small I was drawn to the equipment. The bats, the shoes, the gloves and the pads ... I was always looking at what somebody else had, always picking up bats and feeling them. They are, I suppose, the tools of the trade. If I'd followed through on that building apprenticeship when I left school I wonder if I'd have had the same romantic attachment to what was in the toolbox.

Occasionally you'll meet a cricketer who couldn't give a toss, but most of us, particularly batsmen, are obsessed with our gear. Huss would carry a set of scales with him to ensure the bat was an exact weight. If it was over, out would come the sandpaper and he would start to scrape away. I'd give him a bit of grief about it, but when he wasn't around I'd weigh mine too. Most of us arrive with an arsenal of bats: the lucky one, the one that's almost broken in, the one that's there and about ...

The secret to a good one is how it feels in your hands and the soft tonk sound a new ball makes on good willow. Your ear tells you. I suppose a guitar or a piano is the same, but you'd have to ask a musician if that's right.

My game bat never comes out until the morning of the match, it never gets an appearance at practice. The others are works in progress, bits of willow that will, with a bit of tuning and knocking, make it to game-bat status one day. Like players, bats have to earn a place in a game.

WE PONTINGS ARE WORKING-CLASS PEOPLE from a working-class part of Launceston and our entertainment consisted of footy in winter, cricket in summer and golf whenever we could. It was the same with everybody we knew.

From the time I was old enough to ride my bike past the end of the street I would come down to watch the Mowbray Eagles play. I was always drawn to the cricket ground and the dressing room. Uncle Greg played for the Eagles before he moved on to the Shield side and then to Test cricket. Maybe it was him who got me down there the first time, but I knew Dad had played for the same team and most of the adults in my life had something to do with the club. Every Saturday morning I'd be up early, have a quick breakfast and then climb onto my BMX and race down to here or wherever they were playing. If somebody was around I'd have a hit in the nets while the old blokes of the district went about the serious business in the middle, but the best of the times were in their half-lit dressing rooms.

When they were on the field I'd come in and go through the kits. Weighing the bats in my hands, feeling the grips and the balance and examining the grain. Looking back it was pretty rudimentary gear, but at the time it seemed possessed of some sort of magic. I'd try on the gloves and the inners that were way too big for me and I'd memorise where everything was before I touched it to make sure it went back exactly there, so when they came in hot and sweaty from a couple of hours on the field everything would be where they'd left it, and I'd be in the corner where they expected me to be.

I was small and could hide quietly in a corner so you wouldn't necessarily know I was there. I would spend hours there listening to them talk about cricket as they drank beer and cooled down after play. It was a conversation I longed to join and one that when I did I've stayed engaged with all my life. Back then I was soaking it up like a sponge. Listening to their deep, gruff voices cracking jokes and weaving stories about that place out in the middle where I would long to be.

The Mowbray boys had a reputation for being the hardest cricketers around. When we played Launceston or Riverside it was almost class war and the teams from the other side of the river used to quietly dread crossing into our territory. After the game, however, they were always welcome for a drink in the rooms.

Sometimes Dad would drag me home early, other times someone would say 'come on young fella' and throw my bike in the back of their car and drive me home. Being the first to arrive and last to leave is a habit I've maintained ever since those early days.

And today I'm back here at the cricket club that started it all.

When, as captain of the Australian Test team, I would hand players their first baggy green I would tell them that they were following in a grand tradition and to think about the people who had worn it before, but I would also ask them to think about all the others out there at club and state level and how much it would mean to them.

Cricket's given me everything but it's taken things from me too. I'm a Mowbray boy and it's here I feel at home and it's probably the greatest regret of my life that the game took me away from here too soon. As a boy I just wanted to be one of the men in this dressing room, but I suppose the trade-off wasn't too bad. Instead of sharing victory with these men I shared it with some of the great cricketers of our time and some of my greatest mates. Matty Hayden, Marto, Lang, Gilly, Warne, Pidge ... we ruled the world for a while there, climbed the mountain and we were as close as men can be. Having said that, I am just as close and just as comfortable with the people I met in these rooms when I was still a boy. The blokes who put their hands on my shoulder and pointed me in the right direction.

NATURALLY I'M THE FIRST in the rooms at Invermay Park this morning. Had to open up myself. It's fitting in a way as I've always been the first to arrive. The last to leave. Lately I'd found myself looking up expecting to see Gilly or Marto or Lang only to find they've gone and the spot that was theirs has been taken by someone else. One by one they had all left the dressing room until I was the last one left.

Rianna, my wife, has a way of putting things in perspective. When everybody had become emotional at my retirement ahead of the Perth Test she said, 'He's not dead yet people, it's just cricket,' and I love her for that. I love that sense of balance she brings. Recently she came to me and asked if I had really made that many Test runs. She'd seen something on television. Sometimes I think she's the only person who doesn't know these things. (There are whole villages in the backblocks of India who know more about my career.) And I love her even more for that.

To be honest it all became a bit overwhelming when I retired from Test cricket and I wish I could have had her sense of acceptance. Admitting to myself that I was no longer up to it, saying the words out loud to Rianna and then the team and then telling the world; wandering out to bat for that last time and seeing the South Africans lined up in a guard of honour as I approached the WACA pitch … all the other little things that happened for the last time ever in the few weeks leading up to that moment had been like a series of small deaths.

I only ever wanted to play cricket and I could never bring myself to imagine a time when I wasn't playing the game, but that time is approaching.

Since leaving the Test team I have been like a salmon (Tasmanian, of course) swimming back upstream to where it all started. Before I put this old kit bag away for the last time I had some unfinished business. Cricket swept me up early. One day I didn't know how to get on a plane and then for a long time after I wondered if I would ever get off one.

International cricket expanded to fill every available space in my life. At the academy I had been able to get home occasionally, but after that visits got rarer until there was barely time to swing by and have a hit of golf with the old man, or a cup of instant coffee with Mum at the breakfast bar. My little brother, Drew, and sister, Renee — my whole family I guess — watched me on television and tracked my progress that way. I suppose all of Australia did and a few other nations as well. I was away when my pa died and will never forget the helplessness as I spoke to Dad on the phone from England. I wasn't there for him when he needed me.

I'm fiercely loyal. I'm proud of my background and the values I was taught in this town and these dressing rooms. No matter how many five-star hotels I've slept in, how many first-class flights I've been on, how many politicians and businessmen and celebrities have swept through my life I have never lost the sense that I'm that small-town boy who didn't have much but wanted for nothing.

So, in what's left of this last summer of my cricket life, I am trying to catch up.

It's all rushed as it always is. I trained in Hobart yesterday, drove up to Launceston last night and will head back to Hobart first thing tomorrow. I'm so early for the game I park the car down the road a bit and call Rianna on the phone, even when I've done that I'm still the first there so I open the clubrooms and find a space where I figure nobody else will be, just as I did when I was a boy. It's best to stay out of the way and not be noticed, although that's impossible today.

It's early February and the Mowbray Eagles are playing Launceston on the parkland by the Esk River, next to the footy ground.

There're hundreds at the ground and they line up for autographs and I sign them all when I get a chance. There's a lot of familiar faces, people from my past introducing me to their kids. My mum and dad are playing golf because it's a Saturday and that's what they do and I love them for that. They're set in their ways but I have never for one moment felt they haven't been with me every innings

I've played. They're locals and they like their lives down here. They don't like their routine disrupted so they haven't seen me play that much. They would never think of going overseas to watch a game of cricket. It was hard enough getting them to Perth for my last match. No, there's a golf course down the road and every Saturday Mum and Dad have a date that starts at the first hole.

I STRAP ON MY PADS and make my way out to the middle. Head down at first, trying to block out the crowd like I do whether I'm at the MCG, in Mumbai or at Mowbray. Hitting the grass I try and get a little feeling in the legs, running on the spot a bit. I make it to the middle and take centre, just as I learned all those years back, and I scratch my studs into the surface of the wicket. Marking out my territory again.

I do it really tough. Cricket is such a great leveller. I last an hour, but it's as hard an hour as I've spent at the crease. The council owns the ground and keeps the grass long and it's impossible to hit a boundary along the ground. It's been raining and the wicket is seaming. Finally I shoulder arms to a ball that cuts back a foot or two and takes my off-stump.

This game rarely lets you get ahead of yourself. In the evening we have a few beers in the rooms with our gear all around us and the chat begins all over again.

This is who I am and now this is finishing and I suppose that begs a question I am not too keen to ponder: I might not have been finished with the game, but it was finished with me and am I now the person it has shaped?

Someone said when I walked out of the Australian dressing room the door slammed on a generation of cricket. That might be right, but for me there was something deeper. I had been raised in the game. The dressing room was a cradle, I was formed in these confines, I grew up in them and I have as good as lived in them for all my adult life up to this point. There was only ever the game and the team, the competition and the anticipation, and now it is time to move on.

AFTER MOWBRAY it was back to Sheffield Shield.

Twenty years ago I played my first game for Tassie as a 17-year-old and here I am again. At 38 I get to celebrate for the first time as my home state wins the coveted Sheffield Shield. It's a great feeling and I've had a good year, even knocking up a 200 in the game against NSW that followed my Mowbray visit.

Cricket is a cruel mistress and there she was at me again. I had started the summer in great form in first-class cricket and was the highest run-scorer going into the series against South Africa that would be my last. I felt like my technique, my reflexes, my game were in the best place they had ever been, but when it came time to wear the baggy green I could not make a run. So, going out and hitting a double hundred in the Shield a few months after I had literally landed on my face in Test cricket was a bitter irony, but a sure indication that there's an enormous mental element to this game. No matter how hard I tried — and believe me there is nobody who tries and trains harder than me — I couldn't put all the pieces back together at Test level.

It still hurts to admit I had lost it, but it felt good to end the season giving back to my home state, a place that had given so much but for most of my career had been so far away, so hard to get back to.

While Tasmania was winning the Shield competition Australian cricket seemed to be spiralling out of control during a series against India.

They'd barely missed a beat after I left. In my last game in Perth we had a chance to regain the number one rank in world cricket, but now that seemed so far away. In the first series they played after my retirement they easily accounted for a Sri Lankan side. My only contribution was a lap of honour at Bellerive before the Test.

After that things just seemed to go wrong and it was hard to watch. I know more than most how India can get on top of you. The cricket is like the country — it can be breathtaking, but at times it can close in on you and you feel like you are being smothered. It's easy to lose your way there and the Aussies did. I had never led a team to a series victory in India, but not only did they lose 4–0 on the field, they lost their way off it. The dressing room that I loved had changed in the past few years and as hard as it was to see how bad they were going out in the middle, it was just as hard knowing how much they were struggling off it.

I'd seen the signs. When we lost in Perth I went with the boys to have a drink with the South Africans and I was taken aback by the feeling they had in the sheds. Sure, it's easy to be happy when you've won so well, but they were a tight group, a small travelling band that had gelled together and taken down the enemy and as I looked at them enjoying the afterglow I was gripped with a sense of loss.

We used to be like that, I thought.

Everything has to change in cricket, but I'm not so convinced that all the changes I've seen in the past few years are for the better. I was in that Australian dressing room for 20 years and it seemed every time a legend left his corner another arrived to take that place. I saw Adam Gilchrist replace Ian Healy, and Stuart MacGill pick up a lazy 200 wickets when forced to play understudy to Shane Warne. I remember when a 30-year-old called Michael Hussey first got his shot at the big time and a young bloke called Michael Clarke came into the side.

Michael Clarke's got the captaincy now and it's fair to say that the trend that started in the last years of my time in the job has continued. First-class cricket just isn't bringing up the players, particularly batsmen, it once did. There was a time when guys with 10,000 first-class runs, guys who had scored century after century all around Australia and in England for counties, could not get a look-in. Sure there were a few, myself included, who came in young and relatively inexperienced, but we knew we were always under pressure for our places from others who had equal rights to them.

Anyway, I have to let that go now ...

FIRST INNINGS

*From Mowbray Eagles to
a baggy green*

The baggy green

The baggy green cap is the most powerful symbol in Australian sport. Nothing comes close to it for its tradition, meaning and representation. Only a small number of cricketers have played Test cricket for Australia and been presented with the baggy green. 365 cricketers achieved that honour before I made my Test debut in 1995. My Test cap number 366 is now almost part of my DNA.

Fewer than 450 cricketers have earned a baggy green since Test cricket began in 1877. That's quite phenomenal when you think how many Australians have dedicated their life to cricket but have never reached the level of playing Test cricket for Australia. This is what I've always talked about when presenting brand-new baggy green caps to players making their debut for Australia. You are joining a pretty elite group and have achieved a pinnacle of personal achievement in Australian cricket. You are now part of the baggy green family — an exclusive club. How lucky are we!

During my career, I had two baggy greens. My original cap was stolen out of my luggage on the way home from Sri Lanka in 1999. I'd only played 24 Tests at the time and I was gutted to think that the cap was gone. I was given a replacement baggy green that would stay with me right through to my last Test in Perth in 2012. It was a constant companion on and off the field. After losing my first cap, I carried my baggy green in my hand luggage wherever I went. It was with me in 144 Test matches all over the world and was looking pretty worse for wear when I retired from international cricket. There had been calls for me to change to a brand-new baggy green. Some said I was not treating the cap with the respect it demands, by wearing a faded, torn and out of shape baggy green on which you could hardly identify the Australian coat of arms on the front. But I am traditionalist and my baggy green tells a story — the story of my career. It reflects where I was, where I went and, in the latter years, how it was on its last legs — just like me. To me, my baggy green was a symbol of national pride, a monument to all my predecessors, team-mates and future Australian Test players, and a trophy for all the successes we achieved together. That baggy green was me.

Now it forms part of a very special presentation box that Rianna and the girls gave to me for my first Christmas as a retired international cricketer. It sits beside a brand-new baggy green with the most beautiful images of our family standing on the WACA after my last game. The new baggy green now symbolises the next stage of my life. A time of looking forward while never forgetting the incredible opportunities that 168 Test matches, with my baggy green, gave me.

CHAPTER 1

BACKYARD CRICKET

Launceston, Tasmania, the 1970s

MY NAME IS Ricky Thomas Ponting and I played cricket.

I played junior cricket, indoor cricket, club cricket, rep cricket, state cricket, T20 cricket, one-day cricket and Test cricket. When I didn't play cricket, I trained to play cricket. I played cricket almost everywhere cricket is played and with some of the greatest players there have ever been. I played in what might have been the best team the world has ever seen. I tried to be the best cricketer I could possibly be. I gave everything I had to that cause from the time I was a small boy until long after most of my contemporaries had walked away.

I was born in Launceston, Tasmania, a small town on a small island state that often gets left off the map of Australia. We're proud people who look after ourselves and who figure Hobart is the big smoke and the mainland is another country.

My early years were spent in the suburbs of Prospect and then Newnham, where we lived with my grandparents. When we could afford it, we moved to the housing estate at Rocherlea. I played cricket at school and then for the Mowbray Eagles, just like my dad and just like my Uncle Greg who was Mum's brother. People identify me with Mowbray and that's all right with me because that is where I learned the game.

I was born on December 19, 1974 to Graeme and Lorraine Ponting. My mum reckons I was a 'beautiful baby' but she might be biased. 'No trouble at all,' she tells me. 'Slept and ate, that's all you did.' One of her most prominent early memories of me is when I was sitting on the lounge-room floor, eyes fixed on the television, watching Kim Hughes bat. Kim was my first hero in Test cricket, a batsman who, when he was on, was unstoppable. I remember him taking on the West Indies at the MCG the week after my seventh birthday, their fast bowlers aiming at his chest and head, him hooking and pulling fearlessly. That knock stays burned in my memory and probably set the standard for the sort of cricketer I wanted to become. Australian cricket wasn't going so well then, but he stood up that day and scored 100 out of an innings total of 194. Holding, Roberts, Garner and Croft threw everything they had at him, but he was undefeated at the end of the innings and the Australians went on to win that match. That didn't happen all that often back then. There was no doubt in my mind, even then, that I wanted to be out there doing exactly the same.

One of Dad's early recollections of me is not as flattering as Mum's. 'When you were three, you used to wait out the front for the children walking home from school, and you'd run out and kick them and then run back inside,' he once told me. It was, he reckons, one of the first signs of my 'mischievous' streak. I'd like to think it showed I was never going to be intimidated by anyone older or bigger and for the next 20 years of my life I always seemed to be the youngest person in the room. I was the boy in the men's team, the 16-year-old at the cricket academy with Warnie who already had his own car and his own ways, the kid who was missing the final years at school to play first-class cricket, the 20-year-old walking onto the WACA to make my debut in Mark Taylor's team. Fortunately by then I'd stopped kicking the big kids in the leg …

I have a younger brother, Drew, and a sister, Renee, who is younger again. Today they both live within a couple of minutes of our parents' place. I'm the only one that went away.

Mum also has strong memories of me always being outside playing cricket as a boy. 'You always had to be the batsman and Drew had to bowl or field,' she says. 'You'd bat for an hour before Drew would get a bat. Then Drew would finally have a go, but he'd only last two minutes and you'd go back in.' My little brother was the first to suffer for my love. Most batsmen value their wicket, none like getting out, but I took it to an extreme and it all started in the backyard.

Like all kids we built the rules of cricket around the circumstances of our backyard. Over the fence was out and God help you if the old man caught you wading into his prized vegetable patch to fetch a ball. He loved that garden and it lay in wait from point to long-on, ready to swallow a ball. Drew reckons I mastered the art of hitting the ball over the garden and into the fence. I never let him bat for too long because it seemed part of the natural order of things that I was there doing what my hero, Kim Hughes, had done, although with all due respect to Drew he was no Michael Holding. I'd knock him over with my bowling as quick as I could and then take guard again. I have to admit Drew's ability to bowl endless overs was important to my development and I must thank him some time.

As a kid, growing up, I looked upon Mowbray as being a flash part of town.

We didn't come from the wrong side of the tracks so much as the wrong side of the river. Launceston is divided by the Tamar river, one side was middle class and nice and the other was where we lived. On our side they had the railway workshops, the factories and all the key landmarks of my early life — at the centre of which was the cricket club. In the Mowbray dressing rooms on a Saturday night they used to tell beery yarns about having to fight to cross the bridge into town, they weren't true but they told you a little bit about the 'us and them' nature of where I came from. Our greatest rivals were Riverside; they came from the nice part of town and sometimes complained that we played cricket too hard. It was a complaint I would hear on and off for a lot of my career, but I never heard them say we weren't playing fair or honestly.

My father was born in Pioneer, a mining village in the north-eastern tip of the island. His father, Charlie, was a tin miner who wanted a better life for his family so he worked two jobs, digging tin from the ground all week and then travelling to Launceston to dig foundations for houses on the weekends. With the money he made they moved to Newnham. They were people who knew a different life. Dad would tell stories about trapping rabbits and the like so they could eat, and I reckon that his enormous vegetable garden had something to do with that poor background.

The Pontings had arrived in Tasmania back in about 1890. My great great grandfather was a miner, his son was a miner and so was his son, my grandfather Charlie, but Charlie joined the RAAF when the war broke out and that might have changed things. He married Connie, my grandmother, during the war and sometime later they moved from Pioneer into Launceston and that was the last time our family dug for tin.

Pop kept greyhounds and Dad tells the story that he went to the races one night and an owner said to him, 'You want a dog? I've got one that's no good to me, it can't win a race.' Dad walked five kilometres home with the dog and put it under the house. Fed it some steak. His father said he couldn't keep it, but when Dad came home the next day his father had built a run across the back garden and it all started from there. The dog won its first race and we were away. Or that's how the story goes.

In Rocherlea Mum and Dad rented a small three-bedroom housing commission home on the bend at 22 Ti Tree Crescent. It was a cottage that had a nice front yard and a reasonable backyard dominated by Dad's vegetable garden. We were on the edge of town. It wasn't the best neighbourhood and always had a bad reputation — there were some houses that seemed to be visited by the police on a regular basis and I suppose there was a bit of trouble around but I avoided it. I can't ever remember our house being locked, which tells you a little bit about how life was.

We didn't have much money when I was growing up, but I never remember us wanting for anything. Dad left school early to pursue a life as a golf professional, which didn't work out. He was a great sportsman and I think the interest he took in my life was because he wanted me to have a chance to do the things he didn't. Dad was a good cricketer and footballer and a better golfer; I suppose you could say he was pushy, but that's probably too simplistic. Dad saw I was good and did the right thing by letting me know when I could be better. I always wanted to make him proud and never resented the way he encouraged me. He worked at the railways and other jobs, eventually finding his place as a groundsman. He didn't earn a lot but he loved — loves — the work. Mum and Dad's life revolved around us kids. Mum worked, but always made sure she or Dad was there for us when we were home. She was raised in Invermay and for most of our early lives she worked at the local petrol station there.

I sometimes think that if I hadn't dragged them to the odd game of cricket in the past 30 years that they might never have left Launceston.

From our house in Rocherlea, it was about two kilometres south to Mowbray Golf Club, a bit less than a kilometre further to the racecourse, and another kilometre closer to the city centre to get to Invermay Park, the former swampland that would become the home ground of the Mowbray Cricket Club in the late 1980s. That reclaimed land is why people from around this area have long been known as 'Swampies'.

I am extremely fortunate to have parents who love their sport. My mum represented Tassie at vigoro (a game not too dissimilar to cricket), played competitive badminton and netball, and later in life started playing golf because, as she explains it, her husband was always down at the clubhouse. Taking up the game was her best chance of seeing more of him.

Mum and Dad wanted their kids to be happy, humble, brave and honest. There was a toughness about where I was growing up and my parents never hid me from that, but neither did they use it as an excuse to let me run wild. I was sort of street-smart, and that and a combination of my parents' love for me and my addiction to all things sport kept me out of serious trouble. There was, though, a bit of rascal in my make-up. One evening I came home late, explaining that I'd been at a mate's place doing schoolwork, which was in itself a long bow. Worse, my shoes were covered in mud from the creeks at Mowbray Golf Club, where we'd been searching for lost balls that we could sell back to the members. I'll never forget how Dad belted me as he demanded that in future I tell the truth, and how the message sank in. At the same time, I couldn't believe how stupid I'd been, not cleaning my shoes before I got home.

Honesty was important to Dad and he passed that on.

I was never top of my class academically, but neither was I near the bottom. In Rocherlea, learning to stay out of trouble was as important as learning your times tables. Some might be surprised to learn I was a prefect for two of the years I was at high school. I suppose that shows that even at an early age I showed some hints that there was some leadership capabilities somewhere deep inside this sport-obsessed kid.

Sport was the making of me. From a very early age I knew I could hold my own at cricket or football, which gave me plenty of confidence and a lot of street cred with boys bigger and older than me. Because of the rules governing school sport in Tasmania at the time I didn't play any organised cricket or football until grade five at Mowbray Heights Primary School, when I was 10, and I didn't make my debut in senior Saturday afternoon cricket with the men at Mowbray until 1987, when I was 12. Before then, though, I did take part in some school-holiday coaching clinics, watched the Mowbray A-Grade team play and won a thousand imaginary Test matches against my little brother and whoever else we could recruit into neighbourhood contests.

There were other kids who might have had more material possessions, but living on the edge of town meant we had plenty of open space and in the days before laptops and the like we used it well. It could get icy in winter, but it's never too cold to kick a footy, and Dad found me a set of clubs when I wanted to hit a golf ball. If Drew and I could get down for a round of golf Mum would pack us a flask of cordial and give us enough money for a pack of chips and we were away. There was always cricket gear around the house and when a group of us went down to the local nets or park we always practised with a fair-dinkum cricket ball.

Mowbray boys learned not to flinch from an early age.

Being born in a small town had its advantages as everything was close and parents never needed to worry too much about where the kids were. If I was missing Mum or Dad just had to find the nearest game of cricket or footy and they were comfortable that even if I was in the sheds with the older blokes that they were all neighbours and friends and they were all keeping an eye on me. I had a BMX bike that I used to ride about town, and often to senior cricket matches involving the Mowbray club, my home team, Dad's old team, a club that in the years after it was formed in the 1920s used to get many of its players from the nearby railway workshops or the Launceston wharves. I started following them partly because I just loved the game, but also because my Uncle Greg was one of their best players.

Cricket fans know him as Greg Campbell. He's Mum's brother, 10 years older than me and a man who had a significant influence on my cricket career. Greg encouraged me all the way and spent a lot of time playing cricket with me, but more importantly he set an example. Looking back now I can see how important it was to know that someone from our family could make the big time, could go all the way from Launceston to Leeds, where he made his Test debut in the first Test against England in 1989. That was a huge day in our lives. Not only was Mum's brother bowling for Australia, another local hero, David Boon, was playing too. Our little town provided two Test players. It was like Launceston had colonised the moon, although in my world landing in the Australian cricket team was a bigger deal.

Having someone in the family who could do that made the dream of one day doing it myself all the more real. Here was a bloke in the side who had played cricket with me in the back garden. It meant Test cricket was a viable option for people like us. Greg nurtured my interest in cricket and we could get pretty competitive when we played each other. One day, when he thought I was out and I thought I wasn't, we had to go and ask Dad to come out and decide. The ruling went in Greg's favour, which didn't surprise me because he and Dad were best mates, to the point that when Dad coached the footy team at Exeter (a town 20 kilometres north of Launceston) one year, Greg went there and played as well. If there was one thing that could and still does get the men of our family into an argument it's sport. You should hear Dad and myself when a golf game is on the line. To an outsider these disputes might sound pretty serious. They're definitely earnest, but it's just our competitive nature and I suppose it was something that got me into hot water a few times over the years.

One of my strongest memories involving Greg is the day when Mum told me that his Ashes kit had arrived. I flew around on my bike to his house in Invermay to check it all out, to try on his baggy green cap and even his Australian blazer, which was many sizes too big but felt absolutely perfect. He was a hero of mine then and he remains a hero of mine today; he's a good friend who helped show me the way. Standing in that Launceston house dressed in his gear I knew there was only one way my life was going.

In the early and mid 1980s, when I started watching Greg and his team-mates at the Mowbray Eagles, they played their home games at the ground at Brooks High, the local high school at Rocherlea. Sometimes I'd be down there at nine in the morning, even though the game didn't start until 11. I just didn't want to miss anything. It was the same when I joined the team working the scoreboard at the Northern Tasmanian Cricket Association (NTCA) ground during Sheffield Shield games — I scored that gig after I rode my bike down to the ground, found the right person and asked for the job. They paid me $20 a day, but much more important than that, I had a bird's eye view of the game, the warm-ups, the net sessions, everything.

As I said earlier I loved to sit in the corner of the Mowbray A-Grade team's dressing room. Some of the tactical talks and most of the jokes went over my head, but at the same time I was absorbing plenty. I saw their loyalty and passion for each other and the game. Not least, I saw how those men played hard and fair, enjoyed the wins and hated the losses, wouldn't take crap from anyone and always sought to be friendly with the opposition once the game was done. Most times, that mateship was reciprocated and if it wasn't, we knew who the losers were. Those were lessons in cricket etiquette for me. The men set the standard and they said 'no matter what happens on the field you shake hands and you have a beer after the game'. It was a tradition in Australian Test cricket but one that all nations were keen on. Once it happened after every day's play, then it shifted to the end of the Test and later, because everything was so hectic, it became something that you did at the end of a tour. I know whenever we had a drink with the opposition after a series it was a positive experience. Arguments happened on the field and stayed there, relationships were built off it.

If Uncle Greg was my favourite, everyone else in the Mowbray dressing room was a star, too. I'd seen his fast-bowling partners, Troy Cooley and Roger Brown, bowling in the Sheffield Shield. Brad Jones, later my coach when I played for the Mowbray Under-13s, had played for Tasmania Colts. Richard Soule was the Tassie wicketkeeper. A standout was Mick Sellers, a strong burly left-hander who strode out to bat at the start of an innings and whacked the ball all over the place. He used a big Stuart Surridge Jumbo, four or five grips on the handle, batted in a cap and took on the fast bowlers *every* time. If there was ever a blueprint made of the classic Mowbray Cricket Club player it was Mick. He represented Tasmania in a few first-class and one-day games in the 1970s. He played over 400 games for Mowbray and was the club coach. After he retired, he would still be down at the ground, helping to roll the wicket, put on the covers, anything to help. He remains a legendary figure around the club. He was there, of course, when I came back at the end of my career.

He looked after me in those days when I was a constant in their dressing room. He got me involved when the time was right, and sheltered me at other times. In doing so, he taught me so much. They all did. They were kind and generous men. At the same time, everyone feared playing Mowbray; I could see that from the looks on the opposition's faces, what they said to each other while we were fielding. A game against Mowbray was a tough day at the office, plenty of words spoken, no quarter given. A lot of what you see in me today is a result of learning the game the way they used to play it. When we were truly at our best other sides hated playing Australia. South African cricket captain Graeme Smith admitted as much once, and while a lot of people took this the wrong way, to me and to the others in the side the point was we would not give an inch on the field.

After stumps, if Dad had come from golf to see how the boys had played, he would put down his beer, and bowl to me so I could try to mimic the shots I'd seen played earlier in the day. At home games, we used a big incinerator drum as the wicket and just the same as when they were bowling to me at school my ambition was to never get bowled. Dad was my first coach, at cricket and footy, and he could be a tough marker, but he wanted me to be a winner and I wouldn't have wanted it any other way.

Bravery

You often read or hear of the so-called bravery of sportspeople who overcome great adversity to win. I've certainly seen and been a part of some very brave sporting accomplishments over the years, but I must say that the use of the expression 'bravery' is completely overstated when you are witness to some real acts of bravery in everyday life. Rianna and I have met some of the bravest children and families in our work around the area of childhood cancer. The children, especially, move us. While they fight the most horrible disease in the world, they show incredible resilience to go through their treatment and hopefully survive. Without a doubt, it's even tougher for the families. Parents and grandparents continually ask the question: 'Why our child or grandchild?' They have to be brave for the child while maintaining a sense of normality to support siblings and other loved ones at a time that most of us cannot even start to imagine how difficult it must be. Some of the bravest families we have met had children who didn't survive the battle with cancer.

In our days of supporting the Children's Cancer Institute Australia, I stayed in regular contact with a number of children, exchanging text messages and keeping up to date with their progress. Those close to me know that I'm a bit slack at returning text messages but my contact with these children was different — I always made a point of answering straight away. Sadly, in many situations, a message would come through from parents letting me know their child didn't make it. Over the years, though, we have stayed in contact with many families whose children have survived. One very special child close to our hearts is Toby Plate from Adelaide. I first met Toby and his family on the eve of the Adelaide Ashes Test in 2010. During that series, I had a young cancer sufferer join me at each of the opening ceremonies. Of all the children I met that summer, Toby was the sickest — fighting a brain tumour and undergoing the most intensive treatment. We spent considerable time together that day and he left a lasting impression on me. The next day we stood together and sang the national anthem before the second Test began. Sadly not all the children who stood with me in the anthem ceremonies that summer survived their battle with cancer, but Toby did. We have stayed in touch and last year played cricket together at the MCG with Owen Bowditch, who was with me at the Boxing Day Test opening ceremony that summer. These boys and their families epitomise bravery for me. They are symbolic of what it means to overcome adversity. Not all the stories have a happy ending but the bravery shown by each and every child that is confronted by cancer is overwhelming, to say the least.

CHAPTER 2

PLAYING WITH DAD

Mowbray, 1987–88

MOST KIDS PLAY CRICKET with their fathers in the backyard, but where we came from there was a bit of a tradition of the fathers dropping down in the grades to guide their sons through. We never had a big partnership, but I loved the year I played with my old man.

Dad retired from weekend cricket to concentrate on his golf well before I played my first serious game, but after a number of seasons on the sidelines he was talked into making a comeback, the lure being the chance to play with his son. Up until this time I had played a little at school and some indoor cricket, but all the while I was waiting to join the men and that's what I did on the eve of my 13th birthday.

We were both in the thirds at the start of the 1987–88 season. Dad was captain, I was a tiny but promising novice who struggled to hit the ball off the square. My technique was pretty good, but lofted shots were risky because I was never sure I could get the ball over the fielders' heads and there was just not enough power in my arms to play a forcing shot through the field. Still, Dad put me up near the top of the order, reasoning the experience would be good for me, and eventually the day came when he walked out proudly to bat with me at the other end. It was a home game against South

24

Launceston. Just like my favourite players — Launceston's own David Boon, former Australian captain Kim Hughes and the then Aussie skipper Allan Border — did in the Test matches I watched so avidly on television, I sauntered down the pitch before Dad faced a ball, to tell him the leg-spinner who was bowling, a bloke named Matthew Dillon, was getting a bit of turn.

'Just be careful for a little while,' I suggested. I was all of 12 years old. 'Don't play across the line because he's getting a bit of turn.'

The first delivery was handled without a problem, but the second ball Dad went for the big shot and skied a simple catch to cover. I was really disappointed and a bit dirty that he'd thrown his wicket away, but thinking about it now, I guess this might have been the first time I saw what pressure can do on a cricket field — we'd talked so much about what it would be like to bat together, how we really wanted to have a decent partnership, and that seemed to be what Dad was thinking about rather than just playing each ball on its merits. At least that's what we decided at the inquisition after stumps and it says something about the way we were that we sat down and analysed what went wrong. Ironically, in the matches that followed, it was me, not Dad, who struggled to make a big score. At season's end, he was top of the competition for batting aggregates and averages, and having guided me through my first year, he promptly retired for good so he could get back to playing golf all weekend.

I think part of his motivation to come back was simply to protect me, because he knew what senior grade cricket in Launceston could be like. I was sledged more in my first season with Mowbray than I would ever be sledged again in my life. I'd developed a bit of a reputation as a 'young gun' and some old blokes seemed very keen to put me in my place. There were a number of guys playing third grade who were in a similar boat to Dad — older, former top-grade players who were now helping young guys out and at the same time were eager to 'educate' teenage opponents who stood out. Old bulls out to slow the young bulls down and teach them a thing or two about how the game should be played. It was a time-honoured tradition and one that we might have got away from a little now in the select streams of Australian cricket where the best young players are channelled off into age competitions or lured by scholarships to private schools where they only get to play against people their own age.

You can get put back in your place fairly quickly playing against cranky old blokes who played their first game before you were born. Respect is earned in these scenarios and if you have the talent and character to survive you come out a better cricketer and a better person. I got fearsome sledgings on a few occasions; one that stands out was the wicketkeeper from Riverside who had played some representative cricket a few years earlier and now gave me an almighty serve on their home ground after I made the mistake of responding to something he'd muttered from behind the stumps. If I'd been out of line, Dad would have said so. Instead, he got into this keeper and the language was pretty full-on.

Most weeks someone tried to knock my head off, but nothing about playing with the men harmed me. Some people keep their kids away from real cricket balls and some talent streams lock them into playing in their age groups for fear they will be roughed up and mentally scarred. Fortunately I had no fear and came through unscathed. Indeed, the value of playing against cricketers twice, even three times, my age shone through in the January of that season, when I played for Mowbray in the Northern Under-13 Cricket Week — I scored four separate hundreds in the space of five days, all of them undefeated. To me the other team were just like Drew and there was no way they were going to get me out. It was a simple game in those years — you were either in or out and it was obvious who you were competing with; with age comes the doubts and mental struggles that all sportsmen face.

Apparently at one point during this tournament a few of the parents became a little agitated because their kids weren't getting a bat, so Dad suggested to our coach, Brad Jones, that he give someone else a go. Brad disagreed, saying he'd sort it out later. 'I didn't think it warranted this kid who loved the game so much being denied the chance of batting just because some parents wanted to watch their kid bat,' he recalled when interviewed a couple of years back.

Two weeks later, I was picked in Mowbray's team for the final game in the Northern Under-16 Cricket Week and made another ton, which was enough for me to be selected in the NTCA's Under-16s training squad and the Tasmanian Institute of Sport Under-19 squad, and for me to get my picture in the paper for the first time, alongside an article that was headlined: 'Ricky's Making a Big Hit in Cricket Circles'.

From that time on, I never really thought about a working career outside of sport. When people asked me what I was going to do for a living, I'd reply, 'Play cricket.' I think they thought I was joking, but I was very serious.

I was a student at Brooks High School, Rocherlea, by this stage, and one day at school I was interviewed by journalist Nigel Bailey. Today, the story is stuck in Mum's scrapbook and my responses are exactly what you'd expect from a 13-year-old grade-eight student terrified of embarrassing himself. When asked if I'd like to play for Australia, I replied, 'I'd love to play for Australia.' When Nigel asked me if David Boon was a hero, I responded, 'I look up to David Boon because he's from here.' And that was about it, except when I was asked what I liked to do outside of cricket.

'I like to fish for trout with my dad,' I said.

THE FIRST TIME I threw a line in the water occurred during school holidays at Musselroe Bay, a village on Tasmania's far north-east coast, where my grandparents had a caravan and we'd stay at one of the campsites. Quite often, Dad's sister and her kids used to come up as well and other relatives of Dad's had a shack a couple of minutes down the road, so family gatherings could be huge. You had to drive through old Ponting country to get there, the road running through the town of Pioneer which always had Dad telling stories as we drove.

Getting there was half the fun. Dad had a few cars when we were young and none of them were very flash. There was an old Holden, a Ford Cortina and a Toyota Cressida he bought when he got laid off from the railways. My grandparents had a station wagon and would take most of our gear in the back of that. We'd squash into the family car and hold our breath most of the way, just hoping it would get us there.

In Musselroe I'd watch the Boxing Day Tests on a little black-and-white portable TV, sitting on a couch or lying on the floor. I can remember Dennis Lillee bowling off his long run, Allan Border wearing down the opposition and Kim Hughes playing a brand of cricket that I hoped to emulate one day. At other times we'd go out on Pop's little dinghy fishing for salmon. My childhood memories are of us never failing to bring back at least enough food for dinner that night. These were the happiest days of my childhood.

If we weren't fishing, opening Christmas presents or watching Test matches at Musselroe Bay, the odds were I was involved in a sporting activity of some kind. A couple named Sue and Darrel Filgate had a shack on a large, well-grassed block of land, and it was nothing for me to play cricket all day in summer with the Filgates' two sons, Darren and Scott, who were around the same age as me. There were days when I'd bounce out of bed in the morning, have a slice of Vegemite toast for breakfast, and then be gone for the day. Often, one or more of Mum, Dad, Nan or Pop had to come up to the Filgates' house to get me for dinner, because I had no sense of time when we were on holidays, especially if I was batting.

I thought I was going okay and Nan obviously agreed with me. Around the time of my 10th birthday, it could have been Christmas 1984, she gave me a T-shirt that featured an ambitious message: 'Inside this shirt is a future Test cricketer'. A few people had a friendly go at me whenever they saw that shirt, whether it was that

Christmas or in the next few that followed. To tell you the truth, I couldn't see a problem.

UNTIL I WAS 13, most of the organised cricket I played was at school or indoors. Wherever I played I made sure bowlers worked hard if they were ever going to be rid of me. Drew wasn't the only one who suffered. I don't think I was dismissed in my two years of cricket at Mowbray Heights Primary and I do recall that in grade six they introduced a limit on how long anyone could bat — if a batsman reached 30, he had to retire — to stop me from batting all the time.

Our coach was also the umpire and the scorer too, so whenever I was at the bowler's end I'd ask him, 'How many am I?' My plan was to get to 29 and then aim for the boundary so I'd finish unconquered on 33 or 35. The indoor games were played at the Waverley Area Cricket Arena, at St Leonards in south-east Launceston, known across town as the WACA. I was our team's wicketkeeper. Dad was captain.

I played a lot of indoor cricket, including some big games in Hobart representing the WACA. I loved it, but my old man wasn't so keen on me playing so much because he thought it was bad for my outdoor cricket. The key to indoor cricket is to push the ball into the side netting, which meant we were always hitting across the line. 'You can't play straight in indoor cricket,' he'd sneer, because a drive back to the bowler could lead to a run out if the batsman at the non-striker's end (who was always looking for a quick single) backed up too far. He was right, of course, and eventually I gave the game away for that reason.

THE FIRST 'SERIOUS' BAT I ever owned was a Duncan Fearnley size five that Dad bought for me from a local sports store. Then, one day not long after my 10th birthday, Dad and I went along to watch the Mowbray Under-13 team in action. Within minutes of arriving, we learned they were one player short, because someone had dropped out at the last minute. It was my big chance and not one I hadn't fantasised about. The people at the club were aware I was keen and they knew I could hold a bat and catch and throw, and as there was no one else available, I was drafted in, batting last and with no chance of getting a bowl. I was the most excited kid in the world.

In our first innings I made one not out, but we were soundly beaten and the other team sent us back in, even though there was little chance of an outright result. I had the pads on and the coach said I could go in again if I wanted to, an invitation I wasn't going to knock back. While I was waiting for the umpires to take us out Dad came over and said quietly, 'If you can get to 20, I'll buy you a new cricket bat.'

Years later, this was the knock Dad recalled when he was asked if there was a moment when he realised I was going to be a good batsman. I wasn't much taller than the stumps but I knew how to play straight and I could leg glance and push the ball between the fieldsmen at mid-wicket and mid-on for a single. I certainly wasn't scared. In the end, it was more a matter of whether I'd get to 20 before sunset, but I made it and by the following Saturday I had my Gray-Nicolls 'Super Scoop', a David Hookes signature. A year later, I was given some County gear — a bat, gloves and pads after impressing the right people at indoor cricket — but the Scoop remained my favourite bat until, in early 1988, on the back of those hundreds in the Under-13 and Under-16 Cricket Weeks, I was signed up by Kookaburra, whom I've been with ever since.

This sponsorship deal was instigated by a gentleman named Ian Young, a man who became a family friend. Youngy was the hardest working bloke I've ever met, someone who was passionate about everything he did. I first ran into him when I got the part-time job as a scoreboard attendant at the NTCA ground, where he was the curator, but he really came into my life early in my first season playing for Mowbray. One night when we were using the indoor nets at the NTCA ground, he stopped to watch me bat and then came up to me afterwards and offered to help me out.

Youngy had already devoted a lifetime's worth of work to the game, as a player, mentor and administrator, and now here he was — clad in his King Gee work pants, steel-capped boots and big flannelette shirt — meeting me at Invermay Park on Saturday mornings after he'd worked on his pitches in the early hours, to bowl at me for over after over, all because he believed I was a good cricketer in the making. Not long after, he was appointed coach at Mowbray and our bond grew tighter. If he ever rang and said, 'Let's go have a hit,' I'd be on my way. I'd bat, he'd bowl; as I remember my childhood, he was *always* around to throw balls at me or bowl to me. But he never forced me to go to practice; in those days, I would have batted all day every day if I could have. As long as I worked hard, greeted him with a firm handshake and looked him straight in the eye and listened when he spoke to me — that was all he wanted. When it came to batting technique, he was big on the simple stuff: play as straight as you can and wait for the ball. For me, the biggest buzz was simply that someone of his stature was taking such an interest in me; that he cared as much as Mum and Dad did.

Youngy always stood out in the crowd, and not just because he was a tall bloke. He was confident, assertive, never short of a word but always talking sense. It was so good to have him on my side. He was a coach who, if he saw a problem, he tried to fix it and he was happy to work and work until things were right. He taught me the value of a good work ethic. He'd been an outstanding bowler in his day, and if I made a mistake in the nets on a cover drive, you could guarantee the next ball he'd bowl would pitch in the same spot, to give me the chance to do it better.

Sometimes when he got tired Youngy would invite me back to the indoor nets, where he would feed one of the bowling machines so I could keep working on my technique. Often, we were joined by his youngest son Shaun, who was four-and-a-half years older than me and played his cricket with South Launceston. Two other sons, Claye and Brent, were also excellent cricketers. Claye even opened the bowling for Tasmania one season with Dennis Lillee. Shaun, a gifted all-rounder, and I would play plenty of Shield cricket together and in an Ashes Test at the Oval in 1997, an event that prompted the Launceston *Examiner* to organise a photo of two proud fathers, Ian and Graeme, which they put on the front page of the paper.

In 1988, Youngy was good mates with a bloke named Ian Simpson who was working for Kookaburra at that time, and he told him, 'There's a kid down here who looks like he might be all right.' I was introduced to Ian soon after, when he was in Tassie for the Kookaburra Cup final and about a week later, a kit, complete with bat, gloves and pads, landed on our front door.

As the story goes, Ian Simpson went back to Melbourne and told Rob Elliot, the boss at Kookaburra, 'We've got this kid down in Tassie we've got to look after. I've sent him some gear already.' Rob, who is a terrific bloke but who can be tough to deal with, snarled back, 'Why don't you go back to the local prep school and find a few more kids. We'll sign 'em all up!'

I'd like to think the deal I signed turned out to be a pretty good one for Kookaburra, but Ian Simpson left the company soon after, and within a few weeks he was actually mowing the lawns at the Kookaburra warehouse. Not that he was bitter about this development — his first venture after leaving the cricket-gear business was to take on a 'Jim's Mowing' franchise, which worked out very well for him. One of his clients was Kookaburra and no one greeted him more warmly, if they crossed paths, than Rob Elliot.

I obviously made a good impression in those days. Around that time Tasmanian ABC cricket commentator Neville Oliver told a reporter from the *Examiner* newspaper: 'We've got a 14-year-old who's better than Boon — but don't write anything about him yet, it's too much pressure.'

Back then, I continued working with Ian Young and our bond remained as strong as ever until he passed away, aged 68, in October 2010. He was always a fantastic friend and one of my strongest supporters. I was playing a Test match at Bangalore in

India when Ian died and was on the flight home when he was laid to rest in Launceston. On that plane I had plenty of time to think about everything he taught me, about batting, leadership and life. Like just about everyone connected with the Mowbray club, he was big on loyalty, big on sticking with your mates and on looking after each other. And I thought about his ability to cut to the core of a problem but then help you find the correct answer for yourself, rather than just giving advice and hoping you understood. Wherever I was in the world, he would always call me if he thought he'd spotted something about my game that wasn't quite right, and because he knew my technique so well his advice was inevitably on the money. But I was only one of a great number of promising cricketers he helped on and off the field, which is one of the reasons, in the days after he died, so many people referred to him as a 'champion' and a 'legend'.

The last time I caught up with Ian Young was when we arranged to meet at a restaurant located, appropriately enough, just across the road from Invermay Park. The thing that sticks with me of that final meeting was how we greeted each other: I looked him straight in the eye and gave him a firm handshake, no differently to how we did it when I was just a little kid, all those years ago.

Missing Youngy's funeral because of the demands of cricket was hard, but that was the nature of the job. From an early age the game took me away from the people who introduced me to it and made me the person I am. I did get used to it but I can honestly say it never got any easier, in fact as I got older it got harder but I suppose that's just the way life goes. I know I wouldn't have swapped my lot for anything and I know I was doing something that people like Mum, Dad, Youngy and so many others wanted for me.

Still, it would have been nice to have been there for someone who'd always been there for me.

Family

Words can never express how grateful I am for the upbringing my family gave me. My childhood memories are always front of mind for me and are detailed in the early chapters of this book. They are special memories that have become even more important to me as I have travelled around the world.

The toughest part of leaving home and becoming a professional cricketer was the disconnect from my family back in Launceston. When I first moved away, I didn't realise that my cricket journey would end some 23 years later when I was married with two children and settling down in a new home in Melbourne. But that's now a reality for me and I can't wait to re-connect with the family back in Tasmania. That might sound quite dramatic, but a recent phone call from Dad reinforced the sometimes remoteness of our relationship. 'So I can call you again now!' Dad said with a cheeky chirp in his voice. You see, when I was overseas, Dad would never call me on my mobile. If he or Mum needed me, they'd get Drew or Renee to text or call me and I'd phone home. But that was very unusual. I'd keep up to date with how things were at home through regular texts and infrequent calls from Drew and Renee.

The opportunity to go home was dictated by my cricket schedule. A game in Tassie meant I might squeeze in a quick trip home or more likely, the family would come to Hobart to watch me play and we would catch up for dinner. But that's behind me now, and our move to Melbourne means I'm only an hour away from Launceston.

When I left home, my little sister, Renee, was only nine years of age. Now she is married to Greg, has two children, Thomas and Macey, and we are closer than ever before. My little brother, Drew, has also grown up from our backyard cricket games and is married to Krysta. They also have two children, Josh and Chloe.

Growing up, there was quite a bit of routine in our family. A lot of this hasn't changed, especially around games of golf, family outings and celebrating special occasions. I'm longing to slip back into that routine now and enjoy more time together. No doubt there will be a lot more family golf games ahead, too.

CHAPTER 3

OUT OF TASMANIA

Bloemfontein, South Africa, March 17, 1992

THE WORLD WAS WATCHING South Africa in early 1992 as the country decided if it should end years of white rule and the apartheid system. And, so was I, but from a lot closer than you would think. I had arrived in the country a week before with a side from the Cricket Academy and the day we played Orange Free State in Bloemfontein was the day white South Africans were asked to decide if the process of ending apartheid and sharing power should continue or not. We had our bags packed sweating on the outcome of what may have been the most significant referendums of the 20th century. If it had been defeated we would have been straight out of there and the ban on sporting ties with the country would have resumed. I was all of 17 and learning fast that cricket soon takes you right out of your comfort zone.

It was a long way from Launceston, but life was moving fast. So let me just take you back a step.

ONE OF THE THINGS I remember most clearly about my early games with Mowbray thirds was how big the grounds were and how I often felt as if I couldn't hit the ball out of the infield. My lack of size and power held me back for a while, and it wasn't until near the end of my second season that I was promoted to the A-Reserves — for the grand final, no less — when I was chosen as a specialist No. 8 batsman. It was a bit of luck really. Someone was injured, but you weren't allowed to bring a player back from A-Grade for the A-Reserve final, so they picked me primarily for my fielding. All the indoor games, the fielding practice and the hours my mates and I had spent in the vacant land across the road from home and in the nearby park and surrounding scrub, not just throwing and catching cricket and tennis balls, but also throwing rocks at targets like telegraph poles and tree stumps and, occasionally, each other, had turned me into a pretty fair fielder for my age.

I batted for almost three hours in that final, playing one defensive shot after another, though occasionally I'd tuck one down to fine leg for a single or maybe a quickly run two. It can't have been much fun to watch. A tattered newspaper clipping in one of Mum's scrapbooks describes my knock this way: 'Mowbray was struggling at 6–114 against Riverside in the A-Reserve grand final at the Coca-Cola Ground before 14-year-old Ricky Ponting came to the rescue … the nephew of Tasmania's latest Australian tourist Greg Campbell was finally out with the score at 9–246. Ponting scored 30 in 163 minutes at the crease in his A-Reserve debut. He combined with former state paceman Roger Brown for an eighth-wicket partnership of 65 in 76 minutes and with Ross Clark for 36 in 34 for the ninth.'

Having taken the best part of two seasons to earn a promotion to the A-Reserves, I promptly made my A-Grade debut for Mowbray at the start of the following summer, and in my very first game I snared what might have been the best catch I ever took. Troy Cooley, a Tasmanian opening bowler (and later the bowling coach for England and Australia), was bowling and Richard Bennett, a Tasmanian opening bat, was facing. I was pumped just to be playing. Troy, who was as quick as anyone in his day, bowled a full wide one and Bennett played a half slash, half cover drive, and I dived full length and caught it above eye-height, one handed. Before I knew it, everyone had a hold of me.

I'll also never forget a one-dayer against Riverside, when I came to the wicket at 5–44 chasing 147 and with our wicketkeeper, Richard Soule, put on 91 runs to win with little more than an over to spare. To bat in that situation with Richard, a former Australian Under-19 gloveman who'd been Tassie's Shield keeper since taking over from Roger Woolley in 1985, was thrilling and enlightening, especially the way he stayed calm and smart when the pressure was at its fiercest.

When Richard was away playing state cricket that season, Clinton Laskey took over as keeper, but Clinton had to miss our game against Old Scotch that year, which created my one and only chance to wear the keeper's gloves in an A-Grade match. I was up for anything in those days. I think there was even a suggestion on one of my first tours as part of the Australian squad that I could act as reserve keeper if necessary.

You learn on the job in cricket and I was blessed to get an apprenticeship among such good players. I can't remember now if it seemed strange, but a lot of those guys were so much older than me and so much bigger. If Launceston hadn't been such a small town the other sides would have mistaken me for the team mascot, but word got around pretty quick that I was a young bloke with a bit of talent. Naturally the opposition saw this as an invitation to take me down a peg or two. I can't blame them for that and probably should thank them.

Not long after that experience, I was on a plane to Adelaide for the Australian Under-17s championships, my first interstate tour. It's funny, when I think of all the flights I have been on to all parts of the world since then, how the excitement I felt that day — packing my bag, driving to the airport, checking in, eating on the plane — remains in my memory. Dad was team manager, which was reassuring, because if there was something I wasn't certain about (and there was plenty) I could ask him without fear of being embarrassed, but it also meant I had to stay firmly in line *all* the time. On the field, we defeated South Australia and the Northern Territory, and held our own against the ACT and Queensland.

Cricket was consuming my adolescence. I was easily the youngest guy in the Under-17 squad, and then midway through the year, still six months short of my 16th birthday, I was included in the Tasmanian Sheffield Shield team's winter training squad. I was one of 60 players chosen and it was weird to see my name in the paper alongside prominent Test and Shield cricketers like David Boon, Dirk Wellham, Greg Shipperd, Dave Gilbert, Greg Campbell and Peter Faulkner. I had to grow up quickly, and maybe the men at Mowbray Cricket Club were teaching me a lesson of sorts when early in the 1990–91 season they spiked my one can of beer with vodka. Having had a good laugh at my expense, they then dropped me on our front doorstep, which I'm sure didn't impress my parents at all. But even this time, Mum and Dad knew that when I was with the cricketers I was safe, and if they ever needed to find me they knew exactly where I'd be. Not all parents in Rocherlea could say that about their 14- or 15-year-old sons.

I PLAYED MY LAST full season of football in 1990, the end coming abruptly when I broke my right arm just above the elbow while playing in the Under-17s for North Launceston. The doctors had to put a pin in my arm, which stayed there for 16 weeks and meant I missed the early part of the following cricket season. By this stage of my life, I was confident cricket was my future, so it wasn't hard to give the footy away, on the basis that it wasn't worth risking an injury that might end my sporting dream. I think Dad would have stopped me anyway, if I'd tried to keep playing.

Earlier in that 1990 season, not long after I captained the Northern team at the Under-17 state carnival, I was asked to answer a series of questions for our club newsletter. Mum stuck my responses in her scrapbook …

Player Profile
Name: *Ricky Ponting*
Position: *Wing*
Occupation: *Student, Brooks High School*
Ambition: *To play cricket for Australia*
Favourite AFL club/player: *North Melbourne/John Longmire and John McCarthy*
Favourite TFL club/player: *North Launceston/Todd Spearman and Marcus Todman*
Favourite ground: *York Park*
Other sports: *Cricket, Golf*
Favourite food: *Kentucky Fried Chicken*
Girlfriend: *No one (they give me the poops!)*
Dislikes: *Hawthorn and Essendon supporters*
Most embarrassing moment: *Getting dropped from senior firsts to the seconds at school after being the captain the week before!*

TWO WEEKS IN THE MIDDLE of winter in 1991 changed not just my cricket career but the way my life evolved. I had been selected in the Australian Under-17 development squad following the 1990–91 Under-17 championships in Brisbane, which led to me receiving specialised coaching from two cricket legends: Greg Chappell and Barry Richards.

I left school at the end of Year 10. It was a big move I suppose, but it was pretty clear to everyone by then that cricket was the only thing I cared about. Ian Young got me a job as part of the ground staff at Scotch Oakburn College, one of Launceston's most respected independent schools, located to the immediate south-east of the city centre, and that job confirmed for me that a life in sport was what I really wanted. Then it happened: I spent a fortnight at the Australian Institute of Sport's Cricket Academy in Adelaide courtesy of a scholarship from the Century Club, a group of cricket enthusiasts based in Launceston who had come together in the

1970s with the aim of fostering the game and its players in Northern Tasmania. It is impossible to underrate what that scholarship meant to me and my life.

The Cricket Academy, a joint initiative of the Institute of Sport and the Australian Cricket Board (now Cricket Australia), had been officially opened in 1988. Its policy was to invite the country's best young cricketers, most of them Under-19 players, to work together and learn from some of the game's finest coaches.

The Australian Under-19 team was touring England at the time, which meant there were very few Academy cricketers in Adelaide when another top Tasmanian junior, Andrew Gower, and I arrived.

There had recently been some major organisational changes at the Academy, the most notable being the appointment of the former great Australian wicketkeeper Rod Marsh as head coach. Rod had only been there a couple of months and I can imagine he was battling through any number of administrative issues, so the chance to work with a couple of keen young Tasmanians would have been a godsend for him. He took a genuine interest in us and I quickly came to realise he is a bloke who is very easy to talk to and he knows an amazing amount about our game. We were both in our element: Rod, the wily old pro, encouraging and teaching; me, shy but fiercely determined, listening and learning.

One thing Rod said to us during my first full year in Adelaide has always stayed with me, 'If you blokes aren't good enough to score 300 runs in a day you can all pack up your bags and go home now.' That was the style of cricket he wanted us to embrace, but it wasn't the style of cricket you saw too often in Test matches back in the early 1990s. Rod was perceptive enough to realise that assertive cricketers were coming to the fore, that the game needed to be entertaining if it wanted to survive, and that we — the players of the future — needed to be ready for this revolution. Simply put, he was ahead of his time.

Andrew was a very promising leg-spinner from the South Launceston club. While he never made an impact in first-class cricket he did build up an imposing record in Launceston club cricket, spending a number of years at Mowbray as our captain–coach. As teenagers, we played a lot of junior outdoor and indoor cricket together (I first met him at the Launceston WACA), and even after I'd faced Shane Warne I thought Andrew had the best wrong'un and top-spinner I'd seen. In the years to come, he'd do very well in business, and only recently bought a pub, the Inveresk Tavern, not far from Mowbray's home ground, Invermay Park. It's a small town, Launceston, and before Andrew and I went to the Academy together, Dad and I used to go to the Inveresk most Thursday nights, to have a wager or two (I was betting in 50-cent and one-dollar units) on the local greyhound meetings.

For our first two weeks in Adelaide, Andrew and I lived in a room at the Seaton Hotel, which was located out near the Royal Adelaide Golf Club, right next to a railway line (which meant we could never get any sleep) and not too far from the state-of-the-art indoor facilities at the Adelaide Oval.

During my first day at the Adelaide Oval indoor nets, Andrew and I were introduced to a strapping young pace bowler from Newcastle, Paul 'Blocker' Wilson, who had quit his job as a trainee accountant and apparently had been hassling Rod for weeks about getting an opportunity at the Academy. Beaten down by the bloke's persistence, Rod had agreed to give Paul a try-out, which was at this time, and I was the bunny nominated to face the best he could offer. I guess in a way we were both on trial. The first ball was a quick bumper, and I did the same as I would have done if one of Mowbray's senior quicks, say Troy Cooley, Scott Plummer or Roger Brown, had pinged one in short at practice: I hooked him for four. The next one was even quicker and a bit shorter, and according to Rod, Blocker ran through the crease and delivered it from a lot closer than he should have, but I smashed him again. Later, Blocker and I became good mates, but now he was filthy on the little kid who was threatening to ruin his Academy adventure before it even began.

I had no fear about getting hit in the head — at this moment, when I was batting in a cap — or at any stage in my life. This was true when Ian Young was teaching me the basics of batting technique, when I was 13 playing against 16-year-olds, when I was 15 playing for A-Grade against men, at the Academy taking on Blocker or the bowling machine, or later in my cricket life when I was up against the fastest bowlers in the game, like Pakistan's Shoaib Akhtar or the West Indies' Curtly Ambrose. I had to try and find a way to hold my own. I'm not sure I could have done that if I was frightened, even a little. The combination of no fear and a lot of quality practice is why I ended up being a reasonable back-foot player.

After those two weeks at the Academy in 1991, it was impossible for me not to think very seriously about my chances of playing for Tasmania and Australia. The Academy had been formed in 1987 and guys who had gone there before me had been some of the stars of recent Under-17 and Under-19 Australian championships. By the winter of 1991, 23 graduates had played Sheffield Shield cricket, including Shane Warne (Victoria) and Damien Martyn (Western Australia), who had made their respective Shield debuts while working at the Academy in 1990–91. No one had made the Australian team as yet, but it was just a matter of time. Perhaps the best bet for this elevation was Michael Bevan, who had made such an impact in 1989–90 he forced a rule change — back then, the Academy guys living in Adelaide could be selected in the South Australian Shield team, but when the NSW authorities saw Bevan (who was actually from Canberra, but in reality a NSW player) making a hundred for another state instead of them they quickly decided it wasn't right. By 1990–91, Academy cricketers were playing for their home state. I'm extremely glad the change was made, because the only cap I ever wanted to wear in Australian domestic cricket was the Tassie one.

It felt as if I got years' worth of tuition in those two weeks and they obviously liked what they saw because I was invited back in 1992 to join the two-year program. I was leaving home.

For the first half of my first full year at the Academy, we lived in serviced units called the 'Directors Apartments' in Gouger Street, not far from the city centre, where we ate pub meals every day — chicken schnitzel and chips for lunch and something equally exotic for dinner. We moved to the Del Monte Hotel at Henley Beach halfway through the year and that's where we lived until the end of my second year.

In January 1992 I was part of Tasmania's Under-19 squad at the Australian championships, even though I was still eligible for the Under-17s, and after I scored a few runs Rod was on ABC Radio describing me as 'a heck of a good player' and adding, 'He has a big future in the game if he keeps his head and keeps learning. He has a very good technique and appears to have an old head on young shoulders.' Rod also made a point of praising the Tasmanian selectors for picking me in the Under-19s, saying, 'Too often young players are pigeon-holed by age group instead of being allowed to play to their full potential.'

I'm sure there were some who thought I was being fast-tracked ahead of my time, but in my view my progress through Tasmanian cricket was handled fantastically well by the local administrators. There was always a suspicion where I came from that while many of the best cricketers were from the north of the state, many of the most influential officials were based in Hobart, but I never had any hurdles unnecessarily put in front of me just because I was from Launceston. Maybe the facilities and practice wickets in my home town weren't always as good as those available to the young cricketers in Hobart and on the mainland, but that might have made me a better player rather than worse. The truth is I was encouraged at every level in Tassie. After that, the success of Launceston's own David Boon at Test and one-day international (ODI) level (by 1992 he was as important as anyone in the Australian batting order) and the fact I'd gone through the Cricket Academy, paved the way for me to get a fair shot at the Australian team.

I WAS BACK ON the mainland in February 1992 to represent the Cricket Academy in one-day games against the South African and Indian teams preparing for the 1992 World Cup which was held in Australia and New Zealand, and this was when I came across a batsman I would get to know well over the next 20 years.

We'd spent a morning practising at the Adelaide Oval and were supposed to go back home for lunch but I asked for permission to stay. I wanted to see this Sachin Tendulkar who everyone was talking about, and I took up a position behind the nets while he had a bat. It's fair to say I was going to watch him bat for a long time to come, but that day I was studying his technique, trying to see what it was about him.

And then I was named in a 13-man Academy team that toured South Africa in March.

My head, as you can imagine, was spinning. One day I was walking out to bat for Mowbray, then I was being fitted for junior Tasmanian representative teams, flying to the Academy, flying back for more and then I was being fitted for an Australian team uniform. It might have been only the Under-19s but I was an *Australian* cricketer. Most of the side gathered at Sydney airport; by now I was getting used to all this flying business. We met up with the Western Australian players in Perth and then were met by officials from the United Cricket Board of South Africa in Johannesburg before jumping on the team bus emblazoned with our team name to go to our first team hotel. I didn't want the experience to end in a hurry and looking back I guess it didn't for a long time to come. Most of my adult life has been taken up by such journeys.

On that journey from the airport to our flash hotel, I saw squalor, I saw suburbia and then I saw a city that didn't look too different at first glance from the big cities back home. I'm sure there was much to discover if I ventured out from our hotel, but we'd been told to be very careful if we did go out — these were tense times in Johannesburg — which only reinforced something I'd already decided: I'd stick with the group whenever possible and at other times stay close to home base as often as I could. And to think people thought Rocherlea was hard core ...

In retrospect, it seems a bit amazing that the Australian Cricket Board sent a youth team to South Africa at such a critical time in that nation's history. The country was still governed by a white administration, and no official senior team had gone there in more than 20 years. I was an uncomplicated sports-mad kid from Tassie, so almost all of the politics went over my head, but it was obvious this was a country going through a painful period of change. There was a tension about the place. I can still remember a coaching clinic in Soweto just a week before the referendum in which the white population was asked whether they supported reforms that would eventually lead to fully democratic elections. The enthusiasm, natural ball skills and hand–eye coordination of the kids in that township were special, but the referendum was what everyone was talking about. It was hard even for us not to realise how big this thing was — we'd been told that if the vote went against change, we'd be out of the country on the first available plane. I hadn't been thinking of all those victims of apartheid; I was thinking only of myself.

Cricketers are not politicians or diplomats — hell, I was a teenager who'd left school at 15 — but as I said earlier, the game was already taking me out of my comfort zone and into extraordinary situations.

Cricket was my focus. It was what I knew; it was what I was good at. If the conversation turned away from cricket, most of the time I just listened, but I loved talking cricket or sport of any kind. On the flight to South Africa, I sat for a long time with our skipper, Adam Gilchrist, a keeper–batsman who was originally from the NSW North Coast but was now playing in Sydney — and all we did was yak about sport and play a dice-like game called 'Pass the Pigs' for hours and hours. Getting on the plane, I hardly knew 'Gilly' but by the time we landed in Jo'burg we were best mates. He already had a reputation as a special player and from our first practice session I knew that he was so much more advanced in his cricket and the way he thought about the game than I was. He also had a sense of fun that really appealed to me, and a captain's ability to have a good time but never get himself into trouble. We'd see a lot of each other over the next two decades, and these were skills he never lost. There were a couple of others on that trip who you might have heard of too. One was a long thin farmer's son who was living in a caravan in Sydney to advance his career. Glenn McGrath was a funny bloke even then. He reckoned the only way he could stand up in his portable home was to pop the air vent in the roof. Blocker Wilson was on that trip too and a leg-spinner, Peter McIntyre, who played a couple of Tests in the mid 1990s.

After easily winning a one-dayer at Pretoria to launch the tour, our second game was at the famous Wanderers Stadium in Johannesburg, a three-day contest against the Transvaal Under-23s. In our first innings, I batted at six, and then in our second dig we collapsed to 2–4 and Gilly, our regular No. 4, was feeling crook so someone had to go in at short notice. I put my hand up and went on to bat for nearly three hours for 65. To me, volunteering to bat near the top of the order was nothing exceptional — I always wanted to open or bat at three or four, as it was where I batted in junior cricket in Tassie and it was where I was always keen to bat at Mowbray — but I sensed I earned a bit of respect from my team-mates, and from Rod, too, which set up my whole tour. I finished second on the batting averages, behind South Australia's Darren Webber, and topped the bowling averages, too, taking three wickets for 43 with my part-time off-breaks. More important than any numbers, even though I was younger than my team-mates, I didn't feel out of place. I was heading in the right direction.

Life on the road

Life as a professional cricketer sees you on the road more often than being at home, which sounds glamorous to many — but let me assure you that after doing it for almost 20 years, I'm looking forward to settling down in retirement in our new home in Melbourne.

The highlight without a doubt has always been the tours to England. There's something very special about an Ashes tour when you can spend up to four months on the road with your team-mates. It builds a special camaraderie as you travel around the country by bus, playing at the traditional grounds of cricket and living in a culture that is similar to what we are used to at home. New Zealand is very similar as well, plus it has some amazing golf courses, so it's always been one of my preferred touring spots.

Test cricket tours, despite the length of time away, tend to give you the best opportunity to adapt to life on the road. You can unpack a suitcase and make yourself more comfortable in your home away from home. We would stay in each Test location for at least a week, so we could settle in and create a few little home comforts. But one-day cricket was mostly the direct opposite. Always on the move, travelling from city to city as well as regional and smaller towns to play, made it much more difficult to settle down. But that's life as an international cricketer.

A lot of international cricket is played in developing countries, so I have seen great diversity on my travels around the globe. India is the best example of this for me, where I've seen its grandeur, royalty and wealth but have been really touched and moved by its poverty and its underprivileged areas. Front of mind for me is the work the Mumbai Indians do with the 'Education for All' initiative. It's focused on the 62 million primary school age children who drop out of school before grade eight. They are doing amazing work with these children, and I was most fortunate to see it all first-hand in 2013. Don't get me wrong: I have been so lucky to see some of the most amazing sights, cities and wonders of the world, but it's the diversity and social inequality that has probably left the biggest impression on me. Cricket makes a big difference in these countries and we, as international cricketers, should continue to do everything we can to visit these areas, give the people something to enjoy and aspire to and most of all, do our bit to put a smile on the faces of those less fortunate than ourselves.

CHAPTER 4

PUNTER

Adelaide, 1993

ON THE PLANE HOME from South Africa, I was confident I'd never be going back to the groundsman's job at Scotch Oakburn College. As it happened I was only going back home to leave again.

My year was pretty much mapped out: after just a couple of weeks back with Mum, Dad, Drew and Renee I'd be returning to Adelaide, first to train with the Australian Under-19 Development Squad and then to live for the rest of the year as a full-time resident at the Academy. My life was now wall-to-wall cricket, whether in the nets, playing in games, talking cricket or doing physical work and mental conditioning for cricket. I'd get a little homesick at times but never to the point where I was sitting in my room depressed about the fact I wasn't home. Rod Marsh ran a tight ship and if anyone fell short of his high standards we paid a price, sometimes individually, often as a group. Washing cars and gym sessions that moved from eight to six in the morning were two of his favourite punishments.

One not-so-pleasant memory I have of my time in Adelaide was a job fast bowler Simon Cook and I had to do at the Adelaide Oval. In the years that followed, I never gazed at any of the glorious features of the ground, such as the cathedral that overlooks the field or the famous scoreboard or the Victor Richardson Gates, I just grimaced at the sight of the wooden benches in front of the Members' Stand. That was because Simon and I had to change every nut and bolt in those benches. We had to remove the old ones, replace them with new ones, and then go back and retighten them all one more time, before our work was given a tick of approval. My memory is it took the best part of a year to get the job finished.

Most of the boys used to go out for a big one on Saturday nights and use Sunday to get over it, but in my first year I stayed away from most of that. In those days I was determined not to squander the chance I was given, and I remember Gilly telling me years after that South African trip that he couldn't believe how focused I was and how hard I worked.

Inevitably, with the boys concentrating their drinking to just one night, there were some stories to be told, but I can't recall anyone getting into serious trouble. One of the more bizarre moments concerned a room-mate of mine at the Academy, a guy who would go on to play Test cricket. This bloke used to love going out and was rarely home early on Saturday night, even though we were required to attend coaching clinics with groups of young cricketers every Sunday, starting at 8am. One Sunday morning, we couldn't find this bloke — he wasn't in his room, hadn't been home, so all we could do was leave without him. We had to go across a bridge over the River Torrens on our drive from the Directors Apartments to the Adelaide Oval, and the lanes on that bridge were separated by a wide median strip. That morning, as we approached the bridge, someone spotted a body lying on the middle of that median strip, which on closer inspection proved to be my 'roomie', sound asleep with a big bag of Twisties tucked under his arm. After a big night, he'd realised there was no point going home, so instead he parked himself on the route he knew we'd take to the ground, in a place where he knew we couldn't miss him. We stopped the van, picked him up and five minutes later he was coaching the kids as if nothing unusual or untoward had happened. The grog on Saturday night was part of club cricket back home, so it was hardly surprising that it became part of the culture at the Academy, too.

We were all pretty fair cricketers when we got to the Academy, so the coaches concentrated on fine-tuning our techniques and toughening us up so we'd be ready for first-class matches. One drill we had at the Academy was described as a 'bouncer evasion session', where we put indoor-cricket balls in a bowling machine that seemed like it was set at 100mph. Then the machine fired bouncers at us and the trick was to drop your hands and rock out of the way, or duck. I'd been brought up never to shirk a challenge and as I've already said I had no fear. It's not a boast, because it takes a lot more courage to do something if you are scared than if you are not; I just simply wasn't worried about getting hit. When it came to my turn I would stand there and pick the balls off, hooking and pulling. I'm pretty sure I didn't own a helmet back then and they were only indoor balls, but they could still do some damage. One of the students, Mark Hatton, a slow bowler from the ACT got hit flush in the helmet six times in a row and I remember Marshy dragging him out of the nets before he got hurt. Rod loved my aggression at these sessions and used to invite people down to watch this kid hooking like an old-fashioned cricketer. It got to the point where he would yell out 'in front of square', 'behind square', 'on the up' or 'on the ground' and I would do my best to oblige.

I enjoyed that and those shots remained an important part of my cricket arsenal. If you can pick off a ball that's just short of a length it robs real estate from the bowler. He knows if you pitch it up you will drive and if not you will play the cross bat shot and it leaves him very little room for error. There was a time later in my career when the pull shot let me down and there were suggestions I stop playing it, but it would have been like cutting off a limb.

WHEN I ARRIVED at the Academy in April 1992 I had just a few hundred dollars in my bank account; when I left at the end of 1993 things were pretty much the same. We made a few bucks helping kids with their cricket and I also coached some junior footballers and umpired their games (for $5 an hour), but most of the time I was just about skint. When we were living in the Directors Apartments, we received something like $120 a week as an allowance, and we were required to pay for our own meals, laundry and so on. When we moved to Henley Beach, all that was taken care of, but they reduced our stipend.

In my first year, while I didn't drink at all, I would head to a nearby TAB most Monday and Thursday nights, to bet on the greyhounds. I didn't make a lot of money, but I enjoyed myself and I didn't lose. I couldn't afford to. I'd been following the dogs since I was very young, from the time I'd go to my grandfather's place at Newnham, where he had a few greyhounds of varying ability kennelled in his backyard. There are photo albums of me when I was a baby with a dummy in my mouth on a picnic rug with the greyhounds around me, and we had one of Pop's old racing dogs, which we named Tiny, as a pet. Dad also trained and raced some dogs, and he liked to have a bet as well. I'd sit with him and listen to the races, picking out my favourites and cheering them on, and I was hooked from the first time he took me to the White City track in Launceston. Mum reckons that when I was a kid I spent more time in our family home talking about the dogs than my cricket, and she might be right. One ambition I had was to earn enough money to own my own greyhounds. When that happened I made sure I went into partnership with friends of mine, especially with Tim Quill, my best mate through school, junior footy and junior cricket.

My first dog was named Elected, which won a number of races and made a Launceston Cup final. Like quite a few of the dogs I've been connected with, he was trained by Dale 'Jacko' Hammersley, who I'd met at White City and I also knew from the North Launceston footy club. Tim and I then purchased a pup from Melbourne called My Self, who went on to win the Tasmanian final of the National Sprint Championship. Of all the greyhounds I've raced over the years, a dog named First Innings — which started favourite in the Hobart Thousand in 2007 — probably won the most races for me, but My Self had the best strike rate. She only had about 30 starts and won half of them. I also won a Devonport Cup with Ricky Tim, which like First Innings I raced with Tim Quill and his dad, John.

I've raced a few slow greyhounds too, and I'm the first to admit I haven't made any money out of the hobby, but that doesn't matter to me. I still get nervous whenever I watch one of my dogs race. It was pretty much the same throughout my career — whenever I was away, I'd organise for races to be taped so I could listen to them later over the phone. Of course, these days I can get on the internet and listen to the replays wherever I am in the world, and the buzz is still the same. As Pop and Dad told me when I was young, you shouldn't bet with what you haven't got and if you never sway from that policy, the racetrack is always a good place to be.

Anyone who says you shouldn't go to the greyhounds has never been.

IF I WASN'T IN an Adelaide TAB in 1992 and 1993, most of the time I was giving myself every chance to one day be a Test batsman. I hit as many balls as anybody there and spent my spare time analysing the better players and the international stars who came to use the facilities. I was very, very happy, and made friendships that will last forever, including some with guys who'd go on to stellar careers.

Among the future international cricketers I played or trained with at the Academy were Michael Slater, a precociously talented opener who figured if you were going to have a whack at a ball outside off you might as well throw the kitchen sink at it (he was a dasher but he had an unbelievably good technique, and his 152 on debut at Lords was a master class); Colin 'Funky' Miller, who was a medium pace swing bowler in those days and noted lower-order hitter, turned to spin bowling later and I can recall him opening the bowling in a match with medium pace and then coming back to bowl his offies; Paul 'Blocker' Wilson, who we've already met; Michael Kasprowicz, the mild-mannered fast bowler from Queensland whose heroic efforts in sweltering Indian conditions should never be forgotten (he has a massive heart and is a champion bloke); my mate Adam Gilchrist is reasonably well known; Murray Goodwin was my room-mate at the Academy, a funny bloke who loved a night out and who went on to play for Zimbabwe and scored a gutsy 91 against us in Harare some years later; the leggie Peter McIntyre, who played a couple of Tests before Warnie came on the scene and ruined it for everyone, but had a good career for South Australia after that; Brett's brother Shane Lee, who was a hell of a good all-rounder, I think the best we had until Shane Watson came on the scene; Brad Hodge went through with me and he was a man who would have played 100 Tests in any other era; the fast bowler Simon Cook, who helped me fix the seats at Adelaide and then went on to take seven wickets in his first Test, none in the next — he never played at that level again, probably because of injury (he was an unlucky bloke, managing to run himself over with a steamroller some years later); John Davison passed through and he ended up playing for Canada in World Cups, breaking a record for the fastest century in a match against the West Indies and he popped up later as an Academy bowling coach; and Wade Seccombe, who was a great gloveman but spent his time living in Ian Healy's shadow.

As a keen student of the game I learned so much by being around such diverse cricketing talents and such diverse people. And, it seemed the cricketers I encountered at that formative time would later show up here and there and travel part of the journey with me.

On my final tour with an Academy team — to India and Sri Lanka in 1993 — one of my fellow travellers was Tim Nielsen, a no-nonsense wicketkeeper who later became the Australian team coach. Tim was working at the Academy as a coach and brought with him an approach to the game that made him a good man to have around. He was treated poorly later on, but we'll get to that in due course.

I have vivid memories of Glenn McGrath back then. I wasn't interested in fashion, but it was obvious that the farm boy struggled to get a pair of pants that could fit. His cricket trousers finished closer to his knee than his ankle and consequently exposed a pair of seriously raw-boned legs. He was nicknamed Pigeon because he had legs like a bird. To complement this look Glenn wore huge leather-soled bowling boots that were laced like boxer's boots. He looked like something from a different age, but there is one other thing about him from back then that stays strongly in memory: he was quick, real quick. I can still clearly picture Pidge at the Wanderers in Jo'burg, where the pitch was like Perth, fast and bouncy, and Adam Gilchrist was back 30 metres and taking them above his head. The two of us — Pidge from Narromine in north-western New South Wales and me from the outer suburbs of Launceston — had a certain affinity which came from the reality we were pretty unsophisticated compared to many of our city-slicker comrades. We quickly forged a friendship that remains rock-solid to this day.

This came about even though, in many ways, we were very different. My favourite videos were anything cricket or the 1975 VFL Grand Final (the year North Melbourne won its first premiership, beating Hawthorn by 55 points); his preference was an instructional number that demonstrated how to skin a wild pig. One day in Adelaide, I went up to Pidge's room to discover that he had lined up a collection of empty cereal boxes, side by side, along a window ledge.

'What did you do that for?' I asked.

He didn't say anything, just slowly walked over to his cutlery drawer, from which he dug out all the dinner knives he could find. Then, with a flick of the wrist, he started firing those knives across his bed at the boxes. *How do you come up with this stuff?* I thought to myself, my back safely up against the wall. Then I looked over at the carnage on and around the window ledge. *And how is it that you hit the centre of the boxes every single time?*

Warnie was different again and always seemed a little more mature than the rest of us. In a Warnie sort of way. He had a flash car, while we got around on buses and bikes. He had a contract with the Australian Cricket Board that had numbers on it that we could only dream about. I first met him in the winter of 1992, when he came to Adelaide to work at the Academy with his spin-bowling coach, the former Test leg-spinner Terry Jenner, in preparation for the Australian Test team's tour of Sri Lanka. Shane had made his Test debut the previous January. I was 17 years old; he was 22, nearly 23, but despite the age gap he was headed in the same direction as me and we shared plenty of time together. He and Terry needed someone to bowl to and I put my hand up every time — and not just because I liked them and I wanted them to like me. Warnie was miles ahead of any spin bowler I'd ever faced before. I knew I could improve plenty by working with him.

One day, Shane announced that he had to head down to Glenelg to visit a friend, and he asked me if I wanted to go along for the ride. On the way back, we stopped to get a drink — a frozen yoghurt soft-serve for me and a slurpie of some kind for Warnie — and then we set off, with my drink in my left hand and Shane's in the other, which he grabbed off me whenever he had the chance. We came to an intersection with the lights working our way, but a very old lady driving a gold hatchback Torana wasn't paying attention and she went straight through her lights, Warnie only saw her at the last second, tried to swerve out of the way, but couldn't avoid crashing into the back end of her car. From there, she shot straight across the road up onto the footpath, through the front fence of a house and smashed into a big tree, while the soft-serve and the slurpie went all over the windscreen (though at that moment that was the least of our worries). Fortunately, the other driver and her elderly friend in the passenger seat were okay, if a little shellshocked, and we were fine, though I couldn't stand still from the adrenalin shooting through my body. Warnie, meanwhile, having established that everyone was safe, was staring blankly at the crumpled front of his Nissan Pulsar Vector, which was eventually taken away by a tow-truck. The poor bloke looked like he was farewelling a dear friend going off to war as his car slowly disappeared from view. He wasn't totally bulletproof after all. We had to get a cab home.

Shane was the bloke responsible for my 'Punter' nickname, which he gave me because of my habit of sneaking down to the TAB twice a week to bet on the dogs. Everyone else called me 'Pont' or 'Ponts', but to Warnie that wasn't quite right. I can't remember if Shane ever came with me to the TAB, but he knew where I was and I think he was impressed with my nerve and the fact I liked a bet. What he definitely did try to do was 'corrupt' me by taking me to the nightclubs and casinos he liked to frequent. I had no time for that stuff and resisted for a while. My favourite excuse was that I didn't own a pair of jeans or a decent shirt (which was 100 per cent true), but that alibi only worked for so long. Eventually, he found some gear, dressed me up and out we went. I might not have looked anything close to 18, but even back then there wasn't a doorman in the universe who could resist Shane Warne. I can still remember Warnie saying to me during that night out, 'Well, Punter, what do you reckon?'

And I just replied sheepishly, 'Aw, mate, I dunno.'

I was like a rabbit in the headlights, not knowing which way to run. I realised the disco was all very colourful, even exhilarating, but my gut instinct said the old world I knew was better for me. Suddenly, I was feeling my age and considerable lack of sophistication. I got home in one piece that night and resolved to wait until I was a bit older before I went back. Cricket was my priority.

Planning

Planning is a critical foundation to achieving success. I learned this from a very young age and developed my own preferred process for planning. As Australian captain, I was able to use it to its maximum but it's also been with me in other teams that I've played with. It involves three Vs — Vision, Values and Validation.

The Vision is the over-arching goal of what you want to achieve and how you will get there. It's set by the captain — as leader you must have a vision for where you are heading with your team and what your critical goals are. I've always talked through this with the senior people around me but have set the ultimate goal myself. This is paramount to the position of leader or captain.

The second stage of my planning process is Values. These are set by the leadership group and senior players and are a set of behaviours for how we do things together to ensure we achieve the Vision. The process to create the values empowers the members of the group and ensures that they work with the captain to set the right example and culture for the team.

The third and final part of the process is the Validation. This is where we get the buy-in of the entire team including all the support staff and management. It establishes how we are all going to play a role in achieving the Vision and the principles for how we will go about it. It becomes part of the day-to-day activities of the team as well as the players as individuals. It creates the culture and the standards that the group becomes known for.

Over the years, I've been involved in all types of planning processes but when I'm in charge, I prefer to keep it very simple and straightforward as I firmly believe that's the best way to get full buy-in and validation from the team.

CHAPTER 5

IN THE COMPANY
OF BOONIE

*A hotel room somewhere in Adelaide, 1992,
about 9.30am*

I WAS SOUND ASLEEP and then the phone was ringing. Or was it someone at the door? Maybe it was the alarm. I was confused, didn't know what was happening, but eventually worked out it was the phone and when I picked it up there was an angry voice: 'Where the hell are you?' I looked at the clock and my heart sank. I'd slept in and no matter how fast I moved now there was no escaping the fact I was late. The team was already at the ground.

Welcome to my first game of Shield cricket. I hadn't gotten out of bed on the wrong side, I just hadn't gotten out of bed at all. It was no way to start a first-class career.

AT THE START of the 1992–93 season, most observers of cricket in Tasmania believed the selectors would be wary about choosing a 17-year-old kid in Tassie's Sheffield Shield team. David Boon and Richard Soule had been picked as 17-year-olds, but the pool of players from which the team was chosen was stronger now. Of course, I wanted to be promoted as soon as possible, my expectations fuelled in part by a conversation I'd had with Greg Shipperd, the coach of the Tasmanian team. Greg had brought a group of players to Adelaide for some pre-season training and while he was there he sought me out to say, 'Mate, you're in the selectors' minds. We rate the Second XI games you'll be playing highly and we'll be watching them closely.'

One of the changes Rod Marsh had made to the way the Academy was run was to stop scholarship holders from playing Adelaide grade cricket. Instead, from October to December, we played a series of one-day and four-day games, mostly against state Second XIs and usually on first-class grounds, before going back to our home states until the next Academy 'year' began in April. When I scored 59 and 161 not out for the Academy against the South Australia Second XI in Adelaide I figured — if Greg was fair dinkum — I must have been a chance for the Shield. When I heard that Danny Buckingham, a stalwart of the Tassie batting order, was out with a groin injury my hopes became even stronger. And then, on Recreation Day, a public holiday held each year in Northern Tasmania on the first Monday in November, I made a hundred for Mowbray against Riverside at Invermay Park. It was — remember I had spent most of my time from age 15 away from Launceston — my first hundred in the top grade for the club. The Shield team was due to be announced 13 days later. Now, I was certain to be in the state side according to the *Examiner*'s correspondent at the game.

I'd only returned home on the previous Friday, having been away for the best part of seven months. Mum's first words were to remark on how much fitter I looked, then Dad and I hit Mowbray Golf Course as soon as we could for the first of a number of rounds we played in the following fortnight.

David Boon had been 14 days away from his 18th birthday when he made his first Shield appearance in December 1978, and the local papers were making a fuss about the fact I was in line to make my debut at a younger age (by 15 days). If you had asked me three months earlier if beating Boonie mattered I would have said not at all, but as the first Shield game of the season drew closer and the speculation in the press, around the cricket club and around the family dining table became louder, I suddenly really wanted it to happen. By the middle of the following week I was like the proverbial cat on a hot tin roof, buzzing down the fairways, going for jogs around Rocherlea and out into the bush, anything to keep me occupied. Fortunately — for everyone — I got sent to Canberra to play a four-day game for the Academy, and when I came off at the end of the first day I got the news that I would be playing for Tassie in the first game.

I guess I'm supposed to say that when I heard I'd been chosen I was gripped with a panic, but the truth is I knew I was in good form and I was pretty confident, based on what I'd seen and been taught at the Academy, at Tassie squad practice and in the matches I'd played with Mowbray, that I could step up to the higher standards of the Shield. My debut game would be at Adelaide Oval, a ground I knew so well even the benches in front of the Members' Stand were familiar to me. It was all excitement and eager anticipation, no fear or dread. I don't think this self-belief meant I was brash or cocky, but on the cricket field I was definitely comfortable in my own skin.

In the Tassie dressing room, I did what I'd always done when surrounded by men: sat quietly in the corner, listened, did as I was told, and thought twice before asking a question. In the papers, before the game, Rod Marsh had described me as 'a very sensible, quiet lad'. Still, I couldn't wait to get out of Canberra and catch up with my new team-mates in Adelaide, which I did late on the Wednesday night, about 36 hours before the biggest game of my life to that point was due to begin.

I WAS ROOMING with Michael Di Venuto, who wasn't in our starting XI but had travelled with the Shield team as part of an 'Ansett Youth Cricket Scholarship' he'd been awarded at the start of the season. Hobart-born, Diva is 12 months older than me but we had played a lot of cricket together in the juniors and become great mates. He was a left-hand opening batsman with serious talent. Diva made over 25,000 first-class runs and 60 centuries but only played a smattering of ODIs for Australia. In another era he'd have played quite a few Tests I reckon. Here in Adelaide we were both very keen to impress by doing *everything* right. So we retired to our room early, ordered room service, watched a movie and made sure we set the alarms next to our beds so we'd be down early for breakfast.

Next thing we knew there was a ringing noise buzzing through the room and I stumbled out of bed thinking it was the alarm. But it was the phone. It was Greg Shipperd ringing from Adelaide Oval: 'Where the hell are you?' he shouted down the line. 'What are you doing?'

We looked at our damn clock-radios and saw it was 9.30am. I couldn't believe it … we'd set it for 9.30pm. All we could do was get dressed as quickly as we could and bolt down to the ground. Luckily, it was raining so we hadn't missed anything, but the impression we'd made was appalling. The team had started their warm-up in the indoor centre next door. David Boon had told the rest of the team that if anyone said a word to either of us they'd get fined. If they even looked at us, they'd be fined. We said a sheepish, 'Sorry boys,' as soon as we got there … and there was no reaction. *Nothing.* I tried to start a conversation … no reaction. *Nothing.* This was day one of my Sheffield Shield career. After warm-ups, we explained ourselves and said it was an honest mistake, and Boonie gruffly told us to make sure it didn't happen again. Later, he pulled me to one side and reiterated the message.

I've rarely felt less important in my life.

I SPENT MY FIRST TWO DAYS of Shield cricket either in the field or watching the rain, which actually wasn't a bad way to settle in. South Australia was able to declare at stumps on day two thanks to centuries from Joe Scuderi and Tim Nielsen, but we spent most of the afternoon watching it rain again. I then had a pretty restless night knowing I'd be batting the next day, probably on a wicket with some moisture in it. As it turned out, the pitch was still terrific to bat on, but I was still in fairly early, at 2–50.

There was something very reassuring about being met in the middle by the legend himself ... David Boon. Like me, Boonie is a former player from the North Launceston Football Club. Typical Launceston, he's a master of the understatement and seriously loyal to those he trusts. He'd been there and done that, but didn't overload me with advice. All he did when I came out to bat was to remind me the wicket was nice and we had plenty of time. And, last of all, he said simply, 'Good luck.' Still, I can't begin to tell you how lucky I was to have the reassuring presence of the great man at the other end. I was determined to do the little things right — call loudly, run hard, be assertive. It took me 13 balls to get off the mark, then Tim May came on to bowl, and things changed.

I had never faced an off-spinner of May's class before. The way the ball looped away from my bat and then spun just that little bit more viciously than I'd ever previously seen was a genuine eye-opener. I felt out of my depth; I couldn't get off strike and I started to hear the sledges the fielders were aiming at me. I was fine against the quicks, especially as they were so keen to bounce me, but I couldn't get comfortable against the off-spin and I didn't like it. This was a weird experience for me, one I'd never felt before other than in my first games against the men, but in those situations I knew I'd be okay when I got a little older. This time, the fear was I wasn't good enough.

Boonie took it upon himself to take most of May's bowling and that plan didn't come unstuck until he was caught at first slip for 60. We'd batted together in a little less than two-and-a-half hours. Straight after Boonie was out I hit their quick bowler Damian Reeves, who was also making his debut, for three straight fours to reach my 50. This prompted South Australia's captain, Jamie Siddons, to bring his fastest bowler, Denis Hickey, back on. That proved the end of me. Hickey bowled (another) short one, but this was quicker than anything Reeves had delivered and I nicked my attempted hook shot through to keeper Nielsen. As I walked slowly back to the dressing room, I was more dirty on the hundred missed than happy with the 56 scored, especially as I'd let myself get a little excited by those three consecutive boundaries.

I wasn't a victim of over-confidence so much as I just didn't quite appreciate how intricate the challenges can be at this higher level. Tim May had put me through the ringer, and though I had clearly struggled at times, I sort of came out the other side. Then Boonie was dismissed and suddenly I was the 'senior partner', a situation that created new expectations, at least in my mind. And then I hit those three fours, which did me in. It was natural for my blood to be pumping, but at that stage of my life I didn't have the nous to put a lid on it. I'd never heard of the term 'mental strength' at this point in my life but that's what I was lacking. And experience. Siddons knew what he was doing when he brought his No. 1 quick back and Hickey knew what he was doing when he tested me with that quick bouncer. In junior cricket I'd have gone on to a big score, but this wasn't junior cricket. I still had plenty to learn.

Mentors

When I look back on my career, I realise I had three significant mentors who helped me become the best that I could be as an international cricketer. They all played key roles in my development at different times and I am forever indebted to them for all their support and encouragement.

Ian Young was my first mentor and first real coach. I first met Youngy when I was nine years old, at an NTCA school-holiday coaching clinic. While I was in the nets, I noticed a tall, skinny bloke in a white floppy hat watching me bat. He stayed until I finished and then introduced himself. Straight away I could tell that he was someone who cared. From that first meeting way back in 1983 Youngy was a constant in my life right up until he sadly passed away in October 2010. We spent hours and hours talking together about cricket, practising in the nets and in the field, talking about football and how to be as good a person and sportsperson as you could be. Apart from my family, Youngy made the biggest impression on my life. He was a great motivator, listener and confidant. He had an incredible ability to help me find the answer myself while reinforcing the critical points to become better — as a batsman, leader and person.

Youngy gave me a great foundation, which helped me when I arrived at the Cricket Academy in Adelaide. There I came under the watchful eye of Rod Marsh, who gave me a wonderful opportunity at the Academy and became my second mentor in the game of cricket and life. Rod pushed me very hard from my earliest days with him, and I look back on that now and know that it set the platform for the way I apply myself to training, preparing and playing my cricket. We got on well and spent a lot of time talking about cricket, the difference between good and great, and experiences that Rod had that he felt would help me. And they did. I probably didn't realise it then but my time at the Academy with Rod taught me to grow up as a person, learn to be independent and self-reliant and to always give 100 per cent to my training and preparation. These lessons from Rod have been with me right through my career and it was great to have him back around the Australian team as a selector in my final years with the team.

My other significant mentor is current Victorian and past Tasmanian coach, Greg Shipperd. He made a huge impression on me when I first came into the Tasmanian team, and right through my career was around the most when I needed someone to help me with something in my game. He was also very hard on me and would tell me exactly what he thought — all of which I really appreciated. If I got out playing a bad shot, Shippy would be at the gate as I walked off to tell me. But then he would watch the video with me to break down where I went wrong so that I wouldn't make that mistake again. We have become good mates and he has been great for my batting, especially in the latter years of my career, where I've had a few challenges creep into my technique.

What stands out for me with my three mentors is that they all pushed me hard, taught me to work harder than anyone else and, above all, to aim to be a good person. I am forever indebted to all three of them.

CHAPTER 6

AN ANGRY
YOUNG MAN

Sheffield Shield, 1992–93

THERE WERE A COUPLE of good young players going around in the Sheffield Shield in the summer of 1992–93 and if I was one of them I was a fair way down the pecking order. Today it's hard to believe how much talent was bubbling away in domestic Australian cricket back then.

A half-century in my first game wasn't a bad start, but I struggled a bit after that, getting only 4 in the second innings of that game. I got a few starts after that but didn't get to 50 again until my fifth game, which luck would have it was at Bellerive against South Australia. Against Western Australia in Perth I saw a young bloke called Damien Martyn score a century, he was only 21 and had just made his Test debut against the West Indies and he was one of those setting the standard. He was one of the best batsmen I had seen and to this day I still say the same thing. Justin Langer didn't do too badly either against us.

We went up to Sydney in late January to take on NSW at the SCG, which in those days always helped the spinners. Glenn McGrath was playing his first Shield match and opened the bowling with Wayne Holdsworth, an honest fast bowler who took over 200 first-class wickets. At six was another making his debut for the Blues, my former Academy captain Adam Gilchrist who had been chosen as a batsman because Phil Emery was the wicketkeeper. Gilly was 21 and had been killing them in the seconds and even got a shot playing in the Prime Minister's XI, but until then couldn't force his way into the state side. It still amazes me that he took another seven years to make it to the Test team.

It was, however, a bloke who was a bit older who sticks in my mind from that match. Greg Matthews is one of the more unique people to have ever played for Australia. He was a great bowler and will always be remembered for getting the final wicket in the Madras (Chennai) tied Test but he also made valuable runs. He could be different, but there's no doubt he was talented and on this day he put me through one of the hardest exams of my cricketing life.

Pace bowling never worried me that much, but as you can tell by now it was the spinners who challenged me to knuckle down and do the really hard yards in the middle. I batted for four hours that day, much of the time doing my best to hang on as we went off three times for rain delays. Scoring had been relatively easy at first but then the Blues put on the handbrakes. We lost a few wickets then, but I managed to find the mental energy needed not to throw things away. They extended play for an hour to draw out my pain and Matthews, aided by Emery, really tied me down, but when they eventually did call us in at stumps I had moved to 98 not out. Apparently I spent the best part of an hour in the 90s.

I can't say I wasn't thinking about a century, but the overriding feeling I had as I made my way back to the sanctuary of the dressing room was pride that I had shown so much patience. I was also pretty pleased that my footwork had really improved. Tim May had pinned me to the crease in Adelaide but now I was following the advice of Ian Chappell who had told us during a coaching session at the Academy that you have to get to the ball on the full or the half volley when playing spinners. He'd also advised using the sweep but it wasn't a shot that I ever truly mastered so it wasn't one I was willing to play.

No batsman should sleep soundly on 98 not out, especially one who hasn't scored a Shield 100, but I was the most exhausted 18-year-old on the mainland that night and fell straight into a deep sleep when I got back to my bed. Okay, I admit waking with the cold sweats during a dream where I had run myself out trying to get to three figures, but even then I was so tired I think I just passed out again.

I got there the next morning and it was a great feeling. It wasn't just getting my first hundred, it felt like I had matured as a cricketer and taken my game to another level. When I went home Mum showed me how the papers had covered the innings, and the quote that stayed with me was from Richard Soule, when he said the difference in my batting now to where I'd been before was 'astronomical' in terms of my 'mental application'.

That's how I felt, too.

There was a fair degree of excitement in the papers about that century. I was the third youngest ever in the Shield to reach three figures, Archie Jackson did it at 17 and Doug Walters at 18, but he was about a month younger than I was. The journos must have asked Rod Marsh if I was the 'next Doug Walters', but he was too smart to fall for that. 'There's a touch of Doug Walters about him ... there'll never be another Doug Walters, make that clear, he's Ricky Ponting.' Later that year Launceston cricket writer Mark Thomas shot down comparisons between me and Boonie by saying 'there will never be another David Boon; but there could be the first Ricky Ponting'. It was all starting ...

It's funny looking back, but I think we were all pushing each other onto bigger things then whether we knew it or not. Gilly said later that watching me score the hundred made him think, 'If he can do it I can do it.' When our time did come there was a sense among us that we could do anything because I think we'd seen the talent in each other and watched as our contemporaries took things up to the next level. If he could do it, I could ...

Greg Matthews finally got me in the second dig when I'd got to 69.

Running through someone's Shield stories can be a bit eye-glazing but there was something that happened in the next game against Victoria that I reckon I was reminded about every time Cricket Australia chief executive James Sutherland got to speak publicly with me in the room. Back then he was a long thin medium-pace bowler and while he didn't play a lot of first-class matches he did in this one and as anybody who has been on the receiving end of one of his speeches will know by now, he got me out.

I'll give James his due, he tells a good story and he follows that boast by explaining that I was out 'hit wicket'. I'd actually played a pretty good shot and set off for a run or two, but had made the mistake of wearing a new type of shoe. When I tried to take off, my foot slipped back and I knocked off the bails. I wasn't happy at the time, but it gave the man who was later to become my boss something to talk about for years to come …

In the penultimate game of the year I got back-to-back 100s against a Western Australian attack that included Jo Angel, Brendon Julian and another tall bowler, Tom Moody. It was a nice thing to do as I was playing against a home crowd at Bellerive, but in those days the pitch was a road and if you considered yourself a batsman then Tassie was the place to fill your boots.

Three centuries and four 50s is a pretty good start to a Shield career, but it had me a fair way down the table compared to some of my contemporaries. Damien Martyn played four matches and got four 100s, Matthew Hayden bagged a couple and reached 50 five times playing up at Queensland where the wickets were pretty juicy, Jamie Siddons got four 100s too and Michael Slater scored over 1000 runs in the competition.

There was an Ashes series coming up that winter and some talk that I might get a look-in. Marto and Lang had already made their Test debuts and while Lang missed this time round they took Marto and big Mattie Hayden. My old mate Warnie also made a bit of a splash when he got his first chance to bowl in England. The batting line up for the first Test was M Taylor, M Slater, D Boon, M Waugh, A Border and S Waugh with Marto and Haydos in the wings … I was a lot further back in the pecking order.

I didn't really expect to be picked for that tour, but I went into the next Shield season thinking I could be a long shot to go to South Africa at the end of the summer. I went all right too, scoring three 100s and as many 50s, but on reflection I knew I had let things get to me. The season started well, WA came down to Hobart and in the first innings Justin Langer and Damien Martyn knocked up 100s. In our innings me and Michael Di Venuto both did the same. The pair of us put on 207 and had fun wearing down the visitors.

After that I went through a frustrating run of 'starts' but could not kick on. I felt in terrific form, but was playing some really dumb shots and I can remember more than once sitting in the dressing room after I'd been dismissed thinking, *What did you do that for?*

People kept telling me to be patient, as if I'd forgotten the lessons of my debut season, but with hindsight I reckon my struggles were more a case of me trying to be more than what I was. A pressure was building in my mind for me to be a spectacular player (as some critics were suggesting I could be), which I never was and never would be, rather than just being technically sound and consistent. When I did finally make another hundred, against WA in Perth, it took me the best part of five hours and it was one of the most sensible innings of my life. A win in Adelaide would get Tasmania into the Shield final for the very first time, and I had a field day in an eight-wicket victory, scoring 84 not out and 161.

Unfortunately I failed twice in the final in Sydney. Michael Bevan got a hundred and so did Brad McNamara and that was us done. It was pretty disappointing, but I wasn't 20 yet and I guess at that age you figure there'll be other chances. If you'd told me I wouldn't get there for another 18 years …

Anyway, I came out of the season with my reputation as one of Australia's most promising young batsmen reasonably intact. More importantly, I was a smarter cricketer now. I'd learned to bat within my limitations and felt pretty good about where I was going. Even if taking the next step meant spending the first winter for a couple of years — and the last for decades to come — back at home.

THE REASON FOR THIS was simple. After two years of pretty much constant cricket, I needed a break. An incident at the Australian Under-19 championships in Melbourne was telling. Because of the Shield schedule, I was available to play two games in this championship and the first of these was against South Australia. When we batted I was 83 not out at lunch and absolutely flying. Straight after the break, I was facing Jason Gillespie, a future Test star and at this point one of the best young quicks in the country. The strategy they'd come up with was to put every fielder in a semi-circle on the offside, with *no one* on the legside. It's a ridiculous field and one you don't see too often although MS Dhoni did it to us in India years later when they wanted to stop us chasing runs. I remember that time well: Simon Katich was batting and he was forced to play balls way outside off onto the onside. Eventually he went out and later that night an Indian journalist made the mistake of asking him why he'd been so defensive out there. He blew up and unfortunately that was what happened with me in this Under-19s game. Jason was aiming well wide of the off-stump, so for the first couple of overs I just let everything go, but eventually I went for a cut shot and nailed it … straight to the fielder at backward point.

Of course, they carried on as if they were geniuses while I was extremely annoyed with myself. As I turned to storm off I went to swing my bat over the stumps. I connected with the top of the off-stump, it came clean out of the ground and I knew I was in trouble. At a hearing at the Victorian Cricket Association offices they made the point that it must have been deliberate because I didn't bend down to put the stump back in, but the truth was I was too embarrassed. I just wanted to get out of there. I was suspended for a game, which we thought was over the top — no one got hurt and the only person I'd embarrassed by behaving the way I did was myself — but there was no avenue of appeal. After going out with the boys that night I flew home.

At times I could be an angry young man on the cricket field. Earlier in the season, during our Shield game against WA at Bellerive, their quick Duncan Spencer — next to Pakistan's Shoaib Akhtar, the quickest bowler I've ever faced — was bowling to me with the second new ball. Again, I played a cut shot and Brendon Julian, who was an unbelievable fielder, dived in the gully and took a screamer. I was out and they were laughing and shouting and throwing the ball in the air. But it was a no-ball! Now they were spewing and I was grinning. Spencer was blowing up big time.

Next ball, he charged in and, no surprise, it was a short one, right at my throat. I managed to block the ball down at my feet, it dribbled up the wicket and Spencer grabbed it, looked up at me, I eyeballed him back, and then he threw the ball as hard as he could straight at me. It was all I could do to jerk my head back out of the way as the ball went whistling past my chest. In those situations the adrenalin kicks in. It was on! I dropped my bat and ran straight at him and we banged chests in the middle of the pitch as players, umpires and fieldsmen raced in from everywhere. They had to pull us apart before the game could proceed. Later, I found out he was a pretty good boxer, but even if I'd known that then it wouldn't have stopped me.

I seriously regretted knocking the stumps over in the Under-19 game against South Australia. A large part of that reaction was frustration at the field they set for me, but that was no excuse. I should have worked out a way to outsmart them. Duncan Spencer was different. He was not entitled to throw the ball at me from three or four metres away. The way I reacted might have looked bad and I guess those people who talk about certain things 'not being cricket' will say I was wrong, that I should have left it to the authorities to work out, but that was not how my brain worked in such situations. My natural reflex was to try to set injustices right as quickly as I could, a reaction that was formed in part on the field with my comrades at Mowbray who strongly believed in playing hard but fair. Part of that equation meant if something wasn't fair you'd go hard. I went where my emotions took me, in this case straight up the pitch to confront the bloke who'd done me wrong.

AS THE END of the 1993–94 Australian season approached, I talked to a number of people — Dad, Ian Young, Greg Shipperd, David Boon and Rod Marsh among them — and they all agreed that after two nine-month stints at the Academy, two full seasons of Shield and one-day games with Tasmania, and youth tours to South Africa (March 1992) and India and Sri Lanka (August–September 1993), some time away from the game would do me good.

My life that winter was fairly predictable and really good. On the weekend I went to as many North Launceston footy games with my mates as I could. On Monday nights we went to the dogs, on Thursdays, we played golf ($50 in, winner takes all) and on Tuesday and Thursday nights we were at the gym, in the indoor nets, or just running laps of the oval.

By the end of a winter of playing pennants for Mowbray my golf handicap had dropped from six to four and my head was clear.

I guess I could have done what my good mate Shaun Young — Ian's son — did and sign a deal to play league cricket in England, which he did after being named Tasmania's Sheffield Shield player of the year. But to tell the truth, a little part of me simply wasn't game — I didn't like the idea of being *that far* from home. Going over with a squad was one thing, going over on my own seemed pretty daunting. I guess I was still a Rocherlea boy learning his way around the world and I wasn't going out there unless it was with a tour group.

The plan was to take a complete break from cricket from April to September and I did that except for when Rod Marsh invited me to be part of an Australian XI that played three games against an Indian XI in Sydney, Canberra and Melbourne. It was fantastic to share a dressing room with some of the country's best young cricketers, including Stuart Law, Jimmy Maher, Andrew Symonds, Damien Martyn, Justin Langer, Brad Hodge, Darren Berry, Shane Lee, Matthew Nicholson, and a future Tassie captain in Daniel Marsh, but the real buzz was to play against a team that included some big names in world cricket.

There was a touring group of Indian players, including Sunil Gavaskar, Gundappa Viswanath, Ravi Shastri, Sandeep Patil, Anil Kumble and the best young batsman in the world Sachin Tendulkar.

I made a few runs against the Indians in the first game and Gavaskar, no less, singled me out for praise, saying I reminded him of Dean Jones.

'There's the same aggression, going after the ball, and the way he hits off the back foot,' he said.

That quote was especially topical, because Jones had announced his retirement from international cricket just a few days earlier, at the conclusion of Australia's tour of South Africa. There were also rumours about that Allan Border was going to call it quits as Australian captain, which meant there might be an opening in the Aussie batting order. For a second I thought I was a bolter for the tour of Pakistan that was to begin in August, but the last two batting spots went to Michael Bevan and Justin Langer. At the same time, I was heartened by the announcement that a fourth team, 'Australia A', would be included in the World Series Cup one-day competition for the 1994–95 season, alongside Australia, England and Zimbabwe — getting into that side was an ambitious but realistic short-term goal for me.

In the meantime, I kept having fun with my girlfriend and my old school and cricket mates back at home, and worked on a strength and fitness program that had been specifically drawn up for me by the physios from the Academy. In two years, I'd gone from being on the fringes of Tasmanian selection to being on the fringe of the Australian Test and one-day teams. For a 19-year-old from Rocherlea, that seemed like a pretty good place to be.

Being in the zone

The best sports stars consistently appear to have more than others to execute their skill. They look to be doing it comfortably, seem to be in the right place at the right time, and perform the so-called 'one percenters' when they are most needed. They are also the sports stars who play 'in the zone' — doing what they do best in a 'semi-conscious' state.

Over the years, the best batsmen have been those who give themselves more time to play their shots. They use triggers in the bowlers' run-ups and release points to pick up the line and length of a delivery quicker. They move their feet less, giving themselves more time for shot selection and execution.

For me, I reckon that happened half a dozen times in my entire career. In those knocks, I was seriously oblivious to what was going on — I was in auto-pilot mode. I've seen plenty of other batsmen do the same, and Andrew Symonds' 143 not out in the first game of our 2003 World Cup campaign stands out for me as the best example of this. Symmo was a late call-up for that game after Shane Warne and Darren Lehmann were suspended and Michael Bevan was injured in our preparation. He took his chance and dominated the game for us. I sat with him in the dressing rooms after the knock, and was bouncing all over the place recounting great shot after great shot. But Symmo couldn't remember any of those amazing shots and just took it all in his stride.

Bowlers would give different signals to show that they were in the zone. Shane Warne and Glenn McGrath are the two best bowlers I ever played with but they displayed completely opposite traits when they were in the zone. Glenn had a reputation for being a bit chirpy out in the middle but he did his absolute best when the ball and his bowling did the talking. If he started to chat to the batsmen, I knew it might be time to give him a spell. Warnie was the direct opposite: he thrived on getting under the skin of the batsman at the other end. He would chat away to them as he dished up his variations ball after ball. The more he spoke, the more the batsmen seemed to fall into his trap. That was when Warnie was in the zone.

The game of cricket doesn't present opportunities for players to be in the zone all that often in their career. The game is about intense spells of concentration broken up with the ebbs and flows that go between each ball that is bowled. Staying on top and dominating is not easy.

CHAPTER 7

MAKING THE TEAM

Summer, 1994–95

I CAME IN AT FIVE. Darren Lehmann, Matthew Hayden, Damien Martyn and Justin Langer batted ahead of me and Tom Moody after. Phil Emery had the wicketkeeping job ahead of Adam Gilchrist. And, you know what the amazing thing was? We weren't good enough. We were the B team. Well, they called us Australia A that summer, but we were the ones not playing for the Australian side, the one with Taylor, Slater, Warne, McGrath, Boon, Bevan …

It's remarkable what depth of talent we had in Australian cricket then. There was a bottleneck of players just waiting for their chance, or another chance. I can't stress too highly how important the opportunity to play in an A side against good opposition was and is. Like most of the players I came through with, I benefited greatly from the chance to test my skills against the top rung.

When Australia A took on Australia in the World Series one-day tournament that also included England and Zimbabwe there was as much, if not more, riding on the outcome of the matches between the home sides as those with the visitors. In footy there is no game played harder than an intra-club match and in cricket it has to be said that this was as close to that as you got.

ONE OF THE CRITICISMS I've often heard about one-day international (ODI) cricket is that we play too much of it. A consequence of this over-supply is that too many games are quickly forgotten. There is some fairness in this criticism — mostly, in my view, when there are too many games in a single series or tournament. The seven-game marathons in England in 2009 and against England in Australia in 2010–11 come to mind, or even the 2007 World Cup, which lasted 47 days from opening game to final. I reckon I'm qualified to make observations here as I've played more ODIs than any other Australian ... there's no way I can remember them all.

I can tell you, however, I have never forgotten playing those games against the Australian team. It was a great chance for a few of us young bucks to get out there and try to prove ourselves. While there wasn't an edge to the game in the sense of cricketers from the two teams constantly sledging each other, there were a few words exchanged and the games we played during the summer were extraordinarily competitive. The Australia A team contained a couple of hard-nosed seniors in Merv Hughes and Tom Moody, a few blokes like Martyn, Hayden, Langer and Paul Reiffel who had been in and out of the Test and ODI teams in the previous couple of years, and young blokes like me who were anxious to impress. So there was never any question we'd try and take it up to the blokes on the next level.

In Adelaide we kept them to 202 from their 50 overs. When I came out to join Matt Hayden we were 3–77 and in with a real chance. Time wasn't really an issue and when our keeper, Phil Emery, and I started building a decent sixth-wicket partnership I really thought we could win. However, Shane Warne came back on to bowl, and I found myself in a real battle. This was a different bowler to the skilful spinner I'd faced in the indoor nets when I was at the Academy — this bloke was turning them just as much but now he was the most competitive bowler I'd ever faced. Every ball felt like an exam, no two deliveries were quite the same, and while Warnie's chat to me seemed friendly enough a few things he said seemed to stay in my head. *What was he thinking when he asked Mark Taylor loudly if he could put a man in at bat-pad?* Previously I'd felt we had the run-rate just about under control, but now it seemed to be climbing rapidly and we were under pressure to get things moving. And, when I did middle an attacking shot, there was always a bloody fielder in the road. I'd get to see this relentlessness in Shane's bowling time and again — the remarkable way he could put the pressure back on the batsmen, so he had the whip hand.

Eventually, having scored 42 from 63 deliveries (which sounds awfully slow by 21st century standards but was actually okay for the mid 1990s), I tried to slog-sweep him out of the ground, but the ball wasn't quite there and it ballooned out to Michael Bevan on the fence.

The final margin was just six runs in their favour, but we choked in the end, losing our last four wickets for six runs when we'd needed 13 to win from 21 balls in hand. Afterwards, a number of people said nice things about the way I batted, but I was very disappointed. I thought I'd cost us the game.

Four weeks later, the two teams met again in Brisbane, and this time we were chasing 253 to win and Michael Bevan (who'd been dropped from the top Australian team) and I were going all right. Then, totally unexpectedly, David Boon came on to bowl. If Warne was the Ace in the pack in the previous game, this time Mark Taylor was playing his Joker. It was very good captaincy. Now Boonie didn't really enjoy bowling, he never bowled for Tasmania and in the previous 11 years he had sent down the grand total of 6.4 overs in ODI cricket, and taken exactly no wickets.

I knew he'd come on to bowl for my benefit — they knew how much I idolised Boonie and that I'd probably be too scared to play a shot, for fear of getting out. I figured he'd probably bowl off-breaks, and I think that's what they were. And jeez they were hard to get away. 'Don't you get out, Ponts,' he kept chirping down the wicket, 'If you do, I won't ever let you forget it.'

'Bowled Boonie,' chimed in wicketkeeper Ian Healy, as if he was keeping to Warnie or Tim May.

My fellow 'Swampie' admitted later that it was he who had conned the captain into giving him a bowl. 'He'll be that scared of getting out he might not go for many,' he'd said. Boonie didn't get me out, but my fellow Swampie only went for 17 from four overs, at a time when we needed more than that. They'd outsmarted me. Bevo and I both ran ourselves out as we lost our last eight wickets for 52 runs, and we could only rue another opportunity lost. The real casualty, though, was poor Phil Emery. So impressed was Mark Taylor with Boonie's bowling against me that he used him again in the second of the World Series Cup finals (we'd beaten England once and Zimbabwe twice to finish second on the table after the round-robin games), and this time he bowled five overs for just 13 runs and knocked Phil over with a slow, straight delivery that was somehow inside-edged back onto the stumps. Afterwards, Boonie wouldn't leave our keeper alone, until eventually Phil had to say, 'Piss off, will you, I don't want to hear about it again!'

We lost that best-of-three finals series 2–0, but we ran them mighty close. It came down to the 50th over of their run-chase, and our quick, Greg Rowell, bowled nearly the best last over in the history of the game: five perfect yorkers before a low full toss just outside off-stump was slashed over gully by Heals to win them the game. The second game of the finals series wasn't as exciting, but they still needed 49 of their 50 overs to get home.

The other thing was we beat England in one of the games. Which just goes to show how much depth there was in our cricket.

I think the Australia A experiment was a fruitful exercise, but having gone on to captain Australia myself I can see why Tubby Taylor didn't like the concept (and he certainly wasn't the only one in his team who felt that way). If they won, they were the bad guys, but if they lost, their Test and ODI places were in jeopardy. The guys in the main team told me later they hated getting booed at home and fair enough. Things got heated at times and in one match I remember Matty Hayden and Glenn McGrath going at it before Pidge pushed Matty away. On balance, though, I believe the good outweighed the bad, so if Cricket Australia ever wanted to revive the idea I'd be for it. I didn't have a very productive tournament, but it was still a chance for me at age 19 to share a dressing room with blokes who'd been there, done that, to showcase my technique on a national stage and to come up against the best in the business in matches that mattered. For guys like Greg Blewett (who came into the Australia A team for our last four games and scored a hundred and two fifties) and Paul Reiffel (who was controversially 'promoted' to be Australia's 12th man for the finals), it offered a springboard into the Australian Test team.

My 'lucky break' came three weeks after the one-day finals, when Michael Slater had his thumb fractured by England fast bowler Devon Malcolm in the fifth Ashes Test at the WACA. Australia was scheduled to fly to New Zealand straight after that game for an ODI tournament that would also feature India and South Africa and with Slats injured, a new batsman was needed. Realistically, the selectors could have picked any one of seven or eight players (Stuart Law, Damien Martyn, Justin Langer, Darren Lehmann, Michael Bevan, Matt Hayden, Tom Moody, Shaun Young ...) but I was the bat they went for, which for me, the entire Ponting family and it seemed much of Mowbray, was just unbelievable.

I was home in Launceston when the phone call came late on a Thursday. I have to admit there was a celebration that night and a stack of phone conversations the next day, as friends, family, cricket officials and reporters queued up to offer their congratulations. I was also quickly invited to a lunch in the city organised by the Century Club, but was a little embarrassed when I realised that my jeans and collared T-shirt hardly met the dress code of the club where the function took place. Boonie, much more up on these sorts of things, was wearing a jacket and tie. Mind you, if I'd known more formal wear was required I'm not sure what I would have done, because at that point in my life I certainly didn't own a suit and I'm not sure if I even had a necktie to my name.

With all this activity, it took a little while to sink in that I really was an *Australian* cricketer. The best chance I had to think about what was happening to me came on the Saturday, when I turned out for Mowbray against Launceston, opened the batting, and was out in the second over for a duck. Those who say cricket is a great leveller know what they're talking about. On the Sunday, I was at Bellerive, playing for Tassie against WA in a Mercantile Mutual one-dayer, and this time I made it to 10 when we batted. I tried to cover-drive Brendon Julian on the up but hit a catch to Damien Martyn, my Australia A captain, at cover. 'Take that to New Zealand with you,' Martyn sneered at me as I began the long walk back to the pavilion.

Twenty-four hours later, I was on the plane to Wellington, wearing a blazer with a very similar crest to the one on the blazer Uncle Greg wore to England in 1989, sitting in the same block of seats as some of the biggest names in Australian cricket. It was a happy time. The guys had just retained the Ashes pretty emphatically and their partners and children had all come along too. Mark Taylor was accompanied not just by his wife Judi and son William, but also their new baby Jack, who was less than two weeks old when he set off on his first overseas trip.

I wasn't too intimidated by the whole experience. In a way I had been preparing for it all my life and I had already met most of the guys on the plane somewhere in my travels. Initially, I stuck close to the blokes from the Australia A team, such as Grew Blewett and 'Pistol' Reiffel, but of course I knew Warnie, Boonie and Glenn McGrath pretty well and a guy I found I had plenty in common with was Mark Waugh, who loves talking racing, particularly harness racing. A day out at the Dunedin Golf Club, when I discovered that Blewey and I (the two youngest guys in the team) had the lowest handicaps, was an off-field highlight, not least for the way the senior guys reacted when Warnie claimed he played off 14. I heard the term 'burglar' whispered more than once before we teed off and then shouted by just about everyone after the wonder leggie walked away with all our prizemoney. The vibe through the group was terrific. When I look back on that short tour — indeed, on my first couple of seasons in the Australian set-up — I can't help but think how lucky I was to start my career as a junior member of a team on the rise.

I played in all four of our games, batting six against South Africa and New Zealand (scoring 1 and then 10 not out) but being promoted to first-drop for the game against India, when I made 62 from 92 deliveries. It wasn't the most flamboyant dig of my life, but at the time I felt it was one of the most important because I made this half-century in a fair-dinkum one-day international (remember the Australia A games weren't granted full status) in front of men whose respect I craved. Every time one of them said, 'Well played,' I felt even more important. In the final I was back at No. 6 and I walked to the wicket with us needing 17 to win and more than 20 overs available in which to get them. David Boon was at the other end and he challenged me to be with him at the end, two Swampies together. I was 7 not out when we sealed our six-wicket victory, and after the presentation, back in our dressing room, Boonie led us in a triumphal singing of our team anthem, 'Underneath the Southern Cross', which only happened after a victory in a Test match or a one-day series. As I looked around the room I saw how much it meant to them — even for a minor tournament like this (though, of course, it was miles from 'minor' for me). An amazing rush of pride and humility dashed through me, and, cheesy as it sounds, I really did feel I was the luckiest bloke in the world.

THE REASON FOR MY selection for that New Zealand trip became clear near the end of the tour when the Australian side for the upcoming Test and ODI tour of the West Indies was announced. The final two batting places went to Justin Langer and me, so I had to assume that I'd been given the Kiwi experience as an entrée to the Caribbean main course. I had enjoyed another pretty successful summer with Tasmania, averaging 75 in the Shield and scoring my first double century — an innings of 211 against WA that occupied seven hours and 20 minutes. It was my fifth straight first-class hundred against WA, dating back to the twin hundreds I scored against them at Bellerive in March 1993. I always liked playing against the Western Australians, loved batting on the bouncy Perth pitch, and enjoyed their competitive nature, the way they were always up for the fight. Guys like Damien Martyn and Lang encapsulated this spirit.

Other highlights of 1994–95 for me were an innings of 82 from 86 balls for an ACB Chairman's XI in the opening game of England's Ashes tour, played at Lilac Hill in Perth, and my selection in the Australian XI side that played England in Hobart a week before the start of the Ashes series. The critics described the team as a virtual shadow Test team and the fact the game was staged in my home state meant I felt extra nervous during the lead-up. No way could I get to sleep the night before the game, even though I stayed out with quite a few of the guys for a couple of beers. Next morning, I was up early, worked extra hard in warm-ups, and when we batted I got to 71, enjoying a good partnership with Marto.

I went out for a few beers that night, happy that I'd made some runs in what, for me, was a very important audition. Most of the batsmen were out with me, which was the way it worked in those days — if we were going to be fielding the next day, the guys who'd already batted usually went out for a while. Next morning, however, I slept through the alarm (again) and by the time I got to the ground the boys had left our dressing room and were about to start their warm-up on the field. Bob Simpson, the long-time coach of the Australian Test and one-day teams, was working with the Australian XI and he was out there with them. Simmo was a renowned disciplinarian, but after I'd apologised and said it would never happen again and he replied it had better bloody not, there was nothing more said about it … until the warm-up was completed.

The boys started to walk off, but the coach stayed where he was. 'Ricky, you can stay out here with me till the game starts,' he said.

First up, Simmo had me catching high ball after high ball — he was renowned for hitting balls where you had to sprint as hard as you could for 30, 40 or 50 metres to just get your hands on the catch, and then he'd do it again. And again. That's what we did until the game started, which wasn't good for a bloke with a hangover. I was buggered by the end of it. Later in the dressing room, I guess I should have been thinking about how I'd let myself down, but instead I was preoccupied by the thought that I'd been caught out doing what my more experienced team-mates had also been doing, but they'd got to the ground on time, so the coach was none the wiser, or at least more forgiving.

I liked Simmo. He made you work, he could be hard, but in my experience he was always fair. I quickly came to learn that one of his party tricks was to make hungover, late or ill-disciplined players work doubly hard in practice, and that he was testing me out on that second morning of the Australian XI game. Fortunately, I survived every challenge and we got on well after that. At least he couldn't question my work ethic. In fact, I revelled in his fielding drills, though I never needed anyone to push me with that part of my game. I knew I was a good fielder and catcher, but I was never satisfied. Where this came from, I don't know — but as with batting and golf, once I realised I was good at it, I kept trying to improve. I remember going to training with Mowbray, Tuesday and Thursday nights, and I fielded all evening. As soon as I'd done my batting, I was running around, catching high balls or ricochets off the slips cradle, taking pride in every aspect of it, trying to be better than everyone else. It was the same when I was at fielding practice with the Tasmanian and Australian teams. I didn't care how good the best fielders, guys like Mark and Steve Waugh, were, I tried my best to outdo them. That trait stayed with me right up until my last game.

I found Simmo to be a helpful and perceptive coach, who had a very similar philosophy to Rod Marsh when it came to teaching cricket. Neither man set out to massively change the way I batted on the basis that I was obviously doing a few things right to get to the level I had reached. As a result they restricted their advice to fine-tuning my technique.

THAT FIRST AUSTRALIA A game we played in Adelaide happened in late November. A little more than three months later, I was at Sydney airport, walking into business class of a Cathay Pacific 747, finding my seat for the flight to Hong Kong, from where we'd fly to London for a two-day stopover before heading to Barbados. It was genuinely exciting to be in London for the first time, but what I noticed most was how different the mood was on this tour from the atmosphere in New Zealand, when partners and kids were with us, and the week had a 'holiday' feel. This time, we were serious.

Yes, there was time to walk around London, but we also spent time under team physio Errol Alcott's expert supervision in the gym at the Westbury Hotel, watched some videos of the recent West Indies–New Zealand Test series and had a lengthy team meeting chaired by captain Mark Taylor that established the approach he wanted the team to take in the Caribbean. I was struck by how professionally run this gathering was, and how astute and perceptive many of the comments were — from Tubby, Simmo and a number of the senior guys. This was clearly a team with plenty of cricket nous and a tour that meant a great deal to them. I didn't say anything during the meeting, just listened intently and lapped it all up.

The next morning, we had to be downstairs not long after 6am for the start of the next leg of our journey, and that hour of the morning was not one I usually enjoyed seeing. This time, however, I was the first one ready for the bus.

Building a team

If I had a choice between two very similar standard players, I would always select the player with the right temperament, make-up and personality. While I was never a national selector, nor would this situation be a regular occurrence, my point is that the character of players is really important to building a successful team. We are always looking for the best talent to come through our system and play for Australia. In the most successful teams that I have been a part of, the talent in the team was outstanding and our performances showed that. We had a team of individuals from which you knew there was always at least one player who would stand up and deliver when the team needed something extra.

Success breeds success, and success also builds teams. But teams that do not achieve consistent success require a completely different approach. Sometimes you can't build a team around individual brilliance, group dynamics and group leadership. Sometimes you have to pick players with particular character to support the younger, less experienced players or to add value to the leadership group or simply for their experience.

Over the final third of my time in the Australian team, there was a lot of turnover in our teams. As players retired, a new generation of players made their Australian debuts. Many of these never quite became permanent fixtures in the team and played only a few games. This was a challenge for me as captain. Players would come in to debut and we would have a data bank of information on their technique, strengths and weaknesses and other game data to help me and the team get the best out of them. But we lacked the detail on their character and personality. I had to spend as much time as I could with these guys when they first came into the group getting to know them, working out what made them tick and what I needed to be aware of in the game situation. A lot of this was done on the run and wasn't always a success out on the field.

It's when the pressure comes on that you really find out about an individual and their capacity to perform at the international level. When you are building a team or preparing for a period of change in a team, more time and care needs to be taken to focus on the character and make-up that will be required to balance the critical need for talent and the ability to perform consistently at the highest level.

CHAPTER 8

RETALIATE FIRST

West Indies, 1995

'THOSE HANDSHAKE AGREEMENTS between you blokes, where you don't bounce each other, they don't exist anymore,' he said, looking straight at our pace bowlers: Craig McDermott, Glenn McGrath, Damien Fleming and Paul Reiffel. That sounded pretty fair to me, but then I wasn't one of the late-order batsmen who were about to cop as good as they gave, maybe even worse.

Steve 'Tugga' Waugh had a reputation for being a tough and combative cricketer and he demonstrated it here, arguing that it was inevitable that the West Indies quicks were going to fire bumpers at us, so we had to bounce them too. Furthermore, they were going to attack our tail, so we should do the same to them.

As it turned out, Steve would have a famous tour, most notably when he stood up to the fearsome Curtly Ambrose on a dangerous wicket during the third Test at Port-of-Spain, and then followed up with a brave and brilliant double century in the series decider at Kingston.

Tugga was one of our most experienced players — having come into the Australian team as a 21-year-old in late 1985, when the side was losing more often than it won — and many times in the years we played together he would reminisce about those days, emphasising that we should never take winning for granted. In the days leading up to this Test series, he wanted us to know that during the 1980s and into the 1990s the West Indies played cricket bloody hard and to make this point he'd recount stories of fast bowlers like Malcolm Marshall, Patrick Patterson, Courtney Walsh and Ambrose firing bouncer after bouncer at battle-weary Australian batsmen. David Boon, who would play his 100th Test in Port-of-Spain during this tour, recalled how Marshall had whispered to him at the non-striker's end during his Test debut, 'Are you going to get out, or am I going to have to kill you?' Mark Taylor, Craig McDermott, Mark Waugh and Ian Healy had similar stories, so it was hardly surprising that the senior blokes backed Steve's call to stand up to them this time. We were going to, as old footballers like to say, 'Retaliate first!'

Part of this process was to have our quicks bowling plenty of short stuff in the nets, as a rehearsal for what they'd be doing in the Tests and to get the batsmen used to the reprisals they'd be copping from the Windies' quicks. This helped me, I think, because I was never shy about playing the hook and pull shots. I desperately wanted the leadership to believe I deserved to be on the tour, and whenever Tubby or Steve or Bob Simpson complimented me on the way I handled the short deliveries I felt I was on the way to achieving that.

With Greg Blewett established in the Test line-up at No. 6 (he'd scored centuries in each of his first two Tests at the end of the 1994–95 Ashes series), Justin Langer and I realised we were the two 'extra' batsmen in the squad. Rather than let this situation get us down, we made a pact in Bridgetown, in the early days of the tour, that however much we enjoyed ourselves off the field, when it was training time we'd work tenaciously hard. It was on this tour that I came to realise how hard I needed to work if I wanted to become a very good international player. Justin and I were able to watch how the accomplished players prepared themselves for games, what routines they kept, even little things like what they did as they waited to bat. No two blokes were exactly alike; what I had to do was watch what they were doing, work out why they were doing it and then decide what was best for me.

As it turned out, I made little impact on the actual field of play, chiefly because I had few opportunities. I appeared in the third and fifth ODIs, one other limited-overs game and one three-day tour game, and in all three of the 50-over games we played in Bermuda at the trip's end. I knew, going in, that unless there were injuries I was very unlikely to play in a Test, though I would have loved to have made at least one big score.

I was unlucky in one respect, as an agonising bout of food poisoning in St Kitts forced me out of the three-day game against a West Indies Cricket Board XI that was played between the second and third Tests. On the evening before the game, we'd been invited to one of the island's finest seafood restaurants, but while everyone else went for the lobster or one of the succulent fish dishes, I chose the 'conch chowder' and paid the price, spending all night and most of the following day throwing up at regular intervals. My best innings on the tour was the 43 I scored in the ODI at Port-of-Spain; my only half-century came in the last game before we flew home.

I was pretty disappointed about getting sick as there was an outside chance in that tour game I could press my case for a Test place. I had never been on a tour before where you did nothing and it was a steep learning curve. One of the things that is important on a tour is not to have guys weighing down others. When you get picked or are in the team and struggling to make an impact it is important to stay positive. Self-indulgence is something of a crime and there are many blokes who have had their cards marked as bad tourists and possibly missed the chance of being in the squad because they became a liability. Later, when I was captain, one of the things I would tell every new player coming into the squad was that it was the job of the 12th, 13th or 14th man to keep everybody happy and to bring some energy to the group. If you weren't playing that was your role. Back then David Boon was a great help to me when he saw how upset I was to miss the tour game, telling me to keep my spirits up and to ensure I used the opportunity to learn as much as I could about being part of the squad. I was so fortunate to have him around. He was one of my people, we had played footy for the same club and he was just a typical Launceston bloke. He never had much to say, but when he did it was worth listening to; his humour was dry and devastating. He adopted me in those early days and had a lot of positive things to say about my future. When he released his autobiography Boonie wrote a small piece suggesting I would make more Test runs than him. He had a lot of nice things to say, but couldn't help sledging me about the fact he and Shaun Young had been driving me around for years and I still didn't have a licence. Oh, and he couldn't help but bring up his bowling performance against me that summer. 'The only thing Ricky Ponting fears on a cricket field is facing my bowling. The thought of losing his wicket to me obviously has him petrified.' I suppose I had that one coming.

AT THE START OF THE TOUR, most of the boys were still calling me 'Pont' or 'Ponts' but eventually Warnie got his way and I became Punter, the nickname that will never leave me. I guess my actions on our very first day in the Caribbean might have hastened this evolution, as Mark Waugh and I skipped a fancy lunch so we could get to the races in time for the first. It was Barbados Cup day, an event we believed needed to be savoured in its entirety, so we were on our way to the track as soon as we'd collected our first tour allowance. If we wanted an early introduction to Caribbean culture, this was perfect. There was plenty of calypso, a sea of colour and a strong bouquet of rum that wafted over proceedings. I loved being able to stand back and watch the locals with Tugga and Warnie, who joined us during the afternoon and we were immediately feted like rock stars. I couldn't help but be impressed by how nice and friendly everyone was to us. When the cricket started, however, the locals proved to be not so friendly. The next morning, we played our opening game and the first ball was a beamer to Michael Slater, which nearly decapitated him, and the third was a vicious riser that ballooned off his glove to first slip.

The short stuff would continue throughout the Test series, but just as the boys had promised they stood up to every single bumper, while our pace attack, spearheaded by Glenn McGrath, gave at least as good as we received. The way Pigeon took them on was magnificent and the positive body language of all the boys was so impressive — it seemed to intimidate the West Indies players, which was almost stunning given the manner in which they'd steamrollered all challengers over the previous 15 years or more. When we won the Frank Worrell Trophy in Jamaica our dressing room was filled with TV cameras and reporters and they were allowed to stay to do their interviews while the room was doused in beer and champagne and some of the worst renditions of Cold Chisel's 'Khe Sanh' ever heard were telecast via satellite back to Australia. Eventually, though, everyone except those in or very close to the team were asked to leave, we formed a tight circle, and Boonie led us in a rendition of our anthem that literally had the hairs on the back of my neck standing to attention. Even though I didn't play in the series I still felt part of it all. In the years that followed, there would be some rousing renditions of 'Underneath the Southern Cross' — I'd even get to lead the team in a few — but I'm not sure any had the raw emotion of this one.

That night, we ended up at a hotel next door to the one where we were staying, but most of the guys stayed in their whites and along with a few past players — Allan Border, Dean Jones, Geoff Lawson and David Hookes — who had been savaged by the West Indies in the past, we sat on deck chairs, glasses never empty, and talked about how good it was to win. I hardly said a word, just took it all in. In the years that followed, all the senior guys on this tour would talk about how their memories of the losses they suffered in the 1980s and early 1990s acted as a spur to keep going when the team started winning consistently; how it taught them to be relentless. Coming later as I did, I never experienced those painful setbacks, but I saw how much winning in the Windies in 1995 meant to the older guys. It was a lesson I never forgot.

THE TWO MONTHS WAS an education for me in other ways, too. Rooming with Steve Waugh, for example, meant I could grill him on how he approached Test cricket. Tugga was a cricketer who had thought deeply about the mental challenges of batting against giants like Ambrose and Walsh, and he was also happy to talk about his struggles at the start of his international career, like how he coped with not scoring his first Test hundred until his 27th Test. It wasn't that he was trying to scare me; more that he wanted to stress that success wasn't going to come easily. If I persisted, he explained, I was a chance for a long career.

After Steve, I 'bunked' with Tim May, which was a completely different assignment. Maysie was not in the Test XI and had made the assessment that with the team going well that situation was unlikely to change, so he set out to enjoy the tour as much as possible. What was most remarkable was his rare ability to turn up at breakfast seemingly as bright as a button despite the fact he'd been out until sunrise. He knew there were boundaries and he never crossed them, and rather than get people into trouble his natural instinct was to make sure everyone was sweet. When I said at midnight I'd had enough for the night, Maysie never talked me into kicking on (which, more than once, he easily could have), because he was always in my corner. He is also a born comedian, and remarkably astute at mimicking people and exposing their foibles, which meant that sharing a room with him was a laugh a minute.

As well as a couple of days at the races, the odd spot of deep-sea fishing and a few rounds of golf (especially in Bermuda), there were numerous activities organised by the team's social committee. These ranged from team dinners to beach volleyball to, at the start of the tour, a facial hair–growing competition, where we were given a specific assignment — handle-bar moustache, bushy sideburns and so on — with prizes to be awarded to the best achievers. I was assigned a goatee beard. Apparently, this competition had been a bit of a hit on the Pakistan tour in 1994. This time, however, the guys quickly lost interest, but I kept at it, mainly because I copped such a ribbing during my slow early progress that I was determined to see the thing through. In the end the goatee stayed with me for the best part of the next two years.

In Guyana, where we played the final one-day international of the tour and the first of two first-class games before the first Test, I got my ear pierced, which seemed like a good idea at the time. Dad had always told me if I came home with an earring he'd rip it straight out, and to this day I wonder why he didn't. Maybe the fact Boonie got his ear done at the same time had something to do with it, but it didn't last too long. Another way I confirmed my novice status on this tour came after we were told not to stay on the phone if we called loved ones in Australia. I made a couple of calls home to Mum, kept talking, and was horrified to discover when we checked out of the hotel that I was hundreds of dollars out of pocket.

When we arrived in Bermuda at the tour's end, the boys were ready to party. We hadn't been at our flash resort for long and I was down at the bar with a trio of seasoned campaigners — Boonie, Tubby and Errol Alcott — and after a couple of ales someone proposed we check the island out on the mopeds that were available for guests to use. We didn't get far before we lost Boonie. First, we decided to give him a chance to catch up, but when he didn't reappear we figured we should go back and look for him, and when we couldn't find him we assumed he'd returned to the bar. That seemed like a good idea so back we went. But he wasn't there either. What to do? We ordered a beer, having decided that if he didn't return by the time the drinks were finished we'd organise a search party, and it had reached the stage where that's what we were going to do when our hero finally emerged with blood seeping from cuts to his legs, arm and chin and an unlit cigarette perched precariously on his bottom lip.

It was one of those situations where everyone wanted to ask, 'What happened to you?' But everyone was waiting for everyone else to ask that obvious question. Then, before anyone said anything, Boonie quietly deadpanned, 'Anyone got a light?'

He'd been riding at the back of our pack when he failed to take a turn at high speed and he and bike parted company.

Perhaps his mishap should have been a warning, but there was no holding back when a larger group of us went out that night for some more exploring. This time, Ian Healy stalled his moped and I volunteered, because of the basic mechanics Dad had taught me, to get it restarted, saying, 'Don't worry, I'll catch you all up.' I was able to do that, but then the bludger conked out again on the way back to the hotel and as I tried to get it going the back wheel got caught in a gutter. My response — part bravado, part frustration, part eagerness to return to the pack — was to go full-throttle, and when the bike did free itself it took off on me straight into a pole on the opposite side of the road. I'm not quite sure how I survived, but the bike was a write-off.

This wasn't the only time a moped took a battering while we were in Bermuda. Right at the start, we had to get a permit before we could ride the things, which involved a basic test in the resort car park. A number of the guys had their partners with them for this final leg of the tour — until then, it had been boys only — and the girls had queued up so they could ride around the island too. All each of us had to do was go in a straight line, ride around a tree situated on the edge of the bitumen, and then come back, dodging a couple of witches' hats along the way. I passed the course easily, we all did, except for one of the girls who had no idea how to ride a bike and when she was supposed to slow and turn instead she panicked and accelerated straight up a steep rise behind the tree. Near the top of the rise, the bike flipped back over itself while she kept hanging on, and for a moment it looked like things might turn really messy. Fortunately — and a bit miraculously — she survived, but then, when she picked up the bike, the back wheel was still spinning and as soon as it hit the ground it took off again. The two of them — bike and terrified rider — shot straight across the car park and it was a miracle (again) that she was finally able to get the thing to stop. Despite all this, she was then given a pass and soon we were on our way.

STRICTLY SPEAKING, I SHOULDN'T have been given a permit, because when we were making our applications we were required to fill out a form, and one of the questions was: *Do you have a driver's licence?* The correct answer — if I wanted a permit — was 'yes', so I had to lie.

I could have got my driver's licence any time after I turned 17, but I never felt like I needed one, at least not until I was well into my 20s. From the time I first went to the Academy when I was 15 I was never really in one place for any length of time, so getting an opportunity to do the lessons was tricky. And when I was back in Launceston, there was usually someone able to give me a lift and more often than not at other times I could get to where I needed to go without too much of a hassle. It's not that big a town. Most of the time I was going no further than the golf course, the cricket ground, the footy or the dogs, and I was rarely going to any of those places on my own.

I certainly wasn't scared of driving, more just lazy, I guess. If I'd found myself constantly marooned at home unable to get to places I needed to go, I'm sure I would have got my licence in record time, but the blokes I spent my time with were all happy to pick me up or Mum or Dad were usually there if I needed a lift. And if you arrived at the club on time there was a bus to take you to the away games. Ironically, one of my first sponsors was Launceston Motors, the city's biggest Holden dealership, and they offered me a car as part of the deal. (Perhaps my favourite sponsorship from those early days was with a local bakery. I didn't get anything out of it; instead the funds were used to renovate the clubhouse at Invermay Park.)

When I was 24 I bought a house in Norwood, a suburb in South Launceston, which I shared with my then girlfriend. It was after we broke up early in the 1999–2000 season — and I found myself living in the house on my own — that I finally felt the need to get my L plates.

I suppose I can tell the story of finally getting my licence now. There was a policeman in a small town about three hours' drive from Launceston on the north-west coast who may not have been the strictest when it came to those sorts of things. I don't know how I heard of him, but Mum drove me up there and I basically went for a little drive with him and before I knew it I was a registered driver. If Boonie ever needed a lift all he had to do was call.

SIX WEEKS AFTER WE returned home from the West Indies in 1995, I was in England as a member of a 'Young Australia' team that was captained by Stuart Law. With hindsight, it's easy to say that this was a classy outfit — of the 14 guys in the squad, four had already played Test cricket (Jo Angel, Justin Langer, Matthew Hayden and Peter McIntyre) and eight more of us would before our careers were over (Stuart Law, Matthew Elliott, Michael Kasprowicz, Shaun Young, Adam Gilchrist, Martin Love, Brad Williams and me). The only blokes who didn't go on to win a baggy green cap were the South Australian pacemen Shane George and Mark Harrity, but if you'd told me at the time that they would be the two to miss out, I wouldn't have believed you. They were two excellent quicks.

We were reminded in our first team meeting that an Ashes series would be played in the UK in 1997, so the guys who did well in English conditions on this trip might gain some inside running. To be honest, though, while some blokes might have been planning that far ahead, I think for batsmen like Haydos and Lang, who'd experienced Test cricket, and myself and Stuart Law, who had played ODI cricket in the previous 12 months, we were hoping to crack the top side before the middle of 1997. The problem was, given that the Frank Worrell Trophy was now in the Australian Cricket Board's trophy cabinet, there didn't seem to be an opening. All we could do was make a case to be next in line, and that process began with this tour.

In this regard, I didn't do myself any harm, going past 50 five times in 12 first-class innings, but the other blokes had a good time of it as well, so I never felt as if I was standing out. A highlight for me came at Worcester, when I scored 103 not out against an attack that included the former Test bowler Neal Radford, but the enormity of the task I faced to make the Test side was underlined in our one-dayer against Surrey at the Oval, when I thought I batted really well to score 71 from 87 balls. Trouble was, at the other end Stuart Law was in sensational form, smashing 163 from just 126 deliveries and in the process making everyone forget I was even out there. There were numerous examples of this happening, where one guy would play really well but another would do something even better. Against Somerset, for example, Shaun Young made an excellent hundred, but Adam Gilchrist hit 122 from 102 balls, reaching his ton with a colossal six. The competitiveness among us would serve us and Australian cricket well for the following decade.

The only downer of the tour for me was that in the six weeks I was in England I never once had the chance to get to a dog track or a racecourse. Sure, I got to see iconic tourist attractions like Buckingham Palace and the Houses of Parliament, and to play at famous grounds like the Oval, Headingley and Edgbaston, but a number of blokes back in Launceston had told me how different and interesting horse and greyhound racing can be in Britain and I wanted to experience it for myself. All I could do, as I tried to find some sleep on the long flight home, was to make a commitment to do all I could to get back to England in the near future, preferably with the blokes I'd been with in the Caribbean, this time as a member of an Australian Ashes touring team.

Practice makes perfect

Practice makes perfect is one of those everyday coaching lines that you hear all the time. But for me it goes one step further than that — *perfect* practice makes perfect! You have to train as specifically as you can for what you require and do it at an intensity that is as close as possible to match conditions.

For me, cricket has a long way to go to replicate this specific training. We train away from the centre wicket and outfields — on surfaces that are nothing like what we play on during a match. As a batsman preparing in the nets, you are at the end of a wicket that is almost certainly nothing like the centre wicket for the game. You face four or five bowlers — all of different paces and techniques — bowling in an order one after the other with different balls. Again, nothing like what happens in a game, when you face the same bowler with the same ball — for six balls in a row. Bowlers are faced with similar challenges. Many of them are unable to train with their full run-ups, with a full set of different balls to replicate different times in a game, no field placements to bowl to, and most bowlers are limited to the number of balls they will bowl in training to protect their capacity for a game.

I had a saying 'train hard and play easy' that summed up the need for more specific training. I think this was one of the reasons we weren't at our best in the 2005 Ashes series, where we lacked the specific training we required. We certainly fixed that for the 2006–07 Ashes series, where I demanded that Brett Lee, Glenn McGrath and Jason Gillespie bowl new balls at full pace at me in the nets, day in and day out. The bouncers, movement and sheer intensity of those training sessions helped us all and was a part of the foundation for our 5–0 whitewash of England in that series.

Fielding practice has certainly come a long way since my early days in cricket and it's as specific today as ever. Most days you now get on the outfield of the ground you are playing on. You can replicate a whole range of typical game situations from catching to runs-outs and throws. I had a set routine as part of my one-day training, where I had someone hit balls to me at backward point or extra cover, and I would field the ball and get it into the stumps as quickly as possible. I also had a variation of this where I would attempt to throw down the stumps at either end of the ground. I did tens of thousands of repetitions of this, at high intensity, and it certainly was perfect practice that made perfect.

CHAPTER 9

THE HUNDRED THAT GOT AWAY

NTCA ground Launceston, December, 1995

AT THE START of the 1995–96 season, Justin Langer and I were at the front of the queue to get into the Australian Test team if an opportunity came up, but Stuey Law was one of a number of gifted batsmen who were close behind. Of all of us, he was the one who started the season best in the early Shield and Mercantile Mutual one-day games. Then in early November, I finally found some form in a Shield game at Bellerive against Stuey's Queensland, scoring 100 and 118, but he replied with a stylish 107 in their second innings. At the same time, poor Lang could hardly score a run for WA, until he cracked a second-innings 153 in Adelaide.

It was that old, quiet battle again, all the fringe players pushing each other.

Australia was involved in three Tests against Pakistan, and as that series unfolded concerns grew about the form of the Australian batting order, with most attention being on David Boon and Greg Blewett, who were struggling. In the third Test, which Pakistan won by 74 runs, Boonie and Blewey both missed out, while at the same time I made some big runs against the touring Sri Lanka, whose three-Test series against Australia was due to begin at the WACA on December 8. First, I scored 99 in a one-dayer at Devonport and then 131 not out in Tasmania's first innings of a four-day game against the tourists at the NTCA ground in Launceston with Test selector Jim Higgs watching. I was a little lucky, to be honest, as I had been dropped on 14. The media believed Blewey was gone for the opening Test against the Sri Lankans, and I was the obvious option to take his place. Then it was announced that Steve Waugh was out because of a groin strain, which seemed to make my selection even more likely.

THE DAY BEFORE THE TEAM was announced, the *Examiner* ran a back-page headline which shouted: 'Pick Ponting!' Inside, it pointed out that if I was selected it would be the 'best 21st birthday present he could wish for', because the Test was due to start on December 8, which was 11 days before I would turn 21. The next day, the *front-page* banner headline was more exuberant: 'He's Ricky Ponting, he's ours ... and HE'S MADE IT!'

Underneath was a big photograph of me giving Mum a kiss, while the accompanying story began: 'Tears of pride welled in Lorraine Ponting's eyes yesterday as she told of how her son Ricky had always said he would play Test cricket for Australia.'

The Test side was named on the last day of Tassie's game against Sri Lanka, and that photo of Mum and me was snapped just before the news was announced over the PA system at the NTCA ground. There was something a bit special about learning of my promotion at my home ground with family, some of our closest friends and my Shield team-mates there to share the moment with me. Mum was never keen to watch me play — after I failed a couple of times when she was there, she started thinking her presence might be the cause — so when I saw her in the grandstand when I walked off the field I figured something must have been up. She ran down to meet me at the gate and was the first to tell me I'd been picked for Perth along with Stuart Law. It would be Stuey's first Test as well.

Unfortunately, Dad was working, rolling the pitch at Scotch Oakburn College (Ian Young had teed up that groundsman job for him), but we caught up at home that evening and then, when the phone finally stopped ringing for a minute, the whole family dashed out for a celebratory dinner. After that, I raced over to the greyhound meeting at White City, where I met up with a few mates. It wasn't a late night, but it was a beauty — everyone at the track seemed to know that Tasmania had produced another Test cricketer and I was overwhelmed by the number of people who came up to wish me all the best.

Inevitably, there were plenty of well-meaning individuals who wanted to give me advice. I'm not sure who suggested I get a haircut (probably Mum), but I did as I was told. Of all the suggestions offered, a couple stand out, not so much because of the advice offered but who was giving it: Uncle Greg told me to 'stick to what you know best' and then David Boon said I should just 'go out there and enjoy it'. Nothing more complicated than that. Not long after I landed in Perth, captain Mark Taylor reminded me I was a naturally aggressive batsman and fielder. 'I want you to add some spice to the side,' he said. 'And don't go away from the style of cricket that got you into the team. It's worked for you in the past and it will work for you here.'

I was actually one of three newcomers, with Michael Kasprowicz (for the injured Paul Reiffel) also coming into the 12-man squad, the likelihood being that Kasper would be 12th man, with me batting at five, one place lower than I'd been batting for Tasmania, and Stuart Law at six.

We flew to Perth on the Tuesday, three days before the Test was due to begin, but I honestly can't remember feeling particularly nervous, at least until the day of the game. I guess the fact I'd been with the guys in New Zealand and the West Indies helped me, plus the fact that I'd also come into contact with a number of the players at the Academy, or with the Australia A team in 1994–95 or on the Young Australia tour. It's funny thinking back, but while my memories of the actual game remain strong I recall very little of the build-up — except for my constant modelling of my very own baggy green cap in front of the mirror and the fact I took the stickers off my bats, sanded the blades down and then re-stickered them all and put new grips on the handles. I also knew the occasion was special because my parents, as well as Nan and Uncle John (Mum's brother) and Aunt Anna Campbell flew over. Since he retired from cricket, I could count on two hands the number of times Dad had given up his Saturday golf to watch me play, and he's never been a bloke to move too far away from his comfort zone unless he has a good reason to, but here he was in Perth, a long, long way from home. Pop, however, was too set in his ways to fly all the way to Western Australia.

I do remember going out and buying an alarm clock, to complement the clock-radio next to my bed at the hotel, and the two wake-up calls I organised and the early-morning call from Mum and Dad, all to make sure I wasn't late for a day's play. No way was I earning the wrath of Boonie or Shippy again.

HAVING SAFELY GOT TO the ground on time, we bowled first after Tubby lost the toss, which gave me a day to 'settle in' and also meant I could prove that, as a fielder at least, Test cricket was not going to be a problem for me. More often that not in those days, almost as a rite of initiation, the youngest member of a Shield or Test team became the short-leg specialist (rarely a favourite fielding position for cricketers at any level), and I'd fielded there a few times for Tasmania in the previous couple of years, but Boonie had made that position his own for the Australian team, so I was allowed to patrol the covers, which gave me a chance to burn off some of the nervous energy that was surging through me.

On day two, Michael Slater scored a big century, he and Mark Taylor added 228 before our first wicket fell, not long before tea. I went looking for my box and thigh pad. Boonie was controversially given out just before the drinks break in the last session, so I went and quickly put my pads on and then, as the last hour was played out, I grew more and more fidgety, going to the toilet more than once but never for long. Out in the middle, Slats and Mark Waugh looked rock solid on what had become a perfect batting wicket, while Tubby saw I was getting very edgy, to the point that 10 or 15 minutes before stumps he asked Ian Healy to pad up as nightwatchman if a wicket unexpectedly fell. The move proved unnecessary; my first Test innings would have to wait another day.

I was shattered when I got back to our hotel — it had been a long day, even though I'd never got a chance to bat. (I always found it very difficult having to wait so long to have a hit, and didn't have much practice at it as I rarely batted as low as No. 5 in a first-class game; having to adjust to sometimes waiting around for ages before I got a bat was one of the hardest things I had to do in my early days as a Test cricketer.) I went out for dinner that night with Mum and Dad, and in their company I felt reasonably relaxed. My sister Renee had called from home to say she had scored 48 Stableford points while playing for Mowbray Golf Club against Devonport GC in a competition known as the 'Church Cup' — a colossal effort which would take three shots from her handicap — and it appeared our parents were just as proud about her achievement as they were in me playing a Test match. Mum insisted on an early night, but when I went to bed there was no way I could get to sleep. The strange thing was that whereas in the days leading up to the game I'd been picturing myself doing something positive, playing a big shot, even making a hundred, now I was a fatalist — picturing myself getting out for a duck, run out without facing a ball, or maybe I wouldn't get a bat at all, then get left out of the side when Tugga came back and never play for Australia again. When I woke the next morning I felt as if I hadn't slept a minute, but at the ground I was a lot calmer than I'd been the previous evening and I hit the ball pretty well in the nets before play.

Slats was 189 not out at the start of the day, and there was some talk among the team about him having a shot at Brian Lara's then world record Test score of 375, but in the first hour, totally out of the blue, he drove at Sri Lanka's spinner Muttiah Muralitharan and hit an easy catch straight back to the bowler. Just like that, he was out for 219, Australia 3–422.

I DON'T REMEMBER WALKING out to bat, taking guard or talking to my batting partner, Mark Waugh, before I faced my opening delivery. However, I do recall that from early in my innings I was batting in my cap (rather than a helmet) and I will never forget the first ball I faced in Test cricket … a well-flighted delivery from 'Murali' that did me fractionally for length as I moved down the wicket. I pushed firmly at the ball but it held its line and clipped the outside edge of my bat … and for a fateful second I thought my Test career might be over as soon as it had begun. Fortunately, I'd got just enough bat on it for it to shoot past first slip's hand and down to the fence for four, which took away the possibility of a duck on debut and slowed my heartbeat a little. In fact, it calmed me down a lot — it doesn't matter whether you're batting in a Test match or in the park, if you nick your first delivery and it goes to the boundary you feel lucky, like it might be your day.

For the next four hours, it looked like it was going to be mine.

Initially, I was a little scratchy, but then they dropped one short at me and I belted it through mid-wicket for four. Middling that pull shot was what I needed; it was as if I shifted into a higher gear. From that point on, my feet moved naturally into position, I had time to play my strokes and my shot selection was usually on the money. I'd batted at the WACA a couple of times before and loved the extra bounce in the wicket and the way the ball came on to the bat, and the light, too, which seems to make the ball easy to pick up. All I focused on was 'watching the ball', a mantra I repeated to myself before every delivery, the way Ian Young had told me to do. Being out there with Mark, who always made batting look easy and was a brilliant judge of a run, helped me enormously and then, when he was out for 111 to make our score 4–496 Stuart Law came out. Two of us out there in our first Test. He started very nervously, which in a slightly weird way was good for me as well, because suddenly I felt like the senior partner instead of the rookie.

When I reached my half-century, I looked straight away for my family in the crowd, especially for Mum, and I pointed my Kookaburra in her direction. It was a very satisfying feeling getting to fifty, because I knew — even with Steve Waugh coming back into the team and Stuey now looking comfortable — that I'd get another game. Now, I just wanted to enjoy it. We were already more than 200 in front, so I knew a declaration was coming sooner or later, certainly before stumps, but Tubby never sent a message saying I had a set amount of time to try to get a hundred. So we just kept going.

It was only when I moved into the 80s that I *really* thought the ton was on. By that point, the way Stuey and I were going through the last session of the day, he'd get to a half-century and I'd make three figures about half an hour before stumps, and that seemed a logical time for a closure. But it wasn't to be. Sri Lanka had just taken the third new ball and I was on 96 when left-arm paceman Chaminda Vaas got one to cut back and hit me above my back pad — closer to my knee than groin. They did appeal, quite loudly considering how much it had bounced and the state of play, while I panicked for that split-second after I was hit (as a batsman always does as a reflex when hit on the leg anywhere near the stumps), but I quickly calmed down when I realised the ball was clearing the stumps. Nothing to worry about.

Then, Khizar Hayat, the umpire from Pakistan, gave me out lbw.

I simply couldn't believe it. I looked down at the ground, fought the urge to complain or kick the ground, and began to trudge slowly off. *What else can I do?* The Sri Lankan captain, Arjuna Ranatunga, rubbed me on the head, as if I was a kid who'd just been told to go inside and do some homework, and for a moment I felt a surge of anger, but I managed to let his gesture go. I felt so empty, a feeling accentuated by the mass sigh and stony silence that immediately greeted the decision, though the crowd was very generous in their applause as I approached the dressing room. You only get one shot at scoring a century in your first Test innings and I'd done the hard work … and that opportunity had been snatched away from me when everyone, me included, thought I was home. Apparently sections of the crowd got stuck into the umpire, but I didn't hear it. All I could think of was the hundred that got away.

Tubby declared immediately, with Stuey left at 54 not out, which meant that there was plenty of activity in the room as we prepared to go out for the final four overs of the day. There was still time for the boys to congratulate me on how I'd played and to tell me I'd been 'ripped off', a fact that was confirmed for me as I watched the replay of my dismissal on the television in our room. I was gutted. I felt like I'd got a duck, like everything I'd done was a waste. Back on the field, the fans were now really giving it to umpire Hayat, and this time I heard every crack, from the obvious to the cruel.

Umpiring mistakes, as much as your own, can cost you records and matches, and this one cost me the chance to join that very exclusive club of Australians who have made a century in their debut Test innings. I guess there were extenuating circumstances; it was a really tough Test match. Hayat had been out on the field for five-and-a-half hours on a very hot day, and he was under pressure after reporting the Sri Lankans for ball tampering and then giving David Boon out when he shouldn't have earlier in the Test. Making it worse, we went out and bowled four overs, and in the last over of the day I was fielding bat-pad on the offside for Shane Warne, and Warnie got a ball to fizz off the pitch, straight into the middle of the batsman's glove and it popped straight up to me. All I had to do was catch it and throw it jubilantly up in the air, which I triumphantly did, but umpire Hayat said, 'Not out.'

Afterwards, I said all the things they expected me to say: that I would have taken 96 if you'd have offered it to me at the start of the

Test; that good and bad decisions even out in the end; if the umpire said I was out, I was out … but I was still disappointed and I don't think I truly got over it until I went out for dinner that night with my parents and Nan.

'Another four runs would've been nice,' Dad said. 'But I'm proud of you, we all are.'

Of course, with the Decision Review System (DRS) in place, you'd like to think decisions like that wouldn't happen today. They'd have gone to the replay and then promptly reversed the decision. But at the time, I was not even aware that Hayat felt he'd made a terrible mistake. When he saw the replay at tea, his umpiring partner on the day, Peter Parker, recalled him being shattered he'd made a mistake. When they first introduced the DRS, I was hesitant, because I always worry about tampering with our game in any way on the basis that it's pretty good the way it is. But then someone would ask, 'Don't you remember your first Test?' And I'd think, *Maybe a review system isn't such a bad idea.*

The last word goes to Nan, who couldn't hide the fact she was so thrilled with all I'd done and was doing with my cricket. I was so happy she was there to share my first Test with me. As I batted on that third day, and the possibility of me making a debut ton grew closer, the TV cameras found her in the crowd and a reporter went over to see how she was going. Of course, she was asked about that T-shirt — the one she made when I was nine or 10 that said I was going to be a Test cricketer — and she quipped that she was going to print up another one.

'What's this one going to say?' the reporter asked.

'I told you so!' Nan replied, and everyone laughed.

I'd missed out on the debut ton, but Nan was right: I was a Test cricketer.

AT THE START of the 1995–96 season, I had been awarded a contract by the Australian Cricket Board. To tell the truth, I can't remember what it was worth — if I had to guess I'd say around $50,000, with the potential to make quite a bit more — which reflects the reality that at this stage of my life I just didn't care what they were paying me. Occasionally, I'd hear a senior member of the Australian team muttering about how badly we were being paid, how the ACB was ripping us off, and I'd just nod my head and move on. I just wanted to play. The 'security' a contract brought meant nothing to me, because it didn't guarantee I was going to be involved in the next game. What mattered to me was how well I played, not how my bank account looked.

For me, the best part about getting the Board contract was that it meant the people running cricket thought I deserved it. The combination of their backing, the camaraderie I felt in the Caribbean and the belief I had in my ability meant I felt a genuine sense of belonging when I played top-level cricket, even though I was not yet 21. This was a step up from the confidence the Century Club had in me when they sponsored my trip to Adelaide, that Rod Marsh had in me when he freely told others that he thought I could play, or that companies like Ansett, Kookaburra, Launceston Motors and the Tasmanian TAB were showing in me when they signed me up for cricket scholarships or sponsorship deals.

It was as if I'd moved from standby to actually having a seat on the plane. I felt like I'd never have to work again. And in a sense that's what happened, because playing cricket has always been a joy for me. I've never felt like I had to be there for someone else's sake, or because I needed the money. I think if I'd never played in a grade any higher than park cricket I would have been one of those blokes who kept playing forever, into my fifties, just because I love the game so much. I was getting well paid for doing something I would have done for nothing. Few people get this lucky and I've never forgotten that.

Every year of my cricket life I've had to pinch myself.

Honesty

Being honest shouldn't be that hard. It's a value that every person should have. Honest team members create an honest team — and if you don't have that, then trust and team values break down. Honesty has been a core value of mine for as long as I can remember. It's been essential to me, right through my whole career — being honest to myself and to my team-mates, to the media and, above all, to the Australian public and cricket fans all over the world. It's not a trait that you manufacture; it's a way you live your life.

It's also the way you should play your cricket. Honesty in the way you prepare, in your training, in your interactions with your team-mates and in your mental approach to a game. Honesty is integral to how you play the game. Always giving 100 per cent, being true to the values of the team and of your country, and of your team-mates. It's also about being true to the spirit of the game of cricket. Playing to win, playing within the rules and playing with the integrity that is expected of all cricketers. Honesty is for the public eye but also behind closed doors with the way you communicate and interact with others. For me, honesty is not negotiable.

CHAPTER 10

BEST SEAT IN
THE HOUSE

Australian Test, summer, 1995–96

IN MY FIRST THREE TESTS, I saw a ball-tampering controversy in
Perth, Muttiah Muralitharan no-balled for throwing by umpire
Darrell Hair in Melbourne and David Boon announce his retirement
from international cricket in Adelaide. In between, relations
between the Australian and Sri Lankan teams became pretty ugly,
to the point that the two teams refused to shake hands after we
won the World Series Cup in Sydney.

Simmering in the background was the continuing match-fixing
controversy, which had become a headline story in Australia back
in early 1995 when it was revealed that Mark Waugh, Shane Warne
and Tim May had accused Salim Malik of trying to bribe them
to play poorly in a Test match and a one-day international on
Australia's tour of Pakistan in 1994.

During the following October, Malik was cleared by Pakistan's
Supreme Court. But the so-called Malik affair didn't end there. It
was to be in and out of the courts for another ten years.

Then on January 31, 1996, two days after Boonie's farewell
Test, a huge bomb blast went off in Colombo, where we were

scheduled to play a World Cup match two-and-a-half weeks later. The loss of life was horrifying. Some of the guys received death threats, I was being asked questions about being a possible terrorist target, and not everyone was keen to go to the subcontinent for the Cup. I hadn't been prepared for any of this and wasn't sure what to make of it all.

I was supposed to be soaking up every moment of being a Test cricketer, but there was so much going on around the games it was almost overwhelming.

The ball-tampering episode in Perth was a bit of a joke, because the umpires didn't take the allegedly damaged ball out of the game, so it was a bit hard later on for anyone to determine if the Sri Lankans had done what the umpires reckoned they had. In the Boxing Day Test, Darrell Hair cast his verdict against Murali from the bowler's end, where I would have thought it was harder to make a clear judgment than if he was standing at square. Mark Waugh reckoned Hair's no-ball calls were the worst thing ever, because for the rest of the day every time Murali bowled the crowd was yelling, 'No ball!', which was very off-putting for the batsmen. Mark was eventually bowled, when he gave himself some room and late cut the ball onto his leg stump. Not his off-stump, his leg stump!

In our dressing room, we initially thought Murali had been no-balled for over-stepping the popping crease, but when the umpire kept going we quickly realised something awful was happening and I couldn't help thinking that if there was a problem with his action there had to be a better way to fix it than to slaughter him on such a public stage. There had been some talk among us about Murali's action, with a few guys adamant that his action wasn't right, but I'd say the overriding view was that it wasn't for us to worry about. Our job was to work out a way to counter him. I came to see his action as unusual rather than bent, and because his top-spinner often deviated from leg to off, we had to be wary of him in the same way we'd be careful against a leg-spinner with a good wrong'un. Over the years, scoring runs against Murali would become among the biggest and most enjoyable challenges I'd face as a Test batsman.

As things turned out, the only time Sri Lanka beat us in Australia in 1995–96 was in a one-dayer in Melbourne, the irony for me being that this was the game in which I scored my first ODI century. Batting at No. 4 and in at 2–10 in the seventh over, I lasted until the last ball of the innings, when I was run out for 123. There are two things I clearly remember about this knock. One, I hit a six, which was very rare for me in those days. I wasn't sure I could hit it *that* far on bigger grounds like the MCG and the SCG, which is a reflection on where I was in my physical development and also on the bats we used then compared to today's much more powerful pieces of willow. Here, I charged down the wicket and hit one as hard as I could right out of the middle of my bat ... and it landed three rows beyond the boundary fence. And two, I didn't claim the man-of-the-match award. That prize deservedly went to Romesh Kaluwitharana, who set up Sri Lanka's run-chase with a superb knock of 77 from 75 balls. Ironically, when we talked about the defeat straight after the game we thought his effort was a fluke — it was only his second innings as an opener in ODI cricket and most people in those days still thought it was a top-order batsman's job to build a platform and help ensure there were wickets in hand for a late-innings assault. In fact, Kaluwitharana's smashing innings was the start of a revolution that would gain traction during the 1996 World Cup and explode from there in the hands of dynamic top-of-the-order hitters such as Australia's Adam Gilchrist, India's Sachin Tendulkar and Virender Sehwag, Sri Lanka's Sanath Jayasuriya and South Africa's Herschelle Gibbs.

The best thing about my hundred was that it locked up a World Cup spot for me. I thought I batted really well when I scored 71 in the Boxing Day Test (a game in which I also took my first Test wicket: Asanka Gurusinha, caught by Heals before I'd conceded even a single run as an international bowler and *after* I thought I had him plumb lbw with a big inswinger), but my batting form in the early World Series Cup games was mediocre and with Steve Waugh due to come back into the team, my place might have been in jeopardy if I'd failed again. Instead, Michael Slater was dropped when Steve returned, Mark Waugh went up to opener and I became the new No. 3. I'd stay at first drop pretty much full-time for the next 15 years.

THREE DAYS BEFORE the Adelaide Test, we met with the ACB to discuss the World Cup tour. A civil war in Sri Lanka had been going on for more than a decade, and while Australian teams had toured there as recently as 1992 and 1994 (and I'd been there with an Academy team in 1993), fighting in the country had escalated in recent times and there was a real fear that terrorists might see the World Cup as a vehicle to push their cause. Further, some Australian players and coach Bob Simpson had received threats suggesting their lives were in danger if they went to Sri Lanka, a frightening state of affairs. However, I was still keen to tour and I went into the meeting dreading the idea that choosing not to tour might be an option. With hindsight, thinking this way was naive, and I have to say that not everyone shared my enthusiasm, but I didn't want to miss a minute of being an international cricketer.

Mark Taylor initiated discussions by asking what our alternatives were. Did we have to play every game or could we just go to India and Pakistan, where all our World Cup matches bar the Sri Lanka group game were scheduled? Was it one Aussie player out, all out? The ACB bosses said we could pull out of our pre-tournament camp and opening game in Colombo, but if we did that it would put back relations between Australia and Sri Lanka by a decade.

'Okay then,' said Tubby. 'What security measures will be in place?'

First, we were assured that the ACB had been to Pakistan and was happy with the arrangements that had been promised. For Sri Lanka, we would be treated the same way as a visiting head of state. We would leave the airport from a different exit to the general public, after going through a special passport control. There would be no parked cars on the sides of the roads we'd be travelling on and armed guards would look after us 24 hours a day, patrol the ground at practice and ride with us on the team bus. Our luggage and gear would travel on a different bus to us, and no one else would be allowed on our floor of the hotel. The only time we could escape this protection was when we were in our hotel rooms. It all blew me away, such a total contrast to the days when I used to ride my BMX bike from Rocherlea to Invermay Park.

We were grateful for all this, though that feeling was tempered by the news that the ACB had only just received a fax saying that we would be greeted by a suicide bomber when we landed in Colombo. Craig McDermott had received a chilling message that stated he would be 'fed a diet of hand grenades', Warnie was advised to look out for a car bomber, and a couple of their players had told us on the field during matches that if we went to Colombo we'd be 'blown up'. Our security experts advised us that if we received a suspicious-looking parcel it would be best not to open it.

Before the final day's play of the Test, we had a players' meeting in which we decided unanimously to go, with the one change that our pre-tournament camp would be in Brisbane. But two days later, a huge bomb blast exploded in the centre of Colombo, just a few blocks from what was going to be our hotel, killing more than 100 people. When I heard about that, I suddenly didn't want to go to Sri Lanka. I would have gone if we'd been made to, but soon the call was made by the ACB, in consultation with Australia's Department of Foreign Affairs, to abort the Sri Lankan leg of our tour. We were criticised by some people on the subcontinent and a few dopey columnists in England, and the World Cup organising committee ruled it a 'forfeit' and gave the two points to Sri Lanka, which seemed a bit ridiculous but didn't worry us at all. Thinking about it now, I'm sure not going was 100 per cent the right decision.

SO WE WOULD BE going to the World Cup, but one man who wouldn't be travelling with us was David Boon, who called time on his international career after the Tests against Sri Lanka. It is one of my regrets in cricket that even though we played three times together at the highest level I never managed to bat with Boonie in a Test match. However, that doesn't diminish the huge influence he had on me as a cricketer, how much he helped me from the time he was making it possible for all young cricketers in Northern Tasmania to *realistically* dream of greatness to the days we were together in the same Aussie dressing room.

Of all the things he taught me about big-time cricket, the thing that stands out most for me is patience. I was lucky in that from when I first came into the Tasmanian team, I could observe him closely at training and in games and study the manner in which he made the bowlers come to him, how he would wait until the ball was in his area, and then he'd score his runs. 'You have to know your game,' he would say. 'And try to stay out in the middle for as long as you can.'

I thought I knew what he meant when he advised me to 'know my game', but in fact I didn't really get it for a few more years. And that last line might sound obvious, but in my early days in the Tassie team I often threw away a potential big score by trying to blaze away. A rapid-fire fifty might excite the fans, but Boonie knew it was big hundreds that win games and impress the selectors. After I scored my first ODI century, I really felt a part of the side, much more than I did after making 96 in my first Test. In cricket, the difference between two and three figures can be huge, even if it is a matter of two, three — or four — runs.

Unfortunately, my promotion to the Australian side coincided with Boonie's fight to prolong his Test career. From afar, I'd seen the media pursue out-of-form stars in the past, great players like

Allan Border, Merv Hughes, Dean Jones and Geoff Marsh. But that was when I was a spectator; now I got a whole new perspective on the situation. I was at a stage of my career where everything that was written about me was positive, so I was always keen to head to the sports pages. Boonie, about to turn 35 and — as far as some reporters were concerned — well past his use-by date, probably hadn't read a paper in weeks, but he couldn't avoid the whispers, the well-meaning advice to 'ignore what they're writing about you', the negative tone of the journalists' questions. Watching him in the nets, I wondered if he was working *too* hard, but there was no way a young pup like me was going to say anything. I saw how stoic he was in the dressing room at the WACA after he was fired by Khizar Hayat (I think I'd have flipped in the same situation) and I admired how he fought so hard in Melbourne to score 93 not out on the day Murali was no-balled by Darrell Hair. He went on to his final Test century the following day.

I also was taken by the way he handled his omission from the one-day squad, a decision announced straight after the Perth Test. The sacking of a long-time player always cuts at the psyche of a team, but there was no way Boonie was going to sulk or make it awkward for his mates; instead, as usual, he was one of the first guys down to the hotel bar to toast our Test victory before we headed back to Launceston — me to play golf with my brother, Drew, at Mowbray; Boonie to visit his wife Pip in hospital, where she was recovering from a minor operation. Of all the things on his mind, that was easily the one he was most concerned about.

I'll never forget how good he was to me on that flight, despite all the turmoil that must have been spinning through his head. He told me how proud he was seeing a 'fellow Swampie' making runs in Test cricket, and how determined he was for the two of us to go to England together on the 1997 Ashes tour. It wasn't to be. I think Boonie found it hard to adjust to being in the Test side but out of the one-day team, and when it became clear he wasn't going to make the World Cup squad he pulled the pin. He told us at a team meeting just before the Adelaide Test, reading from notes he'd prepared so he got the words right, emphasising how much playing for Australia meant to him and how he had treasured the camaraderie he shared with his team-mates. For 30 seconds straight afterwards there was silence, before Tubby, Simmo and a few of the boys told Boonie how grateful they were to have shared the ride with him.

I didn't say anything, not then anyway. It was a bit different for me, because Boonie was not so much my team-mate as my hero. One thing he kept saying was that he was very comfortable with his decision to retire, that it was the right time. Well, it might have been the correct call for him, but I'd had visions of playing a lot of Test cricket with David Boon. I wish I could have batted with him in a Test match. One part of my cricket dream was over almost as quickly as it had begun.

CHAPTER 11
HIGH SECURITY

India, February, 1996

I WAS SEATED in an aisle seat for the first leg of our flight, from Sydney to Bangkok, next to Steve Waugh. Michael Slater, who'd been recalled to the squad, was sitting directly across from me, and he noticed me studying the flash Thai Airways International showbag.

'It's just toiletries, mate,' he said helpfully. 'Try the breath freshener.'

I unzipped the bag, went through the soap, toothpaste, breath freshener ... no, that's the shaving cream ... deodorant. Finally, I found the breath freshener, but initially I was worried it might be an elaborate trap. *What was Slats up to?* I took the cap off the small bottle, and gave the button a gentle prod, so that just a smidgen of spray came out.

Hey, that's not too bad, I thought to myself, as I nodded in Slats's direction. Thai's business class was so impressive I was beginning to think they'd be serving Tasmanian beer on the flight. Then I looked to my right and saw that rather than checking out what freebies might be on offer, Steve Waugh was intently studying the new laptop one of his sponsors had given him to help him type his next best-selling tour diary. He hadn't heard what Slats and I had been talking about.

'Hey Tugga, have you tried the breath freshener?' I asked, as I passed a bottle over to him.

'Thanks, mate,' he replied, as he put the nozzle to his mouth and pushed hard.

But it wasn't the breath freshener; it was the shaving cream. I'd done him beautifully. He spat the foam out all over his new laptop, muttered something about me being a 'little prick', and then had to call a flight attendant over to clean up the mess. Once that was done, he looked over at me and said, as seriously as he could, 'Don't worry, young fella. I've got a memory like an elephant.'

He has, too. But while I'm sure Steve would have tried to square the ledger at some point over the following six weeks — and with our first game cancelled he had plenty of time before our opening match — I don't think he ever did.

AUSTRALIA'S RECORD IN WORLD CUPS prior to 1996 was hardly flash: winners in 1987; finalists in the inaugural Cup in 1975; but couldn't get out of the first round in 1979, 1983 and 1992. Still, we thought we were a real chance this time, even if we were giving the other teams in our group (bar the West Indies, who also refused to go to Sri Lanka) a game start.

There was a sense of relief and anticipation among us when we finally set off for India, as if we were bidding farewell to the stresses and turmoil of the previous few weeks. In fact, once we landed, we'd be subject to a fair degree of hostility from the locals, who thought we'd overplayed our hand by choosing not to tour to Sri Lanka, but on the plane, at least, we felt far away from that.

THERE WERE ACTUALLY 13 DAYS between our arrival in Calcutta (now Kolkata) and our first game, against Kenya in Visakhapatnam. Those in the squad like Steve and Glenn McGrath, who like to explore, did venture out on occasions, but the high security that accompanied our every move made that even less inviting for blokes like me who aren't into that sort of thing. As it was I lost a couple of days to a stomach bug and wasn't going too far from the bathroom anyway, but when I was healthy I was jumping out of my skin at training, and this caused a bit of grief at one session where Errol Alcott had us working in pairs, one guy wearing boxing gloves and throwing punches while the other held up a circular pad to absorb the jabs. All was going well until I aimed a straight right but missed the pad and instead struck Paul Reiffel bang on the bridge of his nose. Fortunately, Pistol was stunned rather than hurt. He quickly told me I was a bloody idiot and then we got on with it.

The fact we were treated as 'outcasts' by critics in India helped galvanise the group, to the point that we could belt each other and still be good mates, and our spirits remained pretty high despite the days without on-field action. Interestingly, while some officials and a number of commentators seemed dirty on us, the local fans were mostly positive, and I was astonished by just how many of them squeezed into the ground floor at our hotels — not to harass us, just to wish us all the best and, hopefully, to nab a prized autograph or photograph. Over the years of playing in India this is something I have noticed. The media can be tearing you limb from limb, but the fans are among the most generous in the world and sometimes it pays to remember that.

We were one down before we even started courtesy of missing the first game, but made up for it in matches against Kenya, India and Zimbabwe. Mark Waugh won man of the match in the first two games and Warnie was outstanding in the third.

It was when we headed to Jaipur to take on the West Indies that I started to get some traction and played my best innings of the tournament. Remembering back to our early team meetings in the Caribbean a year before, where Steve Waugh talked at length about not being intimidated by Ambrose, Walsh and company, I went out to bat in my yellow Australian cap. It may have been a reckless show of defiance, but one that had me feeling very good about myself after I survived my first few overs. Mind you, this was after I ducked under the first three balls I faced — all bouncers.

My best moment of the innings came when I charged one of their best quicks, Ian Bishop, and put him into the crowd beyond deep extra cover — this might have been the best shot of my life — and I managed to get to my hundred before our 50 overs were up, but then their captain Richie Richardson and star batsman Brian Lara came together in a match-winning partnership.

Late in the day, we were still an outside chance of winning if only we could dismiss the Windies' skipper. Mark Waugh did him slightly in the air as he went for a slog-sweep over mid-wicket. I was riding the boundary and I back-pedalled and back-pedalled … and held the catch Australian football-style above my head … then stumbled on the rope and fell back into a Coca-Cola advertising hoarding perched just beyond the playing field. Six! Soon after, the game was over, Richardson was undefeated, 93 not out, with my innings from earlier in the day all but forgotten. This meant I'd scored two ODI centuries and we'd lost both times.

In between this loss and our quarter-final against New Zealand in Madras, we flew back to Delhi, attended a function at the Australian Embassy, and then early the next morning set off by bus for Agra to have our official team photograph taken with the Taj Mahal as the backdrop. The photo was taken with us in our canary-yellow uniforms, and when someone produced a footy I was one of a number of Aussie cricketers seen trying to take 'speckies' among the tourists. Four days later the Kiwis set us an imposing 287, but Junior was in imperious form as he made his third hundred of the tournament and we won by six wickets with 13 balls to spare, to set up a rematch with the West Indies, who'd stunned the favoured South Africans in their quarter-final in Karachi.

OF THE MANY ONE-DAY victories I enjoyed over the years, this semi-final against the Windies in Mohali is often forgotten, but it is right up among the best I was involved in. For much of the day it looked like we were going to lose, but there was real spirit about our team and we just refused to be knocked out. I was dismissed for a 15-

ball duck, one of the four wickets to fall in the first 10 overs of the game (Ambrose was charging in with the setting sun right behind his bowling arm), but Stuart Law, Michael Bevan and Ian Healy all batted really well and we managed to set them 208 to win. It looked all over when they reached 2–165 in the 42nd over, but Glenn McGrath and Shane Warne were magnificent, Mark Taylor's leadership was inspirational and Damien Fleming was nerveless at the end. Having failed earlier in the game, my contribution was obviously minimal, but I was very proud of one piece of fielding I completed near the death, when I turned a four into a three with a diving save on the boundary. At that point, every run mattered but I still wasn't quite sure how I managed it — the only explanation being the adrenalin pumping through my body.

Immediately after the game, it was as if everyone needed time to take in all the drama of the final 10 overs. The mood was pretty sedate, at least until Heals got up and led us in a rousing rendition of 'Underneath the Southern Cross'. We don't sing our anthem after every one-day victory, but our vice-captain couldn't resist the temptation this time. We did manage a couple of celebratory beers before we headed back to the hotel, and then back in team manager Col Egar's room we started to party. Too quickly, though, the clock raced round to two or three o'clock, and then someone mentioned we had a final to win. So, reluctantly, we called it an early morning.

Bags had to be packed and in the hotel foyer by 10am. That was the easy bit. Then we had to get to the airport, get luggage checked in — rarely a formality at anything but the biggest Indian airports — then battle through passport checks and customs clearances because the final was to be staged in Lahore, Pakistan. It was early evening before we staggered into our new hotel, which left us with only one full day to prepare for the final. Sri Lanka, our opponents, had arrived 24 hours before us, which was a significant advantage for them. Training on that one day was a bit of a fiasco, because both teams turned up at pretty much the same time, so we each had to make do with a single net, which inevitably prolonged the session. Our pre-final team meeting was conducted in the manager's room, which was hardly big enough for the purpose, and we based most of our strategy on how Sri Lanka had gone against us in the recent Tests and one-dayers in Australia, without taking into consideration how they'd been playing in this World Cup. Muttiah Muralitharan was still their main spinner, but Sanath Jayasuriya and Kumar Dharmasena, who'd been largely ineffective in Australia, had bowled some key overs in their quarter-final and semi-final wins. They would play key roles in the final, not least in the way they and Aravinda de Silva (normally a 'part-time' off-spinner) would slow our run-rate just when Tubby and I were due to press the accelerator. Sure enough they did the same in the game. We were 1–134 after 25 overs, but finished with a below par 7–241 after 50.

Of course, you're always disappointed to get out, but how I fell in this final really nags at me. I'll never forget how I slammed my bat into my locker when I returned to the dressing room. There is no joy in being dismissed for 45 when your job as a top-order batsman, once you've got that sort of start, is to go on to make a big score. As I recall it, I sensed something bad was going to happen. Tubby and I began to struggle to get their spinners away and I could feel the mood was changing. One thing I would learn about batting on the subcontinent is that, when the ball is turning, it can really hurt to lose a wicket, because it's hard for incoming batsmen to come out and keep the scoreboard ticking over. In this instance, I was bowled at 3–152 and soon after Tubby was caught in the deep, which meant *two* new batsmen had to try to maintain our run-rate. That was never going to be easy.

Arguably the worst indication of our lack of preparation related to the fact that this was the first time we'd played a day–night game at Lahore. We had no idea how damp the field would become (a result of the evening dew) and when that happened the ball became desperately hard to grip. It hadn't occurred to anyone in our camp to check if there was anything special about the local conditions.

It's too late for that final now, of course, but as a result of what happened in that World Cup final, changing conditions between day and night is one thing that is *always* talked about in Australian team meetings. We should have known then; we know now.

When Sri Lanka batted, we quickly broke up their opening partnership but de Silva strode out to strike a match-winning century and this time there was no amazing Aussie fightback. At least this time the two teams shook hands after the game, but then we retreated to a very sombre dressing room where we had to concede we'd been beaten by the better team on the night.

WHEN I GOT HOME and I was asked about my World Cup experience, all I wanted to talk about was the semi-final, about just how electric it was being out on the ground for those final few overs and in the rooms after the game, but when I was on my own, on the golf course or maybe in the gym, I thought mostly about the final and how empty I felt after the game.

After we lost a really big game I felt like I'd let a lot of people down: my mates, my fans, myself. And there was no quick fix; the next World Cup was more than three years away.

The difference in the mood of those two dressing rooms — one in Mohali after the semi-final; the other in Lahore after the final — was colossal. I was comforted to a degree by the knowledge that after all the stress and rancour that went with our decision not to go to Sri Lanka, we'd actually done pretty well just to get to the final, but the memory of how I felt after that defeat stayed with me. As my career unfolded, I'd enjoy many big wins and be part of some massive celebrations, but there would also be a few losses along the way that really scarred, where straight after the game and even for a few days afterwards I didn't like being on the front line, where I wanted to be miles away. This was the first of them.

Look at those around you

My cricket journey has been long and fulfilling. From my earliest days playing school and grade cricket right through to my last game in August 2013 in the Caribbean, I've enjoyed so many highs and my fair share of lows. I've developed lifelong friendships, been to some of the most amazing places and had the honour to captain my country. I've played with and against childhood idols, on all the great cricket grounds around the world, and mingled with royalty as well as the poorest of the poor. But for all these great opportunities and happenings, I've always tried to stay as grounded and as true as possible to myself, my family and my team-mates in everything that I've done.

I've always tried to be thinking of other people and doing what I could do to support them, of how my team-mates could improve, do better or enjoy their cricket more, as well as observing what their strengths are and how they could make them even better, plus what their weaknesses are and what I could do to help them both on and off the field. I worked really hard at this support, especially when we were on the road, when we could spend more time together.

Stepping back and looking at those around you and working out what you can do to help them is something all cricket captains, leaders or business people should do regularly. You're only as good as the team around you.

CHAPTER 12

DROPPED

Launceston, December, 1996

I ANSWERED THE PHONE at home a few days before Christmas. As soon as he said, 'G'day Ricky, Trevor Hohns,' I knew I was in trouble. It had become a standard quip among the players that the only time we heard from Trevor was when he called to say you'd been dropped.

'We want you to go back to Shield cricket and score a hell of a lot of runs,' he said. I was out of the Test side and the one-day squad too.

As early Christmas gifts went, this wasn't one of the best I'd ever received.

My manager Sam Halvorsen, a Hobart-based businessman who'd been looking after me since Greg Shipperd introduced me to him in late 1994, had negotiated a number of sponsorship deals and was telling me that I was very much in demand — well, at least I was in Tasmania. All I'd done from mid-March to mid-July was keep myself fit, work on my golf handicap, raced a couple of greyhounds and had some fun. In July, I travelled to Kuala Lumpur to play for Australia in a Super 8s event and soon after that I was in Cairns and Townsville playing for Tassie in a similar tournament involving all six Sheffield Shield teams. Life was good.

I was just 22 years old and batting at three for Australia. I'd filled that position throughout the World Cup earlier in the year and with David Boon retired from international cricket I took his spot at first drop for a one-off Test against India.

After just three Tests at No. 3, I was out of favour and out of the team, confused and a little angry with the way I'd been treated. I wasn't really sure why I'd been cast aside so quickly and still don't know why. Some people wanted to assume it was for reasons other than cricket, but I'd done nothing to deserve that. I've always wondered if they were trying to teach me some sort of lesson, as if that's the way you're supposed to treat young blokes who get to the top quicker than most. I got sick of the number of people who wanted to kindly tell me that everyone was dropped at some stage during their career: how Boonie was dropped; Allan Border was dropped; Mark Taylor was dropped; Steve Waugh was dropped; even Don Bradman was dropped. I nodded my head and replied that I was aware of that and that I would do all I could to fight my way back into the team, but the truth was I was in a bit of disarray. It wasn't so much a question of whether I deserved the sack but that it had come out of the blue. For the first time in my life the confidence I'd always had in my cricket ability was shaken. If someone was trying to teach me a lesson, what was it?

Years later, when I was captain, I would push for a role as a selector because I believed I should always be in a position to tell a player why they had been dropped, or what the selectors were looking for. There were a few times when I was baffled by their decisions but had to keep that to myself as nothing was to be gained by making that public and nobody was going to change the selectors' minds. In the year after I retired I saw batsmen rotate through the team like it was a game of musical chairs. I know what this sort of treatment does to the confidence of players and I found it hard to watch from a distance. If you're looking over your shoulder thinking this innings could be your last then you're adding a layer of unnecessary pressure when there's enough of that around.

A FEW MONTHS EARLIER, in late August, we'd been in Sri Lanka for a one-day tour that was notable for the ever-present security that kept reminding us of the boycott controversy of six months before and for the fact Mark Taylor was not with us because of a back injury. Ian Healy was in charge and I thought he did a good job as both tactician and diplomat, with the tour being played out without a major incident. Heals wasn't scared to try things, such as opening the bowling against Sri Lanka with medium pacers Steve Waugh and Stuart Law rather than the quicker Glenn McGrath and Damien Fleming on the basis that Jayasuriya and Kaluwitharana preferred the ball coming onto the bat, and he also made sure the newcomers to the squad, spinner Brad Hogg and paceman Jason Gillespie, had an opportunity to show us what they could do. We did enough to make the final of a tournament that also featured India, but lost the game that mattered, against Sri Lanka, by 30 runs.

The security was ultra-tight wherever we went, to the point that a 'decoy bus' was employed every time we were driven from our hotel to the ground. This, to me, was just bizarre. There were two buses that looked exactly the same, with curtains closed across all the windows, and the first bus would take off in one direction, while the second went the other way. First, I couldn't help thinking that if someone was planning to attack our bus, we were playing a form of Russian roulette. And then I'd wonder: *Why are we here? Is what we're doing really that important? If we need to be protected this closely, doesn't that mean something is not right?*

Security-wise, touring the subcontinent went to another level after the 1996 World Cup, and it's been that way — maybe even more so — ever since. For almost my entire career, it's been awkward to venture outside the hotel. I was one of many Aussie cricketers on tour who spent most of my time in the hotel, drinking coffee or playing with my laptop. As the internet became more accessible, a few guys became prone to give their TAB accounts a workout, focusing on the races and footy back home. Soldiers or policemen carrying machine guns outside elevators, even sometimes outside individual rooms, became a customary sight. Guests were not allowed on floors other than their own, outsiders were kept away from the hotel lobby. For the 2011 World Cup, friends and family needed a special pass if they wanted to get through the hotel's front door. It was life in a fishbowl and not always reassuring.

Being constantly under guard did wear me down from time to time, but I don't think it's shortened anyone's career. No one ever came to me frazzled, to say, 'I can't cope with this anymore, I'm giving touring away.' That thought never once occurred to me. Rather, a little incongruously, the guys who have retired in recent times have almost to a man kept returning to India to play Twenty20, pursue business opportunities and to seek help for their charities.

I guess, in the main, we became used to it.

A MONTH AFTER THE AUGUST 1996 Sri Lanka tour, we were in India for a tour involving one Test match and an ODI tournament also involving the home team and South Africa. I started promisingly, scoring 58 and 37 not out on a seaming deck in a three-day tour game at Patiala, but after that I struggled against the spinners on a succession of slow wickets. However, I wasn't the only one to have an ordinary tour, which was reflected in our results: we didn't win a game.

During the month we were in India, we criss-crossed the country, playing important games in some relatively minor cricket centres, covering way too many kilometres and staying in some ordinary hotels. It was one of my least enjoyable tours, and not just because I didn't score many runs. To get from Delhi to Patiala and back, for example, we spent upwards of 13 hours on a poorly ventilated and minimally maintained train, and then stayed in accommodation that was frankly putrid. The Indian Board had arranged the warm-up match for us and said we'd enjoy the short trip through some lovely countryside, but it took forever and the train was so filthy you couldn't see through the windows. We've been stitched-up a few times over the years with travel arrangements — such as when we've been on planes that have flown over the city we're going to, continued in the same direction to another airport and then we've landed, got off, got on another plane and flown back a few hours later — but the 'Patiala Express', as we sarcastically called it, was the worst of them. Tugga said it was a good 'team-building exercise', but he was wrong.

Complaining about these things might sound precious, but too often when we were trying to prepare for a series we were sent to play at places that had substandard facilities.

For future tours, we learned not to worry about ordeals such as this, working on the basis that it was just part and parcel of the careers we'd chosen for ourselves. There is no doubt the good times far outweighed the bad. They'd make us travel all over India for ODIs, and we'd feel they were trying to make it hard for us to win, but we'd use it as motivation: *You can send us wherever you want, we'll still find a way to win.*

Most of the time we were well looked after on tour and the team hotels were the best available, but there were always exceptions. You talk to the older guys and they tell terrible stories from earlier tours. Rod Marsh says that for a whole tour of Pakistan he never drank anything apart from soft drinks and beer because there wasn't even bottled water. The one thing as a cricketer you are most scared of is getting sick. I do remember once sitting opposite Adam Gilchrist at dinner in a hotel that is infamous in Australian cricket and seeing something that was simply unbelievable. Gilly's meal came with a small bowl of soy sauce and when the waiter put it down there was a cockroach in it. Gilly pointed it out and the bloke just grabbed it and stuck it in his mouth and said 'there's nothing there'. We were absolutely horrified. The waiter was struggling to talk because he still had it in his mouth and I can tell you we couldn't eat after that.

I came to think that it was a good indication of how the team was going if we were whingeing or fighting with each other on tour and I think you can see that from the outside too. The worse the performance on the field, the more likely you are to hear about things happening off it.

I knew the team wasn't in great shape if there was a lot of griping or squabbling going on. This India tour might have offered proof of that — at a time when we weren't sure where our next win was coming from, on a flight from Indore to Bangalore after about three weeks of touring, I was involved in a dust-up with Paul Reiffel. I still think the catalyst for the blue remains one of the funnier things I've seen while travelling with the team, but the result was anything but amusing and I regret my part in it. We'd just lost our opening game of the one-day tournament and I was sitting across the aisle from Pistol when they brought out our meals. There was a very old Indian fellow on the other side of him, and I could see this gentleman trying to open a tomato-sauce satchel by twisting it this way and squeezing it that way. It was one of those situations where you know what's about to happen. Finally, he decided to bite the satchel open … at the same time he kept squeezing … and, sure enough, the sauce flowed all over Pistol. Our pace bowler, who'd go on to become an international umpire, cried out in a mix of anger and anguish, while I couldn't help but laugh out loud.

'Tone it down, Punter,' he said to me, and then he started cleaning himself up.

After a couple of minutes, Pistol and his sparring partner sat down to continue their meals. Everything was fine until the man decided to try to read a newspaper while he tucked into his curry, at which point, he knocked his cup of water straight into Pistol's lap. Again, Pistol's cries of dismay were heard around the plane, while I just lost it completely.

Maybe you had to be there, or perhaps I'm just a bloke with no compassion …

I tried to rein myself in, but I couldn't. Pistol was spewing, but he couldn't take his rage out on the old bloke. 'What are you laughing at?' he snarled at me, to which I rather naively replied, 'What do you think I'm laughing at?'

Pistol went to tap either the top of my head or the top of my seat, as a way of underlining the fact he wasn't happy, but he missed his target and clipped me across the mouth. Now, I wasn't laughing; instead I tried to stand and confront him, but I had my seat belt on so I couldn't get up and suddenly I was looking like a goose. Embarrassed and angry, when I finally got to my feet I went to grab him by the scruff of the neck, which was an over-the-top reaction, but where I come from you never hit someone unless you want a reaction, and he'd hit me. A few of the boys had to come between us and settle us down, with more than one of them reminding us that the Australian reporters covering the tour were also on the plane. Pistol was happy to let it go but — ridiculously, thinking about it now — I was not, and a little while later, as we waited in the aisle to disembark, I said just loud enough for him to hear, 'You wait till we get off this plane.'

I'd scored 35 batting at three in the game against South Africa we'd played before the flight, and Pistol had opened the bowling, but we were both dropped for our next game. Tubby brought the two of us together and told us that while he understood that touring isn't always easy, and inevitably blokes can get on each other's nerves occasionally, we had to be smarter than to get into a fight in such a public place. When I stopped to think about how I'd reacted, I realised I'd totally underestimated how much the stress of travelling back and forwards was getting to me. Recalling the incident now, it's amazing it never made the papers but those were different times. A great irony for me is that Pistol is a terrific bloke, someone I like and just about the last person I would have imagined myself fighting. Except for this one time, we always got on really well.

I WAS HAPPY to get home, and this showed in my only Shield game before the start of our Test series against the West Indies, when I had a productive game against WA at the beautiful bouncing WACA. I was duly picked to bat at three for the first Test in Brisbane, and at the pre-game team meeting Tubby underlined the same points he'd made before the celebrated series in the Caribbean: how we mustn't be intimidated by them; how we had to be aggressive; how the blokes who like to hook and pull had to keep playing those shots.

My 'baptism of fire' came quickly enough, as I was in on the first morning when there were only four runs on the board, after their captain, Courtney Walsh, sent us in and new opener Matthew Elliott (in for Michael Slater) was out for a duck. At lunch I was 56 not out, with Tubby on 19, and I was flying. Ambrose, Walsh and Bishop had all tested me with plenty of 'chin music' but I went after them, and it was one of the most exhilarating innings of my life, right from the moment the first ball I faced kicked up at me and I jabbed it away to third man for four. All my early runs came through that area, and then I put a bumper from their fourth quick, Kenny Benjamin, into the crowd at deep fine leg. When Bishop tried a yorker I drove him through mid-off for four, and then I did the same thing to Ambrose, while Walsh fired in another bouncer and I hooked past the square-leg umpire for another four. On the TV, Ian Chappell described me as the 'ideal No. 3' but others may have been thinking differently.

Benjamin came back and I moved into the 80s with a drive past mid-on for another four. I was thinking not so much about making a hundred as going on to a very big score, but then he pitched one short of a length but moving away, and I hit my pull shot well but straight to Walsh at mid-on. It was a tame way to get out, and I had one of those walks off the ground where I was pretty thrilled with my knock but upset that it had ended too soon, so I was hardly animated as I acknowledged the crowd before disappearing into the dressing room. I made only 9 in our second innings, caught down the legside, but we went on to win the game by 123 runs and I felt my counter-attack on the first day had played a significant part in the victory.

My bowling had also played a part, after Steve Waugh strained a groin in the Windies' first innings. I was called on to complete his over and with my fifth medium-paced delivery I had Jimmy Adams lbw. This meant my Test career bowling figures now looked this way: 29 balls, two maidens, two wickets for eight.

A week later we were in Sydney for the second Test, but I suffered a double failure, out for 9 and 4, both times playing an ordinary shot. But we won again to take a firm grip on the series — the only way we could lose the Frank Worrell Trophy was for the West Indies to win the three remaining games. I had a month to prepare for the Boxing Day Test and in that time I played in three ODIs, for scores of 5, 44 and 19 run out, a Shield match against Victoria in Hobart, where I managed 23 and 66, and a tour game against Pakistan (the third team in the World Series Cup) where I scored 35 and we won by an innings. Sure, none of this was special, but it wasn't catastrophic either so I didn't expect the bloke on the other end of the line to be chairman of selectors Trevor Hohns when I answered the phone at home a few days before Christmas.

When he told me I was out of both sides I was so stunned I didn't say much. I certainly didn't complain, but I didn't ask any questions either. Matthew Elliott was hurt and Michael Bevan and I had been omitted, with Matthew Hayden, Steve Waugh (returning from injury) and Justin Langer coming into the side. Lang would bat at three, which might have given the best clue as to the team hierarchy's thinking. I would come to learn that both Trevor and Mark Taylor were reasonably conservative in much of their cricket thinking, and I think their concept of the ideal No. 3 was a rock-solid type, what David Boon had given them for the previous few years. At this stage of his career, Lang was like that, whereas my natural instinct was to be more aggressive. Looking back, given the attacking way I played when I was 21, I probably needed to score a lot more runs than what I did at that time to keep the spot for long. But the truth is I didn't know then why I was dropped, because they never told me, and I still don't know now. I was never told anything specific about my original promotion up the order — it just seemed like a logical progression — or why I was abandoned so quickly. If they thought I had weaknesses in my technique or my character, why did they move me to the most important position in the batting order in the first place?

Almost immediately after Trevor's phone call, Mum and Dad took me out to the golf club, in part because they thought we'd escape the local media there. It was good to get out of the house but Launceston is not that big a city and the reporters were waiting behind the ninth green. Over the years, journos learned that if they wanted to find me the golf course was the best place to look. This time, I think I handled it okay and they were sympathetic with their questions, but it was almost bizarre as I watched them walk away. I felt like calling out to them, *Don't forget about me!*

One of the things that nagged at me was that I had been keen to bat at three when Tubby offered me the opportunity. But maybe I signed my 'death warrant' when I took on the challenge. Perhaps it would have been smarter to stay at six to give me more time to settle into Test cricket. Boonie had told me I should bat down the order for a couple of years, had even made me bat at four in that Shield game after the second Test, and maybe I should have listened to him. In fact, a lot of thoughts spun through my head, none of them pretty, all of them amplified because I hadn't seen the sack coming. To tell you the truth, I wasn't quite sure how to feel … sorry for myself … determined to get back … embarrassed … distraught … all of the above …

All I ever wanted to do was play for Australia … and now I've blown it.

Am I ever going to play Test cricket again?

In the end, after only a couple of days, I said to myself, 'I'm going to get myself back in the team that quick it's not funny. I'm going to go back to state cricket and get a hundred every time I bat. I'll train so hard they'll have to pick me again.'

IF YOU LOOK AT MY SCORES in the Shield for the rest of the 1996–97 season, you'd think it took me a while to rediscover my form. But I actually felt good from my very first innings in January, when we played Victoria at the MCG. I went out with the intention of batting all day and reasonably quickly I felt the ball hitting the middle of my bat. But when I was on 26 Tony Dodemaide, the veteran fast-medium bowler, suddenly got one to seam back sharply and I managed to get a faint nick through to the keeper. As I walked off after getting a ball like that I felt like I was the unluckiest cricketer on the planet, but in our second innings I made 94 not out, my knock ending only when Boonie declared in pursuit of an outright victory. Then came a frustrating fortnight, where I was hitting the ball beautifully in the nets but could only make 8 and 6 against WA at Bellerive and then 39 against SA in Adelaide. I thought the world was against me.

Trevor Hohns had told me to score heavily and if I wasn't doing that, I knew I was no chance of making the upcoming Ashes tour. After that Shield game in Adelaide, I thought, *This is not working.* By 'this', I meant working my butt off. We finished early on day four and as soon as I could I booked a short holiday to the Gold Coast. For the next three or four days I didn't think about cricket and I left it as late as possible to get back to Hobart for our next match. When I did get home, I only had time for a couple of training sessions and then I immediately scored a hundred in each innings against South Australia at Bellerive.

I actually learned a lot about myself and what was best for me during this time. Hitting a million balls a day and training as hard as possible was not always the solution, especially if I felt I *had* to do it. Sure, I'd spent a lot of time in the nets before this but I'd never forced myself to go, to do even more, as if that was the only answer. When things weren't working, I was better off trying to freshen up mentally, and the best way to do that was forget about the pressures of the game. I learned there is a difference between letting it happen and forcing it, in trusting my skills rather than searching for something more.

The other thing that was crucial for me at this time was the support I received from Tasmanian coach Greg Shipperd. When I was working hard at practice, hitting ball after ball, he was always in my corner. He also offered what proved to be a critical piece of advice. My confidence had taken a hit, and Shippy was convinced I'd got into the habit of trying to hit my way out of trouble when things grew difficult. Of course, every batsman has rough spots during an innings of any length, especially if you bat near the top of the order and the pitch is offering some assistance to the bowler, but my brain was getting cluttered when this happened to me.

In the first innings against SA, I scored 126 out of 248. Then Jamie Siddons, the SA captain, made a very positive declaration on the final day, which gave me the opportunity to produce an even better effort than my first dig. We had to win to keep our Shield chances alive and I was in at 2–52 as we chased 349 to win. Four hours later, we'd achieved a terrific victory and I had played an important part, finishing 145 not out. Selectors love match-winning hundreds, but even more important than that I'd been intimately involved in a special team victory, which reminded me of just what a great game cricket can be. In all the stress of losing and then trying to revive my international career, I'd forgotten a little of that.

I made another big hundred in our next Shield game, against Queensland and finished the season with scores of 64 and 22 against NSW at the SCG. It was time to wait for the Ashes touring party to be named. I went through all the options available and realised that even with my big finish to the season, I was hardly a sure pick. The Test team had won the home series against the West Indies 3–2 before heading to South Africa, where it was in the process of claiming a hard-fought three-game series 2–1. However, question marks were hovering over the batting order, with Mark Taylor completely out of form and none of the excellent batsmen from my generation on the tour — Matthew Elliott, Michael Bevan, Greg Blewett, Matthew Hayden and Justin Langer — having cemented their spots. But none of them had cruelled their chances completely either. The media in Sydney was campaigning for Michael Slater to be recalled, while it was certain that Adam Gilchrist, who had enjoyed a fantastic season with bat and wicketkeeping gloves for WA before flying to South Africa to bolster the ODI line-up, would be Ian Healy's back-up. What if the selectors looked upon Gilly as a batsman too, and decided to take an extra bowler? What if they decided to look for experience, and opt for either of the Shield's leading run-scorers for the season — Tasmania's Jamie Cox or Darren Lehmann of South Australia — or Stuart Law, who was still playing one-day internationals but who hadn't appeared in a Test match again since we debuted in the same game.

In the end, I think I was very lucky. Looking at the make-up of the squad now, it was top heavy with batting talent. Bevo was picked as the second spinner and Gilly as the second keeper, but the selectors still chose eight more specialist batsmen: Taylor, the two Waughs, Elliott, Blewett, Slater, Langer … and Ponting. I've always wondered, but I've never been game to ask, if that request Trevor Hohns had made of me — to go back to the Shield and score a 'hell of a lot of runs' — was what got me over the line. I'd done what he'd asked me to do, so maybe he and his fellow selectors felt obliged to honour their side of the bargain by giving me another go. It would have been far from illogical to pick one less batsman and one more bowler; as things turned out, a couple of the batsmen hardly had a dig on tour, while we had to call up some extra bowlers after the first choices suffered major injuries.

What I know beyond question is that my career might have turned out very differently if I hadn't been chosen for this Ashes tour. Matty Hayden missed the trip and didn't get another opportunity for two-and-a-half years. Great players like Damien Martyn and Darren Lehmann had been picked for Australia as prodigiously talented young players in the early 1990s, but after being discarded it would be ages before they would be granted another go at the top level. In contrast, I was very fortunate. My second chance came quickly. I was determined not to waste it.

Role models

I'm a watcher, a listener, a learner. I like to sit back
in the corner and take everything in; learn as much
as possible from as many people as I can. I've never
really had any defined role models in my life but there
have been plenty of people who I've watched very
closely to help me be a better person. Bottom line for
me has been that it's up to me to be the best possible
person that I can be. I had an understanding of where
I wanted to be as a cricketer and as a person. I've
always just been me. Anytime I messed up along the
way, I've given myself a kick up the backside and then
got on with things, making sure that each day I got
up, looked in the mirror and asked myself how I could
be a better person today. In many ways, I've been my
own harshest critic but it's helped me respond at times
when I've most needed to. It's helped me be true to
myself and those around me and probably also helped
me be a better role model for those looking to me as an
example for how they might live their lives. That's a big
responsibility in many ways but one I have always been
comfortable with.

CHAPTER 13

HOPE BUILDS, FEAR DESTROYS

The Ashes, England, 1997

IT WAS A WEIRD experience, reacquainting myself with the other members of the Ashes squad for our flight to London via Hong Kong. I felt like I'd been out of the team for ages, rather than just five months, and quickly I discovered that things had changed a little in the time I'd been away.

Mark Taylor had been struggling for runs, but had stayed in the Test team and ODI squad despite his lack of form, a policy that impacted on the positions of a few other players. Most people were talking about the selection of Michael Bevan, a left-arm wrist spinner as well as a fine batsman, who was picked as the fourth bowler for the Tests in South Africa ahead of Paul Reiffel, seemingly to stiffen the batting order, even though the pitches over there suited the quicks.

When Pistol then missed selection for the Ashes tour some critics reckoned his career had been set back for the sake of the captain. At the same time, Steve Waugh replaced Ian Healy as vice-captain, which seemed to have shaken our champion wicketkeeper. You could see, even on the flight to England, that he wasn't his usual chirpy self. That change, we all understood, had been made so that if Tubby was dropped from the Test XI in England, Tugga would be his replacement, but Heals couldn't understand why he couldn't remain the deputy no matter who was in charge. I couldn't either.

In the years since, I have read stories of how the team was split, but I can't recall any major blow-ups, just that mood shift, that sense that things weren't quite right. Looking back over the statistics, it is a little surprising that Tubby survived his run of outs — at the start of this Ashes tour, he hadn't scored a Test fifty since early December 1995 and since I'd been dropped he'd scored 111 runs in 10 Test innings — but I was not the sort of person to get involved in conjecture about another player's place in the team, especially when he was the captain and I was a young bloke lucky to even be on the tour. I've always hated seeing behaviour or hearing talk that might divide my team. This time, my attention was devoted to forcing my way back into the side.

However, there were moments that showed just how much our captain was struggling with the bat, and not all of these were in the early weeks of the tour. The day before the third Test at Old Trafford, I was standing near the entrance to the nets, waiting for my turn to bat, which gave me a close-up view of him struggling to lay bat on ball. It looked like Michael Kasprowicz and Paul Reiffel (who'd been called up as a replacement after Andy Bichel was hurt) were bowling at 100 miles an hour, and when Tubby walked out of the net, he said to me, 'If you can lay bat on those blokes in there you can have my spot in the Test.' In reality, batting in that net wasn't all that difficult. I also recall him saying to Matthew Elliott one day, 'Next time, I'll wear your helmet out. If I look like you out there maybe I'll get a few half volleys and a few cut shots like you're getting.' Tubby had convinced himself his batting was just one long hard-luck story. Everything was going against him.

In fact, if my memory is right, he got a bit lucky. We played Derbyshire just before the first Test and when Tubby batted in our second innings, his former Aussie team-mate Dean Jones dropped him a sitter at first slip, and he went on to make 63. Four days later, the boys were bowled out for 118 after being 8–54 on the first day of the opening Test at Edgbaston. England replied with 478 before Tubby famously saved his career with a sterling 129. Even though we lost the game by nine wickets, the turnaround in our fortunes was massive. Finally, we could stop responding to the rumours that the skipper was about to get dropped and start concentrating on retaining the Ashes.

To this point, my on-field contribution had been minimal. I batted with little success in our first three matches — an exhibition game in Hong Kong and one-dayers at Arundel and Northampton — and then didn't play for a month, missing a limited-overs game against Worcestershire, three ODIs, three-day games at Bristol and Derby, and the opening Test. First, I was told they had to give the guys in the one-day team the playing time; then it was the guys in the Test team. At practice, I often had to wait for ages to get a hit and it reached the stage where I was spending more time bowling off-breaks as a net bowler than I was playing off-drives. When I did eventually get a chance, in a three-day game against Nottinghamshire, the first day was washed out completely, and when we did get on the field I batted at three and was lbw for just 19. Fortunately, they chose me again for the next fixture, at Leicester, and I managed to score 64 in our first innings, when the only other contributors to get past 20 were Heals (34) and extras (48). When Michael Bevan failed with the bat in the third Test, which we won to level the series, I was suddenly in the running for the Test team.

Things really did change that quickly.

Before the first Test, the selectors were auditioning Greg Blewett and Justin Langer for the No. 3 spot, with Bevo certain to bat at six because his spinners added depth to our bowling attack. Greg made a hundred against Derbyshire, while Lang failed in both innings, and from there my little mate from Perth gradually faded from contention while Blewey hit a century in the first Test and locked up his place for the series. There were three weeks between the third and fourth Tests, and after a sojourn to Scotland we found ourselves at Sophia Gardens in Cardiff, for our tour game against Glamorgan. Tubby won the toss and batted first, and I went out and scored 126 not out, while my main rival for Bevo's spot, Michael Slater, was out for exactly 100 runs less.

When we batted again, Slats opened the batting and was out for 7, and I was kept back to give others a knock, as if I was now one of the Test regulars. There was one more game before the fourth Test, against Middlesex at Lord's, and I was picked again, to bat at six after the guys who had batted one to five in the first three Tests, and the strong impression I was given was that this was being seen as a rehearsal for the big game a week later. If it was, I didn't do myself any favours — out for just 5 — but it didn't matter. When they announced the team for Headingley I was in, and I felt the same emotions as when I'd learned I was going to make my Test debut, only this time the stakes were higher. It wasn't just that this was the Ashes, cricket's oldest trophy, the contest all budding Aussie cricketers dream about; this time, I really thought my career was on the line, that if I stuffed up this chance I might not get another.

It's funny how cricket takes you down a rung. By comparison I'd been reasonably confident when I made my Test debut, but from the moment you're dropped the game becomes another proposition and the older you get the harder it becomes to deal with those mental pressures. For that reason I have always been wary of axing young players or any player when it comes to that. If you're going to do it you have to understand the profound effect it will have on the person and be aware that it can genuinely set people back. Greg Chappell always said it was better to give somebody one Test too many rather than one too few and I agree.

THE OTHER BLOKE who might have been a chance to bat at six for Australia in that fourth Test was Adam Gilchrist but, cruelly for him, he wasn't available. Instead, he was flying home, having hurt himself during a training session in the lead-up to the third Test.

We were playing 'fielding soccer', which as its name implies is a game where you pass a cricket ball to a team-mate by throwing it below knee-height and attempt to score. I was standing slightly in front of Gilly when someone threw the ball to his left, and I dived in front of him to try to cut the ball off, he put his left leg in front of my dive, I clipped the side of his knee, and down he went. Within 10 minutes, you could prod your fingers into his leg and it felt and looked like Play-Doh, all the way from his ankle to his knee. The eventual diagnosis was a torn ligament and poor Gilly was on that plane home. We still have a bit of a laugh about my dive being 'deliberate' — that was the only way I was going to get a game on the tour. It would have been a bold call, picking our second keeper as a specialist batsman in the Test team, but he had played in two of the three ODIs as a batsman, so it wasn't completely out of the question.

I was very sorry to see Gilly depart. In the early days of the tour, when morale wasn't as bubbly as it could have been it was almost inevitable that we young blokes would seek refuge in each other's company, and bonds that were first established at the Academy or on youth tours were forged tighter. Gilly and I have a lot in common, from a love of harmless practical jokes to enjoying working hard at practice. But the team-mate I grew especially close to on this tour was Blewey, who shares my passion for golf, and we had time to experience a number of famous courses, including the Belfry, St Andrews, Sunningdale and Royal Portrush.

The day at St Andrews felt almost like a pilgrimage to me; I'm not sure I felt a similar sense of golfing anticipation until the day I visited Augusta for the US Masters in 2010. However, purely from a quality-of-layout perspective, Royal Portrush on Northern Ireland's north coast was superior, as good a links course as I will ever see. In fact, I enjoyed every minute of our three-day trip to Ulster that came near the end of our tour: the local Guinness was superb and I scored an unbeaten hundred and took 3–14 in our one-day game against Ireland. Another enjoyable excursion was to the famous Brands

Hatch motor racing circuit where I met for the first time Australia's future Formula One ace Mark Webber. Mark was a cricket tragic and we would catch up quite often in the following years. For a guy who drives million-dollar racing cars at a million miles an hour he is as laid-back and unassuming as anyone you would ever meet.

Keeping up with the AFL and the greyhounds back home was one of the challenges of travelling, and more than once I'd call home and ask someone to put the radio to the phone so I could listen to an important race. Junior was much the same. In the match against Nottinghamshire, I was dismissed in the first over of the day after he had said to me, 'I'm next in, so don't you dare get out early today. I've got to listen to a race.' He was in a toilet cubicle at the back of the change room and the horses were lining up behind the mobile start when I let him down. He had to hang up with his horse in contention a couple of hundred metres from the winning post.

MY RETURN TO THE Australian team for the fourth Test was confirmed on the same day we met the Queen at Buckingham Palace, a visit I remember most for Michael Kasprowicz's extended conversation with Her Majesty about the virtues of the *Gladiators* television show.

Two days later the critical Test started — the series was level at one-all — and we were in the field on a day that was interrupted by rain and England finished at 3–106. The next morning, Jason 'Dizzy' Gillespie ran right through them, bowling outswingers like the wind and taking 7–37 as we knocked them over for just 172.

Our reply started badly, with Mark Taylor caught behind off Darren Gough for a duck and Greg Blewett going the same way for 1, leaving us at 2–16. At this point, I went to find my box and thigh pad. Matthew Elliott and Mark Waugh steadied the ship a little, until Junior was caught and bowled by Dean Headley, which was when I started putting the pads on. Steve Waugh, fresh off scoring a century in each innings in the third Test, strode out to put things right, but I had only just taken up a position in our viewing deck when 'Herb' Elliott edged a sitter to Graham Thorpe at first slip. The chance went so slowly I was actually up off my seat, ready to get out there, but then I saw the ball on the turf. Not that it seemed to matter, though, because next over Tugga was caught at short leg. My first innings in an Ashes Test was about to begin and at 4–50 we were not in a good position.

I'd been nervous before the game, but not so much now. It's not like I was relaxed, as if it was just another innings, but when I walked out there my main thoughts were about getting us back into the game, rather than what might happen if I failed, or what the wicket might be doing, or how everyone here and back home was watching me. Maybe the fact the experienced guys had been dismissed cheaply took a little personal pressure off me. Mostly, I think the situation of the game was good for me, in that I was in a position to do something really big for the team. The great golfer Peter Thomson once wrote how 'hope builds, fear destroys' and my mindset as I began this innings reflected that. I wasn't thinking about failing, only about fighting back.

I was also lucky in that I'm not sure the Poms were too thorough when they did their homework on me. The ball was seaming about but they seemed keen to test me out with some short stuff and I relished the chance to show them I could hook and pull. To get off the mark, I pulled a bumper from Headley which rocketed to the boundary and the confidence that one shot gave me was liberating. None of the English quicks were very tall, so whereas Pigeon and Dizzy had got the ball to lift a little dangerously from this wicket, their short ones just came onto the bat sweetly. And then my on-drive started working and I knew it was going to be a good day. Herb and I were also helped, I'm sure, by the fact the pitch settled down as the day went on. I reached my fifty just after we passed their first-innings score. The sun had come out and by late in the afternoon the conditions for batting were excellent, the Englishmen dropped their heads, and we reached stumps still together with a lead of 86 (coincidentally, I was 86 not out). Not for the last time, I discovered how much batting conditions at Headingley can change when the sun comes out.

The only time I felt the nerves getting to me occurred on that third morning, when I was in the 90s, but luckily a couple of loose deliveries helped me out. I'd slept better than I'd expected overnight — no dreams about crazy run outs — but then right away I played a streaky shot down to third man to go from 87 to 91, and for a moment I had to fight the memories of Perth and the frustration of falling short there. There was some cloud cover and Headley's outswinger was working, but then he bowled a nice half volley, which I drove to the extra-cover boundary, and then a short one which I hit off the back foot to exactly the same advertising hoarding. The second new ball was due in a few overs, so they had their off-spinner Robert Croft bowling at the other end, and when I got down there I was very keen to take him on. On 99 I actually ran down the wicket and tried to slog one through or over the legside, but all I did was inside-edge it onto my leg and it finished down near the stumps as I rushed back into my crease. *Just calm down!* Now my plan was to nudge one into a gap on the legside any way I could. I'm not really sure it would have mattered where his next delivery pitched, that's where it was going, but Croft helped me out by flighting one into my pads. I called Herb through and as I dashed down the wicket I nearly pulled my right arm (the one holding my bat) out of its socket as I punched the air in delight.

I can think back on a range of emotions. Later, even a few seconds afterwards and certainly that night when I thought back on what I'd achieved, there was a huge sense of relief that I'd reached the milestone and answered those who'd doubted me — you can see it on the video, how I let out a deep breath and then had my tongue out, a bit like a runner at the end of a tough mile. But the first moment after I reached three figures was sheer joy. I was also very, very proud of myself, that I'd made the ton and that I'd fought back successfully from the hurt and embarrassment of being dropped the previous December. From the time I was seven or eight years old I had been dreaming about this moment. All the training, the time at Mowbray and the Academy, the junior and senior and Shield cricket, had all been about making centuries for Australia and scoring runs in pressure situations in Test matches. No, not just Test matches, in *Ashes* Test matches. There is a lot of work that goes into your first Test hundred and I revelled in the sense of satisfaction. And it was so rewarding to see champions like Warnie, Heals and Junior up on the players' balcony, applauding. Those guys, all the guys, were genuinely happy for me and that made me feel very important.

We carried on and on until we'd added 268, one of the best partnerships I was ever involved in (apparently it was the third highest fifth-wicket stand for Australia in Ashes Tests at that time). I was dismissed for 127, Herb went on to become the third man and first Aussie to be out for 199 in a Test. That was the only downer of the whole experience — he batted beautifully, there was no question he deserved a double ton.

We went on to complete an emphatic victory, winning by an innings and 61 runs, and two weeks later we retained the Ashes when we decisively won the fifth Test at Nottingham. Not even a loss at the Oval, when Phil Tufnell spun England to victory on a substandard wicket to make the final series score 3–2, could take the gloss off what had become a brilliant experience. Today, I think back fondly on both the hundred and the way I handled the stress and disappointment of being out of the team as if the two go together.

I also like to reflect on how we retained the Ashes in England, which despite what a few outsiders thought at the time is no easy task. The speculation that had followed the team for the first month of the tour was long forgotten, the credit for which must primarily go to Tubby, for his persistence, the mental strength he showed when under duress, and for his great tactical ability, which during the middle of the series shone brightly time after time. The way the team regrouped under his leadership was remarkable, and I was proud to have played a small part in that.

AT THE CREASE

From lad to leader

Loyalty & trust

Loyalty and trust are two of the most important traits that I look for in a person. They are certainly core values in my life and are becoming even more important as I grow older and wiser. A successful team will have a high level of trust and loyalty built into its values and performance. The individuals within that team will have a strong team ethic as a natural behaviour, having taken themselves out of their individual approach and behaviour. These individuals are conscious of the needs of their team-mates, providing a level of co-operation and trust that helps the whole team perform at its best.

I probably trusted people too much. While I was aware that not everyone shared my views on the importance of putting the team before oneself, I still gave all of my team-mates the opportunity to develop these characteristics to strengthen the team. If players broke mine or the team's trust, I would let them know straight away. I would make it very clear that they had let the group down and they needed to go away and rebuild the team's trust, my trust, and their own trust. Most of the time, this happened, and I'd sit back and watch the players do their best to make up for their indiscretions. If they fell back again, for a second or third time, I was a lot harder on them but overall was probably very forgiving.

My own loyalty to the team and my players was really important to me. I was absolutely willing to back all the players I played with. I wanted stability around the group and would do my best to fight change. I wanted new players who came into the group to feel this loyalty and trust. I treated everyone as an equal and went out of my way to give new players this feeling, in the aim they didn't feel less valued than those players who had been with the group for a long time.

CHAPTER 14

SOLIDARITY FOREVER

England, August, 1997

AS A YOUNG PLAYER, I was often surprised by the self-importance of some cricket officials. Not all of them — there were many smart, hard-working administrators who went way beyond the call of duty for the sake of the game and its players, but there were others who I came to view as nothing more than hangers-on. These people seemed to be there for what they could get out of it, the free lunches and the plum seats in the stands. They were the bosses and we Test players merely the workers who if they had their way would come and go from the tradesmen's entrance. Their attitude whenever a cricketer or group of cricketers sought improvements to wages or playing conditions appeared to be simple: 'If you don't like what you're getting, there are thousands of others out there who'd gladly play for nothing.'

Some, astonishingly, were past top-level players, who'd had this attitude ingrained into them and now fought to preserve the status quo for as long as they could. Here's just one example. In 1997, our manager Alan Crompton agreed to a request from Mark Taylor for the players' wives and partners and children to travel with the team for the month from the start of the second Test match. I was only 22, but even I could see the benefits of this move, not least for how the older guys treasured the chance to share the experience with their kids. Today, few would argue with the concept of families being on tour, but things were different back then. I learned recently that a number of Board directors, one of whom was a former Test player, were vehemently against the innovation, their argument being, I guess, that 'it didn't happen in my day'.

By the mid 1990s, the senior members of the Australian side were sick of this. I might have been new to international cricket, but it seemed to me that in arguing for a better deal my experienced and battle-hardened team-mates had a pretty fair case. And so it was that I was a first-hand witness as men like Tim May, Shane Warne, Steve Waugh and Ian Healy fought long and hard to win Australia's front-line cricketers a much better deal than we might have otherwise enjoyed. Their battle also led to an improved relationship between the players and the Australian Cricket Board, and it increased the professionalism of the Board, too. In the years that followed, the way our administration thought and operated finally moved with the times, and some of the Board's revenue streams— including media rights, sponsorship and merchandise — increased dramatically. This would not have happened, at least not as quickly, if my team-mates, some of the great players of the 1990s, had declined to make a stand or if some of the officials had got their way.

Having gone on to captain the Australian team, and to have enjoyed so much of the fruits of their labours, it would be nice to describe here how I played a major role in the birth of the Australian Cricketers' Association (ACA), but the truth is I was on the periphery. I certainly didn't feel underpaid — I was probably the best-paid 21-year-old in Tasmania — but that didn't stop me being 100 per cent behind whatever direction Maysie, Tugga, Warnie and Heals wanted us to go in. I was young and new to international cricket, but I believed strongly in the concept of 'team' and I had complete faith in the leadership group. 'You can count me in,' I quickly said after the ACA concept was explained to me.

For me, the story began at the start of my first major trip — the West Indies in 1995 — when everyone in the team was invited to a pre-tour meeting in Sydney. Thinking back, it was a pathetically unprofessional scene: the players were lying on a bed or on the floor while then Board CEO Graham Halbish told us how things would be. Some of the players were clearly frustrated with Halbish's responses to their questions on subjects like player payments, personal sponsorships, TV rights and insurance, and there were some terse exchanges.

This was also the meeting when we were officially told that Salim Malik had been accused of attempting to bribe Tim May, Shane Warne and Mark Waugh, a story that had just been broken in the newspapers, and that Mark and Shane had been punished by the Board for 'supplying information' to an Indian bookmaker. Apparently, we were firmly told these matters were not to be discussed with anyone outside the room, but I can't recall that direction being given. I guess I'd tuned out by then.

I was new to debates about player payments. Whatever they wanted was fine by me; whatever they paid me was more than I could have dreamed of when I was pushing lawn mowers for Ian Young at Scotch Oakburn College, and more than any of my mates from school were earning. More than once on that Windies tour I heard team-mates comparing how much we were paid to the huge sums being earned by stars from other sports, how poorly Shield cricketers were being treated and the restrictive nature of the Board's player contracts, but I hardly stopped to listen.

The Australian Cricketers' Association was formed after the tour, with Tim May, whose Test career had come to an end, getting the gig as our union boss. Over the next two years Maysie tried to get the idea of payments for Test and Shield players to be tied to the Board's revenue, but the Board wouldn't have a bar of that. It wouldn't even discuss the concept.

You'd think people would have learned their lesson. Back in the early 1970s Bill Lawry and then Ian Chappell had stood up to the Board (in those days the Board was really just one man, Sir Don Bradman). Bill lost the captaincy after demanding a fair go for his exhausted players and when Ian had no more luck in demanding fair compensation Kerry Packer leveraged the situation to split cricket in half by offering proper pay to anyone who joined World Series Cricket.

Here we were fighting the battle again.

Late in the 1997 Ashes tour, between the fifth and sixth Tests, the ACA organised a get-together in a conference room at our hotel at Canterbury. The thing that stands out most clearly for me about that meeting is how stuffy the hotel was because of a lack of air-conditioning. James Erskine, a high-profile sports businessman, was brought on board to negotiate with the ACB on the players' behalf, and he was introduced to us at the meeting. The Board had been stonewalling, but Erskine was willing to bring not just his negotiating skills but also his considerable financial clout into the battle, on the basis that on top of the commission the ACA would pay him, he could also win a piece of the marketing pie when a settlement was finally reached. If Maysie said hiring Erskine was a good idea, then that seemed like a fair deal to me. The ironic thing about this situation was the same Graham Halbish had left the Board on bad terms and was now working with us. It was a stroke of genius by Tim May. He told us there was plenty of money in the bank and any nonsense the Board told us about it being put away for a rainy day was rubbish, as the revenue streams were pretty good.

When Tim stressed that we had to stick together, it just seemed to be a natural thing to do. You don't need to tell a working-class Tasmanian how these things work. When he explained that part of this was necessary because of Australia's industrial laws, saying how we needed to get the Board to recognise that the ACA was entitled to negotiate on the players' behalf, it went straight over my head. Maysie told us it was inevitable the Board would use the old 'divide-and-conquer' trick by painting our tactics in an unfavourable light, saying the ACA was being unreasonable, that a players' union was bad for the game and by making subtle approaches to individual cricketers who they thought might not be totally committed to our cause.

By the time I returned to Australia a story was out that Denis Rogers, in his capacity as Tasmanian Cricket Association (TCA) chairman (he was also the chairman of the ACB), had told a few guys from the Tassie Shield team that the TCA and the ACB would only negotiate with individual players.

Under these circumstances, you would suspect that Denis might have made contact with me, perhaps to offer me a special deal or to argue that my allegiances should be with him, a fellow Tasmanian, rather than with my Test team-mates. He knew I respected the way he had climbed the ladder to become the first Tasmanian to chair the Board, and how I was grateful for the things he had done for Tasmanian cricket, and I was also aware of the work he had done for the Clarence footy club. But the truth is I don't recall Denis ever trying to get me to break away from the ACA. I reckon that was simply because he knew me well. One time early in my first-class career, he drove me home from Hobart to Launceston, partly because I needed a lift and partly, I'm sure, because he wanted to get to know me better. He knew I would stick solid with my mates.

Denis has always been good to me and for me. I have made sure, whenever I've been back to Tassie, that I've always caught up with him and spent time with him, because I enjoy his company, am grateful for the support he has shown me and recognise the remarkable job he has done for Tasmanian sport. Many of the developments we've seen at Bellerive Oval, for example, have been because of his efforts. He is a very smart and generous man, and if Denis was guilty of anything during the ACA dispute it was that he was too concerned with protecting the Board's interests, but that was his job.

During all the public debates that took place in the early part of the 1997–98 season, Denis and his fellow Board members, along with Board CEO Malcolm Speed, regularly painted us players as being greedy and selfish. They even released the amount top players were being paid, knowing the public would think we were greedy. At the same time they never revealed just how much money was in their bank account. Money they earned from marketing our talents. For a while, with the help of a largely compliant cricket media, it appeared they were winning the public relations war, but at the same time their refusal to come to the negotiating table was stiffening our resolve. The turning point came in the third week of November, during the second Test against New Zealand in Perth, when word got out that a player strike was a real possibility unless the Board got fair dinkum about talking to the ACA. By this time, Channel Nine, Australian cricket's TV network, had become concerned that the players might even be planning to form a rebel competition, but there was nothing in that scuttlebutt and the players who worked for Nine — Tubby, Warnie, Tugga and Heals — were able to set the TV bosses straight. Further, Warnie was allowed to go on Nine's coverage of the Test the next day to explain the ACA's position, and he did it so well there was immediately a massive change in the public's perception of who was right and who was not.

At the same time, however, Tubby sat down with Denis and the pair came up with a possible compromise, a surprise development because by working one-on-one with the Board our captain was going against the wishes of the ACA. Thinking about it now I have no problem with Tubby making that move, because when the players are dealing with the Board, the captain should always have the right to talk to the Board chairman. At the time, though, it did cause some angst within our group.

After stumps on day two Tubby presented the playing group with the results of his meeting with Denis. Our reaction was lukewarm at best. There is no doubt our skipper was motivated solely by his desire to see the impasse solved and as always he was persuasive in his arguments, but by this stage the rest of us were determined to stick with Maysie and see the battle through. Tubby went back to Denis the following morning and then returned with yet another proposal that the two of them hoped would do the trick, but our determination was stronger than ever and when Matthew Elliott asked why we were now negotiating in this way rather than via the ACA it was decided to stop the dilly-dallying, and to put things to a ballot.

Twelve pieces of paper were handed out, with each of us asked to write down 'yes' for strike or 'no' for no strike. A few ODIs in December had been targeted. Quickly, each of the voting slips was placed in a baggy green cap (the symbolism was lost on no one), and Blewey was given the job of returning officer. The result was dramatically decisive: 11 to 1. The boys were serious. We were going to strike.

The irony was that when Tugga rang Maysie to tell him of our decision, the reply was succinct: 'Don't do it! The momentum is swinging our way.' I have no idea what clinched the deal, but my guess is that the powerbrokers at Nine asked the Board to fix the impasse. Or maybe the administrators saw that public opinion was swinging our way. Or was it because Tubby had been rebuffed? Perhaps commonsense prevailed. Whatever the reason, we were relieved, nobody really wanted to strike.

In the following few days, the ACA announced it was postponing the threat of strike action and the Board finally decided to talk to the ACA. This proved to be the starting point for some spirited but constructive negotiations. It would be many months before the first memorandum of understanding between the Board and the ACA was agreed to, one which in part gave players 20 per cent of the first $60 million of consolidated 'Australian Cricket Revenue' and a quarter of every dollar thereafter: 57.5 per cent of that pool was to be allocated to Test and ODI players, the rest to those who performed at interstate level. The top Test players actually took a hair cut on this so extra money could be fed into the Sheffield Shield payment pool.

Since then players have always received what I think is a fair slice of the cricket pie, and our incomes increased significantly as overall revenues continued to rise. As someone whose career was largely post-1997 I have benefited as much as anyone from this, so I will never forget the actions of Tim May and his comrades at the ACA. Furthermore, because of the ACA's persistence, productive dialogue between Australian players and Australian officials finally became a feature of the cricket landscape, and more often than not it felt like we were working together, rather than being from opposite sides of the same fence.

BACK IN THE 1990s, it was rare for an inexperienced member of the Australian cricket team to think about anything that wasn't directly related to how his cricket was going. Even things like team tactics were not that important to me, other than how they impinged on my role in the side. At this stage of my cricket life I wasn't going to be standing up at the next team meeting to tell senior blokes how to play. I knew my place.

There were a number of significant things that happened in my first two or three years in the Australian team — Mark Taylor's form slump, Ian Healy losing the vice-captaincy, the ACA conflict, the match-fixing controversy — and I was aware of all of them and saw how they affected the guys involved. However, I never stopped to think too much about them because they didn't impact directly on what I had to do. I don't think this makes me callous or naive or different to the other young guys. My priority was performing to a high standard because that would keep me in the side. Staying in the side was all I really wanted. With the benefit of time and seniority I realise a few of those things were big issues, in some cases momentous, but at the time, to a large degree, they passed me by.

Later in my career I came to have a different appreciation of these events as I went through similar things. At the start of the 1997–98 season Mark Taylor had the one-day captaincy taken away from him when he was still Test skipper. I didn't see it as a big deal — Tubby hadn't been scoring a million runs in the one-dayers, the team's ODI form in the previous 12 months had been mediocre, the selectors made the call, let's move on. That's how I was thinking. Now, having been Australian captain for a number of years, I realise it was a massive thing to happen to him and that a decision of that magnitude had enormous consequences for the team.

In the years since Tubby retired I have been asked many times, 'How good a captain was he?' When I was Test skipper from 2004 to 2010 the bloke I was most unfavourably compared to was Tubby. 'He's no Mark Taylor,' the critics would say of me.

When I first came into the Australian team it was hard for me not to think of Tubby as a special captain because, compared to the skippers I'd previously played under at club and state level, almost everything we did at the international level was a step-up in class, intensity and professionalism. The amount of thinking that went into training and the analysis the leadership group put into an international match in those days compared to what we did at state level was chalk and cheese.

Yet it is also true that the all-round preparation teams put in today is a million miles ahead of what we did back in the mid-1990s. The biggest change is how inclusive it is. The young players of today are involved in everything the team does and everything the team hierarchy talks about when it comes to planning and meetings. Their input is encouraged, as it is vital everyone is on the 'same page'. In contrast, when I first made it into the side, tactics were the realm of the coach, the captain and the vice-captain, and maybe one or two other senior guys. Most times, we'd only talk about a few specifics in a team meeting that lasted for 15 minutes or half an hour. Then we went out to play.

The most telling example I can give of how it often was back then occurred at the 1996 World Cup, before the quarter-final against New Zealand, when we were discussing the Kiwi batting line-up. After a brief discussion about guys like Nathan Astle and Stephen Fleming, we got to Chris Harris. 'He's hopeless,' said one of the senior players. It could have been Steve Waugh, or it might have been Mark. 'Let's not waste our time talking about him.'

Harris, of course, promptly went out and made 130 from 124 balls. In most meetings involving the whole group, we'd breezed through opponents' strengths and weaknesses, devoting no more than an average of 30 seconds for each player. And then the team meeting was done. See you at the bar at six. Inevitably, there'd be more talk of tactics over a feed or a couple of beers, but unless a formal team dinner had been organised, only a few — usually the senior blokes — would be heavily involved in these informal discussions.

On the field, Tubby was a chatty captain, but these conversations were usually with the bowler or the guys in the slips cordon. If I was fielding at cover or deep point I could only guess as to why a change was made. Maybe, because of what we'd discussed in a pre-game meeting, I might have had a clue to the tactics behind a move, but otherwise I was just a soldier following orders. So when people asked me about his leadership how could I know if a captain was a wizard or just lucky? Tubby certainly had a bit of awe about him and under his leadership we usually felt things were going to turn out right. More than once — the semi-final at the 1996 World Cup and the third Ashes Test of 1997 are two examples — he made decisions at the toss that many questioned but they worked out fine in the end so he looked like a genius. The way he nurtured Shane Warne and Glenn McGrath — helped turn them into champions — was fantastic. Yet it's amazing how little memory I have of Tubby's captaincy style or things he did or advice he gave that made me a better cricketer or person. Perhaps that's more an indictment on me as a young cricketer than it is on him as a mentor of young cricketers. Or perhaps it's just a reflection of the times.

CHAPTER 15

I'M NOT GOING,
I'M STAYING

Equinox nightclub, Kolkata, March 21, 1998

WE PLAY CRICKET almost all the time now. It's difficult to believe that in the past there were years when no international side toured Australia, a time when we weren't rushing from one tournament to another. There were times late in my career when I was lucky to spend two months at home in a year — and they were often comprised of weeks grabbed here and there. The schedule is full because cricket earns big money from television networks and players are (now) well compensated for their time. There was a time when we complained there was too much cricket, then the Indian Premier League (IPL) came along and almost anybody who could ran to that honey pot and the money ensured we stopped complaining.

That said, at times, there is still too much cricket and you can tell when it's getting to us because that's when things happen on the field. Sometimes, in the swirl of airports and buses and hotel rooms and long hot days in the sun the cracks finally open up and what comes spilling out is not always pretty.

I guess that might have been part of the reason I found myself being dragged out of a Kolkata (then, Calcutta) nightclub in 1998, but it is too easy an excuse. In truth I still had a lot to learn and when my Aussie rules team, North Melbourne, beat Warnie's St Kilda I think I might have got a little too excited.

And, as I was about to learn, when you are growing up in the public eye your mistakes become very public.

THE NEW ZEALAND TEST series was the first of a trifecta of three-game rubbers we played in 1997–98. After beating the Kiwis 2–0, we defeated South Africa at home 1–0 but lost 2–1 in India. I was in reasonable form in Australia, the highpoint being my 105 against the South Africans in the Boxing Day Test at the MCG, but I struggled once more on the subcontinent, making 60 after we lost four early wickets on the first morning of the second Test at Kolkata but not much else. I wasn't the only one who had a hard time — poor Greg Blewett hardly scored a run, and when Darren Lehmann finally made his Test debut at Bangalore, replacing the injured Steve Waugh, and made a confident half-century he moved ahead of both me and Blewey in the Test reckoning.

In one-day cricket, on the other hand, I had a fantastic time, failing to reach double figures in only the last of the 22 innings I played in ODIs between December 1997 and April 1998. I scored two hundreds and six fifties in this sequence, which involved games in Australia, New Zealand, India and Sharjah, against South Africa, New Zealand, India and Zimbabwe, and I came home as the 15th ranked batsman in all of ODI cricket and the third-ranked Australian, behind only Michael Bevan and Mark Waugh. The 145 I hit against Zimbabwe in Delhi equalled Dean Jones's then record for the highest score by an Australian in an ODI, but I look back on that knock fondly not so much for the landmark as for the fun I had sharing a big partnership with Mark Waugh. Junior and I had become close mates off the field but this was the first time we shared a really big stand in a major match.

It was a tumultuous time for Australian cricket, with Mark Taylor replaced as one-day captain by Steve Waugh and Adam

Gilchrist taking over from Ian Healy as our one-day wicketkeeper. Near the end of the one-day season in Australia Tugga moved Gilly up to open the batting and straight away I was able to see from my No. 3 position just how effective this was. It took Steve a little while to get the hang of the captaincy, even he will admit that, but when he did he was away. We were almost a separate unit now and we were pushed to have pride in our performance, but also to be positive and have fun. I could also appreciate the positives of having 'two teams', though I could see how it was awkward for stalwarts like Tubby and Heals who were now only playing Test cricket.

By the time we came home from the heat and sandstorms of Sharjah at the end of April 1998 I'd established myself at No. 3 in the ODI line-up but was either just in or just out of the Test side.

I was very confident about my place and ability … some of the time.

INDIA IN 1998 WAS my fourth visit to that country, and while again I didn't have the batting success I'd hoped for, I had felt I was finally getting used to and even liking the place. By 1998, we were staying in better hotels, most of which had good restaurants and that meant the threat of picking up a stomach bug was reduced. But there was still much to get accustomed to. I started this tour in pretty fair form, making 53 and 47 against Mumbai, in a game dominated by Sachin Tendulkar, who hit 204 not out, and then I scored 155 batting at three against an Indian Board President's XI at Visakhapatnam as part of a big partnership with Michael Slater who got 207. Immediately after that knock I felt fine, even exhilarated that I'd made a big first-class hundred on Indian soil, but that night, once my adrenalin dried up, I began to shiver then sweat and then my head started pounding. Then came the constant vomiting. I had sunstroke, big time, coupled with a bad case of dehydration. Even the next day I was unable to focus. We were two days out from the first Test but the last thing I wanted to do was play cricket.

A month later, the first ODI on that tour was played at Kochi, a city on the far south-west coast, and the conditions were oppressive. They said it was 48 degrees Celsius, but out of the shade it was way more than that. They batted first and Ajay Jadeja made a good hundred but it took so much out of him he couldn't focus. We took so long to bowl our overs we only got a 15-minute turnaround and poor Gilly had to take off the keeper's pads, put on his batting ones and just get on with it. I couldn't focus when I batted — not because I was suffering from sunstroke again but simply because I couldn't get the memory of that previous dehydration out of my head. I made 12 from 29 balls, at a time when I was in excellent one-day form, and it was one of the most dismal, drawn-out innings of my life. Like a few others I was sick in the showers in the dressing room. It was ugly on the team bus, but I prepared myself by carrying a plastic bag that some pads had come in. One player was even sick as we walked through the foyer of the hotel.

I got much better at touring India. I had to, we went there every year and I started to enjoy the country and its challenges. Their crowds are incredible and you've never heard anything like it when Sachin was batting. The noise was almost a physical force and it was something we used to gauge how we were going. If the crowd was quiet we were on top. The silence when Sachin was out was almost perfect. The country has never engaged me in the way it did some of my team-mates, most notably Steve Waugh. Just as Steve could never understand why I was happy to potter around the hotel rather than explore the crowded lanes and alleys or visit historic landmarks, I was often perplexed that he wanted to venture out when an important match was just around the corner.

That I didn't go out much didn't stop me discovering India is an extraordinary nation, or wondering how more than one billion people are crammed into an area less than half the size of Australia. Often, it feels to me as if there is nowhere to move, no open space, a feeling exacerbated by the stark signs of poverty and despair that are often easy to find, especially in the cities. The range of smells is extreme and they can be invigorating or rancid or somewhere in between, often depending on your mood. On top of all this comes the locals' extraordinary, all-consuming love of cricket, which is wonderful but can create trouble, like the time in Kolkata on that 1998 tour when three of us decided to walk the short distance to a local market. Within 15 minutes, police had to be summoned, because we'd been surrounded by fans and the immediate vicinity had ground to a halt. I reckon there would have been at least 1000 people there, moving and shaking, just trying to get a look at the Australian cricketers. It wasn't frightening, just relentless, and the only thing that bugged me was that the constables told us to hop on a tuk-tuk and return to our hotel or they'd consider charging us for being a 'public nuisance'. All we'd done was leave the sanctuary of our team hotel.

In the course of many tours there I have been forced to marvel at Sachin Tendulkar's life. If we stood still for 10 minutes there would be a crowd of 1000, if he did half the country would descend on the spot. He has no freedom, no chance to step outside and take a walk. It is so bad that he used to take his sports car out at 4am because it was the only time he would not be hassled — and one of the rare times the roads were relatively empty. I noticed over the years how the Indian players made the most of the freedom they had in Australia where they could go out to meals, go for walks, shop and lead a half-normal life. If I ever felt pressure of expectation from the public as an Australian cricketer it was nothing like what they experienced.

Stuck in our hotel, there was always the fear that boredom would bite one of us, and once or twice this happened to me. But that wasn't an issue when I got myself in trouble at the Equinox nightclub in Kolkata, which happened after a few of us had organised to watch St Kilda play North Melbourne in the 1998 pre-season Ansett Cup final in a bar at the team hotel. This happened just a couple of hours after we'd lost the second Test, and with it the series — the first time Australia had lost a Test series, since

Mark Taylor's first matches as captain, to Pakistan in 1994. Of course, the Kangaroos (my team) won convincingly and as soon as the trophy had been presented a few of us decided to kick on to the nearby Equinox, but when we arrived we discovered that single blokes couldn't enter: it was 'couples night'. It looked like our party was over, but then they recognised us as Australian cricketers so they waved us in. Most of the boys didn't stay too long and eventually I found myself having a drink with an Australian-born physio who was doing some work with the Indian team, and then I was on my own. Not long after a security guard came over and told me I had to go because I was by myself. Unfortunately I had enough alcohol in me to bluntly say, 'I'm not going. I'm staying.'

Security said I had to go.

I said, 'I don't have to go.'

With hindsight, I wish I'd just put down my drink and left, but I'd drunk that one-too-many beer that makes some of us boorish and belligerent. They tried to drag me out, there was a brief skirmish, they won and eventually I stumbled into a taxi and returned to our hotel. I only had a vague memory of all of this, but the next morning I honestly didn't think I'd done anything wrong, other than being a bloody idiot, so I didn't see the need to say anything to anyone. However, someone at the nightclub told a reporter about my clash with the bouncers and it made the next edition of the Kolkata *Statesman* (in a report that erroneously claimed our pace bowler Paul Wilson was also ejected and further incorrectly alleged that I had 'pushed a woman'). After we'd settled into our next hotel in Bangalore our co-manager Steve 'Brute' Bernard called and said, 'We've got a problem, you'd better come to my room.'

There I sat down with Brute, Mark Taylor, coach Geoff Marsh (who'd replaced Bob Simpson after the 1996 World Cup) and the team's other co-manager, Cam Battersby. I admitted I'd been involved in an altercation. After hearing what I had to say they concluded that I had broken the ACB's Code of Conduct in relation to 'unruly public behaviour', and I was cautioned and fined. The team then released a statement that read in part, 'Ricky has issued an unreserved apology for the incident involving a scuffle with security staff. He denies the other allegation.'

The reports that I had 'assaulted', 'groped' or 'shouldered' a woman were dead wrong. I am not like that. But I had let myself down by drinking too much, which left me vulnerable when my team-mates left me to it. Ian Healy sat down with me and explained how he had once got himself into trouble, when after a few drinks he got into an exchange with an abusive England fan and ended up wearing a head-butt; and how that incident had shown him that because he was a Test cricketer he couldn't behave as a 'normal' person. He had to improve as an individual then. Now, he said, I had to do the same. But Heals's wise words didn't sink in. Not immediately.

THIS TOUR IN 1998 was also the first time I faced the then 17-year-old off-spinner named Harbhajan Singh, who bowled with little success in our game against the Indian Board President's XI at Vizag, and made his Test debut in the third Test. We ran into Harbhajan again in Sharjah where we played a tournament against India and New Zealand. It was here we learned for the first time just how annoying he could be on the field. We figured he must have had a fantastic time of it as a young teenage bowler, to rocket to the top so quickly, but frankly for much of the time we saw him on this tour he appeared out of his depth. In our second match against India in Sharjah I hit him for four and six, but was then stumped trying to hit him out of the ground again. It was a dopey shot and I was filthy on myself for getting out to him. Getting out is never great, getting out stumped has an element of humiliation to it. My mood wasn't helped when I looked up and found him right in my face, abusing me, telling me where to go. I hadn't had an opponent this close to me since my early days in club cricket in Launceston, or maybe that day in early 1994 against Duncan Spencer at Bellerive, and just as I did then I stood my ground until a couple of their more experienced players came between us to drag him away and I stormed off the field. Later we were both fined and Harbhajan was handed a one-match suspension on top of that. For each of us, this was the first black mark on our international disciplinary records.

While I was in Sharjah, I was offered the chance to captain an Australian A side that would be touring Scotland and Ireland in July–August, but after giving the opportunity plenty of thought I knocked it back, on the basis that a break from the game would do me good. It wasn't that I felt physically run down. It was a big call and could have been taken the wrong way, but I think the Board appreciated my honesty when I said I needed a breather.

It's been amazing over the years to see how so many of the 'ugly' incidents that occur during a game happen when players are mentally tired after months of non-stop cricket. I think my reaction to Harbhajan's provocation was an example of that. It was a nothing series in a hot country and there'd been a lot of cricket and travelling in the lead-up. The shot I played to get out that day was also that of a batsman not on top of his game and my reaction to his provocation was a clear sign I was cooked.

Still, the captaincy offer was the first indication I'd received from the Board and the team hierarchy that they might be looking at me as future leadership material ahead of more experienced players, such as Matthew Hayden and Damien Martyn. Coming so soon after the Equinox and Sharjah incidents, I appreciated the confidence being shown in me and I'd have further reason to be grateful for officialdom's support a few months later, when the bookie scandal surged back into prominence.

Feedback

From the first time I picked up a cricket bat, I sought feedback. Whether it was from my nan in the backyard acknowledging a big pull shot over the neighbour's fence, or from a coach at Mowbray telling me to concentrate on my movement in the crease or on my learning of a fielding drill. The only way to improve is to learn from what you are doing, either good or bad, and be given feedback on that. Seeking feedback has been with me right through my life in cricket and it's helped me to achieve at the highest level. Feedback also became a critical part of my leadership roles around the various teams I played with, especially when I was captain.

Open and honest communication between team-mates, coaching staff and other support personnel around a team is something that is not negotiable for me, whether I'm the captain or one of the players. It's the foundation that great teams are built on. As I became more experienced and was placed in more senior roles, I quickly learned the importance of understanding my team-mates inside and out. This helped me deliver feedback in a way that gave them the best possible chance of learning from it. I had to understand their individual peculiarities and use language, tone and situation to deliver the appropriate message in a timely and effective way. Everyone is different but we all need regular, open and honest feedback.

CHAPTER 16

BETTING RINGS AND BROKEN HELMETS

Before the third Test, Adelaide, 1998–99

'MATE, IF YOU CAN ever let me know what the Aussie team starting line-up will be the night before the game, I'll organise for some money to be put into an account we'll set-up for you,' he said.

I was a little taken aback.

'You're betting on cricket as well as the races?'

It was 1997 and sports betting had just started to take off in Australia, but it was fairly limited. I had been invited to the greyhounds at Wentworth Park in Sydney after an ODI. There was a group of people there including this bloke who had something to do with an offshore betting agency. He was a sports nut and we'd been chatting for a while, but when he made the offer to me an alarm went off.

'Mate, we bet on just about anything,' he explained.

It seemed like easy money, but it also didn't sound right, especially given the controversies cricket was facing. The memory of the cricket betting scandal was fresh in all our minds, but I didn't knock this offer back completely. I just said, more to be polite than anything, 'I'll think about it.'

The way this bloke had described his plan, it sounded harmless, but the more I thought about it in the cab on the way back to our hotel the more sinister it seemed. As soon as I got to my room, I rang my manager Sam Halvorsen who had been so good to me over the previous three years. Sam was not just a manager, he was a confidant, a friend who was there for me almost all the time as I was feeling my way in the world and he would end up backing me for more than a decade. The first thing Sam said to me after I told him about what had happened at Wenty Park was, 'I hope you didn't commit to anything.'

'No, I didn't,' I replied. 'But I didn't tell him to forget about it either.'

'Ricky, don't go near it,' he said firmly. 'If any phone calls come in, don't answer them.'

When I think about it now, I can't believe how blasé I was about it all. I was incredibly naive, but I suppose we all were back then. To me, it wasn't a big deal, but Sam saw the approach for what it was: an attempt to lure me into a world I had to avoid at all costs. This was how the bookies worked. They'd lure you in with a seemingly innocent and harmless offer and then build the relationship up to a point where you couldn't escape. Maybe this bloke with the offshore connections wasn't that evil, but later I'd hear stories of sharks who'd start with something as simple as an invitation to share a coffee or a beer. Then, they'd pay for the drinks and perhaps even organise to look after your room bill, phone calls, mini-bar, that sort of thing. They'd say they were doing this because they loved the way we played, but what they were really after was a firm grip of you. It wasn't beyond them to bring some girls with them to a hotel bar. Once they had a hold of you they'd ask you to give them some significant information about an upcoming game. If you did that even once it could be terribly hard to get out.

I should have been aware of all this, but I was only 22. I did get another call, but I said flatly that I wasn't interested and please don't call again, and that, I figured, would be the end of it.

WITHIN THE TEAM, we had been aware since early 1995 of brief links between Mark Waugh, Shane Warne and an Indian bookmaker. Junior and Warnie had provided the bookie with what they thought was innocuous information about future selections and pitch conditions in exchange for cash. When the Board found out about it they were fined, but the matter was kept in-house. With hindsight, it's easy to say that the story was going to get out eventually and that's what happened during the 1998–99 Ashes series in Australia.

In fact, the storm broke in the days before the third Test at the Adelaide Oval, by which time we were 2–0 up and well on the way to winning the series, while I was about to be axed from the team again. However, my main concerns were for my two mates who'd made a mistake four years earlier and were now being hammered by sections of the media and the public. The low point came when Junior was booed onto the field in Adelaide. I know that affected him enormously and in my view it was way over the top.

Some critics lost all perspective and pursued the case relentlessly even after all the evidence was out in the open. They saw something sinister in the Board's original decision to keep the matter secret and they desperately wanted an Aussie scalp to go with the high-profile cricketers from elsewhere who'd been busted for match-fixing. They couldn't or wouldn't accept that what Mark and Shane had done was so much less than that. And I was on the fringe of it all, because of a chat I'd once had at the Wentworth Park greyhound track.

When the media found out about Mark's and Shane's fines and were about to publish the story, Steve Bernard organised one-on-one meetings with every member of the Australian team, to put the question: 'Have you ever had any dealings, however vague, with a bookmaker or anyone wanting information on cricket matches, or with anyone wanting you to underperform in a match?'

Because of that conversation I'd had at Wentworth Park, I had to reply, 'Well, yes, I have.'

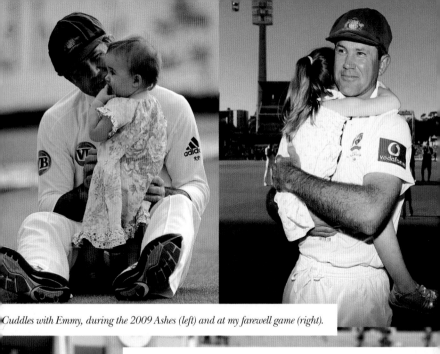

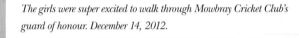

Cuddles with Emmy, during the 2009 Ashes (left) and at my farewell game (right).

The girls were super excited to walk through Mowbray Cricket Club's guard of honour. December 14, 2012.

A suave team. Collecting the Team of the Year Award at the Laureus World Sport Awards ceremony with Shane Warne, Glenn McGrath and Steve Waugh. Monaco, May 14, 2002.

Retiring mates – Damien Martyn, Justin Langer, Glenn McGrath and Shane Warne in the dressing rooms of the SCG for the last time, just after Australia won the Ashes. January 5, 2007.

Once Brute heard the story, he was immediately in contact with Malcolm Speed, who then asked me to come down to the home dressing room at the Adelaide Oval so I could go through my story again. Malcolm asked me why I hadn't revealed the matter earlier and I told him that I didn't think it was necessary because from my perspective there was nothing to it. It was only when Brute explained that he wanted to hear about 'absolutely anything' that might be construed as a connection between a player and a bookie that I mentioned it.

Malcolm thanked me for setting him straight and that was just about the end of the matter. Thinking about it now, he could have hung me out to dry, by putting my experience out there at the same time as he told reporters that Mark and Shane had been fined, but instead he took me at my word and I was grateful for that — not because I had anything to hide, but because I saw how much the turmoil hurt Junior and Warnie and I wouldn't have wanted any of that. When, just before Christmas, the Board announced it had instigated an inquiry into Australia's links to the whole match-fixing scandal, to be headed by Rob O'Regan QC, it also revealed that my story had been investigated and they had found there was nothing more to it than what I had said. O'Regan would also interview me on the subject, and the story was the same. I guess I was approached by the bloke in the betting ring because it was well known that I liked a bet, but that didn't make me corrupt or corruptible.

That this story didn't cause much of a fuss in the media is reflected in the fact that when the Bourbon and Beefsteak affair exploded three weeks later, my 'link' to the match-fixing scandal was never even mentioned. I guess if I'd still been in the Test team it might have been more of an issue because I'm sure the reporters who were following the Ashes series would have been keen for a chance to interrogate me. But my scores in the first three Tests had been 21 in Brisbane, 11 in Perth, and 5 and 10 in Adelaide, so I could hardly complain when they preferred Darren Lehmann for Boxing Day.

Darren had been picked ahead of me for the Tests in Pakistan that preceded this Ashes series, so it had been a mild surprise when I got the nod for the Gabba at the start of the summer, and we all knew that there was so much batting talent about that for just about all of us it was 'one slip and you're gone'. Blewey had been dropped from the Test team after the India tour in 1998 and he, Michael Bevan, Matthew Hayden, Matthew Elliott and Damien Martyn were all waiting for another opportunity. The selectors could afford to choose the men in form.

The one Test I had played in Pakistan had been the game in Peshawar, when Darren was injured and consequently I had the chance to be at the other end as Mark Taylor made his way to 334 not out, which famously equalled Sir Donald Bradman's highest Test score. I finished 76 not out, and what I remember most about batting with Tubby is how physically and mentally exhausted he was during the final hour of his marathon. By the end of it, he was absolutely drenched with sweat and was batting in a white floppy hat when the quicks weren't bowling. It was a truly remarkable innings, echoing Edgbaston in 1997 in that he hadn't been in good touch going into the game, and this was highlighted by some of the shots he played against their good fast bowlers, Shoaib Akhtar and Mohammad Zahid, a tall, skinny bloke who was up there for pace with just about anyone I played against. I don't know how many pull shots Tubby hit but a number of them were from balls that were only a fraction short and might have skimmed the top of the stumps if he'd missed them or let them go.

In almost legendary fashion, he finished the second day unconquered on that score of 334, and there was a bit of talk among us that night as to what he was going to do, but I can't recall if he told us that night or in the morning that he was going to declare.

Eventually he made what I think now was the right call. In all my years with the Australian team, we consistently said that we didn't want to let individual milestones get in the way of what we were trying to achieve as a team. Winning games was more important than setting records.

In the Ashes Test in Adelaide, I went out to bat in our second innings with my immediate Test-match future on the line and a declaration imminent. So I was in a 'no win' position — I could get out, another failure which would definitely mean the sack, but I couldn't make a big score to ensure my place for another game. And when I arrived in the middle, at 4–230, I discovered the ball had just started to 'reverse'.

My first innings began not long after the second new ball had been taken and immediately I tried to stand up and bang one back down the ground off Darren Gough, but only succeeded in edging a sharp chance to Graeme Hick at second slip. It was a shot I didn't need to play — I was trying to be aggressive before I was set. Two days later, we needed quick runs with the closure about to happen, but I was playing for my place in the side, and with the memory of my first-innings demise still strong my brain was scrambled. Often, when the ball started to reverse swing I could work out what the bowler was trying to do by seeing how he was holding the ball. The shiny side is darker than the rough side; which side that shiny side is on will determine how the ball is going to swing (to get conventional swing, you have the shiny side on the 'outside' of the intended curve of the delivery; with reverse, the shiny side is on the 'inside' of the swing). This was all good, but as Gough was running in to bowl and I was trying to watch the ball, I got the sides mixed up and the best I could do was push indiscriminately at an inswinger that bowled me.

When I got back to the dressing room, I took my Australian helmet off and sat it on the ground in front of me … and chopped it in half, right down the middle, with my bat. I knew I wouldn't need my helmet for the Boxing Day Test.

Unlike Christmas 1996, at least this time I still had my place in the ODI team and this meant I wasn't totally out of the picture. And having scored Test hundreds against England and South Africa

I was confident I had the physical skills and technique to succeed in the longer game as well. But in the days and weeks after I was dropped this time, I came to acknowledge that my mental approach was weak, which led to too much inconsistency, too many over-ambitious shots, too many 'starts' that weren't being converted into big scores. Boonie had told me before my Shield debut that I needed to be patient, but I still hadn't nailed that skill, not consistently. I had to toughen up at the batting crease, be more resilient and wait for the bowlers to bowl to my strengths if I wanted to become the prolific Test batsman I'd always dreamed I'd be.

Then, in the New Year, after we defeated England in a one-dayer in Sydney, I decided to go out with a few of the boys to St Patrick's Tavern. From there, I ended up at the Bourbon and Beefsteak. A couple of days later, I was finally acknowledging I had some toughening up to do off the field as well.

The media

If you're involved in top-level business or sport, then the media is part of your everyday life. Like it or not, your every move is open for public scrutiny via all forms of media as well as via Twitter, Facebook and other social media channels. Mobile phones with in-built cameras have meant that the paparazzi for a sportsperson is everyone with a mobile.

I learned from a young age that it was important to understand the media and what they were about to ensure I could manage it as best I could. For years, I've suggested to Cricket Australia that it sets up orientation sessions between young, inexperienced players and the major media journalists so that they can both get a better appreciation of what each of them are about. Too many of our young cricketers today think that cricket writers are always out to get them and write negative stories on them. Sure, that's part of being in the public eye, but journalists more often than not are looking for a positive quote to give them a headline.

I was lucky that aside from a couple of public indiscretions early in my career, most of what was in the media about me was positive. This obviously changed over the past few years, when certain journos had strong opinions on where my career was at. I never really had a problem with that because I knew deep down inside that they were right. But it didn't stop me from getting up every day and working harder to recapture my best form.

As captain, the media were always part of my day and every game. While some of our opposition countries use the media to drive an agenda, I'm very proud of the fact that I was always open and honest with the media and never tried to use the media to set an agenda. Sure, there was always the banter about a certain player or situation, particularly at the start of a big series or tournament, but generally nothing I did with the media was too planned. I was passionate about protecting my team-mates and would often play as straight bat to deflect specific criticism of a player or situation. More often than not, I was able to give the media a quote that would give them the start of the story they were looking for. This was just as important for me as it was for them and it led to me having a long and healthy respect for the media.

CHAPTER 17

THE WRONG PLACE AT THE WRONG TIME

A hangover, January 18, 1999

'WERE YOU TAKING DRUGS?' That was one of the first questions they asked me. I'd never touched drugs in my life, but that was one of the first things they wanted to know. I was so stunned by the implication that for a second I didn't answer. So Malcolm Speed, chief executive of the Australian Cricket Board, asked it again.

'Ricky, were you on drugs?'

'No,' I said quietly, firmly.

'Have you ever taken drugs?'

'Never.'

I knew from this moment they were going to make an example of me. I sat there feeling like a schoolboy hauled in front of the principal, the skin under and around my left eye sore, black and bruised. The same thought kept bouncing around in my head: *Everything I wanted to do — play cricket for Australia and be a good international player — is gone. They're going to dump me.*

The previous year, in India, I'd been fined after the incident at the Equinox nightclub and I'd just been dropped from the Test

XI during the recently completed Ashes series. While my one-day form was okay, I was hardly entrenched in the Australian set-up. I searched for sympathy in Malcolm Speed's eyes but didn't see any. For him, it was a case of finding out how bad things were and then deciding how severe my punishment should be.

The problem was a Sunday paper had photographs. The black eye was evidence I'd got myself in trouble and the word on the street was the photos would show how much trouble. The Board had copped plenty of stick over the recent episode involving Shane and Mark and the Indian bookie, where details of the indiscretions were kept in-house for more than three years until eventually the news leaked out. This time the Board was going to be transparent. So on the Wednesday, three days before the *Sun-Herald* was due to be published in Sydney, the Board scheduled its pre-emptive strike: a media conference at Hobart's Grand Chancellor Hotel ...

THE BOURBON AND BEEFSTEAK was Sydney's best known late-night bar. Back in the late 1990s, even if every other pub in the city was shut, the Bourbon was open. Situated in Kings Cross, it was for many years the preferred drinking hole for some of Australia's most colourful criminals, it had been a hangout for American servicemen during the Vietnam War, and it was a popular venue for State of Origin rugby league teams during the 1980s and 1990s, when pre-match bonding sessions were a way of footy life. Many a buck's party has ended up at the Bourbon, blokes striding into the joint in the middle of the night and then stumbling out into the sunrise a few hours later.

This is where I found myself on the morning of January 18, 1999. How I got there is a story in itself.

It started after we beat England in a day–night one-day international at the Sydney Cricket Ground. Our next game, against Sri Lanka in Hobart, was four days away. The team had a couple of beers in our dressing room, as we always used to do back in those days and then a few of us younger blokes decided to go back to our hotel to get changed and then go out somewhere.

It was a Sunday night and we ended up going to St Patrick's Tavern in the city, a few blocks from the team hotel. Two team-mates, Darren Lehmann and Greg Blewett, were in our group and there were at least one or two others. It would have been the wrong side of midnight when we arrived at the pub, and too quickly it was closing and they were starting to usher people out.

At this point, I made the fateful decision to duck into a toilet. Better to go now, I figured, than hold on until we reached our next destination. But when I surfaced, Darren, Greg and the rest of them were nowhere to be seen. We'd been drinking with a couple of girls and they were still outside. There'd been no talk about going home, so the three of us assumed they'd kicked on to a new venue and I asked the question: 'Where would you go this time of night?' It was late, it was Sunday night; the only places that would be open for sure would be up the Cross. The one pub that kept getting mentioned was the Bourbon and Beefsteak. I'd never been there.

It's amazing how the Cross is so close to the city centre, but when you get there it seems like a different world. The lights are brighter, but at the same time there are more shadows. The bouncers outside the nightclub entrances are bigger, more menacing, and while the place feels grubby, there's that hint of excitement, as though something is always just about to happen. It's a long way from Launceston. Inside the Bourbon, I went looking for Darren and Greg but they were nowhere to be seen. However, we did run into the former Australian player, Greg Matthews, and an English first-class cricketer named Paul Prichard, who I had met previously through Mark Waugh. The younger of the famous Waugh twins had played with Paul at Essex in the late 1980s and early 1990s, and Paul was now playing a summer of grade cricket in Sydney. He and Greg hadn't seen any current Aussie cricketers, and I realised there was no point walking the streets of the Cross trying to find them. So the girls and I decided to stay where we were for a couple more drinks.

Unfortunately, those couple of drinks became three, four or more, to the point that I can't remember what happened from about 4.30am to when I woke in my bed back at the team hotel. The technical term is an 'alcohol blackout'. Obviously, I'd got into trouble and my best guess, supported by some of the more measured media reports, is that I bumped into a bloke at the bar and spilt his drink on him and he reacted by belting me. The girls I was with were quoted in the Hobart *Mercury* as saying, 'He didn't do anything wrong, he was just in the wrong place at the wrong time.' This all happened around 5am, not long after Greg and Paul had left me to it.

I know now and I would have known then if I hadn't been so young and hadn't drunk so much that if you look up a definition of the wrong place at the wrong time you'll see a picture of the Bourbon at 5am.

Despite reports to the contrary, I wasn't knocked unconscious, but it was a king hit and I went straight down. Numerous reports claimed the man who hit me was a Pacific Islander; a story in one newspaper went so far as to identify a Samoan-born former rugby league front-rower who worked as a bouncer. By all accounts, it was one helluva punch, delivered by a man about twice my size. Again, according to newspaper reports, I was immediately helped to the closest cab rank. Where I was unlucky — if that's the right word — was that not only was a press photographer having a drink at the club when I got clobbered but he also got photos of us outside.

We were scheduled to have a team photo for our World Cup sponsors taken at the Opera House that morning. When the alarm woke me I felt my eye, looked in the mirror at the bruising and thought, *What am I going to say?* I rang our team manager, Steve Bernard, and told him a scuffle had broken out at the bar I was at and that I had copped a stray elbow trying to break up the blue. I knew that was probably a lie, but it sounded better than saying I couldn't remember; for a little while it was sweet, but the Board was told a different story on the Tuesday, after we arrived in Hobart, when the *Sun-Herald* rang looking for a comment.

Malcolm Speed and his fellow officials couldn't have been impressed by the sight of me batting in the nets wearing sunglasses, to conceal my black eye from outsiders. It must have looked far worse when they asked me to confirm that the paper was wrong, but I had to admit I couldn't do that. 'I don't know what happened,' I admitted meekly. They'd been told the paper had fairly graphic photos of the incident and the lead-up to it (exactly what, Malcolm apparently wasn't sure, but there were whispers they were bad), and my alibi was flimsy.

'Were you drunk?'

'Yes.'

'Were you punched?'

'I think so.'

'Why?'

'I don't know.'

'Were you taking drugs?'

THE BOARD CAME UP with a spiel they wanted me to say at the press conference they'd organised at the Grand Chancellor Hotel, which is on the waterfront in Hobart. Initially, they suggested I confess to being an alcoholic, but I wasn't going to do that, simply because I knew in my heart it wasn't right. Although I'm sure my prior 'conviction' at the Equinox in Kolkata counted against me. As the cold, hard reality of my situation was hammered home to me, I had to concede I had a problem with the drink, akin to being an occasional 'binge drinker', and it was something I had to acknowledge and then fix if I wanted to be the kind of person I wanted to be, let alone a good cricketer at the top level.

The prospect of facing the media to talk about my situation filled me with dread. The fact it was in my home state made it worse. Malcolm Speed and his Board wanted me to quickly and publicly confess to an alcohol problem and said if I didn't I was out of the team for good. In the end, I was able to come to terms with all that; the embarrassment wouldn't last forever and the most important thing was that I needed to be honest with myself. So I didn't just recite what they told me to say. I worded the key parts of my statement the way I wanted to …

> '*I have to admit to myself I have a problem with alcohol at times and intend to overcome this problem. On occasions I've drunk too much and got myself into situations I don't intend to be in, but I've ended up in them …*
>
> *I believe I've let a lot of people down, particularly my team-mates, my family and people close to me. Tasmanian and Australian cricket as well.*
>
> *I'm very embarrassed about this whole situation and it's certainly something I'm going to work very hard on, to make sure it doesn't happen again …*'

The page-one headline of the *Mercury* the next day was 'MY SHAME', which got it pretty right. Sitting alongside me, Malcolm Speed revealed I was being charged under the section of the ACB's Code of Conduct that stated, 'Players and officials must not engage in public acts of misconduct or unruly public behaviour while representing Australia or their state.' I was suspended from the Australian team pending the results of an investigation, a fine was likely, and I would undergo counselling organised by the Australian Cricketers' Association.

I was big news for a day and still a major story on the Friday, when the scuttlebutt started, including a bizarre piece of gossip aired on a Sydney FM radio station that a girl I'd been dancing with was the drag queen Carlotta! On the Sunday, the *Sun-Herald* duly put two photographs of me on their front page, but all they — and four more photos on pages 10 and 11 — showed were me outside the Bourbon at around 6am among a group of people that included the two women I'd been with for the previous five or six hours. There were no photos of the incident itself or the lead-up to it. One of the girls was described in the caption and story as a 'mystery brunette'. She might have been mysterious to the paper, but not to me or to the Tasmanian journalist Philippa Walsh, who'd tracked the girls down for a report in the *Mercury* that was published 24 hours before the *Sun-Herald* story hit the streets.

If it was hard fronting the public with my black eye and my shame there for all to see it was even harder telling Mum and Dad. I went back to Launceston to tell them and it's fair to say they were pretty rattled. It was a full-on family catastrophe and I was sick to the stomach to think I had let them down. Dad was apparently so worried that I had ruined my career that he cried, and even now I feel terrible to think I did that to him and Mum.

I had great support from my family and from my girlfriend Kellie Sainty. We'd been going out for a few years and had the house in Norwood at the time. The media interest in the story seemed so over the top. I remember somebody writing that it was a turning point for the cricket board. In the past they'd had a reputation for covering things up and copped a lot of heat for keeping the incident with Mark and Shane quiet. From now on they were going to be more open. Starting with me. Kellie and I did an interview with the local paper and I felt a little better to have somebody backing me.

Another person working hard behind the scenes was Sam Halvorsen; he was a person who always seemed to have my back. He was as much a mentor as a manager, advising me about life and cricket.

ONE OF THE MOST common questions I've been asked since January 1999 is: 'What *really* happened at the Bourbon and Beefsteak?' Because I had that alcohol blackout, because the *Sun-Herald* initially claimed its photographs were sensational, because Carlotta got a mention and because the Board came down so quickly and so publicly on me, there has always been a suspicion that there was more to it than what was reported.

The truth is there wasn't any more to the night than how I've told it. A cricketer out on the drink all night is extremely rare now — times have changed and they changed quickly. That's why, when Steve Bernard first asked me what had happened I thought I could come up with any story and get away with it. In retrospect I'm glad I didn't get away with it. If you don't learn from your mistakes you're not getting anywhere as a person. It's obviously not an incident I'm proud of, but it was important that it was not one I shied away from.

It became the kick-up-the-behind that made me change my approach to life. I did more growing up in the course of that difficult week than I'd done in the previous five years or more. As life lessons go, it was a positive.

To understand how I found myself in such a predicament, you need to appreciate the off-field culture of cricket in the 1990s. At every level, from club to Test matches, beer was a regular part of what went on off the cricket field. At Mowbray on a Saturday evening we would walk off the ground, into the dressing room for a few beers and then into town. It was something I was aware of from age 13, when the guys in the first XI would give me a can of beer and I'd sit up at the bar and feel like the king of the world. I discovered at ages 17 and 20 respectively that state cricket and international cricket were little different. In each instance, I joined in eagerly, because I enjoyed it and it was an extension of the cricket culture I loved so much, and if handled properly there is nothing wrong with that.

In the West Indies in 1995, my first overseas Test tour, when I hardly played a game, I was out at night as often as I was in, having a terrific time and never on my own. For blokes not playing, it was almost a habit; even during a Test, if a batsman wasn't expected to put the pads on the next day he might go out for a couple; the bowlers were the same if it was going to be a 'batting day'. We all assumed our performances wouldn't suffer. No hangover had been invented that we couldn't run off at training.

Things didn't really change until a little after my altercation at the Bourbon and Beefsteak, when Steve Waugh was captain. The game was getting more professional, but it also just happened that a large chunk of the team — blokes like Steve and Mark Waugh, Shane Warne, Justin Langer, Damien Martyn, Glenn McGrath, Jason Gillespie and Matthew Hayden — weren't big drinkers. A new culture overtook the old. The rest of the team fell in behind this new example.

I've never been a person who needs a drink — I can go for as long as I want without a beer and it never worries me. But before the Bourbon and Beefsteak incident, when I did go out, I was almost invariably the last one home. I didn't have that mechanism other people have in the back of their brains that says, *Right, that's enough, time to go*. The Bourbon wasn't the first time I'd found myself in strife, just the worst time, the one that got me on the front page of the paper and kicked out of the team. Each time, I'd lost control, something no person can afford to be without, but I usually dodged the bullet. It wasn't until after the Bourbon that I had to admit to myself that in losing control I was opening myself up to all sorts of potential disasters.

This wasn't just about my cricket. Getting drunk to the point that I didn't know where I was or what I was doing was just a dumb thing to do. When I thought about the punch and the shiner and the suspension and the loss of face I just kept thinking about how it wasn't worth it, that I had too much to lose. I resolved to never get myself into that kind of situation again, and I never have.

CRICKET HAS GIVEN ME PLENTY, but it took a few things from me, too. From the age of 15, when I first went to the Australian Cricket Academy in Adelaide, I never spent more than three or four months in any one place, and never has that place been in Tasmania. I didn't go out drinking at all in my first year at the Academy, but I made up for that a little in year two. Mum and Dad weren't there to pull me into line. I never had nights out with my brother, Drew, or my sister, Renee, where I could be the older brother and look after them, set them straight and be conscious of setting a good example. Instead, I was away playing cricket and always the young bloke trying to impress my elders. On January 17, 1999, when we beat England at the SCG and then headed to the St Patrick's Tavern, although I'd been an international cricketer for almost four years, I was three years younger than any other player in the Aussie side. I wanted to score more runs than anyone else, take more catches, drink as many beers ...

At the same time, the attitude of senior players to young guys coming into the side in the 1990s was definitely 'sink or swim'. That's what the senior players had experienced when they came into the side, so that's what a young bloke like me had to face when I made my international debut in 1995. The attitude of the team's leadership group in those days was basically: *Work it out for yourself.* Maybe that's not a bad thing with some young blokes, because it breeds a resilience that can be important when tough times occur later, but I think a few promising players in the 1990s would have appreciated more mentoring from the leadership group.

I went on three tours of India in the 1990s, with little experience of playing quality spin bowling on turning pitches, and never once did any of the more experienced guys come up to me and offer advice as to how I should play. Off the field was the same. The senior players knew what they could and could not do while newcomers had to find out for themselves.

What did I learn from my night at the Bourbon? I imagine many people would expect me to talk about the 'evils' of alcohol, but that wasn't the key lesson. What people need to do when they go out is to know and understand the environment they find themselves in, and not to place themselves in situations where they can get into trouble. Alcohol is part of that — getting yourself in a messy state means you can't be aware of what's happening around you. I've become a big believer in the mantra that anything is fine as long as it's done in moderation. Eat what you want, drink what you want, but do it sensibly.

It's never the beer's fault. It's your fault if you do things that get you in trouble.

IN LATE JANUARY 1999, the cricket caravan moved on at its usual rapid pace. A few of the boys kept in contact — Mark Waugh was one; Shane Warne another — but everyone had their own careers to worry about. On the Saturday, the day before the *Sun-Herald* put me on its front page, Muttiah Muralitharan was called for throwing in a one-day international at the Adelaide Oval and the Sri Lankan captain, Arjuna Ranatunga, threatened to take his team off the field in protest. On the Sunday, Australia's Test skipper, Mark Taylor, revealed he was leaning towards retirement and probably wouldn't be leading the team on its upcoming tour of the West Indies. The next day, I was banned for three one-day games and given a $5000 suspended fine — that news made page one only in Tasmania.

Penance served, my first game back was an ODI against Sri Lanka in Perth. I made a few runs before I was run out, took a catch and also bowled 10 overs, which was a nice and much appreciated gesture by Warnie, who was in charge because Steve Waugh was injured. I hardly ever bowled in matches. Shane gave me those overs even though I hadn't bowled in my four games in the one-day series before my suspension; even though he could have bowled Mark Waugh, Michael Bevan or Darren Lehmann ahead of me; even though Brett Lee only bowled five overs, Brendon Julian seven, Glenn McGrath eight-and-a-half, and Adam Dale six. It was his way of saying, *Mate, you're still an important member of this team*.

Also in Perth, I had a meeting with Steve Waugh and Steve Bernard in which they underlined the fact that I had to change my ways if I wanted to continue in the team. I didn't take that as a threat, so much as smart advice from two colleagues who wanted me to succeed and have a good career. Not that they really needed to tell me anyway, because in my week away from the group I had come to realise that while I couldn't change the past, I could shape my future.

Technique

I'm a passionate student of cricket technique, and studying it has helped me get the most out of my career as a player and captain.

Cricket is a technical game and the more you play it, the more you realise that there's no such thing as perfect technique. Over the years, some of the greatest players have had completely different techniques. For example, great batsmen who hold the bat differently, have different backlifts, go through different routines yet still average over 50 runs an innings. Or great bowlers who have different approach angles for different balls, do something different with their leading arm or have a particular change of arm pattern for a particular ball, yet still average well under 25 runs per wicket.

Having unusual technique does not mean a player can't be one of the greatest ever. Take Graeme Smith's technique, for example. You can't coach his technique yet he's one of South Africa's greatest ever batsmen. His batting stance, grip and the way he opens the face of the bat at the top of his backlift, are not in any 'how to play cricket' books that I've read, but what a great cricketer he has been.

It's fascinating to observe batsmen's techniques over their entire careers. Steve Waugh was very flamboyant in his earlier career, yet after he was dropped from the Australian team, he went away and worked on his technique and returned with a very refined technique. Damien Martyn was very similar and the changes he made to his technique certainly gave him longevity in the game.

My technique didn't change that much from my earlier years right through to when I finished. In my tougher years late in my career, I would spend hours looking at video of my best innings and overlaying it with what I was doing at the time. The big difference, as I've explained elsewhere in this book, is that I was trying to get into position earlier than in the past and this was creating other issues with my technique.

I'm sure that I'll coach in the future, and my ability to understand technique — see little things, pick up what a batsman or bowler is going to do by movement patterns, set fields, have bowlers execute specific plans to each batsman — will give my teams a tactical edge. For anyone who aspires to be the best cricketer or cricket coach that they can be, studying technique is critical. I really started doing it at an advanced level when I was at the Academy with Rod Marsh. He drummed it into me as a 15- and 16-year-old kid but always reckoned that I saw things quicker than most.

Have a vision for what you think is perfect technique but be prepared to work within all sorts of constraints to ensure you get the best out of your team and yourself.

CHAPTER 18
STARTING OVER

February, 1999

MARK TAYLOR'S RETIREMENT as Test captain changed the dynamics of the Australian team. Steve Waugh had been Mark's heir apparent since at least the 1997 Ashes tour, when he replaced Ian Healy as vice-captain, and he'd been the one-day skipper since the start of the 1997–98 home season. I'm not sure there was one person in or close to the team who didn't think Steve would get the top gig when the time came for Mark to step aside.

However, the Australian Cricket Board hesitated when it came to appointing Steve, partly because at the last minute there was a media push for Shane Warne, largely on the back of Warnie's exciting leadership in the one-day series in Australia that preceded the Windies trip. Steve had strained a hamstring and in his absence our legendary leg-spinner led the team in innovative style. Warnie was happy to try the unexpected — such as positioning close-in fielders when other captains would have been protecting the boundary, giving me 10 overs in my return game from suspension or batting Brendon Julian at No. 3 as a 'pinch hitter' — and the team had a real buzz about it as we won the Carlton & United Series. Then the Board announced it was going to formally interview both candidates for the Test captain's position, which suggested each of them had an equal chance, though more likely they were just trying to look thorough. Steve duly got the job, as everyone had expected, but I couldn't help thinking it would have been better if they hadn't mucked around, if they'd named him within 24 hours of Tubby giving it away. That's what would happen 12 years later when I resigned and Michael Clarke took over, and it prevented any mischief makers from promoting the credentials of anyone else.

Steve had made something of a study of leadership, having talked to former captains, coaches from other sports and even some business executives about what it takes to shape a winning team. Yet when he first became Test captain he didn't carry the same sense of authority that Mark Taylor possessed. Few could. The guys in the one-day squad were already aware that Steve was big on tales of mateship and inspiration, but he was something of a contradiction. He was reserved, almost shy and generally not big on having a drink at the bar, but at the same time he was always keen on any type of 'social' event that he thought might boost team spirits. Things like 'Nerds versus Julios' tenpin bowling nights or facial-hair growing competitions on tour really appealed to him, as did books like Mike Brearley's *The Art of Captaincy* and Sun Tzu's *The Art of War*.

He was also a huge believer in major cricket symbols, especially the baggy green cap. Quickly, we'd learn that another of his favourites was the concept of players not just being assigned Test and one-day 'numbers', based on where in the line of Australian cricketers they made their debut, but that those numbers should be sewn into our playing gear: first, on our one-day caps and later on our Test-match shirts. This grabbed us all. I loved the fact I was Australian Test cricketer No. 366 (straight after Stuart Law, who beat me because when two guys debut together alphabetical order comes into play, and before Brad Hogg) and Australian ODI player No. 123 (after Greg Blewett and before Shane Lee).

Some of Steve's other ideas weren't so appealing ... until they started working. It took a while, but Steve eventually built a mighty spirit among the group, which played a strong part in developing the winning culture that would stay with us for nearly a decade.

Warnie's views on captaincy are more pragmatic. To him, things like cricketers reading poems to their team-mates were more a gimmick than a motivating force. I'm sure it surprised him when most of us eventually embraced this idea after Steve proposed it. Shane felt camaraderie came from working hard at training and during games, by giving everyone the chance to contribute on the field and at strategy meetings, and by never letting the game or our tactics get dull or stale. Though he's no big drinker, Warnie saw great value in guys staying in the dressing room after play or getting together at the bar, to yarn and joke and laugh about sport and life. And I'm with him on this: you can discover things about team-mates in those situations that might otherwise stay 'in the locker'. That's how they'd done it in the old days, in cricket and footy, and it worked then so why shouldn't it work now?

Steve had the good fortune to become skipper just as a number of outstanding cricketers were entering their prime. A lot has been made of the fact that guys like Matthew Hayden, Justin Langer, Damien Martyn and Adam Gilchrist all flourished under Steve's leadership, as if one was related to the other, but no one could ever convince me that these great players wouldn't have been stars whoever was skipper. And I say this with confidence because I was in the same boat. What we needed most at this stage of our careers was opportunity, and the retirements of Mark Taylor and Ian Healy in the space of 12 months, and a loss of form suffered by the main rivals for our positions at different times between 1999 and 2001 gave us that. From there, it turned out we were all good for each other and the team blossomed.

Tugga was also very lucky, like the captains who preceded him and those who would follow, to have his bowling attack spearheaded by Shane Warne and Glenn McGrath, two of the greatest of all time. It's one thing to come up with the best-laid plans, quite another to carry them out. With Warnie and Pigeon leading the way we managed to do both for a decade or more.

One of the ways in which both Steve and Shane were usually brilliant as leaders was in the way they let you know they believed in you. 'Back yourself' became one of Steve's mantras; he did this constantly himself and encouraged the rest of us to do the same. In this regard, Warnie was cut from the same cloth to the point that self-belief was probably — next to his prodigious natural leg-spinning talent — his most important trait as a cricketer. It would have been very interesting to see how he went if he'd been given the chance to be Australian captain. All the off-field stuff that comes with being captain might have worn him down, but on the park the key, I think, would have been whether he gave himself the right number of overs. The hardest thing for a bowling captain is to not overbowl himself, because he's always thinking about how *he* can get a wicket, or to not underbowl himself because he wants to give everyone else a go. Shane got everything else right on the field, so he almost certainly would have nailed this one, too.

These two great cricketers had a falling out in the Caribbean when Steve made the brave call to drop Shane for the final Test which we needed to win to square the series. Warnie was only just back from major surgery on his right shoulder and wasn't bowling as well as he could, but he still believed Tugga should have stuck solid. I think that's what should have happened too, on the basis that you should never underestimate a champion, though I respected the fact Steve backed his judgment and made the hard call, when it would have been easier to go the other way. Warnie took his demotion badly, and his relationship with Steve, which to that point had been pretty tight, was never the same.

I WAS JUST ABOUT the last man selected to make the Test squad for the West Indies tour. There were seven batsmen chosen, with Matthew Elliott replacing Mark Taylor, and I was in with Greg Blewett ahead of Darren Lehmann. Blewey and I had both toured the Caribbean in 1995 and I was still the youngest of all the contenders, so maybe those things helped, but I'd made only one half-century for Australia in the five ODI digs I'd had following my return from suspension. In the Sheffield Shield I'd scored a grand total of 28 runs in four innings. I could hardly have complained if the selectors had left me out.

In our first game on tour against a West Indies Board XI in Antigua I batted ahead of Blewey but made 8 and 61 not out to his 52 and 58, and he was picked to bat at six in the first Test at Port-of-Spain. There, both he and Herb grafted really well on the first day, in what turned out to be a low-scoring game that ended with Glenn McGrath and Jason Gillespie bowling out the home team for just 51 when they needed 313 more than that. As Heals led the team in 'Underneath the Southern Cross' following this emphatic win, I couldn't help thinking that I wouldn't be appearing in a Test match any time soon. The Windies had been swept by South Africa in their previous Test series, and this one seemed to be going the same way.

It was more of the same on the first day of the second Test. Before play began, Tugga told us that Brian Lara, the West Indies captain and their one great batsman, had muttered after losing the toss, 'Well, this will be the last five days of this for me.' And when they slumped to 4–37 at stumps in reply to our 256, it looked like that prophecy would come true. But, on day two Lara played a fantastic innings, batting all day to be unbeaten on 212, and though he was quickly out on the third morning, they finished with a first-innings lead of 165 and eventually won the Test by 10 wickets. It was an astonishing turnaround and it prompted a brutal post-mortem in our camp.

At the start of the tour, Steve had laid down his ground rules. He felt we already worked harder than other teams and our net sessions were of a superior quality and intensity, but he wanted us to take that even further. Where we had let ourselves down in the past, he said, was when we grew complacent and he cited the case of the last Test at the Oval in 1997, which came after we'd won three

Tests straight to retain the Ashes, and our preparation was poor. He also talked about Delhi in 1996, when I think we subconsciously rebelled against the conditions and the stitch-up that saw us spend hours on a crappy train to Patiala and back. Steve wanted us to be ruthless and relentless, a team that overcame setbacks, that never gave in to them, but with this series now level at one-all and Tugga desperate not to start his Test captaincy career by losing the Frank Worrell Trophy, he left us in no doubt that he thought we'd gone the other way. He told us our attitude was substandard.

With the support of coach Geoff Marsh and team management, a curfew was introduced and Swamp had us working extra hard at training. Of course, being a junior player, I wasn't game to say anything at the time, but I think Steve made two mistakes. First, he didn't get the rest of us involved in the process that led to this decision, which goes against the maxim that team rules developed collectively are always the most effective and second, he missed a chance to lead from the front by refusing to move himself up the batting order.

Steve was rightly ranked with Lara and Sachin Tendulkar as one of the best batsmen in the world and I think it would have been a huge statement if he'd stepped up to No. 3. I understand why he didn't, because he'd had a lot of success at five and he had become highly skilled at batting with the tail, but I still think it would have been great for team morale if he'd gone up to first drop, even for a short while. He was such a good player, it would have worked. As if to underline this, over the next few weeks he would play a few massive innings that boosted his standing as captain — most notably the 199 he immediately scored in the third Test at Bridgetown and his 120 not out against South Africa at Headingley during the World Cup. Each time he was in after our first three wickets fell cheaply.

After the second Windies Test, we had a few days in Antigua, where we played a West Indies A team in a three-day game. I was in the running for a Test place, with Lang, Matty Elliott and Blewey all under pressure after making low scores in their previous three Test innings. I missed my chance, scoring just 43 and 37, while Lang made a tremendous century in our first innings and Matty did likewise second time around. Blewey was going to keep his place until he suffered a thumb injury at practice the day before the Test. With me the only spare batsman I was suddenly a certainty to play, batting at six. Needless to say, I was determined not to throw away this sudden opportunity and Dad said much the same when I rang him with the news. Then Tugga came up and spoke to me the night before the game to advise me to trust my natural game and enjoy the challenge. He was also very keen for me to be a livewire in the field, to pick the team up through my body language and my energy. This all sounded fine, I could do all that, and then he added, 'This is a real chance for you, Punter. Don't waste it.'

DON'T WASTE IT! THAT thought kept shooting through my mind as I quickly put my pads on in the dressing room. From 0–31 we'd collapsed to 3–36, and Lang and Tugga were trying to stem the tide, while the 'old firm', Curtly Ambrose and Courtney Walsh, were in full cry. Meanwhile, the full house at Bridgetown's Kensington Oval in Barbados, which had needed a mounted police patrol to help squeeze them into the ground before the start of play, was baying for blood, just like the old days. The calypso music was pumping, the rum had kicked in and in the rooms I was feeling a bit like Rocky Balboa before he fought Apollo Creed, just waiting for the call. I'm not sure if I've ever been more 'up' for an innings as I was for this one.

It was probably fortunate that Steve and Justin withstood those two great fast bowlers, and in doing so gradually quietened the mood, because I was so 'hyper', if I'd gone in straight away I'm not sure I would have been able to curb the urge to blaze away, to fight fire with fire. At lunch, we were 3–78 and the next wicket didn't fall until first ball after drinks, an hour into the middle session, when Lang was bowled by off-spinner Carl Hooper. By this time, both the wicket and I had calmed down appreciably. And it was a beautiful day, the light was clear and Tugga looked like he was going to bat forever, so it was an ideal time for me to go out to join him. Second ball, Hooper over-pitched and I drove him past mid-off for three. I was on my way.

Lara made a mistake, I reckon, in that he didn't launch either Ambrose or Walsh at me until I'd been in for more than half an hour. Contrary to the perception at the time, the West Indians would go defensive quicker than other teams, as if a war of attrition was the best way to play Test cricket if the first strike didn't work. A number of teams played that way in the 1990s. We, on the other hand, were usually keen to attack. When Walsh did come back, Steve took him on and I was able to park myself at the bowler's end and observe up close a fantastic duel. At tea, we were 4–195, with the captain 87 not out, and once we'd withstood another barrage from their quicks immediately after the interval the game really turned our way. I was determined not to make a mistake, to the point that at the final drinks break I was 35 from 87 balls, which was slow for me. I'd hit only two fours, a fine leg-glance and a drive through mid-wicket. As the locals lost heart in the final hour, I picked up the pace while Steve just flowed on to be 141 not out at stumps, I was unbeaten on 65 and we were 4–322.

I batted in my sleeveless vest the whole innings. It was stinking hot, but the night before the game I was lying in bed thinking, *I've scored two Test hundreds and both times I wore my vest throughout, so I'm going to do that again this time, whatever the conditions.* I walked out to bat wearing the vest, and after a while I started thinking, *Jeez, it's sticky out here.* But there was no way I was taking it off. Afterwards, I wondered if I was the first person to play a long innings in Barbados wearing a woollen vest. No one else would have been that silly.

Ambrose and Walsh took a couple of overs to warm up at the start of day two and then they switched ends and began firing in the short stuff. They were both giants, but it never worried me because

I'd grown up batting against blokes twice my size whose intention was to knock my block off. Anyway, the wicket had little life in it and I found it easier than I'd expected to withstand the barrage, though I did so cautiously, attempting just one hook shot in the first hour of play. In fact, I added only nine runs before drinks and it took me the best part of two more hours to get to my hundred, as slow a big innings as I would ever play (285 balls to get to the century; just nine fours on a small ground). I never realised being gritty could be so rewarding, but reaching three figures broke the spell. I tried to sweep, that shot I rarely attempted during my career, and top-edged a catch to Hooper at square leg. Losing concentration after reaching a hundred is a far greater crime than falling short in the nervous nineties, and I was so disappointed with myself for doing so, a feeling multiplied many times over when we lost two more wickets — Heals for a duck and Tugga for 199 — in the following 10 minutes.

At Leeds in 1997, I was very keen to celebrate the hundred I made immediately after I regained my Test place, but this time was different. Getting out when the team needed more runs was one of the things that tempered my elation, and the other was that I realised now that one hundred on its own didn't matter all that much unless I could follow it up with an extended run of big scores. I still had heaps to prove. We ended up making 490 in our first innings, led by 161 runs halfway through the Test, but lost because Lara played one of cricket's greatest ever innings, an unconquered 153 out of 9–308, to get them home by one wicket after a thrilling but (from our perspective) deeply frustrating run-chase.

We'd batted badly in our second innings (I was last out, caught at deep cover off Walsh, for 22), but in the end all we could do was tip our baggy greens to the Windies skipper, who was phenomenal, scoring his runs on a wearing fifth-day wicket against an attack that included McGrath, Warne, Gillespie and MacGill, four bowlers who between them would end up with more than 1700 Test wickets. Lara scored another ton in the fourth Test in Antigua, but this time he was a one-man band against our bowlers, who steered us to a 176-run victory that levelled the series. Lang was our batting star, making 51 and 127, while I think I batted as well as I had ever batted in a Test to that point, albeit methodically again. I say this even though I only scored 21 in the first innings, when Ambrose trapped me lbw with a superb late in-dipper 20 minutes before stumps on the first day, and then I was left 21 not out in our second dig as the tail collapsed around me.

FOLLOWING THE TEST MATCHES, we played a vibrant, exciting and often controversial one-day series in which I hardly scored a run, and then we were off to England for the World Cup. I think I suffered a bit of a letdown in the one-dayers, not because I treated them lightly but because I'd been so disciplined with my batting in the Tests, I found it a little awkward having to adjust to forcing the pace from No. 3 in limited-overs games. The good news was that I'd gleaned such a positive vibe out of my Test form that this little run of outs didn't damage one bit the confidence I now had. I knew I was leaving the Caribbean a far better cricketer than what I'd been when I'd arrived.

At our first team meeting after we landed in the UK, Tugga announced he was implementing a complete alcohol ban on all the players, except for immediately after games, on top of his curfew, the argument being that we had to give ourselves every chance of winning the Cup, and this sort of sacrifice was in keeping with that philosophy. He told us his theme for this leg of the tour was 'No Regrets', but I'm afraid my first thought was, *Tugga, you're going to regret this beer ban.* I knew at least a few of the boys simply wouldn't cop it for long.

I looked around the room and I could tell I wasn't the only bloke feeling this way. Interesting times were ahead.

Patriotism

Playing for Australia and the reality of what it means representing your country are two completely different things. When you first get the call-up to play for Australia, you are so excited about what it means for you that you don't immediately come to terms with the great responsibility it brings. When you become an Australian player, expectations go through the roof and you become a public figure representing your great country both on and off the field. As a captain, I was always mindful of how we were perceived as a team both in Australia and overseas. In many countries, the way Australians are perceived is driven by the way we play our cricket and conduct ourselves on and off the field. At times through my captaincy, we were criticised for how we celebrated success on the field or for the intensity with which we played our cricket. I wouldn't change any of that because I believe it is part of the Australian psyche and the way the majority of us live our lives.

Through my career, an immense feeling of national pride was never too far away from my being. Whether it was wearing an Australian blazer or team polo shirt while walking through an airport, spending time in underprivileged communities or royal palaces, or handling media questions about the Australian team, I knew I was representing my country and felt a huge sense of responsibility and patriotism. A lot of this was created by being a part of a Steve Waugh–led team. Steve used national treasures and significant moments of our history to build a culture of great national pride. Under his captaincy we visited Gallipoli, which helped me go back in time to think what it must have been like to be an Aussie Digger in that situation. It also helped us realise how lucky and fortunate we are to play cricket and represent our country.

We are no different from the average Australian except that we are better than others at cricket. That's how we got to the position of representing our country as cricketers. I am proud to be an Australian and will be forever grateful for the opportunities my country has given me. I still get goosebumps every time I sing the national anthem.

CHAPTER 19

MATESHIP MATTERS

The World Cup, June 1999

STEVE WAUGH FIXED THE MEDIA contingent with a fixed glare and before a question could be asked he demanded an answer: 'Who's responsible for spreading that bullshit?'

The captain was one of those blokes who seemed to be at his best or most dangerous when in a corner.

In the team meeting later there was more of the same. Our coach Geoff Marsh was a pretty laid-back guy but he and Steve were tackling this one head on.

'If anyone here has a problem or an issue with anyone,' Geoff said, 'it's coming out now. We're not leaving until this happens.'

THE ALCOHOL BAN HAD LASTED less than a week. Steve Waugh had explained to us that in 1987, the last time Australia had won the World Cup, the whole team had sworn off the grog for the duration of the tournament, and his memory of that was one of the motivating factors for this new embargo. But it was the only other member of that 1987 squad, big Tom Moody, who was first to go to Steve and say this time it was causing more harm than good.

Moods and Tugga were great mates, and I have always believed that Tugga, while not a selector, would have been the one who pushed for Moods to be in our World Cup squad in 1999. Before this tour, Tom hadn't played for Australia since Sharjah in 1998. Our captain resisted change at first, but on the morning of our first warm-up contest, against Glamorgan in Cardiff, he announced that while he didn't want us drinking the day before a game, we could now have a beer or a wine with meals, and have a few straight after a game. We all welcomed this change, but by still not trusting us fully to look after ourselves I felt he was continuing to miss the main point: he was treating men like kids. It was wrong to think that cricketers who were on the road for months at a time, who played Tests and one-dayers one after the other, could suddenly have the same mindset as the swimmers Steve had mixed with at the previous year's Commonwealth Games, when one-day cricket was included in the program and we gained a silver medal, beaten by South Africa in the gold medal game.

That night in Cardiff, after the match was washed out with only 10 overs bowled, quite a few of us went out on the town, and though we'd been told to be home by midnight a few of us might have been a minute or two behind time.

Warnie, meanwhile, was not his usual chirpy self. In the days after being dropped from the Test team, he'd talked about giving the game away. Back in Melbourne his wife was heavily pregnant, and then a story broke in Australia about how he'd been photographed having a cigarette, which went against a sponsorship deal his manager had negotiated for him to promote a 'quit the habit' product.

Nine days after we'd landed in England, we were in Taunton to meet Somerset in our final warm-up match, and the day before the game Warnie kept to himself while most of us played golf, and Steve and paceman Damien Fleming went out searching for some gear for a future 'Nerds v Julios' tenpin bowling night. On the fairways, the main theme of our chat was about how we just wanted the World Cup to start, the hope being that with the tournament underway we'd rediscover the enthusiasm that wasn't quite there.

Unfortunately, our first two games were a scrappy win over Scotland and a five-wicket loss to New Zealand — neither performance was satisfactory. Then, in the lead-up to what was shaping up as a crucial game against Pakistan ABC Radio's Tim Lane broke the story of a 'feud' between Steve and Shane. The 'scoop' was quickly denied by all parties, which would have happened whether it was true or not, but hearing about the subject in the public domain made our leadership acknowledge something wasn't right. Steve seemed to be galvanised by the controversy. It was then that he stormed into the press conference and asked the first question himself. Who was responsible for this 'bullshit'? Lane put his hand up, and the skipper was into him. Then Steve called Shane over and asked him to reject the claims, which Warnie immediately did. The next day, we suffered our second loss in three games, leaving us just one more defeat away from elimination, but the sense I got was that if Steve was sinking (and if we did get knocked out early, he was most likely gone as one-day captain), he was going to go down fighting.

Either he or Geoff Marsh or both called a team meeting before we left the ground, and the gloves were off. 'If anyone here has a problem or an issue with anyone,' Geoff said, 'it's coming out now. We're not leaving until this happens.'

Obviously, a team doesn't have these sorts of get-togethers if things are going swimmingly. It was a good meeting — Steve listened and took a few things on board while we got a better understanding of his thinking. The next day, we travelled north to Durham, where we were to face Bangladesh, and on our first night there a group of us — Steve, Shane, Tom, Allan Border and me — went to a local Pizza Hut and talked the night away.

The dinner might have been Moods's idea, and getting 'AB', Australia's captain from 1984 to 1993 and a bloke we all respected, along was a masterstroke. The choice of venue suited Warnie, whose love of margherita pizzas is world renowned, and I'm still not quite sure why I was invited — maybe they wanted to counter all their experience with a bit of youth; maybe they saw me as being close to Shane, which I always felt I was; or maybe I just got lucky, being close at hand when the meal was being planned — but I'm so glad I was there.

Most of the time I was just listening as my dinner companions yakked about cricket days gone by. They remembered the 1987 Cup, and the 1989 and 1993 Ashes campaigns, talked about how good it was to be an Aussie cricketer and reminisced about some of the characters they'd played with and against. No one directly raised the issue of the current team's struggles, but what this night did was remind everyone at our table that mateship matters and that all we have in common was a lot more important than anything annoying us. It probably wasn't until later in the tournament, after Steve and Shane had a long chat while walking through London's Hyde Park, that they were truly able to put aside their personal differences for the sake of the World Cup, but I reckon the process started in that Pizza Hut at Durham. We beat Bangladesh and the West Indies to qualify for the 'Super Six' segment of the Cup, and the stage was set for one of Australian cricket's great turnarounds.

MY FORM IN OUR early games was good, but in the scorebook I was doing nothing special. One reason for this was that the Cup was being played closer to the beginning of the English season than the end, which meant we were competing on some lively pitches that made batting especially hard for the top of the order. The only time I didn't get to 20 in an innings was against Bangladesh, when I finished 18 not out in a seven-wicket thrashing, but I didn't get to fifty in any of our first seven games, and sometimes I scored quite slowly. I felt I hit top form against Zimbabwe at Lord's, racing to 36 at better than a run a ball but then I inside-edged one back onto my stumps. That should have been a hundred, and at the 'Home of Cricket' too; little did I know how hard it would be for me to make big runs at this famous ground. Still, it was tremendous to feel the ball hitting the middle of my bat.

Even though I had a slight twinge in my hamstring I went into our final Super Six game against South Africa at Headingley — a game we had to win to reach the semi-finals — feeling good about my game and liking the idea that such an important game was being played at a venue that held such positive memories for me.

For a while, though, things didn't look too flash. South Africa amassed 7–271 from their 50 overs and in response we fell to 3–48 in the 12th over, at which point I was joined in the middle by Steve Waugh. The general feeling in the squad was that Tugga had probably saved his job by leading us to the second stage, but if he went down meekly here the selectors might have wanted another look at his future. Maybe that was why he looked so resolute when he joined me in the middle. I was never one who put much value on mid-pitch conversations between the not-out batsman and his new partner, but this time Steve's determination was good for me. 'We need a partnership,' he said to me firmly. 'There's no hurry.'

I'd already hit two sixes — one, off their right-arm quick Steve Elworthy, was a hook that sent the ball slicing through an advertising hoarding perched above Headingley's old dressing room — but we scored only 22 runs in the next nine-and-a-half overs. It was tough, hard cricket, but never at any point in this crucial mini-battle was Steve or I concerned. Our cricket brains were working as one; the key was to thwart the South Africans' momentum, especially with their No. 1 paceman Allan Donald in full cry, so when we talked again at the 21-over mark, with the ask now up to seven runs an over, our mood was still positive. The counter-attack had to start now, we agreed, especially with their 'second stringers' due to bowl.

Immediately we took 13 runs, including two Waugh fours, from one over from the all-rounder Lance Klusener. Their captain, Hansie Cronje, brought himself on, and I smashed him: first a pull shot to backward square; then one of the better straight drives of my life. Their left-arm spinner Nicky Boje started by conceding just a single from his first over, but his second went for 18, including a big six over square leg by Steve and a sweet leg-glance by yours truly. We'd scored 59 in six overs and on the scoreboard the game was back on an even keel, but I thought we were fractionally in front, because from where I was standing my batting partner looked almost bulletproof.

To see close-up how through sheer strength of character Steve turned the game our way was inspirational. The only hint I had that he wasn't in complete control came when out of the blue he lost concentration for a moment and chipped a pretty easy catch to one of the best fielders, Herschelle Gibbs, at mid-wicket. It should have been out, but as everybody knows Gibbs tried to fling the ball in the air in celebration before he caught it and the chance went down. We were always favourites after that.

It was a memorable moment. Legend has it that Steve sledged Gibbs straight afterwards, saying something like, 'You just dropped the World Cup,' but I never heard him say anything like that. It wouldn't have been Steve's style *not* to mutter something quietly between overs as the fielders were moving to their new positions, but my guess is it would have been along the lines of, 'You've just cost your team the game.' I'm also not sure how word got out that there had been an exchange: Steve is not the sort of bloke to publicise his own on-field remarks, working on the admirable principle that what happens on the field stays on the field, so my guess is that one of the South Africans must have spilled the beans, maybe as a way of lauding our captain's ruthless streak and at the same time further embarrassing a team-mate.

Another aspect of the incident that has gone into folklore is that the night before the game Shane Warne saw the dropped chance coming and I can certainly vouch for that. 'Boys, before you go,' Warnie suddenly said as our team meeting was concluding. 'Remember this. If you hit a catch to Herschelle, wait until you're sure he's taken it. Don't walk. He's got a habit of flicking it in the air the second he catches it.'

'Don't walk,' he said again. 'He might stuff up.'

The look on a few blokes' faces reflected most of our thinking: *What is he on about?* And then it happened.

I was dismissed for 69 when we needed 98 from 96 balls, skying a catch as I tried to hit Klusener back over his head, and I'm not sure I've ever been more disappointed to get out. I really had visions of going all the way with Steve, but instead he had Michael Bevan and Tom Moody for company as he took us to a three-wicket win with two balls to spare. He finished 120 not out from 110 deliveries, one of the best ODI innings I will ever see. The celebrations that night were as exuberant as we'd had for a while, and it struck me that it was almost as if we had come out of a fog — that in winning in this fashion, with our beleaguered captain leading the way, we had not just made the semi-finals, but rediscovered our spirit.

The last week of this long tour would be among the most enjoyable of my entire career.

FOUR DAYS LATER, WE met Cronje and his team again, this time at Edgbaston, and prevailed once more, but by an even smaller margin: the game ending in a tie after the last South African wicket fell off the fourth ball of their 50th over. We had finished above South Africa on the Super Six table, and that was the tie-breaker that got us through to the final. This might have been the tensest finish to a cricket game I was ever involved in, the end coming with both batsmen at the non-striker's end and Damien Fleming rolling the ball to Adam Gilchrist to complete a run out.

Gilly knocked off the bails … and then raced the length of the pitch to pull one of the stumps out of the ground as a souvenir — I don't know why he didn't just grab one at his end and neither does he. Afterwards, we didn't celebrate quite as hard as we had at Leeds when we beat the South Africans in the Super Six game, partly I think because many of us remembered what happened in 1996 — when we won a thrilling semi-final but then got beaten easily in the final — but mostly out of exhaustion. The game had been in the balance for just about every one of its 100 overs and it had taken a lot out of us. It was one of those days in the field when you dared not lose focus for even an instant, in case the game found you out. I vividly remember always wanting the ball to come my way, so I could be involved, make a difference. As a fielder, I was always like that.

Just before we'd gone out on the field to defend our relatively small total of 213, Warnie had been a bit weird again, this time saying a couple of times words to the effect of, 'Boys, if we lose this, it'll be the last game for Australia for a couple of us. Let's make sure it's not.'

I'd had a hunch for a week or two that, when we got knocked out of the Cup, Shane was going to follow through on his previous mumblings about retirement, and I wasn't the only one thinking this. But now he chose *this* moment to subtly but still publicly put his plans on the table. That seemed pretty silly to me, but maybe it released the handbrake in his mind that had been stifling his unique talent, because out on the field he was a different bowler.

Tugga had been smart enough to bring him on early, after the South Africans got off to a flyer, and the greatest spinner of them all quickly changed the mood, bowling Gibbs with a mighty leg-break in his second over, and snaring Gary Kirsten and Cronje in his third.

Warnie's reaction showed how big this was for us … and for him! He was roaring, shouting again and again, 'C'mon! C'mon! C'mon!' I'd never seen him react so fiercely when he took a wicket and it was hard not to get caught up in the excitement. He finished with 4–29 from his 10 overs, was named player of the match, and we wouldn't hear him utter the word 'retirement' again for seven-and-a-half years. Like a lot of us, he just wants to be loved and it was hard not to love him when he did things like that.

EARLY IN THE TOURNAMENT, before the New Zealand game, I'd written a poem. Tugga was into that sort of thing, the idea being that a player or a member of our support staff would put pen to paper and then read his literary creation out to the group just before a game, purportedly to inspire us. Initially, I was bit cynical about the exercise, even when some guys used inspirational quotes from the likes of Muhammad Ali, Vince Lombardi or Ron Barassi instead of their own creations, but a few of the boys were right into it and it became strangely addictive, with guys trying to outdo each other, and eventually I came round to thinking it might even work. Reading my poem now, I'm struck by how ordinary it is — I'm sure the English teachers at Brooks High who marked my work so critically in the 1980s won't be changing their minds about my literary skills — yet on the night of June 20, 1999, on the pitch at Lord's, it sounded so bloody beautiful …

> *Every wicket we take, every run we score*
> *Is never enough, we must want more.*
> *And if we do, we will be kings*
> *Then all of us, can have a sing.*
>
> *We'll sing about whatever we please,*
> *'Cause the rest of the world will be at our knees,*
> *And if we win for our great land, we then will sing*
> *'Underneath the Southern Cross' I stand.*

Aside from my attempts at rhymes and verses, I'd been the Aussie one-day team's 'songmaster' since Ian Healy was left out of the ODI side at the start of the 1997–98 season. Heals had rung me a few weeks after he'd been dropped to invite me to have a go, though he reminded me more than once that he was still in charge for the Tests. I was honoured, as if I'd been accepted into a very private club. As I understand it, the tradition of Aussie cricketers singing 'Underneath the Southern Cross' goes back to the 1970s, when Ian Chappell introduced the verse to Australian cricket, Rod Marsh sang it after Test victories and the team enthusiastically joined in. When Rod retired in 1984, he passed on the job to Allan Border, who on being named captain at the end of that year gave it to David

Boon, who in early 1996 gave it to Heals. With the limited-overs games, we didn't sing the anthem too often, only after big wins such as tournament finals, so I'd only had the privilege a couple of times, and it was my call whether we sang or not — which is why we didn't do so after the semi-final tie. As I intimated earlier, I had strong memories of our celebrations after we beat the West Indies at Mohali in 1996, which included a rousing rendition, and have always wondered whether we got a little too excited when we still had a final to play.

Our team for the World Cup final in 1999 had eight players backing up from the side that lost to Sri Lanka in Lahore: Steve and Mark Waugh, Michael Bevan, Shane Warne, Damien Fleming, Paul Reiffel, Glenn McGrath and me. The three 'newcomers' were Adam Gilchrist, Darren Lehmann and Tom Moody (for Mark Taylor, Ian Healy and Stuart Law). The desire to avenge that defeat, added to the momentum and 'never say die' attitude we'd built up in our two games against South Africa, meant that we were always going to be hard to beat at Lord's. To tell the truth, I'm not sure Pakistan had a chance. Indeed, by the time I went out to bat the game was almost over, with Pakistan having been dismissed for 132 (Warne 4–33) and our reply being 1–75 from just 10.1 overs (Gilchrist 54 from 36 balls). I managed 24 from 27 before Wasim Akram had me caught behind, which meant I gave Darren (Boof) Lehmann the chance to hit the winning runs, which he promptly did and that was it.

For the first time in my life, I was a member of the best team in the world.

The game had started half an hour late but it still finished mid-afternoon, so there was ample opportunity for us to enjoy a long celebration in our dressing room. We even had wives and girlfriends in with us for a while, which went against past practices in the Lord's Pavilion, but no one asked them to leave. Once or twice, someone prodded me, and asked when are we going to sing the song, but the sun wasn't setting until after nine so I saw no reason to hurry. My memory is that it was close to dark but not yet night, so it must have been around or just after 8pm when I said to the boys, 'C'mon, let's go out to the middle.' We picked up our drinks and marched down the stairs, through the glorious Long Room and onto the ground. There was hardly a soul there, some of the stands had a ghostly feel to them … it was truly magnificent.

When we got to the pitch, I put the World Cup trophy down just where Boof had square-cut the final four a few hours earlier. Then I motioned to Tom Moody — a bloke who had filled a key all-rounder's role for us on the park and also played such a big part in the triumph through his off-field diplomacy — climbed on his shoulders, said a few words and then reached into my pocket for the special piece of paper I'd been keeping for just this moment. On that paper was my poem and when I read it, boy did it sound good.

And if we win for our great land, we then will sing …

I stopped for a few seconds … and then I started chanting the song, with all the guys quickly, raucously, joyously joining in. I can only imagine how it would have sounded, echoing across this remarkable cricket ground, but where I was, up on Moods' broad shoulders, it was the best thing I'd ever heard.

I was on top of Moods and we were on top of the world.

Mateship

The bond of mateship that is formed between a group of cricketers who spend so much time together is extraordinary. No other sport plays a game that goes for five days and requires players to be out of their comfort zones, to travel to all parts of the world and to be away from home for as long as the game of cricket does. No sport brings a group of people together the way cricket does. The friendships that I've developed over the past 20 years will be with me forever.

My closest mates have been part of my cricket journey. Many of these have come from the most successful years thanks to an even greater bond that comes from achieving success together. I was fortunate enough to play in 168 Test matches, winning more than 100, with various Australian teams filled with some of the greatest ever cricketers, some of the greatest ever guys and some of my closest mates.

I spent a few months playing county cricket with Alec Stewart at Surrey. He is one of England's most celebrated cricketers, who played in 133 Tests for England. But I felt that the sense of camaraderie and mateship in an English team just didn't compare, for me, to that of the 82 Australian cricketers I played with.

When I look back, my friendships were forged in the field of battle but also in the big things that occurred when we were travelling the world together. The birth of a child, the death of a loved one, a strained relationship, home sickness and all sorts of other challenges that brought us all closer together. Team success and individual success are great memories. Representing your country, making an impact on people's lives and doing your bit for the community are the responsibilities that you stand up for. But it's the mateship that you develop that is the most special part of being a cricketer — at any level of the game. It's certainly had a big impact on me.

CHAPTER 20

TEAM FIRST

Heals bows out, October, 1999

WE RETURNED TO AUSTRALIA as mighty conquerors. In 1995, the team had been given a tickertape parade through Sydney after we won the Frank Worrell Trophy, but I missed that because I was in England with the Young Australia team. This time, I was told our reception as we travelled slowly up the main streets of Melbourne and Sydney was much bigger, and from my position in a car with Adam Gilchrist I couldn't have imagined anything grander. People had signs with messages like 'Welcome Home World Champs' and I couldn't help but feel overwhelmingly proud of what we'd achieved. When I was involved in a match, it was always about the team first and the fans after that. That was how I maximised my performance, got the most out of what I did. During some of my best innings, when I was 'in the zone', I was totally oblivious to the noise of the crowd: cheering didn't inspire me; booing never hurt me. When it came to tactics, for me it was always about what was going to give us the best chance to win rather than what might entertain the masses, but because I was a naturally aggressive batsman and because I'd been taught the advantages of keeping a game moving and interesting, these two things were more often than not one and the same.

I always got an enormous kick out of seeing the joy on our supporters' faces, especially young faces, when we'd done something special. I *always* wanted the fans on our side. And I never thought we were 'heroes', as some liked to describe us. To me, the real heroes in life aren't playing sport; they're doing much more important things than that. At the same time, when we were given receptions like those that occurred after the 1999 World Cup, it was hard not to feel more than a little bit special. The challenge was not to let it go to my head.

I think I managed that, this time by once again heading back to Launceston. For the next month I didn't do much at all — again, it was mainly rest, golf, greyhounds.

Exactly eight weeks after the World Cup final, I was in Brisbane playing in a warm-up 12-a-side game, SR Waugh's XI v IA Healy's XI, and a week after that we were in Galle, playing the first ODI of our tour of Sri Lanka. The Australian teams would be on the go, without a break, in Sri Lanka, Zimbabwe, Australia, New Zealand and South Africa, for the next six months, and in that time we would play 46 games (Tests, ODIs and tour games) for 36 wins, six losses, three draws and one no-result. Two of our defeats came right at the start of the adventure, and two more at the end; in between we were nigh on unbeatable. Steve Waugh really stamped his character on the group, and we became a fitter, more professional, more ruthless unit. By the end of this long season the critics were calling us the 'Dominators'.

THE SRI LANKAN TOUR was a bit of a weird experience, in that we played some good cricket, won seven of 11 matches, but the two games we lost were to the home side in the final of the Aiwa Cup one-day tournament and the only Test that ended in a result, so we came away feeling like we'd performed poorly. The image of Steve Waugh (smashed nose) and Jason Gillespie (broken leg) being carted off the field in the first Test at Kandy after they collided at backward-square going for a catch, only added to this perception. Dizzy was out for the season, but Tugga returned for the second Test, playing against doctor's orders and even talking about wearing a helmet in the field to prevent any chance of the nose being reshaped again. A few months earlier, this might have been seen as Steve being selfish, playing only to prevent Shane Warne from being captain even for one game, but now we all took heart from his determination, and from his strong desire to lead by example. He told me years later that his decision to play in the face of adversity in this Test was the making of him as a leader and while I think that process really started during the latter stages of the World Cup, maybe there is a little truth in that.

Warnie himself marked his return to Test cricket by immediately taking five wickets in an innings, while from a personal perspective, the time spent in Sri Lanka was extremely productive, not least because I was named player of the Test series. At Kandy, I was caught and bowled four runs short of a century in a somewhat bizarre fashion — I went down the wicket and tried to block a delivery from Murali, but the ball hit the top of the knee-roll on my front pad, then the face of my bat, and then ballooned back up the pitch. I followed up with 51 in the second. Both knocks were critical as we only managed innings totals of 188 and 140. In the final Test at Colombo I made my fourth Test hundred, an undefeated 105, once again batting with the tail.

Earlier in the tour, in the one-dayers, I didn't make a lot of runs, but I loved the experience of fielding with a newcomer to our ODI team named Andrew Symonds, who was like a tiger shark in the covers or at mid-wicket. I tried my best to match him when I was also in the circle, even outdo him. Together we formed a pretty formidable unit that liked to get in the batsman's mind, trying never to let a ball past and daring them to take our arms on.

Outside of the cricket, my best memory of this tour occurred during the second Test in Galle. I woke on the fourth morning of this game, and I have to confess I was pretty happy to see it was raining heavily outside. We were struggling in the game, but more importantly the Kangaroos were playing Carlton in the AFL Grand Final and while there was no television coverage in Sri Lanka, I was keen to at least listen to the game if I could. As soon as the day's play was abandoned, I dashed back to the team hotel and phoned a mate in Tassie, a Carlton supporter, and asked him to put his phone up next to his TV. And that's how I heard the final quarter, as we won by 35 points. I was paying about $10 a minute for the privilege, so it cost me plenty, but it was worth every cent.

In Zimbabwe, we had a terrific time taking in the sights, and at the same time playing some good cricket even though we were without Geoff Marsh, who had suddenly resigned as coach.

Swamp made the call after days of soul-searching in Sri Lanka following the death of one of his closest friends back home in Western Australia. Over the years we all found that something happening to family or friends could really shake us out of the bubble of cricket life and make us realise just how far away we were and how often we were away. As we got older these things became more important. And so often the best you can do is make a call home because the game demands all of you.

Swamp was older and I think with a family at home he could no longer justify the sacrifices. One look at our schedule showed that he wouldn't be having too many home-cooked meals in the next few months. I was at a stage of my life where as long as I was fit I was happy to be on the road, but when the older guys had their families with them, and I'd stop and play with their kids at our hotel or at the ground, I'd occasionally wonder how hard it was for fathers to be away from home for months at a time.

As the cricket calendar grew ever more crowded, I think a number of us had the same attitude: if we were going to leave our families behind we had to put absolutely everything into our cricket, to make the sacrifice worthwhile. That was the way to turn a negative into something productive. In the old days, wives and families were often seen as a curse or a distraction, but to us, they became an inspiration. Swamp was one of a group of far-sighted blokes who allowed this to happen, just one of the many ways he helped me and the team. Allan Border temporarily filled his role for the Zimbabwe leg of our tour, and we were told we'd have a new full-time coach when we got back to Australia.

A highlight in Zimbabwe was a train journey from Bulawayo to Victoria Falls. It wasn't as if I never went out to see the sights and experience the local way of life, but I am choosy. Some things interest me, others don't, and I'm never going to fake interest. When we toured South Africa and Zimbabwe I was always up for seeing the African wildlife. Anything connected with sport — such as Croke Park in Dublin, the great golf courses of the world, the Manchester United trophy room at Old Trafford or the Garrison Savannah racetrack in Barbados — grabs my interest, while in India, I found the Taj Mahal majestic and was eager to see Gandhi's residence in Ahmedabad, just as in South Africa the day we spent at Robben Island had a profound impact on me. But often on tour, if we were offered the chance to visit another castle or church I tended to say no, on the basis that often, to my eyes at least, if you've seen one, you've seen them all.

However, I've *always* been a bloke who loves to have fun with his team-mates on tour. In 1999, it took us 13 or 14 hours and we stopped a million times along the way before we reached Victoria Falls, but the carriage was first-class, you could see through the windows, it wasn't overcrowded and Stuart MacGill, who organised the trip, went to a lot of trouble, supplying drinks, food, even cigars (which I stayed right away from). We hardly slept, enjoyed a few beers, played cards and instigated a competition during the night where each of us was required to walk through the train and come back with the silliest, best or strangest looking hat being worn by one of our fellow passengers. The only negative was the sounds coming out of Stuey's music box — I would have preferred something a little more modern than 1970s relics like Fleetwood Mac, John Williamson, Carly Simon and the Eagles — but we came away from the experience knowing a little bit more about each other and then there was the exclamation point: the Falls themselves, which are spectacular.

Two days later, the first ever Australia–Zimbabwe Test began, and my contribution was fairly inconsequential: I scored 31 in my only innings and bowled one over, one maiden, none-for-none in each innings, and we won by 10 wickets.

MORE SIGNIFICANTLY, THIS TURNED OUT to be Ian Healy's final Test match, and while we all knew that in Adam Gilchrist we had a ready-made replacement waiting in the wings, I don't think there was one bloke in our set-up who liked the idea of Heals giving it away. He was struggling with the bat and maybe his keeping had declined a fraction, too, but he's such a wise man, a bloke who always put the team ahead of himself, that we worried about the 'intangibles' we'd be losing. I think this was especially true for the younger blokes — he was often the 'go-between' who bridged the gap between senior and junior players.

Heals was one of those cricketers who loved being around the team and the team loved having him around. He was the first one at the bar to have a beer after the game and the first one at training the next morning. We always knew how much it meant for him to be playing for Australia — he never lost sight of that, and he trained as hard as he played. You would often find Heals in the hotel car park practising his keeping by bouncing a golf ball off the wall. There has never been a tougher cricketer, both in the way he competed and in the way he could play through pain, and he was always looking to win games, no matter how we were placed. When I batted against New Zealand at the Gabba in 1997–98, we were chasing quick runs to set up a declaration and I finished 73 not out, from 85 balls. In the first innings, I'd pushed and scraped my way to 26 from 56, and after the second dig, Heals asked, 'Why don't you play like that more often? You can do it, go and play like that.' Not always, he stressed, but more often.

The thing I'll always remember most about Heals was that I always knew he cared about me, that he wanted me to be a successful cricketer. When I screwed up at the Equinox and at the Bourbon, Heals never said anything negative publicly but he was strong enough and shrewd enough to pull me aside and offer his advice — not to become a monk or to give the drink away, but to be sensible. When Heals was in the team, I always felt more comfortable talking to him than I did with Tubby or Tugga. This was something I thought about when I became captain, how I wanted to be as approachable and accessible to the young guys as Heals had been for me, so they could come and talk to me about anything that was bugging them.

Heals wanted to finish his Test career in Brisbane, his home city, in the first Test match of the 1999–2000 Australian summer, against Pakistan, but the selectors wouldn't let him, which we all thought at the time was short-sighted and I still think it was an incorrect call by the powers-that-be. To retire at home would have been fantastic for him. Everyone wants to retire on their terms, and it would have been so much better for him to finish up as he desired rather than in Harare. The thing about great wicketkeepers is that on the field you rarely notice them, because they're never making mistakes, so it would have been nice to put the spotlight on Heals for a change and give the Gabba faithful a chance to bid one of their own a fond farewell.

He rang me in the lead-up to the Test, as he was preparing for his new life as a Channel Nine commentator, and after chatting about nothing in particular we were about to go when he quietly added, 'Oh yeah, Punter, one more thing ... I want you to be the songmaster.' He knew I was hanging out for this (full-time) job, which he had helped build into a great tradition within the Test team, and I was quick to ask him to come down to the rooms after the Test, to lead us one more time. Vivid in my mind was the scene in the Adelaide Oval rooms during my first season as a Test cricketer, when David Boon announced Heals would now be leading us in the singing of 'Underneath the Southern Cross', and then the two of them clambered up on a table and did the job together; Boonie for the last time, Heals for the first, but Heals wanted to stay among the boys after we won the Test, while I led the team on my own, and I have to tell you I found that a very daunting experience.

It was a bit like driving off the first tee with Greg Norman standing behind you, analysing your swing. I had enormous shoes to fill.

CHAPTER 21

GOOD VERSUS GREAT

Summer 1999–2000

BUCK STUCK A BIG SHEET of butcher's paper on a wall in our dressing room with this message: 'TODAY IS THE FIRST TEST OF OUR JOURNEY TO THE INVINCIBLES. LET'S MAKE THE RIDE ENJOYABLE AND ATTAINABLE.'

Initially, I thought this was a strange mixture of arrogance and presumption, but it quickly became a challenge. *Weather permitting, why couldn't we win every game we played?* If Bradman's Invincibles had done it then it could be done again. We promptly beat Pakistan easily at the Gabba and then Adam Gilchrist and Justin Langer produced one of the game's greatest ever partnerships to win the second Test in Hobart (taking us from 5–126, chasing 369 to win, to 6–364). After that, I think most of us believed anything was possible. A phenomenal reflex catch Mark Waugh took at Bellerive to dismiss Inzamum-ul-Haq, one where the batsman half-slashed, half-snicked an attempted cut off Shane Warne and Junior at slip somehow grabbed the ball as it flew past his right hip — only added to this feeling of invincibility. No one else in the history of cricket could have completed that catch — if you can find it on YouTube, you'll see what I mean. Even without Dizzy, who was recovering from his broken leg, we had a fantastic bowling attack and during this season, after a couple of years where our run-getting could be a little hit or miss, the entire batting group sprang to life, making not just hundreds, but big hundreds.

We were taking the game to another level.

JOHN 'BUCK' BUCHANAN, our new coach, joined us at our first team meeting ahead of the 1999–2000 season. He had written a few things up on a whiteboard — mainly about what we could expect from him and what he expected from us. He explained that he went about things slightly differently to other coaches and that he wanted us to be open to all the ideas he had, and to give him a fair go. We quickly learned he was a fan of computers, thinking outside the square and using time shrewdly, but the memory that is most clear for me is when he spoke of his desire to make us *better people* as well as better cricketers.

I was happy to give Buck a go. He is a former first-class cricketer who had been the coach of Queensland for a number of seasons, helping them to their first Sheffield Shield title, and the blokes who'd played under him thought he was excellent, if a little different. Another thing that stayed with me was how open he was to the idea of us winning every game we played.

What I liked most about Buck was that he wanted us to work hard, but to be smart, too. I had learned over the previous couple of years that for me there was no point hitting a million balls in the nets unless you were doing it for a reason and he agreed. He was thorough, sometimes ridiculously so, but gradually — without ever having made a conscious decision to do so — I found myself working harder on my preparation and thinking more about my game, which he had said he wanted us to do. Being meticulous wasn't a grind, but a virtue. His computer stored reams of information on his players and opponents, and for this he copped some criticism from 'old school' thinkers inside and outside the team, but we came to see the value in the information he offered us. The trick was to be able to sift through all he gave you and focus on what could help. Cynics said this type of analysis was just a fad, but every team relies on computer technology today.

In Buck's first home season Australia won every Test and all but one ODI, but at the end of it, as the team prepared to go to New Zealand, he had a new message for us: if we want it badly enough, we can keep getting better. In this regard, he and Tugga were on exactly the same page: *Why be good when we can be great?* In terms of building team spirit, nothing beats winning and we grabbed the challenge with enormous enthusiasm. It was such a wonderful group — while there might have been a decade in age between the oldest (the Waughs and part medium-pacer, part off-spinner Colin Miller) and the youngest (Dizzy, me and a quick from NSW, Brett Lee, who made an immediate impression when he made his international debut in the Boxing Day Test), on and off the field we mostly seemed to mix and match as if we'd all been in the same year at school. Everyone seemed keen to help everybody else, which hadn't always been the way. A golden era had begun.

THE TEST AT BELLERIVE where Gilly and Lang produced their heroics was my second on Tasmanian turf, after the Test against New Zealand in late 1997 when I scored just four. That first time, I'd felt an unbelievable pressure to do well, as if that was when I *had* to repay all the family, friends and fans who had been so good to me, especially all those who'd made the drive down from Launceston. It had all become a bit much for me. I was batting with Mark Waugh, something I usually enjoyed, but that time I struggled to get the ball off the square and there was a sense of inevitability about me getting out, which came when I nicked Chris Cairns through to keeper Adam Parore. I was so out of touch, Mum figured there had to be an explanation away from cricket and was more convinced than ever that she was a jinx. She said wouldn't come again. I argued otherwise, so she ventured down to the Test against Pakistan two years later ... and I made a pair. It'd be years before I could convince her that it was my fault and had nothing to do with her.

It is true that for a player a home Test match is different to any other, especially, I think, for a Tasmanian, because Bellerive doesn't get a Test every year, which makes the occasion when it does occur even more special for the locals. The media zeroes in on the Tasmanian player, seeking a parochial perspective on the game. I was always bombarded by hundreds of well-meaning people, some I knew well but others I didn't, who wanted to say g'day, get my autograph or recall the last time they saw me, and while on their own every one of these approaches was welcome and appreciated, added together they were a little overwhelming.

Inevitably, a lot of people were on to me for tickets and while finding 100 or more tickets wasn't difficult because the other boys weren't using their allocation, it was still time-consuming getting everyone organised. And I had the added disadvantage of not being able to withdraw to my own bed, as guys from the mainland states could when they played in a Test in their home city, because I'm from Launceston and the international games are in Hobart. Having the chance to represent my country in front of my fellow Tasmanians was always one of the great privileges of my career, but it did take me a while to learn that I had to try to treat it like any other game, even though in many ways it was much more than that.

Against Pakistan at Bellerive in late 1999, I received an unbelievable ball in the first innings. I decided to let one go from Waqar Younis, but it reversed so far that even though I saw it clearly out of his hand and felt pretty assured about leaving it alone, it still dived back in and took my off-stump. In the second dig, when I could feel my nerves getting the better of me because I desperately wanted to get off the mark, I played all around a sharp one off Wasim Akram and was lbw. Both times I knew I'd copped a difficult delivery before I had a chance to get my eye in and both times I was very aware of the silence that accompanied me back to the pavilion. I'd also been dismissed for a duck in Brisbane (a horrible lbw decision), so suddenly my place in the side was under a bit of scrutiny again, even though — given that I'd faced only 15 balls so far in the series — it was a bit hard to know just what sort of form I was in.

Brisbane was the first time I'd made a duck, but after Hobart they were starting to become a habit.

WHEN I WALKED OUT to join Lang in the middle on day two of the third Test against Pakistan at the WACA 14 wickets had already fallen in the game for just 209 runs, and I had to face a couple of the best quicks of the modern era: Waqar Younis was injured, but Wasim Akram was raring to go and with him was Shoaib Akhtar, the fastest bowler in the world. They also had Mohammad Akram, who was a very good seamer, and the excellent offie, Saqlain Mushtaq. I was confronted by three slips, a gully, silly mid-off and short leg but immediately I managed to push a ball wide of mid-on for three and what I most feared, another duck, was off the agenda.

Lang had been transformed by his match-winning ton in the previous Test. He had always been a bloke who carried a little self-doubt around with him, despite his huge natural ability, but now he was Buck's biggest disciple, especially when it came to the concept of winning every game. We had been really good mates since we were the spare batsmen on the Windies tour in 1995 who made a pact to get everything we could out of our cricket, and now he was in to me to help him turn this Test around.

'C'mon Punt, let's bat for a long time,' he half said, half pleaded in that earnest fashion of his. 'Anything's possible, mate.'

Under the circumstances, I couldn't have had a better batting partner — I went out there fearing another failure and what that might do to my place in the team, but quickly this anxiety was replaced by a burning determination to not just survive but to make a big score. Lang played a big part in this sudden transformation.

Shoaib Akhtar came on after drinks, to bowl the 15th over of the innings, and he started with four straight no-balls. Then I hit him for two fours, one a straight drive, the other a pull shot. With the last shot, though, I held my breath for a second, because the ball was on to me quicker than I'd expected. I figured he was warming up. Sure enough, the next over was way faster, the highlight being the fourth ball that I tried to hook but only managed to top edge away to the sightscreen. It was pulsating stuff, but after just three overs it seemed he had burned himself out; they brought Saqlain on to bowl and we could really focus on rebuilding the innings. It turned into one of the best, most rewarding and most important partnerships of my career — 327 runs, still the highest stand for any wicket achieved in Tests at the WACA. My little mate made 144 and I went all the way to 197.

For most of the time, I really enjoyed that knock, but there was one brief spell on the third day of the Test when I almost feared for my life. The innings total was getting up towards 350, they'd just taken the second new ball, and it was maybe 40 minutes before tea, when Shoaib suddenly bowled three or four of the quickest deliveries I'd ever face. The fifth ball of the second over with the shiny new pill, he suddenly unleashed this bullet of a bouncer that made a bit of a fool of me. I sort of half hooked at it, but the ball was past me well before I was through with the shot, and I barely had time to turn around to see the keeper, Moin Khan, leap high as he gloved it one-handed. It might have gone for six byes if he hadn't stopped it. All I could do was stand there with a bewildered look on my face, as if I'd seen a ghost, while Shoaib made a weird gesture at me, hands up near his ears, which to me said that he wasn't quite sure where the delivery had come from either. The next two balls were lightning; the first pitched on a reasonable length but Moin still caught it well above his head and the last nearly cut me in half as the ball cut back and flashed over the top of the off-stump. Even though I was 169 not out, I was totally rattled for a second or two and I wasn't helped by having Lang walk down the pitch after each of the three balls to say how exciting it all was watching from the non-striker's end. In the years that followed, whenever I was asked about the fastest bowler I ever faced, I always talked first about those three balls from Shoaib Akhtar.

I was briefly cranky for playing a dud shot to get myself out, caught in the gully, but later on I wasn't that worried by the fact I'd missed the double ton. I was playing for a team that was going on a fantastic journey. After this innings, I knew I was a significant part of it.

I SCORED HUNDREDS in the first and third Tests of our three-game series against India which followed the Pakistan matches, and hours after we'd won that third Test I led the team out to the middle of the SCG with us wearing nothing but jockstraps and the replica Victor Trumper caps Tugga had organised for us to wear as a nod to the new millennium, and we belted out 'Underneath the Southern Cross' just like that.

Then, I was named acting vice-captain while Warnie recovered from a side strain suffered in our opening game of the Carlton & United one-day series, and quickly scored another century against the Indians at the MCG, a knock that took me to No. 4 in the world ODI batting rankings. I felt unstoppable.

My next three digs were all ducks, suffered over five days and involving just eight deliveries.

I felt like the game was teaching me to take nothing for granted. Just a couple of weeks later it did so again. I reckon what happened this time sums up my attitude to competitive sport. We were in total control of the game: we'd scored 7–337 and they'd lost four early wickets in reply. Mohammad Yousuf hit one through the covers and I chased it all the way to the boundary and then slid spikes-first into the advertising board attached to the picket fence that surrounded the ground (there was no boundary rope) ... and my foot got caught, my knee kept going and my ankle was twisted in a way nature never intended. No one would have complained if I'd let the ball run away for four, and if it had we would have won by 151 runs instead of 152, but that's not how I played the game. I managed to half crawl, half stumble over to the ball and throw it back off one leg, but I couldn't walk. They had to carry me off.

We were scheduled to go to New Zealand within a few days of the one-day finals finishing, and I was up all night icing the swollen joint until it was time for me to fly to Melbourne first thing the next morning for a thorough examination. After they did the X-rays and an MRI, I sat down with a specialist who said it didn't look too bad. 'You've got a badly sprained ankle,' he said. 'You'll be batting in three or four days.'

'Bewdy,' I said. 'I'll be right for New Zealand.'

'Can't see why not,' the doctor replied.

A week later, I was home in Launceston and still couldn't put my foot on the ground properly. I'd been ruled out of the first part of the New Zealand trip, the one-dayers, but I was hoping to play in the Test matches, so an official fitness test in Sydney with team physio Errol Alcott had been organised. Before that, I got someone to drive me down to Hobart so I could get a cortisone shot in my ankle, on the basis that this pain relief might be enough to earn Errol's tick of approval and get me across the Tasman. I did this off my own bat, didn't tell anyone from the team or the Board about it.

My doctor took a scan of the joint, which came up on a monitor to ensure he would put the needle in the right spot, and as he was about to put the needle in, he stopped to look at the screen and then asked me, 'Have you ever hurt your ankle before?'

'I've rolled it a few times,' I replied. 'Nothing major.'

'Ricky, you've got a broken ankle,' he said. 'You've got a broken bone in there.'

I thought he was kidding, given that the doctor and physio I'd seen previously hadn't said anything like that, but he showed me the screen and it was obvious he knew what he was talking about. He still gave me the shot and I still went to Sydney, and tried to bluff my way through, but I was no chance. It was all I could do to walk without a limp.

As soon as I started running, Errol said to me, 'Mate, you'll have to go harder than that.' I confessed the ankle was sore. 'Run over there and then zigzag for me,' he ordered. I tried to zigzag and fell over and he said he knew an orthopaedic surgeon who'd be able to sort things out. Soon after, this specialist was taking more X-rays and then he asked me to lie on my stomach while he studied the scans. Then he jabbed his fingers into the back of my ankle and grabbed one particular spot ... and I went through the roof.

'There's a broken bone in there,' he said.

'I know,' I replied.

Two days later I was having surgery.

A piece of bone the size of a 10-cent piece had broken off in the back of the joint, and they had to go in and break it up so they could get it out, because it was cluttering up the ankle joint. What I was originally told would be a three- or four-day injury ended up costing me six months.

I didn't play again until August. After two warm-up games in Brisbane, we played some 'indoor' ODIs against South Africa in Melbourne, which I chiefly remember because the playing surface was pretty loose and I spent most of my time in the field worried I'd go over on my ankle again.

THIS WAS MY FIRST bad injury since I'd shattered my elbow playing footy as a teenager. If you ask most of the trainers or physios I've been around over the years, they'll tell you I never complained about injuries too much. I never saw the point in letting them know about little niggles that weren't going to stop me from playing anyway. I was always worried that if I did tell them, they might err on the side of caution, which is their nature; that they might want to rush me off for an X-ray or MRI that might only bring bad news. The injuries that cost me games were inevitably pretty bad ones.

This time, like any other time, I didn't like being incapacitated for a number of reasons. One was simply that I hated being 'grounded', unable to run around, play golf, be active. This went against all my instincts. It was also disappointing not being able to cash in on what I considered at the time to be the best form of my life. And every time I turned on the TV to watch the boys in New

Zealand, as they continued on our winning ways, I couldn't help but worry about my place in the side. If this sounds like paranoia, then welcome to life as an international cricketer after you've been dropped a couple of times and you know the blokes competing for your spot are all very, very talented. This time, I was replaced by Matt Hayden in the one-day squad and by Damien Martyn at No. 6 in the Test XI. I knew how good these two guys were, how giving them a chance to show what they could do in my place, while inadvertent, was still not a clever move on my part.

I'd taken great heart from my brief run as Tugga's deputy while Warnie was out, because it said the people in charge saw me as a future leader, that they didn't mind my attitude and the way I handled myself on the field, at training and in team meetings, and that I'd won back at least most of the respect I'd lost over the off-field incidents in Kolkata and Sydney. However, none of that was any use to anyone if I wasn't in the team. This was what I kept reminding myself as the new season approached. I'd had a good summer in 1999–2000, but if I wanted to lock up my place in the team I had to keep improving, a philosophy that fitted in very smoothly with the coach and captain's ambitions for the side.

A couple of years earlier, I might have been a bit intimidated by the idea that I had to keep getting better to sustain my life in the Australian set-up, but more and more I saw it as a challenge worth pursuing. I was growing as a sportsman and as a person, just as Buck had planned.

On golf

Those close to me say I'm a golf tragic. Rianna says I've spent more time on a golf course than at cricket and that our storage area at home has more golf clubs in it than cricket gear. Sometimes you can't hide from the truth, can you! You see, I was born into a sporting family. Dad was passionate about most sports but golf was what he was best at. Mum took up golf to spend more time with Dad, and it didn't take long for Drew, Renee and myself to have a golf club in our hands. When Dad worked at the railways and I was still at primary school, he used to take every second Friday off as an RDO to play golf and I would find a way to get off school early to walk around the course with him. He never let me play but I watched him closely and tried to copy what he did when I had the chance. When we lived in Newnham, our home was right next to the Mowbray Golf Club and we would spend hours on the course hitting balls and learning the skills of golf.

With that upbringing, it's probably no surprise that the whole family plays golf just about every week. Dad was a scratch marker at 15 and was a trainee professional at the Riverside Golf Club. He played Division 1 pennant for more than 15 years. Mum took up golf much later than everybody but, with her natural eye-hand coordination, was a very consistent Division 2 pennant player for Mowbray. Drew had more potential than all of us. He did an AIS Golf scholarship in Canberra, represented Tasmania in juniors and colts and is back playing Division 1 pennant again. He's also the head greenkeeper at the world-renowned Barnbougle Lost Farm course in Tasmania. Like Drew, Renee represented Tasmania as a junior and played Division 1 pennant when still in that age bracket.

I'm currently playing off scratch and the lowest handicap I have ever got down to is +1. I play as often as possible, and I love going and hitting balls at a range or putting for hours on a practice green. My golf clubs have travelled with me all around the world many times over and I've played some of the greatest golf courses on most continents of the globe. A day wouldn't go by that I'm not on my iPad researching golf equipment, latest trends and all the news from the various tours. I've been fortunate to meet and stay in touch with many of Australia's best golfers. I'm intrigued by how good they are and what they can do with a golf ball. I've invested in a couple of golf businesses, am exploring some exciting opportunities in golf media, and am also hoping to start up a partnership with one of the world's best golfing brands but still have a bit of work to do on that one.

This book is full of golf anecdotes that are all very special to me. But the one that has an extra special place in my heart was when Dad, Drew and I combined to win a Division 2 pennant game for Mowbray Golf Club in May 2012. I was home for a quick visit and, with Renee as my caddy, we played Prospect in the Northern pennant competition at the Country Club Tasmania. Drew was in sensational form, winning 6 and 5. Dad suffered a rare pennant defeat, while I was able to get on top of my opponent, winning 1 up. It was a very special day, and one which I will never forget.

CHAPTER 22

TURNING PRO

Capital Golf Course, Melbourne, August 15, 2000

I ALMOST BECAME a professional golfer. It was a fantasy of mine there's no doubt, but I can't say there was anything premeditated about this day.

It happened the day before the historic first 'indoor' ODI, against South Africa at what was then called Colonial Stadium (and has since been known as Telstra Dome and Etihad Stadium) in Melbourne. The Australian team had the afternoon off and a number of us were at the Capital Golf Course in Melbourne, which was owned by two of Australia's richest men, Kerry Packer and Lloyd Williams, and is located about 25 kilometres south-east of the Melbourne CBD.

When we arrived, we discovered the Channel Nine commentators were also there for a round, plus a number of other former players, including Dean Jones and Allan Border. Aaron Baddeley, who during the previous year had won the Australian Open golf championship as an 18-year-old amateur and who had turned pro only a few weeks earlier, was playing, too. We got there in time for lunch and while we were eating Kerry Packer walked in and looked us over.

'Seeing as we've got a few people here today, let's have a bit of fun,' he announced. 'I'll put some money up and we'll see what happens.'

'No thanks, Mr Packer,' someone said, 'She'll be right. We've only come out for a friendly round.'

'No,' he said much more decisively, 'this is what we'll do.'

Kerry was not the sort of man who liked to be contradicted.

He organised us in a circle, and then went around the group. 'What's your handicap?' he asked Mark Taylor, and Tubby replied, 'Eight.' Mark Waugh said, 'Ten.' He got to me, and I said, 'Four.' All the time, he was writing these handicaps down, plus the names of our home golf clubs. When we were done, he said to one of his assistants, 'I want you to ring all these clubs and check their handicaps.'

Once this was done, he called us back together and said, 'Right, any one of you blokes who can get 40 Stableford points on my course, I'll give you $5000.'

That spiked our interest. 'Whoever you've got as a partner,' he continued, 'if the two of you can get 80 points between you, that's another $10,000.'

We sensed that Mr Packer was very proud of his Peter Thomson-designed layout (which is seriously magnificent), and he was eager to see how we'd handle it. I'm sure he wanted the course to win. More than once during the round I spotted him driving from fairway to fairway in his golf cart, so he could spy on us from behind trees to see how we were going. I teamed up with Dean, Aaron and AB in our group of four, and I played really well, shooting two under off the stick (enough to beat the reigning Aussie Open champion) and finishing with 42 Stableford points. Deano and I missed the bonus 10 grand by a point.

Back in the clubhouse, Mr Packer went through our cards with the proverbial fine-toothed comb and then he said to me, 'Rightio young fella, go down to the Mahogany Room at the casino tonight and there will be someone waiting for you with your money.'

I felt like I'd won the British Open. As soon as it was polite to do so, I raced back to our hotel, got changed, and took myself down to Crown Casino where, sure enough, there was a big yellow envelope with $5000 cash inside and my name on the outside.

Hardly a word was spoken. I walked out with the envelope folded tightly in my jacket pocket and that might have been the end of it if Deano hadn't got up at a pre-game function the next day and told the whole bloody world about it. The following day in *The Age*, alongside the report of our 94-run victory over the South Africans, was a story about my big payday on the golf course.

Throughout my career, I rarely liked seeing my name in the paper when it wasn't connected with cricket, and this was no different; in fact, on this occasion it created a real problem for me. The day after the three-game series ended all square (one win, one loss, one tie), I flew home to Launceston and not long after I'd unpacked my bag, I took a call from someone representing the Australian Golf Union. When he told me he'd read the story in the paper, I thought he was going to congratulate me, but instead he just inquired flatly, 'Is it true?'

'Pretty much,' I said.

'Well, unless you give the $5000 back,' he said in a school-masterly tone, 'you won't be allowed to be a member of any golf club in Australia for the rest of your life.'

'What are you talking about?' I asked. 'It was a bet.'

'Did you put any money on the table?' he asked. 'The way I read the story, you didn't risk any of your money.'

'No, I didn't,' I said a little feebly.

'Then I'm afraid you've infringed your amateur status. Either you're now a professional golfer, or you've got to give the money back.'

'Fair enough,' I replied. I felt as if someone had just discovered I'd signed for an incorrect score, like Robert De Vicenzo did at the 1968 Masters when they wouldn't let him participate in a play-off.

'But can you do me one favour?' I continued. 'Can you ring Kerry Packer and tell him that you want me to give him his money back? I'd like to see what response you get.'

There was a moment's silence. Then we started talking again. After a bit more amicable to'ing and fro'ing, we both acknowledged there was no escape. Under the 'Rules of Amateur Status' as defined by the Royal and Ancient Golf Club of St Andrews, Mr Packer's money could be considered as either a 'gratuity in connection with a golfing event' or 'prize money in a match, tournament or exhibition'. Either way, it was 'professionalism', so I had to hand the cash over. In the end, I donated the money to a young man from Hobart who had broken his neck playing his first game of senior league footy on the same weekend we were playing the ODIs in Melbourne, which was a much better result than me keeping it anyway.

THE INDOOR ODIs were also the first for Adam Gilchrist as Australia's full-time vice-captain, a promotion for him that had come about after Warnie got himself into a tabloid storm in England earlier in the winter with allegations of sending 'inappropriate' text messages. To tell you the truth, I'm not sure any of the players was too worried about what Warnie had done, on the basis that it was his problem and not ours, but the Australian Cricket Board decided he had brought the game into disrepute and sacked him as Steve Waugh's deputy. I would have looked at all the good things Warnie had done for the team and for cricket and given him another chance; instead, I found myself being invited to Melbourne for what the media described as a job interview with Malcolm Speed and, as I remember it, a number of ACB directors.

When I got there, I was a lot more nervous than I'd expected to be. I knew the vice-captaincy was a stepping stone to the captaincy, so I liked the idea of being appointed but I wasn't desperate for it. I was in no hurry. I think my nerves came mainly from the reality that I was on unfamiliar turf because I'd never actually been involved in a job interview before. Well, that's not exactly true — I did go for a greenkeeper apprenticeship at Mowbray Golf Club when I was straight out of school, before I went to the Cricket Academy, but I think the people at the club had a fair idea I wasn't going to be around much anyway so I was never really a contender. My brother, Drew, actually ended up getting that gig a couple of years later.

One or two media commentators brought the Bourbon and Beefsteak incident up when it was announced I was going to be considered for the vice-captaincy (and they'd do so again a further 18 months on, when the talk started that Steve Waugh was going to lose the one-day captaincy), but otherwise it seemed everyone was happy to consider me as leadership material. I didn't prepare for the interview at all. I never sat down with my manager to think about what sort of questions they'd ask. Instead of going in there aiming to talk my way into the job, I just wanted to survive.

It was true I had more Test experience than Gilly but he was older than me, had been in the one-day squad since 1996, and had been my captain at Under-19 level. We had a very brief conversation after he got the job, when I said flatly, 'Congratulations, let's get on with it.' It was all a bit weird in that I wasn't disappointed that I hadn't got the job, but I would have been happy if they'd offered it to me. In the whole great scheme of things, it really wasn't as important to us as people outside the team might have expected.

I don't think any of us thought, coming out of that process, that Gilly was automatically next in line for the captaincy. We only had to look at Warnie's change of fortunes to realise that you should never look too far ahead. Afterwards, in the days after the Board's decision was announced, my main concern was for Shane, who I knew had strong leadership ambitions that now seemed dashed, but when I spoke to him I sensed he'd come to terms with what had been done to him. Sure, he was filthy on the administrators and thought it was ridiculous that in the 21st century, with all that happens in world sport, he'd been canned for what he felt was none of their business, but he said he wasn't dirty on Gilly or me and that what had happened wouldn't impinge on the way he played or how he would work for the team. And it never did.

MY BRIEF RUN as stand-in vice-captain in 1999–2000 had been the first indication that the selectors saw me as a future leader; the interview for the full-time deputy's job was the second; and a third came in November 2000 when I was asked to captain a Northern Territory Invitation XI in a non-first-class tour game against the West Indies in Alice Springs.

The NT side was a combination of locals and a few first-class cricketers like Colin Miller, Brad Hodge, Daniel Marsh and Michael Di Venuto, and I started well by winning the toss, but it was all downhill from there. Brian Lara scored a superb hundred, I ran myself out for 26 and we ended up losing by 57 runs. My first experience as a first-class captain wouldn't come until 2001–02, when Jamie Cox stepped back so I could lead Tasmania whenever I was available. While I was in the national teams, that wasn't very often, but he still stood aside to boost my chances of one day getting the Australian job.

The home series against the Windies in 2000–01 was very disappointing, played against as poor a major Test side as any I encountered during my career. On paper they were okay — with names such as Lara, Courtney Walsh, Jimmy Adams, Shivnarine Chanderpaul, Ramnaresh Sarwan and Ridley Jacobs — but they were so dispirited, especially during the Tests in Brisbane, Perth and Melbourne when they couldn't get to 200 in either innings, that it sometimes felt like we were involved in something less than a Test match, especially when we compared these games to the red-hot Australia–West Indies clashes of years past. Still, this didn't change the way we played or diminish our effort or enjoyment, and the win in the second Test at the WACA was our 12th in a row, a world record and a tribute to the relentless nature of our cricket. We celebrated by going on a kind of low-key pub crawl, stopping only at venues we were familiar with, and I kept interrupting the journey — 12 times in all — to get the guys to sing the team song.

The only time the Windies were really competitive was in the third Test in Adelaide, when Lara played his one significant innings of the series — a superb 182 that I felt in a way responsible for. Gilly was captain for this game, because Tugga was injured, and I was vice-captain, the first time I'd filled this position in Test cricket, and I was a little fired up to make an impression on the opening day. Lara was in just before lunch and in the overs before and straight after the break he was looking like a Z-grader, struggling mightily to find the middle of his bat. At one point, I ran past him and muttered something like, 'What are you doing out here? Just get on with it.' My plan was to get him to play a big shot to the wrong ball, but all I did was wake him up. We still went on to win the Test, but only by five wickets after we'd claimed the first two games by an innings, and afterwards Lara made a point of thanking me for what I'd said.

'What do you mean?' I replied.

'All I ever try to do at the start of an innings is play 60 balls,' he explained. 'If I get through those 60 balls, doesn't matter how, I feel like I'm okay. When you talked to me, I was up to 60, so I was confident, ready to go. You just made me more determined.'

There was plenty of logic in such a strategy. There's plenty of time in a Test match, especially in the first innings, so it makes sense to use the start of your knock just to settle in, no more than that, on the basis that once you've built a foundation and got used to the pitch and the light and seen a little of the opposition bowlers, then you're in a position to make a big score. And, of course, in Test cricket a big score is almost always much more valuable than a flashy 20 or 30. I guess it doesn't have to be '60 balls', it could be 30 runs or 45 minutes, whatever is your fancy. At the end of the series we swapped shirts and on the front of the shirt he gave me he penned words to the effect of, 'Let's hope we face 60 balls every time we play.'

Of course, no batting plan is foolproof. Warnie had broken a finger just before the start of this series, so Stuart MacGill played in his place and enjoyed some success — except in Adelaide when Lara belted him. At the MCG, we included an extra quick, Andy 'Bic' Bichel, instead of Stuey and when Lara strode out to the middle with their score at 2–6 and Jason Gillespie on fire, Mark Waugh couldn't resist the urge to have a crack at the great West Indian.

I'd told everyone that there was no point talking to him, but Junior ignored me.

'MacGill's not here,' he quipped from second slip. 'Who are you going to get your runs off today?'

Lara stood up straight, turned around, pointed at Bic who was fielding to my left at fourth slip and said bluntly, ominously, 'He's here.' Lara had scored plenty off Bic in a game against an Australia A team in Hobart a couple of weeks earlier and clearly fancied his chances of doing so again.

Dizzy and Glenn McGrath were bowling beautifully, but Lara and Sherwin Campbell survived and after 16 overs the West Indies were 2–15. At this point, Bic came on to bowl and his first two overs to Lara cost just four runs. In Bic's third over, the great batsman from Trinidad cover-drove him for two, was struck on the box by one that nipped back at him and slashed a wide delivery past point for four. And then he half drove a terrific comeback ball and edged it low to, of all people, Junior at second slip. We all enjoyed that one, Bic went on to complete his first five-for in Test cricket and maybe — just as I was after Adelaide — Lara was a little wiser for the experience. Underestimating opponents is never a smart thing to do in international cricket.

Lara could be a strange man on the field, usually laid-back sometimes it was like something in him would snap and he would lose control, but there was no denying his class. He and Sachin Tendulkar were the two best batsmen I fielded against but if I had to pick between them I'd go for Sachin only because of those days we had when I didn't think we were ever going to get him out. Brian was such a flashy player, even when he was blazing there always seemed a chance he'd go for *too* big a shot and get himself out that way. But the way he could manipulate a field was phenomenal; it was almost as if embarrassing opposition captains was his speciality. Against a spinner, for example, he might have been sweeping everything, so we'd move the man at backward point to short fine-leg, to prevent that single and Brian would promptly back away and cut the same ball he'd been sweeping through the gap at backward point. He was also a batsman who consistently made big scores. Not everyone is like that.

But he could get very cranky during a game, which we thought he sometimes did to rev himself up, to get more into the contest. He wasn't the only cricketer who did this; I'm sure Steve Waugh did it once or twice and Glenn McGrath was another player who might initiate an argument with an opponent as much to get himself going as to distract the batsman. In that same Adelaide Test in which he scored his 182, Lara put on a real turn in their second innings after I threw a ball to Gilly from my fielding position at mid-wicket and he thought it went too close to the other batsman, Daren Ganga.

The previous ball, Ganga had edged a catch to Gilly but the umpire said not out, so there was a bit of talk going on and there was a bit of anger in my gesture, but Lara knew I was a good enough thrower to put the ball exactly where I wanted to. For him to suggest I was trying to brand Ganga was just wrong. There were two more overs before lunch, and Lara never stopped whingeing in that time. I have to say we were very excited straight after the break when 'Funky' Miller had him caught by Justin Langer close in on the off-side.

Lara's wicket meant the Windies were 3–87 in their second innings, a lead of 75, but they lost their last eight wickets for just 54 and we ended up getting home by five wickets, to retain the Frank Worrell Trophy. It was typical of this Australian team that we'd find a way to win. During that era, I reckon we got ourselves into as much trouble as more recent Aussie teams have done, but nine times out of 10 we'd recover, sometimes very quickly. From the time we beat Pakistan in Hobart in 1999–2000, when Lang and Gilly got us home, we had a belief in ourselves and each other that we could win from anywhere, and it was amazing how often someone came through for us. In this Adelaide Test it was Funky; in the next Test in Melbourne it was Bic; in Sydney it was Slats and Stuey MacGill.

We'd find out soon enough you can't win *all* the time, but we did win most of the time. And we loved every minute of it.

Brilliance

Brilliance in an individual or team is a trait that I love and it particularly fuels my passion for sport. To watch the brilliance of Tiger Woods as a magician around a golf course is something any keen golfer can do over and over again. As a mad North Melbourne fan, I was always mesmerised by the way that Wayne Carey could impose himself on a game of AFL football and use his individual brilliance to bring his team-mates into a game. While I'm not a huge motor-racing fan, I have watched the film *Senna* and was left with no doubt that Ayrton Senna had qualities of brilliance that might never be matched in that sport.

Brilliance is also a team trait that makes the very best teams great. The long-term dominance of Manchester United in English soccer is built around individual brilliance and a clearly defined culture that created team brilliance. That's what I set out to build when I became captain of the Australian Test team. We had the brilliance of Warne, McGrath, Gilchrist and so many other outstanding players. We already had a clearly defined culture that Steve had developed under his captaincy, so I set out to build on this through our style of play. I wanted opposition teams to look back on a series against us and ask, 'How on earth do we beat them?' I wanted our batsmen to dominate for long periods of time. I wanted our bowlers to execute at the highest level and I wanted our fielding to be the best in the world. Our overall performance during the period 2003 to 2008 was the greatest era of sustained team brilliance and success that I was a part of. We achieved so much, from significantly lifting the run rates achieved in Test cricket, consistently taking 20 wickets a game, to winning matches in less than four days and revolutionising the way one-day cricket was played. It was an unbelievable time in Australian cricket and I was so fortunate to be a part of it.

CHAPTER 23

FROM HARBHAJAN TO HEADINGLEY

Mumbai, India, February 25, 2001

SIR DON BRADMAN'S INNINGS came to an end when, somewhat fittingly, the Test team arrived in Mumbai at the beginning of a three-match series.

There was a sombre mood in the Australian camp when the news came through, but it had been apparent to me from the first time I stepped foot in this country that Indians revered the Australian batsman and often knew more about him than we did. To see his passing marked with such solemnity and dignity in a country so far from home was an experience that left an impression on all of us.

I'd met Sir Donald only once — he spoke to the players during my first year at the Academy and I was in total awe of him and his every word, his presence was extraordinary — yet I still felt a sort of kinship with him, and the news of his death did make me stop and think about what he meant to me. I wasn't sure of my own Test batting average, but like most cricket fans I knew his *precisely*: 99.94. When I was a kid and I used to dream of being an Aussie cricketer, I wondered if there was any way I'd be as good as Bradman. Never better; being as good was as far as I'd dare to dream. In fact, he'd set a standard we could never reach.

Incredibly, Sir Don never played in India. The team's boat stopped in the harbour in Mumbai (then Bombay) when the Invincibles were on their way to England and there is a story of him having to be convinced to come up and wave to the crowds who gathered on the dock, but the greatest batsman of all time definitely held a place in the hearts of almost every Indian cricket fan and player I ever met.

The Mumbai Test started with a minute's silence, and then we bowled India out for just 176. Our reply was stumbling a little on the second day at 4–98 when I strode out purposefully to bat, straight after the first drinks break. Initially, I was up against Rahul Sanghvi, a left-arm finger spinner. There were four balls left in his over, and I handled them comfortably, even driving the last delivery firmly to extra cover, then Matt Hayden took a single from the first ball of my old mate Harbhajan Singh's over.

We'd encountered Harbhajan in our game against the India A team at the start of the tour, when he took a few wickets and I scored 56 and 68. In this Test, he dismissed Justin Langer and Mark Waugh in his first 10 overs, but given the confidence I'd garnered from those twin half-centuries I was hardly quaking in my boots as he moved in to bowl. Maybe I should have been. His first delivery spat up off a length, took the shoulder of my bat, on to the top of my pad and ballooned meekly out to the fielder at short leg. As I walked off, I was in something of a daze, with the same thought going around in my head: *I did everything right … but I got out.* In one ball, the faith I had in my technique was shattered. I can't begin to stress what a profound effect that delivery had on me. When it came to playing off-spin on Indian wickets, suddenly I was shot.

Adam Gilchrist replaced me in the middle, and he and Haydos produced one of great partnerships, with Gilly simply teeing off and racing to a hundred in 84 balls and Matty confounding the Indians by sweeping just about everything. They added 197 in 32 overs and we ended up winning by 10 wickets. My only contribution of note was the catch I took to dismiss Sachin Tendulkar in their second innings, when he smacked a pull shot into Lang's shoulder at short leg, and the ball lobbed out towards square leg. I had just enough time to change direction and run from mid-wicket, dive full-length and catch the ball centimetres off the ground, one of the better catches of my life. That made them 3–154; the next seven wickets promptly fell for 65 runs in 28 overs. We'd now won 16 consecutive Tests, a sequence dating back to Zimbabwe in October 1999.

And we might have won 17 if fate and the umpires had been kinder to me in Kolkata. This was the Test we looked to have wrapped up after three days, but then VVS Laxman and Rahul Dravid batted right through day four, a turnaround that ended with the home team becoming only the third side in Test history to win after following on. It was an extraordinary performance by Laxman and Dravid, especially given that they conjured their miracle against an attack featuring Glenn McGrath, Jason Gillespie and Shane Warne, and they rightly entered Indian cricket folklore (as did Harbhajan, who took 13 wickets for the match). What people don't remember is that the bowler who came closest to breaking their epic partnership was a bloke named Ponting, who would have dismissed Laxman in his second over if only his captain had given him two slips (instead, the edge ran down to third man for four) and who to this day believes he had Dravid plumb lbw in the last over before lunch. How the umpire didn't give that one is something I will never understand …

When Gilly gave the umpires an absolute gobful at the conclusion of this Test — a tirade for which he somehow escaped scrutiny — I don't think he was particularly thinking about this one, more a few lbw decisions on the final day, but he should have included it, because it was just as contentious.

I had bowled a couple more overs straight after lunch, and then didn't come back on until late in the day, when Laxman was in the 250s, Dravid was approaching his 150 and India's lead was almost

300. It was a bowling change that brought a surprising reaction from Dravid, a batsman who was averaging more than 54 in Test cricket at the time. It was unbearably hot and Junior and Warnie had been bowling spinners, so it was hardly a shock that Dravid was batting in a wide-brimmed white hat, but when he saw I was going to bowl he quickly called for his helmet. Maybe his brain was scrambled after batting for so long, or perhaps he thought one of the quicks was coming back on, but I took it as a bizarre compliment to my gentle medium-pace bowling.

It was about the only good thing to happen all day.

Batting-wise, this Test and the one that followed were a disaster for me, but the strange thing was I was making runs in tour games. We played an Indian Board President's XI on a very flat deck in Delhi straight after the first Test and I scored 102 in both innings, the second ton undefeated, but I was all over the place as soon as Harbhajan got the ball spinning in the Tests. In the first innings in Kolkata, I played across the line of a quicker, straight ball and was plumb lbw; in the second, I played an awful, premeditated half-sweep shot first ball and was caught at short leg again. In the third Test, a thriller we eventually lost by two wickets, I tried coming down the wicket and was stumped, and then I decided to go down swinging, but after I lifted Harbhajan for one big six he did me for length and I gloved a catch to the finer of the two short legs.

My dismissal in the first Test still haunted me. *I did everything right ... but I got out.* That thought stayed in my head, and because I felt lonely yet trapped out in the middle, close-in catchers all around me and the ball seemingly spinning like the proverbial top, I panicked. I started sweeping and looked for chances to go over the top, but against a bowler as good as Harbhajan on pitches that were turning that was never going to work.

No one in our set-up was able to help me sort out my problems against an excellent off-spinner on these types of wickets. I certainly wasn't being helped when the captain and coach told me to back myself and to stick to what had worked for me in the past. In the circumstances, they were mere clichés. After the Tests, during a five-game ODI series, I did manage to score a good hundred at Vizag, but because I wasn't confronted by anyone at bat-pad during the 50-over games I knew I hadn't solved anything.

I know now that the problem was that my technique against spinners had been built on Australian pitches, which are usually truer, where a batsman can predict where the ball is going to go and what it is going to do. In India, where the degree of bounce and turn is often less predictable, batting on spinning wickets can be much harder. It wasn't until the day Mohammad Azharuddin, the former Indian captain, showed me how their batsmen handle turning wickets that I began to regain my confidence for batting on the subcontinent. Rather than giving in to the bat-pad catchers, Azharuddin explained, Indian batsmen use their feet and hit the ball before it spins, thus narrowing the margin of error, or if that's not possible they wait until the ball has reached the top of its bounce, after it's spun. They never assume the ball is going to behave in a predictable way. A key skill is being able to read the length. On the rare occasions an Indian batsman uses his feet but doesn't get to the pitch of the ball, he just throws his hands at the ball, not worrying so much where it goes so long as it gets past the close-in fielders. Armed with this information on my later tours of India, I felt I batted pretty well. I went on to score my first Test hundred in India in 2008, and with a bit more luck I could have made three more in the two Tests we played there two years later.

Knowing how much I battled in 2001 and how isolated I felt was something I remembered for a long time and I made sure when I was captain that I was always there to help players who were struggling. Later in my captaincy I felt almost as if I was a part-time batting coach, but it was never a role I resented playing — it was almost like it was a calling.

WE HAD SIX WEEKS at home after India and then it was on to England, via a stopover in Gallipoli, an experience that touched us all. The thing that got me about this visit to the Dardanelles, where troops from a number of countries including Australia and New Zealand clashed with Turkish soldiers defending their homeland, was that the men who went in to battle in 1915 were really just like us, young blokes with so much to live for. Yet while we were soon on our way to London for a few months of sport, they never left this place. The task the Anzacs were set — to clamber up a horrendously steep incline and confront a brave enemy — was ridiculous, yet they never ran away, never gave in. There are often references to war and battles in sport but it is disrespectful to draw any comparison between the two.

I came away from Gallipoli feeling very proud to be Australian. A few weeks later, after we'd won the first Test, someone suggested we get our Test and ODI numbers tattooed on our bodies, and it just seemed like the right and patriotic thing to do ... so Slats, Junior and I headed to a Taunton tattooist, where I had the numbers 366 and 123 and the stars of the Southern Cross permanently inked on my lower back. It was a bit impulsive, sure, but the memory of our brief time in Gallipoli was strong and just about every aspect of my life was going so well — off the field, things were fantastic; the team was firing; we'd just been to Wimbledon, where we wore our baggy greens while watching Aussie Pat Rafter in the men's singles final; and when rain delayed the start of our tour game against Somerset, we were able to watch a live telecast of the Wallabies' gallant victory over the British Lions in Sydney (a win by any of Australia's national sporting teams is always inspirational). The spirit in the group was brilliant, a tribute to Tugga, Buck and the tour management.

THE ONLY PROBLEM I had as the tour entered its final month was my ongoing inability to make a big score in a Test match. It reached the point that I went into the fourth Test at Headingley knowing I needed to turn things around or my place in the side would once again be in serious jeopardy. The team was going super, having already retained the Ashes with three straight wins in Tests at Edgbaston, Lord's and Trent Bridge. I'd been promoted back to No. 3 at the start of the series, with Justin Langer omitted and Damien Martyn coming in to bat at six, but since that promotion I'd hardly scored a Test-match run — just 60 runs in five innings, highest score 17. Before that, of course, I'd struggled mightily in India and I hadn't made a hundred during our clean sweep of the West Indies in Australia that preceded the Indian tour. Steve Waugh was out of the fourth Test because he'd torn a calf muscle, but we expected him back for the next Test at the Oval. Someone would have to miss out ...

The irony was that I'd been hitting the ball beautifully in between my Test failures in India and the Ashes Tests, making a hundred in an ODI at Visakhapatnam and another in a one-dayer at Bristol, as well as run-a-ball seventies in 50-over games at Cardiff and the Oval. I was also scoring runs in the tour matches between the Tests in England, making centuries against Somerset and Sussex, but in my mind — and, I'm sure, in the opinion of the selectors too — that counted for nothing if I couldn't make runs when they *really* mattered: in the Tests.

This game at Headingley was my 46th Test, and I began it with a career Test batting average that was just a fraction more than 40. The best players in the game were averaging better than 50: Steve Waugh, for example, had lifted his average to 51, while Sachin Tendulkar's average was not too far from 60.

Boosting my average to those sorts of heights was for the future ... if I had one. All I could worry about right now was getting some runs, but the lead-up to the start of this game was a little peculiar.

Two days before the Test, Michael Slater missed the bus to training — not a major crime in itself but when Slats got to the ground just a few minutes after the rest of us (he'd hitched a ride with a press photographer) I got into an argument with him, which was probably the last thing I needed. It reflected how jumpy I was going into this match.

I'd known Slats since 1992, when he'd captained the first Academy teams I played for. Back then he was the 'next big thing', a prophecy that came true the following year when he made a spectacular Test hundred at Lord's. Most of the time we were good mates, but occasionally we'd have a blue, such as in Karachi in 1998, after the final Test, when we were celebrating our 1–0 series win. Slats had been stumped for 96 in our first innings of that game — not the first time he'd been dismissed in the nineties — and now he was telling us how he'd fallen victim to some brilliant captaincy from Pakistan's Aamir Sohail. The field had been 'out' for ages, but as our man got close to his hundred, Aamir brought his outfielders in and as soon as they did that, Slats ran down the wicket and tried to loft one down the ground. He missed and was stranded as Moin Khan took off the bails.

'Hang on a minute,' I'd responded. 'You'd got to 96, batted all day. Why not just push four singles to get your hundred. It wasn't great captaincy at all. It was a dumb shot.'

We'd all had a few beers, and my last comment was meant to be funny, just me taking the piss out of him. I should have known better. Slats's personality is a bit like mine in that sort of situation: we get a bit defensive when people question us. He fired back, asking what I knew as I wasn't even in the team. Then he got into Steve Waugh after Tugga suggested we pull our heads in. The thing with Slats was that while he was a terrific bloke, sometimes it didn't take much to set him off. I can remember batting with him once and being worried he was being a little reckless, so between overs I suggested he pull back a little. Instead of even thinking about it, he responded, 'Why don't you go back down the other end and worry about your own batting.'

At Headingley, I'd been trying to help him. Looking after a colleague when they're in trouble is something I've always been big on. When the rest of us were on the bus ready to go to practice and someone said, 'Hang on, Slats isn't here,' I was the one who sprinted back into the hotel and rang his room. He wasn't there.

I tried his mobile … no answer. Then someone else — who was also trying to cover for him — said, 'I think he's got a Gray-Nicolls photo shoot down at the ground. He'll be there already.'

But there was no Slats when we arrived at the ground, and we'd settled into the away team's dressing room when he suddenly came charging in.

'Thanks very much for waiting for me,' he said, which to me was the last thing he should have been saying. I'd done everything I possibly could to try to save him, and I took it personally.

'Mate, don't you come in here blaming everybody else,' I muttered.

That should have been the end of it. However, Slats didn't help himself out on the ground, because when we started running a couple of laps, he lagged a couple of metres behind us, chipping everyone for not looking out for him.

There were a couple of times early in my career when I was late for training or warm-ups, and each time a senior player or the coach reminded me how important it is to have everyone on the same page, doing the same thing, keeping to the same deadlines. A successful team can't afford to be carrying blokes who are not doing the right thing. If I hadn't been the one who'd gone back inside to try to find Slats, and who'd then tried to ring him, I probably would have let it go, but I was annoyed he was blaming the rest of us for his mistake and, as I said, I was on edge, too. That's why I so bluntly tried to set him straight.

Slats's mood didn't improve when Adam Gilchrist, our stand-in captain with Tugga out, told him in front of the entire squad that his tardiness was unacceptable. That led to the two of them having a snappy exchange while we were stretching, which made for an interesting atmosphere for the rest of the session.

Things were better the night before the Test, when we were required to attend one of the better sponsors' functions I've been to: a night on the punt at the Kinsley Greyhound Stadium outside of Pontefract, on the road from Leeds to Doncaster.

On the morning of the game, the weather in Leeds was terrible and it seemed the whole day might be washed out. However, the skies cleared, and as can be the way in these situations, everything was rushed as Gilly won the toss and decided to bat, and Slats and Matthew Hayden were pretty jumpy as the English opening bowlers got the ball to dart around a bit. Still, they managed to get the score to 39 before Slats was lbw to the first ball of Andy Caddick's sixth over. That brought me in, playing for my life.

The first two deliveries struck me on the pad and squared me up a bit as I tried to work Caddick softly to the legside. The third ball was a fraction fuller and pitched just outside off and I tried to drive, but got a thick edge and the ball speared hard and low to third slip, where it looked to me that Mark Ramprakash caught it just *after* it hit the ground. Maybe I was wrong. The England fieldsmen behind the wicket were excited, but Ramprakash wasn't so sure, holding the ball up as if he *might* have caught it, like he wanted someone to tell him he really had grabbed it before it touched the turf. The umpires consulted and then decided to go 'upstairs', while all I could do was wait … and wait … and wait.

It really did feel like an eternity before the verdict came down in my favour, after which I re-marked my guard and patted down the pitch as if everything was sweet. But inside, my heart was pounding … I knew I was lucky in that, while the correct decision had been made, I'd survived by just a few millimetres. Ramprakash was one of the best catchers in England; if the ball had carried to him he most certainly would have held it. Still, feeling lucky can be galvanising, and in the next Caddick over I got off the mark with an off-drive that almost reached the boundary rope. Haydos was lbw four balls later, but Mark Waugh and I then got involved in a long partnership in which I outscored Junior by more than two to one. I faced only 154 balls in my knock of 144, scoring almost a century in boundaries (20 fours and three sixes), and because the pitch was offering a little all afternoon — Junior was dismissed by the last ball of the day, one from Caddick that kicked off a length — I reckon it has to be up there among my most assured knocks. That said, it was probably only the third best dig of the game, after Marto's exquisite 118 from 135 balls that began immediately after I was dismissed and Mark Butcher's memorable last-day 173 not out that won the Test for England.

THERE ARE THREE THINGS from this Test that demonstrate where I was at this stage of my cricket life. First, there was the run-in with Slats. Then, during my century, there was Nasser Hussain, the England captain, having a go at me when I started to hit a few boundaries. 'Nothing's changed, same old Ponting,' Hussain muttered, as if he expected me to play a rash shot at any moment. He kept this up for most of the day. Based on some innings I'd played in previous Ashes Tests there was some merit in his argument, but from that day on I wasn't the same batsman he'd seen in the past.

Then there was our declaration on the fourth evening, which I played a part in, reflecting how I was now firmly part of the leadership group. We set them 314 in 110 overs, which appears mighty generous, but there was plenty of logic in the decision. The clouds had moved in, and we knew from past experience the ball can do some interesting things at Headingley when it's overcast.

'Let's get them out there and put a bit of a hole in them tonight,' I urged Gilly, but we only got two-and-a-half overs before the umpires called play off for bad light.

Next morning, Jason Gillespie bowled a delivery to their opener, Marcus Trescothick, that pitched on a decent length but then jumped over the batsman's head and over Gilly's head, too, and then we took two early wickets and we were looking like geniuses. However, the sun came out and Headingley is a completely different place in the sunshine. Eventually it looked like a really poor declaration on paper, but it might not have been.

The day after the Test we were back in London, where Tugga passed a fitness test and the selectors made the call to omit Slats and Simon Katich (who'd scored 15 and 0 not out while making his Test debut in the fourth Test) and bring back Justin Langer to open the batting. It was a tough call to drop Slats, and I can just imagine how they would have been thinking if I'd been given out third ball at Leeds: *Ricky's not scoring any runs … we're leaving out Slats so let's give Punter a rest as well and that way 'Kato' gets another go.* Instead, I followed up my ton with 62 at the Oval, we won the Test by an innings and 25 runs, and come the start of the 2001–02 Australian summer no one was suggesting my position was in jeopardy.

After a big celebration in the Oval dressing room, which featured an attempted burning of the bails from the just completed Test — the idea being to create our own 'Ashes' — the guys and their partners and families went off in different directions. Some guys went straight home, but a number of us headed to various parts of Europe, and for a brief period in early September there were Aussie cricketers in countries as diverse as France, Italy, Holland, Austria, Greece and the Czech Republic.

My girlfriend, Rianna Cantor, and I went to the island of Mykonos, one of the most beautiful places I've ever seen, and one I will always remember extremely fondly, because it was there, during a candle-lit dinner, while we were looking out over the South Aegean Sea, that I asked Rianna to marry me. We'd been a couple since the previous December, when we first met at a restaurant in Melbourne during the Boxing Day Test against the West Indies. And though, with the cricket tours getting in the way, we hadn't been together all that long, I knew we were perfect for each other.

Rianna's immediate response when I produced an engagement ring was to burst into tears, which wasn't quite what I was after, but then she said 'yes' and I knew I couldn't be more content. When I arrived home, Dad wanted to discuss the cricket and get me on the golf course just as had happened after earlier tours, but that could wait for a minute. I had other things to talk about. Life was changing, all for the better.

CHAPTER 24

LOVE COMES TO TOWN

Southbank, Melbourne, December 26, 2000

MAYBE IT'S TIME to stop talking about cricket for a minute and introduce Rianna.

Fate played a part in our first meeting. A few things had to fall into place for us to run into each other. (I hate to think what might have happened to me if circumstances had kept us apart.) It was a dream of Rianna's grandfather to take his extended family to Melbourne for a Boxing Day Test and this was the year. Rianna, my wife to be, who knew nothing about cricket, joined them anyway. While everyone else watched the first day's play, Rianna went shopping.

By 2000, Christmas time in Melbourne for the Australian cricket team was a real family affair, to the point that only two of us, Andy Bichel and me, didn't have family with us: Bic because his wife Dion was with her family in Queensland; me because I was single.

After the first day's play, Bic and I had just finished a quiet dinner at one of the restaurants at Crown Casino when Rianna's brother Darren, who is a big cricket fan, came over to say hello.

Rianna joined us, but only to try to drag him away. I recognised her immediately, because our eyes had actually met when she'd walked into the restaurant. I insisted she stick around for a drink.

I rang her at 8am the next day and asked her out for dinner that night and also organised some tickets for her family for the third day's play. As Rianna tells the story, her grandfather was horrified to learn that she was keeping one of the Australian players out during a Test match, but I must have created a reasonable impression because the next day she attended a cricket game for the first time in her life. Naturally, I was keen to show them how good I was, but when the fourth wicket fell in our second innings, Tugga came up with the idea of sending our usual No. 10, Colin Miller, out before me to slog some quick runs. Later, I learned that when Funky walked onto the ground, Rianna stood up and started applauding him until someone gave her a nudge and said she had the wrong guy. I batted at seven, faced only 22 balls, and finished 26 not out.

Rianna and I arranged to meet up again when the team was in Sydney for the New Year's Test, and after that we kept in touch as often as we could. I guess with me being from Launceston and Rianna from Bulli, which is a bit more than an hour's drive south of the SCG, most people would have been betting against a relationship working, but we were keen to give it a try.

From mid-February, I was in India and Rianna had returned to her arts/law degree at Wollongong University, but we kept in contact by phone just about every day. During the month and a half before we left for Gallipoli, I made a few flying visits to Sydney, Rianna came down to have lunch with my parents and then she joined us for the final two months of the Ashes tour. More than once we were teased, in a nice way, by team-mates or partners of team-mates for being too 'lovey dovey', but I didn't care. By now Rianna had decided to defer her studies so we'd be together more often. When we were in Mykonos I called Rianna's parents, Brian and Leanne, to formally ask for permission to marry their daughter.

Rianna learned that a jeweller in Hong Kong was a favourite of a few of the partners, so we came up with a plan to find an engagement-ring design in England and then see, on our way home, if the guy in Hong Kong could match it. With this in mind, in the days before the final Test at the Oval, I took Rianna to Hatton Garden, the renowned diamond quarter in London. Initially, we didn't have any luck but then Rianna found exactly what she was looking for.

'That,' she said emphatically, 'is the most beautiful ring.'

She looked at the ring from every angle, memorised the design, and then we were on our way. I could tell she was counting the days until we got to Hong Kong, but I was ahead of her. Later that day I quietly returned to Hatton Garden on my own and ordered the ring there and then. I picked it up after the Test and stuffed it in a pair of cricket socks which I then placed deep in my suitcase.

Earlier in the tour, when we were in Birmingham for the first Test, Rianna said jokingly, 'You'll never propose because you're too lazy and too disorganised. You'll never organise it.' So she wasn't expecting me to pop the question in Mykonos or produce a ring. That was part of the reason for the tears. Mostly, though, it was simply because we were very, very happy.

I KNOW THAT IF you asked Rianna whether she changed me, she'd say no, except for improving my dress sense. In fact, she changed me a lot. She gave me confidence and extra motivation to improve at a time when I was trying to better myself in the wake of the Bourbon and Beefsteak incident. I don't mean improve at cricket; I mean as a person, as a citizen. It took me a long while to get over the embarrassment of that episode and two years on, the classiest, most intelligent woman I'd ever met believed in me, wanted to be with me. It's not too much of an exaggeration to say that where once I was walking down the street with my collar up and gaze down, hoping people wouldn't recognise me, now I had a genuine bounce in my step. I was making her happy and I was so happy myself. The impact on my self-respect was enormous.

From the time I first met her, I thought she had as much drive as anyone I'd ever met. Sure, I'd seen cricketers with incredible passion and determination, who wanted to be No. 1 and would let nothing get in their way, but this was different. She was studying law, had a strong interest in politics and was selected to be a member of the national youth roundtable, where she had the opportunity to meet with government to present her report on issues affecting young people. The people I grew up with in Tassie were not motivated like this, which is no sledge on them, more a reflection on how quick and competitive a young person's life in Sydney can be. Rianna had visions of changing the world, but then I came along and she put those dreams on hold. I had to justify that sacrifice, not by scoring runs so much as by continuing to improve in *everything* I did.

She turned her energy to charity work, first as an ambassador for the Children's Cancer Institute Australia and then as the principal force behind the Ponting Foundation. We were, and still are, a good team, helping each other, pushing each other. We were married in June 2002 at the Quay restaurant on Sydney Harbour, a beautiful night that was organised almost entirely by my new wife. All I had to do was fly in the day before, collect my suit and turn up on time. 'Make sure you call me tomorrow and tell me you're still coming,' Rianna had said to me the night before. As if there was any chance I was going to miss it.

Eighteen months later, we were in Adelaide for a Test against India. Throughout my career to this point, we'd stayed in the same hotel on Hindley Street whenever we were in Adelaide. I'd said to Rianna this was one game she shouldn't miss, because it's such a good city, the Adelaide Oval is one of the most beautiful grounds in the world, and the hotel rooms we stay in were big by typical hotel standards. Unfortunately, Cricket Australia had found us a new hotel and the rooms were tiny. My cricket gear took up every centimetre of space, to the point where Rianna couldn't get her bags in. She had been touring with me non-stop for months.

Gradually, our nerves became frayed. After a couple of nights, she'd had enough. 'I want to go home in the morning,' she told me.

But I wanted her to stay. 'I feel something special is going to happen this week,' I said. 'Please hang around for the first couple of days. I want you here. If nothing good happens, then head home.'

I would have understood if she had kept packing her bags, but she relented and then I went out and scored a double ton. When I reached 200, she was the first person I looked for, because I needed to say thank you. Spontaneously, I blew her a kiss, which was totally unplanned and totally not me ... or at least it wouldn't have been me before I met Rianna. But it felt like the right thing to do and I've not regretted it for a moment. I was in the best form of my life, on and off the field. I was now seen as a leader, not a lout. My wife's love and support and the faith she had in me was a large reason for this turnaround.

Of course, this does not mean that I escaped being sledged for my public show of affection. A couple of team-mates asked me what I was doing, and said their wives wanted to know why, if Ricky could it, they couldn't do the same. I also received a few messages from old club mates at Mowbray, seeking an explanation. I was living in Sydney by this stage, and they wanted to know what the 'big smoke' was doing to me.

It was doing me good.

I had them worried again a week later when I withdrew from a Sheffield Shield game so I could attend Rianna's graduation ceremony in Wollongong. A few people wondered out loud if playing for Tassie had lost its appeal to me, but that had nothing to do with it. I just felt that after everything she had given up for us, how she had put her study on hold for months at a time so we could be together, it would have been wrong for me to miss her big day. I knew that what she had achieved was a huge deal, and that by stopping and starting she had lost that continuity and sense of team from the study groups that must be a big help when you're trying to write a thesis and pass exams. The people who had been there when she started her study graduated a year before her. I was so glad I was there with her family when she received her degree.

Rianna never once gave me advice about my cricket. In fact, she used to surprise me by how little she knew about what I was achieving. Her interest has always been in me as a person. Once, near the end of my career, she started asking me questions about my batting feats, how many runs I'd scored, how many centuries I'd made, that sort of thing. When I explained that my numbers weren't too shabby, she replied with a grin, 'You're pretty clever aren't you?' She had never stopped to think about where my achievements fitted in the history of the game.

I reckon this was a good thing for me. I never came home and talked about cricket. Home was an escape for me. This meant that when I returned to the world of cricket, I inevitably felt fresh and revitalised. And when the cricket was over, I felt good again, because I was heading home. I was in love and being loved. That is always a good place to be.

Communication

Communication is a two-way thing — you have to be able to get your message across in the most appropriate manner, but you also have to be an excellent listener. I always try to be open and honest in all conversations, but that is not always easy. I certainly found it particularly tough when I was captain and not a selector of the team. More often than not, my team-mates wanted to hear of their selection fate from me and not the selectors. It put me in a difficult position when I didn't agree with the selection decisions but was having to communicate those decisions to my team-mates. On one hand I had to respect the selectors' decisions, but in the conversation with my team-mates I had to be as honest as I could. For this reason, I lobbied strongly for the captain of the team to become a selector, and while it didn't happen while I was captaining the side, I was pleased to see it formed part of the Argus report that was delivered in 2011.

I think I am a good listener, and this has been a huge help for me over the years. Listening helps you to better understand the person you are communicating with. It gives them peace of mind that you care and, above all, it sets the tone of any two-way communication. It's certainly worked well for me over the years.

CHAPTER 25

THREE AMIGOS

A batting partnership on and off the field …

WE CALLED OURSELVES the 'engine room'. The rest of the batsmen were dismissed with good-natured derision as 'interior decorators'. The way we saw it, we did all the hard work at the top of the order constructing the innings and then they came in to splash a bit of paint around, maybe put a vase of flowers in the corner and order the curtains.

Justin Langer, Matthew Hayden and I were the closest of mates. We came into cricket around the same time, reached the top of our game at the same time and we enjoyed each other's company wherever we went.

It was interesting how it all came together.

One day, not long after Justin became the Australian team's batting coach in 2009, we were sitting in the dressing room reminiscing, as old cricketers sometimes do. We started talking about the 2001 Ashes tour. Lang was dropped for the first Test on that trip — a decision by the selectors that pushed me back to my preferred No. 3 — and for the next two months the poor bloke couldn't score a run in our tour games. 'I didn't think I could bat anymore,' he told me.

Usually, when a cricketer is recalling times when they were out of form, their face turns into a frown and their voice drops to close to a whisper, as if they're talking about a failed relationship or a disastrous run on the punt. However, in this instance, Lang was more upbeat, because he knows his story has a happy ending. 'I didn't know what to do,' he continued. 'It was like I'd forgotten how to bat.'

Being who he is, a man who almost obsesses about getting everything right, he stayed in the nets all day and hit ball after ball after ball. He wore out John Buchanan's arm, because he kept nagging our coach to ping some more 'throw downs' at him, but doing all this just made his batting worse, which is often the way when things aren't going well. Touring life became a grind; he was missing his wife, Sue, and their kids. Then, as luck would have it, he found himself driving past a park, saw some young blokes playing cricket, and decided to stop for a minute — something I know plenty of top cricketers like to do. I'm certainly like that, especially if it's a kids' game. What shone through for Lang was the fun these guys were having, and how much they were enjoying themselves. They were smiling; Lang wasn't, at least not until then. He realised if he wanted to succeed at the highest level, he needed to get back to being the happy cricketer he'd once been. Soon after, he was back in his hotel room when Steve Waugh rang to tell him he'd been picked for the final Test, as an opening bat, and you couldn't get the grin off his face.

Through that grim spell, Lang hadn't been enjoying his sport. And by 'sport' I don't just mean the on-field stuff (though that, of course, is a big part of it), but also everything else that goes with playing at the top level. Being dropped had hurt more than he'd first thought, and though he'd responded in what I saw as the right way, he wasn't getting the results he thought he deserved for working hard, being a good comrade and not sulking in front of his mates. Worst of all, he'd turned 30 the previous November and had wondered if his career at the top level was over before he'd planned, never a pleasant thought for a professional sportsperson. But he got another chance and went into the opening Test of his new career determined to enjoy himself, which he did in style, scoring a hundred as we won by an innings. The experience turned his cricket life around.

Being happy within yourself is such an important part of being a successful Test cricketer. If you are in a good place off the field, and liking where your life is going, then it's so much easier to score runs, take wickets, be a good team-mate and ride out the tough times.

I was a happily engaged man and a reasonably assured Test batsman going into the 2001–02 season, and my confidence was boosted further when first up I scored 126 and 154 in a Pura Cup game in Sydney against a NSW attack that included McGrath, Lee and MacGill. I was helped here in that I came to the wicket with our score at 1–205 in the first innings (openers Dene Hills and Jamie Cox both scored hundreds) and 1–77 in the second, making my job as No. 3 easier, and this set the mood for the Test season, when I was usually striding out to bat after Matty Hayden and the rejuvenated Lang had well and truly seen off the new ball. The result was a productive home summer for all three of us, especially for Lang and Haydos, who each scored four Test hundreds while I averaged a bit more than fifty. Then at Cape Town, after South Africa set us 334 to win the second Test and my mates started our run-chase with a partnership of 102, I played one of the best innings of my life to get us home.

The three of us adored the game, loved working hard, talking cricket and helping each other out. We never had one worthless on-field conversation while we were batting, only productive ones. There were a few that made me chuckle, such as the day at Sharjah in 2002, when we were playing a Test against Pakistan and Haydos was hit on the helmet by Shoaib Akhtar. Straight back on his feet, he looked down the wicket at Shoaib and snapped, 'Is that the best you've got?' After that, he went on to make 119, on a day when the thermometer soared past 50 degrees Celsius, and then Pakistan were bowled out for 59 and 53 in their two innings, meaning Haydos beat them on his own.

A couple of years later, we were playing Pakistan again, this time in Sydney, and Lang was facing a bowler Rana Naved-ul-Hasan, who like Shoaib opened the bowling but at about half the velocity. Still, he tried a short one, Lang went for the pull shot but missed. The ball struck him just below the stomach and down he went. There he was lying on the pitch, this supposedly tough cricketer, and as I walked down the wicket I couldn't help but laugh.

'You weak little bastard,' I muttered when I reached him, while he gasped for breath. 'Get up. I've seen other batsmen wear bouncers from bowlers twice as quick as this bloke.'

Lang got his own back on me a few years later, as you will see.

We liked each other as people, attacked our cricket in the same style, and placed the same premium on virtues that mattered to us, such as loyalty, courage and not cutting corners. We played the game hard and saw nothing wrong with that and came to understand each other's games really well, in terms of technique and approach. Consequently, we could help each other in the nets *and* out in the middle, and sense trouble before it struck. I used to love discussing the game with Lang and Haydos over a cup of coffee, a beer or a feed, just talking about batting and how we could get better. As a dynamic opening duo, they were special — both statistically (averaging more than 50 in Tests, with 14 century partnerships and six double-century stands), but even more importantly in terms of how they often established the mood of the game and put us in front from the jump. No one appreciated that more than me at No. 3.

I ARRIVED IN SOUTH AFRICA in February 2002 for a Test series followed by seven ODIs as confident in myself as I'd ever been in my life. We'd just beaten the South Africans in three straight Tests in Australia — by 246 runs, nine wickets and 10 wickets — and though I hadn't made an absolute stack of runs, a couple of run outs had hampered me, I knew I was in excellent form. Off the field, thanks largely to Rianna's influence, I'd developed the ability to switch off when I was away from the game, which made me a more focused cricketer when it was time to play and train, and, I'm sure, a better person, too.

About the only thing I didn't like about the way we were going was the pressure we found ourselves under after the one-day team started losing matches at the start of the year, with most of the attention focused on Steve Waugh, whose place in our ODI line-up was suddenly on the line. None of us liked seeing Tugga being put so brutally under the media microscope: one, because until you witness it close-up, see one of your mates go through it, you can't imagine how psychologically debilitating that kind of relentless scrutiny can be for the target; and two, because the team dynamic had been so good, it seemed wrong that outsiders were trying to break us up.

Making it worse for us was that rather than quelling the growing storm, the selectors seemed to be feeding it, first by picking too many batsmen in our squad — which had all of us worried we were about to get dropped — and then by sending different signals as to whether they supported a 'rotation policy', which Steve was keen on. His idea was to give everyone in the squad a game, and at the same time give the team's stars an occasional day off. When the selectors u-turned on this plan, it was impossible not to think that Tugga was losing their support. And as we started wondering if our skipper was for the chop, bit by bit his words lost some of their authority as we experienced our worst run in one-day cricket since Steve's first season as ODI captain.

It happens every time the media starts campaigning for the captain or even for a senior player or two to be dropped, and I bet it's the same in business if a CEO is under threat. That's why these campaigns often become self-fulfilling; and after they've got their man, the people responsible can move on to their next victim.

When Steve's reign as one-day captain ended, at the end of the home season, I couldn't help thinking it had been handled appallingly and that he'd deserved better. When I was a boy, I'd read about Ian Chappell's reaction when they sacked Bill Lawry as Australian captain, how he told friends, 'They won't get me that way.' As I watched the TV coverage of the media conference in Sydney, with the new Cricket Australia CEO James Sutherland and chairman of selectors Trevor Hohns sitting with Steve as they announced his time as ODI captain was through, I felt a bit like that.

I WAS IN POTCHEFSTROOM, a university town about 100 kilometres south-west of Johannesburg, when I took the phone call that told me I was the new one-day captain. Two things stand out from this moment: one, I was sharing a bed that was near enough to a single with Rianna; two, the phone rang at six in the morning. James Sutherland was calling from Australia, and my first thought was that he'd got his time-zones mixed up. But then I thought about all the people James had to contact and how Cricket Australia's decision wouldn't stay secret for long, and I realised he had no option but to contact me as early as he dared.

I honestly didn't expect to get the job. I had kept my nose clean since the Bourbon and Beefsteak incident, and had solidified my place in the side in the 18 months since Adam Gilchrist and I were first interviewed for the vice-captain's position, but I still saw myself as third in line at best, behind Shane Warne and Gilly. However, Warnie was apparently still on the outer when it came to leadership positions — unfairly in my view — and I guess the selectors and Cricket Australia were reluctant to give a wicketkeeper the captaincy, their argument being that the dual responsibility of keeping and leading was too heavy a workload. Keepers, so the story goes, are better as deputies, and I think that's probably right more often than not. That said, Rod Marsh, Ian Healy and Gilly would all have been outstanding Australian captains.

If you'd asked me when I was 13 or 14, I would have said, 'Sure, I want to be Australian captain' but throughout my time in junior rep cricket and at the Cricket Academy, I was usually one of the youngest players in the team, so I never had the chance to be a captain. I made Shield cricket at age 17, and I was a Test cricketer before my 21st birthday, and when all this was happening I never stopped to think about being in charge one day. It was the furthest thing from my mind. I just wanted to learn, to enjoy being in the company of men who'd been among my heroes, and to score enough runs from game to game so I'd keep my place in the side. It wasn't until we were in Zimbabwe in 1999, when, at a media conference, Steve Waugh described me as 'the future of Australian cricket', that I began to think about maybe being captain one day. But I was still one of the youngest blokes in the squad at that time. Only two guys on that Zimbabwe tour, Simon Katich and Andrew Symonds, were younger than me, and each by only a few months.

I certainly never coveted the captaincy, just figured that if an opportunity came up to show a bit of leadership at training or in the dressing room then I'd do my bit. When I took that early-morning call, my feelings were a mixture of stunned, proud and excited. I couldn't help thinking about where I'd come from and the thought occurred to me that it was pretty fantastic that a kid from the backblocks of Launceston could become an Australian cricket captain. I thought of one or two school teachers who would never have thought this possible, and a couple of cricket coaches who might have thought it was. Straight away, I was on the phone to Mum and Dad, and it was wonderful to hear the joy and excitement in their voices. Soon there was a knock on the door of our room and there was Gilly, who'd just been woken by James Sutherland to be told he'd be staying as vice-captain.

'Good on you, mate,' he said to me. 'Anything you need, I'll be there for you.'

'Thanks, mate,' I replied. 'I'll see you at breakfast.'

I was very excited, but there was nothing more to say, the same as had been the case a year-and-a-half earlier when Gilly was named vice-captain. Both of us lived with the 'team first' philosophy, and we knew we had each other's unconditional support whoever was in charge. *Let's get on with it.*

But before we could do that, we had a Test series to win. For me it was awkward to be named the new one-day captain as we were preparing for the upcoming Test series, and I wondered if it would affect my working relationship with Steve, who was of course still the Test captain. As it turned out, I don't think it did.

In fact, Tugga and I didn't talk about the 'handover' until after the Tests were over, when the team had a dinner party after the last day of the series at our hotel in Durban and we chatted for an hour. For most of the time I picked his brains and he certainly had some good things to say. One was about me making sure I didn't worry *too much* about what everyone else was doing and how they were preparing. 'Don't forget you're still a key batsman,' he advised. 'Make sure you give enough attention to your own game.' Steve believes that when he first became one-day captain he went the other way, that he was too focused on everybody else. Of all the things he said, that was the piece of advice that stayed with me.

OUR WIN IN THE FIRST TEST in Johannesburg in 2002 was one of the finest in which I was ever involved, in terms of the sheer scale and ruthlessness of our victory. At stumps on the opening day we'd reached 5–331 on the back of a Matt Hayden hundred, and then on day two we just sat back and watched a wonderful partnership unfold. The contrast between Adam Gilchrist's brutal hitting and Damien Martyn's elegant strokeplay was marked; the main thing they had in common this day was that neither of them ever looked like getting out. Steve Waugh had said during the previous afternoon, just after he was dismissed, 'They [South Africa] won't get 150 on that wicket.' Now this looked absurd as Gilly smashed his way to 204 not out, Marto finished with 133, and Tugga declared at 7–652, but even with all those runs on the board we knew that if we bowled enough balls in the right areas on that pitch we were going to create some chances. Sure enough, they nicked everything and we triumphed by an incredible margin: an innings and 360 runs.

It was a massive win, against a pretty good South African team on their turf. And making it even sweeter, we'd stuck it up a crowd that was as unpleasant and arrogant as any I experienced in my 20-plus years in first-class cricket. Gilly copped the worst of it as a small pocket of supporters kept making snide reference to a crude, defamatory internet posting that had made it into a few newspapers, while Tugga was spat on and Marto had beer thrown over him. The latter two incidents occurred as the players strode up the caged walkway from the field to the dressing room, so after the Test that was where we went to chant 'Underneath the Southern Cross'. For us, singing the song there was 'payback'.

Sixteen days later, I was as excited *on the field* as I have ever been in my life. We were chasing 331 to win on the final day of the second Test and had reached 2–251, so we were looking all right. From there, though, I lost partners at frustratingly regular intervals, and when Gilly was dismissed by Jacques Kallis to leave us six-down we still needed 26 to win. Shane Warne, the new batsman, was playing in his 100th Test match and he'd already marked the occasion by bowling 98 overs (taking 2–70 and 6–161) and scoring 63 in our first innings, and it occurred to me how appropriate it was that he was coming out to help get us home. That's how I was thinking; not nervous, just confident, working out how we were going to win. The contrast with India 12 months earlier was palpable.

Second ball, Warnie top-edged Kallis over the slip cordon for four, but after that, for the next 15 minutes, we managed nothing but a few singles. Kallis bowled with two men deep on the legside boundary and tried to pin us down, as if his best strategy was to wait for us to get ourselves out, while from the other end, they relied on their left-arm wrist-spinner, Paul Adams, who had one of the weirdest bowling actions ever seen in international cricket. The pitch was turning and Adams was capable of producing an unplayable delivery, but he could also bowl a loose one and, sure enough, he overpitched on my leg stump and I drove the half-volley out to the mid-wicket boundary, to take me to 94. I think that shot broke the tension a little. At the end of that over we were 6–319. Twelve to win.

Next over, Kallis went for the bouncer, but it was way too short and ballooned through to their keeper, Mark Boucher. Then, Warnie backed away a fraction and tried a sort of square-cut off middle stump, which had the South Africans excited. The following delivery was a no-ball, unforgivable in the circumstances, and Kallis then came up with a short, wide one which went crashing past cover point for four. From my vantage point at the bowler's end, it was a thrilling moment, but all Shane could say was, 'Sorry, mate.'

'What d'ya mean?' I responded.

'I'm costing you a hundred,' he said.

Last ball of the over, Kallis went for the yorker but he couldn't get it right and the result was almost a full toss that went flying out to the extra-cover fence. We were just about there, but again all Warnie could say was, 'Sorry mate, sorry, sorry.' And he genuinely meant it, which shows what a generous bloke he is and also, I guess, the confidence he had in me.

'Stop hitting fours then and give me half a chance,' I said with a grin. *I don't care if I finish 94, 98 or 100 not out*, I thought, *as long as it was not out*. I wasn't going to risk being dismissed and putting the win in jeopardy. All I wanted was to be out there when we won the game.

But then, first ball of the next over, Adams presented me with a half-tracker, on about the line of the leg-stump. I reckon I would have hit it for six whatever the circumstances, but the sight of this one sailing over the boundary was as beautiful as it gets, and straight away I was jumping all over the place, punching the air again and again. We'd won and I'd got my 100. It was just the second time in my career I'd hit the winning runs in a Test match (the previous occasion had been the fifth Test against the West Indies in Sydney in 2000–01, when the winning four left me 14 not out). This time, the feeling was exhilarating.

I always loved being there at the 'death'. I know it probably sounds trite, but in these instances I really was living out my childhood dreams when I'd imagined myself winning Test matches for Australia with a massive hundred or an incredible catch. As my career unfolded, I rarely enjoyed going out to bat when there was just a handful of runs to get or a few overs to survive, though when this happened, because I batted so high in the order, the game was never on the line, just my reputation. But when we were in the field during pulsating finishes, such as the World Cup semi-finals in 1996 and 1999, I wanted the ball to come to me every ball. In the Test at Cape Town in 2002, even when more experienced batsmen were getting out, I revelled in the moment; the closer the game got to its climax, the more confident I became. And when we won, with me hitting the six that clinched it, I felt as important a cricketer as I had ever felt in my life. The common denominator, with my fielding at the World Cups and my batting in the latter stages at Cape Town, was that I felt assured about what I was doing. I went into this Test, the 55th of my life, with a Test-career batting average of slightly less than 44. In the following five years, I'd play in another 55 Tests and for those matches score almost twice as many runs as I did in my first 55 and average more than 72.

Seven months earlier, Justin Langer had turned around his career with that happy hundred he made at the Oval. Similarly, the confidence this Cape Town hundred gave my cricket was liberating; it was, in a way, the making of me.

AT THE HELM

From World Cup glory to
World Cup failure

Mentoring

I've never really seen myself as a mentor specifically.
I know that players who have played with me might
list me as one of their mentors, but I've never really
singled anyone out for any form of individual attention
or support. My role as a leader and captain was to
ensure that I was available to all my team-mates to
encourage and assist them as often and wherever
possible. I guess if you look at the amount of time I
spent talking, training and working with team-mates
over the years, they would have been influenced more
by my actions than my words. Youngy, Rod and Shippy
all taught me to work hard, and that led to the 'lead by
example' principle that has been with me right through
my career. There's no doubt that the players who I
captained in the period beyond our dominance would
have looked for more support and encouragement. The
great players like Warnie, Gilly, Pidge, Lang, Haydos
and others didn't specifically need the individual
leadership and mentoring support that the younger,
less experienced guys did.

CHAPTER 26

CAPTAIN AND PLAYER

Feroz Shah Kotla ground, Delhi, March 7, 2001

STEVE WAUGH LOOKED AT ME, said 'you can take over' and walked off to the cool of the dressing room. It was almost like Dad throwing you the keys to the family car.

It was in Delhi during a tour game against the Indian Board President's XI in 2001 and Adam Gilchrist, our vice-captain, was not playing. Steve didn't explain why he was leaving or what he wanted me to do in his absence and, before what he had said had sunk in, he was gone.

To tell the truth, I found the experience pretty daunting. I didn't want to appear too eager to change things, so I just let things tick over and tried to give everyone a fair go. The batting collapse that happened while I was acting captain had nothing to do with me.

A few months later, I was given a more formal opportunity to lead the team, when Steve and Adam sat out of the three-day game against Somerset at Taunton during the Ashes tour.

Another five months on, and we were in Sydney for the New Year's Test match, and South Africa were slowly trying to bat their way back into the Test after we'd earned a 400-run first-innings advantage. Their opening bat, Gary Kirsten, was past his century and it seemed to me that we were bowling to him just the way he wanted. What had worked earlier in the series wasn't so effective now, so I walked over to Tugga and quietly made a couple of suggestions. Steve looked at me and said bluntly, 'Why don't you worry about your fielding and I'll worry about the other stuff.'

There was nothing more to this episode than that Steve was a bit stressed, something Test cricket can do to you. In later years, I'd get to know exactly how he felt at that moment. Suitably chastened, I ran back to my fielding position, Kirsten was dismissed soon after for 153 and we went on to win the Test by 10 wickets.

Some people openly wondered in the early weeks of our time in South Africa if our relationship was a little distant, but it wasn't like that at all. Steve was now the former one-day captain and I was his successor; but we were still friends and we still respected each other as cricketers and people. That we just got on with things reflected how cricket had evolved since the days when guys like David Boon, Mark Taylor and Ian Healy struggled to come to terms with having their 50-over careers cut short.

Steve was the guy promoted to the ODI captaincy in late 1997 when Tubby was left out of the team, so he knew he had to be pragmatic about what had happened to him, and while we all knew he was very disappointed and more than a little angry with the way the end of his one-day career had been handled, he never did anything that might have made my new job harder. On the contrary, as I've already mentioned, the advice he gave me when we talked straight after the Test series was insightful and helpful, and the next morning he and his wife Lynette drove away to Sun City and the nearby wildlife park for a safari. In the years that followed, whenever Steve wrote an article or was asked to pass judgment on my captaincy, he was inevitably fair, constructive and perceptive.

When I looked at the one-day team I'd inherited, I couldn't help thinking how lucky and privileged I was to be in charge. Steve had argued that our mediocre form in Australia was an aberration. I believed that too. It wasn't the first time the Australian one-day side had struggled to find top form in the summer immediately after an

Ashes tour. In the 1993–94 World Series, Australia lost three times to South Africa and once to New Zealand; in 1997–98, we actually lost more ODIs (six) than we won (five). This time, we'd lost our first three games in the VB Series, but then we claimed four of our last five — not enough to get us into finals but hardly an indication we were in some sort of catastrophic slide.

I figured as captain my main task was *not* to make too many changes to the way we played. Instead, I resolved to set the best example I could in the way I trained, especially with my fielding, and also I wanted to make sure that whenever I spoke in team meetings that I made sense. Preparation was the key. I was never going to wing it, never going to suggest that talking about an opponent or an idea was unnecessary, never going to dismiss someone else's idea before we had a chance to think about it. In the previous couple of years, I'd become more vocal in strategy meetings and I wanted to encourage others, especially the less experienced guys, to be involved. I was also keen to exploit the cricket brains of some of the guys who'd come into the squad in more recent times, most notably Darren Lehmann and Damien Martyn.

Before this tour, Darren had played only nine ODIs in the previous two years, but I was rapt that he was on my side. 'He's one of the best one-day players in the world,' is how I described him during my first series in charge. 'He loves playing cricket and being part of a successful team and it's good for the young blokes to see that sort of thing, knowing they can come into the team and be themselves.'

And then I added something that I really believed was crucial if we were going to keep winning: 'It's important to have different characters around the team.' Darren was a cricketer who loved winning and enjoyed life. He quickly became one of my most trusted lieutenants, an essential role because not only was Steve Waugh no longer part of our one-day set-up, neither was his twin Mark, which I must confess I found hard to understand. After all, my good mate had scored four ODI hundreds in 2001, but now, because the selectors had suddenly become very keen on generational change, he was on the outer. What was interesting was the way the two Waughs reacted to their demotions. Steve was very determined to force his way back into the ODI squad and prolong his Test career, but I think, subconsciously at least, Mark gave in to his detractors. The result was that Steve enjoyed the best part of another two years of Test cricket and retired on his own terms; Junior played only three more Tests.

I REALLY DIDN'T THINK about it until my captaincy debut got close, but in the couple of days before the game I couldn't get the thought out of my head that I really should have been third in line for the job, after Shane Warne and Adam Gilchrist. The official media conference before my ODI captaincy debut was a weird experience, because I was way more nervous than I'd expected I would be, and the same thought kept bouncing around my head: *What are you doing here?*

I was very proud at the toss (which we won) and couldn't wait until it was time for me to lead the team out. Although that in itself would be a bit weird, because in the past I'd always made a point of being the last one onto the ground. Funnily enough, nine years later, when my time as captain came to an end, one of my first thoughts was, *Now I can walk out after everyone else again!*

We batted first, and Gilly and Matt Hayden put on 50 for the first wicket. When I came in at No. 3, their captain, Shaun Pollock, made a big play of bringing fine leg up and putting deep square leg out. They didn't bounce me straight away, but obviously they were going to and when they did I absolutely creamed a pull shot straight to the bloke on the boundary. My first game as captain and I fell for the oldest trick in the book! Still, thanks to a good all-round batting effort and some terrific bowling and fielding, we prevailed by 19 runs. Two days later, in the second game of the series, with the memory of my first-up batting failure still fresh in everyone's minds, I smashed the first ball I received straight back to the bowler, left-arm spinner Nicky Boje, who took a sharp catch.

We won again, so that was good, but I was starting to get a little anxious. After all, my predecessor as captain had been dropped because he wasn't scoring enough runs. In game three, I managed a single and a two in my first 11 balls, and then I was late taking off for some runs because I had to wait to make sure the bowler didn't stop a Haydos straight drive. As I charged down the wicket trying to complete a third run I sensed the ball was going to the striker's end, and realised that my only hopes of survival were a bad throw or for me to get in the way of the ball. I could see where keeper Mark Boucher was moving to catch it, just next to the stumps … because the throw was coming from in front of the sightscreen I had to run straight at him … Boucher gloved it, whipped off the bails … and all I could do was grit my teeth and go straight over the top of him, like a base-runner crashing into the catcher protecting home plate. My helmet was shoved into my face, the grille was all mangled … I was run out.

Obviously, having made the big call to change captains, the selectors weren't going to make another change, but for my own peace of mind and to give me some credibility when I spoke at team meetings, I really needed some runs. Consequently, I'll always regard the hundred I made in game four as being one of the most important of my career. At one point, I hit Jacques Kallis back over his head for six, something I rarely did against bowlers of his pace, and in winning the game reasonably comfortably we took an ironclad grip on the series, an outstanding performance given we were playing without Warnie and Michael Bevan, who were battling injuries. As a captain *and* a batsman, I was now on very good terms with myself.

With the next World Cup to be played in South Africa in early 2003, the fact we were beating them on their own turf was a nice boost for us and further victories in games five and six only added to our psychological advantage. Unfortunately, we eased down before the winning post and they beat us easily in game seven, a performance I publicly described as 'embarrassing'. Before the game, I'd told everyone I wanted us to be absolutely ruthless, but instead we let ourselves down in that final match, and when the journos asked me about our effort I saw no problem in answering their questions honestly. This would be a policy I'd try my best to adhere to throughout my captaincy career.

AFTER THAT ONE-DAY SERIES in South Africa, Shaun Pollock described the Australian team as 'the Tiger Woods of cricket at the moment'. Given my love of golf, I couldn't help but enjoy the analogy, which Shaun made just a few days before Tiger won his third Masters at Augusta. A month later, I was in Monaco, which is a long way from Mowbray, for the Laureus World Sports Awards (where we were named the 'team of the year'), and my golfing addiction received another boost when I had a meeting with the great Gary Player, who was one of a vast array of sports stars past and present who had gathered for the presentations. Now this was a brief meeting that has been retold many times over the years by people who weren't there, so let me explain what actually happened.

It certainly wasn't as exciting or potentially life-changing as the legend has it. The Laureus World Sports Academy staged a number of events to coincide with their awards ceremony, and one of them was a golf day at the exclusive, picturesque Monte Carlo Golf Club, perched high in the ranges that surround the principality, maybe 15 kilometres from the iconic Formula One street circuit. Of course, I was eager to be involved, but I didn't get to play 18 holes with Player, in fact all I did was hit a few shots in front of him, as did every member of every group when they arrived at the par three where the nine-time major winner was waiting to chat to each and every group as they came through.

When it was our turn, I took a seven iron out of my bag and despite my nerves managed to land it on the green, which prompted Player to shout enthusiastically, 'Son, grab your driver out of your bag.'

I did as I was told and then he pointed to an area wide of the green and said, 'Hit one down there.'

I put a ball on the tee and absolutely murdered my drive.

'Do that again,' Player said, loud enough for everyone around us to hear.

I put another ball down and went bang, smacked it out of sight. This was when he said, 'Ricky, you are wasting your time playing cricket.'

Then he turned and announced to the hundred or so people congregated around the tee, 'He should be a professional golfer, don't you think?'

While I appreciated the compliment, my guess is that he was saying nice things to anyone who hit a good shot in front of him, and not just on this day but on any corporate day when his job is to entertain guests. Maybe he'd seen the recent cricket results from South Africa, and thought his national team might be better off if I wasn't playing. The shots I played were good, but I knew that playing them ultra-consistently for four rounds every week would be well beyond me.

Funny thing is, my old man absolutely idolises Gary Player, to the point that he dresses in black most Saturdays because that's what Player used to wear in the final rounds of the biggest tournaments. If Dad had been in my golf shoes that day, it would have been the most memorable day of his life. But when I came home I never told him what Player had said to me, because he wouldn't have believed me. Dad has seen me play. He would have just laughed and told me that being Australia's one-day captain was going to my head.

Tactical advantage

The expression 'tactical advantage' will normally get the attention of any aspiring sportsperson. In cricket, our game has always been tactical but it's gone to a whole new level over the past decade as technology has enabled teams to build large databases of information on opposition players and teams. We now have real-time access to information on every international player in the world, including a dossier of strengths and weaknesses. The planning and preparation that goes into any international game is now at a more detailed level. We have more people playing a role than ever before. Team management has grown from a small group of support staff including a coach to now having a big group of specialist coaches, analysts, leadership groups and other staff all charged with the responsibility of building the plan for a game. Match preparation has become a 'process' that starts with this larger group of people and ends up with the full buy-in of the team as it heads into a game or series. But like anything, it's the execution of the plan that delivers success.

There is always a need to have a number of plans or tactics for each batsman you're bowling to. Batsmen also have to be flexible in their approach to each bowler — knowing what they're most likely to do, understanding their various balls and looking for trigger signs as to what the next ball will be. You have to be patient and let the plan unfold. Field placements need to fit the situation, batsmen need to dominate for long periods of time, and the bowlers have to execute their plans.

Over the years, it's struck me that the best tacticians come from the teams that may not necessarily be the most skilled. This was particularly so in my early days of playing for Tasmania, where we didn't have the best team in the competition but we certainly were way above average with our tactics and results. If I look back on my international career, New Zealand stands out as the team that didn't have the depth of class or skill that most of the other teams had. But they were exceptional planners and seemed to have plenty of set plays that they were able to execute, especially in the big tournaments, where they more often than not performed above expectation. Stephen Fleming deserves a lot of the credit for this and I rate him very highly in the group of captains and tacticians who I played against. He was always looking for an advantage and had an uncanny ability for getting the best out of his team when it mattered most.

CHAPTER 27

SWIMMING BETWEEN THE FLAGS

Sharjah, October, 2002

SHARJAH WAS BLAST FURNACE HOT but I was in the best form of my life. The 150 I scored in the third game against Pakistan was my third in five Tests, and from the beginning of the Ashes series to the end of our tour of the Caribbean in May 2003 I'd hit another five, one of them a double, in eight more Tests. In the middle of that run, during the 2003 World Cup, I played the most explosive one-day innings of my life.

The team was, more importantly, in even better form and we were masters of the cricket universe. Nobody could touch us and our confidence was supreme.

The record of the Australian Test team in the four years after John Buchanan was appointed coach in November 1999 was phenomenal. Except for the series in India in 2001, we were just about unbeatable, and as I mentioned earlier, at one point winning an historic 16 Tests in a row. A large part of this, of course, was a result of us having a number of genuinely great players in the team at the same time, but the main reason I reckon the team's performance stayed as excellent and consistent as it did was because the individual players in the team were never satisfied with what they had achieved. We always wanted more.

It didn't matter that Shane Warne and Glenn McGrath had each already taken 400 Test wickets, something no other Australian had ever done; they were going to do everything they could do to be even better for the next day, next series, next year, the rest of their careers. We three blokes in the engine room — Justin Langer, Matthew Hayden and myself — might have become best mates on and off the field, and we loved seeing each other do well, but we were competitive, too. Such was our mateship, this competition never led to us keeping things secret; on the contrary, we knew our games so well we were, in a way, batting coaches for each other. Adam Gilchrist's attention to detail was legendary. At a time when Steve Waugh was being informed by people outside the team that his career was just about over, he was telling us his main ambition was to keep improving. John Buchanan had asked us to believe, and now we saw it happening — if individuals in a team keep trying to make themselves better, there really are no boundaries to what that team can do.

There was so much talent in the group, and once we started winning, the confidence and trust we had in each other kept growing. We came to believe we could win from anywhere, which we often did, and when new guys came into the team — whether they were young blokes new to international cricket or seasoned pros who'd finally been given a chance — they bought into our attitude and immediately started playing above themselves. And while we were on the road a lot, we never grew stale, partly because the people in charge were innovative in the way we prepared, never sticking with the same thing too long (which meant we did a lot of fun things and a few weird ones — like chasing albatross in New Zealand or speed-reading a book titled *Who Moved My Cheese?*), and also because cricket is a game that always has a surprise around the next bend. Whenever I think I've seen it all, something new happens that reaffirms my firm belief that it's the best sport in the world.

THE 2002–03 SEASON BEGAN in August in Nairobi, Kenya, where we were involved in a one-day tri-series with the locals and Pakistan. From there, we headed to Sri Lanka for the ICC Champions Trophy. This ODI tournament, which involved all the major cricket nations, had been known as the ICC KnockOut when we were eliminated early in 1998 and 2000, and this time we made it to the semi-finals, where we were handled comfortably by the home team, who won by seven wickets with 10 overs to spare. It was my first setback as ODI skipper and a bad one. Afterwards, a local reporter asked me if the slow pitch was the reason we lost, but I wasn't having a bar of that. 'We were out-fielded, out-batted and out-bowled,' I said. That pretty much nailed it.

A week later, we were still in the same city, Colombo, but at a different ground (the P. Saravanamuttu Stadium rather than the R. Premadasa Stadium), playing a different form of cricket (Test instead of ODI) against a different team (Pakistan). We'd been due to tour Pakistan for a three-match series, but it was less than 12 months since the war in Afghanistan began, and no one was able to guarantee our safety if the games went ahead as planned. The agreed alternative was to play on neutral turf, which was why we found ourselves in Colombo for the opening game of the series and then in Sharjah for the second and third Tests.

The first Test was an exciting contest, in which I again showed my liking for batting in Sri Lanka (scoring 141 on the opening day), but my runs were forgotten as the game evolved into an intriguing battle between two of the highest-profile bowlers of the era: Shane Warne and Shoaib Akhtar. Shane took 11 wickets, including 7–94 in their first innings when we won a first-innings lead of 188, while Shoaib produced an amazing spell that turned the game on its head. In terms of pace and skill it was similar to how he'd bowled in Perth in late 1999. Initially he didn't bowl quick at all but then he came back in the middle of the day to get the ball to reverse at lightning speed and immediately took three wickets in four balls (me; Mark Waugh; dot ball; Steve Waugh).

Up to that point in the Test we'd been belting them, but from 0–61 we crashed to 127 all out, and when they reached 2–173 just before stumps on day four it looked like they might even win. However, Warnie's dismissal of the in-form Younis Khan was crucial, and then Pidge and Jason Gillespie ran through their tail with the second new ball.

In Sharjah, the thermometer said it was 51 degrees Celsius but it seemed hotter than that in the middle. It was crazy to the point that during the first of the two Tests there I wondered if we were actually putting our lives on the line just by going out on the field. I've already mentioned how Matt Hayden scored a hundred in this game — a feat of endurance so remarkable I still can't get my head around how he did it. In all, he was in the middle of the furnace while the Pakistanis bowled 92 overs at us; they wilted so quickly their two innings lasted a total of 56.4 overs. At one point, Andy Bichel bowled a seven-over spell and was next seen wandering deliriously in the outfield, before he was helped off and put in an ice bath. I fielded through the first session (Pakistan 9–50), and then went out to bat just before tea and it was diabolical. Whenever I could, I crouched behind the umpire at the non-striker's end to melt in his shadow, and after I was dismissed, during the last hour of the day (for 44 in 95 minutes), my calf cramped up badly as I stumbled off the ground. In the dressing room my hamstrings gripped tight and my back started to spasm. All the boys could do was pick me up and chuck me an ice bath. Physically, after batting for an hour and a half, I was completely gone. Haydos, meanwhile, kept going.

The heat was nearly as oppressive in the third Test, so I decided to bat in a cap and Mohammad Sami immediately smacked me flush on the jawbone. It was a weird experience, because it had never happened to me on a cricket field before. For an instant, everything went blank. I got up onto my knees, opened my eyes and thought, *Nothing is really wrong here.* I started moving my jaw around. It felt all right. I wasn't dizzy; my vision wasn't blurred. The medicos came out and played around with my jaw for a bit, to check everything out, but they couldn't find anything wrong either. So they left me to it and I faced up to the next ball.

In this game, I got to bat with both the Waughs, which is a memory that has stayed with me. It turned out to be Mark's last Test innings, so for me it was kind of sentimental to be out there, while Steve was as determined as I have ever seen him (no mean feat!), as he withstood the oppressive conditions to score an unbeaten hundred and a guarantee he'd still be captain when the first Ashes Test at the Gabba began 18 days later. Tugga hadn't made any runs in the first two Tests, and there'd been plenty of media conjecture that if he didn't get a score in this innings, his international career was over.

A number of things came together that allowed me to enjoy this golden run. First, a point I have to keep emphasising, I was part of a great side — the way we competed with each other, but at the same time fed of each other's success made for a wonderful recipe. Further, as far as batting at the highest level was concerned, I'd bought into the Waugh and Buchanan mantra that there should be no end to ambition. I was sure of my place in the side, confident I belonged in top-level cricket, and supremely fit, which meant — unless the temperature approached 60 degrees Celsius in Sharjah — I rarely flagged, physically or mentally. I was experienced, having appeared in more than 50 Tests and 150 ODIs, but I was not yet 30, too young to be burning out, too battle-hardened to be complacent. Best of all, I'd become a good learner — I'd worked out that to be a successful batsman I had to 'swim between the flags'.

At the beach, the lifesavers decide where it's safe to swim and they put flags in the sand to mark these boundaries. Drift outside those flags and even the strongest swimmers can get into trouble. I had to work out what shots I could play, when I needed to defend, when it was prudent to be bold. If I stayed within my limits, I was very hard to dismiss and I had the skill to score runs at a reasonable rate. However, if I ventured outside my flags, I might be okay for a while, might even play a big innings or two, but sooner or later I'd get into trouble. Eventually, I'd drown.

I can't recall anyone ever hammering the point about keeping between the flags or playing to my limits or anything like that when I started in big-time cricket. I do, though, recall a conversation with Matt Hayden not long after he scored his first Test hundred, against the West Indies at Adelaide in 1996–97, and he said to me: 'I've just learned how to bat.' I couldn't stop thinking, *What's he on about?* Haydos had made his Test debut three years before this, had been on an Ashes tour and had scored more than 7000 runs in first-class cricket. It wasn't until 2002 that I truly understood what he was talking about. Young batsmen who play a couple of spectacular innings but then suffer a sequence of low scores believe they're just experiencing some 'ups and downs', that their 'luck' will return. It's much more serious than that.

Swimming between the flags became the bedrock for my batting plans. Further, when I was out in the middle, I needed my brain to be focused only on the contest between bat and ball. If I started thinking about anything other than watching the ball when I was batting, I was out. I repeated 'watch the ball' twice a ball, every ball I faced, when a bowler was halfway in his run-up and then when he was in his delivery stride. I blocked everything else out of my mind, made my thinking very clear, very simple. And because there was nothing more to it, I was able to relax between deliveries, which made batting for long periods less taxing. My technique — forged by the good advice I'd received from Dad and Ian Young at Mowbray and fine-tuned by Rod Marsh and his comrades at the Academy — was strong and my eyesight was sharp. It took a long while, but now I was giving myself every chance to be a successful batsman at the highest level.

It was no coincidence that from the day I realised staying within my flags was the way I needed to bat, I became more relaxed out in the middle, more likely to get into a rhythm that suited me. The ultimate extension of this was to get 'in the zone', when I somehow was able to switch off from everything else that was happening and just play every ball on its merits, no matter what the opposition was doing, how they were bowling or what fields they were setting. These days are rare and you can't just call them up when you need them; they find you. I reckon I was in the zone when I made the hundred against Pakistan in Colombo, when Mark Waugh said to me while we were batting together, 'Mate, it's like you're playing school cricket.'

There was plenty happening that day, with Waqar Younis and Shoaib Akhtar charging in, but all I was thinking about was watching the ball, reacting to the ball. Intuitively, I knew where the gaps in the field were. My judgment of line and length was flawless. On other days, when I was struggling for form, I'd think about what the opposition was saying, see devils in the wicket, fret about the run rate; on the worst of days, I'd get involved in confrontations with bowlers or fieldsmen, or even decide what shot I was going to play before a ball was bowled. However, when I was in the zone, there might have been 50,000 people cheering but I didn't hear them. It was as if someone had pressed the 'mute' button. My mind was committed only to the next delivery.

Good preparation played its part. The way I went about things in the days, hours and minutes before a game and innings was so much better than it had been when I made my international debut. The chief benefit of this was that I was usually 'fresh' when I went out to bat. There is no value in being rushed, at practice or on game day. I developed a sixth sense about how much time I needed to spend in the nets to keep my game in order. I also learned that the key to effective training for me was not about the number of balls I hit at training, but the *quality* of the practice I was enjoying. I needed to replicate the challenges I was going to face in a match, but I didn't need to do that for too long, just long enough.

Best of all, scoring runs never stopped being fun for me. I loved the competition: the one-on-one battles I had with the bowlers and with myself at times out in the middle. And I wanted to be a successful part of a successful team; my will to win was all about having and sustaining the drive, courage and smarts to make that happen. It was never just about me; I had to do it for the team's sake as well. I was alway like that, from Mowbray to the end.

THE HUNDRED I MADE against England in Brisbane in November 2002 was my first Ashes century in Australia. I always thought that once you were 'in' at the Gabba it was one of the best places to bat anywhere in the world, mostly because the pace and bounce is so consistent, and despite the early cloud cover that day was always going to be a balmy one, so I was pretty happy when their captain, Nasser Hussain, sent us in.

Matt Hayden and Justin Langer put on 67 in the first 14 overs, and after Lang was caught behind, Haydos and I had a field day. We weren't separated until late in the afternoon, when I was bowled by a ball from their left-arm spinner, Ashley Giles, that ricocheted from my thigh-pad to the ground to the stumps. Haydos went on to 197, then made another hundred in our second innings, and we won by 384 runs. By the time of the Boxing Day Test at the MCG, Steve Waugh was imploring us to stay focused, so we could replicate the effort of Warwick Armstrong's Australians in 1920–21 who won all five Ashes Tests. A five-wicket victory in this game, the fourth Test of the series, meant the clean sweep was definitely on.

It was a weird Test summer in a number of ways. We retained the Ashes in 11 days, winning by such decisive margins our celebrations in Perth after we went 3–0 up were a little muted compared to some of the most raucous days of the past. Glenn McGrath was having a fantastic time, the absolute highlights being a stirring over to Hussain in Brisbane, which ended with the England skipper edging a filthy delivery to me at second slip, and his famous catch to dismiss Michael Vaughan in Adelaide, when he ran, dived and somehow held a ground-level chance in front of the spectators at deep square leg. Jason Gillespie was brilliant and Warnie was Warnie. The Poms didn't stand a chance.

The only negative was that the media quickly revived its campaign to have Tugga removed as captain. He had often told us that it didn't matter if things were going badly or well, you needed to keep going at the same level, not get carried away with success and not get weighed down by failure, but we could tell that things were getting to him. Never the most exuberant of blokes, he was just that little bit more reserved, and it seemed to me he was losing patience with the journalists who wanted to be friendly during media conferences but then would head back to their laptops to sledge him in their columns. In Adelaide, he held back on a cut shot and hit a catch to point, when in the glory days he would have just crunched the ball to the boundary, and in the second innings in Melbourne he played a bizarre innings, got out, and then came off and told everyone that he had a migraine. I'm sure he did have a bad headache, but while most people were being sympathetic I couldn't help thinking that in his heyday he never made excuses. That wasn't him.

It wasn't for the rest of us to worry about what the selectors were thinking, nor was it our way to think ahead to the next series when we still hadn't completed this one. I knew that if Steve's time as captain was up, I was the most likely to succeed him but my attitude was simple, *I'll worry about that if it happens*, and my opinion was that while we were going so well there was no reason to change anything. In a sequence of six Tests — from Sharjah to the MCG — we won four Tests by an innings, another by 384 runs, the sixth by five wickets. Some critics with short memories seemed to think that winning Test matches was easy, when the truth, of course, is it's bloody difficult. Steve never asked me how I — as a senior player or as a friend — felt and I never went out of my way to offer anything other than the total support I always gave him and had always given Tubby before that. We just got on with it.

Of course, he famously shut the critics up with a really good hundred in the fifth Test at the SCG, one which became an epic when he hit the last ball of the second day for four to get to the ton. The thing I'll always remember about the innings, besides the drama of that final over, was how in control he was, how he played plenty of attacking shots but never a reckless one. His display that day was swimming between the flags at its best.

One of the greatest thrills for a dressing room is when one of your own fights back from adversity and this was as good as it gets. Only trouble was, in the dressing room that evening it was like we'd already won — even the Prime Minister, John Howard, came down to savour the moment — but it was all a bit out-of-sync because in fact the Test was evenly poised. When Tugga was dismissed immediately the next morning and then Vaughan scored a big hundred, I knew we were in trouble. The clean sweep would have to wait for another day.

CHAPTER 28

LEADING OUR DEFENCE OF THE WORLD CUP

Sandton Sun Hotel, Johannesburg, February 10, 2003

I WAS HAVING A MASSAGE when our physio, Errol 'Hooter' Alcott came up to me and said quietly, 'Punter, one of the biggest stories in world cricket is about to break.'

My first reaction was to think it was a gee-up and I could do without this nonsense with our first game in the World Cup due to start the next day, but the look on his face told me otherwise. Errol was a no-nonsense guy who kept injury and life in perspective, a miracle worker whose skills had seen many a player perform at his best when he should have been in traction and I could see he wasn't mucking around.

He told me Warnie had received a fax and then a phone call from the Australian Sports Drug Agency (ASDA) informing him he had tested positive.

Warnie will be facing a long suspension, I thought. *How could he be so dumb?*

The masseuse must have felt every muscle in my body lock up, but if my body was tense my mind was going a million miles an hour.

I needed to know exactly what was going on and I needed to navigate a way through it so our campaign wasn't derailed before it began.

I went up to Shane's room and knocked on the door. I'd never seen him so down. He looked and sounded rattled. He immediately confirmed he was in trouble. He'd taken a slimming tablet prior to his comeback game because he wanted to look his best. I know some people thought this was a ridiculous alibi, but if you know Warnie, you know he always wants to look his best. Many was the time he'd turn up at the start of a tour with a newly bronzed tan and his teeth gleaming white. 'I have to clear my name,' he mumbled, and I knew he was not going to play any part in the tournament. It was his 'A sample' that had tested positive. He could have chosen to sit tight until his 'B sample' was analysed, which would have bought him six weeks, but he was guilty (not, I must stress, of taking a performance-enhancing drug, but of taking a drug that was on the banned list, which I reckon is an important difference), and it was too big a story to keep secret. As I looked at him, I saw a bloke shattered by his own naivety and stupidity, not a cheat distraught that he'd just been sprung.

I'LL ALWAYS BE PROUD of the way I handled the crisis. On so many levels, this was a disaster. He was a good mate and I hated seeing him go through the personal grief his mistake inflicted on him. At the same time, I felt let down ... *How could he be so dumb?* From a cricket point of view, Shane was our best player and biggest personality, and all our plans had him playing a crucial role. The added scrutiny on the team, some of which I tried to channel my way, was a very unwelcome distraction. We had a World Cup to win, yet in the hours immediately after I was told the news, this hardly seemed relevant.

I found out about the failed test just after 8am on the day before our opening game against Pakistan in Johannesburg. That evening, at six, we had a team meeting where Warnie tried to explain what had happened. He got his words out, but only just, so I quickly closed the gathering and told everyone we'd meet again at nine. This time, Warnie was more composed, ending his explanation —

which in essence involved him taking a diuretic to boost his physical appearance, not knowing that the pill was on the banned list because it could be used as a masking agent by someone using performance-enhancing drugs — with the words, 'You can and will win the World Cup without me.' He left the room to pack for his return flight to Australia, while I gave everyone the chance to ask their questions and have their say. A number of inquiries were directed at Errol Alcott, our physio, about the drug Shane had taken and what it was supposed to do for him. Manager Steve Bernard was asked about the sort of ban Shane was now facing. Gradually, the chat turned to the Cup itself, and I can still vividly recall Darren Lehmann saying quietly but firmly, 'This'll be a good test for us to see how good and how tough we really are.'

I waited until every question had been asked and every comment had been made. And then I stood up, looked my team-mates in their eyes, and said, 'Right, it's happened, there's nothing we can do about it. I don't want to hear another word about this tonight, at breakfast tomorrow, during warm-ups or at the game. I don't want to hear any more talk about it.' And that's what happened, not just for those 24 hours but for the rest of the World Cup. The guys followed my lead. We moved on.

SHANE HAD DISLOCATED his shoulder the previous December, in a one-dayer against England in Melbourne between the third and fourth Ashes Tests. At first, I thought there was nothing in it — he just dived across the pitch to try to field a straight drive, fell a little awkwardly and came up clutching the top of his arm. But then, when I ran across from cover and heard the pain in his voice, I knew he was in trouble. He'd already taken 15 wickets in the Test series, but he wasn't going to take any more; the initial diagnosis was that he'd be out for up to three months. Our first World Cup game was a little more than two months away.

When, two weeks later, Shane was included in our 15-man squad for the World Cup, no one expressed surprise. The general consensus was that even if he wasn't right for the opening game, he was still a worthy selection, as the tournament was scheduled to run for six weeks and he'd surely be fit for at least some of our games. When the team was announced, most media comment focused on Steve Waugh's continued omission and Andrew Symonds' surprise inclusion.

While we were playing the final two Ashes Tests, Shane and Errol Alcott worked overtime on getting the shoulder right, and such were their efforts he was back playing one-dayers for Victoria by the second week of January, and for Australia in the VB Series finals a fortnight after that. At the same time, he announced he was going to retire from ODI cricket after the World Cup, so he could concentrate on taking as many Test wickets as he could. It was an unbelievable comeback, which had an unintended consequence 12 months later when the actor Russell Crowe injured his shoulder during the filming of *Cinderella Man*, the story of the heavyweight boxing champion James Braddock. Warnie recommended Errol to his mate Russell (one worked in Hollywood, the other was sometimes known as Hollywood, so they were always going to team up), and in no time Hooter was flying first-class to Toronto, where the film was being made, to get the Academy Award-winning actor back in front of the cameras.

ON THE EVE of the World Cup, I was asked who our two standout players would be. 'Warne and Gillespie,' I replied.

Warnie was the obvious answer. I had stayed in contact with him throughout his rehabilitation, so I knew how determined he was. He had set his sights on having a great World Cup, to depart one-day cricket on a high, and I'd seen close-hand how when he set his sights on something he invariably came through. When we landed in South Africa, he was as chirpy as ever, telling the local reporters we had a psychological edge over the home team that they'd struggle to overcome.

There were a couple of major issues buzzing about — one was the matter of whether it was right for us to play in Zimbabwe; the other concerned the suspension of Darren Lehmann, who'd been found guilty of a racial abuse charge during the VB Series. While these were taking up some of my time at media conferences and in conversation with Board and ICC officials, they weren't hurting our preparation. The Board had assured us that the security precautions for the Zimbabwe game were sufficient and I was okay to accept that, especially after I talked to Geoff Marsh, who was coaching the Zimbabweans during the Cup.

At the time we all felt Boof Lehmann had been harshly treated after he was heard shouting a disparaging comment in our dressing room, but there was nothing we could do when the ICC decided to make an example of him, banning him for the rest of the one-dayers in Australia and our first World Cup match. Thinking about it now, I understand where the authorities were coming from, much better than I did back then, when my view was pretty much 'what happens in the dressing room stays in the dressing room'. Boof isn't racist, but anyone who heard him could have concluded he was and some people would have been offended by what he said. On that basis, he deserved to be punished.

In terms of our chances, that controversy was almost immaterial compared to what would happen next.

I KNOW IN THE YEARS since this World Cup, I've received a lot of the credit for Andrew Symonds being included in our squad. The truth is John Buchanan and I both pushed for him to be picked, but in the end it was the selectors who made the call. Throughout my time as captain, I was often surprised by how I was given credit for good selections and blamed for bad ones when I wasn't a selector. There were times when I'd push strongly for a player, but when the team was announced, if that man had not been chosen there was nothing I could do about it. In 2003, Buck was a massive believer in Symmo, as was I, and we'd both expected him to do good things at the top level. But he'd had a few chances and never taken advantage of them, so the selectors were entitled to look elsewhere. Where

Symmo was lucky was that everyone — selectors, coach, captain, senior players — agreed that when it came to picking the support players for the Cup, the guys less likely to make the starting XI, character was going to be an important factor.

We could do this because there were so many great players in the group. We needed our 12th to 15th men to be good enough to contribute on the field if we needed them, but if they weren't playing we didn't want them moaning about a lack of opportunity; they had to be positive, smiling, enthusiastic at practice and between games, happy to do the 'little things' in the dressing room and at training. Symmo, Jimmy Maher, Brad Hogg and Andy Bichel, four champion blokes, fitted what we were looking for.

Then Boof was suspended, Michael Bevan was out injured for a couple of games and Warnie flew home ... Symonds, Maher and Hogg were called into the starting XI. After four games, Dizzy was injured, and Bic, his replacement, had the time of his life.

Symmo's impact on the World Cup was immediate. Buck's theory was that he had never been given any direction, that he didn't have a role. Symmo's play suggested he saw himself as a big hitter who bowled a few overs, but he had the ability to be much more than that, so Buck and I sat him down and told him he was good enough and smart enough to build an innings. He could still play his shots, but he didn't have to go at a million miles an hour; he could pick his moments, wait for the right ball. Against Pakistan, Symmo joined me in the middle with our score at 4–86 after I'd lost the toss and he promptly reeled off one of the best centuries I've ever seen in ODI cricket. Knowing his coach and captain believed in him was akin to having a straitjacket removed.

While I was out there I never talked to him about what Wasim Akram, Waqar Younis or Shoaib Akhtar were doing, I just told him to concentrate on the next ball, that there was plenty of time. Afterwards, as we toasted his unbeaten run-a-ball 143 and our victory by 82 runs, I said, 'Mate, that was an unbelievable innings. What do you reckon were your best couple of shots?'

He stopped and pondered the question for a few moments, and then replied flatly, 'Dunno, I can't remember any of them.' He wasn't being unduly modest, or smug, just admitting that throughout his knock he was in a groove, doing what comes naturally. In fact, he played some explosive strokes, especially the cover drives that dissected gaps in the ring-field and flew across the boundary rope before the fielder at deep extra-cover had time to flinch.

Late in his innings, Symmo was really flying and I was worried he might go overboard with the aggression, so I asked one of our subs to take some fresh batting gloves out to him and at the same time advise him to slow down, but Buck was smarter than that. 'Let him go,' he said. 'He'll be all right.'

Pakistan were so frazzled by the end of it that Waqar was reduced to bowling a couple of beamers. This one extraordinary innings got us our mojo back. I reckon some of us might have been secretly wondering if our chances of winning the Cup had left with Warnie, but no one was thinking that way now.

AS IF TO UNDERLINE the point, having scored 8–310 against Pakistan we then bowled out India for 125, setting up a nine-wicket victory. We were chirpy, a reality reflected at the media conference after the India game when man-of-the-match Jason Gillespie was asked if he minded not being given the new ball.

'Nah, not really,' Dizzy answered, 'I don't even get the new ball when I play for my club side in Adelaide.'

Before anyone else could say anything, I chipped in, sounding like a baseball scout who'd just been told about a child prodigy no one else had heard about, 'Who does take it then?'

'Some old guy who doesn't like bowling with an old ball,' Dizzy replied, and suddenly we had a picture of a balding medium-pacer trundling in with the new ball while one of the best and meanest fast bowlers in the world stood forlornly at mid-on, waiting for his chance.

He's a funny man, Jason, and few of us will forget his words when we played on one of the worst pitches I have ever seen, at

Mumbai, in 2004. Players copped a fine if they told the truth about things like this so he told the media, '*I* can't criticise the pitch, but I just spoke to a *mate* and he said it's an absolute disgrace.'

By the time we faced England in our final Group B match, our record was five wins from five games, following victories over the Netherlands, Zimbabwe and Namibia. By this stage, Dizzy's heel injury had got the better of him, but Bic came into our side and immediately produced the all-round performance of his life — taking 7–20 with the ball and then combining with Bevo in an unconquered ninth-wicket partnership of 73 that won the game with two balls to spare. Our self-belief was incredible. I'll never forget Pat O'Beirne, who'd only just joined the ACB as a media manager, commenting on the mood in our dressing room during the game, especially how there was no panic when we lost early wickets. Instead, we had enormous faith in Bevo and Boof to right our ship, and then in Bevo and Bic to get us home. When your mates truly believe in you, that faith becomes infectious and you can't help but believe in yourself.

How good were we going? Every time a match winner left the team, for whatever reason, another came in.

As had been the case in 1999, the second stage of this World Cup was called the Super Six, where the three teams that qualified from Groups A and B played the teams that had qualified from the other group. Astonishingly, South Africa was one of the teams to miss out, after they got their calculations wrong in a rain-marred match against Sri Lanka and finished a run short when the game ended early. We defeated the Sri Lankans in our first Super Six game, and then, after a very slow start, we overcame New Zealand by 96 runs, with Bevo and Bic combining for another important stand and Brett Lee taking five wickets. My contribution was meagre, out for just 6, but I did have one minor victory following a stoush with their outstanding all-rounder Chris Cairns. After I was dismissed, Cairns had made a point of giving me a gobful as I walked off the field, so when he was out at a crucial point in their reply I took the chance to return the serve. Clearly, he wasn't happy, and he walked over to the West Indian umpire Steve Bucknor to complain about my sledge.

'You started it,' Bucknor responded, which I thought was good umpiring.

A win over Kenya meant we were through to a semi-final re-match with Sri Lanka in Port Elizabeth. Going into this game, we feared what the Sri Lankan spinners might do on what everyone knew would be a slow, dusty wicket, but Symmo was brilliant again, making 91 not out, and then McGrath, Lee and Hogg strangled the life out of their reply.

This was the semi in which Adam Gilchrist famously walked after he was given not out, a peculiar incident in that none of us knew at the time that Gilly had suddenly decided to take the umpiring into his own hands. He said it was a big edge, but Matt Hayden at the non-striker's end told us later that he didn't even think it was out. I was dismissed almost immediately afterwards, and in talking to Gilly in the dressing room — two very disappointed men coming to terms with failing in such an important game — the impression I was left with was that he didn't realise umpire Koertzen had given him the benefit of the doubt. Gilly never said anything to me about walking; that wouldn't come until later, when he explained his actions to us and to the reporters. Whatever the confusion, from that day on he was a walker and he remained true to his convictions for the rest of his career. My view is the umpires are there to make the decisions; my role as a batsman was to try to accept the good with the bad.

WE WENT INTO THE FINAL, against India, with Marto (broken finger) and Bic (shoulder) carrying injuries but also with the enormous confidence that comes with winning 16 games in a row (our last six games in the VB Series and our first 10 here). We were already well past the previous record for consecutive wins (11 by the West Indies in 1984–85) and consecutive games without defeat (14 by Australia in 2000), team records that always resonated more with me than any individual landmarks I reached.

In the lead-up to our big day, we had our regular team gathering but I also called an extra one, because I sensed we needed to address the anxiety that had come over the team. Everyone was edgy, too nervous for their own good, so I asked the guys to express how they were feeling, to get their stress out in the open. I reckon one of the worst feelings in the world is to believe you're the only one who's apprehensive, when most times your team-mates are actually fighting the same anxiety. I wanted everyone to relax a bit, so to lighten the mood I started delivering a speech about how we'd won every game we'd played at this World Cup and now it was time to deliver the 'knockout blow'. I continued, 'To show you what I mean, the boys at Channel Nine have put together a video to demonstrate how it's done ...'

They were expecting a film featuring some highlights from this tournament, or maybe some boxing highlights featuring champions like Ali, Frazier, Foreman and Tyson. Instead, what I had for them was a replay of a somewhat comical bout between Jimmy (Mabo) Maher and the former NSW quick Wayne (Cracker) Holdsworth that had been staged a few months before on Nine's NRL *Footy Show*. The boys had a good laugh while an embarrassed Mabo was looking for an exit, and after that we all had a real good chat about how we were thinking and what was worrying us.

I think mostly we just feared losing, especially after we'd won so many games in a row. One of sport's oldest clichés is that every win takes you closer to your next loss, but Buck argued that there is nothing in the rules that says you have to lose eventually. Indeed, his main concern, he said strongly, was that we might start thinking we were owed a win in the final just because we'd made it this far without losing a match. The general reaction to this comment was one of contempt, which was just what Buck was after. We also took inspiration from Marto being so keen to play despite his busted finger.

I'd asked him flat, 'Mate, I need you to tell me if you're okay to play or not okay to play.'

Marto looked me straight in the eye and said resolutely, 'I'm right to go.'

That was it. I knew he wouldn't let himself or the team down by playing if he wasn't okay.

I couldn't wait for the final to begin. Maybe the captaincy had preoccupied me at times during the tournament, and I think I was weighed down a little by the expectations that came with the fact that my predecessors as captain, Allan Border, Mark Taylor and Steve Waugh, had all led Australia to World Cup finals. Now it was my turn. After struggling to get to sleep the night before the game, I got up for a little while and, as I'd done a few times in the past (and I'd do plenty more times in the future), just scribbled down on paper some catch phrases that were buzzing through my head, things that would help me focus on the task ahead ...

WORLD CUP FINAL
Watch the ball
Play straight
Loud calls
Be patient
Don't overhit
Bat for a long time
Man of the match
BE A WORLD CHAMPION

Next morning, I bounced out of bed at 6.30, got dressed, put that scrap of paper in my pocket and headed off to join my mates for breakfast. We'd been in South Africa for almost two months but I didn't feel stale or weary at all. I just wanted to get on with it.

MY INNINGS WAS ONE of two halves. The wicket was a beauty and after India's captain, Sourav Ganguly, opted to bowl first, I was in at the start of the 15th over, by which time Gilly and Haydos had already taken us just past the hundred mark. For the next hour and a half, I batted nicely, hitting only the one boundary but keeping the scoreboard ticking over, so that after 38 overs we were 2–226. By then Marto was past his fifty, scoring at a run a ball.

At this point, I decided to go for it, to just tee off. We had heaps of batting to come, my batting partner was cruising; if I could smash another 20 or 30 quickly it would set us up for an imposing total. What happened was way better than I could have hoped for, starting with two sixes off my old nemesis, Harbhajan Singh, and then two more in the following three overs. My first fifty took 74 deliveries and included one four. My second took 29 balls, with one four and five sixes. After that, I just went crazy, finishing in style with a six and a four from the final two balls of the innings to be 140 not out. The contrast with what had happened in an earlier World Cup final in 1996, when I was dismissed in the 32nd over and our innings degenerated, was massive. It wasn't just that I got lucky in 2003; I was a better, much more confident, more assertive batsman, especially against the spinners. Marto finished 88 not out, and our partnership was worth 234, the last 131 of those runs occupying just 75 balls.

Later, I described it as 'one of those days when everything goes your way'. At one point they had to call for a replacement ball because they couldn't find the one I'd just smashed out of the park. Soon after, I started to lose my grip as I tried for another massive hit, my bottom hand came off the handle, but the ball still went for six. The adrenalin coursing through my body was incredible, but somehow, maybe because the occasion was so special, I was able to manage it.

Our score of 360 was a colossal target, but I refused to believe we were home. If I could play so well, there was every chance Sachin Tendulkar would counter with the innings of his life, but Pigeon knocked him over quickly, which for me was as thrilling a moment as anything that had occurred earlier in the day. I was also worried about the weather stopping the game too early (if we didn't complete 25 overs the game would be abandoned and we'd start afresh in the morning), and for a while that looked like happening when a storm blew in at the 17-over mark. However, we were only off the field for about half an hour, and my only concern after that was whether they might score some runs in a hurry to boost their run-rate — in such circumstances, if the storms then returned they might have been able to fluke a win under the Duckworth–Lewis method used to calculate results in rain-shortened matches. But while the weather threatened to interrupt us again it never did, and we eased our way to a 125-run victory.

The first thing that hit me after the final wicket fell was an enormous feeling of relief. The pressure of wanting to carry on the winning tradition established by the teams before us and the leaders before me had been huge. I also wanted to embrace every single member of our set-up — not just the men on the field but the other players and the members of our support staff: Buck, Hooter, Steve Bernard, assistant coach Tim Nielsen, fielding coach Mike Young, fitness guru Jock Campbell and massage therapist Lucy Frostick. Usually, after a game the Australian room is a bit of a mess, with players' gear strewn in all directions, but not this time ... during the final overs, as the result became inevitable, Mabo ordered a clean-up so when we started dousing each other in champagne nothing would get drenched and we wouldn't fall over an errant bag or batting pad. They never stopped thinking of us.

I have so many memories of the moments after that game. Rianna had been in South Africa early in the tournament, but flew home the day after we beat Zimbabwe, around the time we learned that Warnie had been officially rubbed out for 12 months — his ban being reduced from the usual two years because he hadn't taken the diuretic to aid his performance. When we reached the final, she decided to come back and it was fantastic to be able to look up into the stands, in the middle of our celebrations, and single her out. She had been more nervous than me in the lead-up to the game, and it meant so much to me that she was there, to know how much she cared.

On the field, Andy Bichel grabbed me in a huge headlock and screamed, 'I love you mate!' One thing I really enjoyed was observing the newer members of our group — guys like Bic, Mabo, Hoggy and Symmo — savour our triumph. I felt a little like a teacher seeing students come of age, which was a whole new sensation for me. After the presentation and a short, dynamic thunderstorm, Gilly — who'd taken over as one-day songmaster after I was named captain — took us out to the middle and we sang 'Underneath the Southern Cross' as loudly and exuberantly as we'd done at Lord's four years earlier. And then we partied like it was 1999! The spirit that had grown among us in the time between our first game and our last had made this triumph one of the best cricketing experiences of our lives.

Criticism

Across my career, I always aimed to handle criticism well. It's part of being a professional sportsperson and it's certainly part of being a captain. Every time you go out to play, your own performance or that of your team is open to public scrutiny.

Generally, personal criticism never bothered me. For most of my career, I was able to go out in the next day or two and put right what I may have been criticised for. This was particularly so when I was playing my best cricket and the team was winning more often than losing. But later in my captaincy and my own career, I found that overcoming adversity or criticism didn't come as easily. I never took criticism personally unless it came from past players whose opinions were important to me. Again this seemed to be more prevalent later in my career and, on reflection, some of that criticism was reasonable.

I became very protective of my team and team-mates when the chips were down and when they were being criticised. I wanted to be the face of the team when things weren't going well, to deflect the direct criticism off my team-mates. I would, more often than not, put myself in front of the media at the end of a bad day or a losing game. I didn't want the media to have easy access to the team when we were going through transition. Media pressure is just another part of dealing with being an international sportsperson but being captain gave me the opportunity to shield the team from as much of this as possible. Perhaps it opened me up for my fair share of criticism when the team was losing but that was part of the role I had as captain and it was the way I wanted to lead. If I had my time over again, I would do it exactly the same.

CHAPTER 29

ONE GAME AFTER ANOTHER

Dressing room, Kingsmead, Durban, March 15, 2003

NOT LONG AFTER WE'D BEATEN Kenya, our ninth straight win at the World Cup, Adam Gilchrist quietly asked me, 'Do you reckon you should be vice-captain for the West Indies tour?' We were scheduled to fly to the Caribbean just a week after the Cup final, for four Tests and then seven ODIs. Gilly argued that as I was Steve Waugh's heir apparent as Test captain, it was logical I should be his Test deputy.

'Don't worry about it,' I said. I couldn't see the point in making a change that would be, in my view, merely cosmetic.

Next day, straight after a lunch-time meeting where Steve Bernard revealed the make-up of the Test side for the Windies but made no mention of the leadership group, Gilly sidled up to me again, and this time he said quietly, 'Congratulations.'

'Why? What have I done?'

'Brute just told me you've been named vice-captain of the Test squad.'

I thought this was a bit weird, as our manager hadn't said anything to me. To tell the truth, I would have liked to have been consulted. *Maybe Gilly knew something when he brought the matter up yesterday? ... Maybe, despite what I'd said, he'd prompted the change?* That afternoon, we were due to fly to Port Elizabeth and I still hadn't been told anything official when we boarded the bus to go to the airport. *Maybe it's a gee-up?* We were actually pulling up at the terminal when Brute came down to the back of the bus and handed me his mobile, saying simply, 'It's Cracker for you.'

'Cracker' was Trevor Hohns, chairman of selectors.

'Is it really necessary?' I asked him.

'If anything happens to Tugga during the tour we want you to be the man to take over the captaincy,' he replied. 'You can only do that if you are vice-captain.'

It was exactly the same scenario that cost Ian Healy the vice-captaincy in 1997, and just as I couldn't see the point of the change back then, it didn't make much sense to me this time. Gilly had done a brilliant job as vice-captain. If Steve was injured or lost all form mid-tour, why couldn't the selectors name me as captain and leave Gilly as vice-captain? If it was a good idea to change vice-captains now, why wasn't it smart when I was first named ODI skipper?

But Cracker couldn't be swayed, so Gilly and I just got on with it. I never did ask him why he'd brought the subject up in the dressing room at Durban. Same as before, same as in the future, the selectors' machinations with the captaincy made no difference to our friendship and working relationship.

WE'D COME HOME FROM the World Cup in 1999 as conquering heroes, but unfortunately there was little of that four years later. Our greeting was warm and we sensed the public was proud of what we'd achieved, but the manner of our win — success in every game, often by big margins — hadn't grabbed the imagination in the way our epic fightback four years earlier had. We certainly weren't tired of winning but perhaps a few of our fans and some of the commentators were. It might have been different if there'd been some weeks or months between the World Cup and our next assignment, but we had to get to the Caribbean so quickly there was no time for a formal welcome home.

This was the first time I started thinking, seriously and often, that we were getting on too many planes, being away from our own beds too much, playing too much cricket.

Today, I recall the 2003 West Indies tour chiefly for the unbelievable batting form I was in — centuries in each of the three Tests I played (I missed the fourth because of a viral infection) — and for the great yearning to get home we all felt once our unbeaten run in ODIs ended at 21 in the fifth one-dayer, at Port-of-Spain. We arrived home in the first week of June, but rather than spending time with Rianna and renewing my relationship with the golf course, we cricketers were too quickly preparing for two 'winter' Tests against Bangladesh, the first in Darwin, the second in Cairns, and three ODIs. That took us into August, when we had another short break before beginning preparations for two home Tests against Zimbabwe, both of which we won comfortably, with Matt Hayden making what was then Test cricket's highest ever score, 380, in Perth. Then we flew to India, for the TVS Cup: seven ODIs against the locals and New Zealand. *Are you tired yet?* Then we were back home, where there was time for me to play for Tasmania in an ING Cup (50-overs) game against NSW at Bellerive, before we began what would prove to be Steve Waugh's final Test series — four Test matches in 33 days, from the opening delivery of the series to the last. Then we played 10 games in the VB Series before we flew to Sri Lanka for five ODIs and three Tests.

It's amazing how a fair chunk of this, especially the one-dayers, is no longer in my memory, how one game just blurred into another. We never really stopped. And if the games started to become blurred and forgettable to the people playing them I wonder how they felt for the general public.

ONE THING I DO recall, and did so especially for a few days until the bruise in my left bicep finally disappeared, was an unlikely 'catch' I held on to during the second Test against Zimbabwe, at the SCG. The pitch was a turner, which led to Simon Katich, who was in the team to replace the injured Darren Lehmann, taking 6–65 with his left-arm wrist spinners. I liked to field close in on the offside when the spinners were bowling, because there I always felt I was in the game and you're unlikely to get clobbered on that side of the pitch, but on this occasion, with Kato bowling, someone had to be the short leg and I volunteered. First ball to their keeper, Tatenda Taibu, was a rank long hop and he got ready to play a big pull shot.

Now I know in this situation the short-leg fieldsman is supposed to duck for cover, make himself as small a target as possible, and pray the ball passes by, but I had a crazy moment, which could only have happened because I didn't usually field in this position. My reflex, all in a split-second, was, *you're wearing a helmet, shin-pads, box, stand your ground*. I did flinch a fraction, turned my body sideways to my right, but I kept an eye on Taibu and saw the ball off the middle of his bat. It was going way too quick for me to catch it, but after it crunched into my upper arm and then onto my chest I was quick enough to get my right hand up and grab it before it got away from me. And then I threw it in the air and ran down the wicket to tell Kato how good he was.

In truth, there was an element of fluke to this catch, so I can't put it up with the best I've ever taken. To this stage of my career, the two I rate my best are the one that dismissed Sachin Tendulkar at Mumbai in 2001, when I was fielding at mid-wicket and had to change direction and then dive full-length to catch a pull shot that had ricocheted off Justin Langer at short leg, and the spectacular dive and grab that got rid of Richard Bennett in my debut top-grade game for Mowbray back in 1989. Other favourites are the catch I took at third slip to dismiss Saqlain Mushtaq in the 1999 World Cup final, way to my right and centimetres off the ground, and one I took in the slips at Adelaide Oval in 2001 to nail South Africa's Boeta Dippenaar. That last one was funny, in that I'd just come back on to the ground after going off to get treatment for a back spasm, but when I saw the ball flying past me I couldn't help myself and dived far to my left to grab it one-handed. I bounced to my feet, threw the ball in the air, ran around a bit, and then remembered I wasn't feeling too good and cringed every time someone slapped me on the shoulder or grabbed me too tight.

In the years to come I'd take a few more I was proud of, including a diving one at cover for the Mumbai Indians in the IPL in 2013 that got noticed on ESPN in America, beating a LeBron James dunk as their play of the day. But maybe my favourite was a catch I took to dismiss the New Zealand opener Jamie How off Brett Lee at Adelaide Oval in 2008–09, which involved a full-length dive to where a conventional third slip would have been and the ball sticking between the thumb and the forefinger of my right hand. I never thought of these grabs as lucky, much more a product of good natural instincts and a lot of practice.

ONE OF THE MORE far-reaching things to come out of 2003 was an initiative from Cricket Australia (CA) (our governing body having changed its name from the Australian Cricket Board): the 'Spirit of Cricket' project, which was designed in large part to ensure that all Aussie cricketers from the park to the Test arena were aware of their obligations to fair play, to understand that the Laws of Cricket required us to play our game in the right spirit. All players contracted to CA signed on to the concept, and I was more than happy to do so. In fact, Tugga and I, as the Test and ODI captains, had been discussing the concept with CA chief executive James Sutherland and chairman Bob Merriman for the previous few months, ever since Glenn McGrath and Ramnaresh Sarwan had got involved in a highly publicised on-field spat during the fourth Test of our recent West Indies tour (an incident I didn't see because I was in a taxi on my way to the doctor at the time). There had been times before this when we players felt the administrators were too quick to agree with media criticism of our conduct rather than recognising there are two sides to most stories, but we were shaken by the public outcry that followed the McGrath–Sarwan incident, and how we were tagged by some observers within and outside the game as a group of players who 'spat the dummy' when things didn't go our way.

Steve Waugh stated firmly, and we all agreed with him, that we wanted to be remembered as a great team that played the right way rather than one renowned as much for bad behaviour as excellent cricket. We knew we weren't as bad as some critics liked to paint us, but we also realised we had an image problem and we wanted to fix it.

Despite what some people think, I reckon in the years that followed we did a pretty good job of sticking to the principles of the Spirit of Cricket.

We weren't perfect, nobody is, but if you take into account how tense and high-pressured international cricket can be and how crowded our schedule could be, our violations were few. Most of the time, our worst transgressions occurred towards the end of a series, when players were tired and tempers got frayed, or when one Test match followed straight after another. Of course, brutal programming doesn't make bad behaviour acceptable, but there were times when we really wished the people devising the international cricket calendar would think more about our interests before they staged one game after another.

STEVE WAUGH'S DECISION to announce his upcoming retirement *before* the home Tests against India made for an interesting summer. His plan was to retire after the final Test of the series, to be played on his home turf at the SCG. I wondered about the logic of making such an early announcement, which went a little against the team mantra that we'd never let personal milestones impinge on what we were trying to achieve as a group. What I didn't know then but know now is that Steve's initial preference was to keep his decision quiet until much closer to the end, but after discussing the matter with the selectors and Cricket Australia his plans were leaked to a journalist or two, which forced his hand.

Steve made his retirement plans public on November 26, eight days before the first Test in Brisbane. I had no prior warning he was going to do so. With these things, it's always hard to work out who should be notified and who can wait, and you end up telling as few people as possible on the basis that everyone you don't tell is one less chance of the story getting out before its time. The next day, I was filming a TV commercial for one of my sponsors when I got a call from Cricket Australia's Michael Brown, who told me his directors had backed a recommendation from the selectors that I should be the next Australian Test skipper. Michael didn't offer me the job, just congratulated me and started explaining what the protocol would be in regards to announcing my appointment.

'We're going to call a press conference for tomorrow,' he explained. 'We don't want any unnecessary speculation and we don't want the news to leak.'

'I'm not sure about that,' I replied. 'If we do it now, won't that make it hard for Steve. He's still the captain. Can't we wait until after the Tests?'

'No, mate,' Michael said. 'Steve agrees making the announcement now is the way to go. And it'll take the pressure off you. This way you won't be getting questions about whether you expect to be the next captain.'

That sounded reasonable and if Steve was sweet with it then I was okay. Still, it was a weird feeling, being named captain but not being captain yet, and I found myself having to rein in my pride and excitement, simply because it would be months before I'd actually lead the team out in a Test match and I knew plenty could happen in that time. I might get injured, lose form or maybe the selectors or Cricket Australia might change their mind.

WE WERE STILL WITHOUT the suspended Shane Warne and now the injured Glenn McGrath, and up against a very good Indian team.

After the first Test was drawn following two days of rain, we got off to a flyer in the second Test in Adelaide, scoring 400 on the opening day and ending up with a first-innings total of 556, of which I made 242. India were then reduced to 4–85. From there, however, Rahul Dravid and VVS Laxman — echoing their mighty partnership from Kolkata in 2001 — inspired an unlikely victory for the tourists, built on their 303-run stand for the fifth wicket and our subsequent batting collapse to be all out for 196. I was out for nought in our second innings, establishing a record for the highest score and a duck made by one batsman in the same Test. I'm still not sure if that's a special achievement.

It's ridiculous to think that this Test, one in which I scored a double ton (prompting the famous kiss blown to my wife), is not one I recall very fondly — mostly because of the loss, but also because of the duck and the catch I dropped off Laxman when he was 65 (he finished with 148). First ball after a drinks break, I had a lolly in my mouth and instead of my sunglasses keeping the glare out they were perched on the top of my cap. I realised I wasn't ready as our paceman, Brad Williams, was running into bowl but rather than stop him, I figured, *you'll get away with it for one ball*. With these sorts of thoughts in my head, I wasn't focused on the game and sure enough the chance came, low to my right, and I split it. Another lesson learned. One down with two to play, the pressure was right on us. Australia hadn't trailed in a Test series at home since Allan Border's last summer as captain, in 1993–94.

Following this defeat John Buchanan produced a paper for our attention that listed all the areas where he felt we were letting ourselves down. He didn't miss us, suggesting our attitude was 'un-baggy green, soulless and immature', and that during the game just lost we were more worried about 'deal-making, sponsors, Tug's farewell to Adelaide, the choice of helmets, what the media is saying about you and domestic games after this Test match'.

Clearly, he was trying to blast us out of what he perceived as our lethargy, but I was one of many from both within and outside our team who wondered whether such criticism might have been best delivered face to face. Instead, a copy of the document was slid under the hotel-room door of each of the players, and was also, somehow, leaked to the media, who had a field day. To say the mood in the Australian camp was tense would be quite an understatement.

Boxing Day in Melbourne was more of the same, as Virender Sehwag scored 195 and India reached stumps at 4–329, but the next morning — even though we were playing without Warne, McGrath and Gillespie — we took the last six wickets for 16 runs and then Matt Hayden and I combined for a big partnership that took the game away from them. It was an important day, that December 27, because a real negativity was starting to impose itself on our group but we managed to arrest it before it took hold. When I finished unbeaten on 31 in our second dig, hitting the four that completed a nine-wicket victory, I'd scored more than 1500 Test runs for the year, in 11 Tests, at an average of fractionally more than 100, and the recent loss in Adelaide was being viewed as an aberration.

I was in the best form of my life, having scored 11 Test centuries in 22 months. However, it would be more than a year until I scored another one.

AFTER WE BEAT INDIA in that third Test, Steve Waugh enjoyed a slow walk around the MCG, the ground where he had made his international debut 18 years earlier. Back in the dressing room, I asked him if he wanted to mark the occasion by leading us as we sang 'Underneath the Southern Cross'. 'Nah, not now,' he said. 'Let me do the last one.'

No worries, I thought to myself. Clearly, he expected us to win in Sydney. I did too.

As it turned out, though, that didn't happen. Instead, after I organised for the team to walk out on the first morning before the captain, so we could form a guard of honour as he ran onto the field, India batted for more than two days. On the last afternoon, we briefly looked a chance to make 443 to win, but after Tugga and Gilly were dismissed in quick succession we had to forget about that and the game ended in a fairly tame draw. Still, the SCG crowd gave their hero a stirring send-off and in the dressing room afterwards I talked to a few of the boys and we agreed it was appropriate, as a one-off, to push tradition to one side and sing the team song — not to celebrate a victory but to mark the end of a genuinely great career.

Leadership

There is an old saying: leaders are born — rarely made. I've thought a lot about that saying, as the potential for leadership is just one of those traits that I seemed to have as part of my make-up, enabling me to assume a leadership role in almost all of the teams that I played in. A big part of that came from leading by example. It's about creating energy around the group, staying ahead of the game and gaining respect for what you do — not for the position that you hold. Leaders have to do a lot of little things that all add up to setting the example for their team. Leadership for me has always been about 'looking out before you look in'.

I made it a policy of mine to always have an open door so that any of my team-mates could come and see me to talk over anything at all. I would be first to breakfast each and every morning we were on tour and always the last one to finish training — making myself available for extra 'throw downs', catching or anything else my team-mates wanted or needed. I did this before, during and after my time as captain — always making sure that I was consistent in all that I did around my team-mates so that they knew I was there for them. I also made sure that I worked every day on all the important parts of my own game to ensure that I played my individual role as the No. 3 batsman — setting an example for everyone else to follow.

Leaders are usually the best problem-solvers — they often solve problems faster than others and with better solutions. This is also achieved by having a good team of people around you who you can draw on for your own problem-solving in a quick and efficient manner. I found this over and over again throughout my career when I would turn to those closest to me and my game. Guys like Lang, Haydos and Marto were a constant help to me.

CHAPTER 30

CHARACTER

High Office, 2004

WHILE HE WAS PRIME MINISTER John Howard famously claimed that his job was only the 'second most important' in the land and it was the one I was about to take over that rated more highly. He may have had his tongue in cheek when he said it, but it's fair to say that being captain of Australia was an extraordinary honour for a boy from the backblocks of Rocherlea.

As a cricketer I guess I was as qualified as anybody, but there were many other elements of the job and those required me learning a number of new skills. From the time Steve Waugh had nominated me as a potential successor my manager Sam Halvorsen had set about preparing me for that possibility.

It is fair to say that as a young bloke I was neither articulate nor polished and you might argue there is not much sign of that now, but it is something I have worked hard at. Sam, whose advice early in my career was invaluable to me as a person and a cricketer, organised for me to do a series of courses where I learned to speak in public and speak properly. I had spent most of my life communicating with cricketers and I think we had almost developed our own language. Sure I could get by in an interview with a journo on the sidelines or after a match, knew how to look them in the eye and from a very early age knew what they wanted and how to deal with it, but I had to take it up a step.

Whenever I gave an interview Sam would watch it at home and ring me, picking me up on this and that. He even arranged for me to learn table etiquette. At our house table manners were important, you sat up straight, used a knife and fork, said please and thank you and all that stuff, but Mum never laid out a table with a spread of dessert spoons, salad knives, red wine glasses, white wine glasses ...

I can speak off the cuff anywhere and anytime now, although I prefer answering questions to delivering a prepared speech. The weeks in the lead-up to the Bradman Oration were the longest in my life as I sweated over what is considered one of the keynote addresses in the cricket calendar, but I was a willing learner back then and to this day remain thankful to Sam for his efforts and foresight.

As captain of Australia you can almost literally dine with kings and queens and spend your time hanging out with all manner of celebrities, wealthy businessmen and the like, and I suppose I have over the time, but it was never something I sought out or craved. I would always prefer a quiet dinner with the team, huddled in the corner of a restaurant or to be somewhere alone with my wife.

The captaincy was an important job, yes, and one that came with a lot of respect and trappings, but the most important part of it for me was the cricket. It was my job to make sure we were as good as we could be and that was what consumed all my time.

And while it is helpful as a captain to be able to stand up and speak well in public, the core task is leadership. I had observed captains in the past, watched how it was done back in Launceston and then under Mark Taylor and Steve Waugh. I made a conscious decision that I would lead by example, establishing benchmarks for others to follow but also I wanted the team to be involved and pushing the direction we took. I wanted to get to know the players and understand what made them tick and I wanted them to feel they could talk to me at any stage and be part of the process. At times I was criticised for seeking others' thoughts on the field, but it was a deliberate strategy.

You can't always be on the same page and one of the early issues I had to deal with involved Warnie, who had been a mate for a long time.

BACK IN EARLY NOVEMBER 2003, when we were in India for the TVS Cup one-day series, Shane came to see me in my hotel room. Shane was in Mumbai for the *Wisden* International Cricketers of the Year awards, where he won the gong for the best Test bowling performance of 2002 (his 7–94 against Pakistan in Colombo). He wanted to clear the air, to explain why he wasn't happy that I'd publicly chastised him for failing the drugs test. I took his point that at a time when he and his family were doing it hard he didn't need his team-mates criticising him at media conferences, which is what happened after he left the World Cup. Someone in a press conference had asked me if he was 'naive', and I answered 'that or stupid'. It was blunt, but a reasonable assessment of what he had done given the impact on the team and on himself.

We talked it through and agreed to move on. I was happy that he came and spoke to me and further convinced that anybody in the team, whether we were old mates or not, should feel the same. At the same time, I was struck by how enthusiastic he was about coming back. There'd been no change of mind about his retirement from ODI cricket but he was clearly excited by the idea of playing more Test matches.

I didn't have too many short-term expectations for him. The previous times Shane had come back after extended absences from the game — after shoulder surgery that cost him a large chunk of the 1998–99 Australian summer and from a broken finger in 2000–01 — he'd taken a while to work into form, which led to him being dropped in the West Indies in 1999 and bagged by John Buchanan for being unfit in 2001. This time the break did him a lot of good, probably extending his career, because it gave him a chance to rest his shoulder, spinning fingers and knees, all of which had been put through the grinder during the first 11 years of his international cricket career.

His first game back was in early February, for a Victorian second XI. Not long after, we were at Crown Casino in Melbourne for the annual Allan Border Medal presentation and not surprisingly there was plenty of talk about how he was going, and how he was likely to perform in the upcoming Tests in Sri Lanka. Most of the talk was positive, on the basis that you should never underrate a champion, but there were a few go-slows for him, from people who wondered if his best days were behind him. I sensed his time on the sidelines had reminded him how much he loved the game, the competition and the mateship. He also clearly liked the idea of proving the knockers wrong. He needed only nine wickets to become the second man to take 500 wickets in Test matches (after the West Indies' Courtney Walsh), but my best guess was that he'd end with a lot more than that.

I was lucky enough to win the AB Medal that night — the fifth recipient of the award after Glenn McGrath (2000), Steve Waugh (2001), Matt Hayden (2002) and Adam Gilchrist (2003). The next morning, after I was woken well before 7am for the first of a series of interviews with various breakfast radio and TV identities, I had reason to think about Shane again, though this time for reasons related to, of all things, fashion. The previous night, I'd strayed away from the traditional black-tie and instead worn a pin-striped suit and wide-lapelled shirt, with no tie, and now everyone wanted to talk about my dress sense rather than my past 12 months of cricket. I was a bit taken aback by all this attention, and couldn't help thinking about how far I'd come since those nights long gone when I had to tell my Cricket Academy mate Warnie that I couldn't go out with him to his Adelaide discos because I didn't own even one smart pair of jeans or shoes, let alone a jacket. (If you suspected the influence of my wife you were probably right.)

BEFORE THE TESTS in Sri Lanka, we played them in five ODIs, winning games one, three and four. We had a good time, the spirit among the boys was terrific, but the bloke I think of first when I recall this series is Brad Hogg, the 'chinaman' bowler who'd done such a brilliant job for us during the 2003 World Cup after Warnie was forced to return home.

Hoggy, or George as his WA team-mates called him, because his name is George Bradley Hogg, is a rare individual, razor keen; a man who thrives on putting his team above himself. I can't stress how important blokes like Hoggy are to the psyche of a cricket team on tour. Sometimes, their off-field selflessness and good humour can be just as important for a team's progress as a hundred made on the park. Hoggy's other rare skill was his ability to get everyone feeling good without him even trying, such as the time we were on the bus to Dambulla, north-east of Colombo, and he looked down at his watch and then asked Steve Bernard how far we had to go.

'Probably another two hours,' Brute replied.

Hoggy stopped for a moment and then inquired, 'So when will we get there?'

Maybe you had to be there. A couple of days later, back in Colombo, we were having a coffee in the café at our hotel but unfortunately the autograph hunters wouldn't leave us alone. It was one of those situations where the first request was fine, the next one was okay but by the 40th intrusion it was getting a bit much, especially as not all the signature seekers were polite. Eventually, there was one too many for Hoggy, and he cried out in frustration, 'Don't you Colombians ever give it a rest?'

Then there was the time immediately after we went 2–1 up in the series, when he was told by Jock Campbell, our fitness trainer, there wouldn't be a net session the next day.

'No mate,' Hoggy replied. 'I want to bowl 12 balls tomorrow.'

'Why 12?' asked Jock, who was keen for the bowlers to have a rest.

'Four leg-breaks, four wrong'uns and a flipper,' our man answered.

'That's only nine,' Jock said with a look of bewilderment on his face. 'What about the other three?'

'They're spares, in case any of the others don't come out right,' Hoggy explained.

And finally, most priceless of all, was the day the selectors announced the 15-man squad for the Tests that followed the one-dayers. They named two spinners — Warnie and Stuart MacGill — which meant there was no room for Hoggy. He'd be going home early. I knew he was disappointed, but rather than spit the dummy he went out a few hours later and spun us to victory in the first game of the series, running through their lower order to finish with 5–41. That's the sort of character you don't forget in a hurry.

BEFORE ALL THIS, at the end of the 2003 VB Series, after we'd thrashed India in the finals, Adam Gilchrist got up to lead us in the team song and this was when it occurred to me that I was unlikely to ever get the chance to do that again. The protocol is that the songmaster is not a job for the captain and as I was now skipper of the Test team I knew I'd have to pass the honour on. But to whom? My first thought was Gilly, but then I figured as good and passionate a bloke our champion keeper might be, there was a fellow in our Test line-up who'd cherish the role a little bit more than any other …

So it was that following our win in the first Test in Galle, amid the laughs, the animated chat, the music and the beers, I walked quietly over to the bench where Justin Langer and assistant coach Tim Nielsen were talking cricket, as they always like to do. 'Hey Lang, you got a second,' I said, but he pretty much ignored me as he tried to bring Tim round to his way of thinking. I tried again but my gentle nudges weren't working.

So there was nothing I could do but place my mobile — the one on which I'd typed a text message but hadn't yet sent — firmly in his hand and say, 'I need you to read this …'

'Mate, I want you to sing the team song' was what I'd written.

Lang quickly scanned the message, then stopped … and read it again … slowly, much more seriously. For a second or two, he didn't do anything, then he looked over at me, smiled, stopped, and then grabbed me on the shoulder and half guided, half pushed me into the vacant shower room and shut the door behind us.

'Punter, I can't believe it,' he said. 'This is the greatest moment of my career.'

'Mate, you're the right man for the job. You believe in it and I know you're going to be part of the team for the next few years,' I responded.

To say Lang was overwhelmed is a major understatement. He hugged me and wiped a tear from his eye. If you ask him today, more than any of his hundreds or our big wins, this was the moment when he truly felt secure in his job as an Aussie Test cricketer, that he *really* belonged. That's how much becoming songmaster meant to him. He hadn't expected the gig but was ecstatic and exhilarated that I'd given it to him. That minute or two we had together remains among the most cherished memories of my cricket career.

'Now mate,' I said to him before we rejoined the group, 'you've got to work out how we're going to sing the song tonight.'

I could almost feel Lang's brain going to work. For the next hour or so, I kept glancing over at him and often he seemed in a world of his own, part of conversations but hardly talking, instead thinking seriously about how he was going to make his debut a memorable one. Finally, I climbed on a table, called everyone together and told them who would now be in charge. Everyone roared their approval, reflecting how popular Lang is, and now it was time for him to jump up and join me. Instead, he said proudly, 'Thanks boys, grab your baggy greens and follow me.'

The little man had been thinking and working. He led us out to the team bus, where our driver had the engine running and inside was an Esky full of ice and beers and a music box, fully charged. We drove out of the car park, through a few streets, past the walls of the city's ancient fort and on to the lighthouse, one of Galle's most striking landmarks, where Lang asked the driver to stop and then he bounced over to the base of the historic old structure that has illuminated Galle Harbour for so many years, beckoning us to follow. 'Shirts off, boys,' he ordered, as if we were pro middleweights about to head into the ring. Then we sang 'True Blue' and 'Khe Sanh', a couple of Tugga's old favourites, before he looked back on the Test just completed, reminding us that Andrew Symonds had just made his Test debut, how our bowlers had stuck at it as Sri Lanka built a substantial first-innings lead, and how Haydos, Marto and Boof had all scored second-innings centuries to turn the game on its head, allowing me to declare late on day four, setting them 352 to win. He homed in on Warnie, who'd taken five wickets in each innings, including his 500th Test wicket, and had combined with Stuey MacGill to spin us to victory, and finally he acknowledged the fact I'd started off my life as Test captain with a win. Then he tugged at the peak of his baggy green cap and began, and we roared with him …

'Underneath the Southern Cross I stand … A sprig of wattle in my hand …'

I couldn't have chosen a better man.

It was time to lead the Australian team for the first time. That meant breaking the habit of a lifetime. I had always liked to be the last onto the field, it was just one of those quirks, but from now on I was up front leading the pack.

THIS WAS ONE of the best Australian Test wins of all time, it had to be, but there were a few reasons why it didn't get the recognition back home it deserved. Even though Sri Lanka had a number of genuinely outstanding players in their side — such as Sanath Jayasuriya, Mahela Jayawardene, Kumar Sangakkara and Chaminda Vaas — plus one of the game's greatest ever bowlers in Muttiah Muralitharan, I'm not sure too many Aussie critics rated them too highly, simply because they were relatively new to international cricket. It was only eight years since their win in the 1996 World Cup, their first major triumph, only 21 years since Australia had first played Sri Lanka in a Test. But within our group we knew how good and hard to beat they were, especially on their home turf. Also, I think we were paying for all the cricket we'd played in the previous three or four years; there has to be a point where the fans need a break, too, and here they might have reached it. ABC Radio's decision not to cover these Tests with a ball-by-ball description might have been a reflection of this, but without that coverage it was inevitable our performance, good or bad, would be a little lost. Maybe this is why I want to devote so many words here to this Test and the rest of the series.

The pitch was so obviously a turner, Sri Lanka included just one quick, and had the off-spinner, Kumar Dharmasena, opening the bowling. When I first saw the wicket, it was so dry and cracked I thought the game would be over in three days, and we couldn't help thinking they'd tailored their wicket to suit themselves, inspired by the reality that they had Murali, and Warnie was first up from a long spell. Before the game, to mark my captaincy debut, Gilly put together a video that featured good luck messages from everyone in the group, which he played at a team dinner two nights before the Test began. He also presented me with a Test-match shirt signed by all the boys, a brilliant gesture. It's such an honour, being Test captain, a step above being in charge of the one-day team, and I was humbled by the opportunity, yet I'm sure my first game as Test captain snuck up on a lot of people, chiefly because we'd been preoccupied with so much cricket since I'd been named the next captain three-and-a-half months before. And I'm not the sort of person to outwardly make a big deal about things, which might have had others downplaying the moment. However, Gilly knew how much the new job meant to me, as did Rianna, who flew over especially for the game.

The next day, my manager Sam Halvorsen arrived and he had a special package with him — the captain's blazer — which I handled with the same kid gloves I used to hold my first baggy green and my uncle Greg Campbell's first baggy green, too. Next morning, I was out in the middle for the toss a little early and it was already pretty hot and sticky … but although I had a good sweat going there was no way I was taking that blazer off until I returned to the dressing room!

Murali took six wickets on the first day, which ended with them 1–81 in reply to our below-par 220. Day two was more of the same, and at stumps they were 6–352. Warnie took three quick wickets the next morning, and we went into day four just two wickets down and with an overall lead of 32. It had been quite a comeback, and when Marto and Boof combined quite magnificently to defy the humidity and bat the Sri Lankans out of the game, we found ourselves in the unlikely position of being able to set them a target. At the time, I thought this was Marto's best ever innings (though he'd go to even more formidable heights in the second Test a week later), while for Boof it was an emotional time, as he dedicated his century to his great friend David Hookes, who had so needlessly and cruelly died following an incident at a Melbourne pub a few weeks before. What was fascinating was to see how these two resilient cricketers countered the turning wicket with different methods but equal effectiveness. Marto was stylish, unhurried, mostly playing back to the spinners, reading their bounce and turn off the pitch, while Boof was gruff and ruthless, often using his feet to get to the pitch of the ball. The common denominator was character; they both have heaps of that.

The stage was set for our great leg-spinner, who on day five was irresistible, the highlight coming when their skipper Hashan Tillakaratne was caught by Symmo: the 500th wicket. It was a simple catch, after a top-edge went straight up in the air, and of course we mobbed him, as always happened when a bowler reaches a big milestone, but what I remember most this time was how emotional Shane became, a reaction, I'm sure, to all he'd been through over the previous 13 months. For a moment, he seemed happy to stay within our embrace but eventually he acknowledged the crowd, including a fair number of Aussies who'd made the trip, by holding the ball up and then giving them a bow.

THE SECOND TEST at Kandy was a thrilling match that featured another stirring Aussie fightback. We played the same XI as Galle, but the pitch seamed all over the place at the start of the Test and we did well to make 120 after I opted to bat first and then have Sri Lanka 7–92 at stumps. But the next morning, Vaas and Murali added 79 for the last wicket, giving them a first-innings lead of 91, and I had to go off because my upper back seized up. I felt a sharp pain when I twisted to grab the ball as I ran in from cover and ignored it, but in the following over when I bent down to pick the ball up, something in my back gripped tight, and I just fell over. There was nothing I could do but lie there and wait for our new physio, Alex Kountouris, to run out and as he tried to manipulate things back into place I found no humour in the boys pointing out that I had gone down in the same part of the field where Steve Waugh and Jason Gillespie had collided in 1999. 'This must be Kandy's equivalent of the Bermuda Triangle,' one of them laughed.

Alex was confident I'd be able to bat the next day, but not before then, which meant we needed a new No. 3. The obvious thought was that we should move everyone up one place in the batting order but John Buchanan suggested promoting Gilly, who so far in the series had scored 4, 0 and 0. Buck's thinking was the change would do him good and further it wouldn't change Marto's routine at No. 4, and I was happy with the plan from the moment Gilly said forcefully, 'Yeah, I'll do it!' Quickly, Haydos and Lang were dismissed, but our new first drop trusted his eye and his instincts, hit straight down the ground a lot, and changed the mood, while Marto was simply superb. They added exactly 200 for the third wicket and we ended up setting them 352 to win, the same target they'd failed to reach in Galle. This time, they got much closer. In fact, more than once, they looked like squaring the series.

It all came down to them needing 51 on the fifth day, with three wickets in hand. I was prepared for a war of attrition, setting reasonably defensive fields for Warne and Gillespie, but Vaas and Kaushal Lokuarachchi were having none of that, and they took three from the first over, 10 from the second, and then a leg-bye and a four between long-on and deep mid-wicket from the first two balls of the third. The small crowd was having a terrific time, and then Vaas hit a sharp catch straight to our best fielder, Andrew Symonds at extra cover ... and he dropped it. For a moment, we were all devastated and poor Symmo had his head in his hands. It was Warnie who revved us back up. Two balls later, he served up what to Vaas must have looked like the very same ball he'd hit for four earlier in the over, but this one was fractionally flatter and maybe it turned that little bit more. He didn't quite get it and instead of it spearing away for another boundary it looped kindly out to Lang at deep mid-wicket who made no mistake. I'm sure plenty of people thought the batsman was reckless but in fact Warnie had been masterful. Again. For him to be back, so brilliantly and so quickly, made my early days as Test captain so much easier. Soon after, he took the final wicket, giving him four straight five-fors. Once again, he was in a class of his own.

A moment from this day that has stayed with me occurred as I walked back from a post-match media commitment, when I saw Darren Lehmann sitting outside our dressing room on his own. There were tears in his eyes. I asked him what was wrong and first up he said he was fine.

'Are you sure, mate?' I asked him. Something had clearly upset him, and as his friend I couldn't let it go.

'I just need a moment,' he said.

Then he explained quietly that winning in Kandy meant so much to him, because this was where David Hookes had scored his only Test hundred. Boof had played with Hookesy early in his career and was there when his mate passed away. He needed some quiet time, and I knew the right thing to do was leave him to it.

I was always really close to Boof, especially in my early days as Australian captain. He carried quite a mental load around with him during this tour, and plenty of inspiration, which is a measure of the man. I played cricket with a lot of extraordinary people but never took that for granted. Boof was dealing with the grief of losing his mate but was still able to contribute so critically to the team and that takes extraordinary character.

Often on tour we had to deal with losing somebody special. It happened to me when Youngy died and happened many other times over the years. It was important as mates and as a captain to keep an eye on how blokes were travelling, talking to them when they needed to talk or giving them space when they needed that. It's true that the best counselling in most situations comes from finding a corner in a bar with a good friend and letting it all out in whatever manner suited. I was blessed during most of my time as a cricketer to be surrounded by my closest friends, it was just the way we were.

A WEEK AFTER THE second Test we again overcame a first-innings deficit, this time six runs, to sweep the series, the first time an Australian team had ever done so on the subcontinent (unless you count our 3–0 win over Pakistan in 2002, when we won the first Test in Colombo and the next two in Sharjah). This time, our victory was built on big hundreds from Boof and Lang, a good all-round bowling and fielding performance, and an important contribution from Simon Katich, which underlined another of the positive characteristics of this team: that when we found ourselves in trouble, it could be any member of the side who helped dig us out of the hole. Kato had scored 125 and 77 not out in his most recent Test, Steve Waugh's farewell in Sydney, but for the first two Tests here, with us playing two spinners and two quicks, Symmo was preferred because he could bowl some medium pace. When we decided to play Brad Williams instead of Stuart MacGill in this third Test, Kato was brought back and made a crucial 86 in our second innings, combining with Lang to add 218 for the sixth wicket after we'd collapsed to 5–98.

Simon hadn't deserved to be dropped in the first place; he was just a victim of circumstances. But like Warnie once he came to terms with his suspension, Brad Hogg during the one-dayers, Gilly when he'd had to wait for Ian Healy to finish up, and guys like Haydos, Lang, Marto and Boof when they were out of the team for extended periods, with Kato there was nothing negative in him, just a sharp resolve to exploit the next opportunity whenever it came.

He is a bloke who I can't help but like and respect. There was something compelling about his straightforward manner. When he was out, lbw to Murali, I thought he was unlucky and I told him so afterwards. 'It looked to me like it pitched outside leg,' I said.

'No, Punter,' he replied. 'It was plumb.'

He was aware, after his recent experiences, that he was not guaranteed his place in the side, even after this gallant knock. And he realised that while I wasn't a selector, I'd be talking to the gentlemen who picked the side, so there might have been some value in him agreeing he was ripped off. But that wasn't his style, or the style of any of the guys who made this team such a dominant Australian outfit. Sure, we could get upset at poor decisions or actions that were wrong by the game, and there were occasions when our responses to such errors were used by others as evidence we were 'bad sports', but we were straight with ourselves, accepted we made mistakes and tried to learn from them. Again, it was that doctrine of always trying to improve. Kato's response confirmed what I already knew: that if his attitude stayed the same, he was going to be a very successful and influential international cricketer before his time was through.

Captaincy

Captaincy in cricket can be a complex role. I always tried to keep it as simple as possible by creating an environment so that everyone in and around our team was part of the direction that we were taking. I often got criticised for my 'captaincy by committee' style, but this was a premeditated approach that was all about being open to ideas and input from the group, developing everyone in the team to think like a leader and above all, to have a flexibility in my approach. I certainly was the final decision-maker, but the consultative environment was a huge advantage for me and the teams that I captained.

I made a point of really getting to know all the players in my team. I needed to understand what made them tick, work out how I could get the best out of them and, importantly, aim always to be a good listener so that they knew I was interested in them and had their backs. Everyone is different and you have to observe them to learn their body language, how they talk, how they respond to pressure, how they will respond to different situations, the best way to motivate as well as criticise them and, of course, know their game inside and out. With this knowledge and information, a captain is well placed to get the best out of his team.

CHAPTER 31

DOING THE
RIGHT THING

Colombo, Sunday, March 28, 2004

THERE IS ALWAYS SOMETHING different about the mood in the dressing room at the end of a series. On-field acrimony is usually forgotten; beers are shared with team-mates and rivals alike. This is when the mood between the teams is closest to how it is on Saturday evenings across Australia after club games, how it is at Mowbray, when whatever the result, the mood is invariably good. I probably didn't revel in this as much as some of my Aussie team-mates, the more gregarious blokes like Gilly and Lang, but that's just because I'm a pretty shy bloke at the best of times, most comfortable in the company of people I know well. Most of my closest friends are people I've known for years, people I trust.

In the dressing room after our Test series in Sri Lanka in 2004, the mood was bubbly, though a little rushed as many of the boys were due to fly out of Colombo late that same evening, either for the UK to play county cricket or home to Australia. I was the odd man out, as I was staying overnight and then heading to India to meet representatives from a cricket website with whom my manager had done a sponsorship deal. Back in the 1990s, when Sri Lanka was captained by Arjuna Ranatunga, the relationship between the two teams had been pretty frosty, but those days were long gone and this night I ended up having a long chat with Muttiah Muralitharan, the great off-spin bowler. Murali was actually a bit down at the time — his team had lost and he'd just learned the match referee was going to report his bowling action to the ICC, a peculiar decision because we all thought the question of whether his delivery was legal or not had been settled.

You could never convince me Murali's bowling action was illegal. Sure, it was unusual and if the authorities had ruled against him I wouldn't have been shocked — no doubt, his slightly bent elbow and wrist work pushed the laws of the game — but to tell the truth I was happy when he was cleared, because he's a good bloke. I thought he was good for the game; he was the main reason Sri Lanka became a very competitive outfit and I always enjoyed the challenge of trying to work him out. What set him apart as an offie was that he spun it both ways *and* it was almost impossible to pick which way the ball was turning out of his hand. If he'd been a traditional off-spinner, spinning it into the right-hander and with a well-hidden arm-ball, he'd have been a really good exponent of his art, but not the lethal wicket-taker he became.

With blatant chuckers, it is hard to pick up the ball out of the bowler's hand, because the delivery is jerky, but I didn't find that with Murali; I could see it clearly enough but struggled to immediately work out which way it was buzzing. In our conversation in Colombo, I congratulated him on taking 28 wickets in the three Tests (Shane Warne finished with 26), and he praised the way we batted, making special mention of Darren Lehmann, who he said played him better than anyone else.

Earlier that same night, another spinner, Stuart MacGill, asked if we could have a private chat in the corner of the room. Stuey is a bloke I've always got on well with and throughout this tour I'd sensed he was enjoying bowling under my captaincy. Now, though, he was extremely serious, even agitated, as he told me he was making himself unavailable for our upcoming tour of Zimbabwe. His view was that Australia shouldn't be playing cricket there while President Robert Mugabe, who had been accused of many human rights crimes, remained in power. He wondered if withdrawing from the tour would put him offside with the selectors but I told him I'd do all I could to make sure that didn't happen. No way was I going to try to talk him out of it — it was a big call and he wouldn't have made it without giving the matter plenty of thought.

THE QUESTION OF WHETHER we should play in Zimbabwe was a difficult one for me as captain. Certainly, in the days before our departure, the matter was much discussed in the media and it caused us plenty of angst. I'd read enough to know that the Mugabe government was corrupt, and that many people were suffering as a result. Some communities were starving, the economy was failing, and if protests weren't banned outright they were certainly discouraged. As far as cricket was concerned, since the 2003 World Cup the politicians had significantly increased their direct influence in the game to the point that they were now picking the Test team — with dire results. Many of their best players, including their captain Heath Streak, had either quit or been sacked, and then Geoff Marsh announced he would be resigning as coach. Part of me figured that if we weren't going to be facing their best side, there wasn't any point playing them at all, but in the back of my mind was a comment Geoff had made to me the previous year, during the World Cup, when there was talk we were going to pull out of our game in Harare.

'Do that, mate,' Swamp said, 'and it'll be devastating for Zimbabwe cricket.'

Twelve months later, if we didn't tour, what was left of the Zimbabwean cricket team would be further disheartened, and would feel abandoned. But if we did go, the Mugabe regime and its cricket cronies might use that as evidence that we supported or at least didn't care about their actions, whatever statements we might make to the contrary. Morally, could we allow that to happen? Of course, we were getting plenty of advice from all angles, but was it right for me to make a stand when I'm hardly an expert on African politics? I knew there were some major problems in the world, far greater than anything concerning sport, but I also knew I'd never been trained to solve them. I am a cricketer. Just because I was the Australian cricket captain didn't suddenly make me a career diplomat, no matter what others might have thought. And did anyone seriously believe Mugabe was going to listen to me? It isn't my way to pretend I have the answers when I don't.

Cricket Australia was committed to the ICC's international cricket program. Zimbabwe was a part of that. Having decided to leave the politics to the politicians, my concern was strictly about security — was it safe for my team to travel there? If the officials said it was, I decided, then I'd get on with my job, which was to play and captain the side to the best of my ability. In all my years as captain, I'd never sway from this policy.

Our first game, against Zimbabwe A, was so one-sided it was almost ridiculous and I came away fearing for the country's future in international cricket. Then the ICC decided to call off the two Tests, essentially because the local cricket administration was in such disarray and so many of their best players were unavailable that the games wouldn't have been a Test at all. Strangely, though, they decided to go ahead with the three ODIs scheduled for after the Test series — it seemed bizarre to me that the Tests were off because they didn't want to cheapen that form of the game but it was somehow okay to play what they must have thought were 'substandard' one-dayers. I guess they were just saving face, trying to get something out of the tour. With the Tests abandoned and the one-dayers lacking excitement and a competitive edge (we won by seven wickets, 139 runs and eight wickets), the controversy about us being in Zimbabwe died away and we started to wonder if our fans back home had even scant interest in what we were doing. I wouldn't have blamed them if they didn't.

MAKING OUR TIME in Zimbabwe even harder, because of the security concerns none of our loved ones were with us. Ever since Steve Waugh and John Buchanan had got together, the Australian team had a genuine family feel to it; it was rare for Rianna not to be with me for at least part of a tour and Cricket Australia encouraged such visits. Occasionally, only when we lost, you might hear the odd criticism of this innovation from people who thought having families along was distracting, but the way we played from 1999 was proof that the benefits outweighed any negatives. By 2004, I was so used to wives and partners (and sometimes kids) being with us, home or away, it felt weird in Zimbabwe when we found ourselves on our own as we waited for the games to be played or put off.

I've always been big on family. Like a lot of young people, I wasn't always good at keeping in touch with Mum and Dad in my early 20s but as I got older, especially after I got married, I really came to appreciate all they had done for me, and made a greater effort to make sure they were okay and to let them know how I was going. I know they were proud of what I'd achieved as a cricketer and more than a little stunned to be the parents of the Australian captain, but I think they were most impressed when they saw me up in front of a crowd, giving a reasonable speech and even getting the occasional laugh. I was amazed myself — public speaking had never been my forte at school or even in my early days as a first-class and international cricketer, and while back then I was never scared of facing the fastest bowlers, talking in front of an audience filled me with something close to dread.

In late June 2004, about three weeks after we returned from Zimbabwe, I was at Sydney airport, waiting to board a flight to Brisbane, from where we would head to Darwin for a winter Test against Sri Lanka, when my mobile rang. It was Mum, telling me that my Auntie Annette, Dad's only sister, was perilously ill. Auntie Annette had been suffering from terminal cancer and we'd been preparing ourselves for this day, but it came quicker than we'd expected. Instead of flying north, I organised a flight in the opposite direction and arrived in Launceston late that evening, with the intention of seeing Auntie Annette first thing in the morning, but sadly, she passed away in the middle of the night.

She'd been one of those important bits of glue that helps keep families together. When we were kids, my sister, Renee, brother, Drew, and I spent plenty of time during school holidays at Auntie Annette's house, when Mum and Dad were working, often playing cricket in the backyard with her and her husband, Uncle Michael. They were both at the WACA for my first Test in 1995–96, mostly because they wanted to be there but also to make sure Dad, the renowned non-traveller, flew to Perth as well. Now, as we gathered to share our grief, I knew there was no way I'd be playing in the upcoming Test. It was going to be my first home Test as captain but that didn't matter at this moment — no way was I leaving my family. I wanted to pay my respects to my much-loved aunt and I wanted to be with Dad and my grandparents, to help them through this difficult time. It was also important to me, to be where I was most needed. Five years later, Pop (Dad's father) would pass away while I was in Worcester preparing for an Ashes series and I was unable to come home. I hated being in that situation, feeling helpless, trying to comfort Dad over the phone when every part of me wanted to be in Launceston.

Maybe in the old days, the cricket hierarchy might have looked down on my decision to miss that Test against Sri Lanka in 2004, but I knew Cricket Australia would support me, as would John Buchanan, Adam Gilchrist and everyone in the team. Although it wouldn't have mattered to me if they didn't. There are more important things in life than one game of cricket. I only have one family. I believe I did the right thing.

CHAPTER 32

THE LAST FRONTIER

Edgbaston, September 21, 2004

I'VE NEVER LIKED GETTING INJURED. The pain is nothing; the time out of the game, the days or weeks needed to get the injury right, is what hurts the most. When a broken thumb led to tears in India in 2004 it had nothing to do with physical pain.

Looking back on my career, I was pretty lucky in that I didn't suffer too much. Two of my worst injuries came early in my life — I dropped a drain cover on my foot and broke my toes on VFL Grand Final day in 1984, and the busted arm that ended my football career in 1990, but neither impinged too much on my cricket. In fact, the second one probably helped, because after it happened Dad insisted I forget about footy and focus on what I did best. For the next 14 years, my only bad one was the broken ankle in 2000, which cost me three Tests in New Zealand and a couple of one-day tours. But then I broke my left thumb at the ICC Champions Trophy semifinal at Edgbaston in September 2004, a genuinely shattering blow because there were Test matches in India just around the corner. Becoming the first Australian team in more than three decades to win a Test series in India had become a grand ambition for us, the 'last frontier' as Steve Waugh used to call it. Now the boys were going to do it without me.

The thought of pain has never scared me; the experience of pain never scarred me. When I dived forward from second slip to try to catch England captain Michael Vaughan, and the ball landed just in front of me and then kicked up and clipped the tip of my thumb, I initially just shrugged the damage off, and asked Errol Alcott to tape it up. The thumb was going black and swollen but we had a game to win. As it turned out, we lost by six wickets. It was only later, after X-rays revealed that the thumb was fractured in three places that the doctors explained that I'd risked doing myself some serious damage by staying on the field. My first response was to beg Errol to let me go to India, saying, 'Ian Healy used to keep with broken fingers, why can't I play with this one?'

But he was having none of that. 'Even Heals couldn't play with a smashed thumb, Punter,' he said. 'You're better off going home.'

'But I want to be with the team, and working with you to get it right,' I replied, knowing I was fighting a lost cause. Still, it was worth a try — we'd all seen Errol do some amazing things working with injuries, such as on the 2001 Ashes tour when he got Steve Waugh back on the field within a couple of weeks of Tugga ripping a calf muscle, or in 2002–03 when he helped fix Warnie's shoulder in world-record time.

'Punter, we all know what you're like,' he said with some frustration in his voice. 'You'll want to get involved, and then you'll cop a knock and be out for months.'

So while the rest of the Test players in the one-day squad and their partners went to the airport to fly to the subcontinent, and Adam Gilchrist got his head around the fact he was going to captain Australia in one of the most anticipated Test series in a while, Rianna and I packed our bags for Sydney. An appointment with the surgeon had been scheduled for the day we landed.

THE TEAM LEADERSHIP GROUP had been planning for this four-Test series in India for many months. It had been the subject of many a conversation during the winter matches against Sri Lanka, as

John Buchanan put the finishing touches on a plan he was sure would frustrate the much lauded Indian batting order. I'd spent four weeks with the England county side Somerset in July–August, partly because county cricket was something I'd always wanted to experience, but mostly because I wanted my batting to be sharp for the Tests in October. As much as we tried to treat the ICC Champions Trophy as an important event in its own right, it was impossible not to think about India, and more than once Buck and I sat down to make sure we had our strategies right. He was convinced the Indian batsmen were almost obsessed with hitting boundaries, and if we let them do that, they'd get on a roll, the crowd would get behind them and they'd be hard to stop. 'Let's take that away from them,' he said.

When I first came into the Australian team, our coaches, Bob Simpson and then Geoff Marsh, used to constantly remind us about the benefits of turning over the strike, something we all bought into. It became so much a part of our game, I used to get a bit fidgety if I was stuck at one end, because neither I nor my partner could get the bowlers away. The scoreboard wasn't ticking over and our opponents were getting into a rhythm, implementing their bowling and fielding plans with alacrity. Buck's plan was to build a similar level of anxiety in the Indian batsmen, but in a different way, because their approach to batting was different.

We asked our pacemen — Glenn McGrath, Jason Gillespie and Michael Kasprowicz — to bowl to the Indians' strengths but supported them with field placements that some observers incorrectly described as defensive. At the start of the innings, Gilly would position only one or two slips, instead of the customary three slips and a gully, and the 'spare' fieldsmen were used to plug the areas, in the ring and on the boundary, where the Indian batsmen liked to hit. 'You can keep hitting your favourite shots,' our tactics were saying to them, 'but if you want to hit boundaries you're going to have to hit the ball harder or aim for places other than those you usually hit to.' Pidge, Dizzy and Kasper were all magnificent, the crowd lost a little of its enthusiasm, and batsmen like Virender Sehwag, VVS Laxman and Yuvraj Singh suddenly looked puzzled and seemed to be struggling for form.

Sehwag was recognised as one of the most dynamic opening bats in the game and he did play one substantial innings in this series, during the drawn second Test, but that knock aside our bowlers stifled him really well. We had fieldsmen out on the boundary at deep point and deep backward square from the very first over, and you could see his frustration grow whenever he played one of his characteristic slashes through the off-side field but only scored a single and lost the strike. As I saw — initially from the comfort of the couch in my lounge room — how effective these tactics were, I couldn't help but wish we'd done the same thing against the Indians at Kolkata in 2001 and at Adelaide Oval in 2003–04, when we started leaking runs but did little to try to arrest the shifts in momentum.

Our batsmen were also magnificent. In the first Test, Simon Katich scored 81 batting in my No. 3 spot and Gilly and Michael Clarke (on debut) hit brilliant hundreds; in the third Test, Damien Martyn made one of his greatest centuries, while Kato made a second-innings 99 and 'Pup' Clarke scored 91 and 73. None of their batsmen went past 60 in one innings during either of these two Tests. By the time I was ready to play again, in the final Test of the series, the rubber had been decided after wins by 217 runs and 342 runs. It was a famous victory.

I wasn't there when Michael Clarke made 151 on his debut, but I had been on the phone talking to the selectors. He looked good in the tour match and there was a good feel about his cricket, and the guys over there liked what they saw. Pup was a little like me, he had always had good reviews coming through and there was a thought he might excel given a chance at the next level. I was pushing to get him into that Test team, as I thought it would be good to get some young blood into the group. In those days they brought energy to the field. Pup could bowl a few overs and he was a bright personality to have around. Most young people who brought that to the team were up for anything, but it wasn't so true later and that was a bit of a concern.

I JOINED THE TOUR a few days before the third Test in Nagpur, though I knew I wasn't going to be able to play for at least another seven days. I didn't quite feel a part of it but I didn't feel out of place either. My role was to be available if Gilly wanted my advice, but mostly to be the best waterboy I could be.

I have to admit, though, that I didn't just accept my fate. I did all the physical training I could leading into the Test, and I'd had a plastic guard made for my thumb, to prevent the joint from moving during fielding practice and when I picked up a bat in the nets. Of course, I didn't tell Errol or Buck that the specialist had said I shouldn't have a hit for a few days; instead, I told them I wouldn't be able to play and then went into the nets hoping I'd put on such an impressive show they'd talk me into playing. All I did was prove I couldn't hold a bat right and was in no condition to participate.

When the third Test began, as Justin Langer and Matthew Hayden went out to bat, I was in my whites, wearing the baggy green, ready to do any 12th-man duties that might come my way. I know some regular starters struggle in these situations, when they're not part of the run-on team, but I'd been dealt this card and I wanted to do my job as enthusiastically as I could. A rumour in the lead-up to the game was that some of the Indian players had fallen out with the curator, which led to a wicket being prepared that might have suited us more than it suited them. One report described it as looking like a 'typical English green seamer'. When their captain Sourav Ganguly and No. 1 spinner Harbhajan Singh pulled out of the Test because of injury and illness respectively, we wondered if the playing surface might have been a factor in their decisions.

Damien Martyn scored one of his very best hundreds in the first innings, a knock that demonstrated how much he was a batsman of the absolute highest class. The most important occasions were Marto's favourites. He came to the wicket at a crucial time, but seemed in total command until late in the day, when he ran down the wicket to Anil Kumble and tried to hit him over mid-on for six. Unfortunately, the ball went straight up in the air. It was a rare lapse of judgment, but that night Buck gave him a spray in front of everyone for throwing his wicket away. The coach reckoned he wasn't hungry enough, which was a silly thing to say. It was a fantastic effort making a hundred on that pitch, in such a huge game. I think Buck's comments reflected his own nervousness more than anything else.

Glenn McGrath was playing in his 100th Test match, and he bowled as beautifully as ever, taking 3–27 from 25 overs in India's first innings as he strangled the life out of them. Jason Gillespie might have been even better, taking five wickets, including Sachin Tendulkar who was making a much publicised return to international cricket after a couple of months out with tennis elbow. The pressure on him, with Ganguly missing and the team struggling, was extraordinary, and I had a different view of it sitting just outside our dressing room, watching the crowd's emotions ebb and flow with his fate. They were almost delirious when he walked to the wicket; silent when he was trapped lbw for 8. Gilly didn't enforce the follow-on and on the back of more superb batting from Marto, Simon Katich and Michael Clarke we eventually set them 543 to stay in the series. They were never a chance of getting anywhere near that.

Before he led us in the team song, Lang jumped on a table and invited each member of the group to get up with him and explain what winning in India meant to him. When it was my turn, I struggled for a moment, because I was not quite sure how to explain how I was feeling. My contribution to the win had been minimal at best and I didn't want to sound like I was talking myself up, so I started by saying that I couldn't describe what it was like to win a Test series on Indian soil. I tried to crack a joke.

'I can tell you what it's like to miss out and not be a part of it.'

I felt the back of my throat tighten.

'But I think I can explain what it means to be part of this group ...'

Then I lost it, started to cry, and couldn't get any more words out. I was part of the team but I wasn't, and my disappointment at missing out was part of the reason for my tears. But pride was a part of it too. From the moment I'd become captain I'd been so grateful for how the team had gelled, so proud of the way we worked for each other, and how they unconditionally backed me, Buck and everyone in the leadership group. It would have been a travesty if this team hadn't conquered the last frontier, and I was lucky to be a part of it. We lost the final Test in Mumbai on one of the worst pitches I ever saw, but that didn't take anything away from everything this superb group had managed to achieve.

Team song

'Underneath the Southern Cross' is a song that every Australian Test cricketer looks forward to singing. It's the victory song blustered out by the entire team as part of an in-house celebration after winning each and every Test match. Rod Marsh came up with the idea and started the tradition of leading the team in singing the song. Rod handed on to Allan Border the job of leading the song. When AB became captain, it was decided that the team song shouldn't be led by the captain of the team, so David Boon was chosen by AB to take over. Boonie led the song in my first three Test matches when we beat Sri Lanka 3–0 in 1995–96. I will never forget that experience and I didn't take long to catch on what the song meant to the team. It was a motivational tool for winning and it definitely made the victory even sweeter. Boonie retired at the end of that summer and he chose Ian Healy to continue the tradition. Heals retired just before the 1999–2000 Australian summer, and I remember very fondly the conversation he had with me when he asked me to take over the role of team song leader.

I was still very young and it was a huge thrill for me to be given such an important team role. I tried to do things a little differently in my time. When I first came into the team, we used to sing the song pretty early on after the end of a winning game, but with the introduction of recovery sessions and other post-game activities, I endeavoured to push the time back to sing it much later after the end of the game. I also looked for opportunities after series or significant wins to get away from the traditional dressing-room environment and go to different locations outside of the ground.

When I became captain, I didn't hesitate in choosing Justin Langer to replace me as team song leader. For me, he encapsulated everything the song stands for. A selfless team-mate who worked hard each and every day to be the best that he could. He treasured every Test match he played for his country and wanted to share success with his team-mates, who meant the world to him.

Lang has always said that having that role was one of the very best things to have happened to him in his career. He led the song through a golden era of Australian Test cricket and put his own style on it. It was a great time, and my memory is full of classic renditions of the team song.

Mike Hussey took over from Lang and led the song for the rest of my career. The last time I sang the song was after the third Test against the West Indies in Dominica in April 2012. At the time, I had no idea that it would be the last time I sang the song, but it does stay front of mind for me as it was the last game that our trainer Stuart Karppinen was with the national team. I made a presentation to Karps and then Huss led the song with extra gusto to pay tribute to the great work that Karps had done with us over the years. In many ways, that's what the team song is about. It's a tradition that takes place after success is achieved by not just the team but also the management that support us.

CHAPTER 33

PLAYING WITH BRIAN

Australian summer, 2004–05

WE RETURNED TO AUSTRALIA in buoyant moods and then spent the 2004–05 summer obliterating our opponents, winning seven of eight Tests against New Zealand and Pakistan at home and New Zealand away, 12 of 14 ODIs against New Zealand, Pakistan and the West Indies, and our first ever Twenty20 international, against New Zealand in Auckland. Many of our players were in irresistible form, but perhaps the feat that remains strongest in the memory was the innings of 61 scored by, of all people, Glenn McGrath. He hit these runs in the first Test against New Zealand at the Gabba, when he and Jason Gillespie combined for a last-wicket partnership of 114.

This partnership so nearly never happened. When Pidge and Dizzy came together, at 9–471 in reply to 353, I was very happy with our position and like everyone else I began to change into my whites, as we fully expected Pidge to do what he usually did when he went out to bat with another late-order batsman: get out. He'd developed an ability to often hang around with someone from the top-order batsmen when that was needed, but in situations like this it was always nine out, all out. This time, the Kiwis couldn't immediately break through, but the first eight overs of the

10th-wicket partnership produced only 20-odd runs and Darren Lehmann leaned over and muttered, 'Skip, this is going nowhere. Do you think we should bring 'em in?'

'Let's give it a few more minutes,' I said. 'If they don't get going, I'll declare.'

Maybe they heard that out in the middle, because almost immediately Dizzy hit a couple of fours, and then Pidge slogged their outstanding left-arm spinner, Daniel Vettori, for the first six of his Test career. After that, you could sense something special was going to unfold; there was no way I was closing because no one would have let me. The partnership went on and on, and not long before the umpires called time for the day, Pidge brought up his first Test half-century by hitting Vettori for two fours off successive balls. I don't think I've been in a more excited viewing area as he approached this milestone, but we all ran a mile when he came in at stumps because we knew he'd be unbearable.

Sure enough, he made a beeline for me, first to point out his score, 54 not out, was three more than what I'd been dismissed for the previous day, then to demand he be promoted up the batting order, at least to No. 8, ahead of Shane Warne, who'd only made 10. Then he proclaimed loudly that he needed to get in touch with Michael Bevan urgently, because he'd been using a 'Michael Bevan-autograph' bat and he needed to know if Bevo would be using a Glenn McGrath bat in future. Not even his batting partner was safe. At that moment, Dizzy's highest Test score was 48 not out, so Pidge sat down next to him and said, in a very matter-of-fact tone, 'Isn't it a great feeling, scoring a fifty in a Test match ...'

Next day, they took their stand past 100, and then Dizzy finally reached his first Test half-century and celebrated like Adam Sandler in the movie *Happy Gilmore*, fulfilling a promise he'd made to his mates at the Adelaide Cricket Club. By the time Pidge was finally out, having established a record for the highest Test score by an Australian No. 11, the spirit in our dressing room was at an all-time high. Our opponents, on the other hand, were shot, and Pidge,

Dizzy, Kasper and Warnie slaughtered them for just 76 as we won by an innings and 156 runs.

IF ONE MOMENT CAPTURED the sort of batting form Adam Gilchrist was in throughout this season, it came in the New Year's Test against Pakistan in Sydney. He came out to bat not long before the close of play on day two. We were already 2–0 up in the three-Test series and we'd just passed their first-innings score with only four wickets lost, and I was keen to get to stumps without losing another wicket. So before the start of the last over of the day, to be bowled by leg-spinner Danish Kaneria, I walked down to Gilly and said flatly, 'Let's just get through this over and then we can press on in the morning.'

He just nodded, patted the pitch down a little, walked back to the batsman's end and played the first four deliveries quietly. To the fifth ball, however, he suddenly jumped down the wicket as if we were in a desperate run-chase and lofted Kaneria for six. The crowd, of course, thought it was fantastic but I wondered what had happened to our mid-pitch conversation, so I strode down the wicket to find out. Before I could say anything, he looked at me with a very serious look on his face, as if he'd let me down big-time, shook his head and said, 'I know, I know, don't say a word.'

The mistake, I'm sure, was mine. We all knew Gilly was a totally instinctive batsman, and to restrict him with any sort of riding instructions, even for the last over of the day, was misguided. The way he batted, attack always being the best form of defence, meant that sometimes he got it wrong, but the often great always outweighed the occasional hiccup. On this occasion, he returned the next morning full of confidence and exuberance, and went on to reach his century in 109 balls as we batted Pakistan right out of the game.

Less than a week later I was batting with Gilly again, but in different circumstances, as he opened and I batted at three for an ICC World XI against an 'Asian XI' in a 50-over ODI at the

MCG that had been quickly organised to raise money for the many thousands of people who'd suffered so horribly when a tsunami struck various parts of Asia on Boxing Day.

Although our schedule was already full, we had no problems making ourselves available for such an important cause — one that was close to the cricket community because of the devastation in Sri Lanka, especially in and around Galle, where we had been playing only months earlier. Sanath Jayasuriya and Muttiah Muralitharan, who both flew to Melbourne for the occasion, had some harrowing personal stories to tell about the disaster, and how they and their families were affected. I also learned that the ground where I had captained Australia in a Test match for the first time had been inundated, which in itself was amazing. Sure, the ground was close to the sea, but the boundary was still a fair way from the high-tide mark and it would have taken an incredible surge of water for such damage to have been done.

What I most vividly recall from this 'Tsunami Match' is the spirit among the players as the cricket world came together in a way I'd never experienced before. I have no problem confessing I was a little starstruck, even if I was the World XI captain. Being at the other end while Brian Lara was crafting his innings or as Chris Cairns bludgeoned sixes was a cricket fan's dream. It's not often I enjoyed watching these guys make runs and I remember batting with Lara for a couple of reasons besides the simple pleasure of seeing from a different angle how he went about his craft ...

First, there was the 'shazam'. Something that had come into international cricket over the previous two or three years was the practice of two batsmen meeting mid-pitch after one had played a nice shot or maybe survived a difficult over and touching gloves. We Australians had seen our opponents doing this and thought it was a bit pretentious, so we sarcastically called it a shazam, which comes, I think, from some state-of-the-art wizardry in the *Captain Marvel* comics. But while we thought this 'fist-pumping' was soft, it had caught on among other teams, and now Lara was walking down the pitch after he stroked another four ... and he wanted to shazam me ... and I was pretending I hadn't seen him because I knew my Aussie team-mates in the World XI — Gilchrist, Hayden, Warne and McGrath — would be in to me if I gave way. I didn't want to be rude, because this was a day when everyone was getting on famously, so eventually I relented and later Haydos promised me he'd never let me forget it. He didn't either, at least not for a while.

When India's Anil Kumble came on to bowl his quick wrist spin I asked the great West Indian how he usually played him, and he replied that in the 50-over games he liked to hit most spinners through or over the gap between cover and mid-off. 'Just watch me,' he said, and then, whenever Kumble overpitched even a fraction, he was after him. It didn't matter if it was a leg-break, a top-spinner or a wrong'un, Brian was happy to trust his extraordinary hand–eye coordination and uncanny judgment of length, and hit to that area in the offside, initially just for ones and twos, and then for a couple of fours. I marvelled at his skill, and also I decided that whenever he came out to bat in the upcoming VB Series matches, I'd push mid-off wider and try to make him play our spinners a little differently to what he was doing here.

LOOKING BACK OVER THAT SUMMER, I am struck by the number of times I pushed hard for a player to be part of our first XI ... and the selectors decided otherwise. The pundits, meanwhile, were writing that I had more influence than was actually the case; try as I might to set them straight the myth that I always got the team I wanted would never be put to bed. In the lead-up to the Gabba Test, I strongly believed Simon Katich, who had batted so well in India, should stay in the side, but the selectors went for Darren Lehmann. Of course, I was a big fan of Boof's batting, so the commentators assumed I was the bloke who'd got him picked.

Seven weeks later, before the selectors picked our team for the VB Series finals, they told me they were thinking about leaving Matt Hayden out. Gilly had been given some time off during January, partly just to give him a break but also so he could fix up a couple of niggling injuries, and in his absence Michael Clarke had done an excellent job opening the batting. Now, with Gilly back, they wanted Pup to stay at the top of the order, but I argued that while Haydos had been down on form I thought I saw some good signs in his last game before the finals, in Perth, when he was leaving the ball well and defending with the full face of the bat. I know it might sound silly, especially in one-day cricket, to judge a guy's form by his defence, but I've always thought you can tell when a batsman is in good nick by the way the ball is coming off the bat, regardless of whether that shot is aggressive or cautious. If a batsman blocks the ball and it just trickles to the edge of the pitch, I quickly think he's lacking confidence, whereas if that same shot is timed sweetly to mid-off the likelihood is that the batsman is bang on form. Same if he's assertively letting some good balls go, rather than jabbing at them or playing and missing a lot — that means he's picking up the line and length quickly, a skill that often leads to a big score.

I couldn't rescue Haydos and a few days later I couldn't save Boof either, when the selectors picked a 14-man squad for the one-dayers in New Zealand and opted to take Michael Hussey instead. We all knew Boof had been struggling with a shoulder problem, but I think I sensed better than the selectors just how much that injury had been hampering him. I was confident he'd come good; instead, his demotion effectively ended his international career, which meant I lost an important ally. Boof is one of the smartest cricket thinkers I have ever met, a bloke with a winning gambler's instinct for when to hold fire and when to go all in.

We swept the ODIs in New Zealand five-zip, and during those games I saw that Brett Lee was regaining his very best form. It had been a frustrating summer for Bing, who couldn't crack the Test side with Pidge, Dizzy, Kasper and Warnie bowling so well, but now I was adamant it was time to give him a go. I've never been one to believe you shouldn't change a winning side if bringing someone new in makes you even better. Part of me was worried, too, that the same guys had been doing the bulk of our bowling since July, and I thought that bringing in a fresh face, especially one as dynamic and gifted as Bing, would benefit everyone. However, the men picking the side couldn't be swayed, and I was so disappointed that I insisted Allan Border, the selector on duty, personally tell Brett why he'd been left out.

This was about the only downer in an otherwise brilliant season. Whenever an omitted player started complaining that he'd copped a raw deal and asked why I hadn't gone in to bat for him, what was I supposed to do? Agree with him that in his case the selectors didn't know what they were doing or tell him something that I didn't believe. For the sake of solidarity, my answer was always the latter, but lying like that went against the way I'd been brought up and who I wanted to be. The ill-founded digs in the media suggesting I was always getting my own way when it came to selections only made this situation more exasperating.

Coaching

I've always been a keen student of technique and the skills of the game of cricket. Over the years, it has given me an advantage to perform at or close to my best for long periods of time and to do the best I could as a captain. In the later years of my playing career, it also led to me playing a far more active role as a leader, mentor or coach of the team-mates I played with — not just in the Australian teams, but also in my time back in domestic cricket for Tasmania, the Hobart Hurricanes, Mumbai Indians, Surrey and Antigua Hawksbills. I've developed an even greater passion for helping others be better. I get great satisfaction out of seeing others improve and I want to do more of that. I probably don't see myself having a full-time role as a national coach, but who knows what might happen in the future. I will stay very close to the game through a series of coaching business concepts that we have been developing over the past few years as well as my work in the media. I will now have more time to study other sports that cricket can learn from and will continue to look for that extra little advantage that can give a team a winning edge. I'm also interested in the business of cricket and how we can build a stronger future for our sport in Australia. I have made several comments within this book about the need for Australian cricket to fast-track its plans for state, grade and junior cricket to ensure our pathway is stronger than ever before. Coaching is a critical part of this, and we need to significantly up-skill our coaches and provide more support to the players in our game. I will be doing my bit to make sure this happens and that every Australian child, male or female, has the opportunity to experience what the game of cricket has given to me.

CHAPTER 34

BEHIND THE TIMES

Eden Park, Auckland, March 29, 2005

THE MOOD ON THE FIELD in Auckland during the final afternoon of the Test series in New Zealand was a little grumpy, as we tried to win the game before stumps on the fourth day by swinging at everything and they tried to stop us by slowing things down any way they could.

If we'd been in their boots, we would have tried to take advantage of the opposition's gung-ho approach, by trying to take a few wickets and sneak an unlikely win, but their ambition was to get to stumps without a result and then pray that rain would wash out the final day. Playing for a draw when there is nothing to be gained from such a result goes against my grain (the Kiwis needed a win to square the series), so I had no problem telling them I thought their attitude was pathetic, especially after one of their young punks tried to explain their tactics to me, as if I didn't know. In the end, the Eden Park floodlights were beaming brightly as Justin Langer and I got the runs by belting 59 runs off the last six-and-a-half overs, and I was still bristling at the post-game media conference when I described their approach as 'stupid'.

A nine-wicket win was a terrific way to finish our superb season. The on-field acrimony was quickly forgotten and in the rooms that night we had an extended celebration, with all of the New Zealand players joining us for beers, chat and pizzas. Before the party, I had a quick message for the boys: 'Well done, enjoy tonight and enjoy the break. But make sure you come back in the best physical condition of your life at the start of the Ashes tour, because I want to hit the ground running ...'

WE DIDN'T HIT the ground running. There was exactly two months between the last day of the New Zealand series and the start of our pre-Ashes tour camp in Brisbane. From there, after landing in London, we made a brief visit to Villers-Bretonneux in northern France, where we tried reasonably successfully to replicate our time at Gallipoli in 2001. So far, so good. Then, after two warm-up games, one 20 overs a side, the other 50 overs a side, which I described at the time as 'reasonably light-hearted' and 'comfortable', we were trashed by 100 runs by England in a T20 international at the Rose Bowl in Southampton. I know a few commentators working with the benefit of hindsight have argued that this one result somehow changed the psychological balance between the two teams, but I'm not sure that's right. We were embarrassed to lose so decisively, but we'd hardly attacked the game with the same intensity as the locals.

Worse for me was our next loss, two days later, in a one-dayer against Somerset. In my diary I didn't hold back, using adjectives like 'humiliating', 'poor', 'woeful' and 'sloppy' to describe our effort. Worse again was the loss to Bangladesh at Cardiff in our first game of the triangular ODI tournament that preceded a one-day series against England and the Ashes Tests. We were simply terrible, in part I'm sure because of the events on the morning of the game, when Andrew Symonds turned up at the ground still drunk after a night out that began with a couple of drinks for Shane Watson's 24th birthday. When I confronted him during our warm-up before the game, Symmo flippantly replied, 'Well, don't pick me then.'

At that moment I was so angry, he was heading home, never to be selected again.

John Buchanan told me that Symmo's response to him had been to argue, 'I've played like this before.'

The next half hour or so went like a blur. I needed to talk to Watto and Brad Haddin, who I knew had also gone for a drink, to clarify exactly what had happened. We had to hold a quick selection meeting to decide who was taking Symmo's place. I was struggling to control my anger, but at the same time my instinct was still to protect a mate. Too quickly, I found myself out in the middle for the toss, and when I was asked about our line-up I tried to cover things up, saying Symmo wasn't playing because he was carrying a cold. That only made things worse when the media got hold of what had actually happened, which of course didn't take too long. No one had made me lie. It was wrong to do so. I felt terribly let down that a bloke I considered a friend had put me in the position where I felt I had to. We batted okay to score 5–249 from our 50 overs, but Mohammad Ashraful made a terrific hundred and they beat Australia in an ODI for the first time with four balls to spare.

That night, the team was split, with John Buchanan wanting to come down hard not just on Symmo but also on the other guys, Watto, Hadds and Brett Lee, who'd had a drink the night before a game. Those three, however, were not in our starting line-up and they hadn't kicked on, so I argued they were entitled to some latitude, provided they made a commitment not to make the same mistake again.

Symmo, now sober, was also contrite, so I was also prepared to give him another chance, though I knew some people back home were after him and they were pretty serious people. A couple of individuals within our group felt that way too, which did little for team morale. From this point on, having handled the episode badly when it first happened, I think we got things pretty right and the affair didn't turn out as disastrously as it could have. I was up most of the night debating the point by phone with Cricket Australia CEO James Sutherland and chairman Bob Merriman. Their instinct was to kick Symmo out of the one-day team (he wasn't in our Test squad for this trip). Mine, shaped in part by my past mistakes, was less brutal and our manager and coach backed me. Eventually, we fined him 20 grand and suspended him for two games. After missing a defeat and a victory against England, he was our best player for the rest of the one-dayers on that tour, which culminated with two Australian victories, by seven wickets at Lord's and eight wickets at the Oval.

After those decisive wins, we were back on track. Or so we thought.

IT WAS JUST BEFORE those two games, while we were at Headingley losing an ODI to England, that the London bombings happened. Rianna was flying into Heathrow that day and I was waiting to bat when the vision of the aftermath of the attack began appearing on TV screens.

Naturally, my first thought was for my wife … *What's happening at the airport?* It seemed the transport system had been attacked, the Underground, the buses … *Will we still be travelling to London tonight?*

Then the full horror started to reveal itself — more than 50 people dead, hundreds more injured — and our problems didn't matter at all. It was, I imagine, in a way, something like September 11 in that no one knew if the blasts that had already happened were the end of it. Just minutes after the last ball of the one-dayer was bowled, we had a meeting in the dressing room, where the only topic on the agenda was what we should do next. Management had tentatively booked us into a hotel at Leicester, halfway to London. Rianna was still at the airport, waiting for our next move. We decided to adhere to our original schedule only after Cricket Australia, acting on advice from the Australian High Commission, told us sometime after 10pm that it was reasonably safe for us to do so. I know that was my preference, but only because that was where my wife was staying. We discovered, as we approached the city's outskirts, that there was no traffic on the road. We checked into our rooms about half an hour after midnight, acutely aware of the extra security outside the hotel and in the foyer.

I'm aware there has been a little criticism of our decision to continue the tour, on the basis that if the bombs had exploded in a different country we might have been on the first flight home. Maybe we would have been, but such a decision would never have been motivated by prejudice or preconceptions. London, as we all knew, had suffered terrorist attacks in the past. This time, as we'd done every other time and would continue to do, we simply took the advice of the experts. This policy served us well. It's what happened in 1996, when we didn't travel to Colombo during the World Cup, in 2002, when we played Tests against Pakistan in Colombo and Sharjah, and in 2003 and 2004, when we went to Zimbabwe. It's what happened here when we were advised that the chances of us being caught up in a further attack were remote.

Once we knew that we got on with it. Our practice session at Lord's 48 hours after the bombings was our best of the tour to date. A day after that, I made a hundred as we thrashed England by seven wickets in our best performance since arriving in the UK. It wasn't that we were callous or didn't care — 56 people had died, countless more were seriously injured, and I felt so desperately sad for everyone affected by the tragedy — but years of being under the watchful eye of tough men with machine guns had made us somewhat immune to the *fear* of terrorism. On most tours, every time I wanted to venture out I had to let security know where I was going and what I was doing. When I walked into the hotel foyer or out of the elevator on my floor, there were guards in army uniforms. They were on our bus and on the street. That was the world we lived in. I was used to it.

THE BUZZ LEADING INTO the Ashes Tests on this tour was a bit like 1997 and unlike 2001, in that the results of the limited-overs games that preceded the five-day games had given the locals a feeling they could win. We remained supremely confident. We knew they'd come hard at us from the jump, but if we withstood that early barrage we'd be fine. Or so we thought.

The opening exchanges were as intense as any I'd experienced during my Test career. Second ball of the series, Justin Langer was struck on the elbow by Steve Harmison and it took a while for the numbness to leave Lang's hands so he could grip his bat. Four overs later, Matt Hayden was sconed as he tried to pull a Harmison short one. Still in the first hour, another riser from Harmison bent my helmet grille and I felt blood seeping out from below my right eye and onto my shirt. Later, England's captain Michael Vaughan and I starting blueing about the English fieldsmen shying the ball in our general direction when we were batting.

First ball after tea, at the beginning of the seventh over of England's reply, Marcus Trescothick became Glenn McGrath's 500th Test wicket. By the close of play, Pidge had taken 5–21 from 13 overs, having produced one of the great spells in cricket history and with England 7–92 we had our noses back in front. Cricketers, spectators, viewers and commentators were all exhausted, after a day in which the adrenalin was pumping pretty much every over. The crazy part is, while we went on to win this Test by 239 runs, our play never attained the same fever pitch again during the series. The Poms were able to raise their game. As a team, Warnie apart, we stagnated, even went backwards.

The main reason for this, in my view, was that we lost just a little of our competitive edge — not in the games themselves, but at practice. It wasn't as if we suddenly stopped working, it might not even have been noticeable to outsiders, but it was enough. Buck and I left it to individuals to decide how much practice they needed and a few blokes subconsciously exploited that. In the Tests, our batsmen were facing four excellent quicks — Harmison, Andrew Flintoff, Matthew Hoggard and Simon Jones — who were charging in, getting good bounce and then reverse-swinging the old ball at nearly 150km/h. The deliveries we top-order batsmen were facing in the nets were often much less threatening, in part because our quicks decided they wanted to be physically and mentally sharp for the Tests, which meant they needed to conserve energy at other times. If that's what they needed, we were happy to comply, but it hurt us in more ways than it helped.

The depth of the home team's support staff gave them a significant advantage at training too. More than once, I looked over at our opponents in the nets and saw my old Mowbray mate Troy Cooley working with their bowlers and I couldn't help but be envious. He was their full-time bowling coach, one of a number of experts England had supporting their campaign. By comparison, we were seriously undermanned, with just Buck and assistant coach, Jamie Siddons, plus a physiotherapist, masseuse and fitness manager. International cricket was moving beyond that and suddenly, we were behind the times.

What happened in this series was one of the earliest signs that Australian cricket had become a little complacent. There was a school of thought that we would always set the pace and the others would have to do their best to catch up by copying us. Nobody seemed to notice that in some respects we had already been passed.

I've heard other issues raised in connection with this tour, but I'm not sure they were the negatives some people have made them out to be. Maybe this Ashes tour wasn't as enjoyable as earlier ones, because of the tight schedule and the constant demands on our time, but we'd been on tours in the past that hadn't been much fun off the field and we'd still played some exceptional cricket. In the years after this series, I've heard rumours there was dissension among our players, but that wasn't true (or if it was, it was trivial, because I never saw or heard anything to get worried about), or that a couple of quarrels among the players' partners upset us, but these sorts of things also happened during series when we dominated on the field. I've also heard suggestions that the team was hurt by the decision of Adam Gilchrist and Matt Hayden to spend time with their families in self-catered apartments they'd booked near the team hotels and not enough at the hotels themselves, but I never saw this as a problem. Similar situations occur during every Australian summer at-home game, when guys from the city where the Test or ODI is being played sleep in their own beds, and it has never caused concern.

No, our chief problems were we underrated the value and importance of meticulous preparation and practice. Up against a talented well-drilled adversary, spearheaded by a tremendous all-rounder, 'Freddie' Flintoff, at his absolute peak, we suddenly found ourselves in serious trouble.

CHAPTER 35

HELMET ON,
HELMET OFF

Edgbaston, August, 2005

IN THE DAYS LEADING up to the second Ashes Test of 2005, we kept being told that the pitch at Edgbaston was going to be a minefield. More than one member of the groundstaff revealed they'd had a tough job preparing the wicket, because of recent storms they likened to a hurricane, and that seemed to ring true when we saw the square, because it clearly had a lot of moisture in it. It had apparently been under covers for most of the previous four or five days. The general consensus among our leadership group was that we should bowl first. The only person who argued otherwise was Shane Warne, though he conceded the rest of us had a strong case. I even took time to talk to Darren Lehmann, who was in Birmingham working as a commentator, and he also thought bowling first was the way to go. My best guess was that the pitch would be difficult early, but because of all the water in it, most likely it would hold together okay and be easier to bat on later in the Test.

However, my leaning towards bowling first went beyond the look and feel of the wicket. One of Steve Waugh's philosophies as captain, that I'd usually believed in, was that if you had an opponent on the back foot, keep them there. As I went to bed the night before the Test I kept thinking about how our bowlers had dominated the England batsmen at Lord's, especially Glenn McGrath and Brett Lee in the first innings, McGrath and Warne in the second. It made sense to get those same batsmen back in as soon as possible, to test their mettle. If they failed, we'd break their spirit.

Nothing happened on the morning of the game to change my thinking, not even McGrath treading on a cricket ball about an hour before the game, which ruled him out of the Test. I didn't see it happen. I was with Adam Gilchrist looking at the pitch when Gilly suddenly quipped, 'McGrath's down.' Our initial thought was it was a ruse of some kind, reflecting Pidge's reputation as a joker, but quickly we realised he'd stuffed up his ankle and wouldn't be playing. Errol Alcott wondered if it was broken. Michael Kasprowicz, who'd played in 16 of my first 18 Tests as captain, was immediately called into our starting line-up. He was ready to play — we had always emphasised that everyone in the squad had to be ready to play in case something like this happened.

Many people — no, most people — believe I should have changed tack at this point, that I should have forgotten about sending England in. I've never been convinced about this, even though it's often brought up as the blackest moment of my time as captain. To have changed my mind and batted first at this point would have surprised our batsmen and shown a lack of confidence in our new man. Kasper was a bloody good bowler and a great person to have in the team. I duly stuck to our original strategy, the wicket was placid and Andrew Strauss and Marcus Trescothick scored more than a hundred from the first 25 overs. We managed to have them all out by stumps, but only after they'd scored 407, the most runs conceded by Australia on the first day of a Test since 1938. We ended up losing the game by two runs.

England, especially Trescothick and then Andrew Flintoff and Kevin Pietersen later in the day, batted extremely well. As a group, their batsmen had clearly decided to be more aggressive than they'd been at Lord's and we helped them by bowling too many loose deliveries. They hit something like 23 fours and two sixes before lunch, which is ridiculous, and when we finally did take a 'wicket' it was from a no-ball. That was exasperating, because we'd bowled too many no-balls in the first Test, identified that as a concern, but nothing had changed.

We had misread the conditions.

The pitch wasn't a minefield, so we shouldn't have expected them to be five or six down after the opening session, but they shouldn't have been 1–132 either. The fault, I will always maintain, was not so much with bowling first but with the way we bowled. Later, there were whispers that Warnie and I had got involved in a fist-fight or a shoving match in the dressing room because I refused to listen to him, but that simply didn't happen. In reply, five of our top seven got to 20, and no one scored a hundred, which meant we trailed by 99 on the first innings, and though we bowled much better the second time around, Flintoff inspired a 51-run last-wicket stand that meant we needed 281 to win.

WHEN I WALKED OUT to bat I thought we were going to win and I was confident I'd play a big part in the victory. Langer and Hayden had taken us to 47 in 12.2 overs, before Lang was bowled by Flintoff. Within five balls, one of them a no-ball, my dream of making a major contribution was over. I'd failed to survive what I now consider to be the best over I ever faced.

It was Flintoff's first over of the innings. A bit ridiculously, given that it was so early in the innings and he had the ball moving around so much, their left-arm spinner Ashley Giles had already sent down three overs from the other end. But there was logic in that, because they wanted to change the appearance and condition of the ball and having Giles bowling helped them do that. The new 'Dukes' balls we were using in this series were heavily coated in lacquer. Gradually, but not quite at this stage, we were learning that to be able to work on the ball, to get into the leather so one side was much more roughed up than the other, you had to get the lacquer off it first. With a spinner on, whenever the ball was pushed to a fieldsman in the ring, that man could pick it up in a way that scraped a little lacquer off the ball. Then the ball would be lobbed to the fieldsman whose job it was to keep one side of the ball shinier than the other. Throughout this series, England looked after the ball much better than we did, often making the ball 'reverse swing' in conditions where we couldn't get it to move off a dead straight line.

When Flintoff was brought on, he and the ball were ready to go. His first delivery to me was a rapid inswinger that bounced more than I expected. The next ball was shorter, quicker, and I jabbed it down into the gully. The third was another inswinger, but I was right forward and though it might have hit the stumps I was struck outside the line. Vaughan moved a man into short leg. The next ball pitched was just outside off-stump, veering further away, and a no-ball, so the over wasn't finished. The last was on the same line as the inswingers that had hit my pad earlier, but this swung the other way, at pace, and I did well to get my bat on it.

I walked off with a look on my face that was half bemused, half great admiration for what Flintoff had just done. Sometimes, you've just got to tip your cap and respect a great opponent. There's no doubt that Freddie rose to big occasions. In this series he bowled fast, he swung the new and old ball, and every one of our batsman came away acknowledging they had rarely faced better bowling. To make matters worse he chipped in with some aggressive batting at different times.

We were a sorry 8–175 by stumps and needed 282 to win, but the next day Warnie, Bing and Kasper almost saved the day, getting us within three runs of completing what would have been a remarkable comeback win. It was an extraordinary day of cricket. Nobody had given us a chance of getting close, but Shane and Brett hung on and got us to 220 before our big-hearted leg-spinner fell. We were 62 runs short when Kasper came out. And so began one of the most exciting hours of cricket you will ever witness. Our viewing area and England's were basically on top of each other. It was strange to be able to see the actions and reactions of both camps. God it was tense. On both sides. Eventually they strangled Kasper down the legside and achieved victory in what was one of the greatest Test matches and the closest results in Ashes history.

Through our long winning run, going back to the 1990s, we had been criticised from time to time for being good 'front runners', but not as good when our backs were against the wall. This was as tough a batting situation as we'd found ourselves in since Kolkata in 2001: having to bat out the final day on a wearing pitch with no hope of scoring the 423 runs we needed to win. At 5–182, 40 minutes before tea and 50 overs still to be bowled, we were up against it, with only Michael Clarke (who'd been struggling with a back problem) and the lower order to keep me company. The crowd, a full house despite it being the final day, was loud and parochial and never let up. Damien Martyn had copped an appalling lbw decision at a crucial time, and it really did look like the world was against us. But we managed to hang on. I'd dreamed of playing this sort of innings when I was a kid, although never imagining just how hard it would be.

I was proud of my clarity of thinking through this marathon: my defensive technique, shot selection and ability to let balls go stayed rock-solid as I sought to take as much of the bowling as possible. Sometimes, not playing shots is harder than going for them, because it goes against the grain, but on this occasion I handled that pressure really well. If they bowled a half-volley, I still drove it like I always did, but I was much more cautious than usual. Later, Lang would say it was the best innings I ever played. I'd always assumed that when you were 'in the zone' it meant you were scoring freely, but this day I proved to myself that you can be in that almost trance-like state while defending too. I felt sick when I got out, leaving us nine down with four overs to go, and couldn't watch the rest of the Test from the balcony, instead sitting in the dressing room, pads still on, occasionally looking at a television, but mostly just listening to the shouts and hushes of the crowd. Fortunately, Bing and Pidge batted out to time, meaning we stayed one-all with two to play.

TRENT BRIDGE WAS THE low point. Glenn McGrath couldn't play and we had to leave out Jason Gillespie too, because he just wasn't bowling well enough. I know Dizzy has said he was disappointed I didn't say more to him after that decision was confirmed, and he might have a point, but on the morning of a game there is a lot for a captain to worry about. Two days before the game we'd told Dizzy he was out and would be replaced by Shaun Tait, and he seemed pretty okay with our decision, saying flatly, 'Thought so.' On the morning of the Test, after Glenn was ruled out, he might have expected a late reprieve but the selectors opted to pick Kasper instead. Soon after, I did ask Dizzy whether Trevor Hohns had spoken to him, to make sure he knew he was out, and he said he had, so I moved on, not realising how much he was hurting.

Dizzy had been a champion bowler for the previous eight years, but he was totally out of form and had been since the start of the one-dayers on this trip. To my eye, he didn't appear to be snapping his wrist and following through like he used to, which meant he'd lost his zip and bounce, and it seemed he couldn't get it back. In his prime, the way he could swing a newish ball away from the right-handers at will and at high speed was unbelievable. More often than not, he pitched it *exactly* where he wanted. In Diz's heyday, you could have found a number of batsmen on the international circuit, especially Englishmen, who would have said he was even better than McGrath. I'm not sure about that, but just to be spoken about in the same sentence as Pidge is an enormous wrap. Diz really was that good, but not on this Ashes tour. If anything, we stuck with him for too long. Leaving players out was always hard.

Flintoff scored a hundred in England's first innings of this fourth Test. They batted until tea on day two and then we had to follow on, which was frankly quite embarrassing. At least we started better in our second dig, but then came the infamous moment when I had my run-in with England's coach Duncan Fletcher.

Throughout the series, we believed the home team had been bending the rules by getting their bowlers off the field a few overs before they'd be called on to bowl. They must have been spending these minutes in the dressing room stretching, maybe getting a massage or filling themselves up with an energy drink, because when they came back to bowl they were flying from the first ball. There were no 'looseners'. At other times, the bowlers might come off after a spell, perhaps for an ice bath or a rub down. Compounding the deception, while a first-team player was off the ground, he was replaced by one of the best fieldsmen in the country. At the start of the Test, the player left out of the England XI was usually sent back to county cricket and the 12th man's job was given to a promising young player who was also a gun fieldsman. We had no problem with that, so long as he wasn't roaming the covers while a regular had his feet up in the dressing room. The England camp said their players were simply relieving themselves, but it was happening way too often to be just that.

We first alerted the match referee, Ranjan Madugalle from Sri Lanka, about this practice before the first Test, which upset Fletcher, who said we were questioning his sense of fair play. That was exactly what we were doing. Madugalle nodded his head and said he'd keep an eye on it, but I'm not sure he ever did. Before every Test, we asked him to stop them doing it, but they kept going. The irony was that when I was run out by a direct hit from Gary Pratt, a substitute at Trent Bridge, Pratt was actually on the field legitimately, because Simon Jones had twisted his ankle and was on his way to hospital for an X-ray but I didn't realise that at the time. In my mind, Pratt had been on the field way too often in the first innings and again now, and Jones wasn't the only English fieldsman who'd left the field of play during this innings. I'd been going really well, but now I was out for 48. We were 3–155, still trailing by 104.

To say I was stewing on the dismissal would be an understatement. I knew I was out but I had to wait on the ground until the video umpire confirmed the inevitable. While I was waiting, I told umpire Aleem Dar how pissed off I was. When I was finally allowed to walk off, the crowd was into me, which I expected. And then I saw Fletcher, up on the home team's viewing area, smiling at me. I've always been able to cop losing, but I struggle when the game is being played the wrong way. When Freddie Flintoff was too good for me at Edgbaston, I was almost proud to be involved, that he'd bowled his very best stuff at *me*. This time, to see Fletcher smugly grinning at me as if he was some sort of genius lit a fuse in me that I hardly had control over. I had plenty of respect for the England players who were beating us at the time, but none for him. I barked in his direction as I walked through the spectators. Part of me really wanted to storm into the England dressing room and settle it there and then. I think it was Lang who eventually calmed me down.

I was later fined three-quarters of my match fee for the way I'd carried on, and I deserved that. I issued a statement apologising for my behaviour. It was sincere and it was to the fans at the ground and watching on television, the people I'd offended. But I wasn't saying sorry to Fletcher. I never will.

This incident reinforced a perception some people had of me as an angry man, which I do regret. This was a consequence of the way I played the game. Helmet on; helmet off. Spectators and opponents saw me with my helmet or my 'game face' on, and from that formed their opinion of what I am like as a person. But that was actually what I'm like as a *cricketer*. The person off the field, not wearing a helmet, is a different man.

IN SO MANY WAYS, this was a tough tour. After the Manchester Test, I was told I'd been sent death threats via the Cricket Australia website. The extra security slowed me down for a day or two. But there were some happy times, too, such as when the accomplished

Aussie golfer Peter O'Malley visited us and presented me with a set of clubs and some caps and balls so I'd be well equipped whenever I had a chance to play. A highlight was a day at Gleneagles in Scotland, when I managed to shoot 76 off the stick despite dropping five shots in two holes. Less amusing was the day I put on one of the caps Peter had given me, to discover they had his nickname, 'POM', embroidered on the back.

At the Oval, Simon Katich was fielding at short leg when the batsman hit a fierce pull shot into his upper body. Kato, a tough man, was quickly on his feet, but then he shuffled over to me and said, 'Punter, I've got to go off. I think I've broken my ribs, I'm spewing blood.' We were all concerned as he spat out some red ink on the edge of the pitch, but within an over he was back, looking extremely sheepish. Even before Errol Alcott could take a look at him, Kato realised that all he'd done was bite his tongue as he took evasive action. Not even the English fast bowlers would have gone off for that.

Another memorable moment occurred when Rianna and I stepped out of our London hotel and ran straight into the actor Hugh Jackman, who was driving past at the time. Hugh was very excited that he had tickets for the Lord's Test; I was able to go even better and get him into our dressing room at stumps on day three. This created the amusing sight of the Hollywood celebrity being clearly nervous in the presence of Aussie cricketers, and our players being just as starstruck as they were introduced to the Hollywood celebrity. Hugh stayed for more than an hour. You'd be hard-pressed to find a more likeable, down-to-earth bloke.

However, the abiding positive memory for me from this tour is how Warnie kept going and going while everyone else was down in one way or another. More than any of us, he was the guy who was entitled to be off-key, given he had separated from his wife, Simone, just weeks before the tour started. Instead, he took 40 wickets in the five Tests and also had his best ever series with the bat. He almost took us to what would have been an extraordinary win at Trent Bridge, scoring 45 in our second innings and then taking four quick wickets as the home team scrambled to win a Test they'd dominated for three days.

I know Shane would have liked to be captain, but the off-field stuff prevented that. I know he didn't get on with John Buchanan. In England in 2005 his marriage break-up was making news. But never once did he not try his heart out when he was playing for Australia; when it was time to play, he was *always* up for it. In the days immediately after the terrorist attacks, near the end of the ODI series when the Test-only players joined us, I kept an eye on him, looking for signs that the pressure might affect his cricket. He wasn't very chirpy, but he wasn't miserable either. On the eve of the first Test, I said to him bluntly, 'Mate, are you right to go?'

'Don't worry about me,' he laughed. 'When it's time to play cricket, I'll play.'

For the next two months, with every ball Shane bowled, the crowd kept singing, 'Where's your missus gone? Where's your missus gone?' I don't think I could have handled it, but he almost seemed to revel in it, on the field anyway. I knew that if we were to win the final Test at the Oval, to square the series and retain the Ashes, he'd have to play a major role. Sure enough, he took another six wickets in their first innings, but then the weather intervened, taking time off us and meaning we went into the last day of the series needing to bowl England out in two sessions and then score the runs we'd then need in the final two hours of the day.

Even at this point, though the odds were clearly against us, I thought we'd win. Warnie and Pidge reduced them to 3–67, but we muffed two chances to dismiss Pietersen and the Ashes were gone. Even at 7–199 we might have been half a chance, but the late-order stand between Pietersen and Ashley Giles couldn't be broken and then we went off for bad light. That was the hardest part, not being able to finish the game. It didn't feel like we'd been beaten, rather that we'd almost surrendered. I know that wasn't the reality — they'd definitely earned their win — but it was how it felt at the time.

Our dressing room was quiet. Dead quiet. We were sitting there in a circle, not even packing our bags, just looking around thinking, *Where did those last four Test matches go?* There was little eye contact. We were in a place we weren't used to. It wasn't grief we suffered, that's too strong a word, but we were bitterly disappointed and emotionally hurt. I felt like I'd let my mates down, an awful feeling. The image of Warnie sitting shattered in a corner stays with me. He was the one guy in our line-up who'd been at his best. For most of the previous decade, whenever one or more of us had been down in form, others in the team always picked us up, got us through. That didn't happen this time, partly because we were up against an excellent team and also because on this occasion too many of us were below our best. Not even Shane Warne could save us.

Eventually, our media manager came up to me and said it was time for my post-game press conference. I sat down, baggy green still on my head, and waited for the first question. It didn't take long in coming, from a bloke who introduced himself as being from ABC Radio. I'd never seen him before.

'Ricky,' he began, 'would Australia have won the series with a more positive and aggressive captain?'

'You tell me, mate,' I snapped, my game face back on. 'You must be the expert.'

Partnership, pressure & patience

Partnership, pressure and patience were the three Ps that formed the basis of our approach under the coaching of John Buchanan. Buck brought a whole new dimension to what went on behind the scenes of our preparation for and review of each game we played for Australia. The three Ps were visually everywhere and we would talk about them a lot. Not all the guys were into this type of stuff but it certainly stuck with me right through to the end of my career. Whatever level of cricket you play, think about the three Ps and how they can improve your game.

PARTNERSHIP is about finding a way to complement the batsman at the other end or the bowler you are working in tandem with, even if it means changing your natural game and instincts.

PRESSURE is about executing the basics of the game at the highest possible level of skill and for the longest possible period of time.

PATIENCE is about taking your time and waiting for exactly the right delivery to play a shot or exactly the right time to attack and try to take a wicket.

In my final few months of first-class cricket playing for Surrey in England, I spent a lot of time with our batting group talking about my experiences of batting in all sorts of conditions and circumstances. The three Ps got a number of mentions as did my 'Swimming between the Flags' philosophy, detailed in Chapter 27. The English boys seemed to relate to the Bondi Beach analogy, as they became more patient in the way they batted as that season progressed. They also learned to overcome the challenges of reverse swing, spin bowling and other deliveries that earlier in the season had been causing them concern. Like most sports, enjoyment comes from improvement. Take the time to think about the three Ps and how you can use them to improve your game.

CHAPTER 36

RESURGENCE

August, 2005

ARE YOU THE RIGHT *man to be captain?* I asked myself on the plane home. The 'Sack Ponting' campaign surged while we were in the air, especially after Dennis Lillee argued in his newspaper column in the *West Australian* that Shane Warne should be the new Australian captain. I was duly interrogated by reporters at Sydney airport when we landed. 'Desperate times call for desperate measures,' Lillee had written, and while I didn't think things were quite that dire, the storm of commentary that followed the legendary fast bowler's analysis left me in no doubt that we needed to get back to our winning ways quickly if I wanted to keep my job. At the same time, Cricket Australia announced it was establishing a committee that included former captains Allan Border and Mark Taylor to work out what went wrong. They'd do much the same again five years later, that time getting Steve Waugh involved as well, after another Ashes defeat.

But I'd come to the conclusion that I still had what it took to be a good skipper. This wasn't arrogance on my part, nor did I have blind faith in my ability, but rather that while I'd made mistakes I still believed in my tactical acumen and I knew I had the backing of my team-mates. I knew losing the Ashes was a serious crime and I had to take a fair share of the blame, but I'd been Test skipper for 18 months, and in that time I'd won series against Sri Lanka home and away, New Zealand home and away and Pakistan at home. My ODI captaincy résumé featured a World Cup victory. Based on my overall record, I could still call myself a winner.

One of the things that I soon learned about being captain was that your job never seemed to stop. Press conferences after games were one thing you had to manage. If things weren't going well you had to take time before going in to cool down a bit and get yourself in the right mood. You couldn't take that level of competitiveness into a press room — you can see what happens when football coaches do and it's not pretty. Overseas tours, however, had an added degree of difficulty. While everyone else got on the plane home ready to unwind, at the back of my mind was what was waiting for me once I got there — what questions I would be asked and what was the best way to handle them. I had to make sure I slept well because the moment I got my bags I would be ushered through a side door at customs and straight in front of the cameras. Like everybody else, all I wanted to do was see my family and my couch, but they had to wait. Tie straight, eyes not too bleary, deep breath, here we go ... You are representing your country all over again and you know you can't put a word out of place. It's a balancing act. Journalists set slip cordons and bat-pads for any slip-up. You can't be too defensive or too aggressive. I learned quickly the best way was to give straight answers. The truth generally served you well and if it didn't there wasn't much you could do about it.

Winners have a beer, losers have meetings, inquiries, campaigns to sack the captain ...

Quickly, I decided everyone had to draw a line under the Ashes tour and start again, but before we could do that we needed to address some of the issues that held us back in England. This we did, behind closed doors.

Having wives, partners and kids travelling with us on tours had been, in my opinion, a great step forward, but now some people were arguing that a few players had spent too much time in England with their families and away from the team. Initially, I feared Cricket Australia might come down hard on the concept of families travelling with the squad, take us back rather than forward, but their eventual response was positive and touring for players with kids became easier post-2005 than it had been before.

Another item on the agenda was the matter of Andrew Symonds' penalty for his all-nighter that ruled him out of the ODI against Bangladesh at Cardiff. The reason we had to revisit this was because Cricket Australia wanted to know if Symmo was ineligible for the Allan Border Medal. Players who receive ICC-sanctioned punishments for on-field transgressions are automatically out of medal contention, in the same way footballers can't win AFL's Brownlow Medal or rugby league's Dally M player-of-the-year award if they are suspended during the season. However, Symmo's punishment had been imposed by us players, not the ICC, so technically he was still okay. We sensed the administrators weren't happy about that.

I'd say the team was split pretty much down the middle. Some guys were adamant that because Symmo had let us all down so badly, he shouldn't be eligible. Others argued that the matter had been dealt with in England; it was time to move on. I was somewhere in the middle, same as I'd been when it happened. 'Whatever you guys decide is all right by me,' Symmo said. We ruled him out, reluctantly.

One subject we didn't debate as a group but which a few of us senior players did discuss was the future of coach John Buchanan. Cricket Australia moved quickly after the Ashes tour to confirm Buck was staying, a move I agreed with, but I think it's fair to say there were a few players who would have been happy if he'd finished up.

He had not had a good tour, a result, I think, of a decision he made at the start of the trip to step back a little — one, to give new assistant coach Jamie Siddons an expanded role; and two, because he felt that we, a side made up mostly of experienced campaigners, could largely 'coach ourselves'. He had said a few times that one of his ambitions was to make himself 'redundant' (his word), because he would have educated us so thoroughly we'd be able to solve our own problems. To tell the truth, I thought this was silly, and it looked more and more ludicrous as we saw how well prepared England were, thanks in the main to the efforts of their much deeper backing band, while we were losing our way. Our bowlers were being no-balled way too often, but instead of actually working to fix the problem, Buck asked us if we weren't as mentally strong as we'd once been.

Our coach's challenge was to reinvent himself. That he went on to do so was, in my view, his greatest achievement as Australian coach.

He was helped in that Cricket Australia expanded our support staff, appointing a full-time bowling coach, employing a full-time statistician/analyst and placing greater value on the role of Mike Young, our American-born part-time fielding coach. This was important, because as much as we appreciated Buck's thoroughness and vision, our experience in England had confirmed that he did not possess the technical expertise to be able to tell different batsmen how to solve problems within the framework of their individual techniques. Buck knew what might work for one batsman might not be right for another, but identifying what needed to be fixed and how to fix it was not his forte. Similarly, he wasn't an expert on ironing chinks out of different bowling actions, a flaw that cost us dearly in England, when Jason Gillespie and Michael Kasprowicz lost form and we didn't have a specialist like Troy Cooley who could set them straight. But as the head figure of a highly qualified coaching crew, I expected Buck's man-management skills to come to the fore, and from October 2005 until the end of his time as coach following the 2007 World Cup this proved to be the case.

I had to make some changes to the way I went about things, too. As captain, I took on board some criticism in the papers from former Australian captain Ian Chappell, who wanted me to back my instincts more and consult with senior players less. Ian seemed to enjoy getting into me in the papers, and sometimes I thought he was being too critical, but in this instance his comments were constructive.

Another thing we changed was when it came to our practice I would demand from then on that our bowlers replicate match conditions when they bowled to me in the nets. Give them a bucket of new balls and if they want to bump me, they can bump me. As a group, our training became more structured and more competitive, something that was apparent from our very first net session of the new Australian season, which took place in early October as we began preparations for three ODIs against an ICC World XI.

Away from training, everything was much more precise. If a meeting was set for 10am, that's when it started and everyone was compelled to be there on time, not sort of on time. Same with warmups, there were no stragglers. The coaches mapped out our schedule and we all stuck to it. In short, we became more professional and immediately things picked up for us.

I was reminded of plenty during this time, and not just about the value of hard work and being organised. When Mum and Dad had told me when I was a kid that 'you only get out of life what you are willing to put in' they were on the money. I also learned that a leader must never assume that things are being done. It's all very well to say 'I want this, this and this', but a captain needs to go the extra mile and make sure 'this, this and this' are actually being accomplished, not just talked about. And if they haven't been accomplished, or if chains are being dragged, it's the captain's job to fire the rocket that makes things happen. I was now a more proactive captain, especially off the field, and I started seeing the profits of this change very quickly. The vibe around the team was much more positive and hungrier than it had often been in England, to the point that when Warnie rang me the night before the first oneday game at home to wish me good luck, I was able to confidently reply, 'Mate, these blokes won't touch us. They might be the best players in the world, but they won't get near us.'

Things really picked up for us that quickly. If losing the Ashes in 2005 was one of the low points of my cricket career, being in the middle of such a rapid and tenacious resurgence was one of the higher ones.

Concentration

The art of concentration in cricket is different from that needed in most sports. For me, it was all about short sharp periods of complete focus. Being able to switch on for two or three seconds then switch off again. As a batsman, I talked to myself twice during each delivery. 'Watch the ball' was the mantra that was with me whenever I batted. I needed just one thought in my head and it was all about looking for triggers in the bowler's run-up, delivery action and release to see the ball early and move into position with the minimum of movement. Once I had played the ball, I would switch off while the bowler returned to the top of his run-up. I'd look around the ground, intentionally trying to get distracted by something going on in the stadium — all aimed at switching my brain off. But then it would be time to return to total focus — watch the ball, watch the ball! I used a very similar process when in the field. The concept of switching on for each delivery and then switching off ensured that I was able to perform at my optimum. As a captain in the field, I endeavoured to think a couple of overs ahead of the game. This was about giving me breathing space and not being rushed into decisions. It also ensured my focus was firmly on each delivery being bowled — being in the zone as a fieldsman.

CHAPTER 37

TEST CENTURY

Australian summer, 2005–06

DAMIEN MARTYN HAS A WAY with words. Whenever I'd complain about the captain having more responsibilities, say I had to do a media conference while everyone else was heading to the golf course, Marto would immediately quip, 'That's why they pay you the big bucks, Punter.'

If our transport was substandard, he'd quickly ask, 'Where's our private jet? Would Manchester United travel like this?'

And if our celebrations after a win were ever a bit low-key, he'd remind us, 'We've got to enjoy this. You never know if it's going to be your last.'

That third example of Marto's philosophy on life as an international cricketer was shaped in part, I reckon, by his own experience, when he was picked for Australia in 1992–93 as a 21-year-old prodigy, but — after failing in Australia's second innings in the Test against South Africa 12 months later — he was dropped and didn't get picked in the Test XI again for more than six years.

When I think about the second chances I was given — most notably the Ashes tour in 1997 and the West Indies trip in 1999, when both times I could easily have been left at home — I couldn't have blamed him if he was envious. Nor did I condemn him for being dirty when he was made a scapegoat for the Ashes loss in 2005, when he was dropped from the Test team for the game against the World XI that opened the next Australian season. There is never a problem with changing a line-up if you can make it better, but making changes for the sake of it, or suggesting a veteran should be dropped when there is no one to replace him is just dumb. Wouldn't you know it, by the end of the 2005–06 Australian summer, with a tough Test series ahead of us in South Africa, Marto was brought back into our side.

Fortunately, he was never dropped from our ODI line-up, and in the lead-up to the games against the World team he made the point that we'd 'gone into our shells' a bit in England. There were times, he argued, that we let the raucous crowds get to us. Marto didn't want any false displays of bravado, but if something good happened, let's enjoy it, let's celebrate. I put this to the group and everyone took it on board. After I caught Daniel Vettori to win the first ODI of the season, I threw the ball miles into the air and we all came together in a genuine group embrace, and straight afterwards the chat in our room was lively and exuberant. No one wanted to get away. I vividly remember, after we swept the three-match series, Michael Clarke at the presentation being up the back of the stage and spraying us with champagne, and it felt and tasted brilliant. The camaraderie among us — call it mateship, if you like — was back.

This was the way I always wanted to play cricket, whether it be in Mowbray, Manchester, Melbourne, or anywhere.

THE WORLD XI TEST was a bit of a non-event. The game was played at the wrong time of the year — a month after the end of the English summer and right at the start of our season, when the weather was coolish and the Sydney wicket a few weeks from its prime — and while we were fired up, trying to kick-start our resurgence. The other team didn't seem to be as committed and some of the overseas stars partied harder than they played. After that, we dominated the West Indies in three straight Tests, a strong precursor for two three-game Test series against South Africa: at home in December–January; away in March–April.

Of all the things that happened in these early Tests, three things stay strong in my memory.

First, there was the imposing form of Matthew Hayden, who followed up the century he made in the final Ashes Test with another hundred against the World XI and two more against the West Indies. In doing so, he reaffirmed one of my favourite batting mantras: that scoring runs is a habit. Justin Langer was the first person to put this to me, when he explained that when he was struggling he'd go back to Shield cricket or club cricket or even the nets and attempt to play exactly the same way he did in a Test. The idea, he said, was to get in the groove, and then once he was back in form, even if it was against net or club bowlers, everything else would look after itself. During the 2005–06 Australian summer Haydos was living proof of how this works, often looking invincible as he averaged 73 with four hundreds in seven Tests.

Second, there was the way Brian Lara's final Test knock in Australia ended, when he was caught in stunning style by Haydos for 17. But as remarkable as that catch was, it was the way Shane Warne went about his business against the great batsman that stood out for me. In the first innings, Lara had made 226 as he cruised past Allan Border's then Test run-scoring record, so he was obviously in prime form, and from the moment he came out in this second dig Warnie went round the wicket, having asked for a field without a man at point or cover. There were bowlers' footmarks outside the left-hander's off-stump, and I assumed that's where Warnie was aiming, but Lara seemed to have the problem covered — straight away, he drove a leg-break through the yawning gap between backward point and extra cover for four and then three; otherwise, he just kept his bat behind his front pad or comfortably pushed the ball away. To me, fielding in close on the offside, the strategy wasn't working, so I went up to Shane and said, 'Warnie, are you sure we've got this right?'

'Yep, yep, it's right,' he replied, the animated tone in his voice revealing how much he was enjoying the tussle. 'Leave it, leave it, leave it.'

When he had the ball in his hand, bowling to a serious opponent, Warnie was the most competitive sportsperson I ever met. In a Shield game in Melbourne, when I made fifty against him, he went up a few gears when he was bowling to me, which I took as an enormous compliment. And his ability to read a game was phenomenal. There were days when we'd be fielding next to each other, he at first slip, me at second, and nothing would be happening until suddenly he'd say, 'Be ready, a catch is coming.' And sure enough, maybe as soon as the next ball, a chance would fly our way.

First delivery of Warnie's next over, Lara drove into the gap to the right of mid-off for a couple of runs. The next ball was played defensively, the third was padded away. Then Warnie bowled exactly the big-spinning, well-flighted leg-break he wanted and Lara couldn't stop himself from going for a slashing cover drive. In close, I dived for cover, so I didn't see the ball fly off the outside edge, but Haydos, at slip, not only held his ground, he thrust out his left hand and grabbed the ball when it really should have flown away to fine third-man for four. This mix of shrewd thinking, superb bowling and brilliant fielding captured part of what made us such a successful team during this period.

The third strong memory of this time concerns how I worked with Brett Lee to change the way he went about his bowling, and in the process helped turn his career around. Bing didn't play a Test in the 18 months before the 2005 Ashes series, and though he bowled well in England, taking 20 wickets in the series, he struggled in the World XI game and then was far from his best in the first innings at the Gabba. When we'd batted on the first day of that game, the West Indies' Corey Collymore was impressive, bowling a good line and length, moving the ball off the seam and taking four top-order wickets. On day two, as Brett prepared to bowl the second over of their reply, we expected him to charge in and bowl quick, and I started to set a field to suit that type of attack. But his thoughts were going in a different direction.

'I'm going to try to bowl the way Collymore just bowled,' he told me.

'But Collymore bowls at 125k,' I responded dubiously. 'You bowl at 150.'

'No, not today, not on this pitch,' he said. 'I want two slips, a gully, point, cover, mid-off, no bat-pad and a man at square leg. That's how I want to start.'

'You can't do that,' I said. He'd never been a bowler who could land the ball on a 20-cent piece, but our fastest bowler was determined. His first two overs went for 16; his first six for 39. About 90 minutes later, during the third over of his second spell, after Brian Lara hit him through mid-wicket for two and then pulled him well in front of square for four, I went up to Bing to suggest he forget this medium-pace stuff and instead do what he does best, but before I could say anything, he muttered grimly. 'Take me off, I'm bowling shit. Take me off.'

No way, mate, you've got to work through this, I thought to myself. Third ball of his next over, still bowling slower than usual and with no addition to the score, he somehow trapped Lara lbw, but it was those exasperated comments at the end of his previous over that betrayed his mindset. It was his only wicket of the innings, and in the dressing room after stumps I approached him and said, 'We've got to do something. You're a better bowler than what you showed today.'

In England, I'd made the mistake of never sitting down with Jason Gillespie when he was struggling for form, because I figured Dizzy was experienced enough to work things out on his own. Here in Brisbane, Brett and I focused on his strengths as a bowler and the 'handbrakes' that were holding him back. His best assets were his rare pace and the fact that he could swing a new ball at high speed, but he admitted he was worried that if he tried to bowl fast he'd concede too many runs. He'd been criticised from time to time for being too expensive, but as I pointed out part of that was simply a by-product of being an express bowler. When a fast man is bowling, the slip cordon is less likely to stop an edge that bounces in front of them, while the man at fine leg has no time to get around the boundary to stop an inside edge or a fine leg-glance. With a medium-pacer, these shots are singles. With Bing, they were fours.

'You tell me where you want the fieldsmen so you can bowl to your strengths,' I said. 'I'll give you that field. But then I want you to bowl the way we know you can.'

His problem was mainly a lack of confidence. In most circumstances Brett comes across as sure and certain, but like all of us he is not always as self-assured as he seems. As captain, I had to give him structure and he had to know we had faith in him, which of course was not as simple as me or any of the guys in the squad offering him a few well-meaning comments. We, his team-mates, had to support him unconditionally — which we did, shouting encouragement, reminding the batsmen of the pressure they were under, staying active in the field, cutting off the singles, holding the catches when they came, celebrating his successes.

Brett's comments about the field he wanted were fascinating. He told me he didn't need three slips or a bat-pad; he'd rather a man at point and one forward of square leg, to keep the runs down. I'd probably been as guilty as anyone of wanting fieldsmen in catching positions, because that's what aggressive captains (which I always wanted to be) do, but I saw where Bing was coming from. In one-day cricket, where he was unquestionably one of the best of all time, he worked with only two slips and no one in close but he was still a dangerous attacking bowler who often took wickets in his opening spell. He really did want to go at top speed in Test matches and get the ball to swing, but to try to do that with confidence he needed a little protection. The man forward of square leg was important because it meant Bing could aim an outswinger at middle-and-off and if it didn't swing he wouldn't as often as not get hit to the boundary. It was a case of addition by subtraction — though his field looked a little negative, everything about his bowling and our approach was dynamic and assertive.

In the West Indies' second innings, Bing was fast and fantastic with his new 'defensive' field, taking 5–33 as we knocked them over for just 129 to complete a big win. He had two caught-behinds, one caught at first slip, one bowled, one lbw; every wicket an aggressive bowler defeating a batsman on the back foot. Afterwards, as I reflected on our conversation, I had this wonderful gut feeling that in seeing he was struggling and getting our response right, I'd done the sort of thing a good captain should do. For the next two-and-a-half years, Brett would be our No. 1 pace bowler in both forms of the game.

UNFORTUNATELY, THE COMMENTATORS WEREN'T always so upbeat about my leadership. The condemnation of my captaincy that followed our Ashes defeat, some of it justified, left a blemish I was never able to erase, which meant that too many times when we didn't win I was criticised, usually for a lack of imagination or for being too defensive. In fact, I heard some suggestions I was too conservative from my very first season in charge of the Test team, after I stacked the boundary when New Zealand's Jacob Oram was bashing us for a spectacular century at the Gabba. A year later, after we only drew the first Test against South Africa in Perth, I was alleged to have delayed our second-innings declaration too long, but I wanted to give Brad Hodge a chance to score a double hundred in just his second Test (he'd replaced Pup in the team for the third Test against the West Indies) and even then we still had 132 overs to bowl the tourists out, with Shane Warne in good form. Unfortunately for us, the wicket died, Jacques Rudolph defended superbly and they were only five down at the end. A few days later, during the second Test in Melbourne, I closed our second dig at about the same time in the game, just before tea on the fourth day, and this time Warnie quickly spun through their top-order and we won with four hours to spare.

Batting-wise, I was in really good form, having made a hundred in both innings at the Gabba, a half-century in both innings at the WACA and then another ton on Boxing Day. This meant that I went into the Sydney Test, my 100th Test match, in a very confident frame of mind, but at the same time I was as nervous as I'd been since my Test debut. As the day of the match drew closer I kept telling myself — same as before any other game — all I could do was prepare as thoroughly as I could, but I desperately wanted my performance to match the occasion.

Sure, in one sense, 100 Tests is just a landmark. However, when I thought about the Australian players who'd got there before me — Allan Border, David Boon, Steve Waugh, Ian Healy, Mark Taylor, Mark Waugh, Shane Warne and Glenn McGrath — and reflected on their greatness as men as well as cricketers I was very proud, and this was where my nervousness came from. Subconsciously, I was convinced I had to succeed in this match to prove I was worthy of joining this exclusive club. There'd never be another 100th Test for me, so I had this crazy now-or-never impulse driving me: I *had* to have a productive game.

Fortunately, beautifully, the Test evolved into a brilliant one for me, as I became the first man to score a century in each innings of his 100th Test and we won the match and the series. I guess I was entitled to dwell on the runs I'd scored, but as I revelled in this outcome, it was still the *victory* that mattered most to me. The twin hundreds were terrific and the way the SCG crowd cheered for me was special, but as Lang led us in another rousing rendition of 'Underneath the Southern Cross', the immense joy I felt about the way we'd prevailed was still what mattered most. Maybe I've written about 'team first' too much in this book, but it was always true. In the same way, a loss was never softened by any runs I might have scored.

One good thing about my 100th Test was that I finally put the family 'jinx' to bed. My parents and sister, Renee, flew up for the game, which confirmed that something important was happening. But Mum and Dad had done so reluctantly — Dad because he never liked leaving Tassie and Mum because she'd convinced herself that if she decided to watch me play in the flesh then something would go wrong. The final proof, she argued, had occurred earlier in this season, during the West Indies Test at Bellerive, when they did the three-hour drive from Launceston for the second day's play. I was 17 not out overnight, but because time had been lost on the first day, play started early and they were still in the queue, waiting to get in, when I was bowled by Fidel Edwards. This time, they arrived at the SCG with plenty of time to spare, saw South African captain Graeme Smith win the toss, and then I spilled an easy catch at second slip off the final ball of the third over. I made a point of not looking over to the Ladies Stand where I knew they were sitting. If you'd told me I was going to make a pair and we'd lose by an innings at that moment, I'd have believed you. Fruit does not fall far from the tree.

Fortunately, things got better. My first hundred was one of my better ones, made after we'd slumped to 3–54 in reply to 9–451 declared, but even though Gilly batted really well with the tail, hitting 86, we still trailed by 92 on the first innings. At this point in the game, the most likely result was a draw or a South African win, but then heavy rain cost us most of day four, and left Smith with a real dilemma. He needed to win the Test to square the series, but as the rain kept falling the only way he was going to get a result was to risk losing by setting us a realistic target. On such a flat wicket, there was no way he could bowl us out unless he gave himself a reasonable amount of time to do so *and* we were going for our shots. We knew he'd be bold, and sensed that — because the South Africans had been criticised in the past for being too conservative — he might even overdo it, as if to prove he could be as bold as the next guy.

At the start of that final day, South Africa were 3–94, a lead of 186. McGrath and Warne opened the bowling, and they set out to make it as hard as possible for the batsmen to score runs, which they did magnificently. Just as we'd hoped, Smith was forced into a corner (he ended up setting us 287 runs to win, in 76 overs), and from the moment the declaration came we were playing to win. Lang was out early, but Haydos and I put the pressure on, the South Africans wilted, and we ended up getting home with eight wickets and 15-and-a-half overs to spare. This was only the second time in Test history that a team had lost after declaring twice, so I guess in a sense they were unfortunate to lose, but the manner in which we went about a substantial run-chase was impressive. I was very excited after I hit the winning four, and part of that was about the fact that the entire last day had worked out precisely as we'd hoped. Once again, just as we'd been before the Ashes, we really felt we could win from anywhere.

The party that night was one of the bigger ones, up with the best we'd enjoyed since I'd become captain. There was less grog consumed than had been done in the old days, but the camaraderie was as strong as ever. I might not have made a hundred on my Test debut, but everything that happened in my 100th Test more than made up for that.

Celebrating success

Success comes from hard work. It comes from long hours of preparation, planning and execution. It also comes from working with other people to achieve team and individual goals. This is typical in all walks of business and life, not just international cricket teams. Celebrating success has been part of the Australian cricket team for a very long time. The culture has developed over many decades and has had a profound effect on the mateship and camaraderie of Australian cricket teams. When you consider that a Test match can last up to eight days with the preparation and planning as well as the game itself, the rewards of winning are really satisfying. When you think that only three or four players will star in a typical winning team, the importance of celebrating on and off the field is part of the core values of our teams. Not only does it build a greater bond between team-mates but it also heightens the motivation to win again — pushing a team to a new level of excellence as it prepares for the next challenge.

Over the years, I found that the time sitting quietly with team-mates after winning a game was where I really learned the most about them. Some of my fondest career memories are from a winning dressing room, recounting the success we achieved together and sharing that experience with family and team-mates.

CHAPTER 38

NO FEAR

South Africa, March, 2006

FROM THE END of the Ashes tour in September 2005 to the start of our tour of South Africa in February 2006 developed into another golden run. We played seven Tests for six victories and a draw, won 13 of 17 one-day internationals and also claimed the first Twenty20 international staged in Australia, a game in Brisbane played three days after the Sydney Test. A big crowd and huge television ratings for the T20 game had some people suggesting this might be the future of cricket, but I wasn't so certain. It was good fun, sure, but deep down we all knew the result wasn't important. It was more exhibition than an international cricket match. If the TV audience left us then the show wouldn't go on, certainly not in prime time.

In South Africa, we started with another T20 game, which we lost by two runs, then a five-match ODI series, which was tied after four games. Game five was eagerly awaited, and remains, at least in some South African eyes, the best ODI ever played. I produced one of my best one-day innings, smashing 164 from just 105 balls, a knock spiced with 13 fours and nine sixes. Yet just thinking about this game now gets me agitated, even angry, because we scored 4–434 in our 50 overs but didn't win. I know some Australians, including blokes in our team, have said how terrific an occasion it was, how because the game was so special losing didn't hurt quite so much. Speaking frankly, that's bullshit, at least that's how I saw it. The difference between losing that meaningless T20 game at the start of the tour and this defeat was massive.

I hated feeling so helpless during the South African run-chase. This time, I hated losing the game, and especially the series. The idea of being captain of the team that conceded a world-record total was embarrassing, so when I saw the people in our dressing room applauding the South Africans off the field, and in my eyes not looking too disappointed, I just lost it. Maybe these team-mates were being good losers, but in the blur of such a dismal defeat I didn't see it that way. In big-time sport, good losers don't participate for long, they watch. As soon as the door was shut, I sailed into the biggest spray I'd ever delivered as Australian captain, to the point that I might have been out of control for a moment. Do I regret that? Not at all. The people who should have regrets are those in our set-up who weren't ashamed by the way we played.

I told the team that not being able to defend such a score was ridiculous, unacceptable, hopeless. As captain, I roared, the buck stops with me, but there was no way any member of the squad was going to duck his individual responsibility for such a dreadful performance. At the presentation, it was announced that Herschelle Gibbs and I would share the man-of-the-match award, but I didn't want any part of it. I didn't want anything positive to come out of the defeat. Because it was the end of the series, the two teams got together for a post-game drink, but though I stayed around for a little while I didn't have a beer because it didn't seem right. Usually, after a hard-fought series, a beer doesn't taste too bad even when you lose, because it represents something of a prize for the effort you've put in, but I didn't feel like we'd fought hard or that we deserved any reward.

Is this being a bad loser? I think I would argue that it was the reaction of someone who didn't like bad losses.

I never took a defeat in a one-day game harder. We'd lost the unlosable match. If being so distraught and pissed off means I'm not a cricket romantic, then I plead guilty. I'm happy to accept that winning isn't the only thing, but I could never cop ineptitude, not from cricketers who could play. The good things we'd achieved when we'd batted were rendered worthless. As the evening went on, and into the next morning, whenever I sensed again that some members of our squad were not as disenchanted with our abysmal bowling and fielding performance as I was, my anger surged once more and I was best left alone.

I know scoring nearly 900 runs in a single 50-overs-a-side game is pretty freakish, something that can only happen if good batsmen have a big day, but it wasn't a great game. The contest was thrilling, dramatic and unique, and it featured some of the most fantastic hitting I have ever seen. The packed crowd got right into it, whipping itself into a frenzy, which no doubt helped get South Africa across the line. However, for a cricket match to be truly great it surely needs to have some decent bowling as well, and there was precious little of that. Bowlers would get hit for six and then bowl the very same ball, which went the very same way. At one point, their medium-pacer Roger Telemachus bowled four no-balls in a row. Our seamer Mick Lewis, who'd done some really good things for us during the previous December's Chappell–Hadlee Trophy games in New Zealand, conceded 0–113 from his 10 overs.

So why the runs fest? The wicket was fast and true, the outfield slick. We were playing at altitude, and you have to play in this environment to appreciate just how far the ball can fly. In both innings, the batsmen started hitting from ball one, this aggression paid off so we kept going, and the bowlers' response was feeble. Another key factor was the 'no fear' mentality that had become a feature of modern batting in the 21st century. Part of this came from the quality of the bats we were now using; part of it was the extra confidence that came from batting in helmets; most of it, I think, was that one-day cricket had taught the best batsmen that they could get away with attacking good length deliveries on flat decks so long as their eye and technique were in top working order. Twenty20 cricket would hasten this evolution still further in the years that immediately followed. Suddenly, bowlers were under enormous pressure, and many of them couldn't cope.

Of all the great batsmen, Sachin Tendulkar embodied this 'no fear' mindset better than anyone, though other stars from this time, such as Adam Gilchrist, Matt Hayden, India's Virender Sehwag and the West Indies' Chris Gayle, weren't far behind him. In this game, Graeme Smith and Herschelle Gibbs were 'no fear' personified, as, I guess, were Mike Hussey and I. Huss, who'd made his ODI debut for us in 2004 but had really come into his own after making his Test debut four months earlier, scored 81 from 51 balls, Smith 90 from 55, while Gibbs was phenomenal in clubbing 175 from just 111 deliveries, with 21 fours and seven sixes.

The previous time I'd batted in Johannesburg in an ODI was in the 2003 World Cup final. This was just more of the same in that everything came off, almost unbelievably. Through the middle overs, Huss did the same thing and we added 158 in 15.4 overs, with runs coming from just about every ball, fours or sixes a feature of every over. The six I deposited in the top deck of the grandstand was the biggest slog of my life.

A month earlier in Sydney, I'd played what I thought was my best ODI innings, a run-a-ball 124 in the second VB Series final against Sri Lanka, after we'd lost three wickets in the first three overs, but this one probably matched it. Back in the dressing room after I was dismissed in the 48th over, Gilly had a friendly chip at me because I'd got out just nine short of Mark Waugh's record for the highest one-day international score by an Australian in an ODI. To tell the truth, I didn't know what the record score was, and later, as I reflected on all the runs scored in this game, I figured it wouldn't have mattered much if I had gone past Junior, because someone was going to score 200 in an ODI before too much longer. As we talked, Andrew Symonds blasted 27 from 13 balls at the end of our innings, but it was as if no one noticed because, like a T20 game, fours and sixes had become so commonplace.

John Buchanan had told us we'd score 400 in an ODI one day, so he was feeling very satisfied because his prophecy had come true.

And then it all went wrong.

Their target was so unlikely they had to go for it from ball one, and when they got off to a flyer it created a momentum we couldn't stop. Gibbs batted better than I did, not least because whereas I just went for it, he had a target to chase and an absurd run-rate to preserve, which as hard as you try is impossible to totally ignore. We guarded the short boundary on the scoreboard side, we stressed the need for yorkers and changes of pace; for a short period, we decided to pitch our deliveries well outside the off-stump with four fielders on the offside boundary.

As the runs still flowed and as a home-town win started to look more likely than not a sense of stress came over me as captain that I'd never felt before. I had nowhere to turn, and having grown more and more exasperated with all the mistakes that we had committed, I dreaded the idea of making one myself. Near the end, their all-rounder Johan van der Wath, who'd gone 0–76 in his 10 overs but by this time had swatted 35 from 18 balls, skied a ball to me in the covers, but instead of just swallowing the catch as I normally would I suddenly felt weirdly anxious as I stood under it. I'd never realised how hard it must be for fieldsmen who have no confidence under the high ball. Somehow I held on. That dismissal meant they required 35 from 21 deliveries, with three wickets in hand, which should have been difficult for them, but the tide was impossible to stop and Mark Boucher got them home with a ball and a wicket to spare.

AFTERWARDS, THE RESULT was described in various quarters as South Africa's equivalent of England's Ashes victory. Now they were going to humiliate us in the Tests. Everywhere I went — to breakfast, to buy a paper, waiting for a lift, checking out of the hotel, walking to the bus, even as I was finding my seat on the plane for our flight to Cape Town, where the first Test was due to start just three days later — the locals wanted to tell me how exciting and inspiring it all was. I'd smiled weakly and agreed it was good for South African cricket, but I was still snarling inside. The best sight I had was that of our opponents on the plane with us, clearly the worse for wear after a big night celebrating their victory. After we landed, we got some messages suggesting a few of them had kicked on some more, so caught up were they in the excitement their win had created. Maybe their hangovers would be worse than ours ...

Not long after we checked into our hotel, the Test squad had its first meeting, and of course we started with some good-natured ribbing from the likes of Warne, Langer, Hayden, MacGill and Kasprowicz, who as 'Test only' players hadn't been part of the carnage. Then we got down to business, and straight away the coach began talking from scribbled notes he'd prepared about the 'plenty of good things' we could take out of the previous day's disaster, but I cut him off.

'Buck,' I said bluntly. 'I'm not hearing one more thing about the one-dayers. It's finished, over, done. We're into Test cricket now, we're starting afresh. Everyone's got to forget that game.'

But hard as I try, I'll never completely forget that game.

Match-ups

Cricket is becoming more about the individual match-ups — bowler v batsman — than ever before.

The information available to teams is so extensive that the best thinkers of the game can now go looking in the most intricate detail for the best possible advantage to get each batsman out. For as long as I can remember, bowlers have always had their 'bunnies'. Harbhajan Singh got me out more times than any other bowler. Warnie had several 'bunnies' but none more so than South Africa's Daryll Cullinan, while Andrew Flintoff always worried Gilly. In recent times, James Anderson has seemed to come into the attack as soon as Michael Clarke comes to the crease, as England believes he has the best chance of removing Pup.

The emergence of the T20 game has played a major role in the individual assessment of match-ups and strategic selection of teams. With the shorter format of the game, each and every delivery counts, and the need to take wickets and slow down over rates is paramount in team preparation. We certainly used this to our advantage at the Mumbai Indians, as we went on to become champions of the 2013 Indian Premier League. I wanted to know every bit of detail on every batsman in the IPL and the team had access to a databank that was even more complex than what I had used as captain of the Australian team. We were able to analyse scoring zones, strike rates, boundary percentages, wicket percentages to all types of bowlers, speeds, variations of deliveries and many other combinations of detail to give us the best chance of limiting a batsman's strike rate or indeed getting him out. It has also led to a more specific approach to team selection, especially around the variation of left- and right-handed batsmen and bowlers. I am sure that this will become part of the norm for international cricket as the databank of information becomes even broader and of greater value. Over by over, match-ups will become even more crucial to the outcome of any game of international cricket.

CHAPTER 39
MIND GAMES

South Africa, 2006

THE 'SILICONE TAPE' DRS (Decision Review System) controversy of
the 2013 Ashes series didn't seem to have much substance to it,
but it certainly had a familiar ring for me. Each year from 2003
to 2010, I published a cricket diary of the season just gone, the
first three ghosted by Brian Murgatroyd, the others by Geoff
Armstrong. It was surprising, going through those books for this
project, just how many issues were headline grabbers for a few
days, and then quickly faded into oblivion, sometimes forever,
occasionally to be beaten up again the following year. A good
example of the former was the debate that briefly took hold
concerning a 6mm-thick piece of carbon graphite that the people
at Kookaburra had stuck on the back of my bat. As a marketing
exercise it was brilliant because the bats sold in big numbers,
and the sticker was totally legal according to the ICC guidelines,
but that didn't stop a controversy emerging once someone falsely
suggested the carbon graphite made the bats better. Kookaburra
would have been well within their rights to force the issue, but
in the end they decided to remove the stickers and move on to
their next innovation, this one having served its purpose. When
I arrived in South Africa, I organised for the stickers to come off

and then used the same bats throughout the Test series. It didn't make a shred of difference.

An example of the latter kind of beat-up — the one that can recur from year to year — was the kerfuffle that emerged when Cricket Australia tried to give Adam Gilchrist a break when the Chappell–Hadlee Trophy games were on in New Zealand in December 2005. First, our manager Steve Bernard told Gilly he could stay with his family; then the powers-that-be changed their minds when a few newspaper columnists on both sides of the Tasman suggested we were cheapening the series by leaving one of our best players at home.

A few weeks later, I took a short break during the VB Series (two games: Adelaide and Perth) and the storm that decision started was unbelievable. You'd have thought the very future of cricket was at stake. A Sydney newspaper sent a photographer out to follow my every move for four days straight, the hope being he'd get a pic of me enjoying a cappuccino while the team was having a bad day in oppressive heat — the implication being that I didn't really care. The benefits of star players having a chance to recharge their batteries were ignored. One writer complained that Cricket Australia had 'completely lost the plot' and was 'blind to the desires of the Australian public', while even as good a judge as Steve Waugh insinuated that I'd shown South Africa and Sri Lanka a 'lack of respect'.

In this case, Steve was just plain wrong, though that didn't stop Cricket Australia ringing me to say that if we lost in Adelaide I'd have to get on the first plane to the WACA. It would be a few years before the value of giving players short breaks at the right times was finally fully appreciated, and no longer did we have to put up with the false allegation that we were somehow less committed than the stars from the 'good old days'.

Having said that, it is still one of those stories that seem to pop up every year as somebody huffs and puffs about somebody not playing a meaningless one-day game somewhere.

It's impossible to underrate how important it is to effectively manage players' workloads. Indeed, we were entering an era where the prevention of injuries was becoming a real science and while sometimes I was confused by some of the advice and instructions we received from the experts — especially when it concerned things like how many balls a bowler could send down at training, or what we could do to reduce the impact of jet lag — I always accepted their advice, on the basis that they know more than I do. The value of getting it right was rammed home to me early in the 2006 South African tour, when we travelled almost 60 kilometres, from Johannesburg to Pretoria, for a training run on the ground where we'd played the first ODI. After we arrived we were ordered to do an extended warm-up to make sure we carried no ill-effects from the bus trip. That was fine, but as we completed our stretches it started to rain, so we had to gather all our gear and then sit around in the dressing room until we were convinced the storm had set in. Only then did a few of us head for the indoor nets, where after standing around for about 10 minutes I found myself facing our rookie left-arm quick Mitchell Johnson, who had a brand-new white ball in his hand and was obviously very keen to impress his new captain. A quick in-dipper had me jumping and hunching at the same time, and as I landed I felt something 'go' in my stomach. If only I'd warmed up again; instead, my abdomen was on ice and I was in the back of a police van (the only transport immediately available), siren blaring for some reason, for a dash to hospital for an MRI scan. I was out for a week, which gave me plenty of time to ponder the reality that as I grew older the more I'd have to look after my body if I wanted to get as much out of the rest of my career as I desired.

OUR VICTORY IN THE OPENING Test at Cape Town remains one of my all-time favourites. After game five of the one-day series, the South Africans were supposed to have all the momentum. We were without Glenn McGrath, who had stayed home to be with his wife,

Jane, who had suffered a relapse in her brave fight against cancer. Pidge's replacement, Stuart Clark, was making his Test debut, he was bowling on the first day on a slow deck that wasn't supposed to suit us, and this was our first Test away from home since we'd lost the Ashes. Yet we won in three days, with Stuart (who is nicknamed Sarf, short for Sarfraz, because his bowling action reputedly resembled that of the former Pakistan quick Sarfraz Nawaz) taking 5–55 and 4–34.

I took a lot of pride from my first-innings 74. I was a bit lucky, but on a pitch like this one, where the ball was doing quite a bit and the bounce wasn't consistent, I needed that. What pleased me most was that after seeing how the ball seamed a lot on the opening day, I came up with a strategy to get as far forward as I could as often as possible, and it worked for me. Sure, I ended up wearing a few on the body, but I expected that; by getting so far forward I was less likely to be beaten by the sideways movement. After the game, our assistant coach, Dene Hills, highlighted the way I approached my batting, comparing this to how the home batsmen were either pinned to the crease against Sarf, Brett Lee and Michael Kasprowicz, or they stayed outside the line of many deliveries. Dene wasn't suggesting the South Africans lacked ticker, and neither would I (you can't play international cricket for any length of time unless you're 'cricket brave'), but what impressed him was that I devised a rational plan and then had the courage to implement it and stay with it.

Our second-innings dismissal of their most dangerous batsman, Jacques Kallis, was another victory for astute tactics. The origins of our plan this time went back to the recent Test in Sydney, my 100th Test, a game in which Kallis had scored 111 and 50 not out even though he was restricted a little by an elbow injury he'd been carrying for months. He looked impregnable when he defended, but when he hit through the offside it often seemed he was aiming a little too square, as if he was compensating slightly for the injury. We wondered if he might be vulnerable to a quick delivery pitched short of a length just outside the line of off-stump. If the bounce surprised him a fraction, we surmised, he might nick one to the keeper or the slip cordon. Kallis was not out going into the third day and after Bing, first up, bowled a brilliant over to him, Sarf nailed him third ball with one that pitched perfectly: Kallis aimed a back-foot drive forward of point, the ball climbed on him, took the outside edge and Gilly's one-glove catch was a ripper.

AT OTHER TIMES, WE were enjoying some spirited discussions with Graeme Smith, which I guess some critics mightn't have liked but I always saw these tete-a-tetes as acceptable and part of the game within the game. Both in Australia and now back in South Africa, Smith had made a number of rather grand pronouncements about what his team was going to do and especially about what we were doing wrong. We'd 'lost our aura' he commented at one point. Shane Warne was 'finding it hard to accept Ponting as captain' he said a little later. After we'd fought back from 2–0 down in the one-day series in South Africa to level things up, he accused us of 'choking', which was a bit weird, if only because of the timing. We knew that many of his big statements were prompted by a desire to take the pressure off his troops, and he was, no question, an excellent opening bat, but he wasn't scoring a lot of runs in the Tests and the self-inflicted pressure kept building.

Perhaps the last straw for him came on day four of the second Test at Durban, after we discovered that overnight the ground staff had repaired what had been a substantial crack on the line of a left-hander's off-stump at the end where their quick André Nel had bowled most of his overs. It was against the rules for these footmarks to be fixed in this way, and the umpires and match referee agreed with us that the surgery had to be undone. Smith argued the other way and was clearly upset when the curator came out at the first drinks break to chisel away the dirt that had been hammered into the damaged surface. Nor did he like how Matt Hayden and I kept tapping our bats on this region as we headed for centuries. I guess he figured we were doing this as a reminder that soon he'd be confronted by Shane Warne spinning his leg-breaks out of those footmarks, and he was exactly right. For 10 minutes or more, while he was fielding at mid-off and I was at the non-striker's end, we snapped at each other.

'Why won't you play the game fairly?' he kept asking.

'We get inside your head, don't we?' I kept replying.

The next day, Warnie had one of his best days as he spun us to victory to seal the series, a result achieved in fading light and with floodlights blazing. He started the destruction by getting Smith lbw.

Then it was back to Johannesburg for the final game of the series, but between these Tests, the members of both teams attended an enjoyable and rewarding (in many different ways) fundraiser for the Desmond Tutu Diversity Trust. At one point during Archbishop Tutu's speech, which at different times was sad, passionate, full of hope and humorous, I saw one of the South African players shedding a tear, and I, too, was moved by the stories of the battles against *apartheid* and for freedom and justice. Archbishop Tutu had something about him — a mix of extreme warmth and determination I'm not sure I'd ever seen in one person before.

Later in the night I bumped into Smith and we had a really good conversation, during which he admitted he'd found it exhausting coming up against us so often in such a short period of time. At the start of the series in Australia, he'd told everyone how he was going to take the game to us and play 'courageous cricket', but it hadn't worked out that way. Instead, we were able to keep asking him when he was going to back up his words by scoring a few runs.

'Six months of cricket against you blokes,' Smith muttered, 'it's just too hard.'

I liked him saying that, because it highlighted what a resilient, uncompromising side we'd become, how far we'd progressed since the low point of the Ashes loss, and how, fortunately, that damn one-dayer in Johannesburg hadn't hurt us.

NO ONE PERSONIFIED our renewed toughness better than Justin Langer. The previous November, Lang had missed the first two Tests against the West Indies because of a broken rib, an injury that gave Mike Hussey the chance to debut, a chance Huss took in prodigious fashion, scoring a century in his second Test and a truly memorable ton in his third, when he was 35 not out as No. 10 Stuart MacGill walked to the crease but then was involved in stands of 93 runs for the ninth wicket and 40 for the 10th. He finished 133 not out, and quickly everyone in and out of the team knew him as 'Mr Cricket'. Huss was as excited and nervous as any Test newcomer I've seen when he made his debut in Brisbane, but an even bigger standout for me was the way Lang handled his injury setback, first refusing to concede there was a problem: 'I'm not trying to be a hero, but it's only pain,' he'd said. 'I'm not going to miss a Test match.' And then, after he was ruled out, how he made sure he was the first person to talk to his replacement, saying simply, 'Huss, I'm out, you're in. Good luck, mate.'

The third Test was Lang's 100th Test match, and his family and a number of close friends flew in to Johannesburg for the occasion. We dismissed South Africa in their first innings just before lunch on day two, so out strode Lang with Haydos to launch our reply. First ball, though, their quickest bowler, Makhaya Ntini, dropped one short and Lang, maybe caught up in the emotion of the moment, lost sight of it and it crashed into the side of his helmet. He had to be helped from the field. In the Aussie dressing room, we sensed immediately he was in trouble, because Lang is one of those men who doesn't get knocked down easily. Later in the day the doctors told him his concussion was so severe he was out of the Test. He needed to forget about playing for at least three weeks.

The Test evolved into a thriller. At the start of the last day, we were 6–248 and needed another 44 runs to win with *three* wickets in hand. Lang had been told, and I and team management were aware, that if he was hit in the head again the blow might kill him. It was that serious. At the same time, we all knew that every competitive bone in his body was telling him that if circumstances meant he was required to bat to save or win the game, he must bat. He played his cricket that seriously. He slept with his baggy green. He couldn't let his mates down, but nor could he forget about his wife Sue and his four beautiful daughters. For a moment, I pondered what I might do in the same situation ... and then I quickly started thinking about something else. I just didn't know.

Before Damien Martyn and Brett Lee walked out to resume our innings, Lang asked me if he could talk to the team, and what followed was one of the most emotional couple of minutes I witnessed during my career. He explained what the doctors had said, talked about his family and how he'd spoken to his dad that morning. He was almost in tears.

'I'm sorry, boys,' he said softly, but with a grim determination in his voice. 'I'm pulling the pin. I just can't do it. The doctors say I can't get out there and bat today. I hope you don't look at me and think ... I've got my kids to think about ... my family to think about ...'

The previous afternoon, Marto had played superbly, finishing the day unbeaten on 93. We hoped that he and Bing could take us to a famous win, but just after he reached his hundred he was lbw to Shaun Pollock. Stuart Clark was the new batsman, and as he walked to the middle I looked around and saw Lang sitting there in his casual team gear, trying to be cheerful. Nearby was Michael Kasprowicz, pads on, bat leaning on his knee, maybe thinking back to Edgbaston in 2005, when he and Bing almost batted us to an amazing win. Back then, Kasper had been last out, unluckily caught behind off the glove, when we needed three to win, two to tie. I figured a part of him would desperately want to get out there, to finish the job, set the record straight. But the other part would be quite happy to stay where he was and let his two bowling mates earn the glory.

The target inched down to 25, and then Sarf hit Ntini for two boundaries. It's funny how these late-order run-chases go, how a couple of fours can change the mood, and then a wicket falls and the tension returns even thicker than before. Last ball of the over, Ntini dropped one a little short and Sarf's attempted pull shot went straight up in the air and he was gone.

Pollock's first three deliveries of a new over were scoreless, but then Kasper drove straight for two, there were three leg byes, and then Bing, often a good late-order hitter, whacked the last ball to the extra cover boundary. Eight to win. I turned around again, to see the look on Lang's face … but he was gone. Instinctively I knew where he'd be. He was up the back of the dressing room, now with his whites on, and his pads, his arm guard, his helmet. He was scuttling around a table, praying he wouldn't become dizzy, trying to convince himself he was all right.

'What are you doing, mate?' I asked.

Lang told me he'd decided that batting *was* worth the risk. I looked around for team manager, Steve Bernard, because I needed Steve to explain that Cricket Australia had a 'duty of care'; that they weren't going to let him bat. I expected Lang to say, 'You'd do the same if you were in my position,' so I needed management to take over if I wavered. But our manager was off on some errand and there was no one else to tell Lang he couldn't bat.

'I'm not letting you do it,' I told him. 'You can't do it.'

'No, mate,' he responded. 'We only need a few to win. I'll be right.'

'You can't do it,' I pleaded. 'If you are hit in the head, you could die.'

'Oh, Punt, what's the chance of me getting hit in the head again?'

At that moment, there was a big shout from the guys in our viewing area, and a muffled roar from the crowd. You get to know what different sounds mean at the cricket and this was definitely not a wicket. We ran to see for ourselves, to discover that Kasper had belted Ntini through the covers for four. I figured at this moment there was no point trying to reason with Lang. As he stood at the back of the viewing area, I started to ponder what I was going to do.

Trying to physically restrain him from going out there if a wicket fell would only cause a scene. He is stronger than me. And he was so set on batting I couldn't have stopped him.

Maybe he could go the non-striker's end; maybe I could ask them to allow him to use a runner.

It's permissible to use a runner if you're concussed, isn't it?

Pollock bowled to Bing, who pushed the delivery into the covers and called Kasper through for a run. Three to win, two to tie. Same as Edgbaston. That was when I decided what I was going to do …

If Lang gets on strike, then I'll call them in.

It was my call. I didn't talk to anyone about it. That was what I was going to do. I'd declare. There was a dot-ball through to the keeper, Kasper poached another quick single, there was a shy at the stumps, and finally Bing went crunch and upper-cut Pollock over cover for four. The Test and the series were a clean sweep.

For everyone else in our viewing area, there was a real sense of euphoria, but I felt a little distant. My overriding emotion was a gigantic surge of relief. Afterwards, Lang came over and said defiantly, 'If you had declared on me, our friendship would have been OVER!' I guess it would have been over then because I would have declared. A little later, Huss put his hand on my shoulder and said, 'Punter, I've never ever seen you so flustered as you were today.'

I looked up at Mr Cricket and sort of laughed. I wasn't dirty on Lang because — knowing how determined a bloke and team man he is — he was always going to try to bat. I should have realised that earlier. It was my job as skipper to make the call for him and I think in the end I would have got it right, for his sake, and for the sake of the team and cricket, too.

Though I'm still not sure what I would have done, if I'd been in his shoes.

Delegation

Some of my team-mates called me a 'control freak' and I know that wasn't always meant as a compliment! Sure, I had high expectations and was probably not a good delegator but I never saw myself as a control freak. I knew what I wanted and what I expected of those around me but often took it on myself to get things done.

For a lot of my captaincy, I was constantly asking Cricket Australia (CA) for more resources to enable us to have more responsibility around the group. I saw this as an important part of continually improving even when we were at our absolute peak as a team. But a high-level CA official once told me that funding for more people was never going to happen while we were winning. So I knew there was nothing I could do about that, other than go out and bat and play at my absolute best and hopefully change the course of a game more often than not. Later in my career, when I wasn't as dominant as a player, I probably did delegate a lot more. And if I look back on my captaincy as a whole, I don't doubt for one second that I could have done some things a bit differently to reduce the 'control freak' tag.

Interestingly, as our performances started to slide and the Argus report was commissioned, large-scale changes were made to broaden the roles and responsibilities around the team, to make more people accountable for the final result and to invest in resources to strengthen coaching at the top of our game. I had been asking for these changes for years but to no avail. My own interview with the committee that delivered the Argus report was over much quicker than I'd expected. I had been Australian captain for almost seven years when the report was commissioned, and my three predecessors were all part of the report committee. Surely my views deserved more than an hour of discussion. The Argus report was far-reaching and it certainly had an effect on the decision-making and delegation process around the Australian teams. I can honestly say I'm not sure if I would have handled this process well. The roles and responsibilities made complete sense to me but it's about putting the right people in the right jobs. If that's what I'd had around me, I'm sure I would have been a better delegator under the Argus reforms.

CHAPTER 40

GETTING DIZZY

Beerwah State Forest, August 23, 2006

OUR BUS PULLED UP at a warehouse and as soon as we got off we were told to hand over our phones and grab the backpack that had our assigned number on it. From this moment until the end, we'd be referred to by our numbers, not our names. Orders were barked in military fashion and a group of cricketers who were used to business-class plane travel and five-star accommodation started to understand what it was like to be a rookie in the army. We were living rough.

I'D BE KIDDING IF I told you that during the 2005–06 season we weren't thinking about the next series against England. As early as the Super Test against the World XI, just five weeks after the draw at the Oval, Justin Langer was reminding us before he sang the team song, 'Everything we are doing now is just a step closer to the Ashes.' However, we weren't the only ones thinking this way, with plenty of media people asking me questions about the old urn. In Cape Town, I did an interview with the BBC's *Test Match Special* team, where they were almost aghast when I told them Stuart Clark was bowling 'as well as Glenn McGrath'. Of course, Pidge was still our No. 1 quick, and we expected him back at the start of the following season, but Sarf's emergence was just one of a number of positive stories I could tell our English friends about.

Following the three Tests in South Africa, we went straight to Bangladesh for two Tests and three ODIs — a ridiculous ask given how long we'd been on the road. It was the tour that never ended and we seemed to have been playing back-to-back cricket since the T20 series that kicked off the Ashes the previous June.

Landing at Dhaka, I was exhausted and everyone else in our group looked to be the same. Physically, a few of the boys were struggling; mentally, I reckon all the guys who'd been in South Africa were shot. I argued at the time that there needed to be a minimum three-day gap between Test matches, an initiative that was eventually adopted, though I know some people in high places didn't think it was necessary. It is true that today's elite cricketers are very well paid and well looked after with excellent accommodation and business-class travel. This is all good and players are grateful for it, but it doesn't change the reality that top-class sportspeople need time to recover after a major performance; if they don't get that recovery time then standards suffer and careers are shortened. There is also the stress and angst that come with travelling, often over fair distances from game to game, plus media and sponsorship commitments. I'm not sure outsiders appreciate how taxing it can be giving press interviews or talking at functions, especially when there is a controversy buzzing about, when you're required to say something interesting without giving anything away, where one innocent but poorly chosen phrase can suddenly become the lead sports story on the evening news.

The irony was that in the years that followed, the administrators did improve their programs, but the quality of the Australian teams' performances declined. These two developments were strictly coincidental. But I do wonder if this says something about the Australian teams who won so often in the early years of the 21st century, when some of our itineraries were crazy. Other teams had it tough, too, but maybe as well as being pretty talented we were also more resilient than our opponents.

In the case of Bangladesh in 2006, it is also true that Cricket Australia offered the Australian Cricketers' Association a choice about how the tour should be programmed. We could have come home from South Africa, stayed in Australia for a few days, and then flown to Bangladesh to play the first Test within two or three days of landing. However, we didn't like the idea of all that flying time or an abbreviated Test preparation, so we okayed the lesser of two evils. For a team on tour, the big cities of India are all about swarms of cricket-mad people trying to get a glimpse — or a photo or an autograph — of one of the Australian cricketers. In Dhaka, the capital of Bangladesh, and our first stop, it was not quite like that: the swarms of people in this super densely populated country were simply going about their business. Security was tight, so all our spare time was spent in or around our hotel.

On the field, we had to produce an impressive comeback to win the first Test. At 6–93 in reply to 427, we were in serious trouble but Adam Gilchrist scored one of his better hundreds and then we knocked them over for 148, which meant we had to make 307 to win. This we did, for the loss of seven wickets, a close call that did us good. We'd had such a successful six months, it was handy for future reference to be reminded that a lot of hard work goes into winning a Test.

We had two days off, and then we were in Chittagong for the second Test, a game we went on to win by an innings, one in which Shane Warne took another five-for in Bangladesh's second innings, meaning in the space of nine months — from mid July to mid April — he captured 102 wickets in 17 Tests. Yet as well as he bowled in this game, it is a match best remembered for the miracle of Jason Gillespie, who'd been recalled for this tour when Michael Kasprowicz pulled out. Dizzy had never scored more than 58 in a first-class innings, and had made just two half-centuries in 70 Tests, but here he became the first nightwatchman to hit 200 in a Test match. He admitted later he'd never even made a hundred in the backyard before. But in a way it wasn't *totally* stunning that he made such a big score, because he had always been a good, sensible defensive batsman and at the end of the first Test of this series he'd stayed with me while we scored the last 30 runs of the game. So he was seeing the ball okay; it was one of those flat decks where once a batsman was in he was set, and because he'd been out of the team since the Ashes, Diz was determined to take every advantage of his opportunity.

He's such a popular bloke, we were all happy for him, though we knew that because he is in the McGrath class as a scoundrel, we'd be hearing about it for days. Any batsman who went near him after that would be in for it. 'So, mate,' he'd say, 'tell me how you deal with nerves when you're getting close to 200 ... oh, sorry, that's right, you've never been there.' One of his party pieces was to pinch another player's new equipment — bats, pads, anything — and sign his autograph in big black texta on the just-arrived gear. It could be that I'd be batting in a Test match and call for fresh gloves, and out they'd come with Dizzy's signature all over them. A young Shane Watson was extremely annoyed one day when he discovered some previously pristine gear from his bag had been 'ruined'. Diz himself was using an almost new bat when he batted at the end of the first Test on this tour, and later he was keen to show off the conspicuous red mark on the blade as he retold how he'd square-cut the winning runs. Of course, he'd used the same bat when he made his double century, but I'm not sure when he discovered that someone in our group had drawn a loud texta circle all the way around that nice red 'cherry'. It could have been at training, could have been out in the middle; either way, every time he acknowledged the applause for reaching a landmark and in all the photographs taken afterwards, there was that big black circle on his bat, almost as eye-catching as the satisfied smile on his face.

AFTER THREE ONE-DAYERS COMPLETED our Bangladesh tour, we finally headed home for what we thought was going to be the best part of four months off. Australia's next scheduled games would be some ODIs against India and the West Indies in Malaysia in

September, a precursor to the next staging of the ICC Champions Trophy, in India. Some guys were going to England to play county cricket, while I was going to spend most of my time with Rianna and see plenty of the golf course.

John Buchanan, however, had another idea. One day in Chittagong, when the Test and ODI squads were together, Buck gathered us in a little room at our hotel to discuss the 12 months ahead, the highlights of which would be the Ashes Tests from November 2006 to January 2007, and then the 2007 World Cup. On a sheet of butcher's paper, he had mapped out our schedule and we all quickly noted that there was plenty of down time between the end of April and early September. The only 'interruption' in this period was a get-together he had scheduled for late August, which would become known as the 'boot camp'. It would take place in the rough terrain immediately west of Queensland's Sunshine Coast, and we were told it would be physically and mentally demanding and that attendance was compulsory, but beyond that the details were sketchy. Because it was so far in the future, most of the guys quickly pushed it into the back of their minds, but I was intrigued. Buck explained to me later that the camp would be designed to see how we'd behave and function as individuals and a group when taken away from our regular lifestyles. I'd heard of footy clubs doing this sort of thing with the players going out on military-style exercises armed with little more than a blanket, backpack and scant supplies. Immediately, the concept appealed to me. The hard work wasn't a turn-off and it would be almost like reliving part of my childhood, camping under the stars with a few of my best mates. I could also see how it might teach us a few things about teamwork and each other.

In the end, the camp was both gruelling and rewarding, but over the years, as some of the guys who participated, me included, raved about what we went through, it has developed a mystique that makes it sound more valuable than it actually was. The fact the spinners, Shane Warne and Stuart MacGill, hated it and have made it clear they thought it was a waste of time has only added to its 'charm'.

For the guys who were playing only Test cricket, the camp was scheduled to take place three months before their next game of international cricket. For those signed with English counties, it involved a flight back to Australia, a few days 'roughing it', then a return trip to the UK. Buck didn't care about that. He wanted this to be the start of our preparation for what he called the 'Big Three': the ICC Champions Trophy (which Australia had never won), the Ashes and the World Cup. The boot-camp concept had been devised by an ex-SAS operative and former Queensland Police tactical operations instructor, the idea being to put us through a serious of back-breaking drills that would 'take us out of our comfort zone' and make us work together to survive. We'd be lugging jerry cans over mountains, pushing broken-down vans through thick scrub, moving camp at short notice in the middle of the night, living on rations of bread and cold soup and suffering sleep deprivation. Everything revolved around people working together.

Having come through one of the most successful seasons ever achieved by an Australian team, we were already a tight unit. My guess now is that if we'd done this boot camp when the team was struggling, it might have brought us closer together but it could have led to some splits in the unit. Instead of just Stuey MacGill and Warnie complaining it was unnecessary, a few other blokes might have been arguing that way too. Stuey hurt his knee when he tripped into a hole, and maybe we were lucky there weren't more injuries, given we were stumbling around the forest in the dark, with only the stars of the Southern Cross to guide us. We were elite cricketers, not mountain men.

One night, as we were trudging from nowhere to nowhere, one of the instructors ordered us to halt and then asked each of us to open up about ourselves. To begin the process, he told us about how torturous his marriage break-up had been, how he desperately missed his kids, and this prompted many of us to reveal a bit about ourselves. As a bonding exercise this was effective. At the same time, players weren't allowed to contact wives and kids during the camp, which was fine for the single blokes, maybe not so good for others. Thinking back now, I'm amazed no one rebelled against this embargo, but we had such a rock-solid 'one in, all in' ethos, no one was prepared to rock the boat too hard.

There were certainly some funny episodes, mostly involving members of our team's support staff who couldn't keep up, or guys who were essentially 'city slickers' and consequently had little or no experience of the bush. It is true that Warnie insisted on having his cigarettes with him on the basis he needed them for medicinal purposes, which made the rest of us chuckle. And there are moments from the camp I recall with great fondness, because they brought out the very best in us. Left-arm paceman Nathan Bracken is scared of heights, and as we trekked along a narrow path with a potentially dangerous plummet lurking on both sides, his fear meant that he had to get down on his knees and crawl through this section with Matt Hayden and me supporting him. He stuck with it and got it done.

Not long after, we had to abseil down a rock face and it was a long way down. When it was Jason Gillespie's turn, he couldn't physically make himself step off the edge of the cliff. The rest of us had completed the task; we were telling him it'd be okay and we eventually got him down. When someone was struggling it was never about us ridiculing him or laughing at him; rather, it was about getting in, getting dirty and doing all we could to help that person out. When Dizzy made it down and Bracks made it up I had nothing but admiration for the manner in which they found a way to get the job done.

The way we supported each other, even though we'd been taken miles out of our comfort zones, became the best single virtue of our camp. I came away more convinced than ever that being part of this particular group of Australian cricketers was like being in an extended family. I always enjoyed that.

CHAPTER 41

UGLY AUSTRALIANS?

Australian summer, 2006–07

TWELVE MONTHS EARLIER my captaincy had been under relentless scrutiny, but I went into the 2006–07 season with my position totally secure. Still, I knew I wasn't everyone's cup of tea. There were still suggestions about that I was too cautious, or too rigid in my thinking, a throwback mostly to that decision to bowl first at Edgbaston. Others reckoned I was too cranky for my own good, replaying video of incidents that had me giving a departing batsman a spray or arguing with the umpires if a bad decision went against us.

Well-meaning people at Cricket Australia asked me to tone it down, but I didn't want to change myself too much, to get too far away from who I am, for fear it would diminish me. I had faith in the cricketer I was. That said, most times I got myself in trouble or was criticised in the papers for my behaviour I regretted my actions afterwards. I knew it looked bad and I could only hope those offended could understand my frustration and maybe forgive me. I think most people did, though you can never please everyone. I never pretended I was perfect.

Back at Chittagong, in Jason Gillespie's Test, I'd lost 25 per cent of my match fee after I was deemed guilty of dissent. On the opening day, their No. 6 Aftab Ahmed tried to hit a full toss through mid-wicket but the ball went off the inside edge of his bat onto his boot, and then ballooned into the air for Adam Gilchrist to make the catch. It was out for sure, but the umpires decided to ask the TV umpire to check if the ball had brushed the pitch at the same time as it hit the batsman's boot. While we were waiting, the umpires informed me there was no doubt Aftab had hit the ball.

'Okay, no worries,' I said.

At the same time, someone ran out from our dressing room with some water and to say they'd seen the replay and the ball had definitely not come into contact with the ground.

In these situations, when it takes a while for the decision to come through, we always feared something strange was about to transpire. Then, finally, incredibly, the green (not out) light was flashing, rather than the red (out) one. This was the second incorrect call in less than a week by a video umpire, after Matt Hayden was inexplicably given out, run out, during the first Test, and quickly I was trying to find out what had happened.

'Did the third umpire know what he was supposed to look at?' I asked the on-field officials. 'Have you got your communication right?'

The only way the ruling could have gone the way it did was if the video umpire concluded there was doubt as to whether the batsman had hit the ball. I'm not sure if it was my approach that made them go back 'upstairs', but they did and soon the correct decision was made. The replay clearly showed the ball had not hit the pitch and Aftab had to go.

There was no indication after stumps that I was in trouble, but 24 hours later, apparently after a complaint from someone in the Bangladesh camp, I had to front the match referee and former New Zealand captain Jeff Crowe, who duly found me guilty. 'Although I have sympathy for Ricky I cannot accept his move towards the on-field umpires as they made a move towards resuming play,' Crowe explained in his statement. 'He did not ask for the third umpire to be consulted but when he made that move and spoke to the officials I believe his involvement played a part in prompting the referral. That is a breach of the ICC's Test-match playing conditions, which states that players may not appeal to the umpire to use the replay system.'

We never received word that the umpires had been fined or admonished for their performance. That's not the way it works.

Five months later, I was in strife again at the DLF Cup in Kuala Lumpur, again for questioning the umpire's decision. Shane Watson bowled a delivery that nicked the thigh of batsman Ramnaresh Sarwan of the West Indies, and then bounced through to our wicketkeeper Brad Haddin, who lobbed it to me as I came running in from my fielding position at mid-wicket. At the same time, the delivery was called a wide and Watto immediately threw his hands up, as if to say, 'That can't be right.' Then he turned to the umpire and added, 'Didn't you hear that?'

To which the umpire promptly replied, 'No, I didn't.'

My first instinct was to support my player, but I did it in an ordinary way, muttering, 'Well, if you can't hear things like that you shouldn't be out here.'

If I'd been fined for the cheap shot I would have copped it sweet. But instead I was reported for approaching the umpire when I shouldn't have, which I thought was unfair given that I'd actually been running in as the ball was bowled the way a fieldsman in the circle always should. It looked worse than what it was. And again, I struggled with a situation where an umpire made a clear error and I was the one tarnished as the bad guy. Because I had two charges within the space of a few months on my rap sheet, I was now tagged by some cynics as a 'serial' offender.

In our second game against India in this tournament, Sachin Tendulkar went for a pull shot, the ball brushed his shoulder and he was given out caught behind. We were actually in a huddle discussing the dismissal when the umpire, Mark Benson, asked me if he could have a quick chat. He'd thought about his decision, he told me, and realised he was wrong, and now he was going to call the batsman back. 'If you're sure Sachin wasn't out, we're okay with that,' I replied. He called the batsman back.

Up in the press box, however, our conversation was interpreted very differently by one Australian journalist, who filed a story in which he accused me of approaching Benson to demand an explanation, which was against the ICC rules. In his world, I was on the brink of a suspension. In fact, I was very impressed that Benson had the guts to do what he did. Surely, it is better to correct an obvious error than to hide behind the facade that the umpire's never wrong.

WE WENT ON TO beat India in that game on the back of a stirring Brett Lee five-for and then we beat the Windies comfortably in the final, with Bing taking another four wickets and Damien Martyn batting beautifully. Bing had reached the point where he was, in my opinion, clearly the best and most consistent one-day bowler in the game, while Marto had become something of a master in batting on Asian wickets. He seemed to be in tremendous form, a real boost for us with the Ashes Tests so close.

When I think back on those matches that led into the 2006–07 Australian summer — the DLF Cup and then the ICC Champions Trophy in India — it is how Marto was going that I remember most. Well, him and Glenn McGrath. Pidge began this trip with his place in the side under some threat, given that he was getting old by fast bowlers' standards and he'd missed the tour to South Africa and Bangladesh. Michael Kasprowicz and Stuart Clark had bowled so well in his place, but he responded beautifully, working himself back into top form. His effort against India in the ICC Champions Trophy game at Mohali, when he dismissed Tendulkar and conceded just 12 runs from his first six overs, was vintage McGrath, and three days later he was simply too good for New Zealand in the semi-final, taking 3–22 in a superb 10-over spell. A crucial piece of our Ashes and World Cup puzzles was falling into place.

Marto was my closest friend in the Australian team at this time. Many was the time on tour when we'd duck out for a coffee or three, to just chat and laugh about things that might have mattered to us, but probably didn't mean much to anyone else. I'd been best man at his wedding earlier that year and I felt I knew him better than just about anyone. From the first time I saw him play I knew he was unbelievably gifted, a batsman with an uncanny ability to time shots better than the rest of us. I was almost bedazzled by the way he'd just lean into a stroke and the ball would rocket away to the boundary. On this short tour, in our ICC Champions Trophy game against England when he scored 78 and was a key figure in our victory, he was 'dead batting' forward defensive shots that blasted the ball through the covers for four. In the dressing room, we were all looking at each other and thinking the same thing: *How does he do that?*

I was a batsman who, if I went forward, I went a fair way forward, to get as close to the pitch of the ball as I could. That's what I'd been taught and it made a lot of sense. Marto liked to bag me about how far forward I'd go, as if it was extravagant and unnecessary, but the differences in our methods were why he didn't hit the ball down the ground like I did, or like Matt Hayden did. He would always wait that extra split-second to hit the ball when it was under his eyes, and more often than not, he'd hit it squarer, between point and cover or forward of square leg, or deflect it down to third man or glance it to fine leg. Maybe only Brian Lara was more adept at pushing the ball into the gaps, to keep the scoreboard moving.

Marto played three major innings in the 2006 ICC Champions Trophy — first against England; an unbeaten 73 against India; and a composed 47 not out as we thrashed the West Indies in the final — which added to his imposing record on the subcontinent. Over the years, there were many times in these parts when we felt a long, long way from home, but I reckon the cricketing side of Marto enjoyed that, in part because the slower pitches suited his game, but mostly because he didn't feel like the eyes of all of Australia were looking at him, scrutinising his every shot, his every move, waiting for him to fail. Once, while we were in a café in India, I was complaining about how gruelling Test cricket can be on the subcontinent. 'Nah, Punter, you're wrong,' he'd responded. 'It's better here than it is in Australia. I'll play here any day of the week.'

We gained a lot of pride from winning that ICC Champions Trophy. The scheduling was hardly perfect for us, coming as it did at the start of our season, but we approached it like an important event (which, of course, it was) and afterwards there was plenty of pleasure coming from the simple fact that all the hard work we'd put in had been rewarded. And we had toiled hard, with Buck keen to implement some of the military discipline of the boot camp into our training sessions. Knocking over England decisively by six wickets, so close to the start of the Ashes series, was a genuine bonus, not least because we achieved minor victories over Kevin Pietersen (dismissed for one from six deliveries, one ball after Mitchell Johnson sat him on his behind with a fierce bouncer), Andrew Flintoff (out for four two balls after Shane Watson pinged him on his helmet) and Steve Harmison (who went for 1–45 from 4.1 overs).

Marto was brilliant against Harmison, cracking him for five fours in two overs, including three in a row at the beginning of the English pace spearhead's opening spell. Less palatable was the controversy that surrounded him at the end of the tournament, which occurred after we gathered on the stage for the customary post-final celebration photograph. Sharad Pawar, the BCCI president and an Indian government minister, was the man designated to hand me the trophy, but when he did so he refused to let go. Instead, he stuck with me as I tried to walk back to my team, I guess because he was keen to get his face in as many 'happy snaps' as possible. Marto put his hands up, to try to keep him out of it, or at least on the fringe, and then Mr Pawar stumbled as he finally left us to it. The result was an international incident and instead of us being lauded for our victory we were the 'ugly Australians' again.

At the time I didn't know Marto had done anything wrong and Marto didn't either, but after we landed in Sydney I rang Mr Pawar to say we were sorry and explain that we'd meant no offence. He was happy to accept our apology, but some of the Indian newspaper editors and a few of their former players weren't so keen, so the matter dragged on for a few days. One light moment was when a group of Indian 'fans' were photographed leading around a donkey that was painted green and yellow with 'Damien Martyn' written on the side.

There were times when these sorts of negative stories against the team got to me. This wasn't one of them; I really thought it was a beat-up, just a few negative individuals trying to take some gloss off our glory. But it did affect Marto, who arrived home to find Dennis Lillee and others having a crack at him. Just how much it affected him, we wouldn't discover for a few more weeks.

The Ashes

The Ashes is the pinnacle of Test cricket; it's the reason that every Australian and English boy wants to play cricket. The Ashes urn may be small in size but it's the biggest prize in cricket. Once you get a taste for it, you realise that it doesn't get any better or any bigger than playing Ashes cricket. It's where real legends are born and heroes are made. It's where reputations can be cemented or ruined forever. Andrew Flintoff was an above average all-rounder but he was a game breaker, a series winner in the Ashes where he saved his best for the battle against Australia.

Winning an Ashes series can rejuvenate a nation, like the English victory at home did in 2005. This had a huge impact on English cricket and English sport, and was the catalyst for a sustained period of improvement and ultimate success. This win also rejuvenated Test cricket and, while our defeat sent a huge ripple through Australian cricket, the administrators were privately smiling because they expected it would revitalise the Australian team's determination to bounce back in 2006–07 and to create the expectation for one of the greatest Ashes series.

These two series were remarkable in every way. The cricket in the 2005 series was as good as had ever been seen at that time. The whole of England got behind their team and I will never ever forget the scenes as we arrived at Old Trafford on the final day of the third Test with just as many people outside the ground as there were inside a full ground. The return series in 2006–07 had everything and was an Australian promoter's dream: sell-out crowds, record TV ratings and a win to the home team. For me, that series was our best ever, an unbelievable couple of months. Our team was so well prepared and that's the way we played. The hunger in the group was phenomenal and our performances just as dominant. The England team in that series was a very good team but they were blitzed by one of the greatest Test teams ever.

While that series is my fondest 'Ashes memory', there are many others that stand out as a player but also as a cricket fan. I got a real taste for the Ashes in 1989, when my Uncle Greg (Campbell) was selected to tour England. Seeing all his Australian team gear at his family home inspired me to one day get a chance to do what he was doing. And I will never forget Warnie's 1993 'ball of the century' bowling Mike Gatting at Headingley. I scored my first ever Test century at the same ground in an Ashes Test in 1997. My favourite win in an Ashes Test, and indeed any Test, was the second Test of the 2006–07 series in Adelaide. That win is said to be one of the greatest Test wins of all time.

Now I've retired, the Ashes will remain one of the great sporting events I'll look forward to. It has that special something that captures the full attention of Australia and England. Everything intensifies — the pressure, the expectation, the outside distractions and the performances. It's the ultimate prize in cricket.

CHAPTER 42

ASHES REGAINED

Woolloongabba, Brisbane, 11am, November 23, 2006

IT STARTED WITH ONE of the worst deliveries in Test-match history. It ended with some giants of our game bidding Test cricket goodbye. In between were some of the most satisfying days of our careers, as we redeemed our Ashes loss in England a year and a half before. And I say *redeemed* deliberately, because that's what it was about. For us, it was never a case of seeking vengeance. There wasn't one team meeting where I, as captain, implored the players to get even with England. We sought more than that. It was about us — as individuals and as a unit — improving ourselves to the point where we could perform at a level no other team in world cricket could match. I told everyone in our group that nothing less would do. In the end, I think, we made it.

As a person, I don't think I changed too much between those two Ashes series. I know that as we kept winning in 2006–07 the commentators liked to talk about my 'steely determination' as if it was something new, but I'd always been like that, even when I was a scrawny kid trying to impress the men. When I want something and it's achievable I'll do all I can to get it. I might have become a more proactive captain, but my predominant mantra was still to lead by example, something that remained true from my first day in charge to my last, and beyond.

It is true that from the end of the 2005 Ashes series to the last of the Ashes Tests 18 months later, I enjoyed one of the most prolific batting periods of my career, but I firmly believe that would have occurred whether we lost the Ashes in 2005 or retained them. I would have prepared the same way for each innings, and sought to make the most of each opportunity. Physically, I was at my peak, fitter and sharper than at any other point of my life, which — with a little more maturity and a bit more cricket know-how — gave me the chance to play some of the best innings of my life.

THE 2006–07 ASHES SERIES was one of the most anticipated cricket events of all time. The phenomenon of modern sports marketing and England's surprise win in 2005 made sure of that. The buzz around Brisbane in the days leading up to the first Test was extraordinary; it seemed like *everyone* in the Queensland capital had developed a keen interest in our sport. As captain, I felt one of my chief roles was to keep a lid on the excitement within our team, to make sure no one got carried away and tried to do extraordinary things, as though that was the least that was expected of them. At training I observed everyone closely, looking for any chinks in our preparation, but the coaches had every base covered and throughout our net sessions and centre-wicket practices, always with shiny red balls, we were cheerful, razor sharp and ultra competitive. About the only hiccup was that Allan Border Field, where we usually trained before a Gabba Test, was unavailable because the administrators had handed it over to corporate entertainment for the week. But ironically the alternative facilities made available to us at Brisbane Grammar School were magnificent, probably better than what we were used to. During one centre-wicket practice, when I faced Brett Lee, Stuart Clark and Mitchell Johnson off their full runs, I was repeatedly thinking: *This is the best preparation I can possibly have.* Bing would bump me, Mitch would bounce me, then Sarf would deliver one of his best leg-cutters, the one that pitched a whisker outside off-stump. Then it was back to Bing, who'd fire in a yorker, Mitch an inswinger, then Sarf would dig in his short one. Meanwhile, I'd taken on board the suggestion we'd been too chummy with the Poms during the previous series. 'This time,' I said to the boys during one of our early meetings before the start of the hostilities, 'we've got to try to impose ourselves on these guys every chance we get.'

The way we could do this was via our *presence* — on and off the field. I've always been a big believer in the power of positive body language and sure thinking, I'd been worried (though not intimidated) by it when I was a boy playing against the men and seen how the strong, confident players would take control of big footy matches. 'If you run into any of them in the hotel, at the ground, in mid-pitch, even walking down the street,' I said to our blokes about their blokes, 'I want you to look them in the eye and call them by their given name. No nicknames. I don't want Andrew Flintoff being called "Freddie" any more. I don't want Andrew Strauss being called "Straussy". Pietersen is "Kevin". Steve Harmison is not to be referred to as "Harmie", he's Stephen. I want us to respect them, but I want to make a statement at the same time.'

Call this what you like … trite, silly, I don't care. It worked. From that moment, whenever I heard one of our guys talking to an English cricketer, or even about an English cricketer in the privacy of our dressing room, it was just as I wanted. I know Pietersen grew to hate Warnie constantly greeting him as Kevin rather than 'KP'. Later, before the fifth Test in Sydney, I was interviewed by Simon Hughes, the former Middlesex bowler turned journalist and television analyst, and he mentioned that some of the English players had said we were harder now than what we'd been in 2005, and that they'd specifically complained about how we'd been calling them all by their first names. That was what I'd been after — for them to realise we were different this time.

Another important change was that Troy Cooley was now on *our* team. After Troy's Sheffield Shield career had been cut short by injury, he studied bowling mechanics, fitness and injury management before he joined the Australian Cricket Academy in 2000, working for Rod Marsh. Three years later, with Rod then involved with the English academy, Troy joined the England team set-up and earned a lot of credit for his new team's success, specifically for his work with Steve Harmison.

In mid-2006, Troy returned home, becoming our first full-time bowling coach, and for me two things about his methods quickly stood out: one, the way he worked one-on-one with the bowlers, letting them know how much he cared and showing an appreciation that no two bowling actions are identical, that what works for one bowler may not be the right thing for another; and two, how he wanted our bowlers to 'hunt as a pack'. For me, this second principle was an extension of something that John Buchanan and I always stressed: that cricket is all about partnerships, and that excellent bowling partnerships are as crucial in the quest for victory as big batting partnerships.

ON THE MORNING of the first Test, as latecomers searched for their seats and Justin Langer prepared to face the opening ball of the series, I picked up my helmet, gloves and a bottle of water (which I always have next to me when I'm waiting to bat) and took my seat in our viewing area. Harmison commenced his run to the wicket and after two or three strides, Troy, sitting nearby, said quietly, 'Watch this … this'll go straight to second slip.'

Which, sure enough, it did. The start of the series in England had been so frenetic, but this was almost slapstick. Harmison looked forlorn, the fieldsmen embarrassed, the spectators were now a strange mix of shocked, excited and bemused. Then our bowling coach spoke again: 'This one will be a massive over correction. It'll go miles down the legside.'

Our bowling coach knew his man, how much the tension of this massive occasion would affect him, and Harmison's second ball barely touched the pitch surface as it speared past the batsman's pads. For the next hour, Lang and Haydos were in command, scoring at a run-a-minute as we began to build an advantage we'd never surrender. We were 1–109 at lunch, 3–346 at stumps, and I went on the next day to 196, one of my most treasured centuries. Not that you would have known it when I was dismissed, however, because I stormed off the ground in an apparent huff without acknowledging the crowd. My celebration the previous day when I got to three figures was probably the most animated of my career — a release, I think, after all the stress and emotion that was a part of the extended build-up to the series — but when I got out I was filthy on myself, not because I just missed a double hundred, but that I'd let everyone down when I was going so well. Of course, I should have waved my bat to the fans who had been so good to me, but throughout I'd been keen to send messages to the Englishmen, by running off with my fellow batsman at the end of each session, that sort of thing. We had to be relentless, keep giving them nothing. Throwing my wicket away went against that, no matter how many runs I'd scored.

I declared not long after tea at 9–602, and then Glenn McGrath was superb as we earned a huge first-innings advantage of 445. Pidge's best moment might have been when he trapped Pietersen lbw when the batsman didn't offer a shot, a wicket achieved at the end of a 22-ball sequence in which the great bowler's line and length were impeccable. No one ever beat McGrath in a battle of patience. At the end of the innings, six wickets in his sack, he grabbed his back and limped off the field, a jibe back at the critics who'd said he was over the hill, that we as a team were too old. The desire was still there, which is what really matters.

The Pietersen dismissal was a beauty, but the memory of this innings I really treasure is how Bing knocked over Flintoff. We'd talked about how, when he first came to the wicket, the new England captain could be susceptible to one that moved away from the bat because he didn't move his feet much but still tried to hit the ball hard, even when playing defensively. The length wasn't so important; it was the line and away movement that was crucial. Bing, typical fast bowler, wanted to bounce him first ball, but the batsman in me sensed that the fast leg-cutter or outswinger was the delivery Flintoff least wanted. As captain, I rarely insisted on an experienced bowler doing it my way but this was one of those times, and Brett got it right straight away. The ball flicked the outside edge and as Gilly threw the ball in the air the Gabba crowd went ballistic. It really felt like the stands were shaking.

I could have enforced the follow-on, but we'd learned over the previous five years, ever since we lost at Kolkata in 2001, that doing this rarely worked to our advantage. I was usually keen to give the bowlers a break, and at the same time we were scoring so much more rapidly in Test cricket by this stage that you could bat again and still have plenty of overs to bowl the opposition out. It wasn't always like before I was born, not when teams batting first were taking more than two days to score 600. Our eventual 277-run victory was completed 90 minutes into the fifth day.

EXCEPT FOR THE FIRST four days of one famous game, the series was mostly one-sided. We came from nowhere to win in Adelaide, and then claimed big victories in Perth, Melbourne and Sydney to match the 1920–21 Australian side that swept a five-Test Ashes series. By the final Test the Poms were a mere shadow of the tough, competitive unit that had beaten us 18 months before, but their decline did nothing to abate our sense of achievement. There'd been stories about before the first Test that they were a fractured group, that not everyone in their team was thrilled with Flintoff as captain, that the loss through injury of Michael Vaughan (and the conjecture about whether Vaughan would return) was cruelling their morale. An on-field spat between Pietersen and Harmison during the final day of the second Test was further evidence they weren't happy.

The best gossip for me had been that a few of their players were questioning the worth of their coach, Duncan Fletcher. Over the previous two-and-a-half years, ever since the ICC Champions Trophy in 2004 (when England knocked us out in the semi-finals), I'd grown more and more disillusioned with some of the things

Fletcher said about us. I still hated the way he'd needled me at Trent Bridge in 2005 and it grated with us how he was given more credit than he deserved for England's win, when Vaughan and Flintoff, to name just two, had been much more influential, in terms of leadership and inspiration. Fletcher is one of those cricket people who isn't as clever as he thinks he is. I think this series proved it.

It was a series with so many Aussie highlights, and just one negative episode, when Damien Martyn suddenly retired in mysterious circumstances after the second Test. Here are a few of the moments from this series that I'll never forget …

We were 1–28 in reply to 6–551 declared going into the third day of the second Test, when I brought the team together and told them I honestly thought we could still win. Two days later, during our warm-up and then for half an hour in the rooms before play re-commenced, we went through all the things we had to do to make that win come true. England were 1–59 in the second innings, a lead of 97.

Warnie took the lead, telling us over and over that anything is possible. He knew, as we all knew, he was the man who'd win it for us, and clearly he was invigorated by the challenge. Afterwards, I was asked if this was the 'perfect stage' for him and I responded, 'Anytime there is a game on the line, it's perfect for Warnie.' He was inspirational on this famous day, never more so than when he knocked over Pietersen with an absolute ripper, one that landed just outside the line of the leg-stump and zipped across to clip the off peg as the batsman tried to work it away to the legside. That made them 4–73, Flintoff was caught Gilchrist bowled Lee just four runs later, and suddenly an Aussie win seemed the likely result. In the last 43 overs of England's second innings they scored just 60 runs, and lost nine wickets.

I reckon Shane took leg-spin bowling to another level this day. He finished with 4–49 from 32 overs, but such was the pressure he exerted he got a few wickets at the other end too. The manner in which he was able to vary his pace and flight, turn the ball appreciably but not give anything away, relentlessly getting into the batsmen's heads, was simply phenomenal. For us, it was such a thrill being out there, seeing the same players who'd beaten us in England now so stressed, watching them react so negatively to what the greatest bowler of my experience was doing to them.

We ended up needing 168 from 36 overs, which we achieved four-down with 19 balls to spare, and afterwards we all agreed it was the best comeback we'd ever been involved in. In the rooms, Lang jumped up and shouted, 'I've heard a bit of a rumour Australia is two up in the Ashes.' And then we were roaring. Most times, we'd chant 'Underneath the Southern Cross' twice, but here it was three times, and on each occasion, especially the third, it was bloody fantastic. Later, a few of the England players came into our room for a beer, which I didn't have a problem with, though a few of our blokes felt a bit uncomfortable, especially seeing as we'd agreed not to get too chummy with them during the series. But as it turned out, I found myself conversing with Harmison about life on the tour. Harmison had a bit of a reputation as a homebody. The way he was talking to me that evening, of how much he missed home — and if the cost of touring was worth it all — at the time it just seemed bizarre. It wasn't until the end of my career, when I had my own young family, that I understood this conversation better.

I learned that Marto had called it a career three days after the Adelaide Test. I was playing golf with Stuart Clark in Sydney and after nine holes decided to check my mobile. I saw I'd missed a call from Cricket Australia's Michael Brown and immediately turned to Sarf and said flatly, 'I reckon Marto's retired.'

I'd sensed something wasn't quite right, but Marto would have come and talked to me if there was a serious problem, or at least that's what I'd figured. Instead, he'd sent Cricket Australia's CEO James Sutherland an email in which he announced he was retiring from all forms of cricket. No formal or informal goodbye to his team-mates, no media conference or message to his captain, one of his best mates, to explain why. The suggestions were that he didn't want anyone to try to get him to reconsider, or that he decided that if he just disappeared the story would quickly slip away with him. One report claimed he'd quit because he was about to be dropped, but I knew that wasn't correct because the selectors had told me Marto was in our team for Perth.

About the only thing I knew for sure was that it wasn't for me to judge whether Marto's decision to retire was right or wrong. Later, he sent me a text in which he basically confirmed that he didn't contact me because he was afraid I'd talk him out of it. At the time, I was disappointed because we had lost an excellent cricketer, and confused and frustrated that very few people seemed to believe me when I said I didn't know what was going on. I had, after all, been best man at his wedding not long before.

I'll always think it was the grind that got to him. A lot goes in to always trying to be the best player you can be, supremely fit, ready for the next game and next tour, and clever enough to avoid the pitfalls of being a celebrity and mixing it with the media. Of course, it can also be very enjoyable, financially rewarding and there is a certain glory that only successful players in major sports can know, but if you feel like the whole world's against you it's hardly fun. With Pup making his century in Adelaide while Marto was dismissed for 11 and 5, his future was being debated and there was that controversy from his clash with Mr Pawar at the Champions Trophy presentation, when he initially didn't realise he'd done anything wrong but still he had copped a hammering in some quarters.

The great shame about the manner of his departure was that we never really had the chance to celebrate his career, to say thanks for everything he'd done.

Marto and I are close still but we've never talked about why he left like he did. I suppose I had another game to play and in a way what was done was done and there was nothing to be gained by going over old ground.

The third Test at the WACA was a strange game, caused partly by a pitch that did a bit for the first day and a half but then turned into a 'road'. We were bowled out for 244 and England replied with 215, with 40 of those runs coming in a last-wicket stand between Harmison and Monty Panesar, two of the worst batsmen in cricket history. It was frustrating at the time when we couldn't shift them, but at least we knew the wicket was mellowing.

On the third day, Huss scored 103 and Pup was well on the way to his second ton of the series when Adam Gilchrist strode out to join him with our total at 5–365. Early in his innings, Gilly was a bit quiet by his standards, taking 22 balls to score his first 25 runs, 32 to get to 40, and 40 to reach 50. After that, however, he went crazy, apparently because he thought I'd signalled I was thinking of declaring before stumps and consequently needed some quick runs. I have no idea where that came from — maybe, he misinterpreted something I did, like an auctioneer who thinks you've bid, but you haven't but, more likely, it was another case of his instincts taking over. His instincts said, 'Go for it!'

He went from 50 to 100 in just 17 balls, failing by a single delivery to match Viv Richards' record for the fastest hundred in Tests. The way Gilly crunched his sixes was unbelievable; he'd swing and I'd instinctively look to where I sensed the ball was coming to earth but it would invariably fly further than that. The image that remains with me is of Flintoff watching open-mouthed as one of those sixes sailed over his head and into the top deck of the grandstand. At one point, someone suggested we get a message out to the middle to tell Gilly he was closing in on Richards' record, but what was the point?

It wasn't like he could have gone any faster.

England were nine down at lunch on the last day at the WACA, which meant we were one wicket from regaining the Ashes. I found a quiet spot in the dressing room and thought for a minute about what was about to happen, how I'd handle it, how I wanted the team to handle it, how I wanted this triumph and this team to be remembered. I decided there were two things I wanted to tell them: that just because we'd swept the first three Tests, there was nothing cheap or easy about our success; and that in celebrating this victory we needed to be 'humble'. Part of this was about respect for our opponents, who had played so well in 2005; it was also for the game, which had taught us over the previous 18 months that you can never take it for granted. Further, our quest at the start of the summer was not to win just these three Tests, but to be as good as we could be. Regaining the Ashes at the earliest opportunity was one step in a longer journey. 'Enjoy the moment,' I said. 'Don't get carried away.'

Shane Warne's second ball after play resumed duly did the trick and immediately we were tight in one of those sincere on-field group embraces that only come after the really big wins. Later, 'Underneath the Southern Cross' was sung with much gusto out on the centre wicket, and a few hours after that, as the sun gradually slipped into the Indian Ocean, Warnie nudged me into a corner and said quietly, 'Punter, sit down here. There's something I want to talk to you about.'

'Mate, I don't want to hear this, do I?' I replied.

'Probably not,' he said. 'But this is it. I'm going to retire after Sydney.'

We chatted for a while, but I never asked him if he was certain this decision was the right one. It wasn't for me to try to talk him out of it, because — just like Marto — retirement is a big call that's never made lightly. I will always believe that Shane would have retired in 2005 if we'd retained the Ashes in England, so maybe his announcement shouldn't have surprised me, but everything was going so well.

That night, we found a nice pub with a beer garden out the back and just sat around a big long table, sharing chips, pizzas, beers and chat. It was bloody good. I'm not sure if Shane mentioned his retirement plans to anyone else, but I don't think he did, because it might have taken a little away from the night and he wouldn't have wanted that. At midnight, we toasted my 32nd birthday, and soon after that I went to bed feeling reasonably sober, extremely proud and very, very satisfied. But just a little melancholy, too, because the band was starting to break up and I didn't like the sound of that.

A few days later, during the Boxing Day Test, we were 5–84 versus England's 159 when Andrew Symonds joined Matt Hayden in the middle of the MCG. Symmo had gone okay as Marto's replacement in Perth, making 26 in our first innings and taking a couple of important wickets, but he was batting at six, so he needed a big score soon or the odds were he'd be an ODI specialist for the rest of his career, something neither he nor I wanted. The pressure, both in terms of the game situation and his cricketing future, was substantial, but it didn't get to him. These two proud Queenslanders put together the one big partnership of an otherwise low-scoring contest, in the process demonstrating as clearly as any one example from the series just how much better we were this time than we'd been in 2005.

In England, if two of our batsmen had been in this situation they might have added a few, maybe 30, 40 or 50, something like that, but just when it appeared we were getting on top, one of them would have been dismissed and our opponents would have regained the initiative. This time, Symmo and Haydos toughed it out against good bowling on a tricky deck, fought to earn a first-innings lead, and then, as the bowlers and fieldsmen compounded, they put the boot in, both going past 150. The mid-pitch celebration when Symmo reached his hundred with a six was stirring, as he leaped into his mate's arms, roaring his lungs out, bat held high. That the two of them got as much joy out of each other's success as with their own captured the genuine mateship that was a feature of our team, at a time when our opponents seemed divided. The Poms could shazam in mid-pitch after every single if they wanted; the bond we shared was much tighter than that.

The thing I loved most about Symmo's knock, beyond how it put us in a dominant position, was how he stuck to his batting plan, not always an easy thing to do. In the past, he'd go for a big shot when it wasn't on, get out, and people would snarl about his over-confidence and lack of cricket nous. But he was insecure, not cocky or daft; these ill-advised slogs were actually an attempt to break the shackles he'd built up in his mind. The great hundred he scored against Pakistan at the start of the 2003 World Cup put his mind at ease as far as ODI cricket was concerned, but this was the first time he asserted himself in a Test match. I really thought this would be the springboard that would launch a long and successful Test career, but unfortunately that didn't prove the case. However, it would be fun for a while, starting with the post-hundred media conference, when he was asked what he had been thinking about as he neared his century.

'When I was a handful away from it, I was thinking, should I do this in ones, or if he slips one up there, should I give it some Larry Dooley,' he answered. 'And I decided if he slips one up there, I'll give it some Larry Dooley.'

The Melbourne Cricket Ground was always my favourite venue for a Test match, and never more so than that season. I always loved the Boxing Day Test, Christmas with the team and family, the sense of history and expectation that something special is *bound* to happen, the massive crowd. It took a while to dawn on me how good this was. At first you take it for granted, but after you have played everywhere else it becomes obvious how much of an event it is. Lord's has the tradition, Indian grounds have a certain atmosphere but the Boxing Day Test is just so big. I shouldn't admit this, but sometimes when you're out there it's hard not to imagine what it would be like to play a big game of footy there, to throw yourself around physically in the contest and experience that excitement. The AFL Grand Final is one of the great sporting events. I reckon they do it better than cricket does. This time, with the Ashes decided and his retirement plan revealed to the public, it was mostly about Warnie, and of course he didn't let his fans down, claiming 5–39. The first of these, Andrew Strauss, was his 700th Test victim.

It took a while for Shane to get a bowl that day, because his captain kept him waiting until the 41st over, my logic being that it was a fast bowler's pitch and I should give the quicks every opportunity on it. With McGrath (who had also announced he was retiring, in his case after the World Cup), Lee and Clark all bowling well, I was also guided by the answer to a riddle I kept putting to myself, *Who would I least like to face?* At the same time, I knew Shane would be stewing, because he never agreed with me that the faster bowlers should get priority on a lively pitch.

'If it seams, it spins,' he argued.

One of the most amazing parts of this passage of play was how, as soon as Warnie started warming up, Strauss's body language changed. The Englishman was nearing his fifty and should have been confident, but instead there was this sudden negativity about him, as if his fate was predetermined. I knew this was something we'd miss when Shane retired, the dread that struck our opponents when they realised that before they could win the game they had to defeat or at least survive him.

I was fielding at mid-wicket when Strauss was bowled off the second ball of Shane's fourth over. The ball drifted slightly away from the left-hander, dipped and then zipped through the gap between bat and pad, and as he began his celebration, he looked over at me for a second, as if to say, *Told you!* Then he ran in a circle, a long extension of his follow-through, right arm pointing skywards, until Lang tackled him in a bear hug behind the umpire at the bowler's end. The noise was unbelievable.

England lost their last eight wickets for 58 runs, and yes, some of their batting was ordinary, but Warnie overwhelmed them with his skill, his smarts, his personality, his *presence*. Two days later, our innings victory complete, he was chaired off the MCG like an AFL champion after his 300th game, on the very broad shoulders of Haydos and Symmo. There was something very appropriate about all this, how the three of them, the heroes of the Test, left the ground together.

CHAPTER 43

MOST TOUGH GUYS CRY

Three farewells and an Ashes, 2006–07

'HEY PUNTER, YOU GOT a minute?' There was a point, late in December 2006, when I felt a chill shoot up my spine every time a senior player said something like that.

First Marto.

Then Warnie.

Then Pidge.

I knew Gilly had pondered giving it away. I would have been stunned if Haydos called it quits, especially after his big hundred in the Boxing Day Test. Lang? Well, he loved playing for Australia more than anyone, but I knew how the concussion in Johannesburg had worried him and how he'd been upset by the pre-Ashes speculation over his place in the side, when a few writers had pushed for NSW's Phil Jaques to be chosen instead.

As early as the previous May, Lang had whispered to me at Marto's wedding that he'd been thinking about retirement. 'Mate, don't you ever say that to me again,' I replied, trying to sound a mixture of surprised and angry. 'We've got to beat England. After that, we'll see what happens.'

I had faith in him and I knew the selectors did too. Lang duly scored 82 and 100 not out at the Gabba, which locked up his place for the series, but I guess the thoughts that his time might have come never truly left him.

After Shane and Glenn revealed their retirement plans in the lead-up to the fourth Test, I'd said to them and then the team, 'I'm not trying to be rude, but I'm not going to talk about retirements at our team meetings.' I wanted everyone to keep playing the way we'd been playing. Life can get complicated if you're trying to be good at it for too many different reasons, or trying to please too many people at the same time. I'll never forget how mediocre we were the summer Steve Waugh retired. Even when Lang told me after the Melbourne Test that he was going too, my attitude was the same.

That said, with all the talk of the 'end of an era', I couldn't ignore it completely. John Buchanan's time as coach was ending after the World Cup as well, and everyone wanted to send everyone off in style. Furthermore, for the first time in my life, I was feeling a little old — of the blokes in the team who were not departing, only Matthew Hayden had appeared in Test cricket before I did. The best I could do was underline how important it was that we keep concentrating on all the things that had served us so well during the first four Tests, and look for signs that anyone might be shifting gears. The desire for the sweep was strong. The loss in 2005 will always be there, but deep down I think we all felt if we could regain the Ashes 5–0 our reputations would be sort of restored.

The contrast between Justin's pre-game media conference and Glenn's was pretty stark. Lang knew he was making the right decision, because he'd thought about it so deeply and discussed it at length with his family, but that didn't mean he had to like it, a fact he emphasised to everyone in the room. Pidge, on the other hand, was very jovial. I was sitting next to him, and at one point I was asked what moments from his career were my favourites, which made me stop and think. Just as I was beginning to answer, he started whispering loudly in my ear, just loud enough for everyone to hear, 'Sixty-one … 61 …'

Here he was, the man who has taken more Test wickets than any other pace bowler, keener to talk about his one Test half-century with the bat than any of his match-winning bowling spells.

'That's one of my worst,' I muttered.

I took the room back to Lord's in 1997, when I was in the dressing room, one of the reserves, as he captured 8–38, and to the same venue in 2005, when he devastated England on the first tea-to-stumps session of the series, taking his 500th Test wicket in the process. Someone mentioned the famous diving catch he took in the deep at Adelaide Oval in 2002–03 to dismiss Michael Vaughan and you could sense the pride in the big bloke. But then I revealed he was actually 30 metres out of position at the time. I was fielding at bat-pad on the off-side and captain Steve Waugh was at short cover, and when the ball was hit we both reacted the same way: *Where is he?* Then Pidge emerged, running hard to his left, and he dived full-length, held the catch, and they were advertising memorabilia the next morning. 'If I had been standing where you and Steve wanted me,' Glenn responded, 'Vaughan wouldn't have gone for the shot in the first place.'

He has a deserved reputation as a nuisance and a funnyman in the dressing room, but when people ask me what comes to mind first in regards to his off-field persona, I always go for the way he has been able to separate his personal life and his sport. The tragic story of his wife Jane's battle with cancer is well known. But he was still able to lift himself whenever he was on the field. It was as if the cricket ground was his haven, his escape. The fact Pidge played so brilliantly and so consistently despite all that Jane went through is unbelievable. There were times on arduous tours when he might have been the only guy travelling without his family with him, but it didn't affect his performance or, outwardly at least, his demeanour.

Instead, he was one of the strongest spokes in our wheel. As a pest, he truly is second to none. He was deadly from 20 metres with a grape in his hand; he'd just flick the fruit and hit you behind the ear every time. Many was the time I'd be minding my own business, maybe reading the sports pages, when there'd be a tap on my right shoulder and instinctively I'd turn to my right. Pidge, meanwhile, was standing to my left with that grin. He'd get me all the time, get everyone all the time, and then he'd stroll away chuckling as if he'd just pulled off some masterful practical joke.

There was similarly nothing complicated about his bowling; he rarely swung the ball much and was not quite express pace, but he knew that if he put the batsmen under sustained pressure the dismissals would come. It helped that he was quick enough, could seam it and could get bounce out of most pitches, but he was essentially just a line-and-length bowler, which is not a sledge — batsmen hate bowlers who can keep finding the right line and length, and Pidge could do that whatever the conditions. He did it in the nets; when I was facing him I was never completely sure whether I should play back or forward, and it seemed to me that he bowled as many full tosses as I've taken Test wickets. Of course, some pitches demand a slightly different line and length than others, but he seemed to instinctively know where the batsman would least like it and if he did get it wrong, it was never for long. If you put all the good line-and-length bowlers from my experience in a line-up, Pidge is the one who batsmen would nervously point at as the greatest of them all. He gave his opponents nothing, putting pressure on them like a python cruelly squeezing the life out of its victims. Warnie did this too, which made the two of them easily the best quick–slow bowling tandem of modern times, most likely the best ever. Pidge was also brave, tough and dedicated, which meant that if he was out of the team because of injury or because he needed to be with Jane, he was able to come back as good as ever. He did this every time.

THE THREE OF THEM — Warne, Langer and McGrath — led us out on the opening day of the fifth Test, with Pidge, the NSW man on his home turf, going first of all. Fourteen years earlier, he'd bowled to me on this same ground during his Sheffield Shield debut, when I scored my maiden first-class century. Three days after this great trio strode proudly onto the SCG, we were on the brink of victory after a game in which our lower-order batted much better than theirs in the respective first innings, and then we knocked them over for just 147 when they batted a second time. We only needed 46 to win, and as the Poms gallantly formed a guard of honour for Lang to walk through on his way to the wicket, I turned to Pidge and asked him if he wanted to put the pads on. There was a big crowd outside and in my mind I could already here the roar if he was announced as the new No. 3.

He looked straight at me and deadpanned, 'Punter, I either bat first or last.'

Earlier, he'd been too good for Kevin Pietersen in the first over of the day, another dismissal that went exactly to plan. We figured Pietersen would be keen to get his first run of the morning as quickly as possible, so we left a couple of tempting gaps in the infield and asked Pidge to aim at a good length, just outside off-stump. Of course, he landed it right, the batsman more prodded than drove at it, and the snick flew through to the wicketkeeper. Then, with Warnie bowling at the other end one last time, Pidge snared the final out, a wicket with his last ball in Test cricket, the perfect farewell.

Haydos finished the game with a six and a single, and quickly we were racing out to the middle to celebrate our triumph. There was a lot of joy about, a bit of relief, and a few tears too, because our dreams had come so completely true. Gilly, sensible as ever, had brought his sunglasses out with him, I had to keep as far from TV cameras and press photographers as I could. Someone said to me later, 'Mowbray boys aren't supposed to cry, are they?'

'I think most tough guys cry, mate,' I replied.

I'd never cried on a cricket field before, not when we'd won or lost, or when I'd been hurt, dropped, dropped a catch, ripped off, scored a big hundred, played 100 times for my country, lost the Ashes, even when I hit a six to win a Test and a series. There was that one time in

Nagpur in 2004 when the emotion of the moment got to me, after the boys had just achieved one of our greatest wins, but I wasn't playing and we were in the dressing room, away from the public eye. This time in Sydney was unique, special, one of the best days of my life.

THE SERIES ENDED A little before one o'clock, but before I could really settle in and enjoy the party, I had to do a media conference where I shared the stage with the three retirees and Buck, too. The mood was jovial, a highlight being my response after I was asked what the coach had said to us before the start of play.

'Buck's never really got a lot to say,' I answered. 'He just mentioned three things to the group this morning: about "controlling the controllables", which is something he's said to us a thousand times, I think; "staying in the moment and playing the moment"; and ... um ... ah ... I mustn't have been listening too close to the third one.'

The journos all thought this was very funny, and I guess it was. 'Whatever Buck has to say is usually spot-on,' I continued. 'And those messages he gave us this morning, or at least two of them, were spot-on.'

Back in the dressing room, the two teams had come together, and I was also pleased to see that Marto had joined us, though I never got the chance to have a chat with him. It would be months before we had a decent chat, a little longer before our friendship got back to where it was. As we'd done a few times in the past after a big win and a couple of ales, Lang and I had a wrestle, no holds barred, and this was one of the better ones, and the last one. And quickly, maybe five hours later, someone shouted, 'It's time!' What this meant was that we had to get ourselves ready for stage two of the festivities: a cruise aboard James Packer's luxury yacht on Sydney Harbour. When this concept had first been put to us, I thought it was a terrific idea because it was so much more professional than the days when we'd just head out into town and the more reckless members of the team would end up at some Kings

Cross nightspot. The only worry was if the game ended late in the day, then with media commitments, the essential drink in the rooms with our opponents and a rush back to the hotel to get changed, it would have been very late when we finally sailed from the wharf. 'No worries,' James had said, 'the boat is there if you want it.' Then the game ended when it did, and everyone in our team quickly realised that a night on the harbour would be ideal.

It turned out to be better than that. There might have been 50 people on board, including everyone in our set-up, plus family and friends, and a highlight was when Lang decided to reveal to whom he was handing the honour of being our new songmaster. Adding a bit of gallows humour to the occasion, Stuart Clark, who earlier in the day had been named man of the match and had finished the series as leading wicket-taker, was not handling the gentle swell at all, and not too long into the voyage he came up to me and muttered, 'Can you tell Lang to get on with it. I don't know how long I'm going to last out here.' But he had to wait. First Lang got all the girls up to sing the anthem, which we all thought was fantastic, though I wondered what Rod Marsh and Ian Chappell might have made of it. Then Mike Hussey was given the big honour, and when he led us for the first time he did so with his predecessor up on the table with him, like Boonie and Heals at Adelaide in 1995–96, while everyone else — cricketers, support staff, wives and partners — eagerly joined in.

THE REST OF THE Australian summer was a bit of an anti-climax, as much as we didn't want to admit that. There was another Twenty20 international that attracted a huge crowd and mega TV ratings, we lost to England in the Commonwealth Bank Series, and the now annual controversy about me resting my body for a few games, this time when I missed the Chappell–Hadlee series in New Zealand, came around as expected. Gilly was given a break at the same time, which meant the team crossed the Tasman without its regular captain and vice-captain, but while this time the complaints were that we'd insulted the New Zealanders, the truth was that if people weren't going to accept the concept of giving players time off, they weren't going to be happy whenever a 'rotation' policy was implemented. For a couple of days, one paper had a photographer at one end of my street and another snapper at the other end, so if I decided to go out at any hour of the day they could get a shot of me, wherever I was going.

I often wondered if a few cricket writers needed a break in January, because this was frequently the month when some strange stories appeared, the ones based more on guesswork or gossip than what was happening in the middle. One of the weirder ones led to a box full of yo-yos being put next to my locker during the one-day series. Initially, I had no idea why. Then I read the enclosed note, which explained that the manufacturer of these yo-yos had read in the papers I was hopeless with the toy and he was giving me the chance to pick up my game. I think what bugged me most here was that I'm actually a superstar yo-yo whiz! I asked a few questions and discovered that there had been a story in one of the papers in which readers were told that there had been a yo-yo in my Christmas bon-bon and I couldn't get it to work.

I have no idea where that story came from, but my reputation had been severely and unfairly tarnished! All I could do was distribute some of the toys to the boys and keep the rest in the bottom of my kit, where they stayed for the rest of the summer and on to the World Cup in the West Indies.

At the same time, there was a real story to be scooped, but no one got hold of it. After Matthew Hayden completed that wonderful hundred in the Boxing Day Test and hit the winning runs in Sydney, he found runs strangely hard to come by in the one-dayers, to the point that he went into the game against New Zealand in Perth needing to make a score to stay in the side. I knew this for a fact because I was privy to the selectors' thinking, though I don't think Matt was aware just how thin his ice was. No one in the press box knew. Fortunately, he made 117, but it was one of the luckiest tons of his life, as he was dropped first ball and could have been out half a dozen times before he finally got going. In New Zealand, he broke the Australian record for the highest individual ODI score when he belted 181 in Hamilton, which confirmed his place in our World Cup squad. He really was just one spilled catch away from missing out.

By the time the Chappell–Hadlee series came around, my back was playing up and it was important I eased up for a few days before we left for the Caribbean. The day after the Commonwealth Bank Series ended, I received three cortisone injections to reduce the inflammation around the bone spurs on my vertebrae, after which the doctors assured me I'd be able to get through the next couple of months. Brett Lee wasn't so lucky, doing such serious damage to his ankle on the eve of the first game in New Zealand that he was ruled out of the World Cup, a major setback that came on top of Andrew Symonds ripping a bicep so severely he'd be missing the early Cup matches. The boys lost three straight to the Kiwis, meaning we'd lost five ODIs in a row, and the pundits were into Buck for the way he'd been working his team so hard at training between matches. His logic was that by working our butts off now we'd be able to lighten the load when the big games came around, a bit like an elite swimmer preparing before an Olympic final, but while I wasn't sure if this sort of 'tapering' worked for cricketers, I did like the concept of us being prepared to the minute.

But then I spoke to Buck after the Chappell–Hadlee games, and he seemed a little down, concerned that he'd gone too far, that we weren't temporarily slumping but burned out. Normally, it's the coach's job to gee up his players, but here I was telling Buck everything was going to be fine. Sure, losing Bing for the tournament and Symmo for a few games was a blow, and winning form is always good form, but we'd overcome far worse in 2003.

'If you coaches do your job when we get to the World Cup,' I said to him emphatically, 'we'll do ours.'

Great Australian players of Test cricket

I played Test cricket for Australia with 82 individual players. I thought it would be a fun exercise to pick two even teams from this group and this is what I came up with. It would be a fantastic game to watch!

In batting order:

1.	Mark Taylor	Justin Langer
2.	Michael Slater	Matthew Hayden
3.	Mike Hussey	David Boon
4.	Mark Waugh	Damien Martyn
5.	Michael Clarke	Steve Waugh
6.	Andrew Symonds	Darren Lehmann
7.	Adam Gilchrist	Ian Healy
8.	Brett Lee	Mitchell Johnson
9.	Peter Siddle	Jason Gillespie
10.	Stuart MacGill	Shane Warne
11.	Glenn McGrath	Craig McDermott

CHAPTER 44

WC2007

West Indies, March–April 2007

I PARTICIPATED IN FIVE World Cups, and if you asked people which was my best they'd probably nominate 2003. I guess that would be right, given we had a number of major setbacks to overcome, we were undefeated, it was my first Cup as captain and I batted so well in the final. But 2007 isn't far behind. This time, just about everything went to plan. John Buchanan had been preparing for this event for at least two-and-a-half years; back in October 2004, during our tour of India, I'd looked over Buck's shoulder at his computer and discovered he was working on a document relating to the next World Cup. At the start of the 2005 Ashes tour, he gave us a booklet titled 'Ashes 2005 … and Beyond' in which he said his vision was that we'd 'arrive at WC2007 the best skilled team the world has seen'. The intensive fitness work we all did in January and February of 2007 was just one small part of a strategy to have us primed for the latter stages of the tournament that mattered.

From the moment we regained the Ashes, Buck became close to obsessed with getting us as well prepared as possible for the Cup. Part of this, I guess, was just that he yearned to end his time as Australian coach in style; mostly it was because he always wanted us to be moving forward, that he wanted us to somehow outdo even our 2003 Cup victory and the Ashes clean sweep. From the moment we checked into our rooms at our first port-of-call, St Vincent, he and his staff made a point of getting to training at least half an hour before the players, so when we arrived at the ground everything was set up for us. Our bags were in a row, nets all ready to go, bowling machines in position and cranked up, fielding stations laid out. For us players, it was just a matter of putting our boots on, having a jog and a stretch, and we were into it. This attention to detail made us feel important and it left us with no excuses. If we weren't fully committed to our practice, it would have been an insult to all the work Buck, assistant coach Tim Nielsen and all his staff were putting in.

I also wanted the guys to be aware of a number of things away from training: eating and drinking smart, looking after niggling injuries, getting enough sleep, keeping negativity out of the group, being punctual. I'd developed a theory that you can tell if players are 'switched on' simply by seeing if they are on time for breakfast. If a player has a piece of toast in one hand and a coffee or juice in the other as he jumps on the bus heading for training he might think he's cool but I'll bet good money his mind is elsewhere.

From the jump, we were working our tails off, as training went off with military precision. Elsewhere, however, the Cup was beset by administrative trouble — bags were lost, flying between countries was awkward, ticket sales were slow, venues were below standard or still being renovated as games began. They even banned musical instruments from the venues, which took the calypso out of the Caribbean. The opinion of the local taxi drivers, always a good barometer for how things are going, was that the event organisers were stuffing up big time. Some teams allowed these problems to affect their performance but we never did, which was a considerable achievement.

ADAM GILCHRIST DIDN'T FLY with us to St Vincent, instead staying in Perth for a few more hours so he could be present at the birth of his third child. He arrived four days after the rest of us, while we were playing our first warm-up game, and that night, after we'd completed an encouraging win over Zimbabwe, we were waiting for him at the bar to share a beer and (for some, but not me) a cigar. Gilly was weary after his long flight, and I had to ponder just how hard it must have been for him to farewell his children, who were aged five, two and a half, and less than a week. His eldest was about to start school.

The next morning, Gilly got stuck into his work as professionally and diligently as ever, and it was good for all of us to have him back among the group. But there'd be times over the next few weeks when he seemed to lack a bit of the spark that had been his trademark, and again I wondered if a part of him really wanted to be back home. I never asked him and he never complained, but his best innings of this tour would be his last one, made just a few short days before he'd be reunited with his wife and kids.

OUR OPENING GAME was a huge win over Scotland in St Kitts and four days later we thrashed Holland at the same venue, but any pleasure we took from that second victory was shattered by the news Pakistan's coach Bob Woolmer had been found dead in his hotel room in Kingston that morning. We were informed when our reserve wicketkeeper, Brad Haddin, ran drinks out after we had taken a wicket and told us the appalling news.

Within a fortnight of Woolmer's death, word had leaked out from the police investigation that he'd been killed and a shiver had gone up my spine. It wasn't long before they retreated from the idea he'd been murdered, and eventually forensics experts concluded he had died from natural causes, but the smear left behind is something that even today I don't like to think about. At the time, one of the loudest whispers was that he'd been killed because he was about to make some specific allegations about cricket corruption and while this turned out not to be true, the spooky thing for me was that this rumour was considered plausible. In the Australian dressing room during the previous decade, we'd heard gossip about star players from the subcontinent and their families being threatened by bookmakers or the so-called 'cricket mafia', and I have to confess my first reaction when I heard the rumour that Bob had been murdered was that this was an extension of those earlier disturbing stories.

In those first couple of days after Bob's death, I found myself thinking about little things that had never worried me before. Rianna was in Sydney and during a late-night phone conversation she suddenly asked, 'When someone knocks on the door of your hotel room, do you look through the peep hole to check who it is?'

There wasn't one time, anywhere in the world, when I'd done that. It never seemed necessary. Maybe it was. One thing that was often stated in the press reports out of Jamaica was that there was no sign of any forced entry into Bob's room. The fact we were in St Kitts, 1500 kilometres from where Bob had died, didn't stop some reporters from asking me questions, as if I somehow had access to inside information. Even when murder was ruled out, the inquiries kept coming. The only certainty was that he was a good man and a good coach. Cricket was a lot poorer for his passing

THE CRICKET CARAVAN MOVED on. I guess it had to. While we prepared for our first big game, our final group match against South Africa, in the 48 hours after Bob's death World Cup games were played in Port-of-Spain, Kingston, St Kitts and St Lucia. Back home, the Pura Cup decider was underway, and I had a special interest because for the first time Tasmania were hosting the final. From the toss, I left my laptop on the updating scoresheet on the Cricket Australia website and I also received a plethora of text messages from people making sure I was aware of the latest developments. Prior to the game, I'd spoken with Tassie coach Tim Coyle, a Launceston native who had played a bit of first-class cricket a couple of years before I made my Shield debut, and to some of the players and the only advice I gave them was 'play to win', on the basis that while a draw would be enough to win the title, because we'd topped the points table after the home-and-away season, to suddenly go defensive was asking for trouble. We batted first against NSW on a sporting wicket, got to 7–283 at stumps, and from there raced away for an emphatic win. Over the next few days, as hard as I tried to find Brad Haddin, the regular Blues captain, for a chat about anything he wanted to talk about, he was nowhere to be found.

Technically, I was the captain of this first Tasmanian team to win the Pura Cup/Sheffield Shield, but of course it didn't feel that way. I had only appeared in one Pura Cup game during the season; since I'd become skipper at the start of the 2001–02 season, international commitments meant I'd only played in four Pura Cup games: two in 2001–02, one in 2002–03 and one in 2006–07. For me, being captain of Tasmania was a considerable honour, but if the people in charge of Tassie cricket had ever asked me to step aside as skipper I would have done so. However, I think because they liked the fact their Tassie skipper was also the national captain, the status quo would continue until November 2007, when circumstances meant I really had to give it away. I led the team in one game at the start of this 2007–08 season, a big win against South Australia in which I scored 96 and 124 and we successfully chased down 349 in less than 70 overs, but then I found myself in a difficult situation a few weeks later. There was a Pura Cup game coming up and I had no international cricket scheduled, but my preference was to take the week off to give myself a break before an important Test series against India. But if I couldn't play when technically I was available, it was surely time for a change and Dan Marsh, who'd done such a terrific job leading the team to victory in the 2004–05 ING Cup one-day tournament as well as the 2006–07 Pura Cup final, replaced me as 'full-time' captain.

'Naturally, I'll continue to play with Tasmania and assist the leadership group,' I explained when I announced this decision. I said 'naturally' deliberately, because I had been asked a few times why I was playing for Tassie when I was now living in Sydney, usually by people with a sense of cricket history who cited examples of champions like Bradman, Miller, Harvey and Border who changed teams when they moved interstate. To tell the truth, it never occurred to me to 'transfer' and I never sensed that anyone in Tasmania, NSW or Cricket Australia reckoned I should have been playing for the Blues.

FROM FIRST GAME TO LAST, we got our tactics right more often than not at the 2007 World Cup. I can think of plenty of times when things panned out just as we wanted, and there were other times when our opponents weren't so 'lucky'.

Take, for example, the way we used Shaun Tait. Many people had been surprised when we chose Taity ahead of Stuart Clark in our original World Cup squad (Sarf was eventually included when Brett Lee was ruled out). But like most captains who are batsmen, I always loved having an express bowler in the team. Steve Waugh was always a believer in sheer pace, which I think went back to his days in the 1980s when the West Indies quicks were always bouncing him, while I've never forgotten my days as a young Tasmanian Shield player, when the mainland states had fast bowlers and we didn't. It was only when I started playing for Australia, and we had Craig McDermott and Glenn McGrath (who was quicker early in his career than he was later on), that I got to enjoy this experience. And then Brett Lee came along in 1999. It was fun seeing opposition batsmen jumping around and exciting to be fielding in the slips a long way from the outside edge, as the ball flew through to the keeper. Only a skipper who has never ducked a rapid bouncer could fail to appreciate the value of having an express quick in his line-up.

Taity had struggled when he made his ODI debut a few months before the World Cup, mainly, I think, because of nerves. He opened the bowling and was quick from the first ball, but a few edges went for fours, suddenly he was conceding a lot of runs and his latter overs were ordinary. In this World Cup, we gave him a specific role and he responded magnificently: just a couple of quick overs at the start of an innings; then he came back later, as an attacking option, and invariably slowed the run-rate. 'Powerplays' (where the bowling team is required to keep more fieldsmen in the circle for five-over blocks) had just been introduced to ODI cricket and we decided to be aggressive rather than defensive during them, on the basis that the fieldsmen were up and the batsmen would put themselves under pressure if they didn't score quickly. There were times when Taity made us look like geniuses as he charged in during these powerplays, such as in our group match against South Africa, when in a high-scoring game he conceded just nine runs from 18 balls in the middle of their innings.

Another example where we played to plan occurred earlier in that same match. The day before the game, Matt Hayden and Adam Gilchrist set up a bowling machine to mimic the high delivery of South Africa's best bowler, Shaun Pollock, and then started smashing the ball all over the place. That evening, at our pre-game team meeting, Haydos told us Pollock's major strength, his consistency, could also be a weakness, because on a flat deck it made him 'predictable'. He and Gilly took 33 from Pollock's first three overs, we were 0–50 after five, and Matty went on to score a century from 66 balls, the fastest hundred in World Cup history.

Haydos produced another superb, tactically brilliant innings in Antigua when we beat the West Indies in front of a half-empty stadium in the first of our Super Sixes games: 158 from 143 balls on a dead pitch, with an outfield that was close to a quagmire. Most of the games in this tournament were played on slow, abrasive pitches, which meant the new ball lost its shine very quickly, but there was some swing at the start of the innings, so to make the big innings totals the top-order batsmen had to play cautiously for a short period before going on the offensive. The run-fest from ball one against South Africa was an aberration. Against the Windies, Matty didn't score a run off any of the first

17 deliveries he faced, but still reached his century from 110 balls. In reply, they crashed to 3–20 against McGrath and Tait, and the game was as good as won.

Eleven days later, we faced England at the same ground, and one of the talking points before the game concerned what we were going to do to Kevin Pietersen. Back in January, during an ODI in Melbourne, Pietersen had made the mistake of charging Pidge and suffered a broken rib when Pidge saw him coming, delivered a short one and struck him under the armpit. Now an English reporter asked me what would happen if Pietersen tried the same approach. 'It'd be good to hit him again,' I grinned, not expecting to be taken seriously. But my line was reported just as I'd said it, as if we'd be ruthlessly targeting the recently healed ribcage.

In truth, the one thing we decided to do differently with Pietersen in this game was not to say a word to him on the field. He is an extrovert and I always thought he was a bit like Steve Waugh and Brian Lara in that he didn't mind a confrontation on the field, because it fired him up and made him concentrate. If we left him alone he might have no one to argue with but himself. It was an extension of the 'call them by their first names' trick that had worked pretty well in Australia. The Poms batted first but lost two quick wickets, so Pietersen was in by the seventh over, and everyone was primed to say nothing, but then Glenn tried a bouncer and it was carefully half-hooked to deep square leg for a single. 'You won't get me bowling at that pace,' Pietersen muttered when he got the non-striker's end. Our man bit back.

'It was good enough to break your ribs a couple of weeks ago,' Pidge responded.

My reflex was to support our bowler, so I said something similar, to which Pietersen replied: 'I read what you said in the papers. I thought you were one of the good guys.'

'Don't worry about me being a good bloke, mate,' I shot back. 'I've heard plenty of stories about you from your dressing room. I'd be looking after my own backyard if I was you.'

It was true that we'd heard reports he wasn't very popular with his comrades. Back in the SCG dressing room after the final Ashes Test, when Andrew Strauss and Paul Collingwood had asked me how we handled difficult egos in our set-up, I knew who they were talking about. But so much for the silent treatment! The rest of the team just looked at Pidge and I, legendary bowler and captain, and wondered what was going on. In this case, the strategy was good, but the application was appalling, and of course Pietersen went on to make an excellent hundred. However, at the end of his innings he seemed more concerned with reaching three figures than maximising the run-rate. He was out for 104 in the 49th over and England only scored 51 runs in their final 10 overs, when they needed much more than that. We eventually got home with seven wickets and 16 balls to spare.

By the time of our semi-final re-match with South Africa in St Lucia, we were supremely confident. Our opponents, on the other hand, changed tack. First, they batted after Graeme Smith won the toss, which was strange because the pitch seemed to have a little in it and also because they usually preferred to bowl first whatever the conditions. Then they came out and swung the bat from the very first ball, as if they needed to score 400 again, but instead they lost 5–27 in less than 10 overs, with a couple of their senior batsmen playing ridiculous shots. Smith tried to charge Nathan Bracken in the game's third over and was bowled, and soon after Kallis was embarrassed by McGrath. It appeared they tried to adopt the old Steve Waugh mantra of 'backing yourself' in pressure situations but they'd taken that to the extreme, trying to play in a way that was so far outside their flags it was more suicidal than smart. Our performance, in contrast, was compelling. I gave Pidge an extended spell with the new ball and he ripped through their top order, Taity enjoyed his best day in Australian colours, and on the back of sensible innings from Haydos and Michael Clarke we cruised to victory just three wickets down.

Best ODI Australian team

I played 261 one-day internationals for Australia and was lucky enough to be a part of three World Cup-winning teams. Over that time, we were the most dominant team in one-day cricket and had a long list of players who left an everlasting impression on this form of the game. Here's my best ever team of ODI team-mates, in batting order:

1. Adam Gilchrist
2. Mark Waugh
3. Damien Martyn
4. Darren Lehmann
5. Andrew Symonds
6. Michael Bevan
7. Michael Hussey
8. Shane Warne
9. Brett Lee
10. Nathan Bracken
11. Glenn McGrath

CHAPTER 45

GOOD TIMES

Kensington Oval, Bridgetown, Barbados, April 28, 2007

I KNEW SOMETHING AMAZING might happen from as early as the first ball of the final. Chaminda Vaas pitched one up to Adam Gilchrist who offered a solid forward defensive stroke and the ball rocketed to mid-off. Pup was sitting next to me in the viewing area outside our dressing room and I slapped him on the leg and said as loud as I dared, 'This could be Gilly's day!' They didn't score but there was something about the way he centred that ball that suggested to me something was on here. You can tell a lot from the way a batsman defends.

This tournament had dragged on and on, but you'd rather hang around than go home early.

THE SEMI-FINAL AGAINST SOUTH AFRICA had been staged on Anzac Day, a full six weeks after our opening game. At different times there had been gaps of eight days, six days and twice five days between our games, leaving us with plenty of down time, which guys filled in a variety of ways, including the usual suspects like gym, golf, sightseeing, internet and computer games, and more exotic pursuits such as trolling for marlin and other forms of deep-sea fishing. In Barbados, before we played Ireland, Buck organised for the great Olympic rower, Sir Steven Redgrave, to talk to us, and two things stayed with me: one, the emphasis he put on his ability to conquer the urge to stay in bed rather than go out in the freezing cold to train, as though that was the difference; and two, how pleased he was that we'd invited him. The England team was staying in his hotel, but to this point he hadn't heard from them.

After we beat Bangladesh in the first week of April, Rianna (who came over for the latter stages) and I spent a couple of days, a sort of 'half-time break', relaxing on the tiny, gorgeous St Barthélemy (also known as St Barts), one of the Leeward Islands, not far from St Kitts.

Before the World Cup final at Kensington Oval in Bridgetown, we had our briefest break between games, three days, which seemed like a strange time to start rushing things. Still, I've rarely felt better prepared going into a big game and I know most of the guys were the same. There was little of the group nervousness that had worried me on the eve of the 2003 final, so my pre-game speech this time was one of my briefest, as I simply reminded the boys we'd done all the hard work and once again asked them to let our opponents know we were confident through our body language. I specifically used that word again: *presence*.

The day before the game, Haydos and Gilly were once again playing with a bowling machine, this time setting it up to mimic the round-arm slinging action of Sri Lanka's exciting fast bowler Lasith Malinga. We'd faced Malinga before and been reasonably impressed by him, but it seemed his game had gone to a new level in this tournament, most notably when he took four wickets in four balls against South Africa, so our opening bats took part of this bowling machine's legs off, positioned it so the balls were coming at them from about head height, directly over the stumps, because that is where the ball leaves his hand, set the speed to explosive, and then strapped the pads on. When they revved up the bowling machine before our first game against South Africa, Haydos hit that incredible hundred. This time, it was Gilly's turn.

He was batting with a squash ball in his left (bottom) batting glove, to help him with his grip, something he'd done from time to time in the nets but not, to the best of my knowledge, in a game. My impression was this was a last-minute call on his part — I won the toss on time but the start of the game was delayed by morning rain, and as we waited for the sun to arrive, Gilly was raring to go. Then, when it was time to walk out at 12.15pm for a day game that had been reduced to 38 overs a side, he suddenly raced back into the room and grabbed the squash ball out of his kit. And then he reached his century in 72 balls, with eight fours and six sixes, on his way to 149 from 104. There was a time when I could lay claim to having made the best innings by an Australian in a World Cup final. Not anymore.

The logic behind using a squash ball is that it stops a batsman gripping the handle too tightly with his or her bottom hand. I would have found it more of a hindrance, because it wouldn't have felt natural, but it obviously works for some, or at least one. Similar in a way to what Gilly was doing, there was a time when I taped two fingers of my bottom hand together, to weaken my bottom-hand grip, because I know one of the things a batsman must guard against is his bottom hand taking over when playing a stroke; it has to be the top hand and the front elbow that lead the way.

We'd decided to stick with our batting strategy of beginning cautiously and then going hard once the ball lost its shine, and the way Gilly clobbered them meant the plan worked like a dream. We were 0–46 after 60 deliveries and then sped along for the rest of the innings at eight-and-a-half runs per over. Early in Sri Lanka's reply, it looked like Kumar Sangakkara and Sanath Jayasuriya, their most dangerous batsmen, might hit them back into the game. However, the weather was closing in again, and Brad Hogg, who for the second World Cup in a row played an important role as our No. 1 spinner, secured the breakthrough when he tricked Sangakkara into chipping an easy catch to me at short mid-wicket, to make them 2–123 in the 20th over. Pup bowled Jayasuriya soon after, and then, with the light deteriorating and Sri Lanka well behind on the 'Duckworth–Lewis method', I brought McGrath and Tait back to pummel them right out of the game. Just five runs came from the next two overs. We were as good as home.

By the time the 35th over of the innings ended it was more like night than day and we were miles in front. I had the ball in my hand as I watched the two umpires, Aleem Dar and Steve Bucknor, confer and immediately I thought: *They're going to offer them the light*. Weirdly, the batsmen accepted the offer and I triumphantly chucked the ball as high and as far as I could, because in my mind this World Cup was over ...

Moments like these always end up being a blur, as a cocktail of adrenalin, joy, excitement and relief takes over. Later, when they asked, 'What were you thinking?' I struggled to put it into words. We all grabbed the bloke nearest to us, then we were in a team hug, but all this emotion was rudely interrupted when Aleem Dar tapped me on the shoulder and said, 'I'm sorry, the game isn't over. We have to come back tomorrow. There are still three overs to be bowled.'

'You've got to be kidding?' I replied incredulously.

Over his shoulder, I could see that the ground staff weren't bringing the covers out; they were setting up the portable stage on which the presentation would be held. Another bloke was picking up the fielding circle markers, while there was still enough light for him to find them. I honestly thought it was some kind of joke or maybe a stuff-up that the officials off the field would soon put straight.

'No, we have to come back tomorrow,' Aleem Dar said again.

'But 20 overs constitutes a game,' I argued, with a look on my face that was more bewildered than angry. 'Once the team batting second faces 20 overs, it's game over.'

'Twenty overs constitutes a game,' I said again.

Aleem Dar was getting advice through the earpiece that connected him with the video umpire's room. 'No, those rules are written for rain,' he said in a measured tone. 'It's different for bad light.'

Sri Lanka couldn't win, whether we played on, went off or came back in the morning, so it wasn't as if they were trying to take the victory away from us. They were stealing a little of our glory. For a while it seemed no one knew what was going on and a tournament that had suffered its share of administrative problems now had its signature piece. The umpires and officials were in conference on the edge of the ground, as the twilight turned to night, and who knows how it would have ended if Sri Lanka's captain Mahela Jayawardene hadn't said firmly, 'Let's finish it. We'll bat out the overs now.'

This grand gesture got the organisers out of a real bind. Later, they confessed they'd misread the rules, that the game should have been over when the offer for the light was accepted, but Symmo and Pup had to bowl three overs in terrible 'light', before we could celebrate a second time. I was fielding at mid-wicket for those last 18 balls and I couldn't see a thing. I know this tame ending took the edge off the game for many neutral observers, but for us it didn't really matter; I just wish I could have engineered it so Glenn McGrath's final over in international cricket was the last of the tournament.

Still, Glenn did get to lead us in the singing of the team song, though this too didn't work out quite the way we'd planned it. As we'd done after the Cup finals of 1999 and 2003, at Lord's and the Wanderers respectively, after some time in the dressing room we swaggered out to the centre wicket to sing 'Underneath the Southern Cross'. This time, clasped in a tight circle, Gilly began proceedings by asking each of us: 'What is your lasting memory of this World Cup?' One by one, we recalled a personal highlight and it was such a terrific time; so much so that none of us were aware some members of the local constabulary had marched up and formed a circle around us.

'Right, it's time to go,' a massively built senior officer barked. 'We're closing up. You must leave the ground.'

'Oh, c'mon mate,' one of us shot back. 'We won't be long.'

'No, you must go now.'

'Hang on,' I butted in. 'We've just won the World Cup. Just give us one f***ing minute?'

That swear word had no sooner left my mouth than I wanted it back. 'You cannot cuss like that in Barbados,' he growled. 'If you do not leave the ground immediately, I will lock you in jail.'

Given my bluster, there was no way they were going to let us finish our reminiscing or allow us to sing our song. I was totally out of line, which I deeply regret, but I still do wonder why they couldn't have given us a little leeway. We traipsed back to the dressing room, packed our bags and headed for our hotel, where we sang our anthem next to the pool, with Pidge in full cry, showing us the way one last time.

After we'd lost the Ashes less than two years earlier, we'd identified what needed to change and then, with the help of the coaching staff and Cricket Australia, a framework was built that allowed those improvements to happen. There was a lot of skill involved in the success we achieved between October 2005 and April 2007, a lot of planning and a lot of character, but more than anything, our victories came about because we were prepared, as individuals and as a team, to work harder than we'd ever worked before. That's why I felt more satisfied in the hours and days after this World Cup than I'd ever felt before or would ever feel again during my cricket career. It wasn't just this tournament; it was all the success I'd been a part of during the previous 19 months. As a cricketer and captain, I'd made a contribution. I'd scored a lot of runs and made more good choices than bad.

I'd been Test skipper for a little more than three years, one-day skipper for five. Once again, we were champions of the world. I liked being Australian captain and felt totally settled in the job. The criticism that had followed the Ashes defeat was a distant memory. Yet I hadn't forgotten it completely, so there wasn't any part of me that was feeling smug. The team's future looked very bright, even if many of the guys I'd played with during the previous decade had retired or were contemplating retirement. We were all assuming that the young guys in or near the squad were good enough to keep the victories coming, and I was looking forward to helping them become our future stars. In the euphoria of our wonderful World Cup victory, as we sat on the deck of another of James Packer's luxury boats and drank and laughed our way through the day after the final, no one stopped to think that an era was ending.

Earlier in the day, Pidge and Gilly, champagnes in hand, and I were on the beach having our photos taken with the Cup, which had somehow survived the night reasonably intact, while out to sea Brad Hogg and Shane Watson buzzed around on jet skis and up on the balcony of one of the rooms at our hotel Mitchell Johnson and Andrew Symonds were wearing no more than jockstraps as they toasted our triumph one more time. As we partied, smiles all over our faces, I think we all thought the good times might last forever.

CHAPTER 46

ZERO TOLERANCE

Australian summer, 2007–08

IN WHAT WAS THE most angry, acrimonious and difficult summer of cricket the Australian cricket team ever faced I needed to know that Cricket Australia was 100 per cent behind me and the team, supporting us when we needed it most, but the truth is it wasn't.

It was a sobering and disturbing lesson amid the many learned when we made the mistake of following the rules we had been repeatedly told we must follow. If it was tough to learn the realities of cricket politics, it was even harder to see a mate suffer and I think lose his love for the game.

THERE HAD BEEN A fair bit for us players to like about our relationship with Cricket Australia in the two years following the 2005 tour of England. The way the administrators — led by Cricket Australia's CEO James Sutherland — reacted to the Ashes loss was mostly fair and helpful. They seemed open to any idea or innovation that might improve our performance. They recognised that there were flaws in the way families were travelling with the team, but they didn't just revert to an embargo, as old-time officials probably would have. The schedules, while still cramped, became a little more manageable.

When the elite players needed a break, or at least a game off, they usually got it.

For me, a large chunk of this goodwill was lost in 2007–08. I'm big on loyalty and supporting your mates, especially when they're under attack. There was an incident on the field, an Indian player was charged, found guilty and suspended by an independent arbiter and we were the bad guys. Indian officials threatened to call off the tour, their captain bad-mouthed us, sections of the media bad-mouthed us and Cricket Australia and its lawyers went looking for a compromise, as if they were the ones who had to save face.

It was impossible for me not to conclude that they considered Australian cricket's relationship with India more important than how they looked after us and communicated with us. They let me down and let the team down.

I'm still struggling to forget that.

RACISM HAD BEEN AN issue in cricket for a number of years. As with other sports, the racist element in cricket mostly involved abhorrent comments from spectators. Occasionally, though, teams from the subcontinent would make allegations against Australian players, which we always refuted. Making comments to opponents on the field, 'sledging' as it's called, was part of the game and had been since the days of WG Grace and Warwick Armstrong. At its best it involved getting into another player's head, getting under his skin. Racial abuse, we were well aware, was completely different. We played hard, but we weren't racist.

For many years we were more bemused than upset by such accusations, as they usually came from players looking for alibis or from ex-players who'd suddenly become cleanskins upon the issue of their first media pass. We knew that many cricketers from India, Pakistan and Sri Lanka actually gave as good as they got. In my first season as a Test player, 1995–96, I saw how the Sri Lankan captain Arjuna Ranatunga would call for a runner when he wasn't injured, just a bit tired, and then whinge about our sledging straight afterwards. I always wondered if the Sunil Gavaskar who kept telling us how rude and unsportsmanlike we were was related in any way to the Sunil Gavaskar who tried to take his team off the field during a Test at the MCG in 1981 when an lbw decision didn't go his way.

Racism was a whole other issue and became a *major* issue during South Africa's tour of Australia in 2005–06, but again this was because of barbs fired from beyond the boundary, when some mugs in the crowd abused a few of the tourists. As part of our game's response, we as frontline players were reminded often and frankly about our responsibilities. Appropriate clauses were added to the ICC's code of conduct, with big penalties for anyone who stepped out of line. I was told that if I witnessed an instance of racism on or off the field while I was leading the Aussie team I had a duty to report it. During our pre-season briefings, racism became a significant topic of discussion, given the same level of importance as the fight against performance-enhancing drugs. If you'd asked me to sum up cricket's approach to both scourges I would have said flatly: 'Zero tolerance.'

IN OCTOBER 2007, WE found ourselves in India for seven ODIs and one Twenty20 international. India at the time was buzzing about cricket, on the back of their team's victory the previous month in the World Twenty20 in South Africa — essentially a T20 World Cup, we'd been knocked out by India in a semi-final. A few days later, after India had defeated Pakistan in the final and we'd landed in Bangalore, we discovered the country was mad for the newest and shortest form of the game. Their players were welcomed home as conquering heroes, as if they'd won something that really mattered. Now they had to prove they deserved this new status. The atmosphere during our one-dayers would have a real edge to it, in the packed stands and on the field too.

This was especially true during the second ODI at Kochi — when incidents involving Michael Clarke and Harbhajan Singh and then Andrew Symonds and their pace bowler S. Sreesanth received plenty of attention — and then in the last three games, at Vadodara,

Nagpur and Mumbai. Most noticeably during these latter three matches, small sections of the crowd took to making monkey noises whenever Symmo walked in their direction. The vibe was pretty unpleasant and then after the final game Symmo, who is of part Afro-Caribbean descent, informed us that while we were fielding, though I didn't hear it myself, Harbhajan had called him a 'monkey'.

We knew that if any of us had chipped one of the Indians about their race they would have been filing a complaint pronto and that would be the right thing to do. The papers would have been onto the story immediately, and we'd have been the bad guys ... again. However, our first reaction, in contrast, was to do what we'd always done. *Just let it go.* Of course that put me in a difficult position as we'd been told to report any offence.

Before the dressing-room debate could go too far, Symmo stood up and said, 'I'll fix it.' He strode over to the Indian team's room, knocked on their door, and asked for Harbhajan. In his book *Roy on the Rise: A Year of Living Dangerously*, published the following year, he recounts this moment, though Harbhajan denied this conversation took place. 'Look,' Symmo recalls having said to Harbhajan, 'the name-calling is fine with me; it doesn't particularly worry me what you call me, but you know what is going to happen. One thing will lead to another and you blokes will end up going to an umpire and it will get out of hand.' Symmo also said he told Harbhajan that the word used was 'offensive and hurtful'. He said Harbhajan then apologised and said it wouldn't happen again, that they then shook hands, and Symmo said: 'That's the end of it.' We figured, naively as it turned out, that it would indeed be the end of it.

WE WON THAT ODI series 4–2, with the opening game abandoned. We were thrashed in a T20 international, which to Indian eyes seemed to balance the ledger, and then back home beat Sri Lanka in Test matches in Brisbane and Hobart, the latter contest featuring a superb innings of 192 by Kumar Sangakkara that was only ended by an incorrect umpiring decision. It was one of those moments when I thought the batsman was out, so I appealed, the umpire fired him and then I started thinking, *Maybe he didn't hit it.* The replay showed the ball hit Sangakkara's shoulder and then his helmet but not his bat. It wasn't the only umpiring error of this series, just the worst of them; one of a number of incorrect decisions that helped wreck the summer. Prior to 2007–08 I was a vocal opponent of using off-field technology to review umpire's verdicts. In my view, cricket had got by pretty well putting faith in the adjudicators on the field, and while they sometimes made mistakes there wasn't a compelling reason for change. By season's end, I'd realised I was wrong.

The Boxing Day Test against India, the first of a four-match series, was one-sided, with our pace attack of Brett Lee, Stuart Clark and Mitchell Johnson overwhelming the visitors after Matt Hayden made one of his best hundreds on the opening day. It was our 15th Test victory in a row, one short of the record for consecutive wins we'd established between October 1999 and March 2001, and it meant we'd gone through 2006 and 2007 winning every Test we played. For me, when I look back on my career, this game also marked the end of my 'golden run' with the bat. I'd averaged 50 or better in 10 of the previous 11 series I'd been involved in, the only exception being the 2005 Ashes. Starting at Leeds in 2001, I'd scored nearly 7000 Test runs at 72, and made 26 hundreds. For the rest of my career I'd average 39. In this big win against India at the MCG I was out for 4 and 3, and after Harbhajan had me caught at slip in our second dig (the sixth time he'd dismissed me in seven Tests) he was asked if there was a flaw in my technique he was exploiting.

'He hasn't batted long enough against me,' he answered. 'So I don't know.'

I actually didn't mind that quip; it was sort of funny and I was always okay with a judicious sledge. Harbhajan was a talented and competitive cricketer who I found harder to combat than Murali. Like the great Sri Lankan, he was an off-spinner who could turn the ball the other way, and at his best he could get the ball to drift and dip and zip off the wicket in a way that confounded just about everyone. Haydos used to sweep him all the time, which worked for him, but same as I'd always done I preferred to get down the pitch to the spinners. However, that was difficult against Harbhajan because his loop was often so hard to nail. Hindsight says I should have practised the sweep more, but I wasn't keen to change what had worked so well for me most of the time.

When Harbhajan dismissed me twice more in the New Year's Test in Sydney, he could hardly contain himself, sprinting away from his team-mates and then rolling on the ground after I was out for 1 on the fourth day. In the press box, the pundits and commentators all chuckled and thought he was terrific; the next day, when we celebrated actually winning the game, they'd say we were rude and arrogant.

Why? Part of it, I think, was simply because they were bored with us winning all the time. The media cycle can be relentless. Maybe some of them saw India as a potential source of income and were tailoring their reports and criticisms for this new audience. I also think some of them had a view of the cricket world that was often divorced from reality; they'd talk among themselves, chat to a few members of the local cricket society and use that small sample to judge how all the fans were thinking.

In the papers and on the radio we heard that we hardly had a friend in the world, but everywhere I went, from the ground to the hotel to my golf club to the coffee shops, just walking down the street, our support was strong. I was consoled by James Sutherland's view in the essay he wrote for my *Captain's Diary 2008*, where he noted that measuring the mood of the public is 'not always as simple as the talk-back commentators and columnists will have you believe'. Such was Cricket Australia's concern about our standing after Sydney that they conducted formal market research on the perception of the team; the findings included 'that the public genuinely rates the Australian team, its individual players, and the way they play very highly'. The research also noted that Australian cricketers 'stood out as sportspeople who are admired and highly respected, ahead of those from almost all other sports'.

ONE OF THE REASONS Harbhajan might have been so excited to get me out might have gone back to the previous day of the Test, when he'd been reported for making what we believed to be a racist comment. It was a repeat of what had happened in Mumbai, and the first I knew of it was when I heard Michael Clarke shout, 'He's done it again! He just called Symmo a monkey again!'

Harbhajan was batting with Sachin Tendulkar in the final session of day three, and had just sliced Brett Lee for four over the slips and then squeezed a yorker out on the legside for a single. As he ran through for the run, he patted Brett on the backside, which prompted Symmo to remind him that he didn't have any friends among us. Soon the two were standing toe to toe, mouthing off, but I didn't care what they were doing; I wanted to talk to Mitchell Johnson about what he was going to do when he bowled the next over. Then I heard Pup yelling in my direction.

I knew what I had to do. It wasn't about giving him a second chance because we'd already done that. The strict instructions about on-field racial abuse I'd received from the ICC and from the match referees before Test and one-day series over the previous couple of years had been explained to me again just a few days earlier, when India captain Anil Kumble and I had met Mike Procter, the ICC match referee, for a formal pre-series chat.

Out in the middle of the SCG, I asked Symmo what had happened. Matt Hayden joined in to say he'd heard the monkey sledge too. I then went over and talked to umpire Mark Benson. Benson went to Harbhajan and Tendulkar and put the accusation to them. Harbhajan denied doing anything wrong. The umpires went back to their positions for the new over, but before another ball was bowled, as I ran back to my fielding position at second slip, I did snap at Harbhajan, 'I hope you haven't said that again.'

'Leave it alone,' Tendulkar responded. 'I'll fix this, I'll sort this out.'

Because we'd already raised the matter with the umpires, it had gone beyond that. The match officials would have to sort it out.

The game went on. Soon we were informed that Mike Procter, a good man and one of the finest all-rounders in the history of the game, would conduct an inquiry at the end of the Test.

At stumps on that third day, James Sutherland asked me what I wanted to see happen.

'If he's guilty,' I said, 'I want him to be accountable for his actions.'

I wanted Symmo to know we were all behind him. I wanted the game to be fair dinkum about eradicating racism. I wanted everyone to be treated the same way.

If one of our blokes had been charged with racial abuse there would have been no second chance, no pressure being turned back on the accuser, no insinuation that the charge was a beat-up. That's what happened to us.

THE TEST TURNED INTO a thriller. With a maximum two overs remaining and three wickets needed I gave Pup a try even though to that point in his life he'd never taken a Test wicket in Australia. He promptly took three wickets in five balls.

The climax came at the end of a day that featured controversy over whether I'd left my declaration too late, controversy over the umpiring, controversy over whether we were right to claim catches that went close to ground, controversy over when and how we appealed, controversy over the Indians' time-wasting late in the day, and continued debate about the upcoming hearing into the racial abuse charge.

Leading 2–0 in a four-Test series, we'd retained the Border–Gavaskar Trophy. We'd won 16 Tests in a row. The crowd went crazy. So, for a minute or three, did we.

We were criticised later for not shaking hands quickly enough with our opponents, but that was unfair. We won, merged into one joyous embrace in the middle, kept hugging each other one at a time, and then we sought the Indians on the field, in front of the Members Pavilion.

In what seemed like no time, I was taking my seat for the post-game grilling by the press boys. Then I was with a small group of my team-mates in the umpires' room, being told by James Sutherland and team manager Steve Bernard when Mike Procter's inquiry would start and how it was going to work. The formalities began around 7.30pm. The best part of seven hours later, after what I'll always believe was a fair hearing, I left the SCG. Procter had heard testimony from the umpires, the two Indian batsmen, plus Symmo, Gilly, Pup, Haydos and me. Harbhajan was banned for three Test matches.

IN THE CAB on the way home, I figured there'd be some controversy over this suspension, but never did I think it would erupt into a firestorm. Maybe I should have, based on what had happened during the media conferences that followed the Test. I went in first, before Anil Kumble, and early on the mood was reasonably bright, as I patted away a couple of tame questions from the local scribes. A few of the Indian journalists were cranky, and they revved me up and I got angry when they started questioning my integrity over a couple of contentious decisions that had gone our way. The umpiring had been terrible, but that was hardly my fault. I was also asked about the relationship between the two teams and I answered, 'There was absolutely no doubt about this match being played in the right spirit. There's been one little issue that's come out of the game that we'll all hear about later, but otherwise the spirit between both teams in both Tests has been excellent.'

A few minutes later, Kumble was in the same seat answering the same questions. When he was asked about the spirit in which the game was being played, he responded differently. It was a rehearsed reply to a loaded question ...

I think only one team was playing within the spirit of the game. We like to play hard on the field and we expect that from Australia as well. I have played my cricket very sincerely

*and very honestly, and that's the approach my team takes on
the field. I expect that from the Australians as well ...*

As I understand it, no journalist in that room, Indian or Australian,
challenged Kumble's assessment of the game. A number of them
cheered. No one observed that the words came from a captain who
had just lost two Tests in a row, who had seen his team lose a Test
despite scoring 532 in their first innings. The few who knew their
cricket history realised the India captain was echoing the remarks
made by Australian captain Bill Woodfull during the infamous
Bodyline series, when he told the English managers, 'There are
two teams out there. One is trying to play cricket and the other is
not.' Those who didn't know their cricket history were immediately
brought up to speed. Often in media conferences during my time as
captain I could sense the pack waiting for me to say something that
would give them the next day's headline; when I said it, deliberately
or inadvertently, they'd all be feverishly writing in their notepads,
grateful their work was done.

Over the course of the next few hours, Mike Procter heard
all the evidence and found Harbhajan guilty. The next day, the
Indians responded by threatening to go home. Because Kumble's
uncontested line about 'Australia playing outside the spirit of the
game' received so much attention, quickly the belief spread that it
was us, not Procter's judgment, that provoked the trouble. Then
a Peter Roebuck article was published in *The Age* and the *Sydney
Morning Herald* and in newspapers all across India saying we were
a disgrace. Roebuck demanded I be sacked as captain and that
Hayden and Gilly also be thrown out of the side.

The journalist's hysterical story was printed on the front page of
the Sydney newspaper. He called us 'a pack of wild dogs' who had
brought embarrassment on our country, I was 'arrogant and abrasive'
and Harbhajan Singh was a 'Sikh warrior' who was supporting a
family of nine and was a victim of our rudeness. Roebuck even went
so far as to question Matthew Hayden's religion.

I had got up early that morning and was playing golf when Rianna rang in tears to ask me if it was true that I was a chance to get the sack. It was the first I knew of the story.

Cricket Australia advised me to lie low, said the storm would blow over. It didn't. Instead, my name and those of my team-mates were trashed by the sceptics in the media. It was hard not to think about it. The Indians withdrew their threat to call off the tour and appealed Procter's decision, two moves which added to the perception that they were the innocent victims. The new hearing, before a High Court judge from New Zealand, Justice John Hansen, was scheduled for Adelaide immediately after the fourth Test. Harbhajan was cleared to play, pending the result of the appeal.

Meanwhile, James Sutherland did make some public comments saying Cricket Australia was 'supportive of the Australian team and the way they play' but his remarks were so tame and formatted they got lost among the bitter sneers and talkback calls that made the headlines. I spoke to James every day during the week after the Sydney Test, asking him to forcefully defend us, to reject Kumble's post-Test jibe and specifically to back us over the racism charge, but most of the quotes I saw from James and Cricket Australia chairman Creagh O'Connor concerned their efforts to save the tour, not the Australian team's reputation.

Not long after we arrived in Perth for the next Test, all the players were obliged to attend a meeting moderated by a 'leadership consultant' employed by Cricket Australia, a bloke who had once been an officer in the Royal Australian Air Force. It seemed to me the motivation for the get-together was for us to discuss and then improve the way we played the game, as if Kumble's allegations against us actually had legs. I hated sitting through this meeting at the time; the memory of it pisses me off now. We were advised not to give the media opportunities to bag us, but when someone asked for examples of where we'd gone wrong they couldn't help us. As I wrote in my diary:

*The trouble is, we can go for six months without putting
a foot out of place — no mean achievement in modern
professional sport — but first time we make a mistake,
we're damned by the Roebucks of this world as 'Ugly
Australians'. Of course, this has been happening since Ian
Chappell was Australia's Test captain, and it frustrated me
that I had to explain this to people who I thought were on
our side. All I could promise to my masters and the masses
was that we would keep playing and preparing to the best
of our ability, and adhere as best we could to the 'Spirit
of Australian Cricket' code we established for ourselves
in 2003. I was confident that if we did this, then our
supporters would be happy to back us unconditionally.*

WE LOST THAT THIRD Test, outplayed by a group that was hungrier
than we were, at least for the first three days.

One of the lowpoints of my cricket career was the time after
Sydney when I felt like I was on trial, exhausted, let down. By day
four at the WACA I could feel some of my enthusiasm for the game
coming back, as we prepared to chase what would have been an
Australian record successful fourth-innings total. I was 24 not
out and keen to make some history, but unfortunately their young
quick Ishant Sharma delivered a fantastic spell in the half-hour
before lunch. I revelled in the contest and nearly survived, but he
got me, caught at slip, in what would probably have been his final
over. Often the line between failure and glory can be a fine one. If
I'd just got through that over, I might have gone on to make one
of my most memorable innings. We ended up 73 runs short. Eight
days later, in Adelaide, I made my first Test hundred in more than a
year, the game was a high-scoring draw, and then we had to go and
introduce ourselves to Justice Hansen.

For me, some of the discussions we had with Cricket Australia
in the days immediately prior to this hearing were farcical. I'd
reached my century on the fourth day of the Test, but during the

innings my back had seized up a little and I needed some treatment and rest that night so I'd be right as we tried to bowl India out on the final day. Instead, I was required at yet another meeting to debate what had become something of a stalemate. Mike Procter had ruled Harbhajan guilty of a 'Level 3.3' (racial abuse) charge but the Indians wouldn't cop that. Cricket Australia's external legal team, who were keen for a compromise, wanted us to concede that Harbhajan's words were offensive and seriously insulting rather than racist. Symmo and I didn't understand why we had do that, so the discussion went round in circles for hours. There was a fear that things would escalate, and a split in world cricket wasn't out of the question. James Sutherland and Creagh O'Connor had informally been told that Harbhajan would accept a 'lesser' charge.

'If Symmo and I do decide to go ahead with a "level 3" charge, will we have the support of Cricket Australia?' I asked.

The chairman said he'd have to speak to his board in the morning. That was where we left it, well after midnight, still in the lurch. It wasn't until the next day's lunch break that Creagh told me Cricket Australia's preference was to compromise, but if we wanted to go ahead they'd back us. I couldn't help thinking that if they were fair dinkum we would have had that support from day one. We decided, on a matter of principle, that we wanted Mike Procter's judgment to stand.

Once we got into the hearing, I knew we had no chance. Maybe that was just my perception, with all the formalities and the legal jargon and after all the negativity and counter-charges of the previous three weeks, but my worst fears came true. In the course of submissions, Cricket Australia's lawyers informed Justice Hansen that Symmo now 'took the language to be offensive and seriously insulting, but did not consider it fell under the requirements of [Level] 3.3'. Justice Hansen accepted that Symmo, Haydos and Pup were certain they'd heard the word 'monkey' and noted that they had immediately confronted Harbhajan on the field. Justice Hansen also saw Tendulkar as a key witness. In his decision, he said:

> *Contrary to reports that Mr Tendulkar heard nothing, he*
> *told me he heard a heated exchange and wished to calm*
> *Mr Singh down. His evidence was that there was swearing*
> *between the two. It was initiated by Mr Symonds. That*
> *he did not hear the word 'monkey' or 'big monkey' but he*
> *did say he heard Mr Singh use a term in his native tongue*
> *'teri maki' which appears to be pronounced with an 'n'. He*
> *said this is a term that sounds like 'monkey' and could be*
> *misinterpreted for it.*

I couldn't understand why Sachin didn't tell this to Mike Procter in the first place.

'I need to "be sure" in relation to the allegations, and if I am left with an honest and reasonable uncertainty then I must make a finding favouring Mr Singh,' the judge concluded. Harbhajan pleaded guilty to the 'Level 2.8' charge they'd been pushing us to accept in the lead-up to the hearing — offensive abuse not amounting to racism — and in place of the three-Test ban he received a fine of half his match fee.

Absurdly, owing to an administrative error, the judge was never told about any of Harbhajan's past offences, which meant the penalty was way less than what it should have been.

As I pondered this result over the weeks and months that followed, I started to think that I needed to be more savvy about off-field politics. But then I thought about the way a number of people in the game had questioned our motives; how they thought we were just seeking an advantage rather than acting on principle. It was much more serious than that. When Darren Lehmann was suspended for a racist comment in the lead-up to the 2003 World Cup, we were criticised as a group for not seeing the seriousness in what Boof had done. Five years later, the roles were reversed. I felt that there was a lot of hypocrisy about the 'Monkeygate' scandal.

I don't think we were mistaken in challenging it. Would I do it all over again? Yes. Because I'm committed to doing the right thing by the game and I would hope that others would feel as passionate about this as I do. I don't think we should have caved in.

The worst of it all was the impact it had on Symmo. I had tried to protect him from most of what was going on in the lead-up to the hearing, but when it was done I reckon it took the wind out of his sails. He had never been one to seek the limelight; he loved his sport and was brilliant at it but the attention that came with it never sat well with him.

In a lot of ways Symmo was gone from this moment on and it still makes me angry.

Mumbai retrospective

Being drafted by the Mumbai Indians and being made captain for the sixth season of the Indian Premier League (IPL) in 2013 was a highlight of the nine months that followed my retirement from international cricket.

I had a taste of the IPL in its first year, when I played for the Kolkata Knight Riders, but my priority to play for Australia meant I chose not to make myself available for the following seasons. I must admit to having a bit of apprehension about joining a team that had the reputation of under-achieving despite its financial wealth and superstar players. On top of this, I was sharing a dressing room with my old adversary Harbhajan Singh as well as Sachin Tendulkar and Anil Kumble, who were all involved in the Monkeygate affair back in 2008. But the experience was an extremely positive one in so many ways, highlighted by us winning the final and qualifying for the Champions League in October.

I started the competition as an opening batsman alongside Sachin but didn't manage to be as successful as I would have hoped, so I decided to drop myself from the team after the first six games. We made Rohit Sharma the on-field captain, and for the rest of the competition I continued to lead the team from the sidelines and in the training and preparation for each game. In many ways, this was a strange experience but at the same time it gave me a real taste for the off-field demands of coaching, mentoring and leadership. I want to do more of this and am looking forward to the opportunities in the future.

Looking back, the two months at Mumbai gave me a great insight into Indian culture, their people and their absolute passion for cricket. I have been to India more than 20 times but just about always in the cocoon of an Australian touring team. To be part of an Indian-cultured dressing room and team environment was an experience I will never forget. Working closely with Anil and head coach, John Wright, we managed to turn the team of champions into a champion team. I got to know all of the players really well, including Sachin and Harbhajan. Sachin and I have always had great respect for each other, and it was a huge thrill to play with him. He was really good to be around, is an even deeper thinker of the game than I realised and his understanding of technique and strategy is why he is the greatest cricketer I ever played against. I spent hours talking with Harbhajan about our on-field rivalry, and what I found was that he is just as competitive a beast as I am, always giving 100 per cent and having emotion and adrenalin in the moment of great cricket contests. We even made positive front-page headlines together when I managed to take one of the sharpest catches I've ever taken — off Harbhajan's bowling. Everyone thought it was really funny that it took a catch to end 10 years of intense rivalry.

CHAPTER 47

IRREPLACEABLE

Farewell Gilly, January 2008

'I'M OUT,' HE SAID quietly. 'The time has come.'

And another one was gone. It was Gilly's turn to up and leave the room.

He'd sent me a text on the second night of the Adelaide Test, asking me to come up and see him. I was having dinner at the time. It was an unusual text, a bit abrupt. I skipped dessert.

'What's going on, mate?' I asked.

Listening to him, I recognised a similar situation to where guys like David Boon, Ian Healy and Mark Waugh had been earlier in my career. The high-class consistency that had been a hallmark of Gilly's game had slipped a fraction — he'd spilled a couple in Sydney and then dropped an easy one in the first innings of this Test — and to get back to greatness he knew he'd have to work bloody hard. He no longer had the desire to do it. Not at this time of his life, with young kids always waiting for him at home. One of the common threads with all of us was that we always wanted to improve; to be 'never satisfied' was a mantra that Steve Waugh and John Buchanan drummed in to us and none of us ran away from. Once the desire to get even better starts to dim, or you realise that no matter how hard you try your best hope is to mark time, that's when retirement stares you in the face.

I realised there was no point trying to talk him out of it, in fact I never tried to talk any of the boys out of going. You don't make a decision like that lightly. In almost all situations it was the biggest decision they had ever made and it wouldn't be fair to try and change it because I knew how hard it was to make it.

Straight afterwards, as I walked slowly back to my room, I compared Gilly's situation to mine and realised that — while all the crap I'd been dealing with was eating away at me — I was in no mood to call it quits. I wanted to support the new blokes in our squad in the same way people like Boonie, Heals and Shane Warne had helped me and I hoped to take my batting and leadership to a new level, but events were conspiring to make that task harder than ever.

Gilly stepping down during the Adelaide Test was only one thing I had to deal with. There were times during that game when instead of being on the field playing cricket and leading the team I was in a room under the old grandstand meeting with Cricket Australia chairman Creagh O'Connor, CEO James Sutherland and general manager of cricket Michael Brown.

There is no way that sort of thing should be happening in the middle of a Test match, but that's what it had got to.

I have little memory of the rest of the 2007–08 season in Australia, when my enthusiasm was diminished because of the disappointment I suffered after the Harbhajan affair was 'resolved'. Then I played four T20 matches for the Kolkata Knight Riders in the inaugural Indian Premier League, which was good in parts — I liked being part of what was an exciting new venture, coped with the glitz, enjoyed helping out a few of the younger players — but it wasn't the best thing for me at the time. I hardly scored a run. The experience was a rush, just like the game, but I needed time.

It wasn't until during the West Indies tour from mid-May to early July, when I was involved in Test and one-day series as a winning captain of a young and enthusiastic Aussie squad, that playing cricket started to feel right again.

OF ALL THE CHAMPIONS who retired during my career, Adam Gilchrist was one of the two we missed the most. Warnie, of course, was the other. Gilly was unique as a cricketer: a very good gloveman, better than most people gave him credit for; most likely the greatest No. 7 batsman in the history of Tests; maybe Australia's most influential one-day player. He was a shrewd thinker on the game, a thoughtful and generous team-mate, and he had a remarkable (and much admired within the group) ability to stay out of trouble. On the field, he was reported as much as any of us, but somehow sustained his good-guy image while the rest of us were slandered if we put a toe out of line. And while he celebrated as hard as anyone, there were never any stories about misdemeanours or late-night shenanigans. He had that sensible gene when he partied that early in my life I sometimes lacked. He could do no wrong.

After Gilly made his retirement announcement in Adelaide, he opted to play out the rest of the international season. This was good for us but probably a mixed blessing for him. I know part of him hated the 'farewell tour' element of those final ODIs, the fact he was being singled out for special attention. He was always big on us working as a group, all of us on the same page. Still, for one more month he could proudly wear the green and gold and continue to enjoy the sometimes simple pleasures that go with playing our game. During our innings against Sri Lanka at the SCG, a couple of overs after I joined him in the middle, he came up to me between overs and muttered, 'I'm going to miss this.'

I figured he was talking about representing his country; playing in front of a big crowd. Or maybe it was simply the buzz of the contest. I gave him a smile.

'I'm going to miss all the good times we've had on the field. I'm going to miss batting with you,' he continued.

If either of us was going to get sentimental, it was going to be Gilly. I was more concerned with building another partnership, to take advantage of the good start Gilly and Matt Hayden had given us.

'Mate, let's not talk about that now,' I replied. 'We can talk about it later.'

I was dismissed soon after, for 9. Gilly went on to 61, combining with Michael Clarke on an awkward pitch to bat the Sri Lankans out of the game.

I reckon there were many similarities in our relationship to that of plenty of Australian cricketers, at all levels. We were the same as plenty of blokes in the park who love training together, driving to the game together, arguing and laughing with opponents together, building partnerships, taking catches, dropping catches, having a beer afterwards, sharing memories of games won and lost. Gilly was our keeper, me at second slip; he was an opening bat in ODIs, me at No. 3; he was vice-captain, I was captain. We did it at the elite level, which meant we also shared extended celebrations after Test and tournament triumphs, weeks away from our families, planes, trains and taxis that weren't always on time, good and bad hotels, applause and abuse, fair and unfair scrutiny, fair and unfair punishment. As we experienced so much of the glamour and grind of professional sport together, we built a bond that was stronger than rock solid. It was inevitable that the day he walked out of the Aussie dressing room for the last time, my cricket life would never be the same. We could still share a coffee or a beer if our paths crossed, still chat on the phone about any sport, any time. But as a player and captain I'd come to rely on him so often it became second nature. *What does Gilly reckon?* For the first few days in the West Indies, as I made plans for the tour and especially as I tried to work out how I was going to communicate with and get the best out of the new players in our squad, I felt a bit lonely.

On the field, our new keeper Brad Haddin performed well in the Caribbean (taking 16 catches and batting consistently without a big score as we won the three-Test series 2–0), but Gilly was irreplaceable. The trend towards Test keepers averaging closer to 40 than 30 with the bat was well underway when Gilly debuted in 1999, but he made it compulsory by being so much better than that. A few exceptional wicketkeepers who weren't so good with the bat have Gilly to blame for not getting an extended run in Test cricket. Chris Read of England is one who comes to mind. For much of his career Gilly's Test average was 60 and more, his runs made in a style that would have been described as cavalier if he didn't do it all the time. He was a mix of smart, fearless and unconventional with the bat in his hand, a one-of-a-kind who specialised in assaulting ODI opening attacks at seven, eight or nine runs an over, and turning a Test innings score of 5–200 into 5–350 or 5–450 at better than a run a ball.

The most extraordinary thing about Gilly's batting record is that it could have been even better, especially in ODI cricket. Whenever I got off to a fast start in the one-dayers, say scored 30 from my first 20 balls, I'd do all I could to make a hundred even if it meant I slowed down a bit to get there. The pragmatist in me reasoned that a big score from the No. 3 was the best thing for the team. Gilly's strategy was to keep swinging. If he was 40 from 20 he wanted to be 80 from 40, which sometimes led to his downfall. Was he wrong or was I? Yes, he should have scored more hundreds, but I can't recall his bravado costing us games and certainly he wouldn't have had so much fun (neither would the fans, neither would the rest of us). He believed in being positive, he believed in winning and he proved time and again the two go hand in hand.

He was the best deputy a captain could have. There was never a minute when he didn't have my back, or a time when he intimated he might do the job better than me. He was a servant to team harmony. In this way, he could have modelled himself on Heals, who was brilliant as vice-captain when I first came into the Test and ODI teams. Gilly was forthright in team meetings, never afraid to offer a contrary view, but once we settled on a plan he was 100 per cent behind it. His time as vice-captain and his experience as captain when I was injured was enough for him to know the pressures that came with being skipper, which meant he was always seeking to make my job easier. One of his pet projects was to get us all together to talk about ourselves, tell a favourite joke or an unusual story, which could have a really galvanising effect on us as a group. These were less effort but more effective, I reckon, than the gimmicky social events that were organised as team-bonding exercises on tours early in my career.

I was fielding at bat-pad on the off-side the moment we regained the Ashes in Perth in 2006–07 and as soon as the last wicket fell I just ran, exuberant, not sure where I was going. Gilly, even at this juncture more composed and rational than most of us, was after me, because he had something he needed to say. He jumped on my shoulders, turned me around and as we hugged he shouted in my ear, 'Mate, I'm so bloody proud of you!' He knew how much losing the Ashes had hurt me and how dedicated I'd become in the quest to get them back. He understood how important this victory was for me. He cared. He always did.

IN MAY OF 2008, we arrived in the West Indies for an eight-week series. We won the three Tests 2–0. I scored a good century in the first Test and Simon Katich, who came back into the side as an opener after being dropped three years earlier, made centuries in the second and third matches to help get us home. Just before the one-day international series started we got word that Jane McGrath had lost her battle with cancer. I can't begin to tell you how hard it was to hear the news, especially on the tour and so far from home, and just how sad it was. It was only a year since Glenn had been with the team in the Caribbean when we'd retained the World Cup. Now it was near the end of June, I was in St Vincent, and all I could think about was what Glenn and the kids must be going through.

Jane was a beautiful person, she lit up every room she entered. I always loved it when she was around the team. I was so upset, I contemplated not playing in that opener and had made up my mind to do so, but on the eve of the five-game series I realised I had to stay. The cricket demanded it and the team needed me to put on my game face and keep going. In Jane's memory, on that first day of play at the Arnos Vale Ground in Kingstown, we all wore pink ribbons and used the pink grips on our bats that Symmo and Haydos had previously used in international matches to promote Jane's work at raising awareness of breast cancer.

Back in Sydney, Rianna went to the funeral and it hurt to know I couldn't be with her.

As it turned out, while batting in the second ODI in Grenada I suffered a wrist injury that was much worse than I'd first thought. I played through the pain but then couldn't complete the next training session and was flown home just prior to the fourth one-dayer in St Kitts for surgery to repair the tissue and tendon damage. I was relieved to be going home early, as it meant I could be with Rianna to be present at the birth of our first child Emmy Charlotte Ponting on July 26.

When I'd shared a celebratory beer with Gilly in St Vincent back in the early days of our 2007 World Cup campaign, to toast the safe arrival of his third child, he didn't know that Rianna and I were having great difficulty starting a family of our own. Hardly anyone did. From the day Rianna and I were engaged in 2001 we talked about starting a family, and soon, but it wasn't happening for us and that caused us a lot of heartache. We'd joined the IVF program (in the process meeting some remarkable doctors and nurses, especially Professor Michael Chapman). But this created all sorts of stresses, especially when it didn't work for us as we'd hoped, and making it harder, we'd told only our immediate families exactly what we were going through, which we had to do, but that created anguish of its own, as keeping secrets always does.

Later on during that World Cup tour, when Rianna and I spent a couple of days in St Barts, we had a coffee in a beautiful little village looking out over some very expensive yachts and crystal-clear water. Twenty-fours hours earlier, she had been in a clinic in Antigua, having some blood tests done and then organising for the results to be sent back to our doctors in Sydney. We were going to a lot of trouble for no progress, and eventually she said sadly, 'If it's just you and me, we'll travel everywhere and we'll have some amazing experiences together. That will be enough for us.'

I said that was enough for me, too. And it would have been.

But we didn't give up, and a couple of months later we finally had the good news we'd been yearning for. At the end of August, I was at a pre-season camp in Brisbane and though I didn't say anything, my mood was constantly bubbly. The intention was that we'd return home for just a couple of days after the camp and then fly to South Africa for the World Twenty20.

Rianna picked me up at Sydney airport and I could tell immediately that something was wrong. Initially, she was quiet, intending to wait until we got home, but before too long she pulled over and told me the bad news: we'd lost the baby. I can't think of the right word to describe how we felt — shattered, devastated — and I knew immediately I wasn't travelling anywhere. I needed to be home with my wife so we could grieve together. Rianna had to have an operation and it was imperative I stay for that and the days after; exactly when I'd resume playing was the least important thing on my mind. We put out a statement that my departure had been delayed because Rianna was 'ill', which was sort of right, but then my manager had a gossip columnist on the phone, asking if we were having marital problems.

I did get to South Africa eventually, but only after Rianna insisted she was okay. A few months later, after our seventh IVF treatment Rianna fell pregnant again with what I now call our 'little miracle'. Such was the anxiety we'd been through in the previous few years, it was a while before we felt brave enough to be truly over the moon, but when Emmy was born, five weeks early, it was an amazing time. I was so proud of her, and so unbelievably proud of Rianna. The love in the room in the hours immediately afterwards was so special. Every day since has been special. Then Matisse came along and made it even better.

I can't say the birth of our first child suddenly gave me a new insight into the stress that dads like Gilly went through when cricket separated them from their loved ones. I think I appreciated this from the start of my international career, when I saw how happy guys like Mark Taylor and David Boon were travelling to New Zealand with their families in early 1995, and then how they coped with missing them a few weeks later when we went to the West Indies. Boonie told me once how hard it was coming home from an Ashes tour – he'd been away so long he was genuinely worried his kids wouldn't recognise him. Never once did I as captain object to a player having his kids with him on tour, no matter how small the hotel was or what we were expecting of him as a cricketer at the time. My view is it is *always* a good time to have your family with you.

In the seasons since that first short trip to New Zealand, I've had some wonderful things happen to me as an international cricketer, but nothing compares to becoming a father and seeing your children grow and develop. Things that might seem simple to single blokes — like dropping Emmy at kindy or reading with my daughters — give me a sense of happiness that is different and in many ways more rewarding than what I've enjoyed on the sporting field. At the same time, the respect I have for Rianna has gone through the roof because of the way she has coped with the stresses that come with raising children, often on her own while I have been away because of cricket.

Having such a happy and settled home life didn't make the game on the field any easier, but it did make my life in the game easier. I know my three girls love me unconditionally and I was aware when I was away playing that they supported my sporting dreams totally. If I'm ever asked if I was a 'lucky' cricketer, having the chance to share my life with Rianna and my kids is what I think of first.

Loss

Loss is a horrible thing as, almost all the time, it's outside of your control. Loss was not a constant in my career but there are a number of moments that will always be with me as I reflect back on my time travelling the world. Loss included being on the road when close family and friends passed away or needed me most. Loss was about some of the greatest ever cricketers retiring at various times while I played on. Loss was also the deepest despair of losing series that we should have won, and loss was often about dealing with adversity. Aside from the sad passing of family and close friends, which I deal with separately in this book, I always tried not to dwell too long on the other loss situations I was confronted with. You can only control what you can, and there's no point over-analysing or getting down when things outside of your control don't go well. You certainly need time to think about what has happened but then it's time to continue on as best you can. In a team environment, communication was always paramount around any situations like this. I spent many a long night with team-mates who knocked on my door wanting to chat about problems in their private lives, feeling homesick or dealing with something else critical to them. I had an open-door policy that I was available to the boys 24 hours a day. Sometimes talking through things made it easier but often it was the change in environment that helped us deal with the problems or loss. Life on the road and being away from loved ones is not easy and it's made even more difficult when you suffer a loss.

CHAPTER 48

OVER-RATED

Fourth Test, Nagpur, India, November 9, 2008

'PUNTER, THE OVER-RATE'S no good,' he said quietly. 'They reckon we might be 10 overs behind.'

If I was hoping to get through a series against India without controversy I was sadly mistaken. We would be accused of cheating by their opening batsman and then I would be accused of putting myself ahead of the team. In my books I'm not sure which is worse, because I prided myself on never doing either.

I had three months off after my early homecoming from the Caribbean. It was almost like long service leave and just what I needed to prepare myself for the four-Test series in India. Immediately after that series we set off on a journey that for the guys like me playing all three forms of the modern game would be 18 months long. We had seven weeks in India, came home for the Australian summer, headed to South Africa for three Tests, two T20Is and five ODIs, then to Abu Dhabi and Dubai for five one-dayers and one T20I against Pakistan and then on to England for a World Twenty20, five Ashes Tests, eight ODIs and two T20Is. After that it was back to South Africa for the ICC Champions Trophy, another visit back to India for seven ODIs and then home again for another summer before finally heading to New Zealand for five ODIs and two Tests.

I didn't play in all the games. No one could. After the Ashes tour I pulled the pin on Twenty20 internationals, not because I really wanted to but simply because something had to give.

Even before the Tests in India, while I was waiting for my wrist to recover from surgery, the boys played three ODIs against Bangladesh in Darwin. On the field, those games were good for us, but elsewhere Andrew Symonds was getting himself in trouble. It was the beginning of the end for Symmo as far as international cricket was concerned, a process that would end with him being sacked from our squad just before the World Twenty20 in England in the first week of June 2009. The cause of his demise was analysed to death in the media, with various experts coming up with a whole stack of possible causes. To tell the truth, I think it was pretty simple really: he just got sick of it.

By 'it', I don't mean the actual cricket, but the grind and the scrutiny. As I said before Symmo was scarred by the Harbhajan affair. Say what you like about Symmo, I've always found him to be a straight-up-and-down bloke. Although I rebounded in the West Indies, got my love of the game back, Symmo didn't. Not completely.

In Darwin, he skipped a team meeting to go fishing, and the leadership group and selectors responded by omitting him from the games against Bangladesh and the India tour; nine months later, in England, he went to watch TV coverage from Melbourne of a State of Origin rugby league game and stayed afterwards for a few beers, which contravened team policy about consuming alcohol away from the dressing room and the team hotel. This was the last of a series of instances where he broke team rules and in total they added up to a man who didn't really want to play for Australia anymore. It was such a shame, because when he was firing he was a highly influential cricketer and a very positive presence in the dressing room. One thing that frustrated me was that when he departed, any number of people said or implied that he wouldn't be missed, as if we had a never-ending smorgasbord of experienced first-class players to pick from, but times had changed. This long season proved that.

Inevitably, there was an edge to our Test tour of India, given that it came so soon after the controversy in Australia. I was aware of this as soon as we arrived at our first destination, Jaipur, when the local reporters got into me about my lousy Test average to that point in India (12.28 in four matches, three in 2001, one in 2004) and how they reckoned Harbhajan had it over me. After the local cricket officials and staff at the Rajasthan Cricket Association (RCA) academy looked after us brilliantly while we prepared for the big games to come, one high-ranking Indian administrator complained publicly that 'the RCA is being a little too obliging to the Australian team'.

Then, about a week into the tour, their great opening bat Virender Sehwag was quoted as saying we'd cheated during the Test at the SCG. 'We'd have won the Sydney Test match if they hadn't claimed catches taken off half-volleys in that game,' was how the papers reported his comments.

Every media interview, I had to be careful not to throw petrol on the fire. If I said the wrong thing, they had their story; if I successfully played the diplomat, the result was a draw. I couldn't win. If I was more of a political animal, I might have grown to enjoy the exchanges, but I just wanted to play cricket the same as I'd always done.

I went into the first Test determined to make a hundred. By this point in my career I'd developed something of a reputation for batting well early in a series, having made a 'first up' hundred in nine opening Tests of a rubber to this point of my career, including four times in the previous three years. This is a case, I guess, of the statistics truly telling a story — as much as I'd like to believe I was as ready and fresh for one game as another, as much as I tried to mimic my preparation from one game to the next, it must have got harder for me as a series was played out. Maybe the gradual build-up of stress and pressure diminished my output, maybe the extended times at the crease in the early Tests took more of a toll than I realised, mentally more so than physically. In the 2006–07 Ashes series, I scored big hundreds in the first two Tests but I reckon my best dig, purely for the quality of batting, came in the fifth Test in Sydney, when I cruised to 45 without playing a false stroke. Every ball pinged off the middle of my bat, until I pushed a ball to Jimmy Anderson at mid-on and called for a single that wasn't there. As far as mental mistakes go, this run out was one of the worst of my career. I doubt I would have made this mistake in the opening Test of the series.

In the opening Test in Bangalore, I scored what would prove to be my sole Test century in India. It wasn't a pretty innings but under the circumstances — made on a slow deck in my first big game back from the wrist surgery, with all the pre-match animosity simmering away and with Harbhajan bowling plenty of overs — it remains one of my favourites. I'm not a goal-setter and revenge is not a motive that works well for me, but I did want to show that I could bat well on Indian pitches and I still hated the manner in which they'd got their way over the racial abuse charge. I had a point to prove to a few people, as well as to myself. When I reached three figures I was very excited and it showed in my celebration, one of the most animated of my career.

This was a Test we could easily have won. Mike Hussey also made a hundred and then we had them seven down and 198 runs behind during their first innings. But Harbhajan and Zaheer Khan put on 80 for the eighth wicket, playing up to the big crowd like a pair of pro wrestlers, and our early momentum was lost, never to return. This wasn't the best hour of my time as captain. We took the new ball and our quicks tried to blast Harbhajan and Zaheer out, but on such a slow wicket this was the wrong tactic. We should have been patient; instead we gave two experienced cricketers a chance to swing away, hit a few fours and change the mood. For the rest of the series, we were playing from behind.

THE INDIAN TEAM WE were playing was a very good one. Sourav Ganguly had announced he was retiring, but Sachin Tendulkar, Rahul Dravid, VVS Laxman and Sehwag were still very hard to get out. MS Dhoni was, post-Gilchrist, the most influential keeper in the game, and Zaheer Khan and Ishant Sharma made for a potent opening attack. Harbhajan took his 300th Test wicket when he bowled me in the fourth Test. At the same time, our bowling lacked penetration. We had come to rely on Brett Lee, and for the first 12 months post McGrath and Warne that worked out all right, because Bing was magnificent, taking 58 wickets in nine Tests. But now, suddenly, he was in decline, as a run of injury, illness and some personal problems overtook him. Our other bowlers couldn't pick him up.

As things turned out, Brett's Test career only had a couple more months to go, and his frustration boiled over during the second Test, when he felt he should have been bowling during India's second innings. Before the start of play on day four, we decided we weren't going to make the mistake we'd made in Bangalore; on another slow pitch we were going to take the pace off the ball, and make it hard for the batsmen to score. So Shane Watson and Cameron White, medium pace and wrist spin, bowled first up. Then I turned to our best two quicks in the first innings, Mitchell Johnson and Peter Siddle, but with every over the game was getting away from us, in more ways than one: India's lead was almost 400, with nine second-innings wickets in hand; Dhoni had been sent out to blast some quick runs; the match referee had told us we were behind our required over-rate and if it got any worse I, as captain, would be suspended for the next Test. That was the law. I decided to bring Huss on to bowl some slow-medium stuff, the logic being that he would be hard to get away and he'd pick up the over-rate, but Brett was upset at not getting a chance. During a break in play he told me so. This was the last thing I needed, so I had a go at him, told him to think a bit about the game and what was best for the team.

'I'm a bowler, I want to bowl,' he snapped at me during the lunch break. 'Just like you're a batsman, you want to bat.'

I understood where he was coming from, but the way he carried on went against how I'd been brought up to always support the captain. I took some of the blame by saying maybe I didn't explain our tactics well enough before the start of the day's play, but everyone else was on the same page. After the interval, Brett did get his chance and even took a wicket as India batted us right out of the game, but it was our on-field spat that gained most of the attention, leading to stories of a 'rift' between us. I never thought it was as bad as that. We'd been mates for a long time and it was going to take a lot more than this to push us apart.

THE OVER-RATES CAME BACK to haunt me again in the final Test, at Nagpur. After a high-scoring draw in Delhi, we needed to win here to retain the Border–Gavaskar Trophy, but for much of the game that task seemed to be beyond us. Jason Krejza, an off-spinner originally from Sydney who'd moved to Hobart and done enough for Tassie to become the latest to audition for the job as Shane Warne's successor, made his Test debut and immediately took eight wickets (for 215) in his first innings. Jason was as talented an off-spinner as any who played for Australia in my experience, but in my view he lacked the consistency to ever nail down the spinner's job. In reply, we fell 86 runs behind, and when the Indian openers, Sehwag and Murali Vijay, added 116 at the start of India's second innings it looked like we were gone.

Then, almost without warning, we were right back in the series. In the middle session of day four, Shane Watson began to get the ball to reverse swing, while Brett Lee briefly rediscovered a little of his best form. When Bing had Sehwag caught behind India were 3–142, a lead of 228, and then, as soon as I brought Krejza back on, Laxman was knocked over by a beauty that zipped between his bat and pad. Ganguly, playing his final Test innings, was out first ball, caught-and-bowled. A few minutes later, with tea almost upon us, Tendulkar ran himself out. India were 6–166, a lead of 252. The atmosphere when we ran into our dressing room was electric; it was as if we'd just been told Santa Claus really does exist. Then coach Tim Nielsen sat down next to me.

'Punter, the over-rate's no good,' he said quietly. 'They reckon we might be 10 overs behind.'

I couldn't believe it. At the drinks break, midway through the session just gone, I'd been told we were three or four overs down. That was manageable; 10 overs down was not.

'Mate, we're checking with the match referee,' Tim said. 'I'll tell you exactly what's happening as soon as we find out.'

There was any number of conflicting emotions spinning around in my head. Jason Krejza had already taken 10 wickets in the Test so he was an obvious choice to keep bowling …

If you go for the win you're going to miss a Test match.

Watto was exhausted after bowling for much of the previous session, so I needed an alternative, preferably someone who could get the ball to reverse …

You can't just ignore the match referee … they'll be into you again for not playing in the right spirit.

If Mitch or Bing bowled like Watto it was possible we'd run through their lower order. But at team meetings, when we'd discussed our over-rate problems, we'd agreed we'd fix the problem without slow bowlers …

Just go for it.

I started with Mitch. Harbhajan handled him comfortably. Out came the bad news: we were nine overs down. Jason bowled the second over, conceding a single. I spoke to Michael Clarke, the vice-captain, and he said flatly, 'Mate, you've got to keep attacking with your best spinner at one end and try and rush through the overs at the other.' At the same time, a left-field idea kept nagging at me …

Cameron White was our first-choice spinner for the first three Tests; he'd bowled 10 overs in their first innings, for 24 runs; they wouldn't be expecting him; his very best leg-spinner is almost Warne-like, only quicker; it'll help the over-rate.

I brought him on.

If this move had worked, they might have called me a genius for backing my gut instinct, but unfortunately Cameron promptly bowled the worst six balls of his life. He conceded 12 runs including five from an ugly legside wide. The mood changed and quickly I grew agitated by the way this happened. In the glory days, we always won these key moments; now I was so bitterly disappointed things had got away from us so quickly. I reacted by bringing Mike Hussey on to bowl slow-mediums off a short run. He could fix the over rate at one end, I figured, while Jason kept trying to get wickets. Simply put, I tried to solve everything and came up empty. After Huss, I tried Michael Clarke's left-arm spin but he couldn't repeat his SCG miracle, and after that I figured there was no point going back to the quicks because then we'd just be in over-rate trouble again.

The runs flowed, no wickets fell, and Dhoni and Harbhajan ended up adding 108 for the seventh wicket. At stumps we were 0–13 needing a further 369 to win. Back on day three, when they'd set some disgracefully defensive fields (at one point having eight fielders on the off-side while the bowlers aimed way wide of the off-stump), we'd scored just 166 runs in 85.4 overs. We couldn't win.

THE CRICKET GRAPEVINE is unforgiving. I knew pretty quickly that my tactics were going to be criticised; indeed, that they were already being ripped to shreds. What I didn't anticipate was how my integrity would be questioned, how I'd be accused of sacrificing a win to escape a suspension. The ABC commentators had been into me. So too had former Australian captain Allan Border while calling the game for Fox Sports. 'I don't know what to make of all this,' AB said. 'They go into the tea break on a high and come out worrying about over rates. I am glad Ricky can't read my mind right now because he is not going to like it.'

Of all the critics and ex-players who had a dig, the spray from AB was the one that stung the most. Like everyone, I know what a terrific bloke he is, and I never enjoy having good people criticise me. But what really annoyed me was that Allan was, at the time, on the board of Cricket Australia, the same Cricket Australia who ever since the Sydney Test had been reminding us about how we had to do the right thing by the game. Now here he was telling the world that I should have just ignored the match referee and worried only about winning.

The next day, after India won the Test by 172 runs, I said what I thought:

> To tell you the truth, I'm disappointed with some of the criticism, particularly from former Australian captains and Cricket Australia board members. As captain of the Australian cricket team, I feel I have a responsibility to play the game in the right spirit. I have an obligation to bowl 90 overs in a day's play and the way we were heading, if the quicks had continued we would have been maybe 12 overs down ...
>
> Everyone has an opinion on the way I captain the team or the way the team plays, but the thing I am most disappointed about is this inference out there that I put myself totally ahead of the team. Anybody who knows me or the way I play my cricket or how I operate around the Australian team would hopefully not say that is the case ...

MY MINDSET IN THE days after Nagpur was as disheartened as I ever got with cricket. I missed my two girls, everyone wanted a piece of me, and too many people believed I was selfish and stupid. Having a tough hide didn't help, because it allowed me to conceal my despondency pretty well — it was only when I was on the phone to Rianna that I confessed to how sad and lonely I was. Outside the team, it felt as if I had precious few mates trying to defend me. A few did, Warnie, Lang and Gilly among them, but not a lot.

One person who did offer support was Cricket Australia CEO James Sutherland, and I was very grateful for that. He had said he wanted to rebuild our relationship after the stresses of the previous January and this was the first real test of that. At a time when it might have been more comfortable to sit with the critics he was out there arguing that my actions were 'very reasonable'. After we arrived home, he said of me, 'Any suggestion that he put himself first ahead of the team last week in Nagpur is completely off beam and can only come from someone who does not know him or understand him.'

It took a while for me to find some perspective. My captaincy on that fourth day wasn't great when it needed to be, because at a vital time I wasn't able to separate what mattered from what could wait. I needed to compartmentalise things better, focus on what was really important. But my motives were honourable; never then, before or since have I put myself ahead of what was best for the team. If anyone doesn't believe that, it's his or her problem, not mine.

At the same time, I realised I was never going to win with the narky section of the cricket media. If I put a foot out of line they were going to be into me. That this was especially true of some past players, including blokes who used to complain incessantly when they were the cricketers being denigrated by some past players, was annoying, ironic and even a little sad. I think my relationship with this section of the media actually improved after this tour, because I came to accept them for what they are.

As for over rates, I came to realise I was part of the problem. I sometimes talked too much with bowlers and team-mates between overs, even between deliveries. I wanted to help and sometimes needed to cajole but this was slowing us down too much. I wasn't the only one who had to alter his ways, and it wasn't just us Australians or just us players who had to improve. Sometimes the drinks breaks, for example, could drag on forever, not because we were overly thirsty but because it took too long for the sponsored refreshment carts to get on and off the ground. But I did have to change. Back in the glory days, our great bowlers didn't need too much on-field input from me; they could put things right themselves. Bowlers like McGrath, Gillespie and Warne used to keep the pressure on and didn't go for many runs, so there weren't as many minutes spent chasing balls to the boundary, and less time required to change the field because we'd conceded a single. Warnie, of course, was a leggie, so he rarely took too long to bowl an over. The longest delays were waiting for the next batsman to come in.

Unfortunately, for the most part, those days were gone.

CHAPTER 49

LAST MAN STANDING

Australian summer, 2008–09

THE SOUTH AFRICAN TEAM arrived in December 2008 having never won a Test series in Australia. They soon put that straight, successfully chasing 414 in Perth and then dominating the Boxing Day Test, two results that did a lot to burn all the wood we'd had over them for the previous 15 years. This was especially true of their win at the WACA, when we outplayed them for three-and-a-half days but could hardly take a wicket after that. If we'd set them 600 they still might have won.

In Melbourne, we had them at 8–251 in their first innings, in reply to our 394, and from there they never looked like losing. JP Duminy, playing in his second Test, made 166. Dale Steyn, who to that point in his Test career had amassed 245 runs at an average of less than 10, scored 76. Despite Steyn taking his second five-for of the game we set them 183, which they reached for the loss of just one wicket. I became the second man in cricket history to score a hundred and a 99 in the same Test; I also became the first Australian captain since Allan Border in 1992–93 to lose a Test series at home. Given the match result, there was no joy in the former; the latter left me despondent. This was different to the Ashes loss in 2005, because I wasn't sure how we were going to turn things around.

The key to my century on Boxing Day was that I managed to work out the pace of the wicket, which was slower than what we'd expected, not your typical MCG pitch of recent times. It was possible to be aggressive, but you had to pick the right delivery, and after lunch, from the moment I hit Makhaya Ntini for three straight fours, my concentration was as good as it had been in two years. I went from 60 to my ton in 37 balls, specifically acknowledged Rianna and Emmy in the crowd, and then fell immediately to Paul Harris, their left-arm spinner. Afterwards, I lamented not going on to make a really big score, which is what the team needed — this was one of those situations when just making a hundred was not enough — and inevitably there were suggestions that I'd lost focus in the wake of celebrating the century. But it wasn't as if I threw the innings away. This was only the third time in almost 10 years that I'd been dismissed between 100 and 110 in a Test match.

The second innings, when I was out one *short* of a hundred, was different. This innings was a real mental struggle, as I fought to save the game while — except for a 96-run stand with Michael Clarke — wickets kept falling at the other end. Steyn was delivering some superb outswingers at pace, demonstrating why so many people rated him the best fast bowler in the game. Having spent most of the previous day in the field watching the South African late-order take the game away from us, I was determined to bat for as long as I could. I'm not sure I'd ever been more determined to put together a really big score.

But as I approached the hundred, my brain became a little scrambled, in an almost bizarre way. Our lead was just past 150, not nearly enough, and we were seven wickets down. There is always something special about getting a century in each innings, but I became almost obsessed about *not* worrying about the achievement. By this stage of the Test, the pitch was a bit up and down. I kept reminding myself that getting out at this time, whether it was just before or just after I reached three figures, would severely diminish the value of my effort, because I had to make 150 or 170 if we were going to set South Africa a decent target. Not only were Steyn's outswingers a severe test, the cutters of Morne Morkel, their tall fast bowler, were becoming more and more awkward ...

Forget about the ton ... if you're going to get out, you've got to be last man out.

Coaches and sports psychologists like to remind players to stay 'in the moment'. It's about process not outcome. I got ahead of myself. Morkel bowled a slower ball and I pushed half-heartedly at it and spooned a catch to Graeme Smith at short cover. The pressure, most of it self-inflicted, had got me, in a way that I don't think it had ever affected me before. Sure, I'd been dismissed just short of a hundred in the past, but I'd never thought of myself as being particularly susceptible to the 'nervous nineties'. The stress of the game situation, the fact we were losing and I was the only man who could save us, is what made this so different, so difficult. I know this will sound arrogant, but the fact is I didn't have much experience of losing, and I was finding out how different a game of cricket can be when you're not on top, or expecting to be on top, or confident that if you're not on top that you or someone else in the team will get you back on top.

THE INCONSISTENCY OF SOME of our new players was maddening. Jason Krejza was terrific in Nagpur but lost his way in Perth. Mitchell Johnson took 8–61 in South Africa's first innings at the WACA, including a devastating spell of 5–2 in 21 deliveries, but hardly looked like breaking through in Melbourne. Most of the guys in the top seven were making some runs, but we were all having off days too. Brad Haddin was good, sometimes very good, with the bat, but he had a few niggling injuries that hampered his keeping.

Worst of all, Matt Hayden was really struggling, which I think had a major effect on us all. Haydos' strength and belligerence as the rock at the top of the batting order had been one of the team's trademarks for the past six or seven years, but now everything was going against him. More than once an umpire fired him and in his 100th Test, the game against New Zealand in Adelaide, he was involved in a mix-up with Simon Katich and was run out for 23. I kept hoping he'd fight his way out of his slump, but things went from bad to worse against South Africa. Not being able to give him the magic bit of advice that would turn things around was so frustrating.

When Haydos was firing, which was most of the time between 2001 and 2008, no opening bat hit more powerfully through the line, or more often took control of the game from the jump. I batted No. 3, straight after him, so I often saw first-hand the sort of devastating impact he had on opposition bowlers. His problem now wasn't technical and it wasn't a lack of desire. When he'd lost a bit of form in the past, he'd always rediscovered it through his mental strength, either by blasting his way back to his best or by bunkering in for a long fight. When neither method worked this time, he lost a little of his self-belief. Kryptonite has a similar effect on Superman. A bit like Boonie in 1995–96, Junior in 2002 and Gilly just a year earlier, if Haydos was 27 he would have practised his butt off to get his greatness back — and in India and at the start of this Australian season he did work bloody hard — but all that continued effort didn't have quite the same appeal it once did. Retirement was just around the corner.

I was the same captain who had once given Andrew Symonds a shot at Andrew Flintoff in a Test in Perth, ahead of McGrath, Lee, Clark and Warne, a move made on a hunch that worked immediately. I was the same bloke who threw the ball to Michael Clarke against India in Sydney when no one else had thought of it and Pup bowled us to a stunning win. I was even the skipper who made the unexpected but ill-fated move to give Cameron White a go at Nagpur. However, on the last day and a half in Perth, when Graeme Smith and AB de Villiers made hundreds, and at the MCG, when we couldn't get Duminy and Steyn out, I was too stubborn and too regimented for the team's good.

The men that made me. Former Mowbray stalwarts Richard Soule, Mick Sellers, Brad Jones and Ian Young.

Two coaches who had a major influence on my career, Greg Shipperd (left) and Rod Marsh (right).

Caught by the Launceston Examiner *sporting a classic '80s mullet.*

Heading off for a single, with then Mowbray captain Richard Soule in a game against Riverside. November 7, 1992.

With Boonie at the MCG. Australia vs Sri Lanka, December 1995.

A proud day. Rianna joined me at the Order of Australia presentation at Government House, Sydney. May 10, 2012.

On the best day of my life with my beautiful bride. Our June wedding, 2002.

The first Christmas at home with my girls and my first one not on Tour in 17 years. December 2012.

Ten days after this double century at Bellerive Oval, Tasmania, I was picked to play for Australia. November 4, 1994 (top left). Aiming for the boundary against New Zealand at Launceston, 1993–94 (top right), and diving for my century against India at the SCG, January 4, 2011 (bottom).

On my way to my century in the ICC Cricket World Cup quarter final, Ahmedabad, March 24, 2011 (top left). Setting the field with Shane Warne in the second Ashes Test match, Adelaide Oval, December 2, 2006 (top right).

I'm no Glenn McGrath, my medium-pacers at the Gabba against the West Indies, November 24, 1996 (bottom left); during my first Test as captain in the slips with the guys, Sri Lanka, 2004 (bottom right).

Diving to catch Jon Lewis of England during game one of the Commonwealth Bank One Day International Series between Australia and England at the MCG on January 12, 2007.

The biggest challenge of my captaincy, Monkeygate (bottom left). Celebrating some of my favourite centuries: one of two at the SCG against South Africa, 2006 (bottom right).

Michael Clarke takes three quick wickets to bowl us to a miracle victory late on day five of the second Test against India at the SCG, January 6, 2008.

Highs and lows. Winning the ICC Cricket World Cup final, 2003 (bottom left), and contemplating the loss to India in the quarter final at Sardar Patel Stadium in Ahmedabad, 2011. It turned out to be my last ODI series as captain.

Bringing up my 100, my last ODI century at the ICC Cricket World Cup quarter final, Ahmedabad, March 24, 2011 (top left). Copping a bouncer on the cheek from Steve Harmison at Lord's (top right)

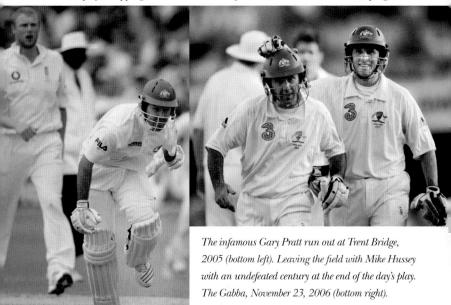

The infamous Gary Pratt run out at Trent Bridge, 2005 (bottom left). Leaving the field with Mike Hussey with an undefeated century at the end of the day's play. The Gabba, November 23, 2006 (bottom right).

Celebration on the field: with Shane Warne, who had just trapped Ian Bell lbw, 2005.

Coin toss in Cardiff with Andrew Strauss, first Test, July 8, 2009; and the long walk back, jeered by fans after being run out by Andrew Flintoff, fifth Test, August 23, 2009.

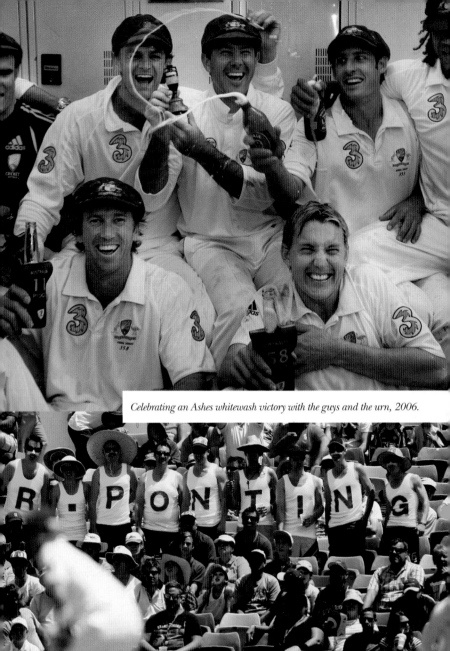

Celebrating an Ashes whitewash victory with the guys and the urn, 2006.

Moral support WACA-style.

Saying farewell from where it all started. WACA, December 3, 2012.

It was a case of loyalty — to our pre-match plan and to the guys I was leading — overriding reality. In fact, changing course might not have made any difference but as captain I had to do more than just hope we'd come good. You never get lucky by standing still.

WE HEADED FOR SYDNEY and promptly earned one of the most enjoyable wins of my time as skipper. It didn't start well — I made my second first-ball duck in three Tests on day one — but I was really happy with the way I hit them during my second-innings 53. My captaincy was pretty productive as well, most notably when I thought I got our declaration just about spot-on. The timing was tricky: I wanted to be aggressive but Test teams are successfully chasing big totals on the final day more often now than they did in the good old days. No team had ever scored more than 288 to win a Test at the SCG, but we'd set that record the previous time we'd played South Africa in Sydney, when we made 2–288 in 60 overs on the last day in 2005–06. I'd been tagged a conservative declarer, even though there aren't too many examples of me costing a team a win by dallying too long. If I was going to be cautious, this would have been a good time, because we were facing a clean sweep, something no Australian Test team had ever suffered at home. Instead, I set the South Africans 376 in more than three-and-a-half sessions, which had some people wondering if I'd let them back into the game, but I felt I knew the Sydney wicket pretty well, and that while defending wouldn't be too difficult, scoring runs at speed would be. We needed plenty of overs to chisel them out.

The next day, with a maximum 50 deliveries remaining, Smith walked out to the middle, batting last because of a broken finger, to try to save the game. He and their regular No. 11, Makhaya Ntini, nearly made it, until Mitchell Johnson delivered the final blow with the second ball of the second-last possible over, a lethal in-cutter that kept low and smashed into Smith's stumps. For the second time in two seasons a Test at the SCG had gone down to the wire. Both times, Australia had prevailed. Both times, the crowd's support for us was fantastic. This time, the umpiring was good and the spirit in which the game was played was excellent, exemplified by the circumstances that saw Jacques Kallis out, caught and bowled, on the final day by our new all-rounder Andrew 'Ronnie' McDonald.

It was one of those ones where the catch was made at absolute ground level, and if it had been left to the umpires it could have gone either way. The video umpire would have given the batsman the benefit of the doubt. I'd been campaigning for years to get the fieldsman's word accepted in these instances, but strangely it seems there are few people who agree with me. Anil Kumble and Michael Vaughan were just two of a number of overseas captains who didn't like taking the fieldsman's word for it. This time, Jacques asked if the catch was fair and Ronnie confirmed it was. He then walked off. If only it could work this way every time.

Much later in the day, with the gloom setting in, just a few overs left and South Africa nine wickets down, Ronnie desperately and successfully ran down a shot that could have reached the boundary, which meant that Ntini, usually a poor batsman, would be at the non-striker's end for the first ball of the following over.

'Why didn't you kick it into the boundary?' I asked him, a mock-stern look on my face.

This was the first time Ronnie had played under my captaincy. He didn't know me well but he was well aware that kicking the ball over the rope in such circumstances is an unsporting thing to do. Of course, me being skipper and him being a debutant, he didn't say that to me; he just looked at me like a kid in the principal's office who was getting roused on even though he hadn't done anything wrong.

Then I grinned … he grinned … and we went back to trying to win the Test. I was sad after Nagpur, Perth and Melbourne, questioning my worth as a captain. Now, quickly, I was chirpy again.

Winning does that for you.

Playing fresh

The world has become a very busy place. Whether you're a family person, high up in the corporate world, work for someone else or play cricket for a living — you're probably doing more than ever before. As professional cricketers, we have certainly seen the world become a smaller place as we travel more often and play more games. The introduction of an additional format of cricket (T20) has also added more tournaments, competitions and games. Don't get me wrong, I'm not complaining about that at all but I certainly had to adapt in the final third of my career to give me the best chance of achieving longevity in the game. I always found that I played better when I was mentally fresh. Sure my body was not always 100 per cent but it was generally always manageable. But mental fatigue is completely different and, from about 2008, it was something that I was very conscious of and worked to minimise.

I decided to not play any T20 cricket so as to give myself the chance of prolonging my international first-class career — only returning after my retirement from international cricket. This gave me forced breaks on all tours, which was fantastic — especially while I was still playing one-day cricket. And it became even easier when the selectors dropped me from the ODI team, meaning all I had to do was concentrate on being the best Test cricketer I could. Over the years, my very best cricket seemed to come in the opening games of a Test series.

My first innings / first Test average was 57.31.

I put this down to going into a series mentally fresh and always a little underdone. I intentionally didn't overdo the work in the nets leading into the first Tests, meaning I had to concentrate even more on my game during the first 20–30 balls I would face. As long as I felt I was moving okay, with good rhythm, then I didn't need to do much in the nets on the day before the first Test. I wanted to take more time and get myself set. I didn't want to go out and attack until I really felt in control of the opposition bowlers.

As series or tournaments progressed, finding a way to get a mental break became important too. It was amazing how a sleep-in till 9.30am every now and then would make a world of difference to how I felt and performed. Mental freshness didn't only help my batting but it also helped my decision-making as captain. There's no doubt that the fresher your mind is, the quicker you see problems and find solutions.

CHAPTER 50

THE OLD BOY

MCG, January 11, 2009

IT WAS IN THE middle of a T20 match — the one where a young buck named Dave Warner attracted the attention of the world — that umpire Rod Tucker pointed out I was the oldest player out there. I'd never thought about it before, but looking around I realised he was right. It was a significant moment: I had always been the youngest guy in the room and now I was the veteran.

Time was moving on.

ANDREW McDONALD AND NSW left-arm quick Doug Bollinger made their Test debuts in that Sydney Test against South Africa. This was the first time since November 1999, when Adam Gilchrist and Scott Muller came into the team together, that two Australians began their Test careers in the same match. It meant eight Aussies had debuted in the year since the end of the SCG Test against India in early January 2008. Comparisons with earlier seasons reflect just how rapidly the team was evolving. In the period from my first Test as captain, at Galle in March 2004, to the end of 2007, 11 men wore the baggy green for the first time. During Steve Waugh's time in charge, from November 1999 to January 2004, seven Aussies made their Test debuts.

Things were moving so quickly in so many ways, sometimes it was hard to keep up. Every time we played an ODI we had the next ICC Champions Trophy and World Cup in the back of our minds — what tactics should we use … which players are best suited to such strategies … who will be our frontline players … which guys have the right skills and character to back up our starting eleven — but as for the individual games themselves, more and more they became a blur. It was the same with the Twenty20 internationals. Ask me today who won or who did what in specific T20 or one-day games in Australia in 2008–09 and I can't tell you much without being prompted.

I do recall a young left-hand bat named Dave Warner making his T20 international debut before he'd played even one Sheffield Shield match, and cracking 89 from just 43 balls in his first innings. Dave hit some massive sixes when I was batting with him, but then struggled when he was chosen for the ODIs that followed. Still, he'd done enough to suggest he was a future star. I thought then and still do now that Dave can forge a dynamic attacking role in Test cricket that could set him apart from other cricketers of his time.

It was in that same T20 game at the MCG, while I was fielding at mid-wicket, that Rod Tucker, who'd played with me for Tasmania in the 1990s pointed out that there was no one my age left in the team.

I looked around the field, hoping to find someone who'd been born before me, but the closest I could find was Mike Hussey, who is five months younger than me. I had just turned 34! I'd never been a veteran. When I was a teenager, I'd always played at least a year or two above my age group. Even at school, being a December baby, there were always a few guys older than me.

Another unusual on-field conversation from those T20 games occurred in Brisbane, when I was 'wired up' so the TV commentators could talk with me. Ian Healy was on air as we chased a win, and he wanted me to premeditate my next shot. It was the last ball of an over, after Huss had hit three fours, a two, then a one. The full house was buzzing …

'C'mon mate, you're on television,' Heals said.

'Sorry mate, we've got a game to win,' I replied.

This was all good fun. Less entertaining for me were the public discussions I was part of concerning our ever-evolving 'rotation policy' and Andrew Symonds' cricket future. As an example, Mitchell Johnson had established himself as a key figure in all forms of the game, but he was rested from the start of the one-day series against South Africa. I thought it was sensible to give Mitch a break, same as when Brad Haddin missed two T20 games and I didn't play in a couple of the one-dayers against New Zealand that followed the South Africa games. At a time when some guys in our squad were signing big-money deals to play T20 cricket in India and county cricket in England, some people wanted to argue that we as a group were soft and didn't realise how good we had it.

The criticism missed the point. The debate, however, would never go away. My strong view is that in the 21st century everyone with an interest in our sport — fans, players, captains, coaches, support staff, officials, media partners, sponsors and so on — have to accept that the human body needs time to rest and recover, and a critical part of that process is managing the elite players' workloads. Due consideration has to be given not just to the playing and how often games occur, but also to the cocktail of training, travel, time zones, supporting sponsors, administrators and media, and doing the right thing by family and friends. As I wrote at the time: 'We actually want to play plenty of cricket — and this is the best time of our sporting lives and we can't waste it — but we also need to be fit and sharp so we can show the world what we can do.'

Part of it was having us players as fit as possible as often as possible. Another part was ensuring all our best players were primed for the big Test matches and the most important ODI and T20 tournaments. Mitch was only five weeks away from a Test series in South Africa when he was rested, four-and-a-half months away from a World Twenty20, six months away from the first Ashes

Test. Missing a couple of T20s and a couple of ODIs made sense. Or at least it did to me.

In mid-February, I announced I was withdrawing from the second year of the IPL.

Symmo's name came up in interviews I was doing after he did a radio gig where he bagged the New Zealand wicketkeeper Brendon McCullum and the fact McCullum had been picked by NSW to play in the domestic Twenty20 final. There were suggestions he might have had a drink or two before he went on air, and questions for me from the press as to whether I still wanted him in my teams. 'Absolutely,' I quickly said to that one, but then I found myself talking publicly about his 'rehab' and his 'counsellor' as if I was his doctor or a character witness. As I tried to answer honestly but at the same time not add fuel to a fire or upset a bloke I considered a close friend, I felt more like a politician than a cricket captain. Same as when Shane Warne failed his drug test in 2003 or when Symmo had his big night in England in 2005, I knew juggling these conflicting elements as I spoke to the media was part of my job.

It was the worst part.

OF COURSE, THERE IS a lot more good to the captaincy than bad. Sometimes, I had to remind myself of this but I guess everyone has to do that at different times, whatever his or her role or occupation. As I write this book, it gnaws at me how often I mention the frustrations I had with the media or cricket politics, as if being an international cricketer is almost not worth the trouble. The injustices that come with the worst parts of the scrutiny the top cricketers are under can be diabolical, but the truth is playing out your childhood dreams, being excellent at something, especially as part of a team, and bringing pleasure not just to your family and friends but also to thousands of people you don't or hardly know is often special and sometimes even better than that. When you're winning, as we did for most of the time between 1999 and 2007, it's incredible.

The rewards are many. Not all are directly related to playing the game. Some of the most emotionally fulfilling moments come during the days when we are able to bring a little comfort to people who are doing it harder than most. For example, organising for Aussie cricketers to say g'day to sick children in hospital is supposed to be for the kids' benefit, but I have found such visits to be a source of enormous inspiration, as their courage and optimism far outshine mine.

My serious involvement with childhood cancer charities started at a corporate lunch in Sydney in 2002. Phil Kearns, the former Australian rugby union skipper, was at the same function. After I responded, 'Anything with children,' to the question, 'What charity most appeals to you?', Phil revealed he was on the board of the Children's Cancer Institute of Australia (CCIA).

'Would you be interested in coming to the Children's Hospital at Randwick, to help the kids out?' he asked me.

The expression 'to help the kids out' stayed with me. What exactly did that mean? What could I do?

Kearnsy arranged for us to have an extended tour, and because it was just Rianna and me, there was time for us to have a few 'one-on-one' conversations with patients, nurses and doctors. Meeting those kids and their carers on this occasion was a life-changing experience.

All the kids were inspirational, but two stand out in my memory. The first child we saw was a six-month-old boy who had just been diagnosed with leukaemia. He was in his parents' arms. The parents had given up their jobs in the country to move to Sydney so they could be close to their baby while he was treated. They had no permanent accommodation in the city; they were making it up as they went. Down the corridor, I noticed a boy aged about 14, who was lying on his bed, having just had his latest chemotherapy treatment. He looked shattered but then our eyes met and his face lit up because an Australian cricketer was in the room. I was hesitant to go over and talk to him, because he looked so pale, but then he elbowed himself up, reached out for his walking frame and began to shuffle towards us. I went over to greet him, but before I could shake his hand the effort became too much for him and he threw up all over himself and the floor. The nurses had to clean him up and get him back into bed before I could have a chat, but when we did talk I quickly discovered he was one of the bravest people I'd ever met. That look of excitement on his face when our eyes first met stayed with me.

Rianna and I kept our emotions in check while we were in the wards, but in the hospital car park and most of the way home we had tears in our eyes. The doctors had explained how dire many of the children's situations were and how brutal the side effects of their treatment could be, yet the kids were so brave and seemingly happy, so full of hope. Their parents were dignified and quietly determined, even though they were going through hell. Their lives had been turned upside down. We promised to keep in touch. And we did. Often the news was cheerful, sometimes it was awful. I'd receive messages from parents telling me their boy or girl was out of hospital and doing fine, but then a month later a message would arrive explaining that their beautiful child had passed away.

Quickly, Rianna and I became ambassadors of the CCIA. For Rianna, this became the primary passion in her life. We set out to make a difference by using our time and my profile as a cricketer to raise money that would help fund research into the early detection of relapse in children who'd been diagnosed with Acute Lymphoblastic Leukaemia, the most common children's cancer, which sounds awful, is awful, but can be overcome (the survival rate in Australia has climbed to more than 90 per cent). I was inspired by my wife's total commitment to this cause. The 'Ricky and Rianna Ponting Molecular Diagnostic Laboratory', which is part of the CCIA's research facilities at the Lowy Cancer Research Centre in Sydney, where kids can be tested to see how likely they are to suffer a relapse, was opened in 2004. After that, we decided to continue to devote our resources to research, but also to try to help the kids and their families in a tangible way. This was how we linked with Redkite, formerly the Malcolm Sargent Cancer Fund for Children, which specifically provided financial grants and practical assistance. Redkite wants the kids and their families to feel they are not alone with their cancer. We wanted to help them in any way we could. We wanted them to not be concerned by the price of petrol when they were driving from their home to the hospital. We wanted them to not have to stress about the next mortgage payment.

In 2008, just before Emmy was born, we launched the Ponting Foundation, the concept being to link up with some of Australia's most respected cancer charities and research groups, including Redkite, the David Collins Leukaemia Foundation of Tasmania, the Murdoch Childrens Research Institute and, of course, CCIA. Our mission continues to be to provide financial backing for essential services that comfort and care for Australian kids with cancer, while also offering emotional support and monetary help for the kids and their families. Aligning our foundation with these fantastic organisations is the best way for us to make this happen.

A GOODWILL EXCURSION of a different kind to a hospital visit, but just as stirring, occurred near the end of the 2008–09 season, when the Australian team visited the victims of the bushfires that had ravaged parts of Victoria in early February. This was Michael Clarke's idea, to show our support by travelling to the fire scene. After the Victorian government agreed it was a terrific concept, Cricket Australia arranged for us to stop over at Whittlesea, a town just north of Melbourne, on our way to Brisbane for the fourth one-dayer of our series against New Zealand.

A bit like when I first visited the Children's Hospital, I wasn't sure how I'd react when I met the victims who had suffered so much. The media were outstanding, keeping their distance as we mingled with the locals, heard their stories and felt a little of their pain. A 10-year-old boy named Koby, who proved he was a pretty good bowler when he bowled to me in a 'backyard' game at the local sports ground, told me his school had been burned to the ground. A teacher told us it was the first time since the blaze ripped through that she'd seen the kids in her class with smiles on their faces. The most confronting moment for me came when a woman kept saying I looked exactly like the son she hadn't seen since the fires struck. I could only hope that things would work out for them. The anguish I saw in people's eyes was heartbreaking, but there was a resolve among these people we outsiders couldn't help but respect.

I came away with a renewed faith in the Aussie spirit and filled with admiration for all the volunteers and charity workers who were operating around the clock for none of the acclaim or income elite sportspeople get for doing far, far less. Similarly, I had total admiration for the firefighters, who'd risked their lives to help others. I was genuinely in awe of all these good people. It was a privilege to be among them and put our day jobs into perspective.

CHAPTER 51

SIX DAYS IN POTCHEFSTROOM

February, 2009

WE TRAVELLED TO SOUTH AFRICA in 2009 for the return series against Graeme Smith's team as clear underdogs. For most observers, the strongest memories of the Tests in Australia were of us struggling to take wickets at key moments in the first two games, and Smith fending us off despite his broken finger in the dying stages of the match in Sydney. The fact they beat us 4–1 in the ODI series that followed the Tests only added to these memories. However, from the day we arrived in Potchefstroom, about 120 kilometres south-west of Johannesburg in central South Africa, where we'd established a base at the start of the 2003 World Cup as well as our tour in 2006 and were doing again in 2009, the boys seemed more relaxed than they'd been back home and I began to believe we might surprise a few people. Home-ground advantage is a funny thing: if you start well, the fans get behind you and sometimes lift you to unexpected heights; start slowly and the second-guessing can be debilitating.

Our team had more new faces. Marcus North, a batting all-rounder, Tassie fast bowler Ben Hilfenhaus and 20-year-old left-hand opening bat Phillip Hughes, all made their Test debuts in the opening Test, essentially replacing Andrew Symonds, Brett Lee and Matt Hayden. It was the first time in 23 years that three Aussies made their debuts in the same game. A fourth newcomer, Victorian leg-spinner Bryce McGain, would make his maiden appearance in the third Test. Mike Hussey and I were the only men to wear the baggy green in this Test series who had played the previous rubber in South Africa, in 2006.

I landed in South Africa with a plan. Partly because of the inexperience of our squad, I resolved to take an even more 'hands on' approach to leadership than the one I'd adopted since the 2005 Ashes series. As I've explained, I learned on that ill-fated trip that a captain can never simply assume that his crew is doing everything right; he or she has to make sure no short cuts are being taken. On this trip to Potchefstroom, where we stayed for six days, I asked the senior players and coaches to make sure everyone knew *exactly* what was expected of them. Every training session was mapped out precisely. Coach Tim Nielsen and I knew exactly what we would say when we addressed the group. There'd be no confusion. At the nets, I stood behind the stumps at the non-striker's end, as if I was an umpire, to be in the middle of things. Of course, I was a big supporter of the guys practising as they played, and in this respect I set the example.

Elsewhere, we formed into small groups to develop 'mission statements' that described how we were going to play. One night, the senior players recalled confrontations, triumphs and amusing anecdotes from earlier tours, in the same way Mark Taylor, David Boon and Ian Healy had done when I first came into the team. Once that was done, I stood up and said, 'Okay, I don't want to hear any more about "senior" guys and "junior" guys in our squad. I don't care if you've played in no Tests or 100, we have to believe in ourselves and believe in our ability as a group.'

It wasn't all hard work, serious talk and sober meetings. We played a three-day game against a South African Board President's XI and started slow but finished strong. There were also convivial chats over coffees and beers, as new guys and old mixed and talked about what we'd done and what we could do. As a team-bonding exercise, these six days were sensational. The set-up in Potchefstroom was perfect, almost cut off from the main cricket highway; we had a terrific blend of youth, experience, talent and cricket nous, and everyone bought into what we were trying to achieve. I spent as much time as I could with the younger blokes, giving them an opportunity to get to know me, and giving me the chance to discover as much as I could about them. There were no disruptions, no injury setbacks. I can't recall a single argument or complaint.

Try as we did, after that tour, we could never quite replicate that atmosphere for the rest of my time as captain.

MUCH OF THE TALK in Jo'burg in the days before the first Test was that South Africa was about to become the No. 1 ranked team in the world. It was amazing how many of the questions I was asked, from fans and local reporters alike, came back to this subject. The home team had won 18 of their previous 25 Tests, including beating us on our home turf; this series was to be their coronation. It was so satisfying, given all this, how we then took control on the first two days of the first Test and never let go.

I won the toss and immediately chose to bat on a pretty juicy wicket; we sunk to 3–38, but Michael Clarke and I scratched and scraped through to lunch and beyond. We took a couple on the body, enjoyed a little luck, but we weren't separated until we'd added 113, one of our most satisfying partnerships. The batsmen behind us built on the platform we'd created, with Marcus North and Brad Haddin adding 113 for the sixth wicket, Northy and Mitchell Johnson 117 for the seventh, and Mitch and Peter Siddle slamming a further 53 for the ninth. Marcus scored a century on debut. Mitch was left stranded on 96, and promptly had Smith caught behind off the fifth ball of their innings. Next over, Ben Hilfenhaus took a wicket with his second delivery in Test cricket. Three days later we were celebrating a 162-run victory.

When I recall our most memorable renditions of 'Underneath the Southern Cross' I usually think back to celebrations after series and tournament triumphs. I think of the three World Cup finals we won: Kingston in 1995, on top of Table Mountain in 2002, Nagpur in 2004, and the Ashes clean sweep in 2006–07. I include Galle in 2004 for different reasons — it was my first Test as captain and Justin Langer's first time in charge of the song. And there's this one: the famous Wanderers ground, where we'd copped plenty of abuse from fans in Tests and one-dayers past, was all but empty. The final wicket had fallen three or four hours earlier, but the image of Mitch shattering the stumps of Dale Steyn, the man who'd dominated the Boxing Day Test two months earlier, was still vivid. Now we were sauntering back to the scene of that magic moment. Dougie Bollinger was carrying an Esky full of beers and ice. Halfway out, I sidled up to young Phillip Hughes and whispered, 'Never forget how good this feels.'

The overwhelming emotion for me was pride: I was proud of the team and our support staff, proud of the way we'd prepared and played, and proud of the things I'd said, the decisions I'd made and the example I'd set that contributed to our success. Eventually, Mike Hussey brought us in tight, to remind us that this was a special victory, but we still had a series to win. 'Don't get carried away!' he shouted. My gut instinct said that wasn't going to happen, because there was no arrogance about us, nothing smug. Still, as captain, I was grateful for Huss's common sense and caution. He and I are two cricketers cut from the same cloth.

THE SECOND TEST IN Durban began four days later and for most of the game it was more of the same. There were only four days between the two Tests, and the danger for us was that we'd let the first-up win go to our heads. The model for me was our previous tour of South Africa, when the home team had celebrated too hard after they'd scored 438 in the final one-dayer to win the series, but then played poorly in the first Test. We had a good night after winning at the Wanderers, took it easy the next day, and then got right back into it. The pitch at Durban looked similar to how it had been three years before, when the fast bowlers took most of the wickets and I scored a hundred in each innings, so I knew there was no need to change our 11. Despite a few whispers doing the rounds, I was confident batting first would be an advantage and I was able to call right at the toss. From there, it was only on day four, when Jacques Kallis and AB de Villiers put together a big third-wicket stand, that we lost even a smidgen of the ascendancy.

For Hughesy, it was the game of his life. In just his second appearance, he became the youngest batsman to score a hundred in each innings of a Test. Simon Katich also made a ton in our first innings, and then Mitch first broke Smith's finger again and then the top of the South African order, leaving them essentially 4–6 in reply to our 352. Our pace bowlers hunted as a pack, in the style of McGrath, Gillespie, Lee and Kasprowicz, and for the second Test in a row I could have enforced the follow-on. Instead, I gave our exceptional new opener a chance to make history before closing early on the fourth afternoon with a lead of 545. The next day, the sun was still shining when someone asked me at the media conference how I felt about winning a series after starting (in other people's eyes) as the genuine outsider, something Australia hadn't done since 1989.

'Mate, I'm as happy as I've been in my whole career as an Australian player.'

This was my proudest moment as a captain.

When the last wicket fell in this Test, we celebrated in the middle and then I deliberately ran about 30 or 40 metres ahead of the team. I stopped near the boundary rope and then looked back so I could see how much it meant to the young blokes. I wanted to see the expressions of joy and satisfaction and pride on the faces of guys like North, Hughes, Siddle, Hilfenhaus, Johnson and McDonald. They had their arms around each other, revelling in each other's success. It's something I'll never forget.

I still get almost an adrenalin kick whenever I think about this series win. We built a spirit and togetherness in the group that was remarkably powerful. I knew it would be premature to believe we were on the threshold of another golden era, but I was certain Australian cricket was in good hands. The guys like Kato, Huss, Pup and me, who had played Test cricket prior to 2007, all had at least three or four years left in them, in Pup's case more than three or four. All we needed was for the young fellas who'd done so brilliantly on this tour to turn their enormous potential into greatness …

WE SANG 'UNDER THE SOUTHERN CROSS' in the rooms that night and then decided to take up an invitation to head to a nightclub we'd been told good things about. To tell the truth, by this stage of my life I was pretty much done with clubs, but the spirit in the group was so vibrant I decided to tag along. It was a Tuesday night, so we assumed the place would be pretty quiet but instead it was packed, with a queue extending down the street. As VIPs, we didn't have to wait to get in and they looked after us really well, which meant I didn't get back to our hotel until much later than I'd originally intended. It was one of the best nights out with the boys I'd enjoyed in a while, which was only appropriate given the scale of our great victory.

Rianna and Emmy were travelling with me, so I knew I had to be quiet when I got in. We were flying out early the next morning, and Rianna had packed all our gear, knowing that with a very young daughter and a dusty husband to contend with, spare minutes in the morning would be hard to find. All our suitcases were packed and Rianna had even been kind enough to leave my tracksuit, travel shoes and so on laid out for me so I wouldn't have to look for them when I woke up. Even better, she'd also left a bottle of water sitting there for me, right next to my gear. I took off my shoes, tip-toed to the toilet, and then came back and decided to guzzle the liquid straight away. I picked up the bottle, unscrewed the cap, had a big swig and instantaneously realised I was drinking poison. My reaction woke up the entire hotel, probably the whole city. It was Emmy's washing detergent. Rianna had used it to wash some clothes in the bathroom sink, and left it out for us to pack in the morning.

Travelling with your family is not always easy.

MAYBE THAT EXPERIENCE was telling me something, because the rest of the tour was something of an anti-climax. I won my sixth straight Test-match toss at Cape Town, but we batted poorly and never recovered. Our quicks looked tired and Bryce McGain, who came into the side when Northy was struck down by a stomach virus, had a nightmare debut. A few people questioned the way I handled Bryce, but the fact was the poor bloke never settled after I gave him a chance early in their innings and Ashwell Prince, who was playing instead of Smith, hit him over long-on on his second ball for six. They planned to attack the leg-spinner as soon as he came on, a policy they continued whenever he bowled, and Bryce didn't handle it. On the second day, I stuck with the quicks until just before the drinks break in the middle session, which was tagged as strange by some but it was something I had done in the past with spinners, even with Shane Warne. First chance he had, Prince was into Bryce again, hitting his first three balls of this new spell to the boundary. His third, fourth and fifth overs cost 14, 10 and 14 runs respectively, and there never seemed to be an appropriate time to bowl him after that.

Prince, Kallis and de Villiers all made hundreds, as did Mitchell Johnson in our second innings. We lost by an innings and 20 runs, a fair reflection of the difference between the two sides in this game, but afterwards I was able to get past this loss and think instead of all the good we'd done in Potchefstroom, Johannesburg and Durban. I was convinced I was a better captain at this point of my career than I'd ever been in the past, and an Ashes series in England was just around the corner.

There was still much to look forward to.

WE LOST BOTH T20 internationals and three of the five ODIs that followed the Tests, but I didn't see either result as a major setback. South Africa was the No. 1 ranked team in 50-overs cricket, but I came away from these games convinced they were beatable, and almost hoping we'd face them in a big game at the next ICC Champions Trophy or the World Cup. Before game five, we'd talked about the need to finish on a winning note and I was pleased that we'd managed to do that via a terrific team effort. Five batsmen scored 40 or more and the wickets were shared around too as we won decisively by 47 runs. An excellent catch by Ben Laughlin — one of two Australians to make their first ODI appearance in this series and one of 12 to make their ODI debut between June 2008 and April 2009 — on the mid-wicket boundary late in their innings sealed our victory.

The team then headed to Dubai, for five one-dayers and a T20 game against Pakistan, but I flew home for some extended rest before our England tour. It was a tumultuous time for cricket on the Indian subcontinent, owing to terrorist threats and domestic conflicts that had nothing to do with our sport. The second edition of the IPL was transferred to South Africa. Our series against Pakistan was being played in the Middle East because the Australian government, the Australian Cricketers' Association and Cricket Australia couldn't guarantee our safety in Pakistan. In late 2008, not long after we flew home after seven weeks in India, there was an attack on two hotels in Mumbai that we were very familiar with: the Taj Mahal and the Oberoi. That was a little too 'close to home'. Then, while we were in South Africa, word came through of an appalling incident in Lahore, where the Sri Lankan team was the victim of a terrorist attack as they travelled to the Gaddafi Stadium for day three of the second Test of the first Test series to be played in Pakistan for two years. Australia had not played a Test there since 1998. None of the cricketers or support staff were killed, but eight people did die, including six policemen and the driver of the bus. A number of people, including some players and the fourth umpire, were injured. ICC match referee Chris Broad was highly critical of the Pakistani security forces. The tour was abandoned.

In Durban, where we were at the time, our protection was increased, even though it was already substantial, but it didn't make any difference to how I went about my business. I was shattered by the loss of life and felt genuine anguish for what the Sri Lankan guys were going through. We sent a message to Trevor Bayliss, the former NSW coach who was now looking after Sri Lanka, asking him to let everyone in Lahore know we were thinking of them. But it was almost bizarre how immune I'd become to the sight of men in army commando gear carrying machine guns looking over us at training and in hotel foyers. In some cities, a police escort on the way to the ground was part of the backdrop, like traffic lights.

I couldn't afford to let it get to me, because if it did I would have been looking at shadows everywhere. International cricketers are public figures, which I guess makes us targets, though not principal targets. We need protection and I always had the utmost faith in the protection organised for us, even on occasions such as the 1996 World Cup when we were upgraded to the same level as a visiting head of state, or in the days after the London bombings in 2005, when the strength of the security looking after us was noticeably increased.

There's no doubt the heightened security made tours less enjoyable than they might have been in previous eras, but I can't recall anyone ever saying it shortened his career. I think I became used to it, to the point a strong man in uniform armed with a machine gun was almost commonplace. He'd be there on the floor of your hotel, at the elevator, on the bus, at the ground, 24/7. Before a tour, we'd always be briefed about the security arrangements, what would be in place and why, but there were still occasions when I saw new players stunned by the scale of our protection and maybe even intimidated by it. We had a security officer with us on all tours, and he had to know where we were going if we left the hotel. Often, one of his team would accompany us when we went to a restaurant, and would sit in a corner and wait until it was time for him to make sure we all got home safely. It was extreme, but necessary. We understood that.

Probably the scariest single moment for me occurred in 2007, after a game in Hyderabad. We were returning to the team hotel in the middle of the city, when suddenly our bus stopped as we drove through a village. This was highly unusual, because our drivers on the subcontinent were under orders to keep moving if at all possible. The roads are invariably cleared for us. I was on my mobile, talking to Rianna, when suddenly there was this colossal BANG!

The sound was like a gunshot, a bomb going off, or at least that's what it was like for me.

Poor Rianna on the other end of the phone didn't have a clue what was happening. All she heard was the bang, me swearing and the chaotic, incomprehensible sounds of players diving to the floor and security guards on their feet, sprinting out of the bus to try to find the little bastard who had emerged briefly from the shadows to hurl a rock or some kind of missile at us. They never found the culprit. The window was shattered, I had a small cut on my ear, and there were shards of glass all over me and the floor of the vehicle. My heart was pumping like never before.

I'll never forget those first few seconds when I thought we were under attack. It scared the life out of me.

Because there was nothing on the bus to indicate it had the Australian cricket team on board and with the tinted windows preventing those on the street from seeing who was inside, our security experts concluded it was just a random attack. This was some comfort for me, though I'm not sure it made Rianna feel any better. When I called her again later that night she was still obviously shaken. We are only cricketers and we all have families back home. If anyone had ever said they didn't want to go on an overseas tour because of the security threats, I would have understood.

Top five English players

ANDREW FLINTOFF

Flintoff was the ultimate Ashes competitor. His overall
record in Test cricket probably doesn't look that
flash, but a couple of the Ashes series he had were
probably as good as anybody's in the history of those
contests. You could say those series were what he
lived and played for; he loved the big stage and the big
moments. 2005 was a remarkable series: he bowled
at 95mph whenever he had the ball in his hands, he
swung the new ball and he reversed too. Our batsmen
walked away from that series saying he was up there
with the best fast bowlers they had ever faced. He
not only made runs, he made positive runs, making a
statement with the bat. At critical moments in the field
he stood up. He ran me out at the Oval in 2009. As far
as competitors go, he was the best English player I saw.

GRAHAM THORPE

I didn't play against Thorpe a lot, but his overall record
is so impressive. When I was at Surrey in 2013, the
English talked about him as the best batsman they ever
produced and the best young player they ever saw.
When he played he was the standout in that English
side, and he had a good record against Australia
when the other guys from his era, you could say,
underperformed.

KEVIN PIETERSEN

We probably thought it was a bit of a hindrance for
England having Pietersen and Flintoff together because
we thought they were two guys who didn't like to share
the limelight, but would you turn down the opportunity
to have both in your team? They were the big boys and
it was their show, their stage whenever they had the
chance to take it. In 2005 Pietersen made a statement
about the way he was going to play his cricket; the
158 he made at the Oval in the last Test was a pretty

special innings, and we tried everything to rough him up: Warnie bowled a lot to him and tried to get in his mind; I remember a spell Bing bowled, where we had two or three fieldsmen on the legside, and I said, 'Run in and bowl bouncers at him for three or four overs,' but he took us on and got the better of us. When he bats, he wants to own the game, and his record is really starting to stack up now. When he's going, he's as good a player as any in the game. With all the stuff that's happened around him it is obvious that England know they have a match winner there, and they want to have him around their team.

ALASTAIR COOK

Not that long ago we thought that if there was a weak link in their top order it was Cook: he always seemed limited and you could bowl good areas to him and dry up his scoring. Then, in the Ashes tour to Australia in 2010–11, he made three hundreds, including a double in Brisbane, and that kick-started what we have seen since then. He's the captain now, and he is in the same boat as Michael Clarke in that his past few years have been outstanding. He's now made the most Test hundreds for an English batsman, and he's got a while left in the game yet. You have to admire what he has made of himself.

DARREN GOUGH

Gough's included here as much for his competitive approach as his record. The other thing was he got me out a lot in Ashes cricket, more than any other English bowler I reckon. With him you always knew it was going to be a red-hot contest; whenever he got the ball in his hand you knew you were in for a battle, you knew he would charge in, bowl quick and try to hit the stumps. He was a low skiddy, quick-through-the-air bowler who was always at your stumps. He could swing the ball and was a very good reverse swing bowler, which he showed with that hat trick in Sydney in 1999.

CHAPTER 52

PUBLIC ENEMY No. 1

The Ashes, England, 2009

THE ASHES DIDN'T START WELL, but it had nothing to do with cricket.

I was in Worcester before the England Lions game when I got a call from Dad telling me that his father had died. Charlie had been a constant in our life, we'd lived with him and his wife Connie when we were young, holidayed with them and they had been my biggest fans. He was a great bloke, a tin miner, as I said earlier, your salt-of-the-earth Tasmanian type. A man of few words but one who left a big impression on my life. Again I was away and suffering that helpless feeling when you can't be where you think you should be. That call with Dad was one of the hardest I have ever had. He was so upset to have lost his father and it was a son's duty to be there for him, but cricket has no time for sentiment and we just had to deal with it as best we could. Pull the helmet on and pretend there's a game face under it.

There were times during the 2009 Ashes series when I felt I'd batted as well as ever: in our first innings at Cardiff and Headingley; our second innings at the Oval. At Lord's, I copped a shocker from the umpire. At other times I got out in ways that didn't happen to me earlier in my career. I'd push too hard at the ball, get caught in two minds, or look for swing or seam that was more feared than real. Why did this happen? I blame it on the pressure. I was desperately keen to do well, and for my new, young team to retain the Ashes. On a good day, when my mind was clear, this ambition inspired me. When I was distracted or under the pump, I tended to struggle.

A feature of the Test matches was how often the momentum shifted, sometimes with brutal speed. Unfortunately, England played better than we did when it really mattered.

They scored 435 in their first innings of the opening Test, at Cardiff, and then Phillip Hughes cracked 28 from his first 30 balls, but this was hardly a sign of things to come for our little opener. Andrew Flintoff started dropping them in short of a length, cramping Hughesy up, attacking his ribs, and suddenly our rising star looked terribly mortal, a shadow of the dynamo who'd done so brilliantly in South Africa. He was eventually caught behind. His technique had been found out and his confidence bent. I replaced him in the middle and for a little while, at least until Freddie finished his spell, the cricket was red hot. After that, though, Simon Katich and I settled right in and by stumps we had made it to 1–249, having hardly played a false shot during the final session. I pinched the single to get me to three figures and for a moment I thought I was dead if the throw was true, but I got there. I was very animated on reaching three figures, betraying how much I wanted to make an imprint on the series, set the right example, do my bit. I went on to 150 the next day, one of four hundreds in our total of 6–674 declared (Kato, Marcus North and Brad Haddin were the other centurions). We had England 5–70 and 7–159 on the final day, with plenty of time remaining, but they held on, nine down at the end, to earn a draw.

Four days later, we were at Lord's, one of my favourite grounds even though I didn't score too many runs there. At least the teams I was a part of usually won: three Test wins out of four; seven ODI wins and a tie out of eight. The one loss was this Ashes Test in 2009, when we batted very poorly on the second day and couldn't recover. I was the second wicket to fall, given out in absurd fashion, caught at slip after what might have been an lbw shout when I clearly didn't hit the ball. Three days later, England were celebrating only their second ever victory in a Test against Australia at the 'home of cricket'. A draw at Edgbaston in the third Test meant they were just one win away from regaining the Ashes.

The fourth Test was at Headingley, scene of my maiden Test century, and finally a game started beautifully for us: England all out for 102; Peter Siddle 5–21, Stuart Clark 3–18. But the pitch was lively and Simon Katich was out for a duck, unable to control a riser from the recalled Steve Harmison. I strode out determined to be aggressive, but the first two balls made me look like a mug: the first one cut me in half; I missed the second one by a mile. Then I called for a quick single that wasn't on. I was as jumpy as the wicket.

At the other end, Shane Watson — who had replaced Hughesy for the third Test — was scoring at a run a ball and finally I caught his mood. Harmison seemed obsessed with getting me on the back foot, which on this pitch suited me fine, and I hit him for two fours. At the other end, Graham Onions came on for James Anderson and I immediately whacked him over mid-wicket for six. Then the next ball was deflected to the fine leg boundary, taking us past 50 in 6.2 overs. Another four and a single and I was 32 from 20 balls, with five fours and a six. We'd taken the life out of the crowd, the bowlers and, it seemed, the wicket. I went on to make 78, which in the context of the match was worth much more than a hundred. It was the best counter-attack of my career. Mitchell Johnson, who'd struggled mightily with his line and length during the first three Tests, took his first five-for of the series in their second innings, and we returned to London needing only a draw from the final Test to retain the Ashes.

Our top-order had collapsed completely twice earlier in the series, leaving us in an impossible position in the second Test and fighting to save the game in the third. At the Oval, it happened again, as we replied to their 332 by going from 0–73 to 160 all out, after which England batted us just about out of the game. When Strauss declared we needed an unprecedented 545 to save the Ashes.

WE WERE 0–80 AT stumps on day three. The pitch was a bit crumbly, with the occasional delivery breaking through the surface, but it was playing better than it looked. In my mind, if we were going to pull off a miracle I needed to make a huge score. I set myself to do just that.

Kato and Watto were both dismissed in the first five overs of the day. Mike Hussey had been battling for runs throughout the series, to the point that — like Justin Langer in 2001 and Matt Hayden in 2005 — he was now probably playing for his Test career. I always enjoyed batting with Huss and this was a reminder why: we worked the singles, stayed positive, and were encouraged by how quiet the fieldsmen and the crowd became. He has this terrific ability to always be enthusiastic without ever sounding like he's part of a cheer squad or just reciting slogans. His advice is always on the money. Occasionally, a delivery gripped, stayed low or jumped, but never outrageously and never enough to change how we reacted to the next ball. I was slow early, watchful, but gradually the runs started to come. Graeme Swann, their off-spinner, is one of those bowlers who's excellent when things are going well for him, but he loses his rhythm when the pressure's on, and here, when he couldn't force a breakthrough, he started mucking round with his pace too much. When he pitched short, I cracked past point for four. Next ball, he overcompensated, and I drove him past a lumbering Harmison for four more. When Flintoff finally came on we handled him comfortably. At lunch we were 2–171, 374 to get, we'd added 81 for the third wicket.

My only ambition was to bat them into the ground. If I had a target it was the drinks break, then tea, then stumps, but really

I just took it as it came, an over at a time. Reaching landmarks like lunch, or my fifty, or the hundred partnership, were satisfying in themselves, but I got more joy out of moments that reflected how we were gradually getting on top: a misfield, a brief argument between two of them, Stuart Broad warned for running on the pitch, Strauss's reluctance to bowl Harmison, presumably because he feared he'd go for plenty. We were past 200, still only two wickets down.

Finally, after I'd cracked Broad for two fours through the off-side, Harmison came on. I'd compare my concentration at this moment to any of my best innings; if I was asked to select one dig as my example of being 'in the zone' it might be this one. My feet were moving beautifully, I was picking up the line and length immediately, never did I find myself playing forward when I should have been back, or back when I should have been forward. I was aware of the crowd but I didn't hear them. If they'd tried to sledge me, it wouldn't have registered. By the time the bowler arrived at the start of his run-up, everything but focusing on the next delivery was forgotten. Every ball, as the bowler was coming in, I said to myself, 'Watch the ball … watch the ball.' Every ball, without fail, I watched the ball right on to my bat. At other times in the series, a variety of conflicting thoughts were buzzing through my head. This was different; there was no more captaincy to do, just batting and scoring runs. Huss, my mate from the glory days, was entrenched at the other end …

Harmison's first two overs were lacklustre, as if to prove his captain's judgment was right. He started his third over with two no-balls, and then I got him away through the off-side field for three runs. Three scoreless balls to Huss, and then he half-drove, half-pushed one to mid-on, to the fieldsman's left hand. Off the bat, I didn't think there was a run in it but Huss called, 'Yes!'

In these situations you back your partner's judgment. You go, but I hesitated for a split second. Then I sprinted for my life. Halfway down the wicket, maybe earlier, I knew I was in trouble, because it was Flintoff, the one member of their team with the strength, talent and charisma to rise to this occasion. It was his farewell Test, and he was hardly the sort of bloke to go out with a whimper. I glanced back once or twice as I ran, praying for a misfield that didn't happen because I sensed from the get-go Freddie was throwing to my end. I contemplated diving but instead I slid my bat as quickly and desperately as I could.

The stumps exploded.

I knew immediately I was gone.

I had to wait for the replay, which was a misery in itself, knowing I'd been kicked in the guts and waiting to be kicked again. I will never feel worse about getting out, about losing. I walked off in a daze, scarcely believing what had happened, and in the dressing room immediately afterwards I wasn't angry or bitter or swearing. Just stunned. I was going to bat forever.

Michael Clarke was run out during the next over and from there wickets fell at regular intervals. Huss was last out for 121. We lost by 197 runs. England regained the Ashes.

IT WAS INCONSISTENCY THAT brought us undone. I thought, after Headingley, we might finally have gained an advantage, but the Englishmen bounced back brilliantly at the Oval, on the back of some superb bowling from Broad, a fine batting effort from Strauss and the debutant Jonathan Trott, and our woeful batting effort on day two.

Three months earlier, we'd arrived in the UK on the back of our tremendous victory in South Africa, but in the World Twenty20 which preceded the Ashes Tests we were drawn in the same group as the West Indies and Sri Lanka, with two to go through, and lost both our games. That result looked bad, and I guess it was bad, but as it turned out our conquerors, spearheaded by Chris Gayle (West Indies) and Kumar Sangakkara (Sri Lanka) turned out to be two of the best teams in the competition. Still, failing to make the second round was hardly good for our psyche. It also created a circumstance where we began our preparation for the Ashes with some of the Test squad, the guys who weren't in the T20 line-up, not even in the country. That was hardly Potchefstroom.

I couldn't fault anyone's dedication to our cause, but injuries and a loss of form by some key players didn't help. Mitchell Johnson and Phillip Hughes, who on the back of their exceptional feats in South Africa were being spoken of as future champions, couldn't reproduce the form that had been so impressive just a few months before, in the process underlining a significant evolution in modern cricket. If the game at the top level is harder today than it was when I started it is because there is less room to hide now. The way teams analyse the opposition is so thorough and the grapevine is so extensive, if a cricketer has a weakness, he'll be found out quick smart. Especially in Hughesy's case — I'm certain that's what happened during this series. Such was his natural talent, I was equally sure he'd eventually fight his way back.

Hughesy had got to England early and made a real statement with a string of 100s for Middlesex, but maybe in doing that he had sown the seeds of his downfall as England's captain Andrew Strauss was also with that county. They got a hint of a weakness in his game against anything short at the body and that was confirmed in a tour match when Harmison found him out at Worcester. I tried working with him on developing a pull shot, but the first time he played it in the second Test he gloved one from Anderson which just compounded matters. It was hard to drop him, but it was the right call because he was struggling. There was a bit of a story around him not playing in the third match when he confirmed on Twitter a report published in Australia that he'd been dropped. We weren't too impressed with this as we were trying to keep our selection in-house and I had a few stern words with him at training before the toss. I think he hadn't actually tweeted himself, that his account back then was run by his manager, but it didn't matter. I guess Hughesy was one of the first cricketers to get into hot water over social media, but he certainly hasn't been the last.

Phillip is a great cricketer with an impressive first-class record. Justin Langer would say he has 'the eye of the tiger' and I agree. He's one of the blokes I would pick and stick with in tough times because he is totally committed to his game and to being a better cricketer. And, as we saw in South Africa, he is an enormous talent.

Until the Test at the Oval, Mike Hussey was often struggling. Brett Lee bowled so well in a lead-up game at Worcester it seemed he was on the verge of a remarkable comeback, but then he tore an abdominal muscle and was lost for the series. Brad Haddin damaged a finger five minutes before the start of the third Test. Nathan Hauritz, our No. 1 spinner, suffered a heel injury in the days before the series decider and we had to rule him out despite the fact the pitch at the Oval looked like it was going to turn.

We should have been able to rise above these setbacks, even though we were up against a strong, well-led, well-balanced team. Our batsmen scored eight individual centuries to their two during the series, but were also involved in three dreadful first-innings collapses: at Lord's (2–103 to 8–152), Edgbaston (0–85 to 8–203) and the Oval (0–73 to 9–143). The common denominator in all three of these failures was that, after 20-odd overs, the quirky Dukes ball they use in England started swinging and seaming, the bowlers rose to the occasion and we fell apart. However, I don't think it was our techniques or our attitude that was flawed, because at other times in the series our top-order showed unequivocally they had the skill, courage and nous to handle whatever the home-team bowlers had to offer. I blame it on the pressure to be excellent, to be as good as our predecessors and to retain the Ashes. As I said at the opening of this chapter, it occasionally got to me during this series. It got to all of us.

I BECAME THE SECOND Australian captain, after Billy Murdoch in the 19th century, to lose two Ashes series in England, an outcome that received plenty of airtime. Earlier in the series, I'd been 'public enemy No. 1' for reasons other than my losing record as skipper, partly as a result of an incident at the end of the first Test, and also because the press and the English public wanted a villain and I fitted the bill. At times, the booing and catcalls directed my way as I walked out to bat were fierce, to the point that before the fourth Test the England and Wales Cricket Board (ECB) put a message in the program asking for the abuse to be toned down. Sections of the media didn't miss me either. The *Daily Mail*, for example, called me 'Ratty Ponting, the grumpiest captain in world cricket'.

The booing and the negative press never worried me. Instead, I wore it as a badge of honour, remembering back to my days as a kid when the players the public didn't like — such as Richard Hadlee and Ian Botham — were usually the best or among the best players in the touring team. Probably what bugged me most was how some people used the events at Cardiff as justification for my bad-guy status. That annoyed me in two ways: one, because we did nothing wrong; and two, because I was burned for comments I made in the emotional minutes after we failed to win a game that for much of the day we thought was ours. What I said was valid, even if I didn't make my point very well.

With just a few minutes to go in the Test, England's final partnership, Jimmy Anderson and Monty Panesar, were trying to save time any way they could: patting down the wicket, mid-pitch conversations, that sort of thing. I was fine with that. However, when their 12th man came out with a change of batting gloves two overs in a row and then a physio strolled out to treat an injury that didn't exist I told the umpires that it was ridiculous and then hurried the interlopers off the field. Anyone watching would have known I was upset. In the end, it wasn't the reason we couldn't force a win, but that wasn't the point. Things like using superior fieldsmen while bowlers are resting in the dressing room and blatant time-wasting are not the way cricket should be played.

At the media conference, I was quickly asked what went on. 'It was pretty ordinary,' I said. 'They can play whatever way they want to play. We'll do everything we can to play by the rules and the spirit of the game. It's up to them to do what they want to do …'

Next day, England coach Andy Flower claimed 'I'd made a meal out of it'. Some of the tabloids suggested I was a pot ranting about a kettle, and within a couple of days you would have thought I was the one who'd been time-wasting. 'Was I that bad after the game?' I asked when the press boys began grilling me about it the day before the Lord's Test. 'That was a one- or two-minute thing that has been made into a five-day thing.'

'But Ricky, that's what your comments encouraged,' one of the scribes replied with a bit of a grin. 'They were a gift from heaven.'

When I walked out the next day for the opening session the Lord's crowd was in to me. Even some of the members joined in. They wouldn't let up until the Oval, when the commentators started saying that this would probably be my last Test in England. It was as if everyone realised at once that the joke had gone a little too far and I was applauded warmly to and from the wicket. In fact, so generous was the reception when I walked out to bat in our second innings, Freddie Flintoff asked me if I'd hired a PR company to coordinate the day.

It's not that I'm an angel. I've never pretended to be. I can get as cranky as the best of them, and occasionally I've seen video of myself getting upset on the field and wished I'd handled myself better. I can't remember ever being so angry that I wasn't ready for the next ball, and I always felt that I was at my angriest when the game was being short-changed, but there were times when, after I'd cooled down, I realised that the attention would be on me for my reaction rather than the real villain for his actions.

During the Lord's Test, for example, Nathan Hauritz took a catch near his toes to dismiss their No. 3 Ravi Bopara, but the umpires referred it 'upstairs', rather than taking Horrie's word for it. Of course, the video umpire gave it to the batsman; they always do with those sorts of catches. Next day, Andrew Strauss caught Hughesy at ground level and the umpires on the field gave him out. To me, the two situations were identical and I couldn't understand the inconsistency. But the way I approached the umpires was deemed by some to be too confrontational, so I was the one under scrutiny.

OFF THE FIELD, the highlight of this tour for me was the 'Ashes to Ashes' dinner the Ponting Foundation staged on London's South Bank in the lead-up to the second Test. The night was a sell-out and we managed to raise a considerable amount of money, a great tribute to the vision and persistence of Rianna, and my manager James Henderson and his team. We were astonished by the number of prominent people who came along to support us, including all of our team, many of the English players and a number of former Test stars. Sir Michael Parkinson interviewed me on stage, when we talked a little about cricket, but more about how I have been inspired by the spirit and courage of kids battling cancer and by their families. Australia's Formula One ace Mark Webber came along too, just two days after he'd won the German Grand Prix. We had some fantastic auction items up for bid, but I think the gloves Mark wore when he won at the Nürburgring might have been the pick of them.

I'd chatted with him earlier in the tour, at Worcester, when he drove up from London for a day while we were preparing for a tour game against the England Lions. At one point, while we were standing near the nets, I threw some pads at him and suggested he have a net against our quick bowlers. He tossed them straight back, saying he wasn't that silly, which I found funny given the way he shows no fear as he flies around the racetracks of the world at lightning speed. In the same week he made it to our dinner, he also attended the first day of the Lord's Test, which he travelled to by train. That said something about the modest nature of the bloke, as did his response when James suggested he might like to come up to our dressing room.

'Will they want me in the room?' Mark replied. 'Or will I be in the way?'

Eventually, James was able to convince him we'd be very happy to see him. As if there was any doubt. He and I talked for a long time — a little about the cricket, but mostly just two mates talking about a whole variety of things, including family, footy and being away from home. And then he bid us farewell, to stroll back up to St John's Wood station to catch the Tube home.

Winning

I played cricket to win. I trained at 100 per cent to give myself and my team the best chance of winning. I demanded an environment and a belief that we were going to win each and every time we played. Winning is reward for the work you do. It's a reward for the planning, the hours of preparation and for the execution throughout a game. I was brought up with a competitive edge, and believing I could win was instilled in me at an early age. Winning is everything! This became more obvious for me at the back end of my career when winning was more difficult following the retirements of so many great Australian cricketers. I never took winning for granted but it meant even more to me when I was either captain or part of the teams through 2007 to 2012. Competing with a new crop of younger and less experienced team-mates brought a whole new experience to winning.

Winning makes you want more. Winning makes you hungrier for more success. Success is achieved through hard work, so the more you win, the harder you should work to always ensure you stay ahead of the opposition. But it is important to stay modest with success. My family taught me to stay grounded and not get too carried away by winning and from success. It's a great lesson in life and one that I will be passing on to my children in the years ahead.

CHAPTER 53

MUG OR MAGICIAN

Australian summer, 2009–10

HAVING LOST IN INDIA, lost at home to South Africa and lost the Ashes, we then went on an almost unprecedented winning run throughout 2009–10, in Tests and one-dayers. It started in England, straight after the Ashes, when we won the first six games of a seven-match ODI series. Not for the first time in my experience, the team that lost the Test matches dominated the one-day series that followed. Still, we didn't feel our wins were a fluke and we proved that on the way home when we won the ICC Champions Trophy in South Africa and in late October to early November, when we were too good for India in an ODI series on their home turf. In Australia, we then won two of three Tests against the West Indies and all three Tests against Pakistan, five straight ODIs against Pakistan and four of five ODIs against the West Indies (the other being washed out). Immediately after, in New Zealand, we won three of five ODIs and prevailed in both Tests.

All up, in this period, from September 1 to March 31, we won seven Tests out of eight and 26 of 31 ODIs.

Australia also won four Twenty20 internationals out of five, but I wasn't part of these games because I'd decided, at the end of the Ashes series, to retire from T20 international cricket. Maybe I was getting old, but Twenty20 hadn't grabbed me in the same way Tests and one-dayers always did. I enjoyed this new form of the game, saw it as a challenge, but it wasn't the same, not at international level anyway. Test cricket and the next World Cup, scheduled for March 2011, were my cricket priorities. I estimated that quitting the T20s would give me as much as four more weeks to rest and recuperate. It wasn't a hard call. Michael Clarke took over.

You might assume I'd look back on this extended season with much fondness, as a time of triumph, but with hindsight I think we were fooled by our success into thinking everything was right with Australian cricket. The ICC Champions Trophy victory, the second time straight we'd won this prestigious tournament, was a fine achievement, not in the same stratosphere as our World Cup wins, but very satisfying all the same. Our victory over England in the semi-final at Centurion, when Shane Watson and I came together at 1–6 in the second over chasing 258 and went all the way, both of us scoring unbeaten centuries, was brilliant. Our victories in India were also very enjoyable, especially the fact we didn't let a series of injury setbacks beat us, but the games didn't have quite the same edge as our matches of the previous two years. Having played six ODIs in India in 2007 and four Tests there in 2008, there was a sense that these games were a little too much of a good thing. Still, the game at Hyderabad was a beauty, as we made 4–350 in our 50 overs, a record ODI total by Australia in India, but Sachin Tendulkar nearly got them home. He scored 175 as we won by three runs with two balls to spare. After that win and a much more decisive triumph at Guwahati, to clinch the series, we outplayed two teams in Australia who were, by usual international standards, mediocre. The New Zealanders were as tenacious as ever, but we handled them comfortably. Pakistan were an enigma, a team with some gifted individuals but also, it appeared, a self-destruct button. At the time, as we kept winning games, we convinced ourselves we were enjoying a revival. In fact, it was a false dawn.

TOO MUCH OF THE talk coming out of the first two Tests of the Australian summer revolved around what came to be known as the Decision Review System (DRS). From the day they decided to introduce video replays, there was going to be controversy, even though there was obviously some use for them. The problem was in the doing. The administrators couldn't get it right. Some countries were for it; some against it. Some wanted to use all the technology; others liked some elements but not others. As I've said, initially I was a sceptic. Gradually, I came to realise there was a place for video reviews, if only to eliminate the 'howler', the umpiring decisions that the TV replays confirmed were obviously wrong.

Unfortunately but understandably when you think about it, DRS was expected to go further than that with teams using it to see if things were a centimetre this way or a centimetre that, as if perfection was possible, while elsewhere, notably in India, there were no reviews at all. Sometimes, the delays as the video umpire studies every replay from every angle were intolerable. Asking the players to refer decisions upstairs led to the system sometimes being used tactically (or desperately, depending on your viewpoint) — we might challenge a tight call if one of our best batsmen was involved, or the opponent was a champion like Tendulkar or Kallis, but hold back for a lesser threat — and also to howlers not being fixed because teams had wasted their referrals earlier.

There were times when we players on the field didn't know what was going on, but when we approached the umpires to find out some people on the other side of the fence said we should have been charged with dissent. This was frustrating. The clearest example of this came in Adelaide, when the West Indies' Shivnarine Chanderpaul was given not out by umpire Mark Benson from England when we were certain he had nicked a catch through to the keeper. I was convinced the video umpire would reverse Mark's call. When it didn't, I asked Mark why and he couldn't tell me, so I then asked the match referee Chris Broad at the next drinks break, who explained that while the replay suggested it might have been out it couldn't prove it so the decision on the field stood. I was sweet with that and we got on with the game. That night, however, Mark decided to pull out of the Test and headed home without giving the media an explanation. Some wondered if he was protesting about the way I'd approached him, but that was ridiculous. If that was true, you can bet plenty I would have been told about it. Maybe he didn't like having his verdicts on close calls scrutinised so ruthlessly by the videos, but I don't think that was the major problem. I think travelling the world umpiring all the time just wore him out. It was ridiculous at that time how few umpires there were on the ICC's international panel. They kept asking the same blokes to turn up day after day, game after game, as if umpiring was the easiest job in the world.

The DRS was a bit of a mess when it was first introduced and it remains confused as I write this, all because the men in charge want it to be more than it can be. The umpires and players have worked out that replays can be helpful, but we also realise they'll never solve every line-ball decision. One day, the administrators will accept this too.

IN PERTH, I HAD to retire hurt in a Test match for the first time in my life. Kemar Roach got me and what happened after he did shows how I react when I get stung. I think the only time I haven't tried to get up after I was injured was when I dropped the concrete grate on my foot when I was nine years old. Roach, a young quick from Barbados, had impressed a little in the first two Tests, because he was lively and potentially an improvement on the pace bowlers who had succeeded Curtly Ambrose and Courtney Walsh in the Windies' line-up. His short ball tended to skid as much as it bounced, which meant he could surprise you. That's how he'd dismissed me during the second Test in Adelaide, when I tried to pull a bumper but was late on the shot and lamely lobbed a catch to mid-wicket. After that, I didn't have to be a genius to realise they'd try to repeat the trick at the WACA.

I made my way to the middle at 1–132, after Roach had Shane Watson caught behind for a superb 89. I knew the first ball was going to be a short one, the bowler did too, and when it came I went straight for the pull shot. But I mistimed it. No run. I roused on myself for premeditating the shot. The next delivery was another short one and this time I started to duck underneath it. But it was skidding ... more chest than head height ... so I stopped ducking ... and in doing so turned my front shoulder and lost sight of the ball. I tensed up, knowing it was going to smash into my left arm or my shoulder, maybe the ribcage, hopefully the helmet. My arm took the full impact, just above the elbow.

For the first few seconds, I was more surprised than hurt. *How on earth did that happen?* I can count on one hand the number of times I'd got myself into this sort of tangle while batting. But then my arm began to throb and my fingers, hand and forearm weren't quite right. A lump began to emerge where the ball had hit me. Our physio, Alex Kountouris, rushed out to check for major damage. He was 'pretty sure' nothing was broken. But I couldn't grip my bat tightly.

'Do you want to come off?' Alex asked me.

'Nah mate, it'll be right,' I replied.

Thinking coldly about it now, maybe I should have retired hurt at that moment, on the basis that the team would have been better off with me in the dressing room getting treatment, so I could bat pain-free later in the day. But the competitive part of my brain insisted that would be giving in. No way was I going to give Roach the satisfaction of seeing me walking off with the physio. For me, at that moment, that would be the same as if he got me out. That he would win.

Of course, I was also able to convince myself it was going to get better. I've seen footballers unable to get up at first, but quickly they're back in the fray. The next delivery, the third ball of my innings, thudded into my ribs and it was all I could do not to rub them, or at least touch them. It was painful, awful and exhilarating.

One more ball in the over and it was a riser, on the line of off-stump, and as the ball met my defensive bat a shot of pain raced up my arm. That was when I knew I'd done some serious damage.

For the next few minutes, my only concern was survival. Dwayne Bravo, a couple of gears slower than Roach, bounced me but that wasn't the same. The slip cordon kept reminding me what was coming next, and by the time Roach began his third over to me I was as fired up as I'd ever been. I was disappointed when he didn't bump me. The pain kept shooting up my arm every time I hit the ball, and twice Alex came out — first, to see if there was anything he could do; then to quietly say, 'Maybe you should come off.'

'No way, mate,' I replied. 'Not yet.'

Second ball of his next over, Roach went for the bumper and I helped it down to fine leg for four. The next one was faster, nastier, and I swung away as if it was beach cricket … for six! You could almost see the fire simmer out of the bowler, as he watched the ball's trajectory and then had to turn and lumber back to his bowling mark. The next ball was noticeably slower; I glanced the fifth ball to fine leg again for four more. My brain was buzzing, my arm felt dead and then I saw the Windies captain Chris Gayle signal to his debutant paceman, Gavin Tonge, to get ready. Roach was done. Bravo continued from the other end and when I tried to hook him the pain was so brutal I nearly lost control of my bat. Tonge handed his hat to the umpire and began marking out his run, while I signalled to our dressing room that it was time for me to go. An X-ray confirmed there was no break, but it was a couple of weeks before the arm was right; longer than that before I truly got it out of my mind.

It's interesting, thinking back, how the guys reacted to me retiring hurt. The young blokes were concerned and made a point of asking if I was okay. The guys who'd been in the squad a while, men like Kato and Huss and Hadds, kept their distance. They knew how indignant and uncomfortable I'd be at having to come off. Justin Langer, now our batting coach and a throwback to an earlier time, was in to me. As I sat in the dressing room, waiting for arrangements for me to head off for the X-ray, I noticed that on a whiteboard someone had written in big black letters ... 'GLENN ARCHER'.

Langer was responsible for that. Glenn Archer is one of my all-time favourite footy players, a legend of my club, North Melbourne. He is also one of the toughest, bravest men to ever wear the blue and white. The dig was clear: Glenn Archer would never retire hurt.

If I wanted to bat again in the Test, Alex Kountouris advised, I needed to get hold of an armguard. I immediately pictured my old team-mates back in Mowbray scoffing and spluttering if I'd walked out to bat wearing that sort of protection. Still, I did what I was told and the armguards duly arrived from my gear supplier Kookaburra just before stumps on day two, while we were fielding (catching and throwing wasn't a problem, just gripping a bat). I grabbed them as quick as I could and tried to hide them in my kit, but as I did I noticed somebody had found them before me and written 'GLENN ARCHER' in texta on the back of them.

Langer had struck again.

I'VE HEARD PEOPLE SAY that I never really recovered from being hit by Kemar Roach. I think that's not true. It is true that I struggled with the bat for the next three weeks, more than once getting out to the hook shot, and the injury played a part in that. I needed to nurse the injury, something I found harder to do from a mental point of view than physically. I told myself to bat naturally, but when I went for certain shots a part of me said, *Whoa, be careful.* That led to indecisiveness, a place no batsman wants to be. In the MCG nets before the Boxing Day Test, I went to cover drive a half-volley, held back a fraction, missed the ball and couldn't keep hold of the bat. It would have landed somewhere between deep fine leg and the square-leg umpire if I'd been batting in a game. I decided that in the Test I'd focus on getting my backswing right, which was a good plan but it went against everything I'd done instinctively for the previous 30 years. I made it to 57 without playing a big shot off the front foot, but then Pakistan's opening bowler Mohammad Asif pitched one up and my reflex was to go for the drive. Then my brain said, *Don't!* I tried to check but my arm didn't react quickly enough and the result was a timid half drive/half push and a catch to second slip. In our second dig in this Test and the first innings at the SCG a few days later, I was caught playing hook shots before I was set and this almost happened to me again in the first innings of the third Test, in Hobart, when I was dropped near the deep fine-leg boundary by Mohammad Amir.

If that catch had been taken, the whispers that it was time to give the shot away, move down the order, even retire, would have grown louder. Instead, I went all the way to 209 in front of my home crowd, my second Test hundred in Tassie. After my lucky escape I played a couple of dud pull shots — one delivery hit the toe of my bat and dribbled out on the off-side after I clubbed too early at it — but then Mohammad Amir tried the bumper again and my reaction, half hook, half pull, was as pure as any pull shot I'd hit when Ian Young was throwing short ones at me in the Mowbray nets two decades before. *Of course you can still play the hook shot*, I said to myself as the ball raced to the square-leg boundary …

Now watch the ball …

Michael Clarke and I added 372 for the fourth wicket. I was so excited when I reached my ton I kissed the coat of arms on my helmet. I'd never done that before and I put my sudden surge of patriotism down to the fact that I was in Hobart, in front of Mum and Dad and any number of mates I knew from days gone by. Later, it struck me that I'd hardly given the arm a moment's thought during the knock, especially once I got into my groove, after I'd scored my first fifty. During my last 70 or so runs I felt as much in control of my game as I had at any time in the previous two or three years. If Kemar Roach had scarred me as badly as some people reckon, I don't think I could have played like that.

WE ENDED UP WINNING that Test by 231 runs, a much more decisive winning margin than we'd achieved a fortnight earlier in Sydney, when we'd won a thriller by 36 runs after Pakistan went from 0–34 in the second innings to 139 all out. Until that dramatic collapse, I was being roundly criticised for my decision to bat first. The pitch was damp and the sky grey when I won the toss, but I still opted to bat on the basis that if we could get through the first 25 overs we'd be in the box seat. Instead, we crashed to 7–62, all out 127, and conceded a first-innings deficit of 206. When we fought back to claim a victory that everyone outside our group thought was lost, I was suddenly vindicated, though of course it's never as cut and dried as that.

In so many ways, a cricket captain is only as good as his team. I always thought that was true of Mark Taylor and Steve Waugh when they were Australian captain; and it was true of me. When Tubby batted first on a bowler's deck at Old Trafford in 1997, everyone thought he was crazy until we took control of the game. The main reason we won was because Steve Waugh defied the tough conditions to score twin hundreds and Shane Warne snared six wickets in England's first innings. Steve liked to send teams in, arguing that it wasn't important who batted first, and it usually worked for him. With an attack featuring Glenn McGrath, Jason Gillespie, Brett Lee and Warnie, the best first-day spinner I've ever seen, at his disposal, of course he could say that. I know I'll always be second-guessed for sending England in at Edgbaston in 2005, but the main reason we lost that Test (by two runs) was not that we bowled first but that we bowled badly. At Johannesburg in 2009 I backed our top-order batsmen to survive on a pitch that was clearly going to be difficult at the start, and we lost only three wickets before lunch and went on to make a match-winning 466. Had we been 6–50 at lunch I'd have been a mug. Instead, for a little while, I was a magician.

We were 8–286 at the start of play in this Sydney Test, a lead of 80, with Mike Hussey on 73 and Peter Siddle on 10, and before they went out I made the point that while few people outside our dressing room thought we could win, I hadn't given up. I'd already spoken to Huss, reminding him that he was in outstanding form, had been ever since he made that superb hundred on the last day at the Oval, and I spent a lot of time with Sidds, telling him how much faith I had in his defensive technique. He'd worked really hard on his batting, to the point that he reminded me of Jason Gillespie in the way he refused to throw his wicket away. In the years to come he'd become even better than that, almost an all-rounder. Out in the middle, the Pakistanis gave the 'senior' batsman the easy singles and attacked the 'tailender', but Sidds could not be moved, Huss went on to another century and our eventual lead was 175.

We were relentless in the field throughout Pakistan's second innings. Brad Haddin and Mitchell Johnson took brilliant catches, and Mitch and Nathan Hauritz bowled really well. My main contribution as skipper came after Horrie took a sharp return catch to dismiss Mohammad Yousuf to leave them 4–77. The Pakistan captain was clearly seeking to smash our frontline spinner out of the attack and had hit him for three fours in one over, but I kept the field up and when he went for another big shot he hit it clean but straight back to the bowler. We were jubilant, until we saw the blood pouring from Horrie's left thumb; in taking the catch he'd ripped off part of his nail. After a couple of minutes of treatment from Alex Kountouris, Horrie muttered, 'I'm going to have to go off.'

'No you're not,' I replied. 'Put a bit of tape on it and fix it up later. You've got to bowl.'

Which he did, finishing with his second Test five-for, achieved a week after his first. To me, these returns were all about confidence. We'd encouraged Horrie to bowl a more aggressive line and length and stick to it even if the batsmen went after him. Previously, if he leaked a few runs, he reverted to the conservative way he bowled in ODIs, where he'd had some success over the previous nine months. Here, such was his control, he allowed me to be clever with the fields I set, pushing fieldsmen back at times to try to block a batsman's favourite shots then bringing them back into the 'ring' to tempt them into going over the top. The Pakistanis panicked under the strain we put on them.

MONTHS LATER, SOME OF Pakistan's players were embroiled in a 'spot-fixing' controversy that eventually led to Mohammad Amir, Mohammad Asif and opening bat Salman Butt being suspended and then jailed. Their crimes — committed during their tour of England in July–August 2010 — were not so much fixing games as doing certain things such as bowling no-balls at specific times for the benefit of gamblers or bookmakers who bet on that sort of thing. At the same time, there were suggestions that some matches might have been thrown, which led to the Sydney Test being investigated by the ICC's Anti Corruption and Security Unit. It found no evidence of match-fixing.

At the time, as we put the pressure on and wickets were falling, none of us thought anything was bent. We did plenty of things right during the last two days of that game, to win a Test most people outside our dressing room thought was lost. That's what I'll always remember.

AT THE
CLOSE
OF PLAY

*From international captain to
everyday domestic player*

Losing

Like it or not, losing is part of everyday life. I've always hated losing — still do — but I learned to accept losing as long as we were outplayed or beaten by a better team. I never accepted losing if we didn't prepare properly, were lazy and were not fully committed to our performance. If we gave it our all and did everything we could to win, but didn't, then there was probably not much more we could have done. Our performance was all to do with us. Generally, I didn't do anything different after a game that we lost or won. Sometimes I'd give the guys both barrels if our standards weren't good enough but fortunately this didn't happen all that often when I was captain. We'd always debrief the game to focus on what we could have done better and what we would do next time to be better. This was no different in a losing or winning dressing room.

As captain, maintaining a consistent mood and predictable behaviour after a win or a loss was really important to me. This was about setting an example for my team and never being too high or too low depending on the result. I was never too analytical in defeat, choosing to keep everything simple, direct and focused on the areas we could do better. Losing is part of being better prepared next time. It's a necessary part of wanting to win more often, building a greater desire to succeed and learning more about your own performance and role as part of a winning team.

CHAPTER 54

TACTICS AND TWEETS

England, June, 2010

'WHAT WILL HAPPEN if you lose?' Paul Newman asked me. We were doing a one-on-one for the *Daily Mail*, where Paul is the cricket correspondent.

'I'll probably be looking for a new job,' I replied. 'It's as simple as that.'

I was in London at the time, talking after game four of a five-game ODI series between England and Australia. It was late June 2010. Our main mission on this trip was a short Test series against Pakistan, to be played on neutral territory because of the continuing security concerns in Pakistan, but all the talk in the UK was about the Ashes series due to start in Brisbane the following November. Later in the interview I told Paul I was about to embark on 'the biggest 10 months of my career'.

'We're playing India, then England and then the World Cup,' I explained. 'Everything I do between now and April will be geared at getting the most out of myself and, most importantly, the group. If I'm able to do that I think there are some pretty special things on the horizon for this team.'

I was genuinely confident we'd go well through all these matches, extending our mostly winning run of the previous seven months. The boys had also reached the final of the World Twenty20, which was staged in the Caribbean in the first half of May. We improved from game to game in the one-dayers against England, losing the first three, winning the last two. Then we handled the Pakistanis comfortably at Lord's, in a game notable for the fact that for the first time three Tasmanians — Ben Hilfenhaus, keeper Tim Paine and me — appeared together in the same Test match. In the second Test, at Leeds, we fell apart on the first morning, all out for 88, but fought back so well we nearly won. Again, I was criticised for batting first and this time it was hard to argue. I'd misread the conditions. I knew as well as anyone that the ball ducks around at Headingley when the clouds roll in, whatever the state of the pitch, so with the weather overcast I should have bowled first. We had, in my defence, consulted the meteorologists, who suggested the clouds weren't going to hang around for long, and when I won the toss the pitch looked more like a day-three deck than a brand new wicket. No way was it going to last five days. Of course, if I had sent them in and the skies had cleared as we'd expected I might have looked silly in the opposite way.

Two months later, we were back on the subcontinent for our fifth away Test series against India in 12 years. This 2010 edition involved just two matches — the first in Mohali, the second in Bangalore. Originally, we'd been down to play seven ODIs and no Tests, which didn't suit India because they'd become the No. 1 ranked Test side in the world and it wasn't helpful for us either because playing 50-over games was hardly the right preparation for an Ashes series. So we were glad the change to the five-day games was made. The cricket was as seriously contested and dramatic as any Australia–India confrontation, but because it was only two games and because it was sort of squeezed in between other cricket fixtures it lacked some of the gravitas generated by previous series.

Further cheapening the action a little, a few players — Mike Hussey and Doug Bollinger for us; Rahul Dravid, MS Dhoni and Suresh Raina for India — arrived in Mohali only a couple of days before the first Test. They'd been in South Africa, playing in the Twenty20 Champions League.

For us, these late arrivals created a number of problems beyond the reality that their preparation for the Test was restricted to a day recovering from a 24-hour flight, a day in the nets trying to come to grips with the local conditions, and limited time to catch up on our game plans. A few of the boys were dirty because they thought Mike and Doug had put cash before country. Michael Clarke even went public, saying, 'You don't have to play IPL. You don't have to play Champions League. For me, personally, right now it is about representing my country, and every game I can play for Australia, I will do that. That's my priority.'

What Pup and the others mustn't have known was that Cricket Australia, who owned a share in the Champions League, had made it mandatory for players to put that tournament first. Huss had told me how he wanted to be with us in India, but it was made clear to him that he was contractually obliged to stay in South Africa until his team, the Chennai Super Kings, was eliminated. Of course, they won the final. When a couple of the blokes started grumbling about Mike and Dougie being absent, I was able to put them straight, but for some reason that message never got through to Pup. I wouldn't say the team was badly split over this issue, but there was some tension that we didn't need. Huss was actually the most upset, to the point that James Sutherland had to issue a public statement confirming that, 'Michael Hussey made it clear to CA before and during the CLT20 that his strong preference and preferred intention was to leave earlier than the final to prepare for the Test series in India.' Worse still, Dougie strained an abdominal muscle on the final day of the first Test. We couldn't help wondering if his abbreviated preparation played a part in that.

The Test evolved into one of the most exciting games I'd played in, yet — because of the cramped scheduling — if you asked Australian cricket fans to recall the game and how it finished I'm sure many would struggle to do so. In a nutshell, this is what happened ... Shane Watson hit a tremendous century on the opening day, Tim Paine made 92 and I thought our 428 total was a fraction better than par. Mitchell Johnson took five wickets as India lost their last six wickets for 51 to give us a lead of 23, but we then crashed from 0–87 in our second innings to 192 all out. Despite the unpredictable way the pitch was playing, I thought we were about 20 or 30 runs short, and so it proved. An outstanding bowling effort reduced them to 8–122, but we couldn't shift our old nemesis, VVS Laxman, who overcame a back ailment to be there at the end, 73 not out. He got them home with a solitary wicket to spare.

Our second-innings disintegration was a throwback to the batting collapses that had ruined our Ashes campaign in 2009. We were patient and sensible for most of the game, but for a short but critical period the surprising bounce of Ishant Sharma and Zaheer Khan's reverse swing did us in. Some of us were too aggressive, and I was as culpable as anyone, caught at backward square trying to hook Sharma before I was set. When Hilfy and Dougie ran through their top order I thought we were going to be okay and there was never a point when it didn't look like we could win, even down to what proved to be the final over. In the end, the game slipped away from us in a few moments of mayhem: we truly thought Mitch had their No. 11, Pragyan Ojha, plumb lbw; umpire Billy Bowden decided there'd been an inside edge; the batsman took off for an unlikely single; Laxman sent him back; our sub fieldsman, the young NSW all-rounder Steve Smith, on for the injured Bollinger, ran in from gully and shied at the stumps; it would have been out but the throw missed by a couple of centimetres and ran away for four overthrows. Two balls later, the ball flicked Ojha's pad, eluded Painey's dive and dribbled down to fine leg for two leg byes. The game was over. The small crowd went berserk. It was the closest I ever came to captaining Australia to a Test-match victory in India.

I couldn't blame Smithy, who was only trying to win when he went for the run out when there was no one backing up. If it had been me in the same situation, I would have done exactly the same thing.

The second Test a week later was in many ways a replica of the first, though it lacked the gut-wrenching climax. We made a big total, they matched us and we started our second dig positively before falling right away. This time, however, there was no stirring fourth-innings fightback by our bowlers, as the Indians cruised to a seven-wicket win. I made 77 and 72 in this game, giving me three 70s in four innings for the series, but what was the point of me batting well in India if I couldn't turn my good form into wins? Sachin Tendulkar, in contrast, scored 214 and 53 not out at Bangalore and was named player of the match and player of the series. If one of my three encouraging starts had evolved into a big hundred, we'd almost certainly have won a Test on this tour. If I'd made two big hundreds we'd have won the series.

MY CAPTAINCY BECAME A debating point again after we lost this series. After so long in the job and with the team not winning, it was inevitable and understandable. Australia hadn't lost three Tests in a row since 1988. However, I was disappointed that the fire was fuelled by Shane Warne, who took to Twitter to sledge the way I handled Nathan Hauritz during the second Test. Horrie was struggling at the time, his confidence down, his mindset dominated by negativity. He'd had a difficult time in Mohali, when he couldn't come through for us after Doug Bollinger was hurt, and by the final day in Bangalore I knew it was time to try something different. I wanted him to be more aggressive; he was more focused on not being hit for four. His solution, essentially, was to bet each way, at one point positioning three close-in catchers, at slip, short leg and leg slip, and three men on the fence, at deep point, long-on and long-off. The logic was that the three men around the bat boosted his chances of a wicket, while the boundary riders would limit the chances of him going for too many runs. I thought it was a reasonable idea, not too dissimilar to what I'd done with Brett Lee a few years earlier, when by putting a couple of fieldsmen in defensive positions it actually gave him the confidence to attack. This time, it didn't work, Horrie's opening two overs went for 22, and Warnie was into me, sending me a text: 'How the hell can hauritz bowl to this field?? … Feeling for hauritz, terrible!! … What are these tactics? … Sorry Ricky but what are you doing?'

The response, among Shane's followers and in the wider media, was predictable. 'Warne Slams Ponting' seemed to be the headline of choice.

Shane posted his tweets during the final day's play, so the first I knew of them was when I was questioned on the subject immediately after the Test. I went into the media conference determined to acknowledge we'd been outplayed, give Sachin due credit for his superb batting and to talk about the positives in our performance, such as Hilfy's bowling, Watto's batting and Tim Paine's glovework. Instead I had to contend with something Warnie had said or done. I knew he couldn't help himself, that he likes to be noticed, and Twitter was his latest thing. I just wish he could have asked us why we set the fields we did before shooting his tweet off. As I sat there being asked for a response to these tweets I felt a little like a parent who had told his child not to do something again, explained why, and then had to clean up the mess after the child promptly made the same mistake again.

In the press conference, I said: 'Every field that Nathan's had to bowl with since he's been here is at his request. It's the field he wants to bowl to. Unfortunately it doesn't appear that Shane would take the time to ask anyone about that. Shane's got his opinion out in the public at the moment, and it's a personal opinion. Different people say things at different times, we don't always agree with all of them. That's life I guess. It would be nice if they were a bit more informed before they made some of their comments though.'

Later that evening, I sent Warnie a text bluntly telling him he wasn't helping. It was the start of an SMS exchange between us that left me frustrated and bemused but okay. When he said he'd meant no harm, I accepted his word. He asked if he was off my Christmas card list and if I'd lost my sense of humour. I looked back at his original tweet, and wondered where the joke was. I fired back with, 'Mate, don't sit back and criticise. Help us out. You can say whatever you want after that.' On TV, the night after his original tweet caused such a storm, he said of our relationship, 'We're mates, we're going to disagree a few times, it doesn't mean suddenly we hate each other.'

That's pretty much how I felt about him. At the time I wished we could have kept our comments between us, because that would have made my life as leader a little easier. In this case, the media furore put my future as skipper back on the agenda much earlier than Paul Newman and I had expected when we chatted at the Oval in June. In Paul's paper, the *Daily Mail*, Warnie was quoted as saying, 'Sometimes as a player, when things are going badly, we can all be a bit sensitive to comments that ex-players or commentators make.' But Warnie had a point. It's lucky I like the bloke and am happy to take him as he is!

Mitch, Watto and I were excused from the three one-dayers that followed the Tests in India, so we could return home early to best prepare for the upcoming Ashes series. Immediately, I went back to a training regimen I had started in August, when I'd worked with the team's former team conditioner Jock Campbell to become fitter than I'd ever been before. Part of this was about me not losing any ground on anyone even though I was now the wrong side of 35. As Jock kept reminding me, 'Linford Christie won the Olympic

100 metres in his thirties.' Furthermore, leading by example had become almost an obsession. I wanted my team-mates to see my leaner, stronger frame, think, *Wow, he's been working hard*, and then go off and work just as hard. If that happened, I was confident the results we craved would come.

CHAPTER 55

EXECUTION

Sydney, November 14, 2010

IT RAINED ON THEIR PARADE and then it rained on ours. I'm not sure whose idea it was to announce a 17-man squad for the Ashes 10 days out from the start of the series. I've never bothered to find out. The gossip was it was Cricket Australia's marketing department that came up with the bright idea of announcing the team early, to add to the build-up, but the selectors wisely wanted to wait until as late as possible, to give all the contenders every chance to press for selection.

The compromise was to announce a larger squad, which would be reduced to 12 or 13 in the days immediately before the Test, but this process left us looking disorganised, as if we weren't sure what we were doing. The truth was the only spot really up for grabs was the spinner, but by nominating 'shadows' a few guys were looking over their shoulders when they should have been focusing on the task at hand. The Sydney-based players were invited to the big announcement at Circular Quay but heavy rain turned the event into a fizzer. The public was invited but a combination of lousy weather and poor promotion meant that fewer than 50 fans showed up.

In a number of ways, our preparation for this series was a shemozzle. The Tests in India were tough and competitive, but then we lost short ODI series in India and at home against Sri Lanka. My lead-up to the first Test centred on Sheffield Shield games in Hobart and Sydney but neither pitch was particularly conducive to batting, especially at the SCG where the game lasted just over two days and nobody managed a half-century. In the groundsmen's defence the weather in eastern Australia at the time was ordinary; but what I would have given for a substantial hit on a good, true Aussie deck! Nathan Hauritz was fighting for his Test career in our game at the SCG, but such were the conditions NSW skipper Simon Katich was only able to give him one over in the entire match. Two weeks earlier, in his first Shield game of the season, Horrie had delivered only two overs in the game because the Blues' quicks rolled Queensland for 75 and 96. He never had a chance to bowl himself into some form. My Tassie team-mate Xavier Doherty was picked as our spinner for the first Test.

There was one other selection issue heading into the Test and to this day it surprises me because it involved a man who was one of our most reliable players. Mike Hussey had been struggling for over a year. He wasn't getting runs and he wasn't looking good at the wicket. I seem to remember him getting hit on the helmet a few times and that isn't something that happens to a batsman in good form, particularly Huss.

He scored three runs in his first Shield game of the summer and everything seemed to rest on how he would perform against Victoria. Huss made a duck in the first innings and the story goes that he came off and slumped in defeat. He figured he had lost his opportunity to play the first Test due to start the next week. Western Australia shouldn't really have batted again in that game, they had a good lead but fortunately for Huss they did and he promptly made a century.

It was great news for him and us.

Something clicked for Huss in that last Shield innings, he thought he was gone and he batted with a freedom he had been lacking. He had told people for the previous 12 months that he was doing nothing different and as he piled up big scores over the next 12 months (he was our leading run-scorer in the Ashes) he repeated that mantra.

There was a lesson in that. You didn't suddenly stop being able to bat when you were at this level, it was something mental that stopped you doing it the way you knew how. These were things I had cause to think of a lot in the last years of my career.

Cricket Australia's decision to go with an early team announcement reflected the reality that this Ashes series didn't have quite the same hype as 2006–07. The reason was simple enough. We weren't as good a team as we'd been four years earlier, and plenty of people feared we were going to lose. I didn't agree with this sentiment and was genuinely looking forward to proving the pessimists wrong.

It started well enough. We knocked England over for 260, made 481 in reply in Brisbane and were sure we had England captain Andrew Strauss lbw first ball of their second innings. Aleem Dar said not out, the video replay agreed with him, and Strauss, Alastair Cook and Jonathan Trott batted us out of the game. We just couldn't take the wickets we needed.

In Adelaide, we won the toss, batted, lost three wickets in the first 13 balls of the Test and never recovered. Simon Katich was at the non-striker's end fourth ball of the morning, but got involved in a mix-up with Shane Watson and was run out without facing a ball. A terrible start got worse when I was gone for a golden duck and then Michael Clarke followed six balls later. There was no coming back from there. Cook made his second big hundred in a row, Kevin Pietersen toyed with us for 227 and we lost by an innings. In two consecutive innings, the Poms had smashed us for 1137 runs at an average of nearly 200 runs per wicket. My scores in the series so far were 10, 51 not out, 0 and 9.

THERE WAS A MOMENT in the lead-up to this Adelaide Test that captured one of the problems I was having with my game at this point of my career. I was searching for my rhythm by having some throwdowns hurled at me at practice, while in the net to my right Michael Clarke couldn't hit a ball in the middle of his bat. Every time Pup miscued, he shouted out in frustration and soon I found myself more concerned with how he was going than with my own batting. A bowler would be running in at Pup and I'd stop to watch. When my session was done, I stood my distance but continued to study him closely.

When, still frustrated, he said he'd had enough I stepped forward and suggested he stay in the net, and I gave him some throwdowns while offering some advice about his stance and balance. I'd seen enough of Pup over the years to know that a couple of tiny but significant bad habits had snuck into his game, maybe the result of him playing with a bad back, a chronic injury which had been bugging him for a few weeks. A couple of years earlier, I'd set him straight after he'd started using a heavier bat but that change wasn't working for him. It was okay for Matt Hayden or Andrew Symonds to use a weighty blade, but not Pup, who's a little shorter and significantly leaner than those two Queenslanders. This time, I think I helped him by getting him to stand a fraction taller, and not lean too far to the off-side when he played his drives; by the end of our little tutorial it certainly appeared that some of his timing was back.

However, by focusing on helping a team-mate, I think I lost whatever gains I might have found from my time in the nets. More and more, as the experienced guys left our group, I found myself feeling responsible for *everything* that happened with the Australian team. This is a criticism of me, not of management or the coach. I couldn't let go.

I've already mentioned how, when I first became one-day captain, the best advice Steve Waugh gave me was to make sure I gave my own game sufficient attention. Early on, I reckon I did that pretty well but as my time as captain progressed and we didn't win as often, I started taking too much on. I wasn't overwhelmed, I just had a lot on my plate, which meant I couldn't give my own game enough attention at a time when that's what I really needed to do. This 2010–11 Ashes season was my worst in that regard. There were a number of sponsors to 'service' (as the people in marketing like to say), reporters to spar with, selections to discuss, practice sessions and team meetings to plan, match referees to meet, travel arrangements to discuss, and the odd internal team problem to solve. I don't think the young blokes would have realised there was a problem. I doubt even Michael Clarke, our vice-captain, realised there was a problem.

As captain, I did everything willingly, always because I wanted to win and I wanted what was best for the team. This ever-burgeoning workload is part of why I now believe an international cricket captain has only a limited shelf-life: three to five years.

Mitchell Johnson had been so out of sorts in Brisbane and selectors decided to 'rest' him for the second Test. At the time, I thought that decision was wrong, to the point that when the press asked me if I agreed with it, I didn't toe the line — as I usually did when the selectors picked a team other than the one I'd hoped for — instead replying, 'Good question. You might have to ask [chairman of selectors] Andrew Hilditch that.'

If there was one main problem I had with selectors over the years it was with them picking fast bowlers who I knew weren't right for the game. Before the Brisbane Test it was obvious that Doug Bollinger was not fit enough and he was duly despatched to a Shield match in Perth to get a bit of first-class cricket in his legs. When Mitch struggled in the first match the first thing the selectors did for Adelaide was get Bolli back halfway through the Shield game.

I knew he wasn't going to be right and wasn't surprised to see his pace begin to decline as the heat rose during the match.

I reckon the selectors had made the same mistake when they'd picked Brett Lee for the match against South Africa in Perth the previous year, he just wasn't right and it was no surprise to me when he struggled in that game and broke down in the next.

To make matters worse for us in the second Test of the Ashes, Simon Katich broke down with an Achilles injury. One of the hardest men I'd ever played with, Kato would not leave the field despite the fact he was basically on one leg. I offered him the chance to go off and even tried to hide him but he was a stubborn bloke and his 43 runs in the second innings were a magnificent act of defiance, but he wasn't playing again this series. In fact that was the last we ever saw of him, but more of that later

The captain's job gets you in the end, in a variety of ways. As I contemplated our heavy defeat in Adelaide, I concluded that whatever I said to the group, the opposite was happening. 'There'll be no more meetings,' I said. 'When we get to Perth [for the third Test], we'll just train and play and see how we go.' That's pretty much what we did. We'd had any number of meetings during this series where the point was reinforced about Alastair Cook and Jonathan Trott being so strong off their pads, but that didn't stop our blokes from bowling the wrong line to them. Cook averaged 127 for the five Tests, Trott nearly 90. It's often not about the plans so much as how you execute them.

WHEN WE ARRIVED IN PERTH, I sought out Mickey Arthur, the former South African coach who was now looking after Western Australia. Mickey had been with South Africa when they'd had some success against us at the WACA, forcing a draw in 2005–06 and scoring 4–414 in the fourth innings to win three years later, so I thought he was the right guy to talk to about how the pitch there was going. In seasons past, I'd got some misleading mail from locals about the square and had annoyed a few of them when I bagged the conditions after a few matches. Every time, my beef was the same: that with the advent of 'drop-in' pitches the WACA square had lost its character, become lifeless, a far cry from the days when it was the fastest deck in the world. Mickey reported that while the surface wasn't back to its bounciest days, it was a good quick pitch that he thought would suit us.

Mitch was back for Perth, and after talking to Mickey, I knew he was the guy who could get us back in the series. He'd had some success at the WACA in the past and this time the wicket would suit him even more.

Ironically, Mitch did his first piece of good work with the bat, scoring 62 from No. 8 to help us to 268 all out. I sensed that boosted his creaking confidence and from his first over he was a much more dynamic bowler than he'd been at the Gabba. His opening spell on day two was explosive, starting with the dismissal of Cook, caught by Mike Hussey in the gully. In five dramatic overs, he took 4–7, with Trott, Pietersen and Paul Collingwood all trapped lbw by fast, swinging deliveries. After the Test I described this spell as 'one of the best in Ashes history' and that still sounds right. There were days like this when Mitch was as lethal a bowler as any in my experience; at other times, however, he was so frustratingly erratic and ineffective. I never questioned his work ethic and commitment, but for someone so talented, such a natural cricketer and so gifted an athlete, I found his lack of self-belief astonishing. He bowls left-handed, plays tennis to a high standard right-handed and scored Test centuries before an optometrist discovered his natural eyesight is not as 20/20 as it could be.

The third day of this Perth Test was our best of the series, though there was a sting in the tail in it for me. At the start of the day we were 3–119, a lead of exactly 200, with Mike Hussey and Shane Watson at the crease, their partnership already past 50. They continued on for much of the first session, with Watto playing some thumping drives and looking completely in command until he was suddenly out for 95. Huss continued on to his second hundred of the series, his judgment of length throughout being exceptional. It's an underrated skill knowing when to leave the ball alone, especially at the WACA when the ball is bouncing. The key, like most things in cricket, is to be assertive. You can often tell if a batsman is in form by the way the ball pings off his bat when he plays a defensive shot; it's the same when he leaves a ball alone with authority, rather than nervously. At the same time, when the English bowlers dropped too short Huss was on to them in an instant, playing some superb hook and pull shots. He was last man out, by which time our lead had grown to 390, and then Mitch, Ben Hilfenhaus and Ryan Harris took five wickets before stumps, leaving us in an almost unbeatable position. The buzz on the field as we took those wickets was similar to how we'd felt in South Africa in 2009, and I was beginning to think the momentum was shifting our way. However, my pleasure was dampened by the broken finger I suffered in the closing stages of the third day, when I made a mess of a slip catch. Fortunately, I managed to pop the chance up for Brad Haddin to complete the dismissal of Trott, but X-rays that night revealed a fracture in the little finger of my left hand. My first question, to the doctor, was, 'How bad?' The second, to physio Alex Kountouris, was, 'What do we have to do for me to be right for Boxing Day?' It didn't occur to me that I wouldn't be playing.

'Your only problem will be if you get hit on that finger again,' the experts told me. 'That might move the fracture and then you'll be in trouble.'

The next day, we duly completed an emphatic victory, by 267 runs, with Ryno finishing with six wickets and Mitch another three. With the feeling in the team so positive and the Ashes on the line, playing in Melbourne was a risk I was prepared to take. If I caused extra damage that meant I missed the World Cup in February–March, so be it. I'd need pain-killers and would have to stay away from the slips to see out the series, but there wasn't a player in either team who in the same position wouldn't have been thinking the same way. I was razor keen to play and after the Perth victory excited by our chances. My confidence was dented only by my memory of the amazing resilience the Englishmen had found in 2009, when they'd bounced back so strongly at Lord's and the Oval, after we'd had the better of the previous Test matches.

This time, it was much, much worse for us, as we were twice humiliated by an innings. Again, we kept the team meetings to a minimum, but Mitch left his Superman cape at the WACA, Ryno suffered a stress fracture in his leg, and no Australian managed an innings of more than 55 in our last four digs of the series. It's almost ridiculous when I think about it now — how fired up I was in the week before Boxing Day; how shattered and deflated we all were by January 7. Unlike 2005 and 2009, there were no 'what might have beens' about this Ashes battle. I scored 10 and 20 at the MCG and didn't play in Sydney, completing my most miserable series with the bat since India in 2001.

AN INCIDENT DURING THE Melbourne Test that did little for my reputation occurred on the second day, while Trott and Pietersen were batting us out of the game and the series. We'd been sent in and bowled out on the first day for 98; in reply, the Poms were cruising at 2–259. We were giving our all but nothing was working for us. Sections of the crowd were into us, and not just the Barmy Army. Pietersen was acting as he always did when he was winning, chipper as anything, reminding us how badly we were going. Then, out of nowhere, we might have found a breakthrough, as Ryan Harris got a ball between Pietersen's bat and pad. Some of the guys' shouts were half-hearted, Shane Watson at slip hardly appealed at all, but Brad Haddin behind the stumps was convinced it was out. Aleem Dar gave the benefit of the doubt to the batsman.

I wasn't sure if it was out. It was impossible to tell for sure from where I was fielding at mid-off, but Hadds was adamant, shouting to me, 'It was an inside edge.' I referred the decision to the video umpire.

Of course, we discussed the likely outcome as a group while we were waiting for the verdict. Hadds continued to insist Pietersen was gone. Up on the big screen, they started to show replays of the ball passing the bat and from one angle there was a 'hot spot' that indicated there had indeed been contact. 'I told you,' Hadds muttered. I was sold, we all were, and then they said, 'Not out.'

I could not believe it.

Aleem Dar was one of the best umpires I played under and he's a good man, too. But he'd made a mistake; I was sure of it. I asked him how they'd come up with the call when the technology said otherwise. He began trying to explain that the hot spot we'd seen did not match where the ball passed the bat; it was down near the toe of the bat, he said, but the ball actually went past the inside edge about 10 centimetres higher than that. 'So where did the hot spot come from?' I asked aggressively. He didn't know but that didn't matter. In the mind of video umpire Marais Erasmus there wasn't enough evidence to overturn the on-field decision. I kept arguing and when Aleem Dar said it was time to get on with the game I went up to the other on-field umpire, Tony Hill from New Zealand, and started debating the point with him. Pietersen came up and quipped that he had hit it, but he didn't need to do that. I was already fully wound up. I'd come to believe in the video-review system but the people implementing it clearly didn't have a clue and I was sick of the whole mess. *All the talk and reports and meetings and bullshit about getting it right had been for nothing.* That's how I was thinking. Up in the commentary box, everyone was agreeing with the TV umpire. The whole episode, from initial appeal to next delivery, carried on for eight minutes.

Truth is, I'd had a brain explosion, and argued the point for too long. In the heat of the moment, with my team playing badly, me not contributing with the bat and the Ashes slipping away, I'd lost it. Aleem Dar tried to help by explaining why the TV umpire ruled the way he did, but I wasn't listening. Later, they fined me 40 per cent of my match fee and I deserved that. I apologised for my behaviour.

But I still think Pietersen was out.

Unsung heroes

Australian cricket is built on a rock-solid foundation of volunteers who give their hearts and souls to their cricket club or association. They are the essence of all things great about cricket. Without these unsung heroes, cricket would not be half as successful as it is as a participation sport in our country. These are the often anonymous people who become office bearers at the local club, roll the pitches, put the covers on and off, make the lunches and afternoon teas, run the fundraisers to keep the clubs financial and everything else that goes into making a cricket club a community hub in our local towns and suburbs.

While cricket has become a highly lucrative professional sport, we should never lose sight of these people and where every cricket career begins and ends. That place for me is the Mowbray Cricket Club, and among all I learned there, I will never forget the people like Mick Sellers, the late Rosemary Tucker, Juan Salter, Simon Howard, Brad Jones and so many other incredible volunteers who lived and still live for that club. There's a Mick, Rosemary, Juan, Simon and Brad in each and every cricket club in Australia, whether it's in the outback or one of the more affluent city suburbs. Each is giving his or her time selflessly to the cricket community so that guys like me can enjoy the game week in, week out. These are the unsung heroes of our game and on behalf of every child, woman or man who plays cricket in our country, I say thank you for all your hard work.

CHAPTER 56
PUNTED OUT

World Cup, 2011

I HAD SURGERY ON my broken finger even before the Ashes series was over, after X-rays showed that the fracture had got worse and wouldn't heal properly without an operation. There was a setback when an infection got into the joint, but by early February, I was back in the nets and two weeks later I was declared fit enough to play in our Cup opener, against Zimbabwe.

We'd arrived in India as the ICC's No. 1 ranked ODI team in the world, though I sensed few critics rated us that highly. We'd been that way for most of the time since the official rankings were introduced in 2002. Only in 2009, when we briefly fell as low as fourth, was our status threatened, but we went back on top when we claimed that year's ICC Champions Trophy and were still there when we beat Zimbabwe easily enough, by 91 runs, in the opening game, in Ahmedabad. That took our unbeaten streak at World Cups to 30, stretching back to the preliminary rounds in 1999. In my absence, the boys had won six of the seven ODIs against England that followed the Ashes Tests, victories that featured strong batting from Shane Watson, Michael Clarke and David Hussey and, perhaps most notably, the successful returns of Brett Lee and Shaun Tait. Whatever the experts reckoned, I felt we could still think of ourselves as being among the favourites.

Unfortunately, an off-field incident during our opening game took some of the attention away from how we'd played. Watto's dismissal in the 32nd over left us 2–140. I was 27 not out and ready to change my game a little, pick up the tempo. Michael Clarke came out and almost immediately I was run out by a direct-hit throw as we tried for a second run. I'd had all the problems with my finger before the World Cup, had worked overtime to get it right, trained really hard, done a lot of different things with my bat handles — put on extra grips and tape on the top part so I didn't have to squeeze too hard with my top hand — and I got out *this* way! I walked off and sat in my chair. A big-screen LCD TV was about three metres away ...

My box is made of titanium. It's designed so it won't break. I took it off and threw it in frustration at my kitbag, but instead of disappearing into the bag it clipped the edge, ricocheted onto the concrete floor of our dressing room and then bounced up into the TV screen. The screen didn't smash, there wasn't glass all over the floor, but there was something wrong with one corner. It had gone completely green. When I touched that part of the screen with my fingers, it was as if it was made of sand.

I owned up to it and volunteered to pay for the damage. Someone came to take it away. That, surely, should have been the end of it. No one had got hurt and the owners of the damaged TV weren't out of pocket. But that's not how it works in cricket these days. The next day photos of the broken TV appeared in the local papers. Amazingly, it was in a significantly worse state than it had been when it had left our dressing room. Of course, the accompanying story revealed I was responsible for the carnage, which had us thinking one of the room attendants had dobbed me in. Various reports described my action as a 'hissy fit', 'petulant' and a 'fit of anger', but it was hardly any of that. The local cricket association secretary told the world via the media that 'an Australian team captain should not behave in this manner'. With the story now in the public domain, the match referee had no option but to fine me for damaging equipment in the dressing room, as that was a breach of conduct according to the rules governing the tournament. I was more bemused than anything. In my view, the relish with which some people sought to nail me was more an indictment on them than me.

We followed up with a comfortable defeat of New Zealand in which Taity and Mitchell Johnson bowled really nicely. But after our game against Sri Lanka in Colombo was washed out, we put in two shockers in a row, against Kenya and Canada. After scoring 6–324, we couldn't bowl the Kenyans out and had to be satisfied with a tame 60-run win. We talked about making a statement against Canada by winning by a massive margin, but our effort in the field was laid-back, almost lazy. I had always struggled with the bat against minnow teams, finding it hard to get up for the contests, but there was something more going on here. We lacked some of the intensity that had been the trademark of the great Australian teams and for the first time in my cricket life I was feeling old. Not in the body but in the message.

My frustration spilled over late in the Canadians' innings. Jason Krejza, who was our frontline spinner for this tournament because of injuries to Nathan Hauritz and Xavier Doherty, was struggling with his line and length. Earlier on, our quicks had bowled too short and too wide, trying to overwhelm them with brawn rather than skill. Now a tailender named Harvir Baidwan was looking more like Bradman, as he slammed long hops from Steve Smith and Krejza for four. I was stunned by just how bad our cricket was and I've never been good with bowlers who can't stick to the plan although I'd had a few years to get used to it.

Baidwan then tried to slog Jason out of the country but only succeeded in hitting it high up in the air. Steve Smith was to my right, but it was my catch and I did everything as per the coaching manual. I called loudly for it and kept my eyes on it. It was basic cricket, except Smithy kept coming and we had a minor collision as I clung on to it. I wasn't dirty on him, these things happen, but it was one too many examples of one of our players not being 'in the game'. I threw the ball onto the turf in frustration, didn't crack a smile and barely acknowledged that a wicket had fallen, after which Mike Hussey came over, put his hands on my shoulders, and told me to relax. To me, it was no big deal, though afterwards — following a negative reaction back home from people who hadn't watched the entire game but did see the episode in isolation — I conceded it wasn't a terrific reaction on my part. 'If it looked bad,' I said after the game, 'I apologise for it.'

Thinking about it now, I wonder if demonstrating my displeasure at our performance publicly was actually something I should have done earlier. I've never been a fan of showing people up when they're going badly, on the basis that they're trying their hardest so it's best to wait for the privacy of the dressing room before delivering any rockets. But maybe being 'Captain Cranky' on the field might have been the jolt that got the team going in the right direction. Nothing else was working.

Having said that, I rate Steve Smith very highly and think he is an important part of Australian cricket's future. This came home to me during the 2013 Ashes when somebody asked me on radio who was a potential next captain and as I quickly went through the list of possible candidates he seemed to be the obvious one. Like Phillip Hughes he is one of the young cricketers who needs support and patience. Selectors have got to back these guys.

Australia had won 34 consecutive World Cup games, but the unbeaten streak was finally broken in our last group game, against Pakistan at Colombo, which left us third in our group and set up a quarter-final match-up with India at Ahmedabad. Finally, after six weeks on the subcontinent, with the knockout matches upon us we felt the World Cup was about to begin. In the lead-up, Tim Nielsen said to me that I was looking better than at any time in the previous two years and I fancied myself to make a big score, but then we looked at the wicket, which seemed remarkably well suited to the bowling attack of the home team. One end, which was much rougher than the other, was obviously going to turn from the start. Sure enough, India's captain MS Dhoni gave his off-spinner Ravi Ashwin the first over and the ball spun a mile. Every over of the innings to that end would be bowled by a spinner. The quicks bowled from the other end.

We actually got off to a pretty good start. Brad Haddin and I added 70 for the second wicket, so we were 2–110 in the 23rd over. Michael Clarke came in, but just as we started to get a partnership going, he hit a catch to deep mid-wicket. This began a trend where every time I felt like I was in a position to get things moving, another wicket fell. My job, until right near the completion of our innings, was to establish a partnership with each new man in. A typical batting plan in ODIs for a batsman like me is to start cautiously, build momentum and then, into the final 10 or 15 overs and if there are wickets in hand, go for more shots, take more risks. This time, I knew I had to be there to the end. Fortunately, Dave Hussey gave me tremendous support in the final overs and we managed a reasonable total, 6–260, though I feared we were 20 or 30 runs short.

Not long after I reached my hundred, in the middle of the 49th over, I decided to play a reverse sweep, a shot I think I might have played only once before in my life. Such an unlikely shot selection suggests that my brain was weary, and I certainly played the shot on an impulse, but there was some logic to it. Dhoni had packed the legside, because I had been hitting with the spin when facing Ashwin. There was a fielder at short third man, but he was covering a stack of ground and I figured that all I had to do was get a little bit of bat on it and it would either go fine or over his head. Sure enough, I cracked it straight to him.

For much of India's reply, we were behind, but only just. They needed 74 from the final 13 overs; pretty much a run a ball with six wickets in hand. Yuvraj Singh and Dhoni were at the crease and we saw them as the key partnership. I brought back Brett Lee and Shaun Tait, thinking they were our best bet to get the wicket we needed; worst case, they wouldn't go for too many runs because both batsmen have a reputation as better players of spin than pace. Third ball, Bing had Dhoni caught by Pup at point and I thought I was clever. The rest of the over was scoreless, a wicket maiden, and I began to believe I was a genius. Sadly, crazily, the next three overs went for 33. I've heard some loud crowds in my time in India and this was right up there. They were still only five wickets down when they won with 14 balls to spare.

I GUESS, GIVEN WE gave the eventual champions a tough game in a quarter-final, you could describe our performance as 'competitive'. That was the adjective I used in the post-game media conference. But I'd been hoping for much more than that. We weren't far away from winning, against a very good team playing on their home soil, but I wouldn't have accepted that in 2003 or 2007, and I didn't want it to be acceptable now. The team needed a rocket — not a spray from an angry captain or coach — but something else to inspire it back to life. It needed something new.

Meanwhile, a bit like what happened at the end of the Ashes series in 2009, now that we'd lost everyone was suddenly very nice to me. One of the local papers, while describing my hundred, wrote about my 'grit, composure under pressure, flashes of brilliance and sheer Aussie single-mindedness'. Another called my knock 'an innings of a lifetime' and suggested that 'no Indian would hate him now'. Shane Warne, of course, went to Twitter, to say, 'Last thought — form temporary — class permanent!!!!', while Michael Vaughan tweeted, 'Outstanding innings from Ricky … That will shut a few up.' I couldn't help but wonder where all these people had been when I'd needed them. As I was about to leave the reporters after the game, one of the local scribes asked if I was a 'tragic hero' and my response was flat: 'I don't feel like much of a hero at the moment.'

Just before that, I'd been asked how I rated India's chances of winning the World Cup.

'Better than ours,' I said.

Top five Indian players

SACHIN TENDULKAR

I have always thought Sachin was the best batsman I ever played against. As an opposition captain you probably lost more sleep when there was a game on the line and Brian Lara was coming out to bat the next day, but Sachin because of his technical genius was something else. He had a couple of gears when he batted. If he didn't want to get out on a certain day, his technique was good enough that he could bat for hours and you would never look like getting him out. You never got one past the outside edge and you never hit him on the pads. His technique was so sound. It didn't matter if you tried bouncing him, going around the wicket, bowling wide of the off-stump with a strong field on that side, spin ... whatever we tried, he found a way to combat it every time. His record against Australia, even when we had the better teams — with McGrath, Warne, Gillespie — would be far superior to any other batsman we played against. Sachin was the best technical batsman I ever played against. And then there's the number of games he's played — it is mind-blowing — he has played three more full seasons than me ...

RAHUL DRAVID

A wonderful person and a wonderful batsman. Rahul is more of a workman than a craftsman at the crease, but his longevity in the game is something you just can't ignore. He was one batsman who never made batting look as easy as some did, but he had that ability to bat and bat and bat and play his game. He ended up with over 13,000 runs and averaged over 50. He probably didn't have the best time of it in Australia, but he did everywhere else around the world. On top of that, he was one of the better slip fielders you will ever see, particularly with spin bowlers, and he took over 200 catches — more than anybody else. It is a hard spot to field and particularly hard for off-spin bowlers. We had

an exchange of messages when he finished and when I
did. That doesn't happen every day in cricket and that
meant a lot to me.

VIRAT KOHLI

It is early in his career and time will tell, but he is a
great batsman. He has got presence and is one of
those new breed of Indian players who are supremely
confident, and he has the game to back it up. He
plays spin bowling well and he plays fast bowling
well, which is unusual for young Indian players. He has
got an unbelievable one-day record already, he has
15 hundreds at an average of about 50, and his Test
average is building. I think in two or three years his
name will be up there as one of the best in Test match
cricket.

HARBHAJAN SINGH

I have to include him because he has got me out so
many times. Our rivalry goes back to about the first
game I played in Sharjah, where we both got reported
and that's where our rivalry began. I made a lot of
runs against India in Australia and runs against them in
World Cup finals but in between, particularly in Tests,
he had the best of our battles.

ZAHEER KHAN

It's in the past four or five years that he has really
matured as a bowler. He has dropped his pace, but
when the ball is swinging, whether it is the new ball
or the old ball, he is a very wily, cagey bowler. He is
as good as anyone with a reverse swinging ball and I
reckon most players around the world think that. He's
learned from years of playing on those wickets that it is
not necessarily how quick you can bowl but the areas
you hit and what you can do with the ball. He's always
used his angles well, he comes around the wicket to
right-hand batters. Every time we have been to India
or he's been to Australia, he has been a handful for our
team.

CHAPTER 57

SOMETHING NEW

Ahmedabad, the early hours of Friday, March 25, 2011

I'D MADE A CENTURY, but the team had lost and it was hard to sleep because as much as I tried to stop the thought going through my mind I just knew it was the end. I decided to resign as Australia's Test and one-day captain after the quarter-final, not before. The game had been on a Thursday and we didn't get back to the hotel until late. It was always hard to shut off after a game and a tournament, but never this hard.

Don't decide until the morning, I told myself.

I kept thinking about where I and the team were at. Three facts kept coming up: (1) this World Cup hasn't gone as we'd hoped; (2) I haven't got that long left in the game; and (3) the team's next big assignments are a fair way down the track.

The last one was the clincher. I couldn't hang on, even for another fortnight. It was the right time to give the next guy an opportunity. I remembered how I'd been introduced to the captaincy: first, in one-day cricket and then two years later in Tests. This wouldn't be quite the same, but we did have a short ODI series in Bangladesh due to start in a couple of weeks. The next Test series would be in Sri Lanka in August–September. The next big one-day tournament would be the ICC Champions Trophy in 2013, the same year we were due back in England to fight again for the Ashes.

This is not to say that standing down as captain was easy. It had been my life for so long. I was quitting arguably the most prestigious job in Australian sport. Only 43 people had led Australia in a Test match. It would have been nice to be departing on the shoulders of my team-mates, victorious, rather than at a press conference after a defeat. One comfort was that it was totally my decision. No one had knifed me; instead, a number of people tried to talk me out of it. Tim Nielsen thought it was vital I stayed in the job for as long as I could while the team was developing. Senior figures from Cricket Australia contacted my manager, James Henderson, who had been looking after me since 2007, straight after the quarter-final to say, 'Don't let Ricky make any stupid decisions. At least make him hold fire until after the games in Bangladesh.'

But my mind was made up.

I can honestly say that I had never considered stepping down before this — not after Cricket Australia let us down in 2007–08, or after we lost to South Africa at home in 2008–09, or after the Ashes in 2009, or even after the Ashes in 2010–11. With that last one, I'd resolved to give the World Cup my best shot and then I'd contemplate the future. Throughout this period I always believed I was the best man for the job. In the aftermath of this decision, I wondered if most cricket captains have a shelf-life, that after a few years in the position it becomes increasingly difficult to keep things fresh, to keep challenging the players in different ways. Maybe the twin pressures of leading a team that wasn't winning and scoring runs at No. 3 wore me down more than I was prepared to acknowledge at the time. Spending more than a day in the field and then, straight away, padding up and going out to bat never got easier, but I didn't want to move down the order. Not while I was captain.

No two situations are ever the same. In my case, whenever the Australian team I was leading was struggling, I knew my obligation was to be a better leader and a better player, for the team's sake not just my own. If, during the toughest of times, I'd felt there was an alternative captain I would have stepped away, but I never felt there was anyone else who could do the job better than me. The people who appointed me thought the same. I couldn't walk away. That would have been the wrong thing to do.

I rang Michael Clarke on the morning I made the announcement I was stepping down. We'd been back in Sydney just a couple of days and I was on my way to the SCG for the media conference. It was only a brief chat, but a good one. It was true that I'd been a little disappointed with some of the things he'd done — or, more accurately, hadn't done — as vice-captain, but I was now comfortable with the idea of him taking over. It wasn't that he was disruptive or treacherous, and publicly he said all the right things, but he had never been one to get too involved in planning sessions or debriefs at the end of a day's play, or to volunteer to take on any of the captain's workload. More than once, Tim Nielsen and I had encouraged him to take on more of a leadership role within the group, but when Pup was down on form or if he had a problem away from cricket, he'd go into his shell. I knew he was an excellent thinker on the game, but for a long time I was concerned that he wouldn't be able to handle the huge variety of 'little things' that go with being Australian captain. I wished him all the best and he thanked me for everything I'd done for him. He also said he hoped I was going to keep playing.

As things would turn out, Pup became a new man with the full-time 'c' next to his name. The leadership, in many ways, would be the making of him.

BACK IN 2004, I'D been the reason Michael made his Test debut. When I broke my thumb and had to miss the first three Tests in India, Pup was preferred to Brad Hodge as my replacement, in what must have been a close call. It was the selectors who made that decision but from back in Australia, where I was working to get my thumb right,

I fully supported their verdict, arguing that it was time to 'give the young bloke a go'. Pup justified his selection in superb style, scoring 151. A few weeks later, when he scored another hundred during his first Test appearance on home soil, it seemed we had found our next great batsman.

However, his progress stalled over the course of the next 12 months, and by the following Australian season, 2005–06, it was obvious he was about to be dropped. He wanted me to be the one who told him he was out, even though I wasn't a selector, which I think showed how close we'd become. I'd taken him under my wing a bit, as a mate and as his captain.

Pup promptly went back to the Shield and scored a double century. He then batted beautifully in a Chappell–Hadlee Trophy series in New Zealand and was picked for the tour of South Africa and Bangladesh at the end of that summer, but it wasn't until he made consecutive hundreds during the 2006–07 Ashes series that his place in the team was assured. At the end of that series, as we walked around the SCG acknowledging the fans, all of us wearing sunglasses to hide our tears of joy, I sidled up to Pup and said with a grin, 'How good is this? This is the way we're going to finish every series against England, right?'

I've always been big on passing lessons on, to make sure future generations are aware of the past and can learn from it, because that was what the senior players did when I first came into the team. Pup and I had been in England in 2005; we knew how it felt to lose the Ashes and now we knew how good it felt to win them back. We'd come to appreciate the value of hard work, playing as a team and sticking strongly to the values the group had bought into. Or so I believed. At that moment, I was sure Michael Clarke would be the man who'd pass these messages on after I was gone.

Over the next couple of years, my view changed. Pup remained a good trainer and we could all see that he loved playing for Australia and was determined to do well. But away from cricket, he moved in a different world to the rest of us. It never worried me if a bloke didn't want a drink in the dressing room, but I did wonder about blokes who didn't see the value in sticking around for a chat and a laugh and a post-mortem on the day's play. This was the time when we could revel in our success, pick up the blokes who were struggling, and acknowledge the guys who were at the peak of their powers. Pup hardly bought into this tradition for a couple of years and the team noticed. At times, he reminded me of a team-mate from earlier in my career, who'd be chirpy and bubbly if he was going well, but appear a bit grim if things weren't working for him. The best team-mates are the ones who can keep their moods in check for the sake of the group.

The blow-up with Pup and Kato after the Test in Sydney in the first week of 2009 wasn't in itself a big deal. I've seen worse arguments involving Australian cricketers. I think the blue I had on the plane with Paul Reiffel back in 1996 was livelier, but it was indicative of an ongoing frustration a number of the senior players, including me, were having with our new vice-captain. We wondered if he'd lost a little of his sense of team. It was our first significant Test win in exactly a year, almost certainly Matt Hayden's last Test, yet Pup wanted to get away. I didn't actually witness what went on, but as I understand it he asked if we could do the anthem sooner rather than later, Mike Hussey said he'd have to wait, the point was pushed, Kato suggested Pup be patient, and when Pup continued to complain Kato grabbed him and again told him to be patient. Okay, it might have been a bit spicier than that, but that was the gist of it. Michael left immediately after the confrontation, while we just shrugged our shoulders and said, 'That's Pup.'

In 2010 Pup briefly returned to Sydney from New Zealand during an ODI series so he could sort a few things out in his life away from cricket. He was back a few days later, clearly grateful for the way we'd closed ranks around him. We'd always been there for him, if only he'd realised. Like Warnie in the UK in 2005, Pup found sanctuary out on the field, the ground he knew best, and he promptly made a big hundred in the first Test against the Kiwis, and then in England batted as well as he'd ever done in his life.

I wouldn't say we were tight after that, but we were better. His official reign as Australian captain started on a high, with ODI wins in Bangladesh and ODI and Test wins in Sri Lanka, and he quickly took his batting to a new level, to the point that it seemed he could almost score big hundreds at will. He was training hard when we were together and obviously doing a lot of extracurricular work on his fitness and his game as well, which was inspirational. He now seemed happy to take on the planning, media and administrative duties that he'd veered away from when he was vice-captain and the mood in the Aussie dressing room was positive. Perhaps I'd been wrong to be so concerned for so long.

I KNEW, WHEN I said I wanted to keep playing for Australia, that a few people were worried I might get in the way of the new captain, but I assured them that wouldn't happen. 'I'll help Pup out as much as I can,' I said. 'But only if I'm asked. If I'm not asked, I'll sit back and prepare and play like an everyday player.'

That was my plan, to slide into the background. Gradually, as time went by, I might begin to offer snippets of advice, but in the short term I decided to go back to the days when I was seen and not heard. Quickly I realised that not being captain was a weight off my shoulders. I no longer had to worry about selections, playing conditions, what time we were seeing the match referee, when the next press conference was, what everyone else was doing, all those sorts of things. Instead, I just had to turn up at the ground, get my fielding work done, my batting done and prepare as well as I could for each game. I was still around to help, but the sense of obligation, that I had to be doing something, was gone.

I was insulted by the critics who thought I might be a bad influence, that having a current captain and a former captain in the same dressing room couldn't work. The people who said this didn't know me, didn't understand that I've always played the game for the team's sake. In fact, I believe the captaincy experience made me an even better team player, because I was now much more aware of what everyone else in the group was going through, how they might be thinking, and what was worrying them and maybe holding them back. I'd learned over the previous nine years that an effective leader has to understand and appreciate all the different characters within his group, what motivates them, upsets them, inspires them. I would never have learned how to do this if I had stayed in my own shell.

I NEVER ADDRESSED THE team formally about the captaincy change. After we arrived in Bangladesh, I asked Tim Nielsen to mention it in passing at the first team meeting, to acknowledge, essentially, that a new era was beginning and we weren't going to dwell on the past. The change-over was largely pain-free. We played three ODIs, won them all, and I got a start in each game: run out for 34; 37 not out and, as an opening bat, lbw for 47.

There were a couple of awkward moments, chiefly of my own making, such as when it suddenly occurred to me, 24 hours into the tour, that no one had told me whether I was required at meetings of the team leadership group. I knew what time the first get-together was starting, and where, but that was all. *What to do?* I was still the most senior player. I had always chaired those meetings. Now, with Michael as captain, I wasn't sure if I was supposed to be there or not. It had never occurred to me to ask and now it was about to start, and my desire to make a good impression was causing me grief. *I can't be late … I can't just not turn up.* The phones weren't working. I couldn't get in touch with anyone. All I could do was go down there, knock timidly on the door and stick my head in. There were four of them in the room: captain, vice-captain, coach, manager.

'Am I required here?' I asked.

'No, oops, sorry, we should have told you.'

CHAPTER 58

UNDER PRESSURE

Argus Review, August, 2011

IN AUGUST 2011, CRICKET Australia released the 'Australian Team Performance Review', a report by a panel it had commissioned to discover why we had suffered successive Ashes defeats. This investigation had become known as the Argus Review, after the panel's chairman, the former long-time chairman of BHP Billiton, Don Argus. Former Australian Cricket Board and ICC CEO Malcolm Speed and former Australian captains Allan Border, Mark Taylor and Steve Waugh were also involved.

I must confess I was worried when the report came out, not because I was concerned they might sledge my performance but because the interview I did with them was so short I thought it was a waste of time. I'd put on my best business suit and was raring to go. As the captain of the Test team for the previous seven years, and of the one-day team for the best part of a decade, I assumed my interview would go for hours. Instead, I was in and out in 30 minutes.

The first question Don Argus asked me was this: 'So Ricky, who do you think is accountable for the Australian cricket team's performance?'

'In my time, the captain of the team is the only person who's ever been accountable,' I replied.

I'm sure if Don had asked AB, Tubby or Tugga they would have said the same thing. In any other major sport, from when I was a kid watching the Boxing Day Test at Musselroe Bay to when I gave it away in 2011, the captain of the Australian cricket team would have been called the 'captain-coach'. The Australian captain was not just the on-field marshal and the driver of tactics, he also had major input into the way the team prepared, how it was motivated, how young players were nurtured, how a team presented itself, and how it sustained and amused itself between games. He was the one who met the match referee before games and the media afterwards. The only thing the skipper was not allowed to do was help choose the men who would follow him into battle, something that had always seemed weird to me.

'I was the one who was accountable, but I wasn't a selector. Until the captain becomes a selector, he can never be truly accountable for what happens in his team.'

This was never about getting the teams I wanted, but about getting the lines of communication right. How could I properly and honestly tell players why they were in or out if I wasn't part of the selection process and privy to the selectors' thinking? If the selectors had concerns about how a player was going, how could I, as captain, act on those concerns if I didn't know about them?

When I met Don Argus's panel, I could have continued on this subject for hours, used examples from my own career in the 1990s and involving a number of players from my years as captain, but time was short. We went on to discuss a wide range of subjects, from coaching set-ups to team culture, but none of them extensively.

I was worried the final report would be scornful of the coaching, that it would essentially repeat the old adage that the only good cricket coach is the one who drives you to the ground. I said as firmly as I could that the team needed to mirror what other countries had done, and employ *full-time* batting, bowling and fielding coaches. I wanted to spend more time talking about what I saw as a decline in standards in the Sheffield Shield, how teams were getting knocked over for low scores too often. That hardly ever happened when my first-class career began. I would have suggested these batting failures were related to the lack of 'long form' cricket kids are playing these days. Most of the batting techniques I was now seeing in Shield cricket were nowhere near precise and consistent enough to guarantee success in Test matches. They were good enough for T20 matches. My guess is that young cricketers aren't learning the right techniques at the right age.

This had become a 'hobby horse' of mine. Growing up — except at primary school when they'd made me retire at 30 — when I began an innings I was batting until a bowler got me out. If it took them a week, that's how long it took. This happened all the time in family contests at Rocherlea, when my brother, Drew, and I had some serious arguments because he couldn't get me out. Mind you, I reckon he developed into a reasonable junior bowler as a result of having to bowl to me all the time! Everything about my development, on the field, in the nets and in the backyard, was about setting me up so I could bat forever. It set me up for the days when I had to grind out hundreds in Colombo, Cape Town, Port-of-Spain and Bangalore.

After my interview finished, James Sutherland asked me how it went. I told him I thought they were kidding, that they'd obviously already made up their minds, but my concerns were misguided. I was reasonably happy with the final report, because many of the things it proposed — full-time assistant coaches, a revamped selection committee that included the captain and head coach, resting players from ODI cricket to make sure they were ready for Tests, better feedback from selectors for dropped players, improving the links between state set-ups and the national teams — were concepts Tim Nielsen and I had been pushing for years. Some were ideas John Buchanan had floated when he'd been Australian coach.

Furthermore, when the review asserted that basic cricket skills were lacking in key areas at Australian and at state level, they were confirming what I believed, but I wish they had also acknowledged that at the national level it wasn't just about Australia falling back. Some countries had caught us up, and a couple had passed us by. The challenge, not for the first time in cricket history, was for Australia to rise again.

I'd had a long chat with Cricket Australia chief executive James Sutherland during the last game of the previous Ashes Test which I'd missed because I was injured. There was a lot of discussion about where the team was at, ahead of the performance review, and I said the problem was as much to do with Cricket Australia as the team itself. For 10 years we had been asking for full-time assistant coaches for the team and better quality coaches at the Cricket Academy, but they wouldn't spend more money. He told me that no one ever spends money when they are going well, but I don't think there are too many successful organisations around that don't make significant investment in their futures, who don't put energy into research and development, and who don't try and keep up with the competition and the changing environment. Rod Marsh had been lost to England's academy, Dennis Lillee had been working in India. It had gotten to the point where states were reluctant to release players to our Academy because they had more faith in their own systems. You only had to look at the coaching staff England had in the 2013 Ashes series with people like Graham Gooch, Andy Flower and Graham Thorpe in their set-up. All successful international players.

There are very few former Test players around the Australian cricket set-up these days and the reason is pretty simple; nobody is willing to pay them enough money to keep them in the system. Maybe Rod Marsh was calling in favours when I was at the Academy, but I had Greg and Ian Chappell helping me out with my batting at different times, Ashley Mallett and Terry Jenner were there helping the spinners and they were the best going around; even Dennis Lillee showed up. We were surrounded by the best that were available at the time. Guys like that aren't coaching in Australia any more because it is not a career, there's not enough money for them in it. Darren Lehmann and Justin Langer are the exceptions in a way.

ONE ASPECT OF THE REVIEW that really annoyed me was when they argued that the team lacked 'a hunger to improve, a hunger to win and a hunger to be the best in the world'. I never believed that. I still don't. We were fitter and had worked harder than any of the earlier Australian teams in my experience. When I first came into the Test side, not all the senior players shared information on how to succeed at the top level. They let you figure it out for yourself. In more recent times, however, we came to pride ourselves on how we encouraged everyone to work as a unit, with the experienced guys guiding the younger blokes as best we could.

To me, this criticism was a cheap shot at Tim Nielsen and I guess it was a shot at me, as captain, too. Soon after the review was published, while we were in Sri Lanka winning Michael Clarke's debut series as Test captain, Cricket Australia announced that Tim would have to reapply for the Australian coach's job even though he'd signed a three-year contract just a year before. Not surprisingly, he told them to shove it. The Australian team was poorer for his departure.

When I look back on the men who coached the Australian team in my time, I think of Bob Simpson and Geoff Marsh as 'old school'. There weren't too many computers in the dressing room back then. Buck went completely the other way — it was all about analysis through technology and statistics, plus some thinking outside the square. He was extremely thorough and an excellent manager of people, but his knowledge of batting and bowling techniques was limited. He was lucky in that most of the players in the Australian squad knew their games pretty well, and that we were able to help each other, too.

Tim improved the way we used stats and video to help our games, was excellent with his technical advice, and shrewd in the way he brought outsiders in to offer specialist advice. No one has ever worked harder or loved the game more. He might not have been quite as adept as Buck at getting the best out of all the different characters in our group and sometimes he might have been too quick to defend guys who weren't performing but whom he truly believed in, but we were big on loyalty and thought it would benefit us in the long run. I rate him very highly as a coach; even higher as a friend and confidant.

It was interesting to see Mickey Arthur dismissed suddenly ahead of the 2013 Ashes campaign.

BEFORE THE OLD SELECTORS departed, they made one of their strangest decisions when, a few weeks before the Argus Review was published, they didn't offer Simon Katich a new contract. This effectively ended Kato's international career, because they were hardly going to pick him for our tour of Sri Lanka in August– September so soon after essentially giving him the sack.

In my view, this was as dumb a non-selection as any during my time with the Australian team. Kato had averaged more than 50 in Test cricket during the previous three years. He had scored six fifties and two hundreds in his most recent 10 Tests. More than any statistics, he was one of the grittiest and most sensible cricketers in my experience, a tough character in the Justin Langer mould, my sort of cricketer.

I knew we couldn't afford to cast such a player aside so easily. If the selectors were now rating potential ahead of performance, this was the first we knew of it. I could only assume they were trying to avoid a situation where a few of us senior batsmen of about the same age — Kato, Huss and me were all born within nine months of each other — all retired at once, but to avoid that by dropping Kato prematurely, when the guys in line to replace him didn't have the runs on the board to do so, was a weird remedy.

KATO'S POOR TREATMENT put us all on notice. For me, from here until the finish, it was all about my batting. Initially, playing without the captaincy was good, like I was a 17-year-old in the Tassie team, free of worry and onerous responsibility. That's how I felt. My first Test after relinquishing the captaincy was at Galle, the same city where I'd led Australia for the first time, nearly seven-and-a-half years before. Back then, I'd scored 21 and 28 as we achieved a famous comeback victory, one of the best of my career. This time, I scored 44 as we prevailed decisively by 125 runs, my 100th Test-match win. This was one of my proudest accomplishments, because I'd always wanted to be tough and durable, to play for a long time, and to be a winner. However, I wasn't able to celebrate too hard, just a couple of beers in the dressing room, before I was driven to the airport. Our second child was due and Rianna and Emmy needed me at home.

CHAPTER 59

MATISSE

Sydney, September 8, 2011

I HAVE NEVER BEEN so frightened by silence. My heart thumped and my ears strained to hear a sound, but there was nothing. Rianna had had a feeling during this pregnancy that it had been all been too easy this time around, so we were nervous that something would go wrong. In a matter of an hour, it felt like everything had. We were in surgery, she was having an emergency caesarean and now where there should have been the sound of a baby crying there was nothing.

Everything had seemed to be working out perfectly when I flew out of Sri Lanka, and I'd arrived home in time to be there for the birth of our second child. The doctors had decided they were going to induce the baby and after they had done what needed to be done I took up a place by Rianna's bed with one eye on the baby's heart monitor and another on a golf magazine waiting for things to happen.

It's always a tense time but I was as relaxed as I could be until I heard the heart-rate monitor change as the baby's heart rate suddenly rose. I knew straightaway that something was wrong and ran out to get a nurse who took one look at what was going on and immediately summoned the doctor.

Things happened so fast. They bundled Rianna onto another bed and rushed her down the corridor to the operating theatre and

I was left alone outside. Nobody had time to tell me anything and I was left there for about 15 agonising minutes.

Then the doctor appeared and said I'd better get in there. I didn't know what was going on but I assumed the worst. It was just the way he'd said it. I prepared myself to hear that the baby hadn't made it, and I prayed that Rianna was okay.

Inside they were preparing her for a caesarean and had given her an epidural anaesthetic but there was no time to wait for the pain relief to kick in. It was a nightmare situation and one I imagine a lot of men can identify with. The umbilical cord had worked its way around the baby's neck twice. As Rianna's contractions had started the baby had begun to choke and that's what I had seen on the heart-rate monitor.

You are totally helpless, the person you love the most is in distress and the life of someone you will love is apparently in the balance. All you can do is be there and try to keep a lid on your rising panic.

The doctor eventually said, 'Ah, here's a baby.' I couldn't see anything; worst of all, we couldn't hear anything.

The silence dragged on for what seemed like minutes but at best guess was probably about 30 seconds and I didn't dare breathe.

Finally we heard a little cry and I went to check. There was Matisse, small, messy, but apparently healthy. I told Rianna that I thought she was okay and we were both so relieved.

I now had three girls to adore.

It seemed the balance of my life was shifting profoundly. For so many years cricket had taken up almost every space in my life, but that was no longer the case. I was no longer captain, I was no longer in the one-day team and to be honest I wasn't the batsman I had once been, but I was a husband and a father. I had another life now and it was the one that mattered the most.

Back at the game, the process of letting go was accelerating, although I was fighting it every inch of the way.

Shaun Marsh took my place at No. 3 for the second Test in Sri Lanka and scored a debut hundred. When I returned, Shaun stayed where he was and I moved down one place in the batting order. It was Pup's call — he told me he made it with one eye on the future — and I was fine with that but had some misgivings.

First drop is the most important place in the batting order. I could accept that maybe I wasn't the exact fit for it, but I believed that whoever was going to replace me had to have their game, body and mind rock-solid. It was a big ask for Shaun that early in his career and his body let him down soon after so for one innings I was promoted back. There has been a steady stream of batsmen come in since I left but none have nailed down the spot. The best batsman has to bat there, it is no use putting in people who are still feeling their way.

In the best of times young batsmen came into the Australian side and started at No. 6 or thereabouts. I did, Lang did, Marto, Pup ... We started our careers with good batsmen around us and good leadership and then, when and if we were good enough, we moved up the order. And, it wasn't unheard of to slide down again as you got a bit longer in the tooth, as I obviously had.

I SCORED 48 AND 28 in the third Test at Colombo, hitting the ball pretty well. A month later, we were in South Africa, the scene of some of my favourite moments as a cricketer — first overseas tour with the Academy in 1992, Cape Town in 2002, World Cup in 2003, clean sweep in 2006, series win in 2009, ICC Champions Trophy in 2009 — and I was desperately keen to do well. Almost immediately, I discovered Graeme Smith's team was fired up to prevent that happening. In at 2–13 on the first morning of the series, I betrayed my nerves a little by getting off the mark with a six, a hook shot off Vernon Philander. That was in the eighth over of the innings. Eight overs later, with the game having been delayed for a while because of rain, I'd played only one more scoring shot. I was getting jumpy. From slip, Smith saw I was pressing, and he shouted to his men, 'C'mon guys, maybe he wants it too much.' Dale Steyn bowled an inswinger, at pace, and my first movement was to push well forward. But as the ball swung in, I was off-balance, my head and front shoulder a little too much to the offside, and instead of playing straight, bat and pad close together, my stroke was slightly across the line. The ball missed my bat, and hit my pad. The video replay didn't save me.

I was out the same way in the second innings, this time to Philander, and suddenly I had a major problem and so too did the team.

A game that featured one of the best hundreds I will ever see, by Michael Clarke, also featured the worst and most inexplicable batting collapse I was ever a part of. The captain's 151 gave us a first-innings total of 284. We were all out just before midday on the second morning. The South African innings started well enough and they went to lunch at 1–49. There was no indication of what was to come.

The afternoon session was as crazy as anything I have ever witnessed. Shane Watson and Ryan Harris took nine wickets and the South Africans were knocked over for just 96. They had only lasted 25 overs. Their last batsman headed back to the pavilion before 2.30pm and we were batting again. They had lost 9–47 and before we knew it we were losing wickets just as fast. If not faster.

The daughter of South African coach Gary Kirsten was born the night of the first day's play. There is a story that goes he left the ground early on day two, not long after Pup was finally dismissed for 151 and the home team's reply began. Their openers, Graeme Smith and Jacques Rudolph, were at the crease. When he returned, not long before stumps, he saw that Smith and Rudolph were batting and assumed South Africa had enjoyed a terrific day. I guess they had. Twenty wickets had fallen in the time he'd been away — in less than five hours.

Australia was all out for 47. We were 9–21 before Peter Siddle and Nathan Lyon saved us from what could have been the worst performance in the history of the game. Thanks to their fighting partnership ours was only the sixth worst ever.

I was out lbw to Philander for a duck, the same way I had fallen to Steyn in the first innings and I suddenly knew I had a problem. I was over-balancing and the South Africans knew it.

I also knew the South Africans were targeting me. I went into the nets and worked overtime on my technique, concentrating on my first movement, trying to stop my head and with it my weight moving forward and across as the bowler was letting go of the ball. That was stuffing up my balance. In the old days, I'd have kept my head pretty still and hit a ball that started on an off-stump line and swung into my pads for four, as I reacted naturally to whatever the bowlers gave me. Now, a flaw had snuck into my technique. The South Africans were exploiting it. I had to fix it, but in the short term, things got worse.

On what should have been the fourth day of the Test a handful of us went down to the nets and attempted to get our games in order. Over and over and over again I played at the full-length ball and attempted to sort myself out.

The following morning we woke up to the news that cricket writer Peter Roebuck was dead. All sorts of strange stories were flying about and it was hard to know what was true. He had apparently jumped out the window of his hotel. We drove past where he had been staying on the way to training the next day — it was on the way to the ground.

Peter and I obviously weren't close, but I knew he was good friends with ABC commentator Jim Maxwell and I made contact with him and a few of the other journalists to extend my sympathy. They looked stunned, but they had shown up at work and got on with it. In a way their lives were a lot like ours, they too were away a lot and had to rely on each other for support. Even when something as terrible as this happened they just had to get on with their work, the sports pages had to be filled every day and the cricket never stopped.

My net sessions in the lead-up to the second Test in Johannesburg were terrible. I told myself I had to make sure they didn't get me out lbw, but I became so obsessed with my first movement that all the instinct went out of my game. At my best, all I thought of was watching the ball. That's not all I was thinking about now.

I think I could have fixed up my batting if this first-movement problem was all that was wrong, but now that I wasn't captain, and now that Kato had been dropped, it was my turn to cop all the speculation about whether I was about to be sacked. In the lead-up to the second Test, there were plenty of whispers about that if I failed again I was gone. When I walked out to bat in our first innings, the game was set up for me: we were 2–192 on a nice batting wicket, in reply to South Africa's 266. Steyn was into the third over of a new spell. I was plumb lbw the first ball he bowled to me.

I can recall pretty clearly what I was thinking about as Steyn bowled that ball. I had a whole range of things buzzing around in my brain: 'watch the ball' was one of them; 'don't listen to them', 'don't get out lbw', 'don't push too far forward', 'you don't want your career to end here', 'you can still play' were others. Most of all, I think, I was looking for the ball that was going to hit me on the pad.

No one in the Australian set-up said anything to me, but as soon as Steyn trapped me lbw in our first innings I was sure I'd be playing for my career in the second. This time, I was in before the end of the third over, with Steyn and Philander in full cry. Once again, Smith was chirping from first slip. 'Maybe he wants it too much.'

I'm sure I did.

CHAPTER 60

EDGE OF THE ABYSS

Wanderers Stadium, Johannesburg, Sunday,
November 20, 2011

I WAS ONE BALL from oblivion. The worst thing was I knew it. Having failed in the first innings at Johannesburg I went to bed that night knowing that my next innings could well be my last. It was the first time in my life that I'd worried about being dropped.

I was in trouble and so was the side. Having been embarrassed in Cape Town we were 2–19 when I started my second innings and we were chasing 310 for a win that would draw the series and restore some credibility. History said we couldn't do it and if that wasn't enough Dale Steyn and Vernon Philander were determined we should fail.

I survived my first ball, from Philander, which I let go through to the keeper and Usman Khawaja took all but the last ball of the next over from Dale Steyn. I was able to stay at the non-striker's end as my heartbeat slowed a little.

Steyn's first ball pitched outside off-stump and swung further away. I was able to let it go with a bit of a flourish. For the next 20-odd minutes, I was a bit of mixture, leaving the ball really well when it pitched outside the stumps, but not so assertive when the ball was on the stumps. My footwork was scratchy and the ball was finding the bat rather than the other way round. I managed just the one single, a tentative prod into the covers, but then Morne Morkel came on and immediately bowled a long hop that I pulled to the mid-wicket boundary. Steyn came back and I hit him for four through cover, then Morkel dropped short again and I had my third boundary of the innings.

As quickly as all that, much of my confidence returned. The South Africans' strategy was to set me up for the well-pitched inswinger or off-cutter that would have hit middle and leg. It was clear what they were doing. I let a lot of deliveries go and I was happy with the way I was picking up the line. Usman and I set about batting us back into the game.

At the close of play on day four of the second Test we'd reached 3–142. I was 54 not out, so it was perfectly set up for me, all I had to do was make a big score and help win the game. Usman and I had added 122 for the third wicket before he was dismissed by their leg-spinner Imran Tahir just before the day's play was abandoned because of bad light. During this stand I began to hit the ball well down the ground, something that hadn't been happening in the nets or during my brief innings earlier in the series.

We didn't get on the next day until around 1pm because of rain and for the next hour batting was pretty difficult, but I managed to survive. It was tough Test-match cricket, which I loved, but then, having done all the hard work, I tried to cut a very wide one from Morkel and speared a tame catch off the bottom of my bat to Rudolph in the slips. Walking off, I was so disappointed I hardly noticed the applause as the crowd acknowledged what was almost certainly my last Test innings in South Africa.

I'd have been shattered if we lost, but fortunately, Mike Hussey, Brad Haddin, Mitchell Johnson and 18-year-old Pat Cummins all batted well and we got home with two wickets to spare. The win prompted Pup to say, 'I remember Punter telling me a while ago that when you're captain and you have a great series like this it's more special than when you perform individually. That's what I probably feel now. It feels like I just got my first double hundred for Australia.'

Five days earlier, Pup had asked me to present Pat with his first baggy green cap, which went well until someone pointed out that the teenager wasn't born until I'd completed my first season of Sheffield Shield cricket. These reminders of just how long I had been in the game seemed to be popping up more regularly. The only advice I gave him was very similar to what Mark Taylor had said to me in 1995: 'Do whatever it was that got you here, you don't have to change a thing.' He became the youngest Australian to bowl in a Test match, the second youngest, after 17-year-old batsman Ian Craig in 1953, to wear the baggy green.

MY SECOND-INNINGS 62 was enough to keep me in the side, but not sufficient to end the conjecture about my future. I suppose it wasn't the first time that commentators had speculated on my future, but it was the first time I had ever thought that if I failed I would be dropped. When it had happened earlier in my career I hadn't seen it coming. I can tell you it is not great putting that pressure on yourself and I did my best to block it out. In a lot of ways I was lucky to get this far into my career without having to battle with the conjecture and the doubt. Justin Langer told me he played every Test of his life thinking he had to make runs or he would be dropped and it is a testament to his mental strength that he could operate like that.

Back in Australia, I felt like I was approaching my best form in the nets, but I knew that wouldn't help me if I couldn't score runs in the middle. Against New Zealand at the Gabba, I continued on from Jo'burg, with the stroke I played to reach my fifty a standout. It was as good a pull shot as any I'd hit in my life. I continued on to 78, my highest score in a Test since the Hobart Test in January 2010. Then, out of the blue I went back to my 'old ways', lbw again, this time to Chris Martin, who is a good bowler but hardly in the Steyn class. A week later, in our first innings of the second Test, another of their quicks, Tim Southee, got me out the same way for 5 — my fifth leg-before in six digs — and I could almost feel them preparing my cricket obituary in the press box. There must have been something going on in my head because when that ball hit my pads I knew I was gone and had started to walk even before the umpire had raised his finger.

That night, my nan, Connie, who nearly 30 years earlier had given me that T-shirt with the message 'Inside this shirt is a future Test cricketer' emblazoned on it, passed away. Next morning, the whole team wore black armbands in Nan's honour, and I took a sharp catch at second slip from the third ball of the day, but when I batted in our second innings I struggled to 16 and then misread the line *and* length of a ball from Doug Bracewell, a medium-pacer. The result was a weak bunt to cover. It looked like I was in about four minds when I played that shot. Thinking back, I probably was.

Connie and my grandfather Charlie had been there for me all my life. I loved them dearly. We'd lived with them for a while and spent our holidays together. They were the people who'd helped out when I'd needed money to go on those youth tours, and along with Mum and Dad had been my greatest supporters. If I took pride in my achievements it was because I felt it was a way of fulfilling their hopes too. I took it really hard when she died.

IF I'D BEEN SACKED at this point, I wouldn't have been stunned. Instead, the selectors omitted two of the younger blokes who had been struggling for runs, Phillip Hughes and Usman Khawaja, and I was given another chance, but I had no illusions about my position: I had entered the 'last chance saloon'.

In a way, I was lucky in that our next opponent was India. With all the cricket we'd played against them over the previous four or five years, I was familiar with their leading bowlers and they had four great batsmen — Sachin Tendulkar, Virender Sehwag, VVS Laxman and Rahul Dravid — who were, coincidentally, also searching for their best form.

It was as if I'd been joined at the bar by blokes my age who were having the same problems at work that I was.

When I walked out to bat on Boxing Day, I was met by a Tasmanian team-mate, our left-handed opener, Ed Cowan, who was making his Test debut. I might not have said much to 'Ted' when I joined him when we were 2–46, just asked him how he was going and told him to keep hitting them in the middle, but I felt a real urge not to let him down, to help him any way I could. Our new opener was a different sort of bloke. He was smart, well educated and earnest, but I could relate to him because he had a burning passion for cricket. Perhaps not the most gifted batsman, but he worked relentlessly on his game and soaked up information by watching and imitating. Where a lot of the younger guys seem a little carefree, like they could take it or leave it, I never got this impression from Ed.

That became my focus and we added 113 for the third wicket before I was out for 62. I felt in pretty good nick for much of this innings, though little things would have betrayed the concerns I had with my technique, how I was obsessed with getting everything in order.

When I saw Dad that night he had a go at me for looking at the replays on the scoreboard too often; he knew that I wasn't admiring my batting, but rather that I was checking that my first movement was in order, that my backlift was right, that my feet and balance were in order. 'You've never done that before,' he complained.

In the second innings, I found myself in the middle after we crashed to 4–27. This time, I had a long partnership with my old mate Mike Hussey, and it was a joy to combine with him to bat India out of the game. Huss had long been my type of cricketer, a bloke who is loyal to a fault, adores the game as much as I do, who played and trained with enormous energy, and who absolutely loved to celebrate a win. After a few beers in the dressing room, this new man would emerge, we called him 'Maurice' Hussey, he was loud, loved to sing and would wrestle in the manner of Healy or Langer. If you play five long, tough days of Test-match cricket and you win, then you must celebrate accordingly, he would say. At other times, when we had a job to do or a game to win, he was so classy and dependable.

Many of the very best and most important innings played by an Australian batsman between 2005 and 2012 were by Mike Hussey. I remember some of his best one-day knocks, when as a 'finisher' he was as good as Michael Bevan, which is the highest praise. I remember also the Test hundreds in his maiden season of Test cricket, the match-winner against Pakistan at the SCG in 2009–10, the Ashes ton on his home turf at the WACA a season later. This knock of 89, which set up our eventual 122-run victory, was another of them.

The frustration for me was that I couldn't turn my second-innings 60 into a big hundred, but that would come in Sydney and again in Adelaide, when I twice enjoyed long partnerships with our new captain. The SCG Test was the next stage in the development of Pup's batting, as he went all the way to 329 not out, the highest individual score ever made at the famous ground. He declared our innings closed when most people watching were wondering if he might break Brian Lara's world record for the highest Test innings, and a few critics got into him for doing so, but I was proud of what he did, because it was the best thing for the team. The next day we completed an emphatic win.

My century in Sydney meant a lot to me. It showed when I finally got there, courtesy of a crazy single that would have been out by a metre, maybe more, if Zaheer Khan's throw from mid-on had been on the money. Given I was looking for my first Test hundred in nearly two years, if I'd been run out for 99 it would have felt like a duck. Instead, I was able to pick myself up, rearrange the grille of my helmet, brush some of the dirt and grit off my face, my shirt and my pants, and then acknowledge the crowd.

Three weeks later, I was probably even more animated when I went past 200 at Adelaide Oval, which prompted some people to ask if I was pre-empting a retirement announcement. No matter what I did the question was always the same. One day I was answering in mournful tones after a failure and the next I was a lot happier, but still responding to reporters who wanted to know if I was going to go out on a high.

Whenever I mentioned that I'd like to get to England in 2013 for another Ashes series, I could almost hear them thinking, *No, we'll get you before then.*

There was no escape.

I WASN'T THE ONLY one feeling this way. I only had to look over to the away-team dressing room to see batsmen of a similar age who were being asked the same questions. One I felt an affinity with was Rahul Dravid. Maybe it was because he was a fellow 'first drop', or maybe simply because he is just a respected figure in our game, such a decent and honest man. He is undoubtedly one of cricket's finest ever batsmen, the second man after Sachin Tendulkar to score 13,000 Test-match runs (averaging more than 53 when he reached the landmark), maker of 36 Test centuries, and taker of more than 200 Test catches. More than 10,000 of his Test runs were made from No. 3. He faced more than 30,000 deliveries in Test cricket.

Back in the angry summer of 2007–08, I felt I had to have a chat with Rahul. Even though we'd been playing Test matches against each other since 1996, I didn't know him all that well. On the field, we were completely different — he *never* got himself in trouble with opponents or umpires — but we were still brothers in batting. Of course, I'd spent many a day in the slip cordon watching him at work, seeing how organised he was and how, at his best, he was just about 'unbowlable'. They didn't call him The Wall for nothing.

During the 'Monkeygate' series, his timing was off a little, and in Adelaide, after the last ball had been bowled and before I headed to the Harbhajan hearing, I quietly said to him, 'I've been watching your batting. I can see you're struggling for runs and some people are after your blood, but you're going better than they think. You've still got plenty to offer. Don't let them get you down. Don't even think about retiring.'

It took Rahul a little time to rediscover his best form, but eventually he went on another typical run-scoring spree. It turned out he had another 12 Test hundreds in him. He also had a sense of batsmen's mateship about him that meant that when I was struggling for runs in 2010–11 he was able to return the favour, sending a text that essentially told me to hang in there, that the runs would come.

Rahul and VVS Laxman announced that Adelaide was their final Test. From an Australian perspective, given what they did to us in Kolkata in 2001 and Adelaide in 2003–04, it was appropriate that they departed together. I was genuinely sorry to see them go. I'd had some blues on the field with Indian cricketers in my time (though not, I should stress, with either of these gentleman), but I don't hold grudges. When we were playing against India, and there were 10 minutes to go on the last day and they needed 10 runs and we needed one wicket, I didn't like any of them. My game face was on and they were standing between us and winning. All that would change as soon as the final ball was bowled.

With helmets off we are all just cricketers who have a lot in common. Sometimes maybe too much in common.

Favourite international players

WASIM AKRAM

Wasim's ability to swing the new and old ball at high speed was second to none. He had a short run-up and a quick delivery, which meant I always felt under enormous pressure when I was facing him, and no matter how well I was going I never really felt truly 'in' when he was bowling. When he knocked me over for a duck one year in a Test at Bellerive, I almost thought it was unfair the way he got the ball to zip and in-dip before I was set.

CURTLY AMBROSE

The first word I'd use to describe Curtly's bowling is 'relentless'. When I first ran into him in 1996 I'd never faced a bowler like him, and I'd never been in a situation before where I honestly didn't know where my next run was coming from. I came to regard him in the same class as Glenn McGrath, only taller and a bit quicker. Surviving a spell from either Curtly or Wasim was an achievement in itself, and I'm very proud of the fact I made a Test hundred against both of them — against the West Indies at Bridgetown in March 1999 and against Pakistan in Perth eight months later.

DALE STEYN

Dale became something of a bogey bowler for me near the end of my career. After I retired from international cricket I was asked where I rated him, and my instinctive reply was, 'I don't know if I've played enough against him,' on the basis that in my view he's only been a truly great bowler in the past two or three years and in that time we only played five Tests against the South African team. But he dismissed me for low scores in three of those five Tests, always bowling to a plan, never easing the pressure, so it would be wrong for me to underrate him. He gets through the crease very quickly and hits the bat hard, and while he's not as consistently relentless as Curtly was, he still has a real presence about him and has built a formidable combination with Morne Morkel and Vernon Philander. Morkel is a bowler I have always rated highly, and when he started pitching the ball up a bit more consistently in 2011–12, more at the length that Curtly and Wasim used to bowl to me, he became even more of a threat.

JACQUES KALLIS

I think Jacques is the best all-rounder who has ever played the game. He doesn't get as much recognition as he deserves, but you have only got to look at his numbers and his longevity. If there has ever been anyone better I would like to know who it was.

CHAPTER 61

THANKS FOR THE MEMORIES

Brisbane, February 20, 2012

I WAS BUZZING AROUND at training at the end of the India series in the same way I'd been at the beginning, to the point that our new coach, Mickey Arthur, went out of his way to congratulate me on my commitment and energy. With my fielding drills, I was just doing what I'd always been doing, trying to be best on ground. In the nets, I didn't want to finish until everything felt right. Often, that took longer than in the good old days.

Unfortunately, I conned Mickey, conned everyone and I even conned myself into thinking I was good to go. In truth, after playing in eight Test matches in 10 weeks, constantly batting for my future, I needed a mental break. Eight days after we completed a 4–0 series sweep over the Indians, we were playing them again in the opening game of the Commonwealth Bank one-day series. Over the next 14 days, I batted five times and never once reached double figures. For the last two of these matches, I was stand-in captain as Michael Clarke recovered from a slight hamstring strain. Then they dropped me.

It happened after we beat India comfortably at the Gabba. I was on the way to Brisbane airport the next morning to fly home when my mobile rang. It was the new chairman of selectors, John Inverarity.

After some very brief chit-chat, he came to the point. 'Ricky,' he said, 'we've decided to drop you.'

It had been a few years since I'd heard that line.

Of course, I knew I hadn't scored any runs, but I didn't see this coming … at least not the way it was done.

A bit less than a week earlier, when John (twice) and then the recently appointed high-performance manager, Pat Howard, had rung to ask me to be captain, I'd said pretty firmly, 'No way, I shouldn't be doing that.'

I didn't hear from Michael Clarke, so I don't know what his view was, but I assume he believed it was the right thing to do. To me, it was wrong, if only because Dave Warner had been named as vice-captain in place of the regular deputy, the injured Shane Watson, so the job should have been his. Furthermore, I had to worry about my own form. 'I'll be playing,' I told John and Pat, 'I'll help Dave any way I can.'

In the end I helped them out.

Never at any stage during those conversations did they mention that my place was under threat, that I needed to score some runs to retain my spot. I guess they figured I knew that, but they never said anything. Everything they said was building me up, how important I was, how they needed my help. You might have thought they were ringing me to thank me the next day, but instead they were telling me I was done. That still annoys me.

THE STORY OF MY sacking hadn't broken when I landed in Sydney. My manager James Henderson suggested we arrange a media conference for the next day, the idea being to get all the questions and answers over and done with. I didn't want to do a series of one-on-one interviews in which I'd keep confirming I was still available for the Test team, recall highlights from my one-day career and explain my plans for the future, whatever they were. Once was enough. Unfortunately this event got out of hand because everybody thought I was about to retire from Test cricket. I think a few of the networks had live crosses back to the studio, but they were going to be disappointed. Behind the microphone at the Sydney Cricket Ground, I said all the right things …

> *All I have left now is Test cricket so I want to be the best I can be in that form of the game. The passion for the international game of cricket for me has not died or changed one little bit.*
>
> *I still don't see a finish line as far as my international career is concerned. Now that one-day cricket isn't there anymore we all know that day is coming closer and closer for me.*

Inside, I was seething. Not for the first time in my career I had to keep a lid on what I was really thinking. These blokes had been appointed as the result of the Argus Review, a document that stressed the need for better communication between players and selectors. John Inverarity's new selection committee never gave me the chance to retire from ODI cricket, which — after 375 games, 50 more than any other Australian — I think I deserved. It had nothing to do with the fact that Australia's next ODI was in Hobart. It wasn't about getting a lap of honour, just departing with dignity. Instead, they used me up, by getting me to captain the team for a couple of games and then flicked me when Pup and Watto were available again.

When I said at that media conference that I understood the decision to leave me out, I was telling the truth. I just wasn't happy with the way it was done. From the moment John Inverarity made that phone call, I was thinking to myself, *They're not going to get me this way at the end of my Test career.* If I thought my hundreds in the India Tests had bought me even a little breathing space, I knew now this was not the case. I had to score runs in every game or I might be gone.

CHAPTER 62

IT'S TIME

Team hotel, Adelaide, November 24, 2012

I SAT ON THE EDGE of the bed, looked at Rianna, and quietly said what I'd been thinking since I'd unstrapped my pads a few hours earlier …

'I'm not sure I can do this anymore. I don't think I can keep putting myself through it.'

Rianna looked at me and summed up the situation in a moment. I never had any doubts that she was the right woman for me and times like this confirmed it.

'You don't have to,' she said gently. 'You don't have to keep putting yourself through this.'

We were in Adelaide, the place where Gilly and Marto had both hit the wall, and now it had happened to me. The day I never thought would come had arrived. I'd held it inside until I got back to the hotel, but the moment I sat on the bed the words spilled out.

FOR A WHILE, MY LIFE as a 'Test only' cricketer went all right. I returned to the Sheffield Shield at the end of the 2011–12 season and promptly scored hundreds against South Australia and Western Australia. I finally got to play in a second Shield final, 18 years after my first (against NSW in 1993–94), but with no better luck as we lost, this time to Queensland. A fortnight later, I landed in the West Indies, and though I never made a big score I batted well in the Tests. I just couldn't catch a lucky break. The Caribbean had always been kind to me, but this time I was dismissed in some weird and wonderful ways.

In the first innings of the opening Test I was run out in a mix-up with Shane Watson. He felt so bad and was so upset that he apologised to me later in the dressing room. It happened in the hour before the lunch break, when Watto turned a ball towards fine leg and immediately thought there was two in it. I wasn't so sure, but he'd already hit two fours in the over, his adrenalin had kicked right in and there was no stopping him. I was easily run out at the non-striker's end. I'd been out there for 20 minutes, was hitting the ball in the middle of the bat and was beginning to think a big score was on the cards. A run out is always such a waste; no matter how good the fielding, you're always left with the thought that the dismissal was avoidable. When it's not your fault, it can be hard to mask the disappointment, for the sake of the team and the not-out batsman. Luckily, we've all been at fault at some time or another, though in this case — with me very keen to make a score and the error of judgment on Shane's part so clear — it was hard to stay sort of composed. Watto spent the next week buying me presents, trying to make up for his brain fade. I'd have preferred it had never happened, or at least he had gone on to a very big score, but instead he was dismissed second ball after lunch, playing such an awful shot it was hard not to think he was still thinking about my dismissal.

It was, though, hard to get too dirty on him. I loved every moment I played with Watto. Some people find him a bit hard to read. But I understand him better than most, and his mix of emotion, work ethic and talent. He's a bloke who needs to know he has the confidence of those around him. I always believed he could be an exceptional opening bat in Test cricket. I think I first said that in about 2007, when I argued that his batting technique was 'as good as anyone in Australia', and I still believe that today.

In the second innings of that first Test I was bowled by one that fair dinkum ran along the ground. In the second Test at Port-of-Spain, on one of the flattest Test-match wickets I ever saw, I received just about the best ball of my career from my old friend Kemar Roach. The delivery wasn't that short, and out of nowhere it took off and nicked the shoulder of my bat as it flew through to the keeper. In the second innings, I got caught hooking as we tried to set up a run-chase. In the final Test, I was 57 and going all right when Roach pitched one so short I was sure it would sail well over my head. I ducked almost as a gesture, but then I realised the ball was skidding not bouncing. I had to get my body lower and lower, my bat stayed at the top of the backlift, exposed, and the ball clipped it as it went through, ballooning a simple catch into the slip cordon. I'd never got out that way in my life, not even in the nets, at the beach, in the backyard or in my worst nightmare. The tour was over and I didn't feel like I'd done anything wrong.

I knew I could still play. There were six-and-a-half months between our final Test in the West Indies and our next, against South Africa at the Gabba, and just about every net I consumed in that time — and there were plenty — had a good feel to it. Stuart Karppinen, the Australian team's outgoing strength and conditioning coach, created a series of fitness programs for me that ensured I was as physically prepared as I'd ever been. I have no doubt I was fitter at age 37 than I had been at 20.

The Sheffield Shield season began early, same weekend as the AFL and NRL Grand Finals and from the opening delivery I was the form batsman of the competition. In my second-last game before the first Test of 2012–13, I scored 162 not out and 60 not out on an ordinary MCG wicket against a Victorian attack that included five bowlers who had played Test cricket — James Pattinson, Clint McKay, Peter Siddle, Andrew McDonald and Cameron White — and two more — John Hastings and Glenn Maxwell — who'd make their Test debuts in the following few months. Never once did I play and miss. I went into the first Test as the leading run-getter in Australia.

Retirement was the furthest thing from my mind. I honestly couldn't see the finish line. I believed I was prepared, mentally and physically, for this series against South Africa, the Ashes series in England in 2013 and the return Ashes series in Australia in 2013–14. After that, I'd sit back and think about where my career was headed. I knew I was only one or two failures away from the media calling for my head again, but I was feeling too good and hitting the ball too well to be overly concerned about that. Or so I thought.

After day two of the Test was washed out, I walked out to the middle on the third afternoon in perfect conditions, with Australia 2–30 in reply to South Africa's 450. Once again, I'd be batting with Ed Cowan. Hashim Amla and Jacques Kallis had already made hundreds and I was determined to do the same. I took guard from umpire Billy Bowden, went down and tapped at the pitch, got into my stance, and as Morne Morkel began to move in I said to myself, same as I always did, *Watch the ball*. My mind was clear. The first ball went through to the keeper; the second was a pretty firm forward defence. Ted then hit Dale Steyn for two fours, both pull shots. Morkel again, and I was determined not to fall for the inswinger aimed at middle and leg, the lbw. The first two deliveries were both wide of the stumps and I let them go. I really wanted to hit the ball again, to feel it in the middle of the bat. *He's going to pitch one on the line of the stumps; be ready for it, don't be leg-before; watch the ball; keep your front shoulder still; watch the ball … so long as you don't fail they can't drop you … watch the ball …*

The next delivery was short of a length and wide of the off-stump. I was drawn to it, couldn't resist it, prodded at it. The edge went straight to Kallis at second slip and I walked off in a daze, unable to come to terms with what had happened … not with the dismissal, so much, as how my brain was working as Morkel had run in to bowl.

I had heard sports psychologists talk about the 'little voice' that sits on athletes' shoulders as they compete. It's a negative voice, one that says you're no good, that you can't win, that's it not worth it, that you should give up. The great athletes are able to ignore that little voice, or tell it to go away. I never heard that little voice during my best batting days, but I couldn't get rid of the little bastard at the end, not when I was trying to bat in a Test match. The line I heard loudest as the bowler was approaching the wicket was, 'You're one game away from being dropped.' It wouldn't have mattered if my next three digs were in the Shield and I made a hundred every time. As soon as I failed again in a Test match everyone would have been saying and writing it was time to go. Knowing that was stifling.

I went into this Test in the best of form. Now, for the first time, I started to think that maybe I'd never come good, not at the top level. I didn't feel inadequate or embarrassed. Instead, I was thinking of myself as being like a kid who'd used all his tokens at the show. It was as if someone had decided that I'd scored all the runs I was supposed to score in Test cricket. The night before this Test I'd still been thinking about going to England for the Ashes. Not anymore; I could no longer think that far in advance.

The second Test in Adelaide was more of the same. I expected them to bowl full and straight to me. I hit the first ball I faced, from Kallis, through mid-wicket for four. The next one was overpitched and well wide of the off-stump, but there was method in the delivery, because he was trying to get me leaning too far to the off-side. I expected the next ball to be aimed at the stumps, I was looking for clues to confirm this as he ran in to bowl, and sure enough he went wider on the crease in his delivery stride … thinking back now, my mind at that moment was so cluttered … I assumed he was going to angle the ball towards middle and leg, to try to trap me lbw, and out of his hand that was the line. But then it started to straighten. My balance was wrong and my response was to just try to get some bat on it. But as the ball started to swing away from the bat a fraction I realised it was going to miss the outside edge, so as a last desperate measure I tried to flick my back pad at it … to no avail … instead, my front foot slipped out from under me and I was on the ground, face first, as the ball crashed into the off-stump. I picked myself up and walked off. It was embarrassing.

In the second innings, I scratched my way to 16, at which point Steyn pitched one short of a length outside off-stump, maybe reverse swinging away a fraction; a ball best left alone. I played a 'nothing shot', indecisive, bat on an angle; if it had found the middle of my bat it would have been a tame push to cover. Instead, the ball took a thick inside edge and ricocheted back into my stumps.

'F***!' I shouted in exasperation.

I looked back at the stumps. 'F***ing idiot,' I said loudly to myself.

The South Africans were jubilant. Tellingly, none of them said anything to me. There was no send-off, no need. The surge of anger I'd felt about my ineptness and what was happening to me dissipated quickly, and I trudged off. There was time to look back at the replay on the big screen, to see just how awful a dismissal it had been, how crooked my bat had been, the way my feet had shuffled. There was indecision in my every movement. It was the first time I'd been bowled in both innings of a Test match since Delhi in 1996.

I wasn't thinking about retirement in the dressing room. I was thinking about the missed opportunity. All I'd had to do was get through the last six overs of the day, a situation I'd thrived on in the past, and then turn up the next day and get a reasonable score. But I hadn't been able to do that. Mickey Arthur came up and said, 'Bad luck, it could have gone any way.'

'It was a horrible shot,' I replied. 'That's not how I play.'

I knew I couldn't sit in the corner and sulk. I hate cricketers who do that. Anyway, by the time I took off my batting gear, packed my kit, had a shower and did my recovery, it was time to go.

But on the bus trip back to the hotel, I kept thinking about how good my preparation leading in to the series had been. I couldn't have asked for anything better, yet the results weren't happening. Instead, I was getting out badly.

Rianna was the first person I dared speak my concerns in front of. When she told me in the hotel room that night that I didn't have to keep fighting she said exactly the right thing. She could have put it off and said something like, 'Let's not think about it until after the game is over.' But Rianna supported me as she had done for the previous 12 years.

Later, she would say that she came to realise during this Test that it wasn't fun for me any longer, that fighting every day to get back to the cricketer I had been had taken its toll. We talked about what life might be like after cricket, and as we talked things kept getting clearer and clearer for me.

Rianna had booked a table for us at a favourite restaurant not far from the hotel, so we decided to go out and talk some more. I think if, in my heart, I was still undecided I would have cancelled the reservation. As it was, we found ourselves sitting in the vicinity of a posse of cricket journalists, so we had to keep our voices down. My inclination was to retire on the spot, make this my last game, but Rianna argued otherwise, that we should go to Perth and make the announcement that I'd be ending my Test career where it all began. 'The fans will want to see you have one last game,' she said. 'Your family will want to be there and I want you to get the send-off you deserve.'

To tell the truth, I wasn't sure if any of that mattered so much. If I wasn't good enough, I shouldn't be playing. But I eventually decided I did want to play at the WACA for two reasons: one, because it felt like retiring mid-series was the easy option, that I'd be deserting my mates before the fight was over; and two, because I wondered if I'd be a different batsman without the pressure of needing runs to retain my place. I'd never have to read another 'Ponting Must Go' headline. Maybe I'd get back to my cracking Shield form and finish on a high.

THE ADELAIDE TEST FINISHED on a Monday and we flew to Perth the next day. I told Michael Clarke of my retirement plans in the lounge at Adelaide airport and he spent the best part of an hour trying to talk me out of them. Eventually, I said, 'Okay, I'll think about it.' John Inverarity contacted me not long after we landed, to say that he'd been speaking to Pup and that Pup said he didn't want me to go, argued that I was still hitting them well in the nets and the runs would come, that the team needed my experience and the Ashes wasn't *that* far away. He almost swayed me.

Maybe you can do it, I said to myself more than once. *Keep pushing for a bit longer and see if you can play well on another Ashes tour.* A counter to this was my treatment from the previous season, when they'd begged me to be stand-in captain and then dropped me straight afterwards. Who knows what the selectors would have been thinking if I hadn't retired and then hadn't scored any runs in the Perth Test?

It wasn't until the Wednesday that I truly locked my impending retirement in. Rianna was horrified when she found out I'd been contemplating going on, because she'd seen how lost and defeated I'd been in Adelaide and knew intuitively that to play on would have been a mistake. So did I, but I loved playing Test cricket so much it was understandable I wavered.

I asked my manager James Henderson to work with Cricket Australia to get a media conference organised for the next day, Test-match eve. James would be a real hero for Rianna and me over the following few days and I'm not sure we could have made it without him. I wanted to be open and thank everyone without taking any of the focus away from what the team needed to do. Consequently, when and where and how we made the announcement was very important and James's advice proved impeccable every time.

The Test after Perth was in Hobart and if I played it would be my 169th Test, breaking Steve Waugh's record. I was *almost* certain I didn't want that extra game, but we still talked about it, went through every possibility, and by the end of it we were 100 per cent sure retiring at the end of the South Africa series was the right thing to do. That was an important discussion because it cleared my head of any last shreds of doubt. I'll always be grateful to James for how he helped bring clarity to our thinking during that time.

I rang Dad, who was watching a Twenty20 Big Bash game on the television.

'G'day Dad,' I said. 'What are you doing?'

'I'm watching blokes make runs, something you haven't been doing lately!' he quipped.

Dad was a constant. It was always good to talk to him. However, his mood quickly changed when I told him I'd decided to retire.

'No, not yet mate,' he said quietly. There was silence. As he tried to keep going, I could sense a tear in his voice. 'No, just go out there and bat,' he mumbled. 'Shut everyone up.'

'It's time, Dad. I need you and Mum and Drew and Renee to come to Perth.'

Mum's initial reaction was to say she couldn't do that because she didn't want to leave her work short-handed with such little notice. It was typical of her to be thinking of someone else, though my suspicion is that part of it was a case of her not wanting to be a jinx once last time. Of course, her boss gave her all the time she needed, Drew organised the flights and their accommodation, and the four of them arrived at the WACA not long before lunch on the opening day, by which time South Africa had already lost three wickets.

I was so glad they'd made it. They'd been there for me at the beginning. I wanted them there at the end.

CHAPTER 63

END OF THE JOURNEY

The WACA, December 3, 2012

WHAT I WANTED MOST of all was to win my farewell Test. That, more than anything, was what big-time cricket was always about for me. The winning. I love the game and I played for keeps.

When it came to my competitive sport, I was never a romantic. I know some people like to talk about playing simply for the enjoyment and the fun, but I'm not like that. I enjoyed it most when we won. It wasn't nearly as much fun when we didn't. Throughout my career, I did whatever I could within the rules to win. It was like that for the cricketers who were closest to me: my dad and Ian Young; the men from Mowbray; Test team-mates like Warnie and Junior and Heals and Pidge; Lang and Gilly and Haydos and Marto. That was me.

At the media conference following my final Test, I was asked if I had any regrets, I said no. 'I don't live my life thinking about regrets. Day in, day out, I've just got up and tried to make myself a better person,' I said.

That was nearly true. I do have one regret ... that I didn't go out with a win.

I was sincere when I said before the Test that I wanted to win this game 'more than any game I've ever played in'. Nothing would have thrilled me more than to see Australia back as the top-ranked team in the world, which is what a victory would have achieved. That would have meant much more to me than a farewell hundred.

TELLING THE BOYS was very hard. I'd asked our manager to organise a quick gathering in a room at our hotel before we set off for training, and the mood quickly turned sombre.

'Boys, this is going to be my last game,' I began. That was just about it. I was able to explain the reasons why, but when I started to tell them how much I loved playing with them, sharing a dressing room with them … there were only tears. I knew retiring was the right thing to do, but still there was a shred gnawing at me that said I was letting them down. I'd been tied to the team for so long, so cutting that cord naturally hurt. I managed to tell them that this game wasn't about me, that I needed them to focus on doing all we could to win the series. But that was it. I had to give up in the end.

There was mostly silence. The boys were a bit stunned to see me so emotional. There were handshakes, a few man hugs, then I stressed again that the game was the thing. Soon after, at the ground, I was hitting the ball beautifully in the nets, feet moving nicely. Mickey Arthur noticed, commenting, 'That's as good as you've batted all year.'

'It's a bit late now, mate,' was all I could say.

AFTER PRACTICE, IT WAS time for the media conference, something I was dreading because I didn't want to betray my emotions, not in public. As it turned out, I handled it okay, largely because I talked mostly about why I was retiring and how much I was looking forward to my final game. James Henderson and Cricket Australia had set up a table and microphone in the WACA gym, the team gathered behind the reporters who were sitting in front of me, and Rianna, Emmy and Matisse were sitting to my left. Word had spread that I was retiring, so I got on with it, first thanking everyone for coming, including 'the boys up the back' — my team-mates, who were there en masse.

I quickly mentioned a few things that meant a lot to me: how important it was for me that we won the Test; that I was pleased I was giving my replacement the chance to start afresh in the first game of a new series; that I hadn't been 'tapped on the shoulder' by the selectors or Cricket Australia; and that it wasn't hurting me that I wasn't going to get the chance to participate in one more Ashes series, even though the next series in England was only eight months away. Which was true, because in the time since Adelaide I'd come to accept the reality, distasteful as it was, that I was no longer a good enough player to get there.

I then explained how much I was looking forward to playing out the season with Tasmania, not least because I hadn't spent a lot of time with them for 'near on 20 years'. The closest I got to choking up was at the end, when I nodded to Rianna, Emmy and Matisse, and said, 'This is my new team here.'

Soon after, with the last question having been asked, I grinned a bit like a kid who'd escaped punishment for not doing his homework, stood up and walked over to my new team. Matisse was sitting on her Mum's right knee. Emmy was to her left. I broke into a huge smile and Emmy gave me a hug and a kiss. Rianna, I knew, was the most nervous of any of us. She was so keen for me to go out on a high, for everything in this last week to end well. I felt pretty good.

ALL THE CUSTOMARY EVENTS of the start of a Test — the drive to the ground, the warm-up, the anticipation at the toss — had special meaning for me this time, because it was the last time. I think I was more nervous going into the game than any other game I'd ever played. But always, I kept reminding myself I had to approach the actual cricket as just another game. A part of my brain was devoted to worrying about Mum and Dad getting to the ground before I went out to bat, though I knew there was nothing I could do to get them into their seats any earlier. The cameras hovered during the national anthem, hoping, I'm sure, for some extra emotion to flick across my face, but I played the proverbial straight bat.

And then, finally, we were fielding and the Test started well for us, as we bowled South Africa out for 225, having reduced them earlier in the day to 6–75. It was good bowling, good fielding, good captaincy, a reminder of how enjoyable being on the front foot can be.

We had the best part of an hour to bat before stumps, which meant I had to get ready, and the nerves really started to kick in as early as the first over, when Ed Cowan was dismissed. Maybe my nerves betrayed me, because it was only a few minutes later when I noticed Nathan Lyon putting the pads on. He'd be our nightwatchman. *That's a bit early*, I thought. It wasn't that I was affronted in any way, simply because we had a reasonably precise policy as to when we'd use the nightwatchman and this was slightly ahead of time. When Watto was dismissed in the sixth over of our innings, I still thought it was my time.

I stood up and quipped to those around me, 'Gotta go.'

But even before I'd taken my first step, Michael Clarke said quickly, 'No Punter, you're not going, Gaz is.'

'Gaz' is Nathan, nicknamed after the famous AFL footballer, now TV personality, Garry Lyon. Pup's decision created a funny scene, because the first-day crowd was keen to give me a big ovation as I walked onto the field. Even Rianna got caught up in it, giving 'me' a rousing reception until it gradually dawned on her and everyone it was a nightwatchman walking out, not me. It was a throwback to the first time she saw me bat, at the MCG back in late 2000. Gaz and Dave Warner safely saw out the final six overs before stumps, which meant my first appearance as a batsman in my final Test was put on hold for one more day.

As it turned out, I wouldn't score many runs in this Test, but each time I hit the ball pretty well during the short time I was out there. In the first innings, I was probably more nervous than I'd been 17 years earlier, when I'd made my Test debut, and just like then I was given out lbw by a Pakistani umpire, this time Asad Rauf. I asked for a video review but unlike 1995–96 this one wasn't too high. The umpire had it right. In the second innings, after Graeme Smith, Hashim Amla and AB de Villiers had batted us out of the game, I was worried I might be too emotional, but I actually felt good and sharp. I was pumped, sure, but I didn't have tears in my eyes or anything silly like that.

IT WAS THE FOURTH DAY, December 3, 2012, five days short of 17 years since I'd made my Test debut on this same WACA Ground. There was a fair crowd in, about half-full, but when I went out to bat in the hour before lunch they made more noise than I thought could be possible from a crowd that size. The only time I choked up even a little was when I saw the South Africans forming a 'guard of honour' for me but that emotion quickly changed to confusion when I couldn't see Graeme Smith at the end of the line, where I assumed he'd be. Instead, he was three-quarters of the way down the left-hand side. When I found him, I shook his hand and said simply, 'Thanks mate, I'll never forget this.'

For a brief moment, the South African captain didn't let go of my hand, and then, as I moved on, he patted me on the back. I went to my end, he had a brief word with his bowler and then, as I started patting down the wicket, he jogged up beside me and said, 'Just don't get too many today.' As Ed Cowan joined me in mid-pitch, Jacques Kallis walked past and wished me luck.

Morne Morkel had dismissed Shane Watson off the last ball of an over. They had left-arm spinner Robin Peterson operating from the other end, maybe to help get the ball a bit scuffed up so it would reverse sooner than later. Ted hit a six off the first ball of the over and a single off the third to get me on strike.

The routine was the same. After a few stretches and a walk down the wicket, I kicked away the dirt to clean my crease, asked for middle stump, scratched my guard. For a moment, my bat went up on my right shoulder as I surveyed the field and adjusted my pad flap. A deep breath and I was fine. I went into my stance. I was excited by the clarity of my thinking. My first shots were two scoreless drives into the covers, then a forward defence.

After that, I faced only one ball in the next two overs, which meant I'd been out there for the best part of 15 minutes without scoring a run. Finally, Morkel dropped one short and I produced as good a pull shot as I'd played all season, which was helpful on two fronts: I didn't fancy getting a duck in my final Test dig and playing such a sweet shot early is always a nice feeling. Aside from this aggressive shot, I was defending with some authority. I was leaving the ball well.

Smith brought on Steyn, which I'd expected, and straight away I hit a crisp on-drive for four. Ted played a maiden from Philander, who'd replaced Peterson, and I did the same with Steyn. There was just five minutes to lunch, and Smith brought the spinner back, most likely to ensure he'd get in two overs before the interval. The second ball was a long hop and Ed clubbed it past cover for four. The third he turned to fine leg for a single. And then I got out, my first mistake, caught at slip by Kallis after I made room to cut a delivery that was pitched too close to the line of off-stump. Just like that, my Test batting career was over.

Everything had been going so well and then, bang, gone! Just like that.

I couldn't believe I'd been dismissed by a spinner at the WACA. With due respect to Peterson, he is no Harbhajan or Murali. I was in a daze, scarcely believing what had happened to me, but all I could do was walk away. Most of the South Africans chased me, to shake my hand, which not only slowed me down but gave me a chance to hear the crowd clapping me off the field and to notice the 'Thanks Ricky' sign on the scoreboard. I was nearly off the ground, but fortunately there was still time for me to turn around and acknowledge all points of the ground. I looked up into the stand to find Rianna, the kids, Mum and Dad, Drew and Renee, all my team-mates and the support staff. Though I mightn't have looked it, I was so grateful for everyone's support. Too quickly, the moment was over, the game went on, with Pup replacing me in the middle and hitting his first two balls for four. I was in the dressing room, more numb than anything. It had ended in a rush. I was cranky, too. I hate getting out. We were 3–102 chasing 632 to win. We were losing.

The first person I noticed in our dressing room was Adam Gilchrist. He was there, right next to me, standing over me, the moment I sat down. I didn't want anyone anywhere near me at that moment, even one of my best mates. Gilly put his arm around me and said, 'I'm so proud of you, well done.' I couldn't look at him. My head was down and I started taking my pads off. I wanted him to go away. It was probably half a minute but it seemed like forever. Eventually, he left me to my disappointment. Then he came back and said, 'I won't hang around all day, but I might catch up with you later.'

Yeah, mate, that would be great, I thought, not knowing when we'd next meet, with the series over.

As it turned out he was going home to put the finishing touches on a party to be held in my honour the night the Test finished. I knew nothing about that at this time, but the way wickets were falling, it looked like it was going to be that night.

THE TEST ENDED JUST before 5pm. We went on to the field to congratulate the victors and stayed for the presentation, some interviews and a walk around the ground, which gave me the chance to enjoy the goodwill of the WACA faithful one more time. I spent some time on the field with Rianna and the kids and then, when it was time to leave, Dave Warner and Michael Clarke insisted on hoisting me up on their shoulders and chairing me off.

I spent a little time with my family out the front of the home dressing room, and then with the rest of the Aussie team I went down to the South Africans' dressing room and joined in with them.

They were playing drinking games, enjoying each other's company, displaying a spirit and culture that had once been exclusively ours. I hope our boys noticed, saw the value in it. I briefly remembered back to another Test in Perth, the game in 2003–04 when Matt Hayden scored 380 against Zimbabwe and afterwards John Buchanan had a go at us for not celebrating properly. He was worried we were taking wins for granted, too worried about ourselves and not enough about the team. We decided to show Buck, to the point that during the party after the next Test in Sydney, Lang and I had one of our fiercest wrestles, which only ended when we crashed into an old bench and there were pieces of timber strewn across the floor. Those were the days.

Back in our dressing room, I noticed a big tarpaulin had been thrown over a table in the centre. Pup asked me to pull the cover back, to reveal a presentation from the team and Cricket Australia: 33 bottles of Penfolds Grange, one for each of my first 33 Test-match hundreds, a swing-tag attached to each on which were the details of the innings (score, opposition, series, venue) and the vintage (the year the same as the one in which the hundred was made). I was assured that as newer vintages are released, I will receive more bottles, to complete a collection to match every one of my 41 Test tons.

My thank-you speech was short and heartfelt. First, I promised to display the wine in a glass cabinet at home, only to be drunk in the company of mates with whom I'd shared a dressing room. I talked about the journey the men in front and around me had in front of them, and about what I thought the team needed to do to be No. 1 again. I used the way South Africa had played in this Test as my example, how when the opportunity presented itself they were good and brave and experienced enough to grab it. The way Smith and Amla played on the second afternoon, scoring at a-run-a-ball after we were all out for 163, quickly turning a slight advantage into a decisive one, was where the Australian team needed to take its cricket.

'Take the challenge on,' I implored the boys. 'Don't think you can't do it.'

I also wanted them to know that every time I'd played with them, as captain and team-mate, they were what mattered most to me. I'd had their backs all the time. If they'd been facing the fastest bowler in the world and I'd been at the other end, I'd had their backs. I'd done whatever I could to get us through. If the media had been all over them, I'd had their backs. If the administrators had let them down, I'd had their backs.

BEFORE ALL THAT, I'd survived my final media conference as a Test cricketer, though only just. I hadn't prepared a speech, though in my mind was a list of all the people I needed to thank. This time, Emmy was on my knee for much of it, because she said she wanted to look after me (though about two-thirds of the way through, she'd had enough and went and stood next to Rianna). I didn't mind because I thought having her there might make things easier for me, by making it more light-hearted. Again, we were in the WACA gym.

Before the Test, I'd worn the team sponsor's cap but this time I had on my baggy green, which was looking as old as I felt. The repair work I'd had done on it in 2009–10 was only just holding it together. A significant hole had formed on the left side of the peak, and there were two more in the cloth, near my ears. The green was much faded, far different to the caps of most of the other guys in the team.

All I wanted was to get through it. Early on, I was okay when they asked me about my career, especially when they asked me about my most admired opponents.

I was asked if I had any regrets, and then I was asked, what would I miss most?

'I'll miss the mateship … I'll miss the dressing room.'

I stopped for a second. I was still sort of holding it together. They stopped asking questions and I took the opportunity to acknowledge the people who'd helped make my dreams come true. No longer was I looking at my audience. Instead, I gazed down at the table in front of me as I first thanked Rianna and our kids. I had to stop for a little bit, bite my lip, rue the fact I hadn't brought a bottle of water with me so I could clear my throat. I'd never needed one for that purpose in the past. I thanked Mum and Dad, Cricket Australia and Cricket Tasmania. Then, with a quivering bottom lip, it was on to Mowbray, which I acknowledged as the place where I learned the game. 'What you've seen over 17 years is a result of my early days at the Mowbray Cricket Club,' I said deliberately.

I acknowledged my management team, Cricket administrators and the Aussie squad's support staff, and thanked the media, asking them to be fair with the team I was leaving, reminding everyone that the Aussie cricket team will always 'try to put on the best show that they can'.

Soon after, I was out of there. I walked off the stage, scooped up Emmy and with Rianna and Matisse we walked out of the room together. After a few steps, in the race that runs up from the gym onto the playing field, I stopped and gave my wife one of the biggest hugs of our lives. As I did, I started sobbing, as all the pressure and stress and tension of the past few days came pouring out.

It's hard to describe how difficult it was dealing with all the scrutiny at a time when my life was changing so dramatically, when the thing I cared most about outside my family was disappearing. I didn't stay sad for long, but I needed the release. It was my turn to cry.

Except for the not winning, it had been a good week. But a tough one.

THE PARTY THAT NIGHT at Gilly's house was superb, one of the best ever. I was tired, relieved, content, but with the formalities of the farewell over I really didn't want the day to end. I knew a function of some kind was being organised, but I'd left Rianna and Cricket Australia to it. If they'd asked me, I would have said my first preference was a few beers in the dressing room with the team and our families. Gavin Dovey, the team manager, acting on behalf of Cricket Australia, was extremely generous, even offering to fly some of my former team-mates in from interstate, an idea that was only euchred when the Test finished a day early. Gilly and his wife Mel were talking with Rianna about what might happen and they suggested maybe going into the city, to which Rianna replied, 'No, Rick's not a nightclub person; he wouldn't want to go to some bar.'

Mel then said, 'Let's have it at our house.' I'm so glad they did. I will always be grateful for what she and Adam did for us.

It was a terrific, relaxed night, with superb food, beer, wine and a guy singing and playing his guitar in the backyard. All my team-mates were there, and a few notable comrades from years gone by, such as Justin Langer and Tom Moody. Steve Waugh, Glenn McGrath and David Boon had written letters, which were read out. Gilly and Lang made speeches, during which they referred to how they, Haydos, Marto and me were like a 'band of brothers'. It's not that I wasn't tight with all the others, but we five have a special bond that came not just with being at the top of the Test and one-day batting orders for six or seven years, but also from the time we spent over coffees and beers, talking about bats and batting and all sorts of other things that might not have been important but always made sense to us. Lang at the end said he'd never been to war, but if he had he'd have wanted me in the trenches next to him. That's exactly how I feel about him, about the members of our cricket brotherhood. I didn't have another speech in me, so Rianna replied on our behalf, talking excitedly about the 'sense of family' she'd felt through the night. Cricket does that to you.

It ended up with a few of us sitting in Gilly's cellar, eating party pies and drinking red wine until five in the morning. There was Shane Watson and his wife Lee, Ed Cowan, Tom and Helen Moody, Rianna's brother Darren, Rianna and me, Mel and Adam. Seeing how happy and content Mel and Adam were was important for us at that time. Life after international cricket was clearly agreeing with them.

If this is what is on the other side, I thought to myself, *we have nothing to fear.*

Retirement wasn't the end. It was a new beginning.

EPILOGUE
WINDING DOWN

*I know I have given cricket my all, it's been my life,
there's not much more I could give*

I HAD BEEN ON THE ROAD 21 years and a journey that started in Mowbray ended at the Sir Vivian Richards Stadium in North Sound, Antigua late on August 17, 2013.

We lost the game and were out of the finals.

It was over now. I had booked myself in to play IPL, county cricket and the Caribbean Premier League because I knew if I was going to have another season of Sheffield Shield cricket in 2013–14 I would have to keep playing. It was a hectic schedule, but I figured once I stopped I would not start again.

By June, however, I knew I did not have another summer in me. The thought of being at home with the girls was far more appealing than another summer on the road.

It had been a process of letting go. I had stood down from the captaincy in March, 2011, played my last one-day international in February, 2012 and my last Test that November–December.

In the letting go, the winding down, I wasn't looking for the exit, rather I was enjoying every minute of it. It might have looked like I'd run away to join the circus, but the reality was far more rewarding.

The Shield season turned into something special. For much of the year, though I was scoring plenty of runs, we struggled for wins but the competition was so even that going into the last round of home-and-away matches any two teams could have made the final. The results went our way and we had the chance to play a Shield final at home. My previous two finals, both losses, against NSW in 1993–94 and Queensland in 2011–12, had been in Sydney and Brisbane. The draw we achieved this time, against Queensland at Bellerive, was enough for us to claim our third Shield title. The previous triumphs had occurred in 2006–07 and 2010–11, when I'd been away at a World Cup when the final was staged.

Playing a full Shield season was fantastic, not least because of the terrific culture Tassie coach Tim Coyle, captain George Bailey and all the boys have developed within the group. A little bit of me was thinking I was giving something back to Tassie cricket by playing on, but in fact Tassie cricket was again offering me plenty, not least a reminder of just how unique and wonderful is the sport that has been the centre of my life throughout my first 38 years.

In the lead-up to the Shield final, I was named the competition's player of the year, having averaged 87.5 over eight matches. I was also picked in the Big Bash team of the year. This confirmed for me what I already knew: that it wasn't a decline in my reflexes or my eyesight or my fitness that stopped me scoring runs in Test cricket. It was the pressure that got me. I admitted that again as I had a beer in the dressing room after the final, and I soaked up the atmosphere. I just wish I'd had longer to celebrate. I was on a flight back to Sydney about lunchtime the next day and the morning after that I was on my way to Mumbai. Another couple of days to celebrate with the boys would have been a lot of fun.

I had dabbled with the IPL when it had first begun but avoided it since. I believed that was the right thing to do as the captain of Australia and the right example to set. The demands of the tournament and the extraordinary money on offer, in my opinion, are a distraction for young players trying to make an international career. It is no coincidence that so many struggle with their technique and I suspect, at times, their motivation. When an emerging player can pick up a million-dollar contract on the back of a few quick 50s in a domestic tournament it offers him a level of comfort and certainty when what is needed is hunger and a drive to achieve.

Having said that I loved my time with the Mumbai Indians. Loved sharing a dressing room with three of my greatest adversaries and three of the people who had been at the centre of the Monkeygate ugliness. The times I spent with Sachin Tendulkar, Anil Kumble and Harbhajan Singh were important. It was helmet-off stuff and in that environment where we weren't locked in mortal combat we found a lot of common ground.

I wouldn't have spoken more than 50 words to Sachin right through our time of playing together. It's amazing to think that, when I have been so close to him on so many occasions, starting in the nets in Adelaide when I was the teenage wannabe and he was the teenage Test star.

One of the reasons I never got close to Sachin was because of the lifestyle forced on him. The way he had to lead his life made it difficult to catch up. He spends most of his time in the hotel on tours because it was so hard for him to get out of his room. Most of the socialising we do with other international players is around the team hotel — in the foyer or dining room, but you just didn't see him. If Sachin steps outside of his door he gets swamped.

Having a drink at the end of a series was an important part of the ritual for me, but it was probably something we did more with South Africa and England, more than, say, New Zealand or the subcontinental teams. In recent years I noticed there was so much on that it became harder and harder. Often we would finish a Test series and there would be a T20 a few days later or a plane to catch the next morning.

When I did sit down with Sachin we talked a lot about batting, preparation and tactics. We talked about what bowlers did that made it hard for us when we were batting, I suppose we couldn't have had those conversations until the end because it might have been giving too much away. Like all batsmen we spoke a lot about our equipment, our bats. Sachin uses a big heavy bat and it tells you a lot about him and most batsmen from the subcontinent. Indians like a bat where most of the weight is distributed in the bottom of the blade because the ball doesn't bounce that much there. With that arrangement you get value for your straight shots and these are Sachin's bread and butter. Australians like the weight distributed along the blade because of the bounce and because we play more cross bat shots. Frankly you wouldn't be able to swing Sachin's bat if you needed to play the pull shot. You will notice he has a very short backlift and tends to punch the ball.

We spent a lot of time in the team dugout, at first because we weren't making runs and then because we weren't in the side. Watching the IPL up close is an incredible experience. The atmosphere at the grounds is something else, but it is the power of the batsmen that really stands out.

It is unbelievable how far T20 batsmen are hitting the ball, absolutely unbelievable. The grounds in India aren't huge, but they are hitting them out of the stadiums. The stands are 40 or 50 metres high and they are clearing them. The batters are developing power-based techniques and you notice that the players are so much stronger these days. They are spending a lot of time in the gym and have turned into power athletes so they can hold and swing bigger and heavier bats.

THE IPL WAS GOOD, bad, frustrating, enjoyable. I was excited to be with Mumbai, one of the biggest franchises in the competition. The team owners had asked me to captain the franchise, which I saw as a privilege and it was a responsibility I welcomed. Anil Kumble had agreed to fill the role of 'chief mentor' and John Wright, the former New Zealand opener and one of the game's most experienced and successful coaches, had also been hired. The owners wanted the three of us to work together to change the culture of the Mumbai Indians. They wanted to win.

I arrived a week before the first game, keen to get on with it. However, a number of players were still elsewhere, completing other commitments, so the squad didn't come together until a day or two before our first game. It's hard to start changing the way an organisation goes about its business when the people who make up the group aren't yet in the building.

WHEN THE TOURNAMENT STARTED, I couldn't score a run. Having enjoyed some success opening the batting for the Hobart Hurricanes in the Big Bash, it seemed a natural fit for me to go out first with Sachin, the plan being that we'd get the most out of the first six overs and build a platform for the big hitters in our middle-order, men like Rohit Sharma and Kieron Pollard. After three wins from six games, I had to concede there were other guys in our set-up who could get us off to a quicker start than Sachin and I could.

Following a discussion with John and Anil, I decided to stand down. I didn't enjoy leaving myself out, but it was the right thing to do. Dwayne Smith took my place at the top of the order and had immediate success, hitting 62 from 45 balls to inspire a win over Kolkata. I realised that night that I mightn't play again in the tournament, which is how it turned out, as the boys suddenly went on a terrific run, winning eight of nine games. I was still the leader around the team, keen to set standards, lead preparations and run player meetings, but now I had more of a coaching role. I was surprised how well I coped with the change, which told me something about how my ambitions as a player were evolving. If this had happened earlier in my cricket life I would have been beating myself up, doing all I could to rediscover my best form. This time I accepted my fate and began to relish my new role, especially when the younger players responded well to my advice and the team went on to win the final. In a way, we achieved what I had been signed to help do: change the culture, turn the team into winners.

It was nice to hear Anil Kumble say at tournament's end: 'Ricky's experience of being part of winning Australian teams has certainly helped. He knows how to motivate the players and what exactly to say to the players.' I'd never really envisaged myself coaching at the highest levels before this IPL experience. It's on my radar now.

Sharing a dressing room with one-time opponents was an interesting experience, and I do admit it took a little while for us to warm to each other. The memories of many battles, especially in early 2008, still flickered, and I knew it was up to me to make the first move. As captain, I was able to almost impose myself on them, but within a week we realised that as cricketers we have much more in common than we might have thought. I might not have been able to make such a move earlier in my life, but my experiences have changed me. An enjoyable part of my time in Mumbai was to see the attitudes of the Indian players in our team towards me evolve. The smiles and man hugs on display at the after-final party were all genuine.

When I took a good diving catch off Harbhajan's bowling in our second game of the competition there were photos in the paper the next day of the two of us with our arms around each other. That was probably as close as we'd got to each other since we were fined half our match fee for shoulder-charging each other during an ODI at Sharjah in 1998. I found Harbhajan to be a good, ultra-competitive person, the same as me in a lot of ways. I got on with him pretty well. If we'd known each other like this throughout our careers, I'm sure we would still have had most of the on-field confrontations that we did, but we would have had a drink and a chat after the game, and shook hands at the end of it.

AFTER INDIA I FOUND myself in England, playing for Surrey. I started with a hundred in a first-class game against Derbyshire and finished with 169 against Nottinghamshire, played a few one-dayers and T20 games, damaged my hand and missed a couple of matches. The cricket roller-coaster kept moving, but I knew it was time for me to jump off and that was when I announced my decision not to play on after the Caribbean Premier League.

Now I am left to dwell on all the game has given me: joy, some pain, excitement, pride, and the opportunity to grow as a person, competitor and leader. Best of all, it has given me lifelong friendships. Guys like Haydos, Lang, Marto, Gilly, Warnie and Pidge will be like brothers to me forever. I think, too, of the lap of honour they gave me at Bellerive a fortnight after my farewell Test, when everyone in the crowd was so kind to me and the Mowbray boys formed a guard of honour, which I walked through with Rianna and our girls. With hindsight, I'm glad we did the Tassie farewell that way, rather than me trying to squeeze out one more game. Mick Sellers was there for me as part of that guard of honour, just as he and all the other men from the Mowbray club had been there for me at the beginning.

When I announced I was retiring, someone asked me just how good a player was I. One of the things I'm proudest of, I replied, is that for most days in my career, and always from 1999 on, I gave myself the best opportunity to win every game and every series I played. All things considered, I honestly think I was as good a player as I could have been.

That's good enough for me.

IT'S TIME TO MOVE ON now. I had been on the road for so long and when I finished that last game with Antigua I didn't bother packing up all my cricket gear. I didn't need it anymore. It was liberating to head towards an airport without my tools and good to know that my family and not a press conference was waiting for me at the other end. While I'd been away Rianna had done all the hard work and moved the family from Sydney to Melbourne where we'd bought a new home.

A new life was waiting.

CAREER RECORD

of

RICKY THOMAS PONTING

Born: December 19, 1974 (Launceston, Tasmania)

Right-hand batsman and
Right-arm medium bowler

DEBUTS

First-class debut:	Tasmania v South Australia at Adelaide, November 20–23, 1992
List A debut:	Tasmania v Victoria at Devonport, December 13, 1992
ODI debut:	Australia v South Africa at Wellington, February 15, 1995
Test debut:	Australia v Sri Lanka at Perth, December 8–11, 1995
T20 debut:	Somerset v Northamptonshire at Taunton, July 15, 2004
T20I debut:	Australia v New Zealand at Auckland, February 17, 2005

MAJOR TEAMS

Australia (Tests 1995–2012, ODIs 1995–2012, T20Is 2005–2009); **ICC World XI** (ODI 2005); **Tasmania** (First-class 1992–2013, List A 1992–2013); **Australian XI** (First-class 1994); **Australia A** (List A 1994–1996); **Australians** (First-class 1995–2011, List A 1996–2010); **Young Australia** (First-class 1995; List A 1995); **Somerset** (First-class 2004, List A 2004, T20s 2004); **Kolkata Knight Riders** (T20s 2008); **Hobart Hurricanes** (T20s 2011–2013); **Mumbai Indians** (T20s 2013); **Surrey** (First-class 2013, List A 2013, T20s 2013); **Antigua Hawksbills** (T20s 2013)

INTERNATIONAL CRICKET: BATTING AND FIELDING

Cricket	Mat	Inn	NO	50	100	HS	Runs	Avg	Ct	BF	SR
Tests	168	287	29	62	41	257	13378	51.85	196	22782	58.72
ODIs	375	365	39	82	30	164	13704	42.04	160	17046	80.39
T20Is	17	16	2	2	0	98*	401	28.64	8	302	132.78

INTERNATIONAL CRICKET: BOWLING

Cricket	Mat	Balls	Runs	Wkts	BBI	BBM	Avg	Econ	SR
Tests	168	587	276	5	1–0	1–0	55.20	2.82	117.4
ODIs	375	150	104	3	1–12	1–12	34.67	4.16	50.0
T20Is	17	–	–	–	–	–	–	–	–

Notes
1. In all tables in this statistics section, * indicates not out unless otherwise indicated. Symbols and abbreviations in table headings include: 'Mat' indicates Matches; 'Inn' indicates Innings; 'NO' indicates Not Out; HS indicated Highest Score; 'Avg' indicates Average; 'BF' indicates Balls Faced; 'SR' indicates Strike Rate; '100' and '50' indicate centuries and half-centuries scored; 'Ct' indicates Catches; 'BBI' indicates Best Bowling in an Innings; 'BBM' indicates Best Bowling in a Match; 'Econ' indicates Economy Rate.
2. The Association of Cricket Statisticians and Historians defines 'List A' limited-overs matches as tour and tournament matches between national/state/county/province/zone teams, including domestic limited-overs competitions.

1. TEST CRICKET

TEAM-MATES

90 Tests with Ricky Matthew Hayden; **88** Adam Gilchrist; **85** Shane Warne, Glenn McGrath; **83** Justin Langer; **81** Michael Clarke; **74** Michael Hussey; **72** Brett Lee; **71** Steve Waugh; **59** Mark Waugh; **58** Jason Gillespie; **53** Damien Martyn; **52** Simon Katich; **45** Mitchell Johnson; **41** Brad Haddin; **37** Stuart MacGill; **35** Michael Slater; **34** Shane Watson; **33** Peter Siddle; **32** Michael Kasprowicz; **28** Ian Healy; **26** Andrew Symonds; **25** Ben Hilfenhaus; **24** Greg Blewett, Stuart Clark; **22** Mark Taylor; **21** Marcus North; **18** Darren Lehmann; **17** Nathan Hauritz; **16** Andy Bichel; **15** Phillip Hughes, Nathan Lyon; **14** Damien Fleming; **12** Paul Reiffel, Matthew Elliott, Colin Miller, Doug Bollinger, David Warner; **11** Phil Jaques, Ryan Harris; **10** Ed Cowan; **7** Brad Hogg, James Pattinson; **6** Brad Hodge, Shaun Marsh, Matthew Wade; **5** Nathan Bracken, Mitchell Starc; **4** Michael Bevan, Martin Love, Brad Williams, Cameron White, Andrew McDonald, Tim Paine, Steve Smith, Usman Khawaja; **3** David Boon, Craig McDermott, Gavin Robertson, Shaun Tait; **2** Simon Cook, Adam Dale, Scott Muller, Jason Krejza, Xavier Doherty, Trent Copeland, Rob Quiney; **1** Brendon Julian, Stuart Law, Peter McIntyre, Shaun Young, Paul Wilson, Dan Cullen, Chris Rogers, Beau Casson, Bryce McGain, Graham Manou, Clint McKay, Peter George, Michael Beer, Pat Cummins, John Hastings

APPEARANCE MILESTONES

Test No.	Series	Versus	Venue	Landmark
1	1995–96	Sri Lanka	Perth	Became Australian Test cricketer No. 366
50	2001–02	New Zealand	Perth	35th Australian to play 50 Tests
100	2005–06	South Africa	Sydney	Ninth Australian to play 100 Tests
150	2010–11	England	Adelaide	Fourth player to play 150 Tests
168	2012–13	South Africa	Perth	Equalled Steve Waugh's Australian record

Notes

1. Ricky made his Test debut in same game as Stuart Law. On the basis of alphabetical order, Law became Australian Test cricketer No. 365.

2. On Ricky's retirement, 11 Australians had appeared in 100 Tests. These men are (with total appearances in brackets): Steve Waugh and Ricky Ponting (168), Allan Border (156), Shane Warne (145), Mark Waugh (128), Glenn McGrath (124), Ian Healy (119), David Boon (107), Justin Langer (105), Mark Taylor (104), Matthew Hayden (103).

3. October 1, 2013, the 10 cricketers with the most Test appearances were: India's Sachin Tendulkar (198), Steve Waugh and Ricky Ponting (168), India's Rahul Dravid (164), South Africa's Jacques Kallis (162), Allan Border (156), West Indies' Shivnarine Chanderpaul (148), South Africa's Mark Boucher (147), Shane Warne (145) and Sri Lanka's Mahela Jayawardene (138). The careers of Tendulkar, Kallis, Chanderpaul and Jayawardene were ongoing.

BY SERIES

Batting

Series	Tests	Inn	NO	50	100	HS	Runs	Avg	Ct	Results
SL in Aust 1995–96	3	4	0	2	0	96	193	48.25	4	WWW
Aust in Ind 1996	1	2	0	0	0	14	27	13.50	3	L
WI in Aust 1996–97	2	4	0	1	0	88	110	27.50	2	WWLWL
Aust in Eng 1997	3	5	0	0	1	127	241	48.20	1	LDWWWD
NZ in Aust 1997–98	3	4	1	1	0	73*	119	39.67	2	WWD
SA in Aust 1997–98	3	5	0	1	1	105	248	49.60	2	DWD
Aust in Ind 1998	3	5	0	1	0	60	105	21.00	3	LLW
Aust in Pak 1998	1	2	1	1	0	76*	119	119.00	0	WDD
Eng in Aust 1998–99	3	4	0	0	0	21	47	11.75	4	DWWLW
Aust in WI 1999	2	4	1	0	1	104	168	56.00	1	WLLW
Aust in SL 1999	3	4	1	2	1	105*	253	84.33	3	LDD
Aust in Zimb 1999	1	1	0	0	0	31	31	31.00	2	W
Pak in Aust 1999–2000	3	4	0	0	1	197	197	49.25	5	WWW
Ind in Aust 1999–2000	3	5	2	1	2	141*	375	125.00	3	WWW
WI in Aust 2000–01	5	8	2	2	0	92	242	40.33	5	WWWWW
Aust in Ind 2001	3	5	0	0	0	11	17	3.40	7	WLL
Aust in Eng 2001	5	8	0	2	1	144	338	42.25	7	WWWLW
NZ in Aust 2001–02	3	5	2	0	1	157*	251	83.67	3	DDD
SA in Aust 2001–02	3	5	1	1	0	54	115	28.75	11	WWW
Aust in SA 2002	3	5	1	1	1	100*	309	77.25	4	WWL
Pak v Aust in SL & UAE 2002	3	4	0	0	2	150	342	85.50	2	WWW
Eng in Aust 2002–03	5	8	0	1	2	154	417	52.13	6	WWWWL
Aust in WI 2003	3	5	1	0	3	206	523	130.75	3	WWWL
Bang in Aust 2003	2	2	0	1	0	59	69	34.50	2	WW
Zimb in Aust 2003–04	2	3	1	1	1	169	259	129.50	2	WW
Ind in Aust 2003–04	4	8	1	2	2	257	706	100.86	1	DLWD
Aust in SL 2004	3	6	0	1	0	92	198	33.00	1	WWW
SL in Aust 2004	1	2	0	0	0	45	67	33.50	2	WD
Aust in Ind 2004	1	2	0	0	0	12	23	11.50	2	WDWL
NZ in Aust 2004–05	2	3	1	2	0	68	145	72.50	4	WW
Pak in Aust 2004–05	3	6	2	2	1	207	403	100.75	4	WWW
Aust in NZ 2004–05	3	5	2	1	1	105	293	97.67	2	WDW

Series	Tests	Inn	NO	50	100	HS	Runs	Avg	Ct	Results
Aust in Eng 2005	5	9	0	1	1	156	359	39.89	4	WLDLD
World XI in Aust 2005–06	1	2	0	1	0	54	100	50.00	1	W
WI in Aust 2005–06	3	6	2	1	2	149	329	82.25	3	WWW
SA in Aust 2005–06	3	6	1	2	3	143*	515	103.00	5	DWW
Aust in SA 2006	3	6	0	1	2	116	348	58.00	2	WWW
Aust in Bang 2006	2	3	1	1	1	118*	191	95.50	2	WW
Eng in Aust 2006–07	5	8	1	2	2	196	576	82.29	4	WWWWW
SL in Aust 2007–08	2	3	1	2	0	56	140	70.00	3	WW
Ind in Aust 2007–08	4	7	0	1	1	140	268	38.29	6	WWLD
Aust in WI 2008	3	6	0	1	1	158	323	53.83	1	WDW
Aust in Ind 2008	4	7	0	1	1	123	266	38.00	3	DLDL
NZ in Aust 2008–09	2	3	0	1	0	79	100	33.33	5	WW
SA in Aust 2008–09	3	6	0	2	1	101	285	47.50	0	LLW
Aust in SA 2009	3	6	0	2	0	83	210	35.00	6	WWL
Aust in Eng 2009	5	8	0	2	1	150	385	48.13	11	DLDWL
WI in Aust 2009–10	3	5	1	1	0	55	136	34.00	2	WDW
Pak in Aust 2009–10	3	6	0	2	1	209	378	63.00	3	WWW
Aust in NZ 2009–10	2	3	0	0	0	41	69	23.00	6	WW
Pak v Aust in Eng 2010	2	4	0	1	0	66	98	24.50	2	WL
Aust in Ind 2010	2	4	0	3	0	77	224	56.00	2	LL
Eng in Aust 2010–11	4	8	1	1	0	51*	113	16.14	4	DLWLL
Aust in SL 2011	2	4	0	0	0	48	124	31.00	3	WDD
Aust in SA 2011	2	4	0	1	0	62	70	17.50	3	LW
NZ in Aust 2011–12	2	3	0	1	0	78	99	33.00	3	WL
Ind in Aust 2011–12	4	6	1	3	2	221	544	108.80	6	WWWW
Aust in WI 2012	3	6	0	1	0	57	146	24.33	1	WDW
SA in Aust 2012–13	3	5	0	0	0	16	32	6.40	2	DDL
Totals	**168**	**287**	**29**	**62**	**41**	**257**	**13378**	**51.85**	**196**	

Notes

1. 'Split' years (such as '1995–96') indicate that a Test series was played in Australia or New Zealand. 'Whole' years (such as '1996') indicate that a Test series was played overseas, with the exception of the series against Bangladesh and Sri Lanka played in northern Australia in July 2003 and July 2004 respectively.

2. 'Aust' indicates Australia; 'SL' indicates Sri Lanka; 'Ind' indicates India; 'WI' indicates West Indies; 'Eng' indicates England; 'NZ' indicates New Zealand; 'SA' indicates South Africa; 'Pak' indicates Pakistan; 'Zimb' indicates Zimbabwe; 'UAE' indicates United Arab Emirates (Sharjah); 'Bang' indicates Bangladesh.

3. Ricky did not play in the following 25 Tests from his Test debut to his final appearance: third, fourth and fifth Tests v West Indies 1996–97 (dropped); all three Tests in South Africa 1997 (dropped; Australia won 2–1); first three Ashes Tests 1997 (dropped); first and third Tests in Pakistan 1998 (dropped); fourth and fifth Ashes Tests 1998–99 (dropped); first and second Tests v West Indies 1999 (dropped); all three Tests in New Zealand 1999–2000 (injured; Australia 3–0); fourth Test in West Indies 2003 (illness); first Test v Sri Lanka 2004 (personal reasons); first three Tests in India 2004 (injured); fifth Ashes Test 2010–11 (injured); second Test v Sri Lanka 2011 (personal reasons).

4. The 'Results' column lists all results in a series. <u>The results of the Tests in which Ricky did not play are underlined.</u>

5. Ricky scored more than 1000 Test runs in a calendar year five times: 1064 runs in 11 Tests in 2002; 1503 in 11 Tests (average 100.20) in 2003; 1544 in 15 Tests in 2005; 1333 in 10 Tests in 2006; 1182 in 14 Tests in 2008. Sachin Tendulkar is the only man to score 1000 runs in a calendar year six times; Ricky, Matthew Hayden, Jacques Kallis and Brian Lara (West Indies) have done so five times.

Bowling

Series	O	M	R	W	Best	Avg	SR	Econ
SL in Aust 1995–96	4	2	8	1	1–8	8.00	24.00	2.00
WI in Aust 1996–97	1.5	1	0	1	1–0	0.00	11.00	0.00
Aust in Pak 1998	5	1	13	1	1–13	13.00	30.00	2.60
Eng in Aust 1998–99	4	1	10	0	–	–	–	2.50
Aust in WI 1999	4	1	12	1	1–12	12.00	24.00	3.00
Aust in SL 1999	4	1	7	0	–	–	–	1.75
Aust in Zimb 1999	2	2	0	0	–	–	–	0.00
Pak in Aust 1999–2000	11	2	31	0	–	–	–	2.82
Ind in Aust 1999–2000	1	0	8	0	–	–	–	8.00
WI in Aust 2000–01	1	1	0	0	–	–	–	0.00
Aust in Ind 2001	14	2	43	0	–	–	–	3.07
Aust in Eng 2001	4	0	8	0	–	–	–	2.00
NZ in Aust 2001–02	7	3	9	0	–	–	–	1.29
SA in Aust 2001–02	1	0	11	0	–	–	–	11.00
Pak v Aust in SL & UAE 2002	1	0	5	0	–	–	–	5.00
Aust in WI 2003	2	0	6	0	–	–	–	3.00
Zimb in Aust 2003–04	5	1	15	0	–	–	–	3.00
Ind in Aust 2003–04	1	0	4	0	–	–	–	4.00
Pak in Aust 2004–05	3	1	15	0	–	–	–	5.00
Aust in NZ 2004–05	4	1	10	0	–	–	–	2.50
Aust in Eng 2005	6	2	9	1	1–9	9.00	36.00	1.50
Aust in SA 2006	2	1	7	0	–	–	–	3.50
Aust in Ind 2008	2	0	11	0	–	–	–	5.50
Aust in SL 2011	4	0	19	0	–	–	–	4.75

Series	O	M	R	W	Best	Avg	SR	Econ
Aust in SA 2011	1	0	8	0	–	–	–	8.00
NZ in Aust 2011–12	1	0	4	0	–	–	–	4.00
SA in Aust 2012–13	2	1	3	0	–	–	–	1.50
Totals	**97.5**	**24**	**276**	**5**	**1–0**	**55.20**	**117.40**	**2.82**

Note
The five batsmen Ricky dismissed in Test cricket were Sri Lanka's Asanka Gurusinha (caught by Ian Healy, MCG, 1995–96), West Indies' Jimmy Adams (lbw, Brisbane, 1996–97), Pakistan's Moin Khan (caught by Healy, Peshawar, 1998), West Indies' Ridley Jacobs (caught by Mark Waugh, Bridgetown, 1999) and England's Michael Vaughan (caught by Adam Gilchrist, Nottingham, 2005).

BATTING: BY OPPONENT

Opponent	Tests	Inn	NO	50	100	HS	Runs	Avg	Ct
Bangladesh	4	5	1	2	1	118*	260	65.00	4
England	35	58	2	9	8	196	2476	44.21	41
ICC World XI	1	2	0	1	0	54	100	50.00	1
India	29	51	4	12	8	257	2555	54.36	36
New Zealand	17	26	6	6	2	157*	1076	53.80	25
Pakistan	15	26	3	6	5	209	1537	66.83	16
South Africa	26	48	3	11	8	143*	2132	47.38	35
Sri Lanka	14	23	2	7	1	105*	975	46.43	16
West Indies	24	44	7	7	7	206	1977	53.43	18
Zimbabwe	3	4	1	1	1	169	290	96.67	4
Totals	**168**	**287**	**29**	**62**	**41**	**257**	**13378**	**51.85**	**196**

BATTING: BY POSITION

Position	Inn	NO	50	100	HS	Runs	Avg
No. 3	196	20	43	32	257	9904	56.27
No. 4	28	1	8	2	221	1086	40.22
No. 5	6	0	2	0	96	189	31.50
No. 6	45	5	8	7	197	1989	49.73
No. 7	11	3	1	0	73*	208	26.00
No. 9	1	0	0	0	2	2	2.00
Totals	**287**	**29**	**62**	**41**	**257**	**13378**	**51.85**

BATTING: HOME AND AWAY

Location	Tests	Inn	NO	50	100	HS	Runs	Avg	Ct
Home	92	154	21	38	23	257	7578	56.98	109
Away	76	133	8	24	18	206	5800	46.40	87

BATTING: BY COUNTRY

Venue	Tests	Inn	NO	50	100	HS	Runs	Avg	Ct
Australia	92	154	21	38	23	257	7578	56.98	109
Bangladesh	2	3	1	1	1	118*	191	95.50	2
England & Wales	20	34	0	6	4	156	1421	41.79	25
India	14	25	0	5	1	123	662	26.48	20
New Zealand	5	8	2	1	1	105	362	60.33	8
Pakistan	1	2	1	1	0	76*	119	119.00	0
South Africa	11	21	1	5	3	116	937	46.85	15
Sri Lanka	9	16	1	3	2	141	723	48.20	9
United Arab Emirates	2	2	0	0	1	150	194	97.00	0
West Indies	11	21	2	2	5	206	1160	61.05	6
Zimbabwe	1	1	0	0	0	31	31	31.00	2

Note

Ricky's Test batting on Australian grounds is as follows:

Venue	Tests	Inn	NO	50	100	HS	Runs	Avg	Ct
Adelaide	17	31	2	6	6	242	1743	60.10	23
Brisbane	17	26	5	10	4	196	1335	63.57	24
Cairns	2	3	0	1	0	59	126	42.00	4
Darwin	1	1	0	0	0	10	10	10.00	0
Hobart	7	12	3	2	2	209	581	64.56	9
Melbourne	15	28	5	7	4	257	1338	58.17	18
Perth	17	26	1	6	1	197	965	38.60	17
Sydney	16	27	5	6	6	207	1480	67.27	14
Totals	**92**	**154**	**21**	**38**	**23**	**257**	**7578**	**56.98**	**109**

CENTURIES (41)

Season	Test No.	Opponent	Venue	Inn (of 4)	Position	Score
1997	7	England	Leeds	second	No. 6	127
1997–98	13	South Africa	Melbourne	first	No. 6	105
1999	23	West Indies	Bridgetown	first	No. 6	104
1999	27	Sri Lanka	Colombo	first	No. 6	105*
1999–2000	31	Pakistan	Perth	second	No. 6	197
1999–2000	32	India	Adelaide	first	No. 6	125
1999–2000	34	India	Sydney	second	No. 6	141*
2001	46	England	Leeds	first	No. 3	144
2001–02	49	New Zealand	Hobart	first	No. 3	157*
2002	55	South Africa	Cape Town	fourth	No. 3	100*
2002	57	Pakistan	Colombo	first	No. 3	141
2002	59	Pakistan	Sharjah	first	No. 3	150
2002–03	60	England	Brisbane	first	No. 3	123
2002–03	61	England	Adelaide	second	No. 3	154
2003	65	West Indies	Georgetown	second	No. 3	117
2003	66	West Indies	Port-of-Spain	first	No. 3	206
2003	67	West Indies	Bridgetown	first	No. 3	113
2003–04	71	Zimbabwe	Sydney	second	No. 3	169
2003–04	73	India	Adelaide	first	No. 3	242
2003–04	74	India	Melbourne	second	No. 3	257
2004–05	85	Pakistan	Sydney	second	No. 3	207
2004–05	88	New Zealand	Auckland	second	No. 3	105
2005	91	England	Manchester	fourth	No. 3	156
2005–06	95	West Indies	Brisbane	first	No. 3	149
2005–06	95	West Indies	Brisbane	third	No. 3	104*
2005–06	99	South Africa	Melbourne	first	No. 3	117
2005–06	100	South Africa	Sydney	second	No. 3	120
2005–06	100	South Africa	Sydney	fourth	No. 3	143*
2006	102	South Africa	Durban	first	No. 3	103
2006	102	South Africa	Durban	third	No. 3	116
2006	104	Bangladesh	Fatullah	fourth	No. 3	118*
2006–07	106	England	Brisbane	first	No. 3	196
2006–07	107	England	Adelaide	second	No. 3	142
2007–08	116	India	Adelaide	second	No. 3	140

Season	Test No.	Opponent	Venue	Inn (of 4)	Position	Score
2008	117	West Indies	Kingston	first	No. 3	158
2008	120	India	Bangalore	first	No. 3	123
2008–09	127	South Africa	Melbourne	first	No. 3	101
2009	132	England	Cardiff	second	No. 3	150
2009–10	142	Pakistan	Hobart	first	No. 3	209
2011–12	160	India	Sydney	second	No. 4	134
2011–12	162	India	Adelaide	first	No. 4	221

Notes

1. 'Test No.' indicates Test number of Ricky's career in which the hundred was scored.

2. As at October 1, 2013, there have been 72 instances of a batsman scoring a century in two innings of a Test. Nineteen of these instances have involved an Australian. Eleven players across all teams — England's Herbert Sutcliffe, West Indies' George Headley and Clyde Walcott, Australia's Greg Chappell, Allan Border, Matthew Hayden and Ricky Ponting, India's Sunil Gavaskar and Rahul Dravid, Sri Lanka's Aravinda de Silva, and South Africa's Jacques Kallis — have achieved this feat at least twice. Gavaskar and Ponting have done so three times; Ricky's three instances being 149 and 104* versus West Indies at the Gabba in 2005–06, 120 and 143* versus South Africa at the SCG in 2005–06 (his 100th Test), and 103 and 116 versus South Africa at Durban in 2006.

HIGHEST PARTNERSHIPS

Stand	Wkt	Partner	Versus	Venue	Series	Inn	Score	Result
386	4th	Michael Clarke	Ind	Adelaide	2011–12	1	3–84	Win
352	4th	Michael Clarke	Pak	Hobart	2009–10	1	3–71	Win
327	5th	Justin Langer	Pak	Perth	1999–00	2	4–54	Win
315	3rd	Darren Lehmann	WI	Port-of-Spain	2003	1	2–56	Win
288	4th	Michael Clarke	Ind	Sydney	2011–12	2	3–37	Win
281	5th	Steve Waugh	WI	Bridgetown	1999	1	4–144	Loss
272	2nd	Matthew Hayden	Eng	Brisbane	2002–03	1	1–67	Win
268	5th	Matthew Elliott	Eng	Leeds	1997	2	4–50	Win
248	2nd	Justin Langer	WI	Georgetown	2003	2	1–37	Win
242	3rd	Damien Martyn	Eng	Adelaide	2002–03	2	2–114	Win
239	5th	Steve Waugh	Ind	Adelaide	1999–00	1	4–52	Win
239	2nd	Simon Katich	Eng	Cardiff	2009	2	1–60	Draw
234	2nd	Matthew Hayden	Ind	Melbourne	2003–04	2	1–30	Win
221	3rd	Mark Waugh	Eng	Leeds	2001	1	2–42	Loss
210	4th	Michael Clarke	Ind	Adelaide	2007–08	2	3–241	Draw
209	4th	Michael Hussey	Eng	Brisbane	2006–07	1	3–198	Win
201	2nd	Matthew Hayden	SA	Durban	2006	3	1–49	Win

Notes

1. 'Inn' indicates the innings of the Test (of four) in which the partnership occurred; 'Score' is the team score at the start of the partnership.

2. Ricky's highest partnership in the fourth innings of a Test was 182 with Matthew Hayden against South Africa, Sydney, 2005–06, when they came together at 1–30. Australia won the Test by eight wickets.

3. Ricky's highest partnerships for wickets not listed above are:

Stand	Wkt	Partner	Versus	Venue	Series	Inn	Score	Result
144	6th	Adam Gilchrist	Ind	Melbourne	1999–00	1	5–197	Won
145	7th	Shane Warne	NZ	Hobart	2001–02	1	6–336	Draw
107	8th	Jason Gillespie	SL	Kandy	1999	1	7–60	Loss
14	9th	Brett Lee	Eng	Manchester	2005	4	8–340	Draw
17	10th	Glenn McGrath	SL	Kandy	1999	1	9–171	Loss

FIELDING MILESTONES

Catch	Season	Versus	Venue	Test No.	Batsman	Bowler
First	1995–96	Sri Lanka	Perth	1	Aravinda de Silva	Shane Warne
50th	2001	England	Lord's	44	Ian Ward	Glenn McGrath
100th	2004–05	Pakistan	Melbourne	84	Mohammad Yousuf	Shane Warne
150th	2009	England	Cardiff	132	Andrew Flintoff	Mitchell Johnson
196th	2012–13	South Africa	Adelaide	167	Graeme Smith	Ben Hilfenhaus

Notes

1. Ricky was the eighth Australian non-wicketkeeper to take 100 catches in Test cricket, after Bob Simpson, Ian Chappell, Greg Chappell, Allan Border, Mark Taylor, Mark Waugh and Steve Waugh. Shane Warne, Matthew Hayden and Michael Clarke have also now reached this landmark.

2. Ricky took his 196 Test catches off 36 different bowlers, the most being off Shane Warne (36), Glenn McGrath (23), Jason Gillespie (16), Brett Lee (14), Mitchell Johnson (14), Peter Siddle (11), Stuart MacGill (10), Ben Hilfenhaus (9), Stuart Clark (7) and Damien Fleming (5).

3. The batsmen Ricky dismissed most often as a catcher in Tests were India's Rahul Dravid, VVS Laxman and Harbhajan Singh, and England's Mark Butcher and Paul Collingwood, each 'caught Ponting' on four occasions.

CAPTAINCY

Cricket	Matches	Won	Lost	Drawn	Tied	Win%
Tests (2004–2010)	77	48	16	13	–	62.34

Notes

1. Ricky was Australia's 42nd Test captain and the 14th man to lead Australia in at least 20 Tests, after Joe Darling, Bill Woodfull, Don Bradman, Lindsay Hassett, Richie Benaud, Bob Simpson, Bill Lawry, Ian Chappell, Greg Chappell, Kim Hughes, Allan Border, Mark Taylor and Steve Waugh.

2. Ricky captained Australia in every Test he played from the first Test v Sri Lanka in 2004 to the fourth Ashes Test of 2010–11.

3. Of all captains with more than 10 Tests as captain, Ricky ranks third in winning percentage behind Steve Waugh (71.93% in 57 Tests) and Sir Donald Bradman (62.50% in 24 Tests).

4. Ricky's 77 Tests as captain is fourth highest, behind South Africa's Graeme Smith (102 Tests as at June 30, 2013), Allan Border (93) and New Zealand's Stephen Fleming (80).

PLAYER-OF-THE-MATCH AWARDS (16)

Season	Opponent	Venue	Scores
1999	Sri Lanka	Kandy	96 & 51
1999	Sri Lanka	Colombo	105*
1999–2000	Pakistan	Perth	197
2001–02	New Zealand	Hobart	157*
2002–03	England	Adelaide	154
2003	West Indies	Port-of-Spain	206 & 45
2003–04	Zimbabwe	Sydney	169 & 53*
2003–04	India	Melbourne	257 & 31*
2004–05	New Zealand	Auckland	105 & 86*
2005	England	Manchester	7 & 156
2005–06	West Indies	Brisbane	149 & 104*
2005–06	South Africa	Sydney	120 & 143*
2006–07	England	Brisbane	196 & 60*
2006–07	England	Adelaide	142 & 49
2009	England	Cardiff	150
2009–10	Pakistan	Hobart	209 & 89

Notes

1. Ricky was named the Allan Border Medallist four times, in 2004, 2006, 2007 and 2009 (shared with Michael Clarke). This award, given to the Australian cricketer of the year as voted by players, umpires and the media, was inaugurated in 1999–2000, when it was won by Glenn McGrath. Other winners to 2013 were Steve Waugh (2001), Matthew Hayden (2002), Adam Gilchrist (2003), Michael Clarke (2005, 2009, 2012, 2013), Brett Lee (2008) and Shane Watson (2010, 2011).
2. Ricky was one of *Wisden*'s Cricketers of the Year in 2006. He was *Wisden Australia*'s Cricketer of the Year in 2004.
3. Ricky is the only man to have participated in 100 or more Test-match victories. His first Test win came in his debut match, against Sri Lanka at Perth in December 1995. His 50th Test win was versus Zimbabwe in Sydney in October 2003; he became the 12th cricketer to be a part of 50 Test wins, after the West Indies' Vivian Richards, Gordon Greenidge, Desmond Haynes and Courtney Walsh, and Australia's Allan Border, Steve Waugh, Ian Healy, Mark Taylor, Mark Waugh, Shane Warne and Glenn McGrath. Ricky's 93rd Test victory, breaking Warne's world record for most Test wins, came in the Boxing Day Test against Pakistan in 2009–10. His 100th Test win occurred at Galle in the opening Test versus Sri Lanka in September 2011. His final Test win, number 108, was the third Test against the West Indies in April 2012, at Roseau, Dominica.
4. As at October 1, 2013, Ricky was one of 25 men to have participated in 50 or more Test victories, and one of 13 Australians. The top 10 for most Test wins was Ponting (108), Warne (92), Steve Waugh (86), McGrath (84), Jacques Kallis (80), Mark Boucher (74), Adam Gilchrist (73), Mark Waugh (72) and Matthew Hayden (71).

MOST SUCCESSFUL BOWLERS

Bowler	B	Ct	CB	LBW	St	HW	Total
Harbhajan Singh (Ind)	1	5	–	3	1	–	10
Darren Gough (Eng)	1	3	1	3	–	–	8
Anil Kumble (Ind)	1	3	–	2	1	–	7
Ishant Sharma (ind)	1	5	–	1	–	–	7
Jacques Kallis (SA)	1	2	1	2	–	–	6
Morne Morkel (SA)	1	4	1	–	–	–	6
Makhaya Ntini (SA)	1	3	1	1	–	–	6
Chaminda Vaas (SL)	–	1	3	2	–	–	6
Steve Harmison (Eng)	–	1	3	1	–	–	5
Andrew Flintoff (Eng)	–	3	2	–	–	–	5
Kemar Roach (WI)	–	4	1	–	–	–	5
Zaheer Khan (Ind)	1	2	1	1	–	–	5
Jimmy Anderson (Eng)	–	3	1	–	–	–	4
Chris Cairns (NZ)	1	2	1	–	–	–	4
Rangana Herath (SL)	–	4	–	–	–	–	4
Chris Martin (NZ)	–	1	2	1	–	–	4
Mohammad Amir (Pak)	–	3	1	–	–	–	4
Shaun Pollock (SA)	–	2	–	2	–	–	4
Dale Steyn (SA)	1	–	1	2	–	–	4
Courtney Walsh (WI)	–	2	1	1	–	–	4

Notes

1. The table above lists those bowlers who dismissed Ricky most often in Test cricket. Thus, Harbhajan dismissed Ricky on 10 occasions, Darren Gough eight times, and so on.

2. 'B' indicates Bowled; 'Ct' indicates Caught; 'CB' indicates Caught Behind; 'LBW' indicates Leg Before Wicket; 'St' indicates Stumped; 'HW' indicates Hit Wicket.

3. Ricky was dismissed 258 times in Test cricket. He was bowled 36 times, caught by a fieldsman other than the wicketkeeper 111 times, caught behind 42 times, lbw 47 times, run out 15 times and stumped seven times.

4. Mark Boucher was the wicketkeeper to dismiss Ricky most often in Tests (nine times; all caught), followed by England's Alec Stewart (six times; all caught) and Geraint Jones (four times; all caught). No keeper stumped him more than once. The non-wicketkeeper to catch Ricky most often was Rahul Dravid (five times). Jacques Kallis, VVS Laxman and Andrew Strauss (England) caught him four times.

2. ONE-DAY INTERNATIONAL CRICKET

TEAM-MATES

245 One-Day Internationals (ODIs) with Ricky Adam Gilchrist; **189** Glenn McGrath; **179** Michael Bevan; **172** Brett Lee; **171** Damien Martyn, Michael Clarke; **167** Andrew Symonds; **144** Michael Hussey; **130** Matthew Hayden; **122** Shane Warne; **120** Mark Waugh; **111** Steve Waugh, Shane Watson; **109** Brad Hogg; **108** Darren Lehmann; **92** Nathan Bracken; **84** Mitchell Johnson; **83** Jason Gillespie; **68** Brad Haddin; **65** Damien Fleming, Ian Harvey, James Hopes; **64** Cameron White; **55** Andy Bichel; **46** Nathan Hauritz; **41** Paul Reiffel; **38** Michael Kasprowicz; **37** Tom Moody; **36** Simon Katich; **34** Stuart Law; **33** Shane Lee; **31** Ian Healy; **30** Doug Bollinger; **29** Mark Taylor, Shaun Tait; **28** David Hussey; **27** Stuart Clark; **24** Jimmy Maher, Shaun Marsh; **22** Brad Williams; **20** Ryan Harris, Tim Paine, Steve Smith; **19** Brendon Julian; **18** Adam Dale, Callum Ferguson; **17** Clint McKay; **16** Brad Hodge, Peter Siddle, Xavier Doherty; **13** Michael Slater, David Warner; **12** Adam Voges, Ben Hilfenhaus; **11** Greg Blewett, Paul Wilson; **9** Craig McDermott; **8** Gavin Robertson; **7** Jason Krejza; **6** Brad Young, Mick Lewis; **5** David Boon, Tim May, Matthew Wade, Dan Christian, Mitchell Starc; **4** Graham Manou, John Hastings; **3** Stuart MacGill, Phil Jaques, Brett Dorey, Dan Cullen, Ben Laughlin, Pat Cummins, Peter Forrest; **2** Michael Di Venuto, Ryan Campbell, Mark Cosgrove, Luke Ronchi, Moises Henriques, James Pattinson; **1** Jo Angel, Chris Cairns, Stephen Fleming, Chris Gayle, Darren Gough, Brian Lara, Daniel Vettori, Justin Langer, Ashley Noffke, Shane Harwood, Brett Geeves, Josh Hazlewood, Mitchell Marsh

Note
The above list includes Ricky's team-mates in the ICC World XI that played an Asian Cricket Council XI at the MCG on January 10, 2005, to raise money for the victims of the tsunami that struck parts of Asia on Boxing Day 2004. That World XI team was (in batting order): Chris Gayle (West Indies), Adam Gilchrist (Australia), Ricky Ponting (Australia; captain), Brian Lara (West Indies), Chris Cairns (New Zealand), Glenn McGrath (Australia), Stephen Fleming (New Zealand), Matthew Hayden (Australia), Daniel Vettori (New Zealand), Shane Warne (Australia), Darren Gough (England).

APPEARANCE MILESTONES

ODI No.	Series	Versus	Venue	Landmark
1	1994–95	South Africa	Wellington	Became Australian ODI cricketer No. 123
50	1998	Zimbabwe	Delhi	Scored 145
100	1999–2000	Pakistan	Melbourne	13th Australian to play 100 ODIs
200	2004	Zimbabwe	Harare	Fifth Australian to play 200 ODIs
300	2008	West Indies	Grenada	Second Australian to play 300 ODIs
326	2009	India	Nagpur	Broke Steve Waugh's Australian record
375	2011–12	India	Brisbane	Ranked fourth all-time for most ODIs

at the close of play

Notes

1. Ricky made his ODI debut in same game as Greg Blewett. On the basis of alphabetical order, Blewett became Australian ODI cricketer No. 122.
2. Ricky's 145 in his 50th ODI equalled Dean Jones's then record for the highest innings by an Australian in ODI cricket.
3. On Ricky's final ODI appearance, 10 Australians had appeared in 200 ODIs. These men were (with total appearances in brackets): Ricky Ponting (375), Steve Waugh (325), Adam Gilchrist (287), Allan Border (273), Mark Waugh (244), Glenn McGrath (250), Michael Bevan (232), Brett Lee (221), Damien Martyn (208), Michael Clarke (206). Clarke's career is ongoing; as at June 30, 2013, he had appeared in 227 ODIs.
4. At October 1, 2013, the 10 cricketers with the most ODI appearances were: India's Sachin Tendulkar (463), Sri Lanka's Sanath Jayasuriya (445), Sri Lanka's Mahela Jayawardene (404), Pakistan's Inzamum-ul-Haq (378), Ricky Ponting (375), Pakistan's Shahid Afridi (362), Pakistan's Wasim Akram (356), Sri Lanka's Kumar Sangakkara (354), Sri Lanka's Muttiah Muralitharan (350) and India's Rahul Dravid (344). The careers of Tendulkar, Jayawardene, Shahid Afridi and Sangakkara were ongoing.

BY TOURNAMENT/SERIES

Batting

Tournament	ODIs	Inn	NO	50	100	HS	Runs	Avg	Ct
Centenary Tournament in NZ 1994–95	4	4	2	1	0	62	80	40.00	0
Australia in West Indies 1995	2	2	0	0	0	43	43	21.50	0
B&H World Series in Australia 1995–96	10	10	0	3	1	123	341	34.10	2
World Cup in SL, India & Pak 1996	7	7	0	0	1	102	229	32.71	1
World Series in Sri Lanka 1996	4	4	1	1	0	53	116	38.67	1
Titan Cup in India 1996	3	3	0	0	0	35	52	17.33	0
C&U Series in Australia 1996–97	3	3	0	0	0	44	68	22.67	0
C&U Series in Australia 1997–98	9	9	1	3	1	100	462	57.75	3
Australia in New Zealand 1997–98	4	4	1	0	0	30	76	25.33	1
Pepsi Triangular Series in India 1998	5	5	0	2	1	145	335	67.00	1
Coca-Cola Cup in Sharjah 1998	4	4	0	1	0	52	132	33.00	1
ICC Knockout in Bangladesh 1998	1	1	0	0	0	41	41	41.00	0
Australia in Pakistan 1998	3	3	1	1	1	124*	195	97.50	2
C&U Series in Australia 1998–99	9	9	2	2	0	75*	322	46.00	4
Australia in West Indies 1999	5	5	0	0	0	43	74	14.80	3
World Cup in England 1999	10	10	1	1	0	69	354	39.33	6
Aiwa Cup in Sri Lanka 1999	5	5	1	0	0	38	103	25.75	2
Australia in Zimbabwe 1999	3	3	2	2	0	87*	185	185.00	4
C&U Series in Australia 1999–2000	10	10	0	3	1	115	404	40.40	1
South Africa in Australia 2000	3	3	0	0	0	39	60	20.00	0
ICC Knockout in Kenya 2000	1	1	0	0	0	46	46	46.00	0

Tournament	ODIs	Inn	NO	50	100	HS	Runs	Avg	Ct
Carlton Series in Australia 2000–01	9	9	1	4	0	93	393	49.13	3
Australia in India 2001	4	4	0	0	1	101	137	34.25	2
NatWest Series in England 2001	5	5	2	2	1	102	298	99.33	2
VB Series in Australia 2001–02	8	8	0	2	0	80	254	31.75	3
Australia in South Africa 2002	7	7	1	1	1	129	283	47.17	4
Pakistan in Australia 2002	3	3	0	0	0	14	27	9.00	1
PSO Tri Nations in Kenya 2002	4	3	2	1	0	65	115	115.00	3
Champions Trophy in Sri Lanka 2002	3	3	1	0	0	37	49	24.50	0
VB Series in Australia 2002–03	9	8	1	0	2	119	306	43.71	4
World Cup in SA & Zimbabwe 2003	11	10	2	1	2	140*	415	51.88	11
Australia in West Indies 2003	7	7	2	2	0	59	200	40.00	1
Bangladesh in Australia 2003	3	2	0	0	1	101	130	65.00	4
TVS Cup in India 2003	7	7	1	1	1	108*	257	42.83	4
VB Series in Australia 2003–04	9	9	0	2	0	88	315	35.00	4
Australia in Sri Lanka 2004	4	4	0	4	0	69	257	64.25	1
Australia in Zimbabwe 2004	3	2	0	1	0	91	101	50.50	3
Videocon Cup in Netherlands 2004	2	2	0	0	0	26	51	25.50	0
NatWest International v Pakistan 2004	1	1	0	0	0	4	4	4.00	0
Champions Trophy in England 2004	3	3	1	0	0	29	51	25.50	0
Chappell–Hadlee Trophy 2004–05	2	2	0	0	0	32	61	30.50	1
Tsunami Appeal in Australia 2004–05	1	1	0	0	1	115	115	115.00	1
VB Series in Australia 2004–05	8	8	1	1	0	78	184	26.29	4
Australia in New Zealand 2004–05	4	4	1	2	1	141*	266	88.67	1
NatWest Series in England 2005	7	6	0	1	0	66	135	22.50	3
NatWest Challenge in England 2005	3	3	0	0	1	111	168	56.00	1
ICC World XI in Australia 2005–06	3	3	0	2	0	68	157	52.33	4
Chappell–Hadlee Trophy 2005–06	3	3	0	2	0	75	166	55.33	1
VB Series in Australia 2005–06	9	9	1	2	1	124	345	43.13	5
Australia in South Africa 2006	3	3	0	1	1	164	233	77.67	1
Australia in Bangladesh 2006	2	2	0	0	0	14	19	9.50	0
DLF Cup in Malaysia 2006	4	4	0	1	0	54	83	20.75	4
Champions Trophy in India 2006	5	5	0	2	0	58	118	23.60	6
CB Series in Australia 2006–07	8	8	2	3	2	111	445	74.17	3
World Cup in West Indies 2007	11	9	1	4	1	113	539	67.38	7

Tournament	ODIs	Inn	NO	50	100	HS	Runs	Avg	Ct
Australia in India 2007	5	5	1	1	0	57	199	49.75	3
Chappell–Hadlee Trophy 2007–08	3	2	2	0	2	134*	241	–	1
CB Series in Australia 2007–08	10	10	0	0	1	124	191	19.10	6
Australia in West Indies 2008	3	3	0	1	0	69	87	29.00	1
South Africa in Australia 2008–09	5	5	0	2	0	64	214	42.80	1
Chappell–Hadlee Trophy 2008–09	4	4	0	0	0	16	38	9.50	1
Australia in South Africa 2009	5	5	0	1	0	53	158	31.60	0
NatWest Series in England 2009	4	4	0	1	1	126	233	58.25	1
Champions Trophy in South Africa 2009	5	5	1	2	1	111*	288	72.00	2
Australia in India 2009	6	6	0	3	0	74	267	44.50	1
Pakistan in Australia 2009–10	5	5	0	1	0	55	125	25.00	2
West Indies in Australia 2009–10	5	5	1	2	1	106	295	73.75	1
Chappell–Hadlee Trophy 2009–10	5	5	0	2	0	69	164	32.80	4
Australia in Ireland 2010	1	1	0	0	0	33	33	33.00	1
NatWest Series in England 2010	5	5	0	1	0	92	144	28.80	3
Sri Lanka in Australia 2010–11	1	1	0	0	0	10	10	10.00	0
World Cup in India & Sri Lanka 2011	7	6	0	0	1	104	206	34.33	3
Australia in Bangladesh 2011	3	3	1	0	0	47	118	59.00	0
Australia in Sri Lanka 2011	5	5	1	2	0	90*	196	49.00	1
Australia in South Africa 2011	3	3	0	1	0	63	84	28.00	1
Comm Bank Series in Australia 2011–12	5	5	0	0	0	7	18	3.60	3
Totals	**375**	**365**	**39**	**82**	**30**	**164**	**13704**	**42.04**	**160**

Notes

1. Only Sachin Tendulkar, with 2278 runs and six hundreds in 45 ODIs, has scored more runs and more hundreds in World Cup matches than Ricky's 1743 runs and five hundreds in 46 ODIs. Ricky's 46 appearances is a World Cup record.

2. Ricky is the only non-wicketkeeper to have taken more than 25 catches in World Cup games. Next best to Ricky's 28 catches at the World Cup is Sanath Jayasuriya's 18, then Chris Cairns, Brian Lara and Inzamum-ul-Haq with 16. Next best Australian is Steve Waugh with 14.

3. Ricky scored more than 1000 ODI runs in a calendar year on six occasions: 1166 runs in 24 ODIs in 2002; 1038 in 32 ODIs in 1999; 1154 in 34 ODIs in 2003; 1191 in 29 ODIs in 2005; 1424 in 27 ODIs in 2007; 1198 in 29 ODIs in 2009. Sachin Tendulkar is the only man to score 1000 or more runs in a calendar year seven times; Ricky and India's Sourav Ganguly have done so six times. Sri Lanka's Sanath Jayasuriya, Kumar Sangakkara and Mahela Jayawardene and Pakistan's Mohammad Yousuf have done so four times. Next best Australians are Adam Gilchrist, Matthew Hayden, Shane Watson and Mark Waugh, who have each achieved this feat twice.

Bowling

Tournament	O	M	R	W	Best	Avg	SR	Econ
Australia in Pakistan 1998	4	0	21	0	0–21	–	–	5.25
C&U Series in Australia 1998–99	10	0	41	1	1–41	41.00	60.00	4.10
Aiwa Cup in Sri Lanka 1999	1	0	2	0	0–2	–	–	2.00
Carlton Series in Australia 2000–01	10	0	40	2	1–12	20.00	30.00	4.00
Totals	**25**	**0**	**104**	**3**	**1–12**	**34.67**	**50.00**	**4.16**

Note
The three batsmen Ricky dismissed in ODI cricket were Sri Lanka's Arjuna Ranatunga (caught by Adam Gilchrist, Perth, 1998–99), West Indies' Brian Lara (caught by Gilchrist, Brisbane, 2000–01) and Zimbabwe's Heath Streak (caught by Michael Bevan, Sydney, 2000–01).

BATTING: BY OPPONENT

Opponent	ODIs	Inns	NO	50	100	HS	Runs	Avg	Ct
ACC Asian XI	1	1	0	0	1	115	115	115.00	1
Bangladesh	14	11	3	1	1	101	361	45.12	10
Canada	1	1	0	0	0	7	7	7.00	1
England	39	38	5	8	5	126	1598	48.42	17
ICC World XI	3	3	0	2	0	68	157	52.33	4
India	59	59	5	9	6	140*	2164	40.07	18
Ireland	2	1	0	0	0	33	33	33.00	2
Kenya	4	3	0	0	0	36	60	20.00	3
Namibia	1	1	0	0	0	2	2	2.00	2
Netherlands	2	1	0	0	0	23	23	23.00	2
New Zealand	51	50	7	12	6	141*	1971	45.84	25
Pakistan	35	35	5	8	1	124*	1107	36.90	13
Scotland	2	2	0	0	1	113	146	73.00	0
South Africa	48	48	1	13	2	164	1879	39.98	11
Sri Lanka	46	45	6	10	4	124	1649	42.28	16
USA	1	1	1	0	0	8*	8	–	0
West Indies	45	45	4	12	2	106	1475	35.98	23
Zimbabwe	21	20	2	7	1	145	949	52.72	12
Totals	**375**	**365**	**39**	**82**	**30**	**164**	**13704**	**42.04**	**160**

BATTING: BY POSITION

Position	Inn	NO	50	100	HS	Runs	Avg
Opening	6	1	3	0	87*	272	54.40
No. 3	330	32	74	29	164	12662	42.49
No. 4	17	2	5	1	123	646	43.07
No. 5	6	1	0	0	18*	49	9.80
No. 6	5	3	0	0	46*	65	32.50
No. 8	1	0	0	0	10	10	10.00
Totals	**365**	**39**	**82**	**30**	**164**	**13704**	**42.04**

BATTING: HOME AND AWAY

Location	ODIs	Inn	NO	50	100	HS	Runs	Avg
Home	154	151	12	32	14	134*	5521	39.72
Away	221	214	27	50	16	164	8183	43.76

BATTING: BY COUNTRY

Venue	ODIs	Inn	NO	50	100	HS	Runs	Avg	Ct
Australia	154	151	12	32	14	134*	5521	39.72	62
Bangladesh	6	6	1	0	0	47	178	35.60	0
England & Wales	38	37	4	6	3	126	1387	42.03	16
India	46	46	2	9	5	145	1736	39.45	21
Ireland	1	1	0	0	0	33	33	33.00	1
Kenya	5	4	2	1	0	65	161	80.50	3
Malaysia	4	4	0	1	0	54	83	20.75	4
Netherlands	2	2	0	0	0	26	51	25.50	0
New Zealand	20	20	4	7	1	141*	752	47.00	7
Pakistan	4	4	1	1	1	124*	240	80.00	2
South Africa	33	32	4	7	5	164	1423	50.82	18
Sri Lanka	23	22	4	7	0	90*	740	41.11	5
UAE	4	4	0	1	0	52	132	33.00	1
West Indies	28	26	3	7	1	113	943	41.00	12
Zimbabwe	7	6	2	3	0	91	324	81.00	8

Note

Ricky's ODI batting on Australian grounds is as follows:

Venue	ODIs	Inn	NO	50	100	HS	Runs	Avg	Ct
Adelaide	15	15	3	4	1	107*	445	37.08	4
Brisbane	18	18	2	2	1	106	464	29.00	7
Cairns	2	1	0	0	0	29	29	29.00	2
Darwin	1	1	0	0	1	101	101	101.00	2
Hobart	7	7	1	1	1	134*	272	45.33	1
Melbourne (Docklands)	12	12	0	3	0	68	334	27.83	8
Melbourne (MCG)	41	41	4	15	7	123	2108	56.97	18
Perth	15	15	0	1	1	111	442	29.47	5
Sydney	43	41	2	6	2	124	1326	34.00	15
Totals	**154**	**151**	**12**	**32**	**14**	**134***	**5521**	**39.72**	**62**

CENTURIES (30)

Tournament	Opponent	Venue	Inn (of 2)	Score
B&H World Series in Australia 1995–96	Sri Lanka	Melbourne	first	123
World Cup in SL, India & Pakistan 1996	West Indies	Jaipur	first	102
C&U Series in Australia 1997–98	New Zealand	Melbourne	first	100
Pepsi Triangular Series in India 1998	Zimbabwe	Delhi	first	145
Australia in Pakistan 1998	Pakistan	Lahore	second	124*
C&U Series in Australia 1999–2000	India	Melbourne	first	115
Australia in India 2001	India	Vishakhapatnam	first	101
NatWest Series in England 2001	England	Bristol	second	102
Australia in South Africa 2002	South Africa	Bloemfontein	first	129
VB Series in Australia 2002–03	England	Melbourne	first	119
VB Series in Australia 2002–03	Sri Lanka	Melbourne	second	106*
World Cup in SA & Zimbabwe 2003	Sri Lanka	Centurion	first	114
World Cup in SA & Zimbabwe 2003	India	Johannesburg	first	140*
Bangladesh in Australia 2003	Bangladesh	Darwin	first	101
TVS Cup in India 2003	India	Bangalore	first	108*
Tsunami Appeal in Australia 2004–05	ACC Asian XI	Melbourne	first	115
Australia in New Zealand 2004–05	New Zealand	Napier	first	141*
NatWest Challenge in England 2005	England	Lord's	second	111
VB Series in Australia 2005–06	Sri Lanka	Sydney	first	124
Australia in South Africa 2006	South Africa	Johannesburg	first	164

Tournament	Opponent	Venue	Inn (of 2)	Score
CB Series in Australia 2006–07	New Zealand	Perth	first	111
CB Series in Australia 2006–07	New Zealand	Melbourne	second	104
World Cup in West Indies 2007	Scotland	St Kitts	first	113
Chappell–Hadlee Trophy 2007–08	New Zealand	Adelaide	second	107*
Chappell–Hadlee Trophy 2007–08	New Zealand	Hobart	first	134*
CB Series in Australia 2007–08	India	Sydney	first	124
NatWest Series in England 2009	England	Nottingham	second	126
Champions Trophy in South Africa 2009	England	Centurion	second	111*
West Indies in Australia 2009–10	West Indies	Brisbane	first	106
World Cup in India & Sri Lanka 2011	India	Ahmedabad	first	104

Notes
1. Ricky's first ODI century was scored from No. 4 (when he was in at 2–10). The remaining 29 were scored batting at No. 3.
2. Ricky is one of the two captains to have scored a century in a World Cup final (140 not out in 2003), after West Indies' Clive Lloyd, who scored 102 against Australia in 1975.

HIGHEST PARTNERSHIPS

Stand	Wkt	Partner	Versus	Venue	Series	Inn	Score	Result
252	2nd	Shane Watson	Eng	Centurion	2009	2	1–6	Win
237	4th	Andrew Symonds	SL	Sydney	2005–06	1	3–10	Win
234*	3rd	Damien Martyn	Ind	Jo'burg	2003	1	2–125	Win
225	2nd	Adam Gilchrist	Eng	Melbourne	2002–03	1	1–15	Win
219	2nd	Mark Waugh	Zimb	Delhi	1998	1	1–2	Win
219	2nd	Matthew Hayden	India	Visakhapatnam	2001	1	1–6	Win
200	2nd	Matthew Hayden	NZ	Perth	2006–07	1	1–28	Win

Notes
1. Ricky's partnership of 252 with Shane Watson occurred in a Champions Trophy semi-final. His unbeaten stand of 234 with Damien Martyn occurred in the 2003 World Cup final.
2. Ricky's highest partnership in an ODI at Hobart was 135: with Shaun Marsh for the second wicket against South Africa in 2008–09.

FIELDING MILESTONES

Catch	Season	Versus	Venue	ODI No.	Batsman	Bowler
First	1995–96	West Indies	Melbourne	8	Sherwin Campbell	Michael Kasprowicz
50th	2001	Pakistan	Nairobi	144	Shahid Afridi	Brett Lee
100th	2005–06	South Africa	Melbourne	243	Mark Boucher	Brett Lee
150th	2009	England	Southampton	347	Kevin Pietersen	Shane Watson
160th	2011–12	India	Adelaide	373	Ravindra Jadeja	Xavier Doherty

Notes

1. Ricky was the fourth Australian non-wicketkeeper to take 100 catches in ODI cricket, after Allan Border, Mark Waugh and Steve Waugh. Michael Hussey reached this landmark in 2012.
2. Ricky took his 160 ODI catches off 36 different bowlers, the most being off Glenn McGrath (18), Brett Lee (17), Mitchell Johnson (11), Nathan Bracken (10), Brad Hogg (9), Shane Watson (9), Ian Harvey (8) and Michael Kasprowicz (8). He took three catches off Shane Warne's bowling, in 122 ODIs.
3. The batsmen Ricky dismissed most often as a catcher in ODIs were India's Sachin Tendulkar (five times), New Zealand's Lou Vincent (four times), and New Zealand's Daniel Vettori, Nathan Astle and Scott Styris, West Indies' Wavell Hinds and Pakistan's Shoaib Malik (each three times).

CAPTAINCY

Cricket	ODIs	Won	Lost	Drawn	Tied	NR	Win%
ODIs (2002–2011)	230	165	51	–	2	12	75.68

Notes

1. 'NR' indicates No Result. These games are not included when calculating the winning percentage.
2. Ricky was Australia's 16th ODI captain and the sixth man to lead Australia in more than 20 ODIs, after Greg Chappell, Kim Hughes, Allan Border, Mark Taylor and Steve Waugh.
3. Ricky captained Australia in every ODI he played from the first ODI in South Africa in 2002 to the quarter-final v India at the 2011 World Cup.
4. Of all captains with more than 30 ODIs as captain, Ricky ranks second in winning percentage behind Clive Lloyd (77.11% in 84 ODIs).
5. Ricky's 230 ODIs as captain is the most by any captain. Next best is 218 by New Zealand's Stephen Fleming.
6. Ricky's 29 matches and 26 wins as captain are World Cup records. He led Australia to victory in his first 22 World Cup matches as captain (from Australia's opening game of 2003 to the group game against Pakistan in 2011). He and West Indies' Clive Lloyd are the two men to have twice led their teams to victory in a World Cup final.

PLAYER-OF-THE-MATCH AWARDS (32)

Season	Opponent	Venue	Score
1997–98	New Zealand	Sydney	84
1997–98	South Africa	Sydney	76
1998	Zimbabwe	Delhi	145
1998	Pakistan	Lahore	124*
1998–99	Sri Lanka	Perth	39
1999–2000	India	Melbourne	115

Season	Opponent	Venue	Score
1999–2000	Pakistan	Sydney	78
2000–01	West Indies	Melbourne	73
2001	Pakistan	Cardiff	70
2001	England	Bristol	102
2001	England	The Oval	70*
2002	South Africa	Bloemfontein	129
2002–03	Sri Lanka	Melbourne	106*
2003	Sri Lanka	Centurion	114
2003	India	Johannesburg	140*
2003	West Indies	Kingston	59
2003	Bangladesh	Darwin	101
2003–04	India	Melbourne	88
2004	Zimbabwe	Harare	91
2004–05	ACC Asian XI	Melbourne	115
2004–05	New Zealand	Napier	141*
2006	South Africa	Johannesburg	164
2006–07	New Zealand	Perth	111
2006–07	New Zealand	Melbourne	104
2007	Scotland	St Kitts	113
2007–08	New Zealand	Adelaide	107*
2007–08	New Zealand	Hobart	134*
2007–08	India	Sydney	124
2009	England	Nottingham	126
2009–10	West Indies	Brisbane	106
2011	Sri Lanka	Hambantota	90*
2011	South Africa	Centurion	63

Notes

1. Ricky is the only man to have participated in 250 or more ODI victories. His first ODI win came in his debut match, against South Africa at Wellington, New Zealand, in February 1995. His 100th ODI win was versus England at the MCG on December 15, 2002 (when he scored 119). Ricky's 200th ODI victory came during the Super Eights stage of the 2007 World Cup, against Sri Lanka at St George's Grenada; he became the third man to achieve 200 ODI wins, after Inzamum-ul-Haq and Sanath Jayasuriya. He became the cricketer with the most ODI wins when he was part of his 234th victory, against Pakistan at the SCG on January 24, 2010, going past Jayasuriya. Ricky's final ODI, against India at the Gabba in February, 2012, was his 262nd ODI win.

2. As at June 30, 2013, Ricky was one of 15 men to have participated in 170 or more ODI victories, and one of four Australians, alongside Adam Gilchrist (202 wins), Steve Waugh (196) and Glenn McGrath (171). The top 10 for most ODI wins was Ricky Ponting (262), Sachin Tendulkar (234), Jayasuriya (233), Inzamum-ul-Haq (215), Mahela Jayawardene (213), Jacques Kallis (206), Adam Gilchrist (202), Muttiah Muralitharan (202), Wasim Akram (199) and Shahid Afridi (197).

MOST SUCCESSFUL BOWLERS

Bowlers	B	Ct	CB	LBW	St	HW	Total
Shahid Afridi (Pak)	–	4	4	1	–	–	9
Shane Bond (NZ)	–	4	3	–	–	–	7
Chaminda Vaas (SL)	1	4	–	1	–	–	6
Daniel Vettori (NZ)	–	2	–	4	–	–	6
Johan Botha (SA)	–	5	1	–	–	–	6
Kyle Mills (NZ)	–	2	2	1	–	–	5
Jerome Taylor (WI)	2	1	–	2	–	–	5
Lance Klusener (SA)	1	3	–	1	–	–	5
Roger Telemachus (SA)	1	2	1	1	–	–	5
Shoaib Akhtar (Pak)	1	4	–	–	–	–	5
Mervyn Dillon (WI)	1	3	–	–	–	–	4
Ajit Agarkar (Ind)	–	3	–	1	–	–	4
Praveen Kumar (Ind)	2	1	–	1	–	–	4
Irfan Pathan (Ind)	–	1	2	–	1	–	4
Lakshmi Balaji (Ind)	–	2	1	1	–	–	4

Notes

1. Ricky was dismissed 326 times in ODI cricket. He was bowled 34 times, caught by a fieldsman other than the wicketkeeper 176 times, caught behind 36 times, lbw 34 times, run out 31 times and stumped 15 times.

2. The wicketkeepers to dismiss Ricky most often in ODIs were New Zealand's Brendon McCullum (four times; three catches, one stumping) and South Africa's David Richardson (four times; two catches, two stumpings). McCullum also caught Ricky once as a non-wicketkeeper. The fieldsmen to catch Ricky most often were Stephen Fleming (six catches), followed by Rahul Dravid and Sachin Tendulkar with five. Two of Dravid's catches were taken while he was wicketkeeping.

3. TWENTY20 INTERNATIONAL CRICKET

TEAM-MATES

14 Twenty20 Internationals (T20Is) with Ricky Michael Clarke, Michael Hussey; **13** Nathan Bracken; **11** Brett Lee; **9** Andrew Symonds, Adam Gilchrist; **8** James Hopes, Mitchell Johnson; **7** Matthew Hayden, Brad Haddin, Stuart Clark, David Hussey; **6** Cameron White, David Warner; **5** Brad Hodge; **4** Damien Martyn, Shane Watson, Ben Hilfenhaus; **3** Simon Katich, Shane Harwood, Shaun Marsh, Luke Ronchi; **2** Glenn McGrath, Michael Kasprowicz, Mick Lewis, Brad Hogg, Shaun Tait; **1** Jason Gillespie, Brett Geeves, Callum Ferguson, Ben Laughlin, Nathan Hauritz

BY TOURNAMENT/SERIES

Batting

Tournament/Series	T20Is	Inn	NO	50	100	HS	Runs	Avg	Ct
Australia in New Zealand 2004–05	1	1	1	1	0	98*	98	–	1
Australia in England 2005	1	1	0	0	0	0	0	0.00	2
South Africa in Australia 2005–06	1	1	0	0	0	27	27	27.00	0
Australia in South Africa 2006	1	1	0	0	0	6	6	6.00	0
England in Australia 2006–07	1	1	0	0	0	47	47	47.00	0
ICC World Twenty20 in 2007	4	4	1	0	0	27	61	20.33	2
Australia in India 2007	1	1	0	1	0	76	76	76.00	1
Australia in the West Indies 2008	1	0	0	0	0	–	0	–	0
South Africa in Australia 2008–09	2	2	0	0	0	38	59	29.50	0
Australia in South Africa 2009	2	2	0	0	0	1	2	1.00	1
ICC World Twenty20 in 2009	2	2	0	0	0	25	25	12.50	1
Totals	**17**	**16**	**2**	**2**	**0**	**98***	**401**	**28.64**	**8**

Notes

1. Ricky captained Australia in all 17 of these matches. Australia won seven of these games and lost 10.
2. Ricky did not bowl in a T20 international.

BATTING: BY OPPONENT

Opponent	T20Is	Inns	NO	50	100	HS	Runs	Avg	Ct
Bangladesh	1	1	1	0	0	6*	6	–	2
England	3	3	0	0	0	47	67	22.33	2
India	1	1	0	1	0	76	76	76.00	1
New Zealand	1	1	1	1	0	98*	98	–	1
Pakistan	1	1	0	0	0	27	27	27.00	0
South Africa	6	6	0	0	0	38	94	15.67	1
Sri Lanka	1	1	0	0	0	25	25	25.00	1
West Indies	2	1	0	0	0	0	0	0.00	0
Zimbabwe	1	1	0	0	0	8	8	8.00	0
Totals	**17**	**16**	**2**	**2**	**0**	**98***	**401**	**28.64**	**8**

BATTING: BY POSITION

Position	Inn	NO	50	100	HS	Runs	Avg
No. 3	14	1	1	0	76	303	23.31
No. 4	1	1	1	0	98*	98	–
No. 6	1	0	0	0	0	0	0.00
Totals	**16**	**2**	**2**	**0**	**98***	**401**	**28.64**

BATTING: HOME AND AWAY

Location	T20Is	Inn	NO	50	100	HS	Runs	Avg
Home	4	4	0	0	0	47	133	33.25
Away	13	12	2	2	0	98*	268	26.80

PLAYER-OF-THE-MATCH AWARDS (1)

Season	Opponent	Venue	Score
2004–05	New Zealand	Wellington	98*

4. FIRST-CLASS AND OTHER CRICKET

FIRST-CLASS BATTING AND FIELDING

Cricket	Mat	Inn	NO	Runs	HS	Avg	100	50	Ct
First-class	289	494	62	24150	257	55.90	82	106	309

FIRST-CLASS BOWLING

Cricket	Mat	Balls	Runs	Wkts	BBI	BBM	Avg	Econ	SR
First-class	289	1506	813	14	2–10	1–0	58.07	3.23	107.57

FIRST-CLASS BATTING AND FIELDING: BY TEAM

Team	Years	Mat	Inn	NO	Runs	HS	100	50	Avg	Ct
Australia	1995–2012	168	287	29	13378	257	41	62	51.85	196
Australians	1995–2011	35	57	10	2784	155	9	15	59.23	34
Australian XI	1994	1	1	0	71	71	0	1	71.00	0
Tasmania	1992–2013	71	127	18	6667	233	27	22	61.17	61
Young Australia	1995	7	12	2	460	103*	1	4	46.00	7
Somerset	2004	3	4	1	297	117	2	1	99.00	7
Surrey	2013	4	6	2	493	192	2	1	123.25	4
Totals		**289**	**494**	**62**	**24150**	**257**	**82**	**106**	**55.90**	**309**

Notes

1. Tasmania won the Sheffield Shield three times during Ricky's career, in 2006–07, 2010–11 and 2012–13, and made four other Shield finals, in 1993–94, 1997–98, 2001–02 and 2011–12. He played in three Shield finals, in 1994, 2012 and 2013. He was with the Australian team in India in 1998, South Africa in 2002 and at the World Cup in 2007 and 2011 when the other four finals were played.

2. Ricky scored nine double centuries in first-class cricket:

Score	Team	Versus	Venue	Season
211	Tasmania	Western Australia	Hobart	1994–95
233	Tasmania	Queensland	Brisbane	2000–01
206	Australia	West Indies	Port-of-Spain	2003
242	Australia	India	Adelaide	2003–04
257	Australia	India	Melbourne	2003–04
207	Australia	Pakistan	Sydney	2004–05
209	Australia	Pakistan	Hobart	2009–10
221	Australia	India	Adelaide	2011–12
200*	Tasmania	New South Wales	Hobart	2012–13

3. As at October 1, 2013, Ricky's 82 first-class centuries ranked equal third on the Australian all-time list for most first-class centuries, behind Sir Donald Bradman (117) and Justin Langer (86) and level with Darren Lehmann. Other Australians with 70 or more first-class centuries are Mark Waugh (81), Matthew Hayden (79), Stuart Law (79), Steve Waugh (79), Greg Chappell (74) and Allan Border (70).

4. As at October 1, 2013, Ricky ranks 10th on the list of Australians with most runs in first-class cricket, behind Justin Langer (28382 runs), Donald Bradman (28067), Allan Border (27131), Stuart Law (27080), Mark Waugh (26885), Darren Lehmann (25795), Michael Di Venuto (25200), Matthew Hayden (24603) and Greg Chappell (24535). Of the 18 Australians to have scored more than 20000 first-class runs, three have a higher batting average than Ricky: Bradman (95.14), Lehmann (57.83) and Bob Simpson (21029 runs at 56.22).

5. Ricky's final game for Tasmania was the 2012–13 Sheffield Shield final, versus Queensland at Bellerive Oval, Hobart, on March 22–26, 2013. He scored 35 and 1. The final was drawn, Tasmania winning the Shield by virtue of finishing top of the Shield table at the end of the home and away matches.

6. Ricky's final first-class match was played on July 8–11, 2013, for Surrey versus Nottinghamshire in a County Championship game at the Oval. He scored 29 and 169 not out.

'LIST A' BATTING AND FIELDING: BY TEAM

Team	Years	Mat	Inn	NO	50	100	HS	Runs	Avg	Ct
Australia	1995–2012	380	370	42	83	29	164	13710	41.80	162
ICC World XI	2005	1	1	0	0	1	115	115	115.00	1
Australians	1996–2010	7	7	0	2	1	103	279	39.86	2
Australia A	1994–1996	9	9	2	0	0	42	166	23.71	1
Tasmania	1992–2013	49	49	8	10	2	111*	1640	40.00	21
Young Australia	1995	3	3	0	2	0	71	136	45.33	3
Somerset	2004	4	4	1	2	1	113	298	99.33	5
Surrey	2013	3	2	0	0	0	17	19	9.50	0
Totals		**456**	**445**	**53**	**99**	**34**	**164**	**16363**	**41.74**	**195**

Notes

1. This table is correct as at October 1, 2013. On June 21, 2013, Ricky announced that he would be retiring from all forms of cricket following the Champions League Twenty20, scheduled to run from September 17 to October 6, 2013.

2. The matches for Australia involve his 374 official ODIs for Australia, plus one match against Australia A in 1997–98 and five games at the 1998 Commonwealth Games in Kuala Lumpur, when the Australians won their first four matches but were beaten by South Africa in the gold medal game.

3. Tasmania won the Australian domestic limited-overs competition three times during Ricky's career, in 2004–05, 2007–08 and 2009–10. He did not play in any of these finals. His only appearance in an Australian domestic one-day final occurred in 2011–12, when the Ryobi Cup final at Adelaide Oval ended in a tie, with Ricky stranded at the non-striker's end. South Australia won the trophy by virtue of their top-place finish on the competition table.

4. Ricky's highest score in a limited-overs match for Tasmania was 111 not out against NSW in a Ford Ranger Cup game at North Sydney Oval in 2007–08.

5. Ricky bowled a total of 349 deliveries in List A matches, taking eight wickets for 269 runs at an average of 33.62. His best return was 3–34 from 8.1 overs in a Mercantile Mutual Cup match against WA at Hobart in 1996–97.

TWENTY20 CRICKET

During his career, Ricky played T20 matches for Australia (2005–2009); for the Hobart Hurricanes in the Australian Big Bash League (2011–2013); for the Kolkata Knight Riders (2008) and Mumbai Indians (2013) in the Indian Premier League; for Somerset (2004) and Surrey (2013) in English domestic T20 competitions; and for Antigua Hawksbills in the Caribbean Premier League (2013).

Ricky's highest score in these matches was 98 not out, scored from 55 balls during his T20I debut, versus New Zealand at Wellington in 2004–05.

In eight matches for the Hurricanes (one in 2011–12; seven in 2012–13), he scored 253 runs at an average of 36.14, with two half-centuries. His strike rate in these matches was 118.22. He also bowled two overs for 23 runs, his best figures being 1–11 against the Sydney Thunder at Hobart on December 23, 2012.

Sources
The statistics included in this section were correct as at October 1, 2013, and were derived from a variety of sources, including the websites ESPNcricinfo.com, cricketarchive.com and Howstat.com, the *ABC Australian Cricket Almanacs* (1993–1995), various editions of *Wisden* and the four volumes of the *Wisden Book of Test Cricket* (1877–1977; 1970–1996; 1996–2000; 2000–2009).

5. THE RECORDS

MOST TEST RUNS

Batsman	Country	Tests	Inn	NO	Runs	HS	100	50	Avg
Sachin Tendulkar	India	198	327	33	15837	248*	51	67	53.87
Ricky Ponting	Australia	168	287	29	13378	257	41	62	51.85
Rahul Dravid	India	164	286	32	13288	270	36	63	52.31
Jacques Kallis	South Africa	162	274	40	13128	224	44	58	56.10
Brian Lara	West Indies	131	232	6	11953	400*	34	48	52.89
Allan Border	Australia	156	265	44	11174	205	27	63	50.56
Steve Waugh	Australia	168	260	46	10927	200	32	50	51.06
Shivnarine Chanderpaul	West Indies	148	251	42	10830	203*	28	61	51.82
Mahela Jayawardene	Sri Lanka	138	232	14	10806	374	31	45	49.57
Kumar Sangakkara	Sri Lanka	117	200	16	10486	287	33	42	56.99
Sunil Gavaskar	India	125	214	16	10122	236*	34	45	51.12

MOST ONE-DAY INTERNATIONAL RUNS

Batsman	Country	ODIs	Inn	NO	Runs	HS	100	50	Avg	SR
Sachin Tendulkar	India	463	452	41	18426	200	49	96	44.83	86.24
Ricky Ponting	Australia	375	365	39	13704	164	30	82	42.04	80.31
Sanath Jayasuriya	Sri Lanka	445	433	18	13430	189	28	68	32.36	91.21
Kumar Sangakkara	Sri Lanka	354	331	36	11798	169	16	79	39.53	76.33
Inzamum-ul-Haq	Pakistan	378	350	53	11739	137	10	83	39.53	74.23
Jacques Kallis	South Africa	321	307	53	11498	139	17	85	45.27	72.98
Sourav Ganguly	India	311	300	23	11363	183	22	72	41.02	73.71
Mahela Jayawardene	Sri Lanka	404	378	38	11354	144	16	70	33.29	78.36
Rahul Dravid	India	344	318	40	10889	153	12	83	39.17	71.25
Brian Lara	West Indies	299	289	32	10405	169	19	63	40.49	79.51

Ricky comments: 'I think many cricket people think of Sachin Tendulkar and Brian Lara together, because they began their Test careers at about the same time — Sachin in 1989, Brian a year later — and then, for a number of years in the late 1990s and early 21st century they were rated by most experts to be the best two batsmen in the game. They were very different players, which makes it hard for me to rank one ahead of the other; whenever I was asked I always quietly went for Sachin but what nagged at me whenever I made this assessment was the feeling I often had when we played against the West Indies: that Brian was capable of taking the game away from us on his own.

'When Sachin was at his best, his defence seemed impenetrable, because he was so well organised, so good a judge of line and length, and so in control of his emotions despite the obsessive support he receives from his millions of fans. He could make runs in any conditions and was prolific in all forms of the game. With Brian, we always thought we had a chance, especially early on, because he might just go for a shot that wasn't really on. But if we didn't get him before he'd faced his first 60 balls, then we were in big trouble. Once set, he played the way *he* wanted to play. He was a master at manipulating fields, in the process putting bowlers, fieldsmen and captains under pressure, which made it easier not just for him, but for his batting partners as well. Whenever the Windies challenged us, it was inevitably because of Brian.

'What probably puts Sachin fractionally in front of Brian is the sheer scale of his achievements. When he scored 175 against us in Hyderabad in 2009, he went past 17,000 ODI runs and I was astonished by the fact he was about 3600 runs in front of his closest challenger (which at that time was Sanath Jayasuriya). Now the gap is even greater and he keeps pulling further away, establishing records that might never be broken. To do all that he has done, you have to be fit, strong, smart and brave. Sachin is all of those and more. It was a privilege to play against him, to try to counter him, and then, right at the end of my career, to be his team-mate at the Mumbai Indians.'

MOST TEST HUNDREDS

Batsman	Country	Tests	Inn	NO	50	100	HS	Runs	Avg
Sachin Tendulkar	India	198	327	33	67	51	248*	15837	53.87
Jacques Kallis	South Africa	162	274	40	58	44	224	13128	56.10
Ricky Ponting	Australia	168	287	29	62	41	257	13378	51.85
Rahul Dravid	India	164	286	32	63	36	270	13288	52.31
Brian Lara	West Indies	131	232	6	48	34	400*	11953	52.89
Sunil Gavaskar	India	125	214	16	45	34	236*	10122	51.12
Kumar Sangakkara	Sri Lanka	117	200	16	42	33	287	10486	56.99
Steve Waugh	Australia	168	260	46	50	32	200	10927	51.06
Mahela Jayawardene	Sri Lanka	138	232	14	45	31	374	10806	49.57
Matthew Hayden	Australia	103	184	14	29	30	380	8625	50.74
Don Bradman	Australia	52	80	10	13	29	334	6996	99.94
Shivnarine Chanderpaul	West Indies	148	251	42	61	28	203*	10830	51.82
Allan Border	Australia	156	265	44	63	27	205	11174	50.56

Ricky comments: 'During my final Test, when South Africa's top-order was batting us out of the game, I happened to look up at the WACA scoreboard at a moment when it was displaying Jacques Kallis's Test record. It is hard not to be blown away by the sheer scale of his numbers: the longevity (he made his Test debut in 1995), the runs, the average, the hundreds, more than 550 wickets and more than 300 catches in international cricket. As I write this, he's been involved in 80 Test victories.

'What I've come to admire most about Jacques' cricket is the way he has worked out what is best for him and stuck solidly to it. He has a complete understanding of his own game and what he can and cannot do, and has the mental power to play to his strengths whatever the circumstances. Once or twice, I've wondered if he could have been more assertive with the bat, that maybe he could have been even better than he's been, but when I think about the load he's carried I realise such criticism is unfair. Stats don't always tell the story but in Jacques' case they do; he has to be one of the greatest all-rounders the game has ever seen.'

BATSMEN WHO HAVE PLAYED 100 TESTS WITH A 50 BATTING AVERAGE

Batsman	Country	Tests	Inn	NO	50	100	HS	Runs	Avg
Kumar Sangakkara	Sri Lanka	117	200	16	42	33	287	10486	56.99
Jacques Kallis	South Africa	162	274	40	58	44	224	13128	56.10
Sachin Tendulkar	India	198	327	33	67	51	248*	15837	53.87
Brian Lara	West Indies	131	232	6	48	34	400*	11953	52.89
Javed Miandad	Pakistan	124	189	21	43	23	280*	8832	52.57
Rahul Dravid	India	164	286	32	63	36	270	13288	52.31
Ricky Ponting	Australia	168	287	29	62	41	257	13378	51.85
Shivnarine Chanderpaul	West Indies	148	251	42	61	28	203*	10830	51.82
Sunil Gavaskar	India	125	214	16	45	34	236*	10122	51.12
Steve Waugh	Australia	168	260	46	50	32	200	10927	51.06
Matthew Hayden	Australia	103	184	14	29	30	380	8625	50.74
Allan Border	Australia	156	265	44	63	27	205	11174	50.56
Viv Richards	West Indies	121	182	12	45	24	291	8540	50.24

Ricky comments: 'In November 2007, at Hobart, Kumar Sangakkara played one of the finest Test innings I ever saw, maybe the best I ever saw by a batsman who was running out of partners. We'd set Sri Lanka more than 500 to win, but Kumar batted beautifully to reach his hundred just before stumps on day four. The next morning, while wickets fell at the other end, he launched into us, smashing Brett Lee, Stuart Clark and Mitchell Johnson to all parts of Bellerive. A six over deep cover off Mitch was a spectacular highlight. We knew he was a shrewd, well-organised batsman who was as good at 'swimming between the flags' as anyone. This day, he showed how inventive and dynamic he can be.

'The only thing that surprises me about Kumar topping this table is that he's done so even though he's also kept wicket for Sri Lanka in almost 50 Tests, which should have made making runs that little bit harder. Like Adam Gilchrist but like no one else, he has handled the dual roles with distinction. What also impresses me is the way many of his hundreds have led to Sri Lankan wins. To me, stats that reflect whether a player is a winner or not are the most important numbers of all. As at October 1, 2013, that classic century Kumar scored against us in Hobart is one of only four he has made in a losing cause. Eighteen of his tons have helped Sri Lanka to victory.'

MOST TESTS AS CAPTAIN

Captain	Team	Career	Tests	Won	Lost	Drawn	Tied
Graeme Smith	South Africa	2002–2013	102	50	26	26	0
Allan Border	Australia	1978–1994	93	32	22	38	1
Stephen Fleming	New Zealand	1994–2008	80	28	27	25	0
Ricky Ponting	Australia	1995–2012	77	48	16	13	0
Clive Lloyd	West Indies	1966–1984	74	36	12	26	0
Steve Waugh	Australia	1985–2004	57	41	9	7	0
Arjuna Ranatunga	Sri Lanka	1982–2000	56	12	19	25	0

Captain	Team	Career	Tests	Won	Lost	Drawn	Tied
Michael Atherton	England	1989–2001	54	13	21	20	0
Hansie Cronje	South Africa	1992–2000	53	27	11	15	0
Michael Vaughan	England	1999–2008	51	26	11	14	0
Viv Richards	West Indies	1974–1991	50	27	8	15	0
Andrew Strauss	England	2004–2012	50	23	11	16	0
Mark Taylor	Australia	1989–1999	50	26	13	11	0

Ricky comments: 'I wasn't quite sure what to make of Graeme Smith when we first played against him. He was one of those cricketers who talked a good game, but we wondered if he had the mental strength to back up his words. As I documented in these pages, at the end of 2005–06, when we beat South Africa five Tests out of six, he told me playing game after game against us was "too hard". But rather than giving in, he and his team toughened up and within three years he was firmly in charge of the first South African team to win a Test series in Australia.

'During my career, I came to learn just how hard it can be to bat in the top-order and also captain a team, especially when you're on the field for more than a day and then you have to put the pads on and go straight out to bat. Initially, we thought Graeme had a weakness outside off-stump, but he tightened up that part of his game while continuing to hit powerfully through the legside and hammering anything short. He's averaged just under 50 while appearing in more than 100 Tests, but even more impressive for me is how he's continued as South African captain for so long while his team has kept improving. Of course, South Africa's winning run over the past few years has had a lot to do with the quality of their line-up, which has featured names such as Dale Steyn, Hashim Amla, Jacques Kallis, Mark Boucher, Morne Morkel and AB de Villiers. But the overall contribution of Graeme Smith, his runs and his leadership, might have been the most important factor of all.'

BOWLERS WITH 300 TEST WICKETS AT AN AVERAGE OF LESS THAN 24

Bowler	Country	Tests	O	M	R	W	Avg	Best	5w	10w
Malcolm Marshall	West Indies	81	2930.4	613	7876	376	20.95	7/22	22	4
Curtly Ambrose	West Indies	98	3683.5	1001	8502	405	20.99	8/45	22	3
Fred Trueman	England	67	2447.4	522	6625	307	21.58	8/31	17	3
Glenn McGrath	Australia	124	4874.4	1470	12186	563	21.64	8/24	29	3
Allan Donald	South Africa	72	2586.3	661	7344	330	22.25	8/71	20	3
Richard Hadlee	New Zealand	86	3460.4	809	9611	431	22.30	9/52	36	9
Dale Steyn	South Africa	65	2277.4	471	7469	332	22.50	7/51	21	5
Muttiah Muralitharan	Sri Lanka	133	7339.5	1792	18180	800	22.73	9/51	67	22
Imran Khan	Pakistan	88	3106.0	727	8258	362	22.81	8/58	23	6
Shaun Pollock	South Africa	108	4058.5	1211	9733	421	23.12	7/87	16	1
Waqar Younis	Pakistan	87	2704.0	516	8788	373	23.56	7/76	22	5
Wasim Akram	Pakistan	104	3771.1	871	9779	414	23.62	7/119	25	5
Dennis Lillee	Australia	70	2834.1	652	8493	355	23.92	7/83	23	7

For **Ricky's comment**, see page 614.

MOST ONE-DAY INTERNATIONAL WICKETS

Bowler	Country	ODIs	O	M	R	W	Avg	Best	4w
Muttiah Muralitharan	Sri Lanka	350	3135.1	198	12326	534	23.08	7/30	25
Wasim Akram	Pakistan	356	3031	236	11812	502	23.53	5/15	23
Waqar Younis	Pakistan	262	2116.2	143	9919	416	23.84	7/36	27
Chaminda Vaas	Sri Lanka	322	2629.1	277	11014	400	27.54	8/19	13
Shaun Pollock	South Africa	303	2618.4	313	9631	393	24.51	6/35	17
Glenn McGrath	Australia	250	2161.4	279	8391	381	22.02	7/15	16
Brett Lee	Australia	221	1864.1	141	8877	380	23.36	5/22	23
Shahid Afridi	Pakistan	362	2637	70	12184	359	33.93	7/12	13
Anil Kumble	India	271	2416	109	10412	337	30.90	6/12	10
Sanath Jayasuriya	Sri Lanka	445	2479	45	11871	323	36.75	6/29	12
Javagal Srinath	India	229	1989	137	8847	315	28.09	5/23	10

Ricky comments: 'What made Muttiah Muralitharan so difficult to play against was that he spun it both ways and I, like most other batsmen, could rarely pick the difference between these two deliveries as the ball left his hand. Knowing that he could turn the ball the "other way", away from the outside edge of my bat, meant I couldn't use my feet against him in the way I tried to do against a traditional offie. If I went down the wicket but didn't get right to the pitch of the ball, and it spun away from me, I'd be gone. With me pinned to my crease and he being supremely accurate, he could then build pressure and bring his bat-pad fieldsmen into play. Batting against him was mentally exhausting. In one-day cricket, Murali didn't have the close-in catchers to help him, but such was his control he was still extremely hard to get away. To take all his ODI wickets at a better average than champions such as Wasim Akram, Waqar Younis, Shaun Pollock and Brett Lee is no mean trick.

'When I said at my final media conference at the WACA that Harbhajan Singh was the best spinner I'd faced in international cricket, even harder to play than Murali, I think most people thought I was kidding. But I was fair dinkum, though I probably should have stressed I was thinking mostly about Test matches, where he has taken more than 400 wickets. I had my special problems with Harbhajan in Tests (he dismissed me 10 times in 14 matches) and not just because at times he could be so annoying. Like Murali, he was an off-spinner who could turn the ball the other way, and while I don't think he was as hard to pick at his best as the great Sri Lankan he could get the ball to drift and dip and zip off the wicket in a way that confounded just about everyone. Matthew Hayden used to sweep him all the time, which worked for him, but my method was always to get down the pitch to the spinners. Harbhajan's "away spinner" didn't worry me so much, but his loop was often so hard to nail. That and his fierce competitiveness were what made him such a difficult proposition for me.'

INDEX

PHOTO CREDITS

FINAL WORD

I'M FORTUNATE TO HAVE been surrounded by so many wonderful people and organisations across my career. As a young cricketer in Tasmania, I had no comprehension of what lay ahead of me from a support and business perspective. Sponsorships were about getting gear given to you, media was as simple as answering a few questions after a day's play and smiling for a photo, and my diary was all about training and playing.

But as I made my way through the ranks to eventually play for and captain Australia, the demands grew significantly both on and off the field. In the early days, the people I trusted for advice and direction were all immediately involved in cricket — either at club, state or national level.

When things took off for me I appointed Sam Halvorsen as my manager after an introduction from Greg Shipperd. Sam managed me up until early 2008 and was a huge influence on so many aspects of my life. He taught me so much, and his experience, network and advice helped set me in the right direction. As my life became busier and more demanding, Sam was always there to take care of all the non-playing matters so I could concentrate on my cricket.

With his help, I started working with a number of the biggest companies in Australia, became more comfortable in front of the media, learned to deal with political and business leaders who I came in contact with, had someone to tell me where and when I needed to be so I didn't miss a commitment and, importantly, started to build an investment portfolio that would support me and my family beyond my playing days.

The start of 2008 was a pretty tough period for me. The Sydney New Year Test against India became infamous for the 'Monkeygate' affair. My world got turned upside down at a time that I was also considering a move to the newly formed Indian Premier League and had decided to change managers by appointing DSEG (Dynamic Sports and Entertainment Group). It was really difficult to move on from Sam, who had been such a major part of my life. However, I felt I needed the support of a business that was bigger and more active in the marketplace that would help Rianna and me build a plan for retirement and beyond.

DSEG is owned by James Henderson, a fellow Tasmanian whom I had first met when he was Chairman of the Tasmanian Greyhound Racing Board, before he moved to Melbourne. We got to know each other well and he was very supportive of my business and charity endeavours, working closely with Sam and our partners.

James took over my management affairs from 2008 and has done a fantastic job at growing our interests inside and outside of cricket while working closely with all the stakeholder groups that we are involved with. Many of these are sponsors that we consider part of our family. Companies like Kookaburra (Rob Elliot), Swisse (Radek Sali), Rexona (Sharon Parker) and Valvoline (Michael Porter and Peter Besgrove), who have been on my journey and have shown great faith to partner with me beyond my playing days.

Along the way, there's been numerous other sponsors that have been incredible supporters of mine and I have been extremely proud to represent them. These include Pure Tasmania, adidas, Nike, Albion, Smorgon Steel, One Steel, National Foods, Tasmaid, SEP, Codemasters, Sony and many others.

I've had media deals with the Nine Network, News Limited and a number of overseas newspapers as well as my publishing deals with HarperCollins. I've recently signed a deal to join the Ten Network's coverage of the Big Bash and can't wait for that to start. I've also worked closely with the many companies that have sponsored and supported Australian cricket. In my wildest dreams, I never imagined that I would become a business in my own right but that's what cricket has done for me. I've learned about the importance of brand, relationship building and investing for the future. Fortunately, I've had a great team off the field to support me and, importantly, it's not changed the way I am as a person.